Handbook of Qualitative Research Methods for International Business

Handbook of
Qualitative Research
Methods for
International Business

Edited by

Rebecca Marschan-Piekkari

Helsinki School of Economics, Finland

Catherine Welch

University of New South Wales, Australia

Edward Elgar
Cheltenham, UK • Northampton, MA, USA

Published by
Edward Elgar Publishing Limited
Glensanda House
Montpellier Parade
Cheltenham
Glos GL50 1UA
UK

Edward Elgar Publishing, Inc.
136 West Street
Suite 202
Northampton
Massachusetts 01060
USA

This book has been printed on demand to keep the title in print.

A catalogue record for this book
is available from the British Library

Library of Congress Cataloguing in Publication Data
Handbook of qualitative research methods for international business / edited by
    Rebecca Marschan-Piekkari and Catherine Welch.
        p. cm.   1005566549
    Includes index.
    1. International business enterprises—Research—Methodology. 2.
International trade—Research—Methodology. I. Marschan-Piekkari, Rebecca,
1967– II. Welch, Catherine, 1971–

HD2755.5H3718 2004
338.8'8'072—dc22   2004040439

ISBN 1 84376 083 5 (cased)
ISBN 1 84542 434 4 (paperback)

Contents

PART I: TRENDS AND PROSPECTS IN INTERNATIONAL
           BUSINESS RESEARCH

PART II: CASE STUDY RESEARCH

v

List of Figures

List of Tables

Contributors

Poul Houman Andersen   Aarhus School of Business, Denmark.

Christos Antoniou   University of Leeds, UK.

Russell Belk   University of Utah, USA.

Julian Birkinshaw   London Business School, UK.

Jean J. Boddewyn   City University of New York, USA.

Tommy Borglund   Stockholm School of Economics, Sweden.

Mary Yoko Brannen   San José State University, USA.

Mark V. Cannice   University of San Francisco, USA.

Malcolm Chapman   University of Leeds, UK.

Stewart R. Clegg   University of Technology, Sydney, Australia.

John D. Daniels   University of Miami, USA.

Hans De Geer   Stockholm School of Economics, Sweden.

Giana M. Eckhardt   Australian Graduate School of Management, Australia.

Magnus Frostenson   Stockholm School of Economics, Sweden.

Hanna Gajewska-De Mattos   University of Leeds, UK.

Pervez Ghauri   Manchester School of Management, UMIST, UK.

Karen Grisar-Kassé   Free University of Berlin, Germany.

Bo Hellgren   Linköping University, Sweden.

Suzanne Hosley   Shinawatra University, Thailand.

Leila Hurmerinta-Peltomäki   Turku School of Economics and Business Administration, Finland.

Jan Johanson   Uppsala University, Sweden.

Victoria Jones   Fundacao Getulio Vargas, Brazil.

Geoffrey Lewis   Melbourne Business School, University of Melbourne, Australia.

Valerie J. Lindsay   University of Auckland, New Zealand.

Stuart Macdonald   Sheffield University Management School, UK.

Sara L. McGaughey   Copenhagen Business School, Denmark.

Rebecca Marschan-Piekkari   Helsinki School of Economics, Finland. Administration, Finland.

Dirk Matten   Nottingham University Business School, UK.

Paul Matthyssens   Limburg University Center, Belgium and Erasmus University, Netherlands.

Snejina Michailova   Copenhagen Business School, Denmark.

Nancy K. Napier   Boise State University, USA.

Thang Van Nguyen   National Economics University, Vietnam.

Niels G. Noorderhaven   Tilburg University, Netherlands.

Niina Nummela   Turku School of Economics and Business Administration, Finland.

Arvind Parkhe   Temple University Fox School of Business and Management, USA.

Pieter Pauwels   Maastricht University, Netherlands.

Heli Penttinen   Helsinki School of Economics, Finland.

Richard B. Peterson   University of Washington, USA.

Cristina Reis   Swedish School of Economics and Business Administration, Finland.

Robert W. Scapens   University of Manchester, UK and University of Groningen, Netherlands.

Diana Rosemary Sharpe   Monmouth University, USA.

Maria Anne Skaates Aarhus School of Business, Denmark.

Marja Tahvanainen Helsinki School of Economics, Finland.

Janne Tienari Lappeenranta University of Technology, Finland.

Eero Vaara Ecole de Management de Lyon, France.

Catherine Welch University of New South Wales, Australia.

Denice E. Welch Mt Eliza Business School and University of Queensland, Australia.

Lawrence S. Welch Mt Eliza Business School and University of Queensland, Australia.

Robert Westwood University of Queensland Business School, University of Queensland, Australia.

Ian Wilkinson University of New South Wales, Australia.

Elisabeth M. Wilson University of Manchester, UK.

Henry Wai-chung Yeung National University of Singapore, Singapore.

Louise Young University of Technology, Sydney, Australia.

Tatiana Zalan University of Melbourne, Australia.

Acknowledgements

During this Handbook project, we have received valuable assistance from many people to whom we would like to express our gratitude.

The initial idea to write a book on qualitative research methods in international business came from our colleague, Ulf Andersson (Uppsala University, Sweden). Following a presentation of one of our conference papers on this topic, he encouraged us to write a book proposal and proceed with the idea. Encouragement was also received from participants at the annual Nordic Workshop in International Business. We have also greatly appreciated the confidence and support showed by Edward Elgar and his team right from the beginning of this project.

The book proposal was reviewed by Ingmar Björkman (Hanken, Finland), David Ford (University of Bath, UK), Sid Gray (University of Sydney, Australia) and Monir Tayeb (Heriot-Watt University, UK), all of whom provided us with helpful suggestions and many lessons from experience. We were fortunate to benefit from their expertise and knowledge about book publishing at an early stage of the project.

Through our own professional and personal networks, as well as through several calls for papers, we were able to select 28 contributions to the Handbook. We have very much enjoyed working with these 44 contributors from various parts of the world. Moreover, we were able to include eight vignettes written by other well-established scholars in the field to enhance the profile of qualitative methods and provide personal perspectives on the research process. We would like to thank Mary Yoko Brannen (San José State University, USA) for the original idea of soliciting vignettes.

The diversity of qualitative methods in international business has allowed us to familiarise ourselves with a number of methodological issues, including those with which we were less familiar in the early phases of the Handbook. Therefore, in the review process of the chapters, we involved experts whose knowledge and expertise we have been able to rely on. Many thanks go to Pat Bazeley (Research Support, Australia), Hau-Le Nguyen (Ho Chi Minh City University of Technology, Vietnam), Tho Nguyen (Ho Chi Minh City University of Economics, Vietnam), Anne-Marie Søderberg (Copenhagen Business School, Denmark), Denice Welch (Mt Eliza Business School, Australia) and Lawrence Welch (Mt Eliza Business School, Australia) for their helpful and thoughtful reviews. We would also like to acknowledge the assistance of Joan Nordlund (English for Business, Finland), who meticulously carried out language checks under tight schedules.

During the project, we have exposed the emerging themes of the Handbook to various conference audiences in Australia, Europe and the USA. At these conferences, we have had a chance to meet our contributors personally, which has been an important source of encouragement and inspiration. As co-editors, we also had the opportunity to work together in Sydney, Australia for three months during the most intensive phase of reviewing and editing. This visit and the conference trips were financed by the Academy of Finland (the project on Managing Knowledge Creation and Transfer in Multinational Corporations: A Finnish Perspective); Emil Aaltosen säätiö; Ella ja Georg Ehrnroothin säätiö; Liikesivistysrahasto; Stiftelsen Svenska Handelshögskolan; and Marcus Wallenbergin säätiö. We wish to thank these foundations for the financial support and confidence that they expressed in our work.

Throughout the book project, when struggling with tables, figures and page set-ups, we have had the professional and personal support of Grace Setiawan and Ben Aveling. We deeply appreciate their professionalism and enthusiasm they showed for our book project. We are also grateful for the last-minute logistical assistance provided by Sara McGaughey and Bent Petersen (both of the Copenhagen Business School, Denmark).

Finally, we would like to thank our families, our parents Marina and Alexander, and Denice and Lawrence, who were an infinite source of support and encouragement during the entire book project. They have provided us with both professional and parental advice as we have been learning the role of a hands-on editor. Moreover, their provision of babysitting services for Johanna is gratefully acknowledged. Lastly, we would like to thank Lauri and Ben for their patience during this never-ending project. Despite our absent-mindedness and even absences, they were highly committed to this project. Today is the day they have long been waiting for. We would therefore like to dedicate this Handbook to them.

Observations from a Lifetime of Interviewing

Jean J. Boddewyn

Observation 1: The screening of researchers requesting interviews is sometimes more systematic than it appears. Most large firms subscribe to 'clipping' services about everything said about them in the press. Although I was on very good terms with a multinational parent company, I was once turned down for a further set of interviews overseas because a press report had given the impression that I was critical of that firm when, in fact, I had cited its name in connection with more general issues shared by many MNEs. In other words, be careful about what you say to the press!

Observation 2: I conducted many interviews in the United States and abroad during the 1970s when MNEs felt prosperous and were eager to take you out to copious lunches with cocktails, wine, liqueur and cigars! My point is that these 'hedonistic' circumstances generated greater candour after a few drinks – compared to sipping a Perrier and not smoking (another relaxant). Also, if you could schedule an interview for late afternoon (up to 6 pm in France), you would occasionally find a more relaxed respondent sometimes willing to cry on your shoulder. In other words, respondents are alert and brisk early in the day when they want to get over your interview which they may regret having granted; while, at the end of the day, the job is over and they can be more relaxed and open.

Observation 3: It is difficult to get meaningful interviews at corporate headquarters, but expatriate managers abroad are more open and interested – especially if you interviewed their counterparts in other subsidiaries of the MNE and are willing to share notes in a confidential manner. A good approach is to throw a dilemma rather than a straight question at them – for example: 'I have heard different answers ... I cannot understand the answer someone else gave me ... What do you think they meant?'.

Foreword

I am delighted to have been asked to contribute the Foreword to this Handbook. Qualitative methods have the potential to transform the research agenda in international business and, indeed, can be said to have already done so in some areas of the literature on the subject. As this book shows, however, there are obstacles in the way of pushing this forward. Qualitative research is not an easy option. It can often be expensive, time consuming, risky and even dangerous to the health of the researcher! Those of us who have done 'fieldwork' will (almost universally) extol the insights provided. My first experience of real fieldwork was during my PhD research (at Lancaster University) on foreign direct investors in Ireland. I had dutifully read the literature, decided my objectives, constructed my questionnaire and boldly set off to the Irish Republic. The encounter with real managers in real foreign firms transformed my understanding. As I read this volume, smiles of recognition appeared on my face many times. So, too, did new levels of understanding.

This book conveys the sense of actual researchers (of different genders, nationalities and outlooks) genuinely confronting real philosophical and practical problems. It will be an inspiration to confused researchers (admit it, all researchers are confused – that's why we do research). It is full of practical advice ranging from the philosophy underlying the research to when to use a tape recorder in interviews.

The editors and authors are to be commended for an engaging, useful and thought provoking end product which will be read with pleasure (and I hope will provoke some anger too) and will be a useful guidebook. It is my hope that this book will stimulate more, and better research in the international business field.

Peter J. Buckley
Centre for International Business
University of Leeds (CIBUL)
October 2003

Interviews: A Key Data Source in International Business Research

Arvind Parkhe

Ask Bob Woodward and Carl Bernstein, the legendary *Washington Post* reporters who broke the Watergate story that led to the downfall of the Nixon presidency, about open-ended interviews. They are likely to tell you that, triangulated with other modes of data collection, interviews with key informants located at important nodes of knowledge flows are an invaluable way of connecting with empirical reality.

There are important lessons here for researchers of international business, in particular, for qualitative researchers of international business. In many areas of rigorous empirical investigation, there is simply no satisfactory substitute for interviews. Certainly, paper-and-pencil surveys are far less costly in terms of time and money, and secondary data require far less commitment from the researcher, than do interviews. And certainly, interviews are subject to potential problems of self-reporting bias, poor recall, selective memory, and so on. Yet as I discovered in the area of international alliances, there is no data source as rewarding as interviews, in order to tap into the brain of the person(s) within each organisation under study who are most directly responsible for the phenomenon being researched.

As for international alliances, so for numerous other branches of international business research. With appropriate safeguards and precautions for language, context, interpretation and meaning, interviews with key managers can add rich insights to most studies. OK, so what are the major issues that an international business qualitative researcher is likely to face in using interviews? In no particular order, these would include: gaining access to suitable people and getting them to agree to do interviews; confidentiality; permission to tape record and transcribe; travel expense; language skills of the researcher and/or interviewer; and triangulation of interview data with archival data and other sources. Try it, you'll like it!

PART I

Trends and Prospects in International Business
Research

Theory is not Reality

Jan Johanson

In the 1960s I was supposed to write a thesis about the foreign markets of the Swedish special steel industry. I travelled around and interviewed directors and other managers who were responsible for the international marketing of these companies. My main theoretical background was in microeconomics, which I believed in, but I was also interested in marketing theory and the emerging organisation theory.

My interviews could be called lightly structured open-ended interviews which perhaps most resembled discussions. My questions stemmed from microeconomic theory. The interviewees' knowledge was almost entirely based on their practical experiences of selling special steel internationally. The interviews revealed an enormous gap between our worldviews. The managers obviously thought I was completely ignorant of reality. And I never got answers to my questions. During the interviews, there was tension in the air that the experienced interviewees broke up towards the end by proposing that I should stick to my theories, which probably were fine, but they would continue working as before. Their industry was probably so special that the theories didn't fit.

It did not quite turn out like that. My belief in theory was shattered, but not broken, and I ended up devoting the rest of my life to trying to explain why my respondents did what they said they did.

In the 1970s, before we really got the IMP (Industrial Marketing and Purchasing Group) project going, we did a number of pilot studies in Uppsala to test our ideas about industrial markets. We had some preliminary thoughts about interaction and longstanding relationships, and for a number of years we had been teaching marketing to sales engineers at ASEA. They were ambitious, intelligent and frustrated. They were frustrated about their schizophrenic experiences of tension between top management's stipulations and the requirements posed by their customers.

In these first pilot studies we were out in the field conducting interviews with marketing planners of companies. In these interviews we received descriptions which in terms of the key points largely matched the views presented by Phillip Kotler and other established textbook authors in marketing. It became evident that all our respondents had fairly recently graduated from MSc (Econ.) programmes. They had not been confronted with real customers and markets, and they believed that reality corresponded with the picture portrayed in these textbooks. The lesson we learned for the future was to always avoid staff who are not on the front line. They have time but no experience. It is only those who have 'dirt under their fingernails' who understand where the important problems lie.

These few lines represent my experiences of empirical research. They are very limited, but they have had a considerable impact on my subsequent life in the academic world. I got tired of empirical work fairly soon because I felt I got to hear almost the same stories again and again regardless of the topic of the discussion. It was coincidence and contacts that the interviewees brought to the fore. I learnt that theory and reality do not at all resemble each other. Nor perhaps should they.

1. Qualitative Research Methods in International Business: The State of the Art

Rebecca Marschan-Piekkari and Catherine Welch

INTRODUCTION

Qualitative research[1] has always had a place in the field of international business (IB). Early contributions on firms' internationalisation processes, such as the Uppsala model (Johanson and Vahlne 1977) and regional management (Daniels 1986), typically drew upon a range of techniques, including qualitative methods, in order to generate theory and new insights. Vernon (1994, pp. 144–5) went so far as to comment that since questionnaires are often inadequate instruments for the complex issues that are the subject of IB, 'some of the most provocative work of researchers ... has come from those who have plumbed in depth the behaviour of individual firms, or the interplay of a limited cluster of firms competing in a well-defined product market'.

However, qualitative research still remains a minority and even marginalised pursuit within IB, and one which often carries the stigma of being a poor career move. Therefore, qualitative researchers tend to be on the defensive, and find themselves having to argue the case for the relative merits of qualitative research. Yet at the same time as qualitative researchers continue to battle for recognition, literature on the use of qualitative methods in IB has been steadily accumulating over the past 20 years. This literature has mapped out issues of concern to IB scholars that are often absent in methodological texts aimed at a more general readership.

The present Handbook continues and consolidates the methodological literature on the use of qualitative methods in IB, aiming to reflect the range of approaches to qualitative research in our field. It is designed to go beyond the 'qualitative versus quantitative' debate and provide innovative, even challenging perspectives. It aims to 'demystify' the methodological process

5

by capturing the experiences and practices of qualitative researchers at all stages of the research cycle.

The purpose of this chapter, then, is to review prior research on the use of qualitative methods in IB and shed light on some important issues of concern to those in the field who are already engaged in qualitative research, or who are considering it as a viable research method. Rather than reviewing the contributions of this volume, we aim to place them in the broader context of existing debates about using qualitative methods to research IB topics. We use 'method' in its broadest sense, following Alvesson and Deetz (2000, p. 4), to mean 'a mode and a framework for engaging with empirical material'.[2] Method and theory in a discipline are closely intertwined, with the choice of method shaping and constraining the research agenda in path-dependent ways (Kogut 2001).

Qualitative methods have been defined as procedures for 'coming to terms with the meaning not the frequency' of a phenomenon by studying it in its social context (Van Maanen 1983, p. 9). While qualitative research is often conflated with interview-based case studies (Easton 1995), qualitative methods for data collection and analysis may include participant observation, content analysis, discourse analysis, focus groups, narrative interviews and unobtrusive methods such as archival research.[3] The use of such methods is sometimes, although not necessarily, accompanied by some form of interpretive and anti-positivist paradigm that rejects the pursuit of scientific laws in favour of the *Verstehen* of socially constructed realities (Prasad and Prasad 2002).[4]

The remainder of the chapter is organised as follows. First, we discuss the paradoxical role of qualitative research in IB: the fact that while its status remains stubbornly low, its benefits are nevertheless widely acknowledged. Thereafter, we examine current understandings about conducting qualitative research in an international setting. Finally, we draw some conclusions based on our literature review. In this chapter, we do not review empirical IB studies employing qualitative methods, leaving this task to other contributors to this volume.

QUALITATIVE RESEARCH: STILL SECOND BEST?

In a review of articles published in six leading IB journals in the 1991–2001 period, Andersen and Skaates (Chapter 23 this volume) found that only 10 per cent of all published IB research used qualitative methods. A similar dearth of qualitative research in the field or its sub-domains has been found in other reviews (Mendenhall et al. 1993; Peterson, Chapter 2 this volume; Welch and Welch, Chapter 27 this volume; Werner 2002).[5] In the light of available evidence it seems that qualitative research in IB remains undervalued, beset by its low status. A commonly held assumption is that researchers end up choosing a qualitative approach because a survey is not possible to implement or because they have not mastered statistical techniques. As a methodological alternative, it is considered second best – even unscientific and too 'feminine'. As a result, doctoral students may regard qualitative research as a poor career move with an unattractive future.

One potent reason for the low status of qualitative research is that it is by no means universally accepted as 'legitimate' science. In a recent review of comparative empirical research methodology in IB, qualitative methods are not discussed, despite the fact that the aim of the article is to 'construct a compendium of generic methodological problems and recommended remedies' (Cavusgil and Das 1997, p. 72; see also Schaffer and Riordan 2003). Moreover, the authors look forward to a time when IB will have sufficiently matured as a discipline that it will be less reliant on qualitative and conceptually-based studies. Similar sentiments are expressed by Aulakh and Kotabe (1993), who in their review article on international marketing research class case studies and exploratory research as 'descriptive' rather than 'theoretical'. The assumptions that qualitative research is only suited to exploratory research (for example, Wright et al. 1988), and does not constitute a theoretical contribution, are fairly deeply ingrained.

Another explanation for the low status of qualitative research in IB is sometimes sought in the particular 'cultural' and 'institutional' features of the North American 'system of knowledge production' (Graham and Grønhaug 1989, p. 179; see also Berry 1996). The preference for 'hard science' and cultural assumptions that equate rigour with quantifiable data; the 'publish or perish' system of career advancement upheld by universities; the requirement that research leads to immediate results for practitioners; the socialisation process that is the PhD programme; the research methods demanded by leading journals: all these factors have been identified as militating against the complex topics commonly tackled by qualitative researchers in IB (Berry 1996; Graham and Grønhaug 1989; Usunier 1998). In contrast, the European academic environment is regarded by one commentator as more receptive towards qualitative research in IB (Berry 1996), thus reflecting the transatlantic divide in management studies generally (Bengtsson et al. 1997; Koza and Thoenig 1995).

Paradoxically, at the same time as qualitative research continues to be marginalised in practice, calls for more research of this kind are made at regular intervals (for example, Boddewyn and Iyer 1999; Parkhe 1993; Redding 1994; Vernon 1994; White 2002; Yeung 1995). As a result, certain arguments in favour of qualitative IB research have been popularised. The first is that IB, lacking the sophisticated theory development of a mature discipline, requires more exploratory and theory-generating research rather than empirical testing (Mendenhall et al. 1993; Osland and Osland 2001; Wright 1996).

The second justification is that qualitative research allows for deeper cross-cultural understanding and is less likely to suffer from cultural bias and ethnocentric assumptions on the part of the researcher than survey instruments (Goodyear 1982; Osland and Osland 2001; Wright 1996). Qualitative research takes an 'emic' perspective (for example, Peng et al. 1991) and examines other organisations and societies 'on their own terms', rather than imposing one's own culturally bound concepts and theories (Boyacigiller and Adler 1991, p. 281). Compared to quantitative methods, qualitative research takes a more holistic approach to the research object and studies a phenomenon in its context (see, for example, D'Iribarne 1996–97).

The third argument takes a contingency approach, namely that research instruments need to be chosen to suit the particular location in which the research is being conducted. In particular, it is argued that qualitative research may be preferable in developing countries, where the secondary data required for random samples may be lacking and respondents may be unfamiliar with questionnaires, and in those cultures in which particular emphasis is placed upon the development of social, face-to-face relations and trust (see, for example, Harari and Beaty 1990).

The fourth benefit is that qualitative research goes beyond the measurement of observable behaviour (the 'what'), and seeks to understand the meaning and beliefs underlying action (the 'why' and 'how') (Buckley and Chapman 1996). As Wright (1996, p. 70) explains, qualitative research provides answers to 'messy' problems and complex issues that are typical for international management research. Qualitative methods can take advantage of rich data and in this way allow the researcher to obtain more meaningful results about 'soft' inter-relationships between core factors.

CURRENT DEBATES IN QUALITATIVE IB RESEARCH

In the following sections, we shall examine existing debates surrounding the use of qualitative research in IB. These were generated as an outcome of our literature review and the editing process of this Handbook. The debates centre on four challenges:[6] contextualisation of the research process; design and management of cross-national collaborative research; rethinking current and alternative research methods; and the quality, codification and publication of qualitative research. In our discussion, we also explain how this current volume contributes to these debates, and draw comparisons between methodological developments in IB and those in qualitative research generally.

Contextualisation of Qualitative Research Methods

An analysis of articles published in the *Journal of International Business Studies* between 1984 and 1993 concludes that IB consists, for the most part, of research 'conducted by scholars from the United States, Canada and Western Europe about the United States, Canada and Western Europe' (Thomas 1996, p. 492; see also Peng et al. 1991). Any attempt to remedy this and 'globalize our mental maps' (Thomas et al. 1994) entails confronting the question of whether the 'textbook' approaches to research design and methods, derived from a Western context, can be applied to a wide range of locations. The crossing of national borders means that researchers, no less than companies, cannot assume that what works at home will work abroad. Yet, with the possible exception of anthropologists, the authors of the most-cited qualitative research methodology texts (for example, Miles and Huberman 1994; Yin 1994) do not consider how their prescriptions may need to be adapted as a result of external conditions.

A research design must therefore take into account 'environment characteristics, resource constraints, and cultural traits' to fit the conditions of a particular location (Thomas 1996, p. 497). Punnett and Shenkar (1994a, 1994b) argue that IB researchers need to adopt a 'contingency approach' to their research. The greater the difference between the researcher's home country and the foreign research site, the less likely research methods used at home will 'fit' the foreign field site (Punnett and Shenkar 1994a, pp. 41–2). Adaptations may range from rewording interview questions to radical changes in terms of switching to another research method or using a multi-method approach (see, for example, Adler et al. 1989; Yeung 1995; for a useful summary, see Shenkar and von Glinow 1994). Moreover, since in much qualitative research the researcher is understood to be the 'instrument' (Flick 2002), the researcher's identity and role as perceived in the foreign field site will have an impact on the processes of data collection and interpretation (Tsang 1998).

While there has been a steady accumulation of literature on the challenges of conducting cross-cultural surveys (see, for example, Cavusgil and Das 1997), there has been less debate on the adaptation of qualitative methods. Yet the need for cross-cultural understanding and adaptation is a constant demand when, for example, conducting in-depth interviews in foreign locations (Ryen 2002). In order to address this gap, experiences of the cross-cultural interviewing are analysed in this volume by Daniels and Cannice (Chapter 9), Marschan-Piekkari and Reis (Chapter 11), and Wilkinson and Young (Chapter 10).

As well as cultural differences, researchers are likely to encounter other challenges in a foreign location. Perhaps the most challenging research site consists of 'insecure', or physically dangerous, locations. George and Clegg (1997, p. 1022) caution that research in such locations is likely to prove costlier and more time-consuming than anticipated, and is likely not to meet 'the truisms of standard-method texts'. Another form of political 'insecurity' may be encountered in politically repressive systems, where governments may well seek to control the research process and outcomes, and academic research is not well-established as a legitimate activity (Michailova and Liuhto 2000). This means that certain research topics may be banned, access to organisations and people may be restricted, and respondents may apply self-censorship when answering questions. For example, Shenkar (1994) mentions the problem in China of 'invited' samples.

While George and Clegg (1997) discuss the insecurity brought about by political violence and the threat of physical danger in Sri Lanka, they argue that 'a state of insecurity' may also characterise a country in which research is not a well-established and legitimate activity. They encountered a high degree of suspicion and anxiety from respondents who did not understand the purpose of academic research. Respondents were often unwilling to answer questions for fear of repercussions, and only two out of 350 respondents consented to their interviews being tape-recorded. Other researchers operating in less-developed countries report encountering a similar level of insecurity, or anxiety, since local respondents perceive research as an alien activity (for example, Hofmeyr et al. 1994; Thomas 1996).

The challenge of conducting research in locations 'forgotten' by the US-dominant academy (Thomas 1996) is taken up by several contributors in this volume, such as Grisar-Kassé on Senegal (Chapter 7), Michailova on Eastern Europe (Chapter 18), Eckhardt on China (Chapter 20), Napier et al. on Vietnam (Chapter 19), Wilson on India (Chapter 21) and Jones on Latin America (Chapter 22). Research in such settings may mean selecting appropriate research themes (see, for example, Napier at al., Chapter 19; Wilson, Chapter 21); adapting the interview format in a culturally fitting way (see, for example, Eckhardt, Chapter 20; Michailova, Chapter 18); defining suitable units of analysis (see Eckhardt, Chapter 20); switching to another research method (see Wilson, Chapter 21); learning and utilising the local language (Chapman et al., Chapter 14; Grisar-Kassé, Chapter 7; Michailova, Chapter 18; Marschan-Piekkari and Reis, Chapter 11); managing relationships with key informants in a locally responsive and sensitive manner (see, for example, Jones, Chapter 22; Grisar-Kassé, Chapter 7; Michailova, Chapter 18; Napier et al., Chapter 19; Wilson, Chapter 21); and challenging one's own cultural and paradigmatic assumptions (Grisar-Kassé, Chapter 7; Wilson, Chapter 21).

Contextualisation of the research process, as it is analysed in this volume, is therefore multi-faceted. It may involve adapting research design and methods to local conditions, taking an emic perspective and altering research questions to incorporate local meanings and concerns, problematising the role and identity of the researcher in the foreign location, and even adopting interpretive approaches. Rather than approaching the research act as a fixed set of methods and procedures controlled by the researcher, it can be seen more as an enacted, negotiated, adaptive and serendipitous process (for example, Wilkinson and Young, Chapter 10 this volume).

Turning from external environmental conditions to organisational dimensions, another set of challenges for many IB researchers stems from their research site, the geographically dispersed firm (Marschan-Piekkari et al., Chapter 12 this volume; Yeung 1995). It is well recognised that logistical hurdles are often magnified for researchers conducting research at a distance. The problem of gaining access to firms, which has been ranked as the qualitative researcher's greatest challenge (Gummesson 1991), tends to be accentuated due to the global reach, complex headquarters–subsidiary relationships and the political nature of the multinational corporation (MNC). These characteristics of the organisation are likely to affect the entire research process even once access has been secured. For example, the researcher may have to change the timing of data collection, compromise the scope and focus of the study, and limit the dissemination of findings due to key informants' concerns of anonymity. Mezias et al. (1999, p. 324) advise researchers to 'double check' what headquarters inform them about subsidiary units, since headquarters staff 'may know little of the reality on the ground in these locations'. Attempting to include subsidiary as well as headquarters staff in a research design may unwittingly involve the researcher in internal organisational struggles and divisions. Clearly, managing the relationship with powerful elite informants of the MNC is a critical skill for the qualitative IB researcher (Welch et al. 2002). Like diverse national contexts, the MNC as an organisational context strongly influences the research process. It puts pressure on IB researchers using qualitative methods to be flexible and willing to make adaptations along the way.

Challenges of Cross-national Collaborative Research

IB researchers often recommend the use of cross-national research teams as a way of meeting both environmental and organisational challenges of contextualisation (for example, Boyacigiller and Adler 1991; Peterson, Chapter 2 this volume; Steers et al. 1992; Usunier 1998). The local research team in a collaborative project is assumed to have an intimate knowledge of the local culture. As an insider, it has a name and 'face' in the local community which is likely to facilitate access to local firms.

Interestingly, however, most of the extant literature on international research teams reports on quantitative collaborative projects involving large-scale surveys (for an exception, see Easterby-Smith and Malina 1999). As a result, there has been some discussion of developing and translating a survey instrument, achieving a random and comparable sample in each participating country, and making the decision on how to administer the questionnaire (for example, Milliman and von Glinow 1998; Teagarden et al. 1995). In some cases, the project may also include a qualitative component, but this is usually not discussed in detail (for example, House 1998). Consequently, issues pertaining specifically to collaboration on qualitative projects remain largely unexplored.

It is, nevertheless, likely that the characteristics of the project, including the research methodology, affect the nature of collaboration among research participants. For example, Cheng (1996) and Peterson (2001) note that a cross-national collaborative project seeking to replicate an existing study is likely to be tightly controlled by the leader of that study, with foreign researchers being accorded the subordinate role of adapting instruments for use in their own countries. In contrast, Easterby-Smith and Malina (1999, p. 80) speculate that qualitative collaborative projects tend to be less centralised in terms of control than quantitative projects that utilise a single instrument. They report that in their cross-national qualitative project, considerable differences emerged when designing the project, and when collecting and interpreting data. The British academics on the project team, for example, were startled to find that 'interviews' in China 'were more like lectures, with managers reading from prepared reports in day-long meetings'. Similarly, Søderberg and Vaara (2003, pp. 37–8) observe that, in the context of a Nordic research team, 'in spite of a negotiated interview strategy and a certain degree of standardisation concerning the issues to be touched upon and the questions to be raised, the interviews did not all take the same form' due to differences in nationality, gender, fieldwork experience and so on. Due to such differences in data collection and interpretation, centralised control was neither possible nor desirable.

Needless to say, multinational research teams present challenges of their own. The success of a multinational collaborative research project depends on a range of factors that ultimately are difficult to control (Geringer and Frayne 2001; Nason and Pillutla 1998; Teagarden 1998). Researchers from different countries operate in distinct institutional and professional environments, which may affect their motives for, and desired rewards from, collaboration. They may not necessarily share the same research paradigms or referential systems (Turati et al. 1998). It is thus important that cultural stereotyping and ethnocentrism is avoided, since 'in the context of international collaboration, contentious issues often take on nationalistic overtones which make them harder to resolve' (Peterson 2001, p. 66). In other words, group heterogeneity may be a liability as well as an asset: on the one hand, it can lead to better research outcomes, on the other hand, it can also negatively impact upon the functioning of the team and significantly increase coordination costs (Nason and Pillutla 1998).

The cross-national collaborative research project is, then, by no means an easy fix; nor does it neutralise cross-national and cross-cultural dilemmas. Moreover, it raises broader issues concerning the extent to which research should be done by 'insiders'. The pattern for many cross-national projects is to delegate the collection of data to local researchers. This means that there is limited scope to compare, challenge and synthesise 'insider' and 'outsider' perspectives. The whole process of contextualisation may be sidestepped as a result. Many collaborative projects thus run the risk of being 'multi-domestic' rather than truly international.

Rethinking Research Methods

The selection and application of qualitative research methods follow a fairly fixed pattern in IB. In particular, the positivist assumption that qualitative research is only suited to exploratory research is fairly deeply ingrained, even among qualitative researchers (for example, Wright et al. 1988). Some researchers are, by contrast, redefining perceptions of the role and value of qualitative research. Harari and Beaty (1990) argue that qualitative research has an important role to play in theory testing, particularly in cross-cultural research. They argue that 'naive listening' in the form of unstructured interviews or focus groups should come *after* questionnaires, as a way of confirming a researcher's interpretations of quantitative data that has been collected. In a similar vein, Chetty (1996) demonstrates how case studies can be used to generate causal explanations of export performance.

Qualitative research in IB is still largely dominated by case studies based mainly on data collected from in-depth interviews (Ghauri, Chapter 5 this volume; Osland and Osland 2001). Nevertheless, the nature, limitations and complexity of this reliance on interviewing are rarely examined critically. This is in sharp contrast to developments in qualitative methods generally, in which the interview as a research act has come under close scrutiny. Alternative conceptualisations of the interview have been debated (Alvesson 2003; Silverman 2001); and different strategies for conducting and analysing the interview have been explored (for example, the narrative or ethnomethodological interview; see Gubrium and Holstein 2002).

While interviews are potentially a rich source of data, they suffer from biases and limitations (Macdonald and Hellgren, Chapter 13 this volume), as is true of any method. Yeung (1995, p. 322) summarises some important and well-recognised limitations of interviews: as a 'social process', qualitative personal interviews are strongly influenced by the relationship that develops between the researcher and researched; and are 'communicative events' in the course of which the interviewer can easily slip into imposing his or her norms and frameworks on the interviewee rather than aiming for 'empathetic understanding'. But, as Macdonald and Hellgren (Chapter 13 this volume) argue, these limitations are often downplayed or poorly understood in published management and IB research.

In response to the inherent limitations of interviews, some IB researchers turn to anthropology, with its long tradition of cross-cultural research, as a way of enriching research practice in IB (Sharpe, Chapter 15 this volume). The anthropological tradition of ethnographic research, which is most often closely associated with participant observation but commonly involves the simultaneous use of a range of methods, allows for a 'holistic' analysis of an organisation or setting that uncovers the understandings and shared meanings of the group or community under study (Buckley and Chapman 1996). Brannen (1996, p. 117) and Osland and Osland (2001, p. 206) argue that ethnography is 'perhaps the most effective method for gaining insights into microlevel cultural phenomena'. The use of observational techniques in a foreign field site is, however, highly demanding. The presence of a foreign researcher may be disruptive, and observation requires a high degree of familiarity with the context (including language fluency) often not possessed by the outsider (Lawrence 1988; Punnett and Shenkar 1994a; Usunier 1998).

Moreover, IB researchers wishing to use ethnographic methods face hurdles that are not traditionally encountered by anthropologists (Chapman et al., Chapter 14 this volume). Companies can be notoriously difficult to access and may, even once access is granted, impose restrictions on the publication of results. Company research is 'done *by permission,* [which] somewhat changes the nature of the enquiry, and the possible results' (Buckley and Chapman 1996, p. 239; their emphasis). These differences mean that while the use of methods from other disciplines is one way to broaden the practice of qualitative research in IB, such methods may need to be adapted to the particular contexts in which IB researchers operate. Buckley and Chapman (1996, p. 242) report that the compromise they reached in the case of their ethnographic study was 'long, repeated, unstructured interviews together with participant observation where the company can tolerate it'. In a similar vein, De Geer et al. (Chapter 16 this volume) discuss how the traditional interview study can be augmented, even without undertaking a full-scale ethnographic study.

One explanation as to why a broadening of qualitative research methods is yet to materialise may lie in the lack of alternative research paradigms. Unlike management studies generally, IB research has remained largely untouched by recent trends such as postmodern philosophy, postcolonialism, hermeneutics and critical theory (Noorderhaven, Chapter 4 this volume; Westwood, Chapter 3 this volume). This affects the types of research questions that are posed: IB researchers tend to limit themselves to describing the existing social order (Osland and Osland 2001), and have largely steered clear of theories that are critical of capitalism and globalisation. It also affects the epistemological and ontological assumptions that underpin research. IB research has remained resolutely positivist, objectivist and functionalist (see also Osland and Osland 2001). As well, the lack of alternative research paradigms affects decisions made at every stage of the research cycle: the methods used for data collection and analysis, with techniques such as discourse analysis, narrative inquiry and critical hermeneutics remaining outside mainstream IB research (Vaara and Tienari, Chapter 17 this volume); approaches to validity and reliability, with positivist rather than interpretive standards dominating (Andersen and Skaates, Chapter 23 this volume); and modes of representation (McGaughey, Chapter 26 this volume).

Quality, Publishing and Codification of Qualitative Research

A crucial issue for IB research is what constitutes 'quality' qualitative research. However, this is often not addressed by qualitative researchers themselves – perhaps not surprisingly, given the space limitations dictated by most journals. In such publications, qualitative researchers seldom specify exactly what their data collection methods entailed (Zalan and Lewis, Chapter 25 this volume), what adjustments they made as a result of the location in which they conducted the research, or how they validated their findings (Andersen and Skaates, Chapter 23 this volume). For example, as Buckley and Chapman (1996) suggest, unstructured personal interviews may in fact refer to quite different forms of data collection. At one end of the spectrum, an interview may consist of a 'one-off' questioning of a single company representative. At the other end of the spectrum, a researcher may be referring to an extensive process of repeated interviews over a period of time with multiple informants within a company, as well as with external stakeholders and industry experts.

Consequently, the whole question of how to evaluate qualitative research is often neglected entirely. Possibly the most common answer to this question in the IB literature is that triangulation is a good guide, if not to convincing theory, then at least to the rigorous verification of data (Osland and Osland 2001). Triangulation is a term mainly used to refer to the concurrent use of both qualitative and quantitative data, although the use of multiple qualitative methods has also been discussed (McDonald 1985). Usunier (1998, p. 134) contends that qualitative and quantitative research are 'complementary' rather than 'competing' traditions, and should be merged in the search for 'meaning as differences in nature and differences in degree'. However, even if this argument is accepted, it does not address the dilemma of how researchers should respond if their qualitative and quantitative data yield contradictory and irreconcilable results (for an example, see Brannen 1996). While qualitative research might be branded 'messy' (to paraphrase Parkhe 1993), the use of multiple methods is 'messier' still. It can be conjectured that while mixed methodologies are often advocated, they are rarely used for this reason. Nevertheless, as Hurmerinta-Peltomäki and Nummela (Chapter 8 this volume) show, there are many possible (yet under utilised) strategies for combining qualitative and quantitative data in a research design. Moreover, many such designs challenge the traditional assumption that the role of qualitative research is properly limited to a pilot study.

However, as Andersen and Skaates (Chapter 23 this volume) discuss, triangulation is only one possible validation strategy – moreover, it is one that is increasingly contested in the wider literature on qualitative research, especially by postmodernists and anti-positivists (for a review, see Flick 2002). Even more fundamentally, as Andersen and Skaates show, criteria for ensuring and validating quality are ineluctably tied to paradigmatic assumptions. In the qualitative research literature more broadly, validity and reliability have become intensely fought territory in the paradigmatic wars. There is widespread agreement that positivist definitions of validity and reliability are not appropriate standards for qualitative research (see, for example, Seale 1999). However, what (if anything) should replace these measures has provoked much debate. Some (most prominently, Lincoln and Guba 1985) have suggested alternative criteria, while others deny the possibility of 'valid' knowledge altogether (for a discussion, see Smith and Deemer 2000).

Of course, one surrogate measure of 'quality' research is its publication in top-tier journals. It would appear at first glance that qualitative IB research performs poorly on this measure, given its minority representation in top IB journals such as the *Journal of International Business Studies* and *Management International Review*. However, there are of course other explanations besides the possible poor quality of qualitative research. First, it may be that, given the institutional and cultural disincentives that apply, fewer researchers conduct qualitative research. Certainly, one survey of IB researchers supports this first proposition (Graham and Grønhaug 1989).

The second explanation for the poor representation of qualitative research is that the review process is systematically biased against it (Welch and Welch, Chapter 27 this volume). While anecdotal evidence from qualitative IB researchers would almost certainly support this proposition (although see Steers et al. 1992 for an alternative view), systematic bias is of course difficult to prove. One recent review of publishing IB research (Pierce and Garven 1995) does not even canvas the issue. In their review of three IB-dedicated journals during 1990–2000, Welch and Welch (Chapter 27 this volume) found a wide gap between the stated and actual editorial policy of these journals in favour of positivist, quantitative approaches. Bengtsson et al.'s (1997) analysis of the reviews of five case study-based papers submitted to prominent American management journals (ones also targeted by IB researchers) also provides some evidence for the existence of a quantitative bias (compare Beyer et al. 1995).

A third reason may be that qualitative data is very context specific, and thus perhaps harder to bring into conformity with universalist assumptions of scientific rigour, and make internationally appealing and publishable, than quantitative data. In order to validate our interpretations, we typically present supporting qualitative data in the form of examples or excerpts from interview transcripts at the 'local level' (Alasuutari 2004, p. 595). However, Alasuutari argues that qualitative interview data collected in a peripheral location such as Finland can be too 'exotic' for English-speaking, British or North American publishers. When preparing the English version of his qualitative methods textbook, he had to replace several research examples with work that had been published in English to make 'the English language reader feel at ease with the presentation' (Alasuutari 2004, p. 595). This potentially leaves qualitative researchers with a dilemma: while contextualisation may improve the quality of their research, it may also make it harder to have their findings accepted for publication.

In response to these obstacles, Bengtsson et al. (1997) advise qualitative researchers to take the North American research culture into account when preparing manuscripts for submission. They recommend that qualitative researchers clearly justify the need for more qualitative theory building in their literature review, explain why the research questions are not more clearly defined, and discuss the method and case selection in detail. Moreover, they argue that papers 'should not diverge from a conventional research design more than is absolutely called for' (Bengtsson et al. 1997, p. 488), and that the results of the study can potentially be presented in the form of propositions. In other words, they advise qualitative researchers to apply the style and form of a traditional, North American quantitative study as much as is feasible. Additional perspectives on the publishing dilemma are offered by Birkinshaw (Chapter 28 this volume) and Welch and Welch (Chapter 27 this volume).

Alasuutari (2004, p. 595) adopts a broader perspective on the development of qualitative research and argues that we are witnessing the globalisation of qualitative research where 'the same theories, methods and ideas about how to do qualitative research and how to make sense of human phenomena on the basis of empirical qualitative data' are shared across countries. Moreover, globalisation affects not just the researcher but the researched, with the gradual spread of the modern 'interview society' in which individuals are comfortable with the notion of furnishing strangers with their opinions

(Gubrium and Holstein 2002). Globalisation of the research community would perhaps suggest sharing of best/common research practices and developing common, methodological anchors, as well as a more standardised and transparent approach to writing about methods in qualitative research (as advocated by Zalan and Lewis, Chapter 25 this volume). It could also mean more explicit guidelines and benchmarks for both authors and journal reviewers. Examples of the codification of qualitative research practices and standards can be found in this volume: Pauwels and Matthyssens (Chapter 6) on case study research; Lindsay (Chapter 24) on data analysis; and Andersen and Skaates (Chapter 23) on validation strategies.

This suggests another paradox faced by qualitative researchers: how to deal with convergent or globalising demands, at the same time as balancing requirements for localisation and contextualisation? If qualitative research is to be locally authentic and meaningful, are not standard criteria for research quality counter-productive? Certainly, the production of a standard set of tests for quality overlooks differences in research paradigms, strategies and locations. However, codification can also be viewed as a more open-ended process that promotes 'methodological awareness' and reflexivity among researchers rather than a return to positivism (Seale 1999). Thus, Alasuutari (2004, p. 606) hopes that the 'globalisation' of qualitative research will not result in a single toolbox being applied, but rather will lead to 'increasing knowledge and circulation of tools developed in different parts of the world'. The globalisation of business may entail that IB research can be carried out in a more standardised fashion; however, the location is still likely to affect the nature of the data set and what you see depends very much on where you sit.

CONCLUSION

Research on the application of qualitative methods to IB has accelerated in past decades. Such research bridges the traditional divide in the social sciences between sociology and anthropology, which rely to a greater extent on qualitative methods, and management studies, including IB, which have tended to follow their closer cousins, psychology and economics, in adhering much more rigidly to quantitative methods (Wright 1996, p. 63). Given the frequent calls for more qualitative research in IB, one can speculate whether the ties to sociology and anthropology will be strengthened and the profile of IB as a field of study will change as a result.

Yet despite these developments, as has been discussed in this chapter, a variety of issues of concern to qualitative researchers in IB remains to be explored in depth. What guidelines should be used when adapting methods to fit the particular environmental context in which research is being undertaken? How should collaboration on cross-national qualitative research projects be approached? How can ethnographic methods be applied to the organisational context of IB research? How might IB researchers respond to emergent philosophical and methodological trends in the social sciences, such as postmodernism? How should qualitative research be validated and evaluated? What is 'best practice' in qualitative IB research? Addressing such questions promises to enrich the field of IB and broaden the research agenda – or even revitalise it, to take the perspective of those such as Buckley (2002) who argue it has 'run out of steam'.

Accordingly, this book aims to provide a range of perspectives on such issues, encourage reflection on the different stages of the research cycle, and represent the diversity of qualitative research as it is practised by IB researchers. Ultimately, any book focusing on methods is more than just about method; rather, it involves analysing, challenging and rethinking how a particular area of research is constituted as a community of discourse and practice. The following pages therefore represent different conceptions of the IB research community. The aim in assembling these contributions is not to advocate a single approach to qualitative research; rather, it is to explore existing practices and alternative paths, and provide inspiration for future inquiry.

ACKNOWLEDGEMENTS

We would like to thank Jeff Hearn for his valuable feedback on an earlier version of this chapter. We also received thoughtful comments on earlier versions of the chapter at the annual conference of the Australian and New Zealand International Business Academy, November 2002, and the 7th Vaasa Conference on International Business, August 2003.

NOTES

1. As with so many aspects of research methodology, there is extensive debate about the most appropriate definition of 'qualitative research'. As Prasad (2003) observes, qualitative research is in no way a uniform set of procedures for data collection and analysis, and can be conducted within a variety of intellectual traditions. Even the distinction between qualitative and quantitative research is not clear (Hammersley 1992). Moreover, qualitative research is often defined by what it is not, that is, non-numerical data and non-statistical analysis. Denzin and Lincoln (1994, p. 2) try to move beyond this by defining qualitative research as involving a multi-method approach to 'study[ing] things in their natural setting, attempting to make sense of, or interpret, phenomena in terms of the meanings people bring to them'.

2. Other contributions to this volume, however, do draw a more precise distinction between 'method' and 'methodology', with method referring to the tools to collect and analyse data, and methodology a discourse or theory of inquiry (Schwandt 2001).

3. However, data generated from, for example, open-ended interviews or archival material, can

be quantified and statistically analysed. Thus, as Schwandt (2001, p. 214) observes, 'what precisely comprises a qualitative method is not all clear [*sic*]'.

4. Terms such as 'positivist', 'interpretive' and 'paradigm' are not applied consistently in the methodological literature. In this chapter, we follow Guba and Lincoln (1994) and Lincoln and Guba (2000) by using 'research paradigm' to mean a set of beliefs, or worldview, about ontology, epistemology and methodology. Unlike Lincoln and Guba, however, we do not attempt to distinguish in detail between alternative nonpositivist paradigms.

5. The sub-domain of international human resource management would appear to be an exception, with Clark et al. (1999) reporting that 29.6 per cent of the articles in the journals they surveyed from 1977 to 1997 were case studies, while 1.5 per cent used mixed methods.

6. Many of these challenges are common to both qualitative and quantitative IB researchers, but we emphasise the qualitative perspective. Moreover, some of the concerns we raise are also relevant to the broader community of qualitative researchers, not just IB researchers.

REFERENCES

Adler, N.J., N. Campbell and A. Laurent (1989), 'In search of appropriate methodology: from outside the People's Republic of China looking in', *Journal of International Business Studies*, **20** (1), 61–74.

Alasuutari, P. (2004), 'The globalization of qualitative research', in C. Seale, G. Gobo, J.F. Gubrium and D. Silverman (eds), *Qualitative Research Practice*, London: Sage, pp. 595–608.

Alvesson, M. (2003), 'Beyond neopositivists, romantics, and localists: a reflexive approach to interviews in organizational research', *Academy of Management Review*, **28** (1), 13–33.

Alvesson, M. and S. Deetz (2000), *Doing Critical Management Research*, London: Sage.

Aulakh, P.S. and M. Kotabe (1993), 'An assessment of theoretical and methodological development in international marketing: 1980–1990', *Journal of International Marketing*, **1** (2), 5–28.

Bengtsson, L., U. Elg and J.-I. Lind (1997), 'Bridging the transatlantic publishing gap: how North American reviewers evaluate European idiographic research', *Scandinavian Management Review*, **13** (4), 473–92.

Berry, M. (1996), 'From American standard to cross-cultural dialogues', in B.J. Punnett and O. Shenkar (eds), *Handbook for International Management Research*, Cambridge, MA: Blackwell, pp. 463–83.

Beyer, J.M., R.G. Chanove and W.B. Fox (1995), 'The review process and the fates of manuscripts submitted to *AMJ*', *Academy of Management Journal*, **38** (5), 1219–60.

Boddewyn, J.J. and G. Iyer (1999), 'International business research: beyond déjà vu', *Management International Review*, **39** (special issue 2), 1–14.

Boyacigiller, N.A. and N.J. Adler (1991), 'The parochial dinosaur: organizational science in a global context', *Academy of Management Review*, **16** (2), 262–90.

Brannen, M.Y. (1996), 'Ethnographic international management research', in B.J. Punnett and O. Shenkar (eds), *Handbook for International Management Research*, Cambridge, MA: Blackwell, pp. 115–43.

Buckley, P.J. (2002), 'Is the international business research agenda running out of steam?', *Journal of International Business Studies*, **33** (2), 365–73.

Buckley, P.J. and M. Chapman (1996), 'Theory and method in international business research', *International Business Review*, **5** (3), 233–45.

Cavusgil, S.T. and A. Das (1997), 'Methodological issues in empirical cross-cultural research: a survey of the management literature and a framework', *Management International Review*, **37** (1), 71–96.

Cheng, J.L.C. (1996), 'Cross-national project teams: toward a task-contingency model', in B.J. Punnett and O. Shenkar (eds), *Handbook for International Management Research*, Cambridge, MA: Blackwell, pp. 507–20.

Chetty, S. (1996), 'The case study method for research in small- and medium-sized firms', *International Small Business Journal*, **15** (1), 73–85.

Clark, T., H. Gospel and J. Montgomery (1999), 'Running on the spot? A review of twenty years of research on the management of human resources in comparative and international perspective', *International Journal of Human Resource Management*, **10** (3), 520–44.

Daniels, J. (1986), 'Approaches to European regional management by large US multinational firms', *Management International Review*, **26** (2), 27–42.

Denzin, N.K. and Y.S. Lincoln (1994), 'Introduction: entering the field of qualitative research', in N.K. Denzin and Y.S. Lincoln (eds), *Handbook of Qualitative Research*, Thousand Oaks, CA: Sage, pp. 1–17.

D'Iribarne, P. (1996–97), 'The usefulness of an ethnographic approach to the international comparison of organizations', *International Studies of Management and Organization*, **26** (4), 30–47.

Easterby-Smith, M. and D. Malina (1999), 'Cross-cultural collaborative research: toward reflexivity', *Academy of Management Journal*, **42** (1), 76–86.

Easton, G. (1995), 'Methodology and industrial networks', in K. Möller and D. Wilson (eds), *Business Marketing: An Interaction and Network Perspective*, Boston, MA: Kluwer, pp. 411–92.

Flick, U. (2002), *An Introduction to Qualitative Research*, 2nd edn, London: Sage.

George, R. and S.R. Clegg (1997), 'An inside story: doing organizational research in a state of insecurity', *Organization Studies*, **18** (6), 1015–23.

Geringer, J.M. and C.A. Frayne (2001), 'Collaborative research: turning potential frustrations into rewarding opportunities', in B. Toyne, Z.L. Martinez and R.A. Menger (eds), *International Business Scholarship*, Westport, CT: Quorum, pp. 117–34.

Goodyear, M. (1982), 'Qualitative research in developing countries', *Journal of the Market Research Society*, **24** (2), 86–96.

Graham, J.L. and K. Grønhaug (1989), 'Ned Hall didn't have to get a haircut', *Journal of Higher Education*, **60** (2), 152–87.

Guba, E.G. and Y.S. Lincoln (1994), 'Competing paradigms in qualitative research', in N.K. Denzin and Y.S. Lincoln (eds), *Handbook of Qualitative Research*, Thousand Oaks, CA: Sage, pp. 105–17.

Gubrium, J.F. and J.A. Holstein (2002), 'From the individual interview to the interview society', in J.F. Gubrium and J.A. Holstein (eds), *Handbook of Interview Research: Context and Method*, Thousand Oaks, CA: Sage, pp. 3–32.

Gummesson, E. (1991), *Qualitative Methods in Management Research*, Newbury Park, CA: Sage.

Hammersley, M. (1992), *What's Wrong with Ethnography?*, London: Routledge.

Harari, O. and D. Beaty (1990), 'On the folly of relying solely on a questionnaire methodology in cross-cultural research', *Journal of Managerial Issues*, **2** (4), 267–81.

Hofmeyr, K., A. Templer and D. Beaty (1994), 'South Africa: researching contrasts and contradictions in a context of change', *International Studies of Management and Organization*, **24** (1–2), 190–208.

House, R.J. (1998), 'A brief history of GLOBE', *Journal of Managerial Psychology*, **13** (3–4), 230–40.

Johanson, J. and J.-E. Vahlne (1977), 'The internationalization process of the firm: a model of knowledge development and increasing foreign market commitments', *Journal of International Business Studies*, **8** (1), 23–32.

Kogut, B. (2001), 'Methodological contributions in international business and the direction of academic research activity', in A.M. Rugman and T.L. Brewer (eds), *The Oxford Handbook of International Business*, Oxford: Oxford University Press, pp. 785–817.

Koza, M.P. and J.-C. Thoenig (1995), 'Organizational theory at the crossroads: some reflections on European and United States approaches to organizational research', *Organization Science*, **6** (1), 1–8.

Lawrence, P. (1988), 'In another country', in A. Bryman (ed.), *Doing Research in Organizations*, London: Routledge, pp. 96–107.

Lincoln, Y.S. and E.G. Guba (1985), *Naturalistic Inquiry*, Beverly Hills, CA: Sage.

——— (2000), 'Paradigmatic controversies, contradictions, and emerging confluences', in N.K. Denzin and Y.S. Lincoln (eds), *Handbook of Qualitative Research*, 2nd edn, Thousand Oaks, CA: Sage, pp. 163–88.

McDonald, M.H.B. (1985), 'Methodological problems associated with qualitative research: some observations and a case analysis of international marketing planning', *International Studies of Management and Organization*, **15** (2), 19–40.

Mendenhall, M., D. Beaty and G.R. Oddou (1993), 'Where have all the theorists gone? An archival review of the international management literature', *International Journal of Management*, **10** (2), 146–53.

Mezias, S.J., Y.-R. Chen and P. Murphy (1999), 'Toto, I don't think we're in Kansas anymore: some footnotes to cross-cultural research', *Journal of Management Inquiry*, **8** (3), 323–33.

Michailova, S. and K. Liuhto (2000), 'Organization and management research in transition economies: towards improved research methodologies', *Journal of East–West Business*, **6** (3), 7–46.

Miles, M. and A.M. Huberman (1994), *Qualitative Data Analysis: An Expanded Sourcebook*, Beverly Hills, CA: Sage.

Milliman, J. and M.A. von Glinow (1998), 'Research and publishing issues in large scale cross-national studies', *Journal of Managerial Psychology*, **13** (3–4), 137–42.

Nason, S.W. and M.M. Pillutla (1998), 'Towards a model of international research teams', *Journal of Managerial Psychology*, **13** (3–4), 156–66.

Osland, J. and A. Osland (2001), 'International qualitative research: an effective way to generate and verify cross-cultural theories', in B. Toyne, Z.L. Martinez and R.A. Menger (eds), *International Business Scholarship*, Westport, CT: Quorum, pp. 198–214.

Parkhe, A. (1993), '"Messy" research, methodological predispositions, and theory development in international joint ventures', *Academy of Management Review*, **18**

(2), 227–68.

Peng, T.K., M.F. Peterson and Y.-P. Shyi (1991), 'Quantitative methods in cross-national management research: trends and equivalence issues', *Journal of Organizational Behavior*, **12** (2), 87–107.

Peterson, M.F. (2001), 'International collaboration in organizational behavior research', *Journal of Organizational Behavior*, **22**, 59–81.

Pierce, B. and G. Garven (1995), 'Publishing international business research: a survey of leading journals', *Journal of International Business Studies*, **26** (1), 69–89.

Prasad, A. and P. Prasad (2002), 'The coming of age of interpretive organizational research', *Organizational Research Methods*, **5** (1), 4–11.

Prasad, P. (2003, forthcoming), *Crafting Qualitative Research: Working in the Post-Positivist Traditions*, New York: M.E. Sharpe.

Punnett, B.J. and O. Shenkar (1994a), 'International management research: toward a contingency approach', *Advances in International Comparative Management*, **9**, Greenwich, CT: JAI Press, 39–55.

——— (1994b), 'Preface: broadening research horizons internationally', *International Studies of Management and Organization*, **24** (1–2), 3–8.

Redding, G.S. (1994), 'Comparative management theory: jungle, zoo or fossil bed?', *Organization Studies*, **5** (3), 323–59.

Ryen, A. (2002), 'Cross-cultural interviewing', in J.F. Gubrium and J.A. Holstein (eds), *Handbook of Interview Research: Context and Method*, Thousand Oaks, CA: Sage, pp. 335–53.

Schaffer, B.S. and C.M. Riordan (2003), 'A review of cross-cultural methodologies for organizational research: a best-practices approach', *Organizational Research Methods*, **6** (2), 169–215.

Schwandt, T.A. (2001), *Dictionary of Qualitative Inquiry*, 2nd edn, Thousand Oaks, CA: Sage.

Seale, C. (1999), *The Quality of Qualitative Research*, London: Sage.

Shenkar, O. (1994), 'The People's Republic of China: raising the bamboo screen through international management research', *International Studies of Management and Organization*, **24** (1–2), 9–34.

Shenkar, O. and M.A. von Glinow (1994), 'Paradoxes of organizational theory and research: using the case of China to illustrate national contingency', *Management Science*, **40** (1), 56–71.

Silverman, D. (2001), *Interpreting Qualitative Data: Methods for Analysing Talk, Text and Interaction*, 2nd edn, London: Sage.

Smith, J.K. and D.K. Deemer (2000), 'The problem of criteria in the age of relativism', in N.K. Denzin and Y.S. Lincoln (eds), *Handbook of Qualitative Research*, 2nd edn, Thousand Oaks, CA: Sage, pp. 877–96.

Søderberg, A.-M. and E. Vaara (2003), 'Theoretical and methodological considerations', in A.-M. Søderberg and E. Vaara (eds), *Merging across Borders: People, Cultures and Politics*, Copenhagen: Copenhagen Business School Press, pp. 19–48.

Steers, R.M., S.J. Bischoff and L.H. Higgins (1992), 'Cross-cultural management research: the fish and the fisherman', *Journal of Management Inquiry*, **1** (4), 321–30.

Teagarden, M.B. (1998), 'Unbundling the intellectual joint venture process: the case of multinational, multifunctional interdisciplinary research consortia', *Journal of*

Managerial Psychology, **13** (3–4), 178–87.

Teagarden, M.B., M.A. Von Glinow, D.L. Bowen, C.A. Frayne, S. Nason, Y.P. Huo, J. Milliman, M.E. Arias, M.C. Butler, J.M. Geringer, N.H. Kim, H. Scullion, K.B. Lowe and E.A. Drost (1995), 'Toward a theory of comparative management research: an ideographic case study of the best international human resource management project', *Academy of Management Journal*, **38** (5), 1261–87.

Thomas, A.S. (1996), 'A call for research in forgotten locations', in B.J. Punnett and O. Shenkar (eds), *Handbook for International Management Research*, Cambridge, MA: Blackwell, pp. 485–505.

Thomas, A.S., O. Shenkar and L. Clarke (1994), 'The globalization of our mental maps: evaluating the geographic scope of *JIBS* coverage', *Journal of International Business Studies*, **25** (4), 675–86.

Tsang, E.W. (1998), 'Mind your identity when conducting cross-national research', *Organization Studies*, **19** (3), 511–15.

Turati, C., A. Usai and R. Ravagnani (1998), 'Antecedents of coordination in academic international project research', *Journal of Managerial Psychology*, **13** (3–4), 188–98.

Usunier, J.-C. (1998), *International and Cross-Cultural Management Research*, London: Sage.

Van Maanen, J. (1983), 'Reclaiming qualitative methods for organizational research: a preface', in J. Van Maanen (ed.), *Qualitative Methodology*, Beverly Hills, CA: Sage, pp. 9–18.

Vernon, R. (1994), 'Research on transnational corporations: shedding old paradigms', *Transnational Corporations*, **3** (1), 137–56.

Welch, C., R. Marschan-Piekkari, H. Penttinen and M. Tahvanainen (2002), 'Corporate elites as informants in qualitative international business research', *International Business Review*, **11** (5), 611–28.

Werner, S. (2002), 'Recent developments in international management research: a review of 20 top management journals', *Journal of Management*, **28** (3), 277–305.

White, S. (2002), 'Rigor and relevance in Asian management research: where are we and where can we go?', *Asia Pacific Journal of Management*, **19**, 287–352.

Wright, L.L. (1996), 'Qualitative international management research', in B.J. Punnett and O. Shenkar (eds), *Handbook for International Management Research*, Cambridge, MA: Blackwell, pp. 63–81.

Wright, L.L., H.W. Lane and P.W. Beamish (1988), 'International management research: lessons from the field', *International Studies of Management and Organization*, **18** (3), 55–71.

Yeung, H.W.-C. (1995), 'Qualitative personal interviews in international business research: some lessons from a study of Hong Kong transnational corporations', *International Business Review*, **4** (3), 313–39.

Yin, R. (1994), *Case Study Research: Design and Methods*, 2nd edn, Beverly Hills, CA: Sage.

2. Empirical Research in International Management: A Critique and Future Agenda

Richard B. Peterson

INTRODUCTION

Having entered academia in the mid-1960s, I have a fairly strong sense of most of the postwar research in the broad field of international management. I define international management as encompassing the sub-areas of international strategy, human resource management (HRM), organisational behaviour, ethics, industrial relations, and international joint ventures (IJVs). Thus, we preclude those areas more commonly falling under the area of international business or other functional areas than management. A given study may be limited to a country other than the home country of the researcher (for example, a study of German codetermination carried out by a British researcher), or comparative international (for example, a study including Japanese, American and British samples).

Based on a review and critique of international management research published in three major North American journals over a ten-year period, it leads me to argue the merits of larger-scale research carried out by teams of cross-national researchers using both qualitative and quantitative research methods over time. In the past 30 years quantitative methods have dominated the field of international management. I would argue that the inclusion of qualitative methods such as interviews, ethnography and grounded theory would add to our understanding of international management, while also being a cross-validation of our quantitative insights.

This chapter is written from a North American perspective, from which international management includes two sets of empirical research. The first compares two or more countries which may have included the United States or not. I refer to them as comparative, cross-cultural studies. The second, smaller number of studies is limited to one country other than the United States or Canada. I refer to them as international, non-comparative research.

More specifically, I reviewed all empirical research articles published by the *Journal of International Business Studies, Academy of Management Journal* and *Administrative Science Quarterly* from 1990 through 1999. The first journal is the top-rated journal in the areas of international business and international management. The second and third journals rank within the top three academic journals in the broader area of management. I do not include the third one, the *Academy of Management Review*, because it does not publish empirical research articles.

My review and critique of the empirical research in international management is followed by a discussion of a few multi-year, multi-member research teams that provided more insights about their subject over a much greater range of countries than we typically find in most of the recently published empirical research. Next, I look at some of my own research in international management in which I share how a particular body of research would have benefited from pilot interviews and insights gained by using qualitative methods. Finally, I lay out an agenda for future international management research that would allow both academics and practitioners to gain more in-depth insights into the phenomena that we study. I believe that the field of international management would gain greater exposure and stature by doing so.

REVIEW OF RECENT INTERNATIONAL MANAGEMENT RESEARCH

I included three, rather than one, academic journals in order to gain a broader perspective of the type of studies published on international management. It is possible that the journal editors would favour some types of empirical studies more than others. During this ten-year period one found multiple editors responsible for each of the three journals I reviewed and critiqued. One might ask why we did not include such journals as *Management International Review*, the *Journal of World Business*, or the now renamed *Thunderbird International Business Review*. The first journal is published outside North America. The other journals have reached out both to academics and international management practitioners so their articles are focused on a broader audience.

I have reviewed a total of 124 articles using a coding of number of authors, number of countries, sample and methods. By doing so, it provides some common yardsticks for evaluating and comparing across the various studies and journals. These measures give us insight into how international this sample of international management research is, and how diverse its methods.

Journal of International Business Studies

Table 2A.1 (see appendix) identifies those empirical studies published in the *Journal of International Business Studies* (*JIBS*) from 1990 through 1999. The time period covers three editorships and an expanding number of editorial board members and *ad hoc* reviewers. During this period 78 empirical studies were published in the area of international management. This represents approximately one-quarter of all articles and notes published by *JIBS* in those years.

Approximately 70 per cent of the empirical articles on international management had only one or two authors. An additional 20 articles had three authors. Only four of the studies had four or more authors. In many cases, it appears that the authors were associated with North American universities, or had done their doctoral work there, even if they may have grown up in a country outside North America.

Table 2A.1 also shows the number of countries represented in the 78 empirical studies. More than one-third of the studies were limited to one or two countries (N = 30). In the case of three studies, results were reported from American samples, in addition to samples from a non-North American country. An additional 11 studies included three or four countries. Thirty-two of the studies were defined as using five or more countries, but in many cases the researchers were studying American expatriates elsewhere or Western European expatriates in the USA. However, there was little or no breakdown analyses for the American expatriates assigned to the given Western European countries, or for the particular expatriates from a given Western European country in the USA. Where native managerial and/or employee samples were used, they varied considerably in numbers across the chosen countries.

The overwhelming number of studies were limited to three countries. They were the United States (N = 49), Japan (N = 16), and China (N = 13). Not uncommonly, the American sample was matched with one of the two Asian countries in the same study. Representation from the larger Western European nations would have been higher, had the authors specified the countries chosen, rather than mention that they included a set of Western European or European countries.

The three most common sub-areas covered were international HRM/expatriates (N = 29), cross-cultural management (N = 21), and international strategy (N = 16). With the exception of international joint venture research, no other topic or sub-area was covered in at least ten studies.

Over two-thirds (N = 54) of the *JIBS* studies used surveys developed by themselves or other researchers as the primary or only method of collecting the data.[1] Ten of the studies used data sets published by various governmental agencies in the United States and abroad; while another five used scenarios, laboratory simulations, event analyses or observation. Only seven of the 78 empirical studies used qualitative methods. Of this number, three studies each relied on interviews and case studies.

Academy of Management Journal

I was able to identify 30 empirical articles on international management published by the *Academy of Management Journal* (*AMJ*) during the same 1990–99 period (Table 2A.2 in the appendix). This ten-year period covered four separate editorships. Twenty-one of the studies published in *AMJ* during those years were sole (N = 5) or dual-authored (N = 16). Only two of the international management articles had more than four authors. In both cases, the authors were drawn from a large group of countries. However, one of the articles was an interim report on the state of their cross-national study. Almost two-thirds of the studies were confined to sample data from one (N = 11) or two (N = 8) countries. The samples included college students, employees, managers, organisations, firms or sub-firms.

The two most common research methods employed analysis of records/data and surveys/questionnaires. However, compared to the articles in *JIBS*, a wider number of research designs/methods were employed. Some of them included scenarios, quasi-experimental designs, event studies, role-playing exercises, grounded theory, panel data, causal maps and simulations. However, only four articles reported using two or more research methods.

Administrative Science Quarterly

The final journal I reviewed was *Administrative Science Quarterly* (*ASQ*). *ASQ* tends, on the whole, to publish articles focusing on organisations, companies, and sub-units, rather than individual employees, managers, or college students. I uncovered 16 articles that fall under the category of international management. This is an impressive number, in light of the fact that the average number of articles per issue falls somewhere between five and six.

Table 2A.3 (see appendix) reports all empirical articles on international management topics using the same summary format. Once again, almost two-thirds of the articles were authored by one (N = 6) or two (N = 4) people. Only two articles had four or five authors. If we look at the number of countries represented by the data, all but three of the studies used one (N = 11) or two (N = 2) nations. The samples were diverse, but usually the respondents represented parts or all segments of an organisation or company. Finally, the interview and data record analyses were the most often mentioned methods. Only one study used three or more research methods (archival data, interviews, observation, and survey).

Critique of International Management Studies

What conclusions can we draw from our review of these 125 empirical research studies? The most impressive conclusion is that a growing number of articles in *AMJ* and *ASQ* focus on countries other than the United States when compared to earlier years. This is even truer for the 1995–99 period, when compared to the first five years of the 1990s.

However, there are problems connected with exposure to international management topics or issues across all three academic journals. The first set of issues is related to the choice of within-country samples. Many of the studies use convenience samples from within one or more countries that cannot be considered as representative of their national sample. For example, the sample population may have been limited to managers and/or employees of a small number of companies or industries in the given country. Almost all of the studies used college students or employees and managers (for example, Abramson et al. 1993; Dawar et al. 1996; Francis 1991; Mueller and Clark 1998) as a sample. Where student samples were used, they were drawn from one or two universities in a particular location in the one or two countries. Where employees or manager samples are used, the sample does not represent sampling by industry, size of employer, and so forth. Moreover, these studies report results based on a relatively small number of respondents located in a given part of the national samples used. That makes any national generalisation questionable.

Second, 60 of the 125 articles reported data from only one or two nations. Those research studies limited to one country are not too unlike a study limited to the United States. If two countries are used, it is comparative in nature, but one country may be much larger and more diverse than the other (for example, Johansson et al.'s 1994 study in *JIBS* comparing data from Russia and Belarus). This may be a problem because of the very different circumstances facing the two countries. Where a number of European countries are included in the sample population, the analysis is not necessarily broken down by nation or culturally similar nations (for example, Allen and Pantzalis 1996; Hannon et al. 1995; Kim and Mauborgne 1993; Oliver and Craven 1999).

Third, there are only one or two authors in the case of 82 of the 125 published articles (approximately 66 per cent). In many cases the author(s) are from only one country – typically the United States. Even when more than one country is represented (for example, China and the USA), one or more of the authors may have taken their doctoral studies in North America.

Fourth, one rarely finds any detailed treatment of the cross-cultural literature as a prelude to why the researchers expected that their results for one country (say the Netherlands) should be different from another (say Denmark). In addition, little is said about how different political or economic systems may lead to cross-national differences.

Finally, we note that the overwhelming number of studies published in *JIBS*, *AMJ* and *ASQ* confine themselves to using only one research method, most commonly surveys or research questionnaires, followed by public documentation like government reports. This means, in many cases, that they relied on surveys or research instruments to tell the story without collaboration by another method such as interviews, observation, or a quasi-experimental model, for instance. Furthermore, the most common statistical analyses were correlations and regressions. Thus the authors rarely could support causal relationships between their independent and dependent variables, nor could they gain additional independent insights that might explain the statistically significant findings, or go beyond the survey analysis to better understand the phenomena.

The field of international management has progressed well beyond the stage it was when Roberts and Graham (1972) came down hard on the field based on their thorough review of the then existing research. They found that many of the studies they reviewed lacked any theoretical framework; did not include any insightful discussion of the national or business culture in the country or comparative countries that might explain cross-national differences in the study results; and often depended upon convenience samples that were not really representative of the broader managerial or employee universe in the country or countries used. We are more likely to test theories, use hypothesis testing, and employ more sophisticated statistics than Anovas and *t* tests, but we still have a fair way to go if academic research is to accomplish some or all of the following aims: (1) identifying theories that provide both commonalities and differences in employee/managerial behaviour across national contexts; (2) providing an adequate sample within and across countries to provide comfort that we feel justified in stating our results; (3) obtaining more insights than we would have if we only used one research method. More will be said about this later in this chapter.

MODELS OF INTERNATIONAL MANAGEMENT RESEARCH: A RETROSPECTIVE VIEW

There are several past studies that provide examples of the type of research that offers more to the reader in terms of insights. Perhaps the largest and longest team research project was carried out by Kerr, Dunlop, Harbison and Myers and their colleagues in the 1950s and early 1960s. Their research on industrialism and the industrialisation process was originally funded by the

Ford Foundation. The researchers sought to show how the industrialisation process impacted workers, unions, management, and governments in developed, developing, and underdeveloped countries. Three major books were published by the key research team (Dunlop 1958; Harbison and Myers 1959; Kerr et al. 1964) and 30 additional books were written by other academics (for example, Ehrman 1957; McGivering et al. 1960). Over 40 articles were published related to the same project.

Most of this research was descriptive in nature, but it provided academics in our field with a solid understanding of the diversity of management systems both within the industrialised and developing world at that time. Many of the authors spent considerable time conducting interviews with managers, union officials and governmental officials in the given country. While the key assumptions of the research team members regarding the economic imperatives of the industrialising process were not supported over time, the study provided a real understanding of the dynamics of economic development in the early postwar period (Dunlop et al. 1975). What these studies provided academics at the time was the sense of diversity in how managers varied in terms of background, managerial values, and the relationship between managers, union officials, employees and workers, and government officials. Their findings provided an important basis for the field of comparative management, and the role of both industrialisation and national culture in explaining both similarities and variation across countries.

The second major project focused on the theme of industrial democracy. The multi-member research team was headed by Bernhardt Wilpert. Their cross-national research team in the 1960s and 1970s studied the varying nature of participation schemes in nine countries including the United States, various Western European countries, as well as Yugoslavia. The team members were natives of the country they studied. The research team met on a regular basis to compare their findings. Books and articles were written based on the insights the researchers gained through surveys, interviews, observation, and reviews of the literature. Considerable divergence was found in how each nation implemented its own model of industrial democracy.

What was shared across these two sets of studies? The various researchers shared a common theme in terms of what they were studying, the methods that would be used, and, in most cases, a common set of variables to be studied. This differentiates them from almost all narrower studies of a given comparative management nature, which use different samples, variables, and often surveys and research instruments themselves. The studies represented major contributions to the fields of international management, as well as the broader area of management itself.

The Use of Qualitative Methods in My Own Research

My review of international management published in the *JIBS*, *AMJ* and *ASQ* provides a sense of where our research is currently. Now let me share with the reader some insights I have gained from looking back at my own research in the international management field over 30 plus years. I have chosen to share my experience in doing research in international management that encompassed the use of qualitative research methods alone, in tandem with quantitative methods, or where the use of qualitative research methods would have proven useful. Not surprisingly, I learned a great deal in retrospect of what I would have done differently had I started the particular research project again.

I chose as my dissertation subject the topic of managerial rights in Swedish collective bargaining that I would define as international management research. The field research involved over 40 interviews with union and employer officials at the confederation and federation levels, as well as reading the key labour court decisions involving managerial rights. The interviews allowed me to check for consistency of answers within side (union or management), as well as across side (union versus employer). Surveys were ruled out early in the proposal development stage.

Gaining insights from Swedish Labour Court decisions proved more difficult. While I had taken two years of Swedish at the University of Wisconsin, I found that literal translation of the court cases was not particularly helpful. Fortunately, the then Director of Labour Law for the Swedish Employers' Confederation, and a long-time friend over the years, was able to critique my translation and give me the key findings in the particular cases because of his excellent command of both Swedish and English (see Peterson 1968).

My first excursion into international research as a faculty member was a survey sent out to the president, managing director, or chief executive officer of larger corporations located in Western Europe, Latin America, Japan and the United States (Peterson 1971). Having no money to do interviews with such people beforehand (a pilot study), I was naive to expect a high response rate. While I had read much of the international culture literature ahead of time, my analysis was limited to F tests run on their answers to individual statements. Not a very sophisticated way of studying such phenomena.

Next, while teaching in Norway during the 1971–72 academic year, I undertook two survey-based studies (one of which was eventually published as Peterson 1975). In both cases, the survey was written in the language of the respondent, but no back translation was carried out by an independent person. While I had a large number of respondents in both surveys, I suspect that I might have gained further insights had the surveys been supplemented with interviews.

Upon my return to the United States, I began to make contacts with officials of the Washington Education Association, as well as their national counterparts in Sweden, to gain their support for a survey study of teacher viewpoints of professionalism, job satisfaction and collective bargaining when compared to that of school principals in the two countries (for example, Peterson 1976). We had usable responses from 1054 teachers and principals for a response rate of 48 per cent. Not surprisingly, we had many significant differences between teachers in the two countries, as well as between teachers and principals in the same country. What did I learn? I was aware of the cross-sectional nature of the study, and the questionable matching of teachers in one state (USA) with a national sampling of teachers in Sweden. I know that follow-up interviews would have proven more insightful in trying to understand the results. I gave a report to all of the interested parties, but never had the money to explore our results deeper with the sample of interviewees in each of the four sample populations.

Another study in the 1970s (Peterson and Schwind 1977) involved a comparative study of personnel problems in international companies and joint ventures in Japan. I am rather proud of this early study of HRM, in large part because Hermann Schwind, an MBA student at the University of Washington at the time, had received a General Electric grant to live and study in Japan for six months. Thus, unlike some of my earlier studies reported above, we had an academic researcher on site to conduct interviews with both expatriates, third-country nationals, and native Japanese regarding their 'reading' of personnel problems encountered by American, Western European and Japanese managers in such subsidiaries and joint ventures in Japan. The interviews were supplemented by surveys (in English). Because of lack of money, as well as the variety of Western European expatriates and third-country nationals, it was not possible to interview each person in his or her native language. However, we could compare and contrast the responses by research method and nationality. Not surprisingly, we found that the nature of the personnel problems varied by whom one interviewed or surveyed. Unfortunately, it was cross-sectional, rather than longitudinal, so we have no way of knowing whether the problems were reduced or not over time.

A study was conducted by three of us (Peterson et al. 1988) approximately ten years later with a group of Japanese students attending a long-term management course in Japan, as well as a sample of alumni of the training centre. The strength of the study was related to the chance to compare results between younger and somewhat older employees and managers. However, it was a survey without complementary interviewing to dig deeper into the reasons the respondents gave for their particular answers on the scale. Had we been able to do in-depth interviews with the students and alumni, no doubt we could feel more confident of the results. In addition, we could answer more 'whys'.

Perhaps the most comprehensive field study that I have participated in over my career dealt with expatriate management. Four of us were involved in different phases of the project covering the years 1991–94 in the field (Peterson et al. 1996b). We began by testing the link between corporate expatriate policies, internationalisation, and four measures of firm performance in 150 of the largest multinationals in the world as of 1991 using the survey method. While we did find a number of significant results, not unexpectedly, we also found that such corporate-level expatriate policies could only explain a small variance in our four measures of firm performance.

Since that initial study, we decided to go deeper into the subject by contacting and interviewing one or more corporate international HRM officials in 29 Japanese, German, British and American multinational corporations (MNCs) (Peterson et al. 1996a). We found that we could differentiate between the MNC corporate policies and practices regarding expatriates of the American and British multinationals (fairly similar) and those of their German and Japanese counterparts on a number of issues. Furthermore, there were distinctive features between the German and Japanese multinationals.

Our most recent publication (Peterson et al. 2000) compared the 29 corporate-level international HRM (IHRM) interviewees and interviewees in 56 foreign subsidiaries and joint ventures in Western Europe, the United States, Japan, South East Asia and Latin America. While there were similarities between what we were told by corporate-level officials and those in their foreign operations, there were also differences conveyed between the two levels of the particular multinational. I doubt that we could ever have had the deeper insights we gained through the interview process, had we tried to use surveys instead. In some parts of the world we gained entrance through the personal contact that likely would have been missing had we relied on surveys. Moreover, the interview guide questions did not lend themselves to the respondent answering a survey on a Likert-type scale. I suspect that we have a better, and deeper, understanding of the expatriation and repatriation process now than by relying only on surveys. However, even this study suffered from being cross-sectional, rather than longitudinal over the three-year field research.

Speaking for myself, I much prefer to meet my respondent face to face, rather than rely on statistical analyses of a large number of surveys and questionnaires. The nature of the semi-structured interview (in some cases as a pilot test, in others a follow-up to a survey) allows the researchers to ask each interviewee essentially the same set of questions, but also allows the interviewee to share insights on topics or issues that would never come up using only surveys. Often a sense of friendship and trust emerges during the interview process. This feeling is mutual, as I found recently in a study on American and Western MNCs in the Czech Republic (Peterson 2003). After completing my interviews in the Czech Republic, my attempt to add more firms by mailing a survey to 20 additional MNC operations resulted in a zero response rate. Clearly, the key persons preferred a face-to-face encounter to a non-personal survey mailed to them.

A PROPOSED MODEL FOR FUTURE INTERNATIONAL MANAGEMENT RESEARCH

In this section I identify the major elements that would move the field of international (and comparative) management ahead in terms of our contributions to fellow academics, policy-makers, and management practitioners in the private, non-profit, and public sectors across national borders. I also believe that such efforts would encourage higher participation rates by organisations willing to commit to such longitudinal studies. I use expatriate management as a research topic to illustrate how these elements can be implemented because of our recent work in that field.

It should be noted by the reader that the following proposal is not designed to replace the many research studies on various facets of international management that may have a more narrow focus because of the particular interests of the researcher(s). There is room for those types of studies that have a more limited focus and/or way of studying the particular topic. What I am advocating here is an approach to broader topics within the domain of international management, whether they be at the individual employee, work team, business unit, company/organisational level, or across industry level. If we are going to test meaningful theories in our field, it is almost imperative that most or all of these elements be incorporated into such research.

The first element includes focusing on broader research questions using larger sample populations across a number of countries over a period of at least 5–10 years in order to address the shortcomings of cross-sectional studies with narrow sample populations that permeate much of our management and international management research. By doing so, such research would come closer to the major studies in the 1950s through the 1970s discussed earlier in this chapter.

While there have been numerous studies of expatriate management in recent years, much of it has relied on the experience of American expatriates in a variety of foreign postings. The sample is usually drawn from a relatively small number of large American multinationals or convenience samples drawn from a wider swathe of American firms. Present research also fails to separate out the expatriation process used by such export-oriented countries as Switzerland, Sweden, Taiwan and South Korea. Our own research (Peterson et al. 1996a), if generalisable, shows that American and British multinationals have more in common, while their Japanese and German counterparts have crafted somewhat different models of expatriate management from the other three countries. This finding was only possible because we had a sufficient number of MNCs from all four countries.

Follow-up studies would provide us with some indication whether such multinationals maintain or change their corporate expatriate policies and programmes over time. For example, expatriation research in the 1960s through 1980s would not have captured the more recent move by some German multinationals to revise their expatriate compensation systems so that assignment to neighbouring European countries would no longer have all of the traditional perks.

The second element is that the sample would be drawn from the entire country, rather than a particular town or region (for example, major sections of Spain, as opposed to only Madrid, the Basque country, or Catalonia). Addressing this element is particularly important when including very large and diverse countries in the sample, where there may be very different responses based on the inclusion of only certain regional sampling within the larger nation.

The third element would be the use of cross-national research teams so that we could gain from the insights of those people knowledgeable about the culture, systems, literature and personal contacts in their own country. As the situation is today, most researchers are located in one, or at best, two countries. This means that the overwhelming number of studies (for example, those done by Black et al. 1992) have relied on surveys mailed from the United States to American expatriates located in various areas of the world. Many expatriate studies have relied on English, limiting our knowledge of the experiences of other national expatriates. It is desirable to have a cross-national research group include expatriates from a variety of countries. That way each member of the research team could be responsible for issues regarding translation–back translation, making personal contacts with MNCs and international human resource associations to procure wider support for the study, and interviews with corporate IHRM staff in their own country. If expatriates are included, perhaps the same person could carry out a sample of interviews in the expatriate's native language. To be effective though, the research team needs to be active in the earliest stages so that the theories tested, samples used, and research methods chosen are collaborative in nature, rather than replicating a given study in one nation to the other nations represented by the research team members. Otherwise, the broader study of nations will better be defined as a series of domestic-based studies.

The fourth element is the periodic meeting of the cross-national research teams at national and international conferences. Even ten years ago this was not possible, but today one finds an increasing number of foreign attendees at the Academy of Management and Academy of International Business annual meetings. Furthermore, there are an increasing number of joint or regional meetings in Asia and Europe where the cross-national research team could meet to discuss and coordinate their individual contributions to the research project. E-mail and Internet access also make such cross-national collaboration easier than in the past.

One of the real benefits of such meetings would be the interchange among the group members based on their own particular insights on the expatriation process that go beyond the survey data. For example, we know that some multinationals are using fast-track executive potentials for expatriate assignment as part of their succession planning systems in Germany, while our Japanese set of MNCs showed no such use of expatriates (Peterson et al. 1996a).

The fifth element is that the research team can promise more to the companies when they ask for their participation than one typically finds in the published research in the international management field. For example, if the research team designs a comprehensive multi-stage or longitudinal study of IJVs, and can tell multinationals that they are surveying and interviewing a good cross-section of corporations engaged in IJVs from the major economies (for example, Britain, France, Germany, Switzerland, the USA, Japan and China with operations in other countries), the results are far more useful to the firms' executives than if only IJVs involving, say, Germany and Japan are used.

Similarly, if we look at expatriate management, it would seem far more useful to include the study of expatriation by breaking the sample down into expatriates assigned to, say, the United States, Japan, Germany, China, as well as analyses based on whether the receiving country is defined as a first-, second-, or third-world economy. Expatriates sent to Bangladesh are likely to have a far different experience than if they were assigned to Austria, for example.

A sixth element would include the use of standardised surveys or research instruments. Expatriate research, like research in many other fields, has relied on each researcher preparing his or her own survey so that it is next to impossible to compare the results of one study with others. We would encourage members of the research team to begin their project by interviews with knowledgeable people using a standardised interview guide as a preliminary step to designing the questionnaire in order to cover as many national nuances as possible. Then the research team will develop a common instrument that is supplemented by a set of extra questions or statements that encompass particular nuances in a given country covered or satisfy the needs of the multinational companies in their country as a means of enticing their support and higher response rate.

Having participated in multi-stage research projects since the early 1990s (Peterson et al. 1996a, 1996b, 2000), we have learned a great deal more in retrospect. Our research instruments would have covered more topics in a more structured way had we conducted interviews preceding our preparation of the survey and interview guideline.

Finally, the seventh element, and the most important one, is that the cross-national research team would benefit from the use of multiple research methods. We have already shown how the vast majority of recent research studies in international management have relied on only one research method: namely, surveys and previously developed research instruments.

The review and critique has made it abundantly clear that we need more, and different, methods to more thoroughly understand the phenomenon of interest. As this volume attests, there are a broad array of qualitative research methods to employ, including in-depth case studies, grounded theory, ethnography, simulations, event studies and interviews from which to choose. As it is now, surveys allow us only to provide associational relationships between independent and dependent variables. By using surveys exclusively, we have no way of cross-validating the results by an independent research method. Well-constructed interview guidelines could provide benefits such as: interview insights that help in the preparation of the field survey; new or different insights that emerge from post-survey interviews that help to explain the meaning of the data at a deeper level than otherwise; and finally, a way of cross-validating the survey results to determine if the statistical associations are valid.

A real benefit to the individual members of the cross-national research team is the give and take that results when its members come together to share their results from a study that provides multiple sources of data input, as well as providing the possibility for national cultural differences to emerge than would be the case if the research relied only on survey feedback. Similar arguments could be made on behalf of the merits of ethnography, grounded theory and other qualitative research methods. Overall, we learn much more by using a multi-method approach that usually becomes too costly if the researchers cannot rely on in-country members who can be there to translate the survey into the native language, make contacts with international companies, and use interviews or other research methods.

Are such cross-national teams possible? I am convinced that they are or can be. A colleague who is presently the editor of *AMJ* notes that the journal is receiving a growing number of papers submitted by cross-national research teams, and that the quality of some of these papers is quite high. The reader may raise doubts based on the likely delays when perhaps 5–10 researchers are involved. That can be a problem, but can be overcome or minimised by clear understandings of responsibilities ahead of time. Translation of research instruments in-country would likely make this stage shorter than if the same researcher had full responsibility for finding translators and back translators for multiple language copies. Authorship could be resolved by means of assigning one person to be the research manager and thus first author, or in the case of multiple articles and books emerging from the project, first authorship could be shared among the researchers. Finally, each national member of the research team would have ownership of their own national data if they wished to report their data separately too.

If more of our published research could incorporate most, or all of the seven elements into our design, researchers, corporate executives and managers, and their staff could all gain in a way that would enhance our findings, conclusions and implications for policy and practice, while reducing the limitations of our present research.

SUMMARY

I have reviewed and critiqued all the 124 empirical articles on international management published by the *Journal of International Business Studies*, the *Academy of Management Journal*, and *Administrative Science Quarterly* over a full ten-year period. I then spelled out some of the deficiencies in the present state of international management research. This was followed by analysis of several past studies in the field (including my own) that helped to identify the seven elements in a proposal for more significant research in the coming years.

This proposal does not exclude the continued publication of the narrower, cross-sectional studies, that most, if not all, of us have undertaken in the past. Rather, our proposal advocates complementarity by journal editors encouraging academics in the international management field to form such cross-national research teams that employ most, or all, of the elements spelled out earlier in this chapter.

I believe that this strategy provides a win–win situation for its participants, journal editors and practitioners in the field of international management. Why? The members of the research team gain by: combining their efforts; gaining greater insights; and increasing the likelihood of their papers and books being published. Journal editors that include articles on international management can report broader studies in terms of topic covered, countries included, time covered and multiple research methods employed. The field of international management, as well as the Academy of Management and Academy of International Business, will gain to the degree that our colleagues see our research contributions as important, and our field of increasing value.

Finally, executives and managers in the larger multinational corporations will see more opportunity to gain valuable information from our studies because of the wider national and organisational population samples used, methodologies employed, and conclusions that can be drawn. Finally, follow-up studies by the same research team will provide us with longitudinal data that allows comparison and contrast with the initial study by the cross-national team.

The review of empirical research studies in *JIBS*, *AMJ* and *ASQ* was done in 2000. Perhaps subsequent issues of the three journals would show progress in terms of addressing previous shortcomings. Hence, I have reviewed all issues of the three journals for 2000, 2001 and through the middle of 2002. I have not reported them in table form, but certain conclusions can be made.

If we compare the review from 1990–99 with the most recent period, we find certain commonalities. The most recently published articles in the three management journals continued the earlier situation where: (1) most of the empirical studies were authored by one or two researchers; (2) the sample was drawn primarily from one or two countries; and (3) the studies relied primarily on surveys and questionnaires rather than qualitative research or a combination of research methods. It would seem, then, that the field of international management is ripe for change.

APPENDIX

Table 2A.1   International management articles published by JIBS,
1990–1999

Author(s)	Number of authors and countries		Sample	Method(s)
Abramson et al. (1993)	4	2	Canadian and Japanese MBA students	Research instrument
Agarwal (1993)	1	2	American and Indian salespersons	Research instrument
Agarwal et al. (1999)	3	2	American and Indian salespersons	Research instrument
Allen and Pantzalis (1996)	2	*	Foreign affiliates in the USA	Modelling through data
Bailey et al. (1997)	3	3	American MBA students Japanese and Chinese employees	Survey
Banai and Reisel (1993)	2	4	Expatriates in US, Dutch, and Israeli banks in the UK	Survey
Barkema and Vermeulen (1997)	2	1	Dutch MNCs with operations in 72 countries	Analysis of records
Beechler and Yang (1994)	2	2	Japanese subsidiary managers in the USA	Interviews, case studies
Bigoness and Blakely (1996)	2	12	Alumni of major Western European business program	Survey
Bird and Beechler (1995)	2	2	Personnel managers in Japanese subsidiaries in the USA	Survey
Birdseye and Hill (1995)	2	*	American expatriates	Survey
Birkinshaw and Morrison (1995)	2	6	President or managing director of foreign subsidiaries	Survey
Black and Gregersen (1991)	2	8	American expatriates	Survey
Black and Porter (1991)	2	2	US and Hong Kong expatriates located in other countries	Survey
Borkowski (1999)	1	5	Transnational corporations from USA, Japan, Canada, Germany and UK	Survey
Boyacigiller (1990)	1	*	Expatriates of US multinational bank	Survey
Brouthers and Bamossy (1997)	2	6	Key IJV stakeholders in Hungary and Romania	Interviews (case methods)
Cullen et al. (1995)	3	12	Japanese and local partners in IJVs	Survey
Dawar et al. (1996)	3	*	MBA students in European business school	Survey
Dyer and Song (1997)	2	2	US and Japanese managers	Research instrument
Feldman and Thomas (1992)	2	*	Expatriates in Saudi Arabia, Japan and other countries	Survey

Author(s)	Number of authors and countries		Sample	Method(s)
Feldman and Tompson (1993)	2	26	Alumni of an American graduate school of business	Survey
Francis (1991)	1	2	MBA students in USA and Korea	Scenarios
Geringer (1991)	1	*	Executives in Japanese and Western European IJVs of US-based firms	Survey
Geringer and Herbert (1991)	2	2	US and Canadian IJVs	Survey and follow-up interview
Gibson (1995)	1	4	Norwegian, Swedish, Australian and American employees	Research instrument
Gomez-Mejia and Palich (1997)	2	1	US Fortune 500 firms	Research instrument, survey
Graham et al. (1992)	3	2	Russian and US business negotiations	Laboratory
Gregersen et al. (1996)	3	1	US multinationals	Survey
Hannon et al. (1995)	3	*	Larger foreign subsidiaries in Taiwan	Survey
Harpaz (1990)	1	7	Employees by occupational level categories	Survey
Harvey (1993)	1	1	Members of American Society for Human Resources Management International	Survey
Harvey (1997)	1	*	Dual career expatriates	Survey
Hennart and Larimo (1998)	2	*	Foreign firm entries into the USA	Databases
Husted et al. (1996)	4	3	American, Spanish and Mexican MBAs	Survey
Johansson et al. (1994)	3	2	Russian and Belarus farmers	Interviews, surveys
Kim and Hwang (1992)	2	1	Senior-level officials of US MNCs	Survey
Kogut and Zander (1993)	2	1	Swedish companies	Survey
Langlois and Schlegelmilch (1990)	1	3	CEOs of large British, German, and French corporations	Survey of codes of ethics
Lin and Germain (1998)	2	2	US and Chinese IJV managers	Survey
Lubatkin et al. (1997)	3	2	Senegalese and Hungarian managers	Survey
Luthans et al. (1993)	3	1	Managers and their subordinates in a Russian firm	Observation
Makino and Beamish (1998)	2	*	Multiple partners IJVs between Japanese and foreign firms	Databases
Millington and Bayliss (1995)	2	*	IJVs involving EU nations	Survey, case studies

Author(s)	Number of authors and countries		Sample	Method(s)
Money and Graham (1999)	2	2	American and Japanese sales representatives	Survey
Morosini et al. (1998)	3	10	Firms engaged in cross-border acquisitions in Italy	Survey
Morris (1998)	10	4	American, Chinese, Filipino and Indian MBAs	Survey
Morris and Pavett (1992)	2	3	US maquilladoras in Mexico	Survey
Naumann (1993)	1	4	US expatriate managers in South Korea, Taiwan, Hong Kong and People's Republic of China	Survey
Newman and Nollen (1996)	2	18	A large US multinational in European and Asian countries	Surveys
Oliver and Cravens (1999)	2	*	Non-US firms operating in America	US government required form analysis
Pan (1996)	1	*	EJVs in China	Analysis of data sets
Pedersen and Thomsen (1997)	2	12	MNC executives	Database
Pillai et al. (1999)	3	6	MBA students and professionals in the USA, Australia, India, Columbia, Saudi Arabia, and Jordan	Survey
Pornpitakpan (1999)	1	3	American firms selling to Japanese and Thais	Experimental design
Ralston et al. (1993)	4	3	US, Hong Kong and Chinese managers	Survey
Ralston et al. (1997)	4	4	US, Russian, and Japanese managers	Survey
Ralston et al. (1999a)	5	1	Chinese managers and professionals in state-run enterprises	Research instrument
Ralston et al. (1999b)	3	1	North and South Vietnamese, South Chinese and Southwest Chinese, and US managers/professionals	Research instrument interviews
Rangan (1998)	1	9	Foreign affiliates of US MNCs, US affiliates of foreign MNCs	Databases
Rao and Hashimoto (1996)	2	2	Japanese expatriate managers in Canada	Survey
Reuber and Fischer (1997)	2	1	Founders or members of top management of Canadian software product firms	Survey
Rosenzweig and Nohria (1994)	2	*	MNC foreign affiliate managers in the USA	Survey
Roth and Morrison (1992)	2	6	President or managing director of foreign subsidiaries	Survey

Author(s)	Number of authors and countries		Sample	Method(s)
Roth et al. (1991)	3	1	President or CEO of business units	Survey
Sanyal (1990)	1	1	Foreign-owned firms in the USA	Government records
Sanyal and Neves (1992)	2	16	Foreign firms in the USA	Government data
Schlegelmilch and Robertson (1995)	2	4	Senior executives in the USA, UK, Germany, and Austria	Survey
Schuler and Rogovsky (1998)	2	12	Use of 3 previous international HRM research studies	Available data sets
Shaffer et al. (1999)	3	*	Expatriates of 10 large US MNCs	Survey
Shenkar and Zeira (1992)	2	1	IJVs in Israel	Surveys
Smith (1996)	3	3	Chinese, British, and American managers	Event analysis, research instrument
Soutar et al. (1999)	3	2	Japanese and Australian expatriates in the other country	Survey
Sullivan and Peterson (1991)	2	1	Japanese executives and human resource directors	Survey
Taggart (1997)	1	*	MNC subsidiary chief executives	Surveys
Townsend et al. (1990)	3	28	Companies in 41 manufacturing industries	Analysis of US government reports
Tse et al. (1994)	3	2	Chinese and Canadian executives	Experimental design scenario
Whitman et al. (1999)	3	9	Business school students in the USA, Europe, and Asia	Scenarios

Note: Number of countries marked as * indicates multiple but unspecified number.

Table 2A.2   *International management articles published by* AMJ, *1990–1999*

Author(s)	Number of authors and countries		Sample	Method(s)
Barkema and Vermeulen (1998)	2	1	Large Dutch non-financial firms	Analysis of Amsterdam stock exchange records
Barkema et al. (1997)	4	1	Large Dutch companies	Analysis of company annual reports
Brett and Okumura (1998)	2	2	American and Japanese managers	Simulated negotiations

Author(s)	Number of authors and countries		Sample	Method(s)
Chang (1995)	1	1	Japanese lines of business in the USA	Analysis of records
Chen (1995)	1	2	Employees in US and Chinese companies	Surveys, role playing exercises
Earley (1993)	1	3	Chinese, Israeli, and American managers	Field experimental design
Easterby-Smith and Malina (1999)	2	2	Chinese and UK employees	Demographic field study
Ezzamel and Watson (1998)	2	1	British non-financial companies	Analysis of Times 1000
Gregersen and Black (1992)	2	8	American expatriates	Surveys
Hundley et al. (1996)	3	2	American and Japanese companies	Panel data
Janssens et al. (1995)	3	3	Employees of an American MNC in USA, France, and Argentina	Survey
Jegers (1991)	1	1	Belgian companies	Analysis of financial records
Kim and Mauborgne (1993)	2	5	Managers and top managers in USA and 4 European countries	Surveys (2)
Kim et al. (1990)	3	3	American, Japanese and Korean college students	Scenarios
Markoczy (1997)	1	4	Hungarian, American, British, and Australian managers	Causal maps
Meznar et al. (1994)	3	1	American firms in South Africa	Event study
Meznar et al. (1998)	3	2	US firms operating in South Africa	Event studies
Mueller and Clarke (1998)	2	6	College students in USA, Croatia, Slovenia, Czech Republic, Romania and Poland	Research instrument
Ogden and Watson (1999)	2	1	British companies	Analysis of firms' financial data
Osborn and Baughn (1990)	2	2	Multinational alliances	Record data analysis
Park and Ungson (1997)	2	2	US–Japanese IJVs	Event history analysis
Peterson et al. (1995)	23	21	Middle managers	Surveys
Roth and O'Donnell (1996)	2	5	American, British, Canadian, Japanese, and German foreign subsidiaries	Surveys
Swan and Ettlie (1997)	2	1	Japanese firms investing in the USA	Analysis of secondary records

Author(s)	Number of authors and countries		Sample	Method(s)
Teagarden et al. (1995)	14	10	International companies	Demographic case studies, grounded theory
Welsh et al. (1993)	3	1	Workers in one part of a Russian firm	Experimental design
Wiersema and Bird (1993)	2	1	Executives in Japanese firms	Analysis of demographic and personnel records
Xin and Pearce (1996)	2	1	Chinese executives in one Chinese city	Interviews
Yan and Gray (1994)	2	2	Four manufacturing Chinese–US IJVs	Case study interventions, archival data
Zaheer (1995)	1	*	Trading rooms in New York and Tokyo stock exchanges	Surveys

Note: Number of Countries marked as * indicates multiple but unspecified number.

Table 2A.3   International management articles published by ASQ, *1990–1999*

Author(s)	Number of authors and countries		Sample	Method(s)
Allmendinger and Hackman (1996)	2	1	East German orchestras	Archival data, interviews, observation, surveys
Appold et al. (1998)	3	3	US and Japanese firms and domestic Thai companies	Surveys
Boisot and Child (1996)	2	1	Chinese	Conceptual
Earley (1994)	1	3	US, Chinese, and Hong Kong firms	Laboratory study, field experiment
Farh et al. (1997)	3	1	Chinese employees	Survey
Gerlach (1992)	1	1	Japanese firms	Data analysis
Gooderham et al. (1999)	3	6	European countries	Analysis of surveys
Hofstede et al. (1990)	4	2	Dutch and Danish organisation units	Interviews
Holm (1995)	1	1	Mandated sale organisation	Interviews analysis of records
Lazerson (1995)	1	1	Italian firms	Interviews, observations
Martin et al. (1998)	3	1	Japanese suppliers	Analysis of records

Author(s)	Number of authors and countries		Sample	Method(s)
Murnighan and Conlon (1991)	2	1	British music quartets	Interviews
Nelson (1993)	1	2	US and Brazilian church denominations	Analysis of records
Porac et al. (1995)	5	1	Scottish wool mills	Interviews, surveys
Simons and Ingram (1997)	2	1	Israeli kibbutzim	Analysis of records
Warhurst (1998)	1	1	Israeli kibbutzim	Ethnography

NOTE

1. I consider the use of the term 'survey' to apply to a questionnaire prepared by the author/researcher, while the term 'research instrument' applies to an already existing questionnaire (for example, Geert Hofstede).

REFERENCES

Abramson, N.R., H.W. Laine, H. Nagai and H. Takagi (1993), 'A comparison of Canadian and Japanese cognitive styles: implications for management interaction', *Journal of International Business Studies*, **24** (3), 575–87.

Agarwal, S. (1993), 'Influence of formalization on role stress, organizational commitment, and work alienation of salespersons', *Journal of International Business Studies*, **24** (4), 715–40.

Agarwal, S., T.E. De Carlo and S.B. Vyas (1999), 'Leadership behavior and organizational commitment: a comparative study of American and Indian salespersons', *Journal of International Business Studies*, **30** (4), 727–44.

Allen, L. and C. Pantzalis (1996), 'Valuation of the operating flexibility of multinational corporations', *Journal of International Business Studies*, **27** (4), 633–54.

Allmendinger, J. and J.R. Hackman (1996), 'Organizations in changing environments: the case of East German symphony orchestras', *Administrative Science Quarterly*, **41** (3), 337–69.

Appold, S.J., S. Siengthai and J.D. Kasarda (1998), 'The employment of woman managers and professionals in an emerging economy: gender inequality as an organizational practice', *Administrative Science Quarterly*, **43** (3), 538–65.

Bailey, J.R., C.C. Chen and S.G. Dou (1997), 'Conceptions of self and performance-related feedback in the U.S., Japan, and China', *Journal of International Business Studies*, **28** (3), 605–26.

Banai, M. and W.D. Reisel (1993), 'Expatriate managers' loyalty to the MNC: myth or reality? An exploratory study', *Journal of International Business Studies*, **24** (2), 233–48.

Barkema, H.G., O. Shenkar, F. Vermeulen and J.H.J. Bell (1997), 'Working abroad, working with others: how firms learn to operate international joint ventures', *Academy of Management Journal*, **40** (2), 426–42.

Barkema, H.G. and F. Vermeulen (1997), 'What differences in the cultural backgrounds of partners are detrimental for international joint ventures?', *Journal of International Business Studies*, **28** (4), 845–63.

——— (1998), 'International expansion through start-up acquisition: a learning perspective', *Academy of Management Journal*, **41** (1), 7–26.

Beechler, S. and J.Z. Yang (1994), 'The transfer of Japanese-style management to American subsidiaries: contingencies, constraints, and competencies', *Journal of International Business Studies*, **25** (3), 467–92.

Bigoness, W.J. and G.L. Blakely (1996), 'A cross-national study of management values', *Journal of International Business Studies*, **27** (4), 739–52.

Bird, A. and S. Beechler (1995), 'Links between business strategy and human resource management strategy in U.S.-based Japanese subsidiaries: an empirical investigation', *Journal of International Business Studies*, **26** (1), 23–46.

Birdseye, M.C. and J.S. Hill (1995), 'Individual, organizational/work and environmental influences on expatriate turnover tendencies: an empirical study', *Journal of International Business Studies*, **26** (4), 787–814.

Birkinshaw, J.M. and A.J. Morrison (1995), 'Configurations of strategy and structure in subsidiaries of multinational corporations', *Journal of International Business Studies*, **26** (4), 729–54.

Black, J.S. and H.B. Gregersen (1991), 'The other half of the picture: antecedents of spouse cross-cultural adjustment', *Journal of International Business Studies*, **22** (3), 461–78.

Black, J.S., H.B. Gregersen and M.E. Mendenhall (1992), 'Toward a theoretical framework of repatriate adjustment', *Journal of International Business Studies*, **23** (4), 737–60.

Black, J.S. and L.W. Porter (1991), 'Managerial behaviors and job performance: a successful manager in Los Angeles may not succeed in Hong Kong', *Journal of International Business Studies*, **22** (1), 99–114.

Boisot, M. and J. Child (1996), 'From fiefs to clans and network capitalism: explaining China's emerging economic order', *Administrative Science Quarterly*, **41** (4), 600–628.

Borkowski, S.C. (1999), 'International managerial performance evaluation: a five country comparison', *Journal of International Business Studies*, **30** (3), 533–56.

Boyacigiller, N. (1990), 'The role of expatriates in the management of interdependence, complexity, and risk in multinational corporations', *Journal of International Business Studies*, **21** (3), 357–81.

Brett, J.M. and T. Okumura (1998), 'Inter-and intracultural negotiations: U.S. and Japanese negotiators', *Academy of Management Journal*, **41** (5), 495–510.

Brouthers, K.D. and G.J. Bamossy (1997), 'The role of key stakeholders in international joint ventures negotiation: case studies from Eastern Europe', *Journal of International Business Studies*, **28** (2), 285–308.

Chang, S.J. (1995), 'International expansion strategy of Japanese firms: capability building through sequential entry', *Academy of Management Journal*, **38** (2), 383–407.

Chen, C.C. (1995), 'New trends in rewards allocation preferences: a Sino-U.S.

comparison', *Academy of Management Journal*, **38** (2), 408–27.

Cullen, J.B., J.L. Johnson and T. Sakano (1995), 'Japanese and local partner commitment to IJVs: psychological consequences of outcome and investments in the IJV relationship', *Journal of International Business Studies*, **26** (1), 91–116.

Dawar, N., P.M. Parker and L.J. Price (1996), 'A cross-cultural study of interpersonal information exchange', *Journal of International Business Studies*, **27** (3), 497–516.

Dunlop, J.T. (1958), *Industrial Relations Systems*, New York: Henry Holt.

Dunlop, J.T., F.H. Harbison, C. Kerr and C.A. Myers (1975), *Industrialism and Industrial Man Reconsidered*, Princeton, NJ: The Inter-University Study of Human Resources in National Development.

Dyer, B. and X.M. Song (1997), 'The impact of strategy on conflict: a cross-national comparative study of U.S. and Japanese firms', *Journal of International Business Studies*, **28** (3), 467–94.

Earley, P.C. (1993), 'East meets West meets Mideast: further explorations of collectivist and individualistic work groups', *Academy of Management Journal*, **36** (2), 319–48.

——— (1994), 'Self or group? Cultural effects of training on self-efficacy and performance', *Administrative Science Quarterly*, **39** (1), 89–117.

Easterby-Smith, M. and D. Malina (1999), 'Cross-cultural collaborative research: toward reflexivity', *Academy of Management Journal*, **41** (1), 76–86.

Ehrmann, H.W. (1957), *Organized Business in France*, Princeton, NJ: Princeton University Press.

Ezzamel, M. and R. Watson (1998), 'Market comparison earnings and the bidding-up of executive cash compensation: evidence from the United Kingdom', *Academy of Management Journal*, **41** (2), 221–31.

Farh, J.L., P.C. Earley and S.C. Lin (1997), 'Impetus for action: a cultural analysis of justice and organizational citizenship behavior in Chinese society', *Administrative Science Quarterly*, **42** (3), 421–44.

Feldman, D.C. and D.C. Thomas (1992), 'Career management issues facing expatriates', *Journal of International Business Studies*, **23** (2), 271–93.

Feldman, D.C. and H.B. Tompson (1993), 'Expatriation, repatriation, and domestic geographical location: an empirical investigation of adjustment to new job assignments', *Journal of International Business Studies*, **24** (3), 507–30.

Francis, J.N.P. (1991), 'When in Rome? The effects of cultural adaptation on intercultural business negotiations', *Journal of International Business Studies*, **22** (3), 403–26.

Geringer, J.M. (1991), 'Strategic determinants of partner selection criteria in international joint ventures', *Journal of International Business Studies*, **22** (1), 41–62.

Geringer, J.M. and L. Herbert (1991), 'Measuring performance of international joint ventures', *Journal of International Business Studies*, **22** (2), 249–64.

Gerlach, M.L. (1992), 'The Japanese corporate network: a blockmodel approach', *Administrative Science Quarterly*, **37** (1), 105–39.

Gibson, C.B. (1995), 'An investigation of gender differences in leadership across four countries', *Journal of International Business Studies*, **26** (2), 255–80.

Gomez-Mejia, L.R. and L.E. Palich (1997), 'Cultural diversity and performance of multinational firms', *Journal of International Business Studies*, **28** (2), 309–36.

Gooderham, P.N., O. Nordhaug and K. Ringdal (1999), 'Institutional and rational determinants of organizational practices: human resource management in European firms', *Administrative Science Quarterly*, **44** (3), 507–31.

Graham, J.L., L. Evenko and M.N. Rajan (1992), 'An empirical comparison of Soviet and American business negotiations', *Journal of International Business Studies*, **23** (3), 387–418.

Gregersen, H.B. and J.S. Black (1992), 'Antecedents to commitment to a parent company and a foreign operation', *Academy of Management Journal*, **35** (1), 65–90.

Gregersen, H.B., J.M. Hite and J.S. Black (1996), 'Expatriate performance appraisal in U.S. multinational firms', *Journal of International Business Studies*, **27** (4), 711–38.

Hannon, J.M., I.C. Huang and B.S. Jaw (1995), 'International human resource strategy and its determinants: the case of subsidiaries in Taiwan', *Journal of International Business Studies*, **26** (3), 531–54.

Harbison, F.H. and C.A. Myers (1959), *Management in the Industrial World: An International Analysis*, New York: McGraw-Hill.

Harpaz, I. (1990), 'The importance of work goals', *Journal of International Business Studies*, **21** (1), 75–93.

Harvey, M. (1993), 'Empirical evidence of recurring international compensation problems', *Journal of International Business Studies*, **24** (4), 785–99.

——— (1997), 'Dual-career expatriates: expectations, adjustments, and satisfaction with international relocation', *Journal of International Business Studies*, **28** (3), 627–57.

Hennart, J.F. and J. Larimo (1998), 'The impact of culture on the strategy of multinational enterprises: does national origin affect ownership decisions?', *Journal of International Business Studies*, **29** (3), 515–38.

Hofstede, G., B. Neuijen, D.D. Ohayv and G. Sanders (1990), 'Measuring organizational cultures: a qualitative and quantitative study across twenty cases', *Administrative Science Quarterly*, **35** (2), 286–316.

Holm, P. (1995), 'The dynamics of institutionalization: transformation processes in Norwegian fisheries', *Administrative Science Quarterly*, **40** (3), 398–422.

Hundley, G., C.K. Jacobson and S.H. Park (1996), 'Effect of profitability and liquidity on R&D intensity: Japanese and U.S. companies compared', *Academy of Management Journal*, **39** (6), 1659–74.

Husted, B.W., J.B. Dozier, J.T. McMahan and M.W. Kattan (1996), 'The impact of cross-national carriers of business ethics on attitudes about questionable practices and forms of moral reasoning', *Journal of International Business Studies*, **27** (2), 391–411.

Janssens, M., J.M. Brett and F.J. Smith (1995), 'Confirmatory cross-cultural research: testing the viability of a corporate-wide safety policy', *Academy of Management Journal*, **38** (2), 364–82.

Jegers, M. (1991), 'Prospect theory and risk–return relations: some Belgian evidence', *Academy of Management Journal*, **34** (1), 215–25.

Johansson, J.K., I.A. Ronkainen and M.R. Czinkota (1994), 'Negative country-of-origin effects: the case of the New Russia', *Journal of International Business*

Studies, **25** (1), 157–75.

Kerr, C., J.T. Dunlop, F.H. Harbison and C.A. Myers (1964), *Industrialism and Industrial Man*, New York: Oxford University Press.

Kim, W.C. and P. Hwang (1992), 'Global strategy and multinational's entry mode choices', *Journal of International Business Studies*, **23** (1), 55–76.

Kim, W.C. and R.A. Mauborgne (1993), 'Procedural justice, attitudes, and subsidiary top management compliance with multinationals' corporate strategic decisions', *Academy of Management Journal*, **36** (3), 502–26.

Kim, K.I, H.-J. Park and N. Suzuki (1990), 'Reward allocations in the United States, Japan, and Korea: a comparison of individualistic and collectivist cultures', *Academy of Management Journal*, **33** (1), 188–98.

Kogut, B. and U. Zander (1993), 'Knowledge of the firm and evolutionary theory of the multinational corporation', *Journal of International Business Studies*, **24** (4), 625–46.

Langlois, C.C. and B.B. Schlegelmilch (1990), 'Do corporate code of ethics reflect national character? Evidence from Europe and the United States', *Journal of International Business Studies*, **21** (4), 519–39.

Lazerson, M. (1995), 'A new phoenix? Modern putting-out in the modern knitwear industry', *Administrative Science Quarterly*, **40** (1), 34–59.

Lin, X. and R. Germain (1998), 'Sustaining satisfactory joint venture relationships: the role of conflict resolution strategy', *Journal of International Business Studies*, **28** (1), 179–97.

Lubatkin, M.H., M. Ndiaye and R. Vengroff (1997), 'The nature of managerial work in developing countries: a limited test of the universalist hypothesis', *Journal of International Business Studies*, **28** (4), 711–34.

Luthans, F., D.H.B. Welsh and S.A. Rosenkranz (1993), 'What do Russian managers really do? An observational study with comparisons to U.S. managers', *Journal of International Business Studies*, **24** (4), 741–62.

Makino, S. and P.W. Beamish (1998), 'Performance and survival of joint ventures with non-conventional ownership structures', *Journal of International Business Studies*, **29** (4), 797–818.

Markoczy, L. (1997), 'Measuring beliefs: accept no substitutes', *Academy of Management Journal*, **40** (5), 1228–42.

Martin, X., A. Swaminathan and W. Mitchell (1998), 'Organizational evolution in the interorganizational environment: incentives and constraints on international expansion strategy', *Administrative Science Quarterly*, **43** (3), 566–601.

McGivering, I.C., D.G.J. Mathews and W.H. Scott (1960), *Management in Britain*, Liverpool, UK: Liverpool University Press.

Meznar, M.B., D. Nigh and C.C.Y. Kwok (1994), 'Effects of announcements of withdrawal from South Africa on stockholder wealth', *Academy of Management Journal*, **37** (6), 1633–48.

—— (1998), 'Announcements of withdrawal from South Africa revisited: making sense of contradictory event study findings', *Academy of Management Journal*, **41** (6), 715–41.

Millington, A.I. and B.T. Bayliss (1995), 'Transnational joint ventures between UK and EU manufacturing companies and the structure of competition', *Journal of International Business Studies*, **26** (2), 239–54.

Money, R.B. and J.L. Graham (1999), 'Salesperson performance pay, and job satisfaction: tests of a model using data collected in the United States and Japan', *Journal of International Business Studies*, **30** (1), 149–71.

Morosini, P., S. Shane and H. Singh (1998), 'National cultural distance and cross-border acquisition performance', *Journal of International Business Studies*, **29** (1), 137–57.

Morris, T. (1998), 'Conflict management: accounting for cross-national differences', *Journal of International Business Studies*, **29** (4), 729–48.

Morris, T. and C.M. Pavett (1992), 'Management style and productivity in two cultures', *Journal of International Business Studies*, **23** (1), 169–78.

Mueller, S.L. and L.D. Clarke (1998), 'Political-economic context and sensitivity to equity: differences between the United States and the transition economies of Central and Eastern Europe', *Academy of Management Journal*, **41** (3), 319–29.

Murnighan, J.K. and D. Conlon (1991), 'The dynamics of intense work groups: a study of British string quartets', *Administrative Science Quarterly*, **36** (2), 165–86.

Naumann, E. (1993), 'Organizational predictors of expatriate job satisfaction', *Journal of International Business Studies*, **24** (1), 61–80.

Nelson, R.E. (1993), 'Authority, organization, and societal context in multinational contexts', *Administrative Science Quarterly*, **38** (4), 653–82.

Newman, K. and S.D. Nollen (1996), 'Culture and congruence: the fit between management practices and national culture', *Journal of International Business Studies*, **27** (4), 753–80.

Ogden, S. and R. Watson (1999), 'Corporate performance and stakeholder management: balancing shareholder and customer interests in the U.K. privatized water industry', *Academy of Management Journal*, **42** (5), 526–38.

Oliver, E.G. and K.S. Cravens (1999), 'Cultural influences on managerial choice: an empirical study of employee benefit plans in the United States', *Journal of International Business Studies*, **30** (4), 745–62.

Osborn, R.N. and C.C. Baughn (1990), 'Forms of interorganizational governance for multinational alliances', *Academy of Management Journal*, **33** (3), 503–19.

Pan, Y. (1996), 'Influences on foreign equity ownership level in joint ventures in China', *Journal of International Business Studies*, **27** (1), 1–26.

Park, S.H. and G.R. Ungson (1997), 'The effect of national culture, organizational complementarity, and economic motivation on joint venture dissolution', *Academy of Management Journal*, **40** (2), 279–307.

Pedersen, T. and S. Thomsen (1997), 'European patterns of corporate ownership: a twelve country study', *Journal of International Business Studies*, **28** (4), 759–78.

Peterson, M. et al. (1995), 'Role conflict, ambiguity, and overload: a 21-nation study', *Academy of Management Journal*, **38** (2), 429–51.

Peterson, R.B. (1968), 'The Swedish experience with industrial democracy', *British Journal of Industrial Relations*, **6** (2), 185–203.

——— (1971), 'A cross-cultural study of chief executive attitudes', *Industrial Relations*, **10** (2), 194–210.

——— (1975), 'The interaction of technical process and perceived organizational climate in Norwegian firms', *Academy of Management Journal*, **18** (2), 227–39.

——— (1976), 'Cross-cultural study of teacher professionalism, job satisfaction, and attitudes toward collective negotiations', *Journal of Collective Negotiations*, **5** (2), 113–24.

—— (2003), 'HRM in MNC operations in Central and Eastern Europe since the wall came down', *Journal of World Business*, **38**, 55–69.

Peterson, R.B., R. Adams and H.F. Schwind (1988), 'Personal value systems of Japanese trainees and managers in a changing competitive environment', *Asia-Pacific Journal of Management*, **5** (3), 169–79.

—— (2000), 'Expatriate management and the relationship between headquarters and overseas subsidiaries', *Thunderbird International Business Review*, **42** (2), 145–66.

Peterson, R.B., N.K. Napier and W.S. Shim (1996a), 'Expatriate management – the differential role of national multinational corporation ownership', *The International Executive*, **38** (4), 543–62.

Peterson, R.B., J. Sargent, N.K. Napier and W.S. Shim (1996b), 'Corporate expatriate HRM policies, internationalization and performance in the world's largest MNCs', *Management International Review*, **36** (3), 215–30.

Peterson, R.B. and H.F. Schwind (1977), 'A comparative study of personal problems in international companies and joint ventures in Japan', *Journal of International Business Studies*, **8** (1), 45–55.

Pillai, R., T. Scandura and E.A. Williams (1999), 'Leadership and organizational justice, similarities and differences across cultures', *Journal of International Business Studies*, **30** (4), 763–80.

Porac, J.F., H. Thomas, F. Wilson, D. Paton and A. Kanfer (1995), 'Rivalry and the industry model of Scottish knitwear producers', *Administrative Science Quarterly*, **40** (2), 203–29.

Pornpitakpan, C. (1999), 'The effects of cultural adaptations on business relationships: Americans selling to Japanese and Thais', *Journal of International Business Studies*, **30** (2), 317–38.

Ralston, D.A., C.P. Egri, S. Stewart, R.H. Terpstra and Y. Kai-cheng (1999), 'Doing business in the 21st century with the new generation of Chinese managers: a study of generational shifts in work values in China', *Journal of International Business Studies*, **30** (2), 415–29.

Ralston, D.A., D.J. Gustafson, F.M. Cheung and R.H. Terpstra (1993), 'Differences in managerial values: a study of U.S, Hong Kong and PRC managers', *Journal of International Business Studies*, **24** (2), 249–76.

Ralston, D.A., D.H. Holt, R.H. Terpstra and Y. Kai-cheng (1997), 'The impact of national culture and economic ideology on managerial work values: a study of the United State, Russia, Japan, and China', *Journal of International Business Studies*, **28** (1), 177–207.

Ralston, D.A., N.V. Trang and N.K. Napier (1999b), 'A comparative study of the work values of North and South Vietnamese managers', *Journal of International Business Studies*, **30** (4), 655–72.

Rangan, S. (1998), 'Do multinationals operate flexibly? Theory and evidence', *Journal of International Business Studies*, **29** (2), 217–38.

Rao, A. and K. Hashimoto (1996), 'Intercultural influence: a study of Japanese expatriate managers in Canada', *Journal of International Business Studies*, **27** (3), 443–66.

Reuber, A.R. and E. Fischer (1997), 'The influence of management team's international experience on the internationalization behaviors of SMEs', *Journal of International Business Studies*, **28** (4), 807–26.

Roberts, K.H. and W.K. Graham (1972), *Comparative Studies in Organizational Behavior*, New York, NY: Holt, Rinehart & Winston.

Rosenzweig, P.M. and N. Nohria (1994), 'Influences on human resource management practices in multinational corporations', *Journal of International Business Studies*, **25** (2), 229–52.

Roth, K. and A.J. Morrison (1992), 'Implementing global strategy: characteristics of global subsidiary mandates', *Journal of International Business Studies*, **23** (4), 715–36.

Roth, K. and S. O'Donnell (1996), 'Foreign subsidiary compensation strategy: an agency theory perspective', *Academy of Management Journal*, **39** (3), 678–702.

Roth, K., D.M. Schweiger and A.J. Morrison (1991), 'Global strategic implementation at the business unit level: operational capabilities and administrative mechanisms', *Journal of International Business Studies*, **22** (3), 369–402.

Sanyal, R. (1990), 'An empirical analysis of the unionization of foreign manufacturing firms in the U.S.', *Journal of International Business Studies*, **21** (1), 119–32.

Sanyal, R.N. and J.S. Neves (1992), 'A study of union ability to secure a first contract in foreign-owned firms in the USA', *Journal of International Business Studies*, **23** (4), 697–714.

Schlegelmilch, B.B. and D.C. Robertson (1995), 'The influence of country and industry on ethical perceptions of senior executives in the U.S. and Europe', *Journal of International Business Studies*, **26** (4), 859–81.

Schuler, R.S. and N. Rogovsky (1998), 'Understanding compensation practice variations across firms: the impact of national cultures', *Journal of International Business Studies*, **29** (1), 157–77.

Shaffer, M.A., D.A. Harrison and K.M. Gilley (1999), 'Dimensions, determinants, and differences in the expatriate adjustment process', *Journal of International Business Studies*, **30** (3), 557–81.

Shenkar, O. and Y. Zeira (1992), 'Role conflict and role ambiguity of chief executive officers in international joint ventures', *Journal of International Business Studies*, **23** (1), 55–76.

Simons, T. and P. Ingram (1997), 'Organization and ideology: kibbutzim and hired labor 1951–1965', *Administrative Science Quarterly*, **42** (4), 784–813.

Smith, P.B. (1996), 'The manager as mediator of alternative meanings: a pilot study from China, the USA, and U.K.', *Journal of International Business Studies*, **27** (2), 115–37.

Soutar, G.N., R. Grainger and P. Hedges (1999), 'Australian and Japanese value stereotypes: a two country study', *Journal of International Business Studies*, **30** (1), 203–17.

Sullivan, J.J. and R.B. Peterson (1991), 'A test of theories underlying the Japanese lifetime employment system', *Journal of International Business Studies*, **22** (1), 79–98.

Swan, P.F. and J.E. Ettlie (1997), 'U.S.-Japanese manufacturing equity relationships', *Academy of Management Journal*, **40** (2), 463–78.

Taggart, J.B. (1997), 'Autonomy and procedural justice: a framework for evaluating subsidiary strategy', *Journal of International Business Studies*, **28** (1), 51–76.

Teagarden, M.B., M.A. Von Glinow, D.L. Bowen, C.A. Frayne, S. Nason, Y.P. Huo,

J. Milliman, M.E. Arias, M.C. Butler, J.M. Geringer, N.H. Kim, H. Scullion, K.B. Lowe and E.A. Drost (1995), 'Toward a theory of comparative management research: an idiographic case study of the best in international human resources management project', *Academy of Management Journal*, **38** (5), 1261–85.

Townsend, A.M., K.D. Scott and S.E. Markham (1990), 'An examination of country and culture-based differences in compensation practices', *Journal of International Business Studies*, **21** (4), 667–78.

Tse, D.K., J. Francis and J. Walls (1994), 'Cultural differences in conducting intra- and inter-cultural negotiations: a Sino-Canadian comparison', *Journal of International Business Studies*, **25** (3), 537–56.

Warhurst, C. (1998), 'Recognizing the possible: the organization and control of a socialist labor process', *Administrative Science Quarterly*, **43** (2), 470–97.

Welsh, D.H.B., F. Luthans and S.M. Sommer (1993), 'Managing Russian factory workers: the impact of U.S.-based behavioral and participative techniques', *Academy of Management Journal*, **36** (1), 58–79.

Whitman, M.E., A.M. Townsend and A.R. Hendrickson (1999), 'Cross-national differences in computer-use ethics: a nine country study', *Journal of International Business Studies*, **30** (4), 673–88.

Wiersema, M.F. and A. Bird (1993), 'Organizational demography in Japanese firms: group heterogeneity, individual dissimilarity, and top management team turnover', *Academy of Management Journal*, **36** (5), 996–1025.

Xin, K.R. and J.L. Pearce (1996), 'Guanxi: connections for formal institutional support', *Academy of Management Journal*, **39** (6), 1641–58.

Yan, A. and B. Gray (1994), 'Bargaining power, management control, and performance in United States–China joint ventures: a comparative case study', *Academy of Management Journal*, **37** (6), 1478–517.

Zaheer, S. (1995), 'Overcoming the liability of foreignness', *Academy of Management Journal*, **38** (2), 341–63.

3. Towards a Postcolonial Research Paradigm in International Business and Comparative Management

Robert Westwood

INTRODUCTION

This chapter is not about qualitative research methods. It is about the discursive conditions that are constitutive of, and a resource, foundation and location for, such methods in international business and comparative management studies (IBCMS). It sees methodology as ineluctably embedded in ontological and epistemological assumptions, as well as in the motivations and values of the researcher. These are in turn enfolded in a historically, institutionally and ideologically informed discursive context. It is a context containing particular discourses that claim to speak definitively, authoritatively and exclusively through specific representations of reality. Like all discourses they participate in a knowledge–power nexus that shapes the intellectual and pragmatic spaces in which action is formulated, delineate the boundaries of what is legitimate, proper and truthful, and mark off the illegitimate, improper and untruthful. We cannot reflect on methodology without reflecting on matters epistemological, ontological and ideological. Research methods are not innocent: they are political.

This chapter, then, is concerned with the discursive space in which research methods in IBCMS have developed, offers a critique of it and points to an alternative. It argues that methods are currently located in a very particular, constrained space offering limited and delimiting opportunities for exploration and understanding. The chapter examines the genesis of that discursive space, delineates its contours, explores its consequences and opens it up so that alternative methods are given room.

The chapter is structured as follows. The first section introduces the notion of a postcolonial reading of IBCMS. It discusses postcolonialism as a critical practice, revealing the persistence of the colonial project in contemporary modes of knowing and acting. This is followed by an illustration of how a postcolonial reading of IBCMS reveals the perpetuation of universalist, essentialist and exotic representations of the Other.

The second section explores the ontological, epistemological and methodological foundations for IBCMS and the institutional arrangements that support them. These foundations are, at one level, constituted by a particular discursive matrix consisting of the structural functionalism of Parsonian sociology and early cultural anthropology, the ideologically and materially informed interests of Western trade and business – and the academic institutions that served them – and that triumvirate of post-Second World War projects accompanying those interests: modernisation, development and industrialisation. At another level these conditions are themselves rooted in a particular view of science that developed in conjunction with the colonial project.

The final section draws out some of the implications of this reading and these conditions for contemporary IBCMS research. The postcolonial critique raises important questions and suggests alternative ways of viewing and conducting research that avoids the representational difficulties generated by current practice and offers a more open, inclusive and legitimate research practice; one that is not appropriative, repressive and controlling.

A POSTCOLONIAL READING OF IBCMS

Postcolonialism has emerged as a powerful critique and intellectual practice applied to diverse discourses. While by no means a homogeneous and consensual project, postcolonialism is concerned with revealing continuities and persistent effects of the colonial project and colonial experience in *contemporary* ways of knowing and acting in the world. I shall argue that the contemporary ways of knowing – particularly epistemological, methodological and representational practices – and acting of IBCMS have resonance with the colonial project and are thus open to a postcolonial interpretation.

The Postcolonial Critique

The seminal work for postcolonial analysis is Said's *Orientalism* (Said 1978). Applying a Foucauldian analysis, it meticulously documents the ways in which the West constructed and appropriated the 'Orient' so as to represent it to the West in ways facilitative of control and dominance. Said focused on the West's encounter with the Middle East, but postcolonial analysis encompasses all of Europe's global colonial expansion. Those encounters with difference entailed a need to account for and represent the Other to Self in ways that rendered the Other accessible, understandable and manageable. In the same moment *Self* is constructed and reaffirmed in relation to Other.

Said challenges these strategies of representation and attempts to show how other cultures can be analysed and described from a standpoint that is not appropriating, repressive or manipulative (Dallmayr 1996). The problematics of representation and authority have been recognised in anthropology for some time (for example, Clifford, 1988; Clifford and Marcus 1986), and increasingly in organisation studies (Chia and King 2001; Cooper 1992; Jeffcutt 1993), but have hardly surfaced in IBCMS. Such lack of reflection is worrying given that methodology *is* largely a matter of strategies and modes of representation. Anthropological methodology, following an intense period of reassessment and influenced by postcolonialism, took a radical turn (Clifford and Marcus 1986), fundamentally questioning what is at stake when researchers represent their supposed 'knowledge' of the Other. What is actually so represented, and what is done to the Other in these representational strategies? The second, related question, is what is the warrant for making such representations? Despite the fact that IBCMS research practice is ineluctably concerned with representations of the Other, these questions are barely acknowledged.

Analysis shows that reactions to, and representations of, the Other have always been ambiguous and heterogeneous. For example, MacKerras (2000) painstakingly documents the varied and changing representations of China that the West has constructed throughout the history of their engagement. Despite the heterogeneity there has been a consistent pattern of diminishing and exoticising the Other which Dirks (1992, p. 9) summarises with the themes of 'decline, degradation and decadence'. Prasad (2003b) categorises the West's representation of its various Others by three interrelated discourses. First, and most widely known, is the *orientalist* discourse constructed primarily in relation to the Arab world, and exemplified by Said (1978). In addition there are the discourses of *primitivism* in relation to Africa, and *tropicalisation* in relation to Latin America and the Caribbean. In each the Other is represented on the one hand as exotic and an object of desire, but on the other by various negativities.

Two general forms of negativity predominate: the Other as (1) dangerous and threatening or (2) as suffering from lack or deficiency. In relation to (1), representational strategies are designed to reduce the menace, primarily by representing the Other in codes and categories already familiar to the West (Prasad 1997, pp. 293–4). The Other is appropriated, refracted through the West's discursive lens, and reproduced in the imaginary images of the West's devising. In relation to (2), the Other is variously represented as uncivilised, decadent, barbaric, despotic, corrupt, irrational, indolent and/or ungodly and thus in need of the benefits of colonisation and the guiding administration of the European. In either case the representations serve to position the Other in ways that legitimated and served the interests of the coloniser.

Discourses of alterity are relational and construct oppositional binaries. As the Other is negatively represented, so Self is positively constructed in relation to that negativity. Indeed, Oseen (1997) argues for a pervasive linguistic tendency to privilege sameness and denigrate difference, to situate difference as 'less than'. Any lack, decadence or inferiority constructs the self – the West – as in plenitude, as moral and as superior. This provided the West with a discourse that asserted its moral right and the knowledge to exercise a dominance *vis-à-vis* the rest of the world. It enabled Europe to assume the 'right and duty to appropriate the bounty of nature wasted by the natives to benefit its industrial classes and feed its hungry; a utilitarian discourse joined to a teleological one' (Parry 1987, p. 54).

A key representational strategy is to essentialise the Other, in which totalising categories are constructed which seek to apprehend, capture and homogenise the Other. The Other's heterogeneity and difference are repressed by monolithic and stereotypical representations (Parry 1987). It enables abstracting and objectifying labels, such as 'Chinese', or 'Scottish', to be applied which become reifications standing for the characteristics and qualities of each case/person to whom the category is applied. Essentialising categories also pretend to explain. When a category is applied, the attributes and qualities presumed to attach to it are taken as explanations of the behaviour of the individual case so labelled. For example, applying the label 'Chinese' to an individual enables the attribution of the behavioural characteristic of 'conflict avoiding' and hence an explanation of an instance of conflict behaviour is supplied by invoking the label – the person behaved like that *because* they are 'Chinese'.

Essentialising leads to a tendency to exoticise, that is to amplify or exaggerate differences. Methodologically this can lead to overinterpretation (Keesing 1989), to the elevation of the mundane to levels of specialness, and to a foregrounding of difference and backgrounding of similarity. It has the effect of amplifying the distance between self and Other and further facilitates the delegitimation and marginalisation of the Other.

These representational and appropriation strategies are related to the notion of governmentality: a matrix of practices – including regimes of surveillance and discipline – devised at knowing, using and mastering others (Foucault 1979a, 1979b). Thomas (1994) sees colonial discourse as the governmentalisation of culture – adducing cultures of difference to the centralising and homogenising practice of Western administration and governance. As we shall see, science itself was at the service of the expansionist project, providing representations that apprehended, appropriated, and incorporated, making the Other accessible to the West's knowledge/power systems and governmentality regimes. Reflexively, the capacity to so appropriate and represent reaffirms the efficacy of the West's knowledge system and representational apparatus.

The postcolonial critique has been applied to a range of fields, discourses and texts (Chambers and Curti 1996; Loomba 1998; Thomas 1994; Young 2001). I argue that IBCMS show continuity with the colonial project and are constituted by discourse(s) amenable to postcolonial critique. The next section applies that critique to some key IBCMS texts, revealing the representational strategies of universalism, essentialism and exoticism that echo the postcolonial analysis.

Applying the Postcolonial Critique to IBCMS: Strategies of Representation

A postcolonial interpretation can be approached by asking what is it that IBCMS seek to do? An examination of texts in the field suggests that it explores the management, organisational and business systems of different countries, relative to home systems, in order to improve practice. However, that glosses over the power dynamics attendant on any field of investigation and their knowledge claims. As Foucault (for example, 1973, 1980) has shown, any claim to knowledge is always an exercise of power and a knowledge/power nexus can never be elided. There is always directionality and a will to power associated with social research practice, including IBCMS. It is not, therefore, an innocent, detached, neutral activity; it is research undertaken by one party in order to extract information from and construct knowledge in relation to another. Given the contemporary geo-politics of institutionalised knowledge systems, this means that IBCMS are essentially a Euro-American[1] project directed at the rest of the world for the purposes of apprehension, prediction and control.

Postcolonialism provides an analytic for examining these issues and for exploring the epistemological and methodological implications. It suggests that IBCMS entail subjecting the Other, and specifically their organising systems, to 'scientific' scrutiny in order to appropriate and represent 'knowledge' about that Other. Simply and pragmatically put, IBCMS are conducted by and for the Euro-American 'centre', and function to make accessible and understandable the management and business practices of others so as to facilitate the centre's trade and business practices.[2] To do so, they engage in the same kind of representational strategies and discursive practices that were deployed in the service of the colonial project and for purposes of governmentality.

IBCMS have, throughout their short history, deployed representational strategies that have essentialised and exoticised the Other. As Punnett and Shenkar (1996, p. 116) point out, IBCMS have tended to 'utilise reified categories like "the Italians", "the Japanese" or "the Americans" as explanatory variables'. There is a presumption that these constructions can meaningfully capture the Other and speak in a totalising and authoritative way about their essential nature, characteristics and qualities. This practice ignores the particular, the contextually specific, the differentiations of the local, and the proliferation of instances. It also ignores any self-representations the Other may have available. There are also numerous instances where the Other is exoticised. The West, amplifying differences rather than noting similarities, exaggerates different perspectives and practices, which are often extracted from mundane local contexts and elevated as the marvellous and the unique. The current fascination with Sun Tzu's *The Art of War*,[3] *feng shui*, and the Chinese family business model are examples of exoticisation. I note here only some examples of essentialising and exoticising; further elaboration can be found in Westwood (2001) and Prasad (2003a).

The tendency was pervasive from the outset in Harbison and Myers's (1959) foundational text, which includes references to the 'aristocratic' values of the 'British', the low levels of trust among the 'Italians', 'German' authoritarianism and 'Indian' paternalism. Almost 20 years later, Weinshall's (1977) influential text is still replete with essentialist statements, and remains so through subsequent editions down to the present.

One pervasive essentialist representation – prevalent in Harbison and Myers and similar works – centres on binaries such as democratic/authoritarian and freedom/despotism. Typically, modes of leadership and governance in, for example, India, Chile, Egypt, Japan, and even France, Germany and Italy, were consistently represented as more autocratic, authoritarian and/or paternalistic than in the USA. Other countries' management systems are not only depicted as patrimonial and authoritarian, but also as dysfunctional, irrational, inefficient, incompetent, unsophisticated and so on. The binaries recursively elevate Self while denigrating Other. Harbison and Myers go so far as suggesting that successful management must be based on 'leadership in a democratic setting' (1959, p. 32). Indeed, 'modern' management is contrasted with personalistic leadership based on personal or family ownership, which they castigate as 'the most primitive system' (p. 119). An impositional strategy is advocated wherein the West supplants the leadership and governance structures of developing countries entailing profound changes, especially when accompanied by other shifts in social structures, values and behavioural patterns. For example, industrialisation requires that workers shift loyalties from traditional relationships to the enterprise and its management. The values presented as underpinning 'modern' management are 'individual initiative, consent, persuasion and self-direction' (p. 119), values closely approximating those associated with the USA.

This is not merely historical analysis. Harbison and colleagues' work, and the language, orientation and ideology they initiated in the 1950s and 1960s, has been formative for the whole of IBCMS and these modes of representation persist contemporarily. Some illustrative examples from key texts include:

- The essentialisms and simplifying stereotypes that riddle Weinshall's (1977, 1993) texts (as noted).
- Similar autocratic/democratic binaries and other essentialisms in Richman (1977) and Farmer and Richman (1970) – other IBCMS founders.
- An extensive literature that talks of Chinese management and leadership as paternalistic or autocratic (for example, Chen 1991; Chen 1995; Komin 1990; Wong 1985). Such representations are present even in Redding, despite a more considered and ethnographic account of Overseas Chinese management (see Redding 1990; Redding and Wong 1986).
- Essentialising representations in Hickson and Pugh (1995); for example, describing leadership in Arab countries as a *Sheikocracy* or *Bedo-aucracy* and referring to the culture's personalism, suggesting it inhibits 'commitment to abstractions such as goals and projects' (p. 191).
- Countless binary representations that disparage the Other in Hickson and Pugh (1995): paradoxical/non-paradoxical, intuitive/logical, concrete/abstract, *ad hoc* and inconsistent/consistent and systematic, personalism/impersonalism, autocratic/democratic, stagnant/dynamic, corrupt/incorruptible, nepotistic/impartial, irrational/rational and so on.
- Particularly stark East–West oppositional binaries provided by Gatley et al. (1996), such as contrasting the West's 'atomism' with the East's 'holism', which they then link to differences in brain function according to split brain theory.[4]
- Similar psychological reductionism in Redding (1990; Redding and Martyn-Johns 1979), claiming differences in cognitive style and ways of thinking between the Chinese and the 'West' – including reference to 'oriental fatalism'.
- Convoluted arguments about cross-cultural value differences and their impact by Hofstede (1991; Hofstede and Bond 1988), concluding with the assertion that the 'Western' cognitive paradigm is characterised by the search for 'Truth' while the 'Eastern' paradigm is dominated by a search for 'Virtue'.

It is vital to recognise what is at stake here. These essentialising and exoticising representations occur as the management and organisational practices of others (in China, Japan or wherever) are scrutinised and conceptualised through the refracting lens of Western categories, constructs and theories. The methodologies employed either directly copy 'normal' Western practice or are devised expressly for this scrutinising and extractive process. The Other is so scrutinised and described precisely so that relevant Western audiences – academics, business leaders, consultants, policy-makers – can construct representations of the Other in forms recognisable and amenable to comprehension, prediction and control. The representations pretend to a value-free, objective, accurate status, but ineluctably they derive from the application of an interested, ideologically informed, historically anchored, and localised knowledge system and practice. It is broadly the West's system and practice, and specifically a manifestation of the dominant ontological, epistemological and methodological predilections of Western IBCMS. It also needs to be noted again that such representational strategies are an exercise of power. They are appropriative and exclusionary strategies that lay claim to authoritative representations and a disavowal of alternatives.

Having introduced the postcolonial critique and illustrated how it can be applied to the texts of IBCMS to reveal their essentialising and exoticising representational practices, it is now necessary to analyse the conditions and context that gave rise to these tendencies. This entails excavating the ground upon which the Western discourse of IBCMS rests and, more importantly, its ontological, epistemological and institutional foundations.

THE ONTOLOGICAL, EPISTEMOLOGICAL AND INSTITUTIONAL CONDITIONS FOR IBCMS

I have already noted that Western science was at the service of colonial expansion and contains representational strategies for appropriating the Other. It is argued that Western science co-evolved with the colonial project constituting a relationship that was instrumental in sedimenting ontologies, epistemologies and methods that came to characterise the 'scientific' and that have continued to inform research practice in contemporary IBCMS. This section of the chapter first explores the complexities of these relationships.

This section also explores more recent conditions that have informed IBCMS. While the roots of IBCMS lie in the scientific project that emerged in tandem with colonialism, IBCMS emerged more formally in the post-Second World War period as the major Euro-American economies extended their international trade and deepened their concerns with the issues of modernisation, development and industrialisation. These were the enabling institutional and discursive conditions for the emergence of IBCMS.

Finally, the section notes that IBCMS also emerged into a specific intellectual climate, one where structural functionalism held the orthodox ground. The pioneers of the field were adherents of that orthodoxy and it has provided a dominant legacy, which sustains particular ontological, epistemological and methodological preferences that drive research practice.

Science and the Colonial: Forging the 'One' Science and its Methods

As Said (1978) and others have demonstrated, the non-West has been systematically subjected to the West's intellectual and scientific technology which has scrutinised, labelled, categorised, taxonimised, codified and in other ways laid out the Other in an abstracted and invented discursive space. This space became the ground from which all manner of material practices have been launched: from colonial administration to globalising management and trade practices today. Western science was deeply implicated in those practices, providing systematic modes of representing and claiming to 'know' the Other together with a justificatory rationale.

Recent analysis in postcolonial/feminist studies reveals Western science's reliance on that of others and its co-evolution with European expansion and colonialism (Haraway 1989; Harding 1991, 1996; Jasanoff et al. 1995; Lennon and Whitford 1994; Nelson and Nelson 1996). Scientific development was often in response to the exigencies of the colonial project; in that sense science was serving the colonial project (Kochhar 1992; McClellan 1992). Indeed, Harding (1998, p. 45) concludes that, 'important parts of European organised scientific research were fundamentally in the service of establishing and maintaining colonialism and slavery'. European expansion was facilitated, if not enabled, by what it extracted from the knowledge systems of others it encountered. The colonised world was a resource base for Europeans, not just for raw materials and goods, but also for knowledge. As Kochhar (1992, p. 694) dramatically puts it: 'India was added as a laboratory to the edifice of modern science'. Not just India obviously, the colonial project drew on the world's knowledge resources and incorporated what was useful into its own developing science.

In this analysis, the West's claims for a unified and superior science are shown to be an ideological claim, one requiring a rhetorical masking of its reliance on the knowledge systems and methods. It sees modern Euro-American science[5] not as a unified and universal knowledge and method, but as a historically situated, particular and local knowledge system (Harding 1996; Wong-MingJi and Mir 1997). The old assumption that there is one reality, one truth about that reality, and one science capable of delivering the truth about that reality has been undermined. There is no 'one' science and no one scientific method (Dupre 1993; Galison and Stump 1996).

The postcolonial critique undermines the idea that Western science's success is a function of its own distinctive internal attributes, such as objectivity rules, mechanical models, verification principles, use of probabilistic theory and particular forms of rationality (Harding 1996, 1998).

It is a flawed claim since it ignores Western science's reliance on colonialism and a long intercultural exchange process. Flawed too, through erasing external contextual factors – political, economic and social – that shaped modern science. Postcolonial epistemology disavows science's[6] claim of neutrality and points to the culturally distinctive interests or discursive resources of any society producing research and making scientific claims (Harding 1998, p. 3). Rather science and society (culture) are seen as mutually constituting and co-evolving. There are culturally specific ways of knowing, and these epistemological practices help shape the distinctive contours of a culture. As Harding (1998, p. 20) puts it: 'Cultures generate scientific and technological projects to serve distinctly local interests and needs in the first place'. If we step outside the self-referentiality of Western discourse circuits and see science as 'any systematic attempt to produce knowledge' (Hess 1995), then clearly there is a plurality.

The culture-boundedness of science has been noted in IBCMS (Adler et al. 1989; Boyacigiller and Adler 1991; Hofstede 1980; Kanungo 1990). As Wright (1996, p. 74) says, 'The North American predilection for the deductive approach to theory building, hypothesis testing, and statistical analysis is itself rooted in North American culture, which assumes that the nature of organisations is an objective one, amenable to impartial exploration and discovery'. Such recognition, however, has had little impact on research approaches in the field and barely any reflexivity acknowledging that insight exists.

It is also clear that knowledge systems systematically produce not only knowledge, but also ignorance (Harding 1996). They are always an exercise of power that in constituting knowledge at the same time constitutes non-knowledge. 'Modern science' positions other knowledge systems as non-scientific, pre-scientific, pseudo-scientific, pre-logical, superstitious, magical, alchemical, or folk science. More damagingly, other systems are limited to the purely local and therefore as lacking the generality or universality 'modern science'. Postcolonial epistemology questions the warrant for such claims and demonstrates that modern science is as locally anchored as any other knowledge or belief system. Lepenies (1981) argues that the distinction between science and belief is outmoded and Western scientific knowledge is only one kind of belief embedded in a wider set germane to a particular culture.

Postcolonial analysis, then, shows European 'science's' dependence for development on colonial expansionism, and how this resulted in the destruction or demotion of non-European knowledge systems and traditions (Harding 1998; Reingold and Rothenberg 1987; Sardar 1988). Furthermore, there is a wilful amnesia about this interpenetration of cultures and knowledge systems in the development of 'science'. This is facilitated by a false 'tunnel view' of history in which European civilisation in general, and its science in particular, is traced back through an exclusively European track to ancient Greece. All engagements outside this trajectory are effaced: such as those with sophisticated knowledge systems of the Arab world during the 'middle ages' or with the advanced scientific achievements of the Chinese so richly re-presented by Needham (1969). It is a Hegelian teleology whereby Europe imagines a historical process placing it at the vanguard, moving towards a more 'developed' and 'civilised' state with the rest of the world following behind (Prasad 1997).

It is not much of a leap from there to define progress, development and modernisation in European terms, and to see the colonial project as the legitimate export of such 'benefits' to the rest of the world. It supports the view that colonialism was impelled by a conception of 'receipt-by-diffusion' of European civilisation (Blaut 1993). Modern science is the apotheosis of this historicity, and as such is legitimated in claiming its premier location as the knowledge system *par excellence*, displacing all others. Harding (1998, p. 58) argues that this process continues today through 'the science and technology components of so-called development that are controlled by the cultures of the North'. I would argue that the same can be said for IBCMS.

'Development' is a Western construction that mirrors its self-defining state of advancement. The institutional apparatus concerned with 'development' that emerged in the West in the twentieth century shows clear continuity with the preceding colonial project. Some suggest that so-called 'development' is really a continuation of colonialism by other means (for example, Sachs 1992; Sardar 1988). As colonialism was facilitated by the appropriation of the knowledge systems of the colonised and the simultaneous devaluation/ destruction of indigenous knowledge systems, so 'development' often proceeds via methods serving the West's interests and the de-development of the rest of the world (Bandyopadhyay and Shiva 1988; Brockway 1979; Haraway 1989; Kochhar 1992; Kumar 1991). Indeed, development policy in Europe and the USA post-Second World War was organised by the same people and out of the same offices that had only recently overseen colonial administration (Harding 1998, p. 36). Development policies again rested on assumptions of Western superiority, the correctness and the universality of its methods, and on a diffusion process from the developed West to the underdeveloped Third World.

The notion of 'development' shows clear discursive, ideological and even administrative continuity with colonialism, with science again implicated in facilitating its policies and projects. IBCMS emerged directly into the institutional and intellectual sphere occupied by the adjacent discourses of 'development', modernisation and industrialisation. We now return to the emergence of formal IBCMS research into that institutional and intellectual sphere in order to explore a different aspect of its historical and discursive context, albeit one that reverberates to this colonial account.

The Institutional and Discursive Context for IBCMS

Although IBCMS have clear resonance with scientific practices under colonialism, IBCMS *research* proper emerged in the post-Second World War period. Much of the early work had a strong economics orientation and was part of a growing discourse equating societal development with economic efficiency and rationalism. The orientation was towards abstract, decontextualised, economic-system levels of explanation with accompanying universalistic assumptions about human behaviour. However, these early texts also cohabited a discursive space populated by other projects that had a major impact. Specifically, IBCMS conjoined with that triumvirate of problems and processes labelled modernisation, development and industrialisation. There was intense interest post-Second World War in differential rates of development. The Euro-American capitalist complex needed other countries at a level of development facilitative of its production and trade strategies. Debates about the three processes focused on economic and other structural factors, but cultural factors were also posited (Bendix 1964; Inkeles and Smith 1974; Levy 1966; Lewis 1955; McClelland 1961).

One perspective emergent from this milieu that crystallises a number of issues was the 'industrialisation thesis'. This suggested a common pattern of industrialisation would roll out from the developed West accompanied by certain imperatives. Harbison and Myers (1959, p. 117) expressed the guiding sentiment, 'Industrialisation is an almost universal goal of modern nations. And the industrialisation process has its set of imperatives: things which all societies must do if they hope to conduct a successful march to industrialism. This is what we call the logic of industrialism'. Embedded in the argument was a convergence thesis, suggesting an inherent logic within industrialisation that ensures a shared experience and convergence to a common model of management, organisation and business. Harbison and Myers see this universal logic involving particular forms of organising, modes of leadership and authority, and changes in regimes and related attitudes. Beyond the organisational level the impact encompasses a reconfiguration of society – including its power structures and systems, social divisions, occupational stratification, mobility and dwelling patterns, educational priorities, and value and behavioural requirements. A cultural change is implied and Theodorson (1953) maintains that industrialisation involves shifts along the Parsonian pattern variables towards more universalism, achievement, and specificity, and the suppression of emotionality.

Like its colonial predecessor, the industrialisation thesis is a discourse that points to the inadequacies of other's systems, particularly power and authority relations, and is prescriptive about the adoption of Western models. It advocates a socio-political shift towards a very specific model – that of the industrialised, democratic West, and specifically the United States (Blumer 1960; Jamieson 1980; Nash 1966). Jamieson argues that it involves not just the effects of a technical industrialisation process, but also the values of a modern industrial capitalist system. There is a discursive strategy here that is a recurrent theme in this chapter, that is, the promotion of a very specific and localised worldview, constructed at a particular historic moment, and driven by specific and localised interests, masquerading as a universal and deterministic imperative.

In terms of the institutional context, it is clear that from the outset that IBCMS were a Western – if not a US – project. The emergence of IBCMS coincides with the major expansion of US international trade, but also the growth of US business schools. Regarding the latter, the USA was the first to formalise management and business administration as academic subjects and knowledge domains about which to research and theorise.[7] The former naturally led to an interest in differences in management systems and practices. This was codified by the mid-1950s in a burgeoning literature, reflected most strongly in the work of those in the Inter-University Study of Labor Problems in Economic Development[8] – notably that of Kerr, Harbison and colleagues (for example, Harbison and Myers 1959; Kerr et al. 1960).

The patently Western origin of IBCMS is reaffirmed in accounts of its own history. One influential scholar locates the field's birth in the era beginning in 1500 and then constructs an unashamedly Eurocentric periodisation shaped by a set of business/trade motives that animated the major Western economies (Robinson 1964). In his overview, Ronen (1986) makes cursory mention of the 'ancient' Egyptians, Phoenicians and Greeks[9] before adapting and updating the Robinson periodisation. These are not unusual instances, but typical of the systematic erasure of almost all non-Euro-American representations of the field's history. Indeed, Ronen (1986, p. 4) claims that for all four of Robinson's periods (1500–1970) 'international business was almost entirely a Western phenomenon' – surely a distortion. This prejudiced bit of history is fortuitous since 1492 – the year Columbus made landfall in the Americas – is used by postcolonialists to symbolically identify the perimeter of colonial discourse (for example, Blaut 1992; Crosby 1972).

More generally it is the West (specifically the USA) that has developed a discourse about management/organisation and assumed a privileged position with claims of truth, universality and certainty. It is a position occupied almost totally and its boundaries are policed with vigour. Jamieson (1980) indeed argues that management theory is a US construction, albeit one that has been extensively 'exported' around the world. For example, the MBA, heavily imbued with US research and theorising and materials, is the preeminent educational and socialisation vehicle for managers globally. The institutions and politics of publishing also perpetuate US dominance of the field. Most major journals are US-published and getting into them requires adhering to expectations and rules of research and theory as dictated by US editors thus framing research agendas, questions, and methods. As Thomas (1996, p. 492) concludes 'the foundation of the international business literature largely comprises studies conducted by scholars from the United States, Canada and Western Europe about the United States, Canada and Western Europe'. She also argues that the Euro-American publishing dominance creates barriers to entry for non-Euro-Americans. The methods, models, citation practices, and editorial composition and predilections of the Euro-American academic publishing regime are disadvantageous to externals.

As illustration, a survey of the 16 top IBCM-related journals showed that most authors were either from the USA or from a limited number of European countries and the dominant focus was on issues of concern to the USA with a lesser focus on Europe and Japan (Wong-MingJi and Mir 1997). Analysis of the *Journal of International Business Studies* for the 1984–93 period reveals similar authorship and issue patterns (Thomas 1996). Even when the research is more focused, US dominance is apparent. An analysis of research on Chinese organisation and management in leading international journals showed that 80 per cent of the authors of the most-cited papers were from the USA, Canada or the UK (Li and Tsui 2002).

The field, then, is dominated by the Euro-American centre, who set the research agenda in line with the conceptualisations, models and interests prevailing therein. Western theoretical positions directly shape the types of research questions asked and drive methodology, and in consequence alternative agendas and research questions are marginalised or ignored (Khandwalla 1990). Wong-MingJi and Mir (1997) note the restricted research agenda, but add that the epistemological options also tend to be circumscribed. It is a recursive process since the delineation of agenda, theoretical approach and epistemology drives research practice, which in turn delivers knowledge outcomes that fit with and reinforce that delineation. The circuit of knowledge production is self-reinforcing, and at the same time continues to marginalise, exoticise or exclude alternatives. Other locations rarely get the opportunity to make adequate and full self-representations. It is always the Euro-American centre appropriating and representing the Other, resulting in 'across-the-board romanticisations, essentialisations, reifications, and generalisations' (Wong-MingJi and Mir 1997, p. 351). A number of commentators have noted this Euro-American dominance, the self-interested nature of the research, and its parochialism (Boyacigiller and Adler 1991; Prasad et al. 1997; Wong-MingJi and Mir 1997).

The institutional and discursive context is clear. IBCMS have a heritage in the appropriating and representational strategies of colonialism, a foundation in the business interests of the West (particularly the USA), an intense engagement with the invasive projects of modernisation, development and industrialisation, and an entrenched position in the institutional paraphernalia of academic practice. Furthermore, it emerged into a discursive space in which structural functionalism was the dominant paradigm and provided a rationale for the construction of universalistic levels of explanation. This was facilitated by the industrialisation and convergence theses, which also provided a teleological historiography implying a common trajectory. Some of the ontological, epistemological and methodological implications derived from this institutional and discursive context will now be explored.

Ontological and Epistemological Foundations for Orthodox IBCMS

In addition to the emergence of IBCMS into the discourses of colonialism, development and industrialisation, it also emerged into a particular intellectual space with distinct paradigmatic ontologies and epistemologies. One of these was the structural functionalism of mainstream sociology, exemplified by Parsons (1951, 1964, 1971; Parsons and Shils 1951), which has formed the paradigmatic root for much of mainstream management and organisation studies, including IBCMS, ever since (Burrell and Morgan 1979; Donaldson 2003; Gioia and Pitre 1990). Focusing on the functionality of cultural values in sustaining societal equilibrium, Parsons also founded the basis for most culturalist explanations of management, culminating in the models of Hofstede (1980, 1991), Trompenaars and Hampden-Turner (1993) and Triandis (1982–83).

The intellectual space was also occupied by functionalist anthropology, which again sees explanations of cultural phenomena in terms of the contribution of cultural elements to the functional viability of the total system. It was anthropology's dominant paradigm, exemplified through the works of Radcliffe-Brown (1965), Malinowski (1954), and Kluckhohn and colleagues (Kluckhohn 1951; Kroeber and Kluckhohn 1952; Kluckhohn and Strodtbeck 1961). IBCMS shared an interest in the anthropological enterprise of seeking to observe, explain and appropriate the Other for the benefit of stakeholders in the developed countries. However, it was an anthropology largely restricted to a functionalist, universalising and dimensionalising epistemology.

Orthodox IBCMS are still rooted in those functionalist traditions and continue to engage in research practices involving appropriating representations of the Other. They also participate in the continued Western presumption of the uniqueness, unity and veracity of its science while disavowing alternative knowledge claims and knowledge systems. Indigenous accounts or self-accounts outside of the Euro-American centre rarely find space and are misrepresented and/or marginalised.

A consequence is a reliance on orthodox methodologies deemed appropriate in the domestic setting without questioning their appropriateness in other locations or for cross-national/comparative research. Together with these practices comes a universalising tendency, which results in the promulgation of a single, homogenised model of business and management practice (Boyacigiller and Adler 1991; Wong-MingJi and Mir 1997). A universalist epistemology, fed by the positivist, structural functionalism of Parsons, was apparent early in the field. It was apparent, too, in the industrialisation thesis, which 'supported the view that the logic of industrialism was indeed a fact, and a fact which legitimated the development of a universal management theory' (Jamieson 1980, p. 12). IBCMS were in step with the universalism and functionalism apparent in general management/organisation theory from the outset,[10] and sedimented into the field via contingency theory as championed by the Aston Studies (Hickson et al. 1974; Hickson and McMillan 1981) and their 'culture-free' assertions. It pursued a trajectory that much of general management/organisation theory made, away from the idiographic, particularistic methods of Max Weber and others and towards the structural–functionalist, nomothetic, universalistic approach of Parsons and Emile Durkheim. It is an exclusionary position and so constructivist or interpretivist epistemologies, and nomothetic and qualitative methods, are squeezed out.[11]

In deploying the language of universality the field remains reflexively blind to its own ideological animus and localised and historically situated status. Or as Calás and Smircich (1999, p. 661) note, Western analysis creates categories that 'are blind to their own ethnocentrism'. Nkomo (1992) sees universality claims as an exercise of power in which a totalising coverage of a domain of knowledge is presumed and alternative knowledge claims disallowed. Western management/organisation theory has been written as if written for all – as if it were inherently universal. Echoing the postcolonial view of science, Parry (1987) argues that there has been a cultural hegemony wherein Western norms and values are equated with universal forms of thought. Anyone seeking to publish an account of management/organisation from outside the Euro-American centre is required to provide caveats concerning the specificity of the context of which they write and the limitations on generalisation claims. In short, they must signify that they are dealing with the particular, not the universal. Writers from the centre are not so required; they talk *as if* their pronouncements have universal validity. US management discourse rarely attenuates its findings or representations with caveats acknowledging the particularity of the context or the situatedness of the accounts on offer. There is a tendency to 'treat management as an unsituated and therefore universal discourse' (Wong-MingJi and Mir 1997, p. 354).

The views of Sjöberg (1970, p. 45) and others since, that a set of culture-neutral, universal categories could be identified that were not 'merely reflections of the cultural values of a particular social system' has increasingly been contested. Similarly, Parsons's claim that his pattern variables represented universal and culture-free constructs is counterpointed with the view that they are, in fact, nothing more than the product of a particular cultural orientation and moment in history (Habermas 1970). Indeed, Harding (1998) argues that the search for value neutrality – as well as abstractions and formality – in science itself reflects a value orientation.

There is a poverty of studies from within indigenous contexts exploring local management and organisation issues using constructs developed in and relevant to those contexts. Western researchers typically enter foreign locations with their own agendas, theories and methods and proceed to make observations informed by them. There is little deep analysis of the setting, and any knowledge of it is typically extracted through and represented in relation to the Euro-Western knowledge schema. Substantial, detailed, in-depth single-country or -culture studies are rare, and such studies undertaken indigenously rarer still. IBCMS research is crucially hampered by the lack of such studies, and of theories and concepts developed emically and in relation to the specificities of particular local contexts.

A further consequence of the field's epistemological heritage is the predominant use of methods that are abstractive, decontextualising and quantitative. Studies that measure culture or dimensions of it are exemplars and result in the abstraction, objectification and reification of cultures and cultural phenomena; including persons, identities and subjectivities. This contributes significantly to the construction of essentialising and objectifying categories such as 'Chinese' and 'Arabic', as discussed earlier. Further, patterns of particular behaviour are universalised and decontextualised into instances, for example, of 'uncertainty avoidance', 'specificity' or other dimensional labels. More generally there is a tendency to transform phenomena into variables that are accessible via extant and preferred methods and fit Euro-American theories. There is, as Punnett and Shenkar (1996, p. 6) note, an inclination towards 'the simplification and the reduction of the problem to a few variables, which are stripped of "confounding noise" variations as we attempt to fit them into our preconceived hypothetical understandings'. The drive to quantification particularly facilitates this tendency. Anthropologists have long warned of the dangers of abstracting phenomena from their natural context and analytically decomposing them into component parts (for example, Geertz 1973; Rosaldo 1989).

The vast majority of studies in the field are quantitative. An analysis of international management articles for the 1984–90 period showed only 14 per cent using qualitative methods and 4 per cent joint methods (Mendenhall et al. 1993). There has been little change since (see Andersen and Skaates, Chapter 23 this volume). The reliance on neo-positivistic epistemology and related methods, with concomitant concern for quantification, internal validity, and atomisation of phenomena has, however, come under increasing scrutiny (Boyacigiller and Adler 1991; Redding 1994). Indeed, Wright (1996, p. 70) argues that quantitative methods fail to progress IBCMS because they are unable to address the 'non-linear, interactive, interdependent phenomena that make up the field'. IBCMS have also been criticised for being atheoretical (Boyacigiller and Adler 1994; White 2002); particularly with respect to culture which is often invoked *post hoc* as a residual variable, and treated monolithically and statically (Redding 1994). The field also invariably fails to consider cultures *in interaction*, which is really where the interest should lie (Adler and Graham 1989; White 2002).

The historical, intellectual and institutional context for IBCMS precipitated a particular trajectory with implications for epistemological and methodological preferences that persist in the field. A functionalist epistemology continues to dominate, and universalising, decontextualising and essentialising tendencies and modes of representation persist. The type of turn that is needed if the field is to respond to the postcolonial critique and pursue methods that avoid these tendencies is now considered.

IMPLICATIONS FOR AN ALTERNATE METHODOLOGY

Given the postcolonial critique of knowledge production and representation, it is vital that methods are adopted that do not engage in the type of 'epistemic violence' so apparent in orientalism and other appropriating discourses of the West. Methods that pretend to be neutral and detached from their situated specificity and that appropriate the Other need replacing. It has been shown that traditional epistemologies and methodologies in IBCMS result in essentialising and exoticising practices in which the Other is misrepresented. There is even a taxonomising zeal that locates the Other on one sort of categorical schema or another, be that on dimensions of cultural difference or some statistically derived clustering.

Underlying these tendencies is the persistence and dominance of the structural–functionalist paradigm. The accompanying epistemological frame entails methods that are abstractive, objectifying, reifying and universalising. Methods are often reductionist, or else severely decontextualising, incorporating simplifying representational strategies that do violence to the inherent complexity of the social systems they pretend to represent. Work based on cross-cultural dimensions is typical in this regard. Complex and situated behaviours are reduced to numerical points on bipolar dimensions, which are then presented as an explanation for the behaviours. The paradigm also encourages the quantification of phenomena, which amplifies the decontextualisation.

Methods are needed that avoid these problems, are more suited to the issues faced by the field – ones that do not damagingly decontextualise and appropriate. The positivistic, structural–functionalist and quantitative preferences of the orthodoxy in IBCMS perpetuate these difficulties. For many, the need is a turn to qualitative methods including those developed in anthropology and particularly ethnographic ones (Brannen 1996; Redding 1994; Wright 1996). The contributions in this book bear witness to that need to so turn.

Methods are needed capable of providing meaningful insight into the complex, dynamic, interrelated nature of social systems and the processes by which they are produced and reproduced. This provides a clear case for qualitative methodologies (Cassell and Symon 1998). In particular, there is a strong case for the pursuit of ethnographic studies since they offer the best prospect of retaining contextual integrity and providing insight into the lived realities of complex social systems. However, ethnography is a diverse research practice with versions that are as likely to engage in decontextualisation, impositional and appropriating representational strategies as any structural–functionalist–informed quantitative methodology (Clifford and Marcus 1986; Hammersley 1992; Snow and Morill 1993). It should be remembered that early ethnographies were directly implicated in the colonial project and the appropriating and representational strategies that served it (Fardon 1990). What are needed are reflexive ethnographies and ones that pursue the reflexively aware writing practices advocated by Clifford (1988) and others (Linstead 1993).

As with postmodernism, another concern of postcolonial critique and the search for alternative ontologies, epistemologies and methods is the move to avoid totalising narratives and grand theories. More specifically, universalistic explanations and the attempt to provide general, all-encompassing representations are challenged. Instead there is acceptance and valuing of the locally situated and contextually contingent. In anthropology, for example, the notion that cultures exist and can be represented as monolithic, homogeneous, autonomous and enfolding systems is rejected. The alternative is to view culture as 'historically situated and emergent, shifting and incomplete meanings and practices generated in webs of agency and power' (Ong 1987, pp. 2–3). Cultures are no longer considered as if they developed in splendid isolation from one another, but dynamically as ongoing constructions through their engagements and intersections. When viewed in this manner culture is seen as a process rather than entitatively (Chan 2003).

Postcolonial critique also makes clear that IBCMS need to be mindful and self-reflexive about their own localised, situated, interested and socially constructed nature. The issue of reflexive research practice has increasingly come to the forefront in the social sciences (Steier 1991). As Clifford and Marcus (1986) make clear, there is no escape from the circuits of discourse in which the researcher is located, no innocent and neutral point of observation from above, no value-free research practice, and no standing outside the language through which we represent the Other. It is imperative therefore that we are deeply attendant to the representational strategies we engage in – to the way we *write* the Other. This is a call for a profoundly reflexive research practice of the kind advocated and described by Clifford (1988) and others.

Reflexivity has become an imperative in vanguard social science research and increasingly in organisation studies (Alvesson and Sköldberg 2000; Gergen 1992; Hardy et al. 2001; Tranfield 2002). Reflexivity is virtually *sine qua non* for good, contemporary qualitative research.[12] However, it is neglected in much IBCMS research, or else 'skillfully avoided' (Chia 1996). It reflects a rejection of the innocence and presumed objectivity of science, and requires researchers to factor into their analysis the constitutive effect of their own representational strategies. The researcher must engage in a research practice in which 'research structures and logics are themselves researchable and not immutable, and by examining how we are part of our own data, our research becomes a reciprocal process' (Steier 1991, p. 7).

The analysis has shown that the co-evolution of science and the colonial entailed the marginalisation, destruction or degrading of other knowledge systems. Postcolonial analysis questions the hegemonic, unitarist and exclusive assumptions of Western science. In particular, universalistic assumptions – supported by a structural–functionalist paradigm – need to be dispatched and methods located that honour the meanings and understandings within which particular, local, situated lifeworlds are enacted and experienced. This would include accepting and incorporating the knowledge systems within these localised situations. Such systems are, after all, the means by which the local reality is typically apprehended, understood and acted upon by those within it. At a minimum, local knowledge systems need to be taken into account; they may also, however, be incorporated into research practice as a legitimate mode of researching, knowing and making meaningful representations.

Research practices are needed that are not merely foreign importations but provide space for indigenous research approaches and accompanying knowledge systems that have thus far been denied or marginalised. Given the prevailing geo-politics of academic research this will not be easy, but a prerequisite is greater openness and receptivity to alternate knowledge systems and their modes of representation. More pragmatically, shifts in the politics and institutional framework of publishing are required wherein Western journals adopt more open policies offering greater access to non-

Euro-American work. More broadly the field's institutional practices need to become accommodative of non-Euro-American researchers' pursuit of their own ontological, epistemological and methodological inclinations. I acknowledge this to be an idealistic expectation. An alternative is to establish different research and publishing institutions outside of the orthodoxy, but such 'ghettoisation' brings its own problems. A different strategy is the formation of cross-cultural teams, a desirable strategy for some (Adler et al. 1989; Doktor et al. 1991; Easterby-Smith and Malina 1999). Such teams provide an antidote to impositions and misinterpretations from a purely outsider-in perspective and offer potential synergies derived from combined insider–outsider analysis.

In summary, IBCMS need to break with their historical and discursive legacy and reconfigure their research practice. A postcolonial reading reveals the need to locate methodologies that avoid appropriating, essentialising and exoticising representational strategies. The task of a postcolonial research practice is to resist those tendencies and locate modes of representation that allow for polymorphism and full individuation. The field's heritage in the colonial, development and industrialisation discourses of the past has facilitated a continued inclination towards not only essentialism but also universalism. In addition, the historical and discursive embeddedness of IBCMS in a structural–functionalist paradigm is still reflected in the epistemological and methodological choices of much research and in radically decontextualised, reified and objectified representations. The field must find ways to transcend these approaches and develop epistemologies and methods that are deeply reflexive, authentic with regard to the peoples and systems they seek to represent, and give space to the knowledge, knowledge systems, and modes of representation of those Others with whom it engages. Many of the chapters in this book provide a path forward in this regard.

NOTES

1. Even Euro-American is a misnomer since it is primarily the USA, Britain and some of the more powerful, colonising and early industrialising countries that are really incorporated under this rather clumsy rubric.
2. That the IBCMS project is ineluctably a Euro-American, or even primarily a US, project will be clearly demonstrated later.
3. This ancient Chinese text on military strategy has been repeatedly re-presented in the West to supposedly provide guidance on matters of business strategy in recent times.
4. Possibly one of the most strident and flamboyant examples of essentialising found in contemporary IBCMS.
5. Harding tends to prefer the label 'Northern' science (see Harding 1996).
6. It is important to recognise the extremely limited notion and use of 'science' in this Western discourse. Science in this sense was not even used by the Europeans until William Whewall's usage in 1840. Prior to that the term 'natural philosophy' was more prevalent.

7. The Harvard Graduate School of Administration was established in 1809, but the real growth was post-Second World War with the key journals, the *Administrative Science Quarterly* and the *Academy of Management Journal*, being established in 1956 and 1958, respectively.
8. The universities of Harvard and Princeton were the major protagonists.
9. Even then, oddly, there is no mention of China or India.
10. Exemplified initially by the likes of Henri Fayol, Luther Gulick and Lyndal. F. Urwick.
11. This is not to suggest an absolute dominance and indeed, the exclusion was never total. In the early days, for example, Dore (1973) provided a more ethnographic, social constructivist account of Japanese organisational practices and Child (1972) critiqued the Aston groups culture-free assumptions.
12. See the extensive discussion throughout Denzin and Lincoln (1994).

REFERENCES

Adler, N.J., N. Campbell and A. Laurent (1989), 'In search of an appropriate methodology: from outside the People's Republic of China looking in', *Journal of International Business Studies*, **20** (1), 61–74.

Adler, N.J. and J.L. Graham (1989), 'Cross-cultural interaction: the international comparison fallacy', *Journal of International Business Studies*, **20** (3), 515–37.

Alvesson, M. and K. Sköldberg (2000), *Reflexive Methodology: New Vistas for Qualitative Research*, London: Sage.

Bandyopadhyay, J. and V. Shiva (1988), 'Science and control: natural resources and their exploitation', in Z. Sardar (ed.), *The Revenge of Athena: Science, Exploitation and the Third World*, London: Mansell, pp. 213–34.

Bendix, R. (1964), *Nation Building and Citizenship*, Englewood Cliffs, NJ: Prentice-Hall.

Blaut, J.M. (ed.) (1992), *1492: The Debate on Colonialism, Eurocentrism, and History*, Trenton, NJ: Africa World Press.

———— (1993), *The Colonizer's Model of the World: Geographical Diffusionism and Eurocentric History*, New York: Guilford Press.

Blumer, H. (1960), 'Early industrialisation and the laboring class', *Sociological Quarterly*, **1**, 1–24.

Boyacigiller, N. and N.J. Adler (1991), 'The parochial dinosaur: organizational science in a global context', *Academy of Management Review*, **16** (2), 262–90.

———— (1994), 'Insiders and outsiders: bridging the worlds of organisational behaviour and international management', in B. Toyne and D. Nigh (eds), *International Business Inquiry: An Emerging Vision*, Columbia, SC: University of South Carolina Press, pp. 396–416.

Brannen, M.Y. (1996), 'Ethnographic international management research', in B.J. Punnett and O. Shenkar (eds), *Handbook for International Management Research*, Oxford: Blackwell, pp. 115–43.

Brockway, L. (1979), *Science and Colonial Expansion: The Role of the British Royal Botanical Gardens*, New York: Academic Press.

Burrell, G. and G. Morgan (1979), *Sociological Paradigms and Organisational Analysis*, London: Heinemann.

Calás, M.B. and L. Smircich (1999), 'Past postmodernism? Reflections and tentative directions', *Academy of Management Review*, **24** (4), 649–71.

Cassell, C.M. and G. Symon (eds) (1998), *Qualitative Methods in Organisational Research*, London: Sage.

Chambers, I. and L. Curti (eds) (1996), *The Postcolonial Question*, London/New York: Routledge.

Chan, A. (2003), 'Instatiative vs entitative culture: the case for culture as process', in R. Westwood and S. Clegg (eds), *Debating Organisation: Point/Counterpoint in Organisation Studies*, Oxford: Blackwell, pp. 311–20.

Chen, C.S. (1991), 'Confucian style of management in Taiwan', in J.M. Putti (ed.), *Management: Asian Context*, Singapore: McGraw-Hill, pp. 177–97.

Chen, M. (1995), *Asian Management Systems*, London: Routledge.

Chia, R. (1996), *Organizational Analysis as Deconstructive Practice*, Berlin: De Gruyter.

Chia, R. and I. King (2001), 'The language of organisation theory', in R.I. Westwood and S. Linstead (eds), *The Language of Organisation*, London: Sage, pp. 310–28.

Child, J. (1972), 'Organisational structure, environment and performance: the role of strategic choice', *Sociology*, **6**, 1–22.

Clifford, J. (1988), *The Predicament of Culture: Twentieth Century Ethnography, Literature and Art*, Cambridge, MA: Harvard University Press.

Clifford, J. and G.E. Marcus (eds) (1986), *Writing Cultures: The Poetics and Politics of Ethnography*, Berkeley, CA: University of California Press.

Cooper, R. (1992), 'Formal organisation as representation: remote control, displacement and abbreviation', in M. Reed and M. Hughs (eds), *Rethinking Organisation: Redirections in Organisation Theory and Analysis*, London: Sage, pp. 254–72.

Crosby, A. (1972), *The Columbian Exchange: Biological and Cultural Consequences of 1492*, Westport, CN: Greenwood.

Dallmayr, F. (1996), *Beyond Orientalism*, New York: State University of New York Press.

Denzin, N.K. and Y.S. Lincoln (eds) (1994), *Handbook of Qualitative Research*, Thousand Oaks, CA and London: Sage.

Dirks, N.B. (ed.) (1992), *Colonialism and Culture*, Ann Arbor, MI: Michigan University Press.

Doktor, R., R.L. Tung and M.A. von Glinow (1991), 'Future directions for management theory development', *Academy of Management Review*, **16**, 362–5.

Donaldson, L. (2003), 'Position statement for positivism', in R. Westwood and S. Clegg (eds), *Debating Organisation: Point/Counterpoint in Organisation Studies*, Oxford: Blackwell, pp. 116–27.

Dore, F. (1973), *British Factory–Japanese Factory*, London: Allen & Unwin.

Dupre, J. (1993), *The Disorder of Things: Metaphysical Foundations for the Disunity of Science*, Cambridge, MA: Harvard University Press.

Easterby-Smith, M. and D. Malina (1999), 'Cross-cultural collaborative research: toward reflexivity', *Academy of Management Journal*, **42** (1), 76–86.

Fardon, R. (ed.) (1990), *Localising Strategies: Regional Traditions of Ethnographic Writing*, Edinburgh: Scottish Academic Press.

Farmer, R.N. and B. Richman (1970), *Comparative Management and Economic Progress*, Bloomington, IN: CedarWod Pub.

Foucault, M. (1973), *The Order of Things*, New York: Vantage.

——— (1979a), *Discipline and Punish*, New York: Viking.

—— (1979b), 'On governmentality', *Ideology and Consciousness*, **6**, 5–21.
—— (1980), *Power/Knowledge: Selected Interviews and other Writings 1972–1977*, edited by C. Gordon, New York: Pantheon.
Galison, P. and D.J. Stump (1996), *The Disunity of Science*, Stanford, CA: Stanford University Press.
Gatley, S., R. Lessem and Y. Altman (1996), *Comparative Management: A Transcultural Odyssey*, London: McGraw-Hill.
Geertz, C. (1973), *The Interpretation of Cultures*, New York: Basic Books.
Gergen, K. (1992), 'Organisation theory in the postmodern era', in M. Reed and M. Hughs (eds), *Rethinking Organisation*, London: Sage, pp. 207–26.
Gioia, D.A. and E. Pitre (1990), 'Multiparadigm perspectives on theory building', *Academy of Management Review*, **15** (4), 584–602.
Habermas, J. (1970), 'Technology and science as ideology', in *Toward a Rational Society*, translated by J. Shapiro, Boston, MA: Beacon Press.
Hammersley, M. (1992), *What's Wrong with Ethnography? Methodological Explorations*, London: Routledge.
Haraway, D. (1989), *Primate Visions: Gender, Race, and Nature in the World of Modern Science*, New York: Routledge.
Harbison, F. and C.A. Myers (1959), *Management and the Industrial World: An International Analysis*, New York: McGraw-Hill.
Harding, S. (1991), *Whose Science? Whose Knowledge?*, Ithaca, NY: Cornell University Press.
—— (1996), 'European expansion and the organisation of modern science: isolated or linked historical processes', *Organisation*, **3** (4), 497–509.
—— (1998), *Is Science Multicultural? Postcolonialisms, Feminisms and Epistemologies*, Bloomington and Indianapolis, IN: Indiana University Press.
Hardy, C., N. Philips and S. Clegg (2001), 'Reflexivity in organisation and management theory: a study of the production of the research subject', *Human Relations*, **54** (5), 531–60.
Hess, D.J. (1995), *Science and Technology in a Multicultural World: The Cultural Politics of Facts and Artefacts*, New York: Columbia University Press.
Hickson, D.J. and C.J. McMillan (eds) (1981), *Organisation and Nation: The Aston Programme*, IV, Farnborough, Hants: Gower.
Hickson, D.J., C.J. McMillan, C.R. Hinings and J. Schwitter (1974), 'The culture-free context of organisation structure: a tri-national comparison', *Sociology*, **8** (1), 59–80.
Hickson, D.J. and D.S. Pugh (1995), *Management Worldwide*, London: Penguin.
Hofstede, G. (1980), *Culture's Consequences: International Differences in Work Related Values*, London: Sage.
—— (1991), *Cultures and Organisations: Intercultural Cooperation and its Importance for Survival*, London: McGraw-Hill.
Hofstede, G. and M.H. Bond (1988), 'The Confucius connection: from cultural roots to economic growth', *Organisational Dynamics*, **17**, 4–21.
Inkeles, A. and D. Smith (1974), *On Becoming Modern*, London: Heinemann.
Jamieson, I. (1980), *Capitalism and Culture: A Comparative Analysis of British and American Manufacturing Organisations*, Farnborough, Hants: Gower.
Jasanoff, S., G. Markle, T. Pinch and J. Peterson (eds) (1995), *Handbook of Science and Technology Studies*, Thousand Oaks, CA: Sage.

Jeffcutt, P. (1993), 'From interpretation to representation', in J. Hassard and M. Parker (eds), *Postmodernism and Organisations*, London: Sage, pp. 25–48.

Kanungo, R.N. (1990), 'Work alienation in developing countries: Western models, Eastern realities', in A.N. Jaeger and R.N. Kanungo (eds), *Management in Developing Countries*, New York: Routledge, pp. 193–208.

Keesing, R. (1989), 'Exotic readings of cultural texts', *Current Anthropology*, **30** (4), 459–79.

Kerr, C., J.T. Dunlop, F.H. Harbison and C.A. Myers (1960), *Industrialism and Industrial Man: The Problems of Labor and Management in Economic Growth*, London: Heinemann.

Khandwalla, P.N. (1990), 'Strategic developmental organisations: some behavioural properties', in A.N. Jaeger and R.N. Kanungo (eds), *Management in Developing Countries*, New York: Routledge, pp. 23–42.

Kluckhohn, C. (1951), *Toward a General Theory of Action*, Cambridge, MA: Harvard University Press.

Kluckhohn, F. and F.L. Strodtbeck (1961), *Variations in Value Orientations*, Evanston, IL: Row, Peterson & Co.

Kochhar, R.K. (1992–93), 'Science in British India', parts I and II, *Current Science*, **63** (11), 689–94; **64** (1), 55–62.

Komin, S. (1990), 'Thai value system and its implication or development in Thailand', in D. Sinha and H.S.R. Kao (eds), *Social Values and Development: Asian Perspectives*, New Delhi: Sage, pp. 151–74.

Kroeber, A. and C. Kluckhohn (1952), *Culture: A Critical Review of Concepts and Definitions*, Cambridge, MA: The Museum.

Kumar, D. (1991), *Science and Empire: Essays in the Indian Context (1700–1947)*, Delhi: Anamika Prakashan and National Institute of Science and Technology.

Lennon, K. and M. Whitford (1994), *Knowing the Difference: Feminist Perspectives on Epistemology*, New York: Routledge.

Lepenies, W. (1981), 'Anthropological perspectives in the sociology of science', in E. Mendelsohn and Y. Elkana (eds), *Sciences and Cultures: Anthropological Studies of the Sciences*, Dordrecht: Reidel, pp. 245–61.

Levy, M. (1966), *Modernisation and the Structure of Societies,* Vol. 1, Princeton, NJ: Princeton University Press.

Lewis, W.A. (1955), *Theory of Economic Growth*, London: Allen & Unwin.

Li, J. and A. Tsui (2002), 'A citation analysis of management and organisation research in the Chinese context: 1984–1999', *Asia Pacific Journal of Management*, **19** (1), 87–107.

Linstead, S.L. (1993), 'From postmodern anthropology to deconstructive ethnography', *Human Relations*, **46** (1), 97–120.

Loomba, A. (1998), *Colonialism/Postcolonialism*, London/New York: Routledge.

MacKerras, C. (2000), *Western Images of China*, 2nd edn, Hong Kong: Oxford University Press.

Malinowski, B. (1954), *Magic, Science and Religion*, Garden City, NY: Double Day Anchor.

McClelland, D.C. (1961), *The Achieving Society*, Princeton, NJ: Van Nostrand Reinhold.

McClennan, J.E. (1992), *Colonialism and Science: Saint Domingue in the Old Regime*, Baltimore, MD: Johns Hopkins University Press.

Mendenhall, G., D. Beaty and G.R. Oddou (1993), 'Where have all the theories gone? An archival view of the international management literature', *International Journal of Management*, **10** (2), 146–53.

Nash, M. (1966), *Primitive and Peasant Economic Systems*, Chicago, IL: University of Chicago/Chandler.

Needham, J. (1969), *The Great Titration: Science and Society in the East and West*, Toronto: University of Toronto Press.

Nelson, L.H. and J. Nelson (eds) (1996), *Feminism, Science and the Philosophy of Science*, Dordrecht: Kluwer.

Nkomo, S.M. (1992), 'The emperor has no clothes: rewriting "race" in organisations', *Academy of Management Review*, **17** (3), 487–513.

Ong, A. (1987), *Spirits of Resistance and Capitalist Discipline: Factory Women in Malaysia*, Albany, NY: State University of New York Press.

Oseen, C. (1997), 'The sexually specific subject and the dilemma of difference: rethinking the different in the construction of the nonhierarchical workplace', in P. Prasad, A.J. Mills, M. Elmes and A. Prasad (eds), *Managing the Organisational Melting Pot: Dilemmas of Workplace Diversity*, London: Sage, pp. 54–79.

Parry, B. (1987), 'Problems in current theories of colonial discourse', *Oxford Literary Review*, **13**, 25–58.

Parsons, T. (1951), *The Social System*, London: Routledge & Kegan Paul.

―――― (1964), *Social Structure and Personality*, New York: Free Press of Glencoe.

―――― (1971), *The System of Modern Societies*, Englewood Cliffs, NJ: Prentice-Hall.

Parsons, T. and E.A. Shils (1951), *Towards a General Theory of Action*, Cambridge, MA: Harvard University Press.

Prasad, A. (1997), 'The colonising consciousness and representations of the Other: a postcolonial critique of the discourse of oil', in P. Prasad, A.J. Mills, M. Elmes and A. Prasad (eds), *Managing the Organisational Melting Pot: Dilemmas of Workplace Diversity*, London: Sage, pp. 285–311.

―――― (ed.) (2003a), *Postcolonial Theory and Organizational Analysis: A Critical Engagement*, New York: Palgrave.

Prasad, P. (2003b), 'The return of the native: organizational discourses and the legacy of the ethnographic imagination', in A. Prasad (ed.), *Postcolonial Theory and Organizational Analysis: A Critical Engagement*, New York: Palgrave pp. 123–45.

Prasad, P., A.J. Mills, M. Elmes and A. Prasad (eds) (1997), *Managing the Organisational Melting Pot: Dilemmas of Workplace Diversity*, London: Sage.

Punnett, B.J. and O. Shenkar (eds) (1996), *Handbook for International Management Research*, Cambridge, MA: Blackwell.

Radcliffe-Brown, A.R. (1965), *Structure and Function in Primitive Society*, New York: Free Press.

Redding, S.G. (1990), *The Spirit of Chinese Capitalism*, Berlin: de Gruyter.

―――― (1994), 'The comparative management theory zoo: getting the elephants and ostriches and even dinosaurs from the jungle into the iron cages', in B. Toyne and D. Nigh (eds), *International Business Inquiry: An Emerging Vision*, Columbia, SC: University of South Carolina Press, pp. 416–39.

Redding, S.G. and T.A. Martyn-Johns (1979), 'Paradigm differences and their relation to management, with reference to Southeast Asia', in G.W. England, A.R. Negandhi and B. Wilpert (eds), *Organisational Functioning in a Cross-Cultural*

Perspective, Kent, OH: Comparative Administration Research Institute, pp. 34–46.

Redding, S.G. and G.Y.Y. Wong (1986), 'The psychology of Chinese organizational behaviour', in M.H. Bond (ed.), *The Psychology of the Chinese People*, Hong Kong: Oxford University Press, pp. 267–95.

Reingold, N. and M. Rothenberg (eds) (1987), *Scientific Colonialism: Cross-Cultural Comparisons*, Washington, DC: Smithsonian Institute Press.

Richman, B. (1977), 'The significance of cultural variables', in T. Weinshall (ed.), *Culture and Management*, Harmondsworth: Penguin, pp. 15–38.

Robinson, R.D. (1964), *International Business Policy*, New York: Holt, Rinehart & Winston.

Ronen, S. (1986), *Comparative and Multicultural Management*, New York: John Wiley & Sons.

Rosaldo, R. (1989), *Culture and Truth*, Boston, MA: Beacon Press.

Sachs, W. (ed.) (1992), *The Development Dictionary: A Guide to Knowledge as Power*, Atlantic Highlands, NJ: Zed.

Said, E.W. (1978), *Orientalism*, New York: Pantheon Books.

Sardar, Z. (ed.) (1988), *The Revenge of Athena: Science, Exploitation and the Third World*, London: Mansell.

Sjöberg, G. (1970), 'The comparative method in the social sciences', in A. Etzioni and F.L. Dobow (eds), *Comparative Perspectives: Theories and Methods*, Boston: Little, Brown & Co. pp. 43–67.

Snow, D.A. and C. Morill (1993), 'Reflections of anthropology's ethnographic crisis of faith', *Contemporary Sociology*, **22**, 8–11.

Steier, F. (1991), *Research and Reflexivity*, London: Sage.

Theodorson, G.A. (1953), 'Acceptance of industrialisation and its attendant consequences for the social pattern of non-Western societies', *American Sociological Review*, **18** (5), 476–85.

Thomas, A.S. (1996), 'A call for research in forgotten locations', in B.J. Punnett and O. Shenkar (eds), *Handbook for International Management Research*, Oxford: Blackwell, pp. 485–506.

Thomas, N. (1994), *Colonialism's Culture: Anthropology, Travel and Government*, Cambridge: Polity Press.

Tranfield, D. (2002), 'Future challenges for management research', *European Management Journal*, **20** (4), 409–13.

Triandis, H.C. (1982–83), 'Dimensions of cultural variations as parameters of organisational theories', *International Studies of Management and Organization*, **12** (4), 139–69.

Trompenaars, F. and C. Hampden-Turner (1993), *Riding the Waves of Culture: Understanding Cultural Diversity in Business*, London: Nicholas Brealey.

Weinshall, T. (ed.) (1977), *Culture and Management*, Harmondsworth: Penguin.

—— (ed.) (1993), *Society Culture and Management*, Berlin: Walter de Gruyter.

Westwood, R.I. (2001), 'Appropriating the Other in the discourses of comparative management', in R.I. Westwood and S. Linstead (eds), *The Language of Organisation*, London: Sage, pp. 241–62.

White, S. (2002), 'Rigor and relevance in Asian management research: where are we and where can we go?', *Asia Pacific Journal of Management*, **19** (2–3), 287–352.

Wong, S.L. (1985), 'The Chinese family firm: a model', *British Journal of Sociology*, **36** (1), 58–72.

Wong-MingJi, D. and A.H. Mir (1997), 'How international is international management? Provincialism, parochialism, and the problematic of global diversity', in P. Prasad, A.J. Mills, M. Elmes and A. Prasad (eds), *Managing the Organisational Melting Pot: Dilemmas of Workplace Diversity*, London: Sage, pp. 340–64.

Wright, LL. (1996), 'Qualitative international management research', in B.J. Punnett and O. Shenkar (eds), *Handbook for International Management Research*, Oxford: Blackwell, pp. 63–81.

Young, R.J.C. (2001), *Postcolonialism: An Historical Introduction*, Oxford: Blackwell.

4. Hermeneutic Methodology and International Business Research

Niels G. Noorderhaven

INTRODUCTION

International business has over the past decades gradually matured into a distinct field of research. The research community has its own academy, conferences and scholarly journals. At the same time, it can be said that the field is victim of a prolonged identity crisis. What exactly distinguishes the *international* business field from business *tout court*? If international business research is just an application of theories and research methods on issues that happen to include cross-border aspects, we may ask ourselves the question whether it makes sense to regard it a separate research field. Parkhe (1993, p. 243) called upon management theorists to recognise 'the challenges unique to international management'.

The main point of this chapter is to introduce an approach which does justice to the challenges formed by the unique character of international business or international management as a field. This unique character can be indicated with the concept of 'distance'. Distance plays a double role in international business as an object of inquiry. First there is the distance experienced by the actors in the field: the geographical, social, political, economic, cultural and linguistic distance between buyer and seller, subsidiary and parent company, division A and division B, manager X and manager Y. If this distance were not of crucial importance, why regard international business as a separate field? How these various distances are bridged is the basic issue with which international business occupies itself, and which sets it apart as a field of study. But distance is also important for international business research in a second way. Researchers in the field of international business almost always study a social reality which is much more distant to them than if they were studying domestic organisations or management processes. Even when studying their own society, international business researchers typically do so from an implicitly or explicitly comparative perspective. In this case there is the advantage that the researcher has an intimate familiarity with the society in which the phenomena studied are embedded. However, in order to acquire a comparative perspective, the researcher has to overcome the prejudices that prevent him or her from seeing the things that are taken for granted. This tension between the advantages and disadvantages of familiarity with the national context is described in Michailova (Chapter 18 this volume).

The field of international business calls for a methodology that does justice to the fundamental problems of bridging distance, for practitioners and researchers alike. In this chapter the hermeneutic approach to social reality and social research is put forth as such a methodology. In philosophical hermeneutics, the problem of bridging the distance between the interpreting subject and the phenomena interpreted is given a central position. Hermeneutics (from the Greek *hermeneuein*, to explain, put in words, or translate) refers to the interpretation of phenomena as signs. Interpretation is an act of understanding in which phenomena are taken to be signs referring to a meaning. For an interpretation to be successful it is not enough to observe the signs; their meaning should also be established. Signs can be understood if we can reconstruct and make their meanings our own. This, in essence, means that we try to integrate the sign that we want to understand within our own semiotic horizon, that is, the general, more or less coherent system of signs that forms our worldview (Grondin 1994).

In the following section, the applicability of hermeneutics to the study of organisational phenomena is first discussed. Subsequently, hermeneutics is briefly outlined. This overview does not aim at completeness, but concentrates on particular aspects of philosophical hermeneutics as developed by Hans-Georg Gadamer (1999), and laid down in his *magnum opus, Truth and Method*. After that, previous applications of hermeneutics to management research are briefly discussed. In the third section the relevance of issues of distance and meaning in international business is illustrated with examples from case studies of international alliances. Conclusions follow.

APPLICABILITY OF THE HERMENEUTIC PERSPECTIVE

Organisational Phenomena as Signs

Organisations are not natural phenomena. They are constructed, and constantly reconstructed, by the people within and around them. Consequently, these people also regard them in a different way to natural phenomena. Organisational phenomena are seen as existing for certain reasons, as referring to the purposes of those who produce them. They are regarded as having meaning. Put differently, organisational phenomena are interpreted as signs. A sign can be defined as something that, in somebody's view, stands for something else. A sign is considered to consist of a signifier and a signified, while the relationship between signifier (the organisational phenomenon) and signified (the underlying meaning) is arbitrary. Moreover, the status of the sign is not given, but exists in the eyes of the beholder. What is a sign to one need not be a sign to another. However, man, being a sensemaking creature (Geertz 1973), has a strong tendency to interpret phenomena as signs, in particular in the social world, where social objects can be seen as 'intrinsically meaningful' (Sayer 1992).

Hence, organisational phenomena are bound to be interpreted by the people around them as signs. This is important because the meaning one attributes to an organisational phenomenon has a bearing on one's behaviour. Research on 'framing' and 'cognitive schemata' provides evidence that the way people see the world has a strong impact not only on what they perceive to be rational behaviour, but also on the actual behavioural choices that they make (Barr 1998). To understand the meaning of an organisational phenomenon means having reconstructed the motives, intentions, aims or expectations which have produced that phenomenon (Albert 1988; Weber 1968). This, in turn, will strongly influence one's reaction to that organisational phenomenon. An example will help to make this more clear.

The French researcher Alain Henry (1991), in one of his papers, describes the Régies Nationales des Eaux de Togo, the national drinking water company of the West African state of Togo.[1] In this company, a manual is used which, for all employees, from the *Directeur Général* down to the junior clerk, stipulates what they are expected to do in almost all possible circumstances. Of course, the rules are more detailed further down the hierarchy, but at all levels, the circumstantiality of the rules and procedures and the inclusiveness of the manual are remarkable. Technical tasks as well as management duties are described; not just work processes, but also times of prayer, and leave of absence in the case of the death of a relative and other family circumstances, are mentioned. There is even a procedure for organising the personnel party at the end of the year (Henry 1991, p. 470).

What is the impact of this manual? How do the employees of the Régies Nationales react to it? Is the Régies Nationales to be seen as an extremely Tayloristic organisation, in which all discretion is taken away from lower-level employees and tasks are impoverished? Does it lead to alienation and loss of motivation? Apparently not, for the Régies Nationales des Eaux de Togo is mentioned as an example of 'best practice' in Africa in a study published by the World Bank (Dia 1996). According to Henry (1991), the manual increases rather than restricts the leeway of lower-level employees. In ambiguous situations, lower-level employees will always ask for the opinion of their supervisor. African traditions of respect for authority and seniority may play a role here, but a well-founded fear of being scapegoated if things go wrong is also of importance (Nnadozie 2001; for an opposing view, see

Ugwuegbu 2001). When subordinates have exact instructions, they can work much more independently, and much more decentralisation is possible. The rules also protect employees against pressure for preferential treatment by relatives and acquaintances. And what about the motivation of the workers? Henry (1991, p. 455) quotes a manager of the Régies Nationales, who argues that the manual improves employee motivation by increasing their 'self-importance'.[2]

The example of the Régies Nationales des Eaux de Togo shows that a particular organisational phenomenon – the formalisation of organisational roles – may be interpreted in radically different ways, and, as a result, also have radically divergent behavioural consequences. If extreme formalisation of one's organisational role is interpreted as a sign of distrust of one's intentions or one's skills (or both), a likely response will be alienation and loss of motivation. However, if the same phenomenon is construed to be a protection against the whims of supervisors and others, and to provide a basis for autonomous action within the confines of the organisational role, the behavioural response may be an increase of involvement, initiative and motivation. In general, important elements of organisations (for example, authority structures and rules and procedures) are socially constructed and need to be interpreted, and, hence, can easily be misinterpreted when interpretation takes place across geographical, social, political, economic, cultural and linguistic distances.

The example of the Régies Nationales des Eaux de Togo demonstrates that organisational phenomena, like social phenomena in general, are fundamentally equivocal (Daft and MacIntosh 1981). They can be interpreted in many different ways, since there is no unambiguous link between the sign and its meaning. This creates an uncertainty that people in and around organisations have to cope with, and it creates an even larger uncertainty for researchers of organisations, who are usually outsiders to the organisational reality they study.

In their constant struggle to make sense of their worlds, people look at each other. The formation of an interpretation of reality is a social process, in which one's interpretation of the world, and one's actions based on that, influence the other's interpretations and actions, and vice versa (Weick 1979). The fundamental equivocality of signs opens up a wide scope of possible interpretations. In the world of signs, there is no transcendent reality ordered in a particular way; actors have to make their own order. Choosing a particular interpretation, which will bring immanent order to equivocal sensory inputs, is a creative act, called 'enactment' by Weick (1979, 1995). By making an interpretation and basing one's behaviour on it, one creates new signs for others, which they will take into account in their own sensemaking processes. In this way, meaning is constantly created and re-created in a process of circular causation (Feldman and March 1981; Thomas et al. 1993; Weick 1979, 2001). What a social phenomenon is depends on what it means to the members of a social group, and this social nature of the interpretation and enactment process puts limits on the creation of meaning. Interpretations and the behaviours based on them 'reciprocally confirm' (Llewellyn 1993) other interpretations and behaviours. The one who drifts too far apart effectively places him/herself outside the community of meaning.

Hermeneutics as a Methodology

The social nature of the process of sensemaking underscores the additional difficulties encountered by an outsider trying to make sense of a social reality that is exterior to him or her. Social reality is constructed within communities of people that can be indicated as 'cognitive communities' (Berger and Luckmann 1966), such as groups of individuals working closely together in an organisation (Daft and Weick 1984). The problems of interpreting a social phenomenon within a cultural group are never trivial, given the complexity and equivocality of the social world. However, these difficulties are much increased when one tries to make sense of social phenomena across boundaries of cultural groups. This is always the case in international business – for both practitioners and researchers.

My guess is that few readers from Western countries, unfamiliar with the case of the Régies Nationales des Eaux de Togo, would expect much good to result from the Manual. At the same time, understanding what organisational phenomena mean to incumbents remains of utmost importance in international business research. Interaction processes in international business can only be understood if we carefully 'read' the meanings produced, communicated and negotiated by the practitioners involved in these processes. Hermeneutics, a methodology based on the assumption that social reality has to be understood by reading it as a system of signs, is of particular relevance here. We shall, therefore, now turn to a brief discussion of hermeneutics.

Hermeneutics as a method of interpreting texts, in particular Biblical texts, has a history of at least three centuries, and a pre-history in which the word 'hermeneutics' was not yet used going back to the Hellenic period (Grondin 1994). However, hermeneutics not as a method but as a methodology (which is customarily referred to as 'philosophical hermeneutics') is of much more recent origin, and is associated with the work of the twentieth-century philosophers Martin Heidegger, Hans-Georg Gadamer and Paul Ricoeur. Originally, it was intended that hermeneutics would offer the sciences of the mind an alternative to the logical empiricism of the natural sciences. In the natural sciences, hypotheses derived in accordance with the rules of logical inference are tested against relevant data, with the goal of identifying general regularities or 'covering laws'. Especially in the German tradition, this model was seen as unfit for the sciences of the mind, like the arts and history. As an alternative to the empirical cycle of logical positivism, hermeneutics proposes the hermeneutic circle. In the hermeneutic circle, the interpreter moves from an understanding of single elements to an understanding of the whole. In interpreting texts, the elements are the individual words which, alongside their general meaning, have a specific meaning within the text. The meaning within the text can only be understood by looking at the context, but the meaning of the context, of course, can only be grasped with reference to the meaning of the words out of which it consists:

> Thus the movement of understanding is constantly from the whole to the part and back to the whole. Our task is to expand the unity of the understood meaning centrifugally. The harmony of all the details with the whole is the criterion of correct understanding. The failure to achieve this harmony means that understanding has failed. (Gadamer 1999, p. 291)

As stated in the introduction, hermeneutics refers to the interpretation of phenomena as signs, and considers understanding to take place if a sign can be integrated into the semiotic horizon of the interpreter.[3] This is possible only in a 'dialogue' between the worldview of the self and the worldview on which the object to be interpreted is based. This process always has to start at a prior position that is, by definition (otherwise the understanding would not have to be sought because it would already be there), based on insufficient knowledge of the phenomenon studied. Gadamer uses the word 'prejudice', but not in the conventional pejorative sense. A prejudice, for Gadamer, is nothing more or less than a pre-judgement made at the beginning of the dialogue (Gadamer 1999, p. 270). As our prejudices are confronted in more and more depth with the phenomenon we try to understand, we can see which of them are misguided and have to be altered (How 1995). Interpreting a product of the human mind implies a fusion of horizons: the horizon of the interpreter and the horizon(s) of the individual(s) whose product we try to understand. This fusion is possible only if, from the start, there is some overlap, some common ground. The possibility that different horizons can be fused lies in the fact that they are already implicitly joined 'in the depths of tradition' (Gadamer 1999, p. 306).

If we inevitably start from prejudice this also means that we inevitably are subjective, because we are part of a tradition. The tradition of which the interpreter is a part determines the prejudices from which the interpretation will start. We cannot simply step out of 'the historical field of our tradition' (How 1995, p. 37); 'our foundations lie deeper than we can say' (Caputo 1989, p. 259). In that sense, tradition defines what we can and what we cannot see: our horizon. However, our place in the tradition and the prejudices that stem from it are also a condition of understanding: without it, no understanding would be possible, because there would be no semiotic system within which to integrate the phenomenon to be understood. To stand outside of one's historicity would not mean having an objective view – it would mean having no view at all (Francis 1994).

Interpretation in the hermeneutic view is not a passive process. For the philosopher Friedrich Schleiermacher, understanding is an act: 'misunderstanding follows automatically and understanding must be desired and sought at every point' (quoted in Gadamer 1999, p. 185). When confronted with a phenomenon which is not immediately accessible to interpretation, understanding much be reached through engagement in a dialogue, in which the alien reality is drawn within one's own horizon, which consequently moves and expands. The projective character of understanding revealed by Heidegger and endorsed by Gadamer (1999, p. 260) is equivalent to that of Weick's 'enactment'. Hermeneutics can help us understand these activities of interpretation through dialogue in the field of international business.

Hermeneutics and Management Research

The relevance of a methodology for the interpretation of texts (biblical texts, literary texts, historical texts, juridical texts) to research in the social sciences lies in the generalisation of the concept of text, using this term to mean anything from letters on a sheet of paper to any coherent whole of signs. If texts are seen in this more general way, understanding of social action is a form of reading (Lachmann 1991; Ricoeur 1991; Thompson 1993). Just like the letters on the paper are taken to refer to something else, such as ideas formed by the author, so actions or social phenomena can be taken for signs of the intentions or beliefs of their 'authors'. In this sense, Gadamer's well-known statement that 'being that can be understood is language' (Gadamer 1999, p. 474) has to be read, and this makes hermeneutic methodology applicable also to the field of (international) business.

A growing number of hermeneutically inspired papers have been published in recent years (for a review, see Prasad 2002), for example in the fields of organisational culture (Mercier 1994), the labour process (Ezzy 1997), information systems (Boland et al. 1994; Butler 1998; Klein and Myers 1999; Myers 1995), consumer behaviour (Arnold and Fischer 1994) and accounting (Arrington and Francis 1993; Francis 1994; Llewellyn 1993). In international comparative management, there is one specific approach that can be seen as implicitly hermeneutical (Noorderhaven 2000). This is the so-called societal effect approach, which tries to explain the particular characteristics of management and organisation in different countries on the basis of the reciprocal, interactive constitution of actors and institutions (Maurice et al.

1980; Maurice and Sorge 2000; Sorge 1991; Sorge and Warner 1986).

Notwithstanding the papers referred to above, as well as others not mentioned here, it can be concluded that hermeneutics still has a peripheral position in the field of business research as a whole, as well as in the field of international business. Judging by what is published in the major research journals, it seems fair to say that the majority of international business researchers implicitly or explicitly adhere to a philosophy of science that is closer to logical empiricism than to hermeneutics.

In logical empiricism, rooted in the logical positivism developed in the 1920s and 1930s by the Vienna Circle, knowledge is created by the application of the empirical cycle. Theories deducing refutable hypotheses from basic assumptions through series of analytic propositions are tested against empirical data. If the hypotheses are refuted, new theories are built, and, possibly, new basic assumptions made. But the confrontation with 'data' is not unproblematic. How do we know that something is true or not, and, thus, whether a hypothesis is corroborated or falsified? Observations entirely free from theory do not exist. Perception brackets certain sensory inputs as signals and others not, based on some prior idea of what is and what is not relevant (Lavoie 1991). And empirical research, at least in the social sciences, is very much a social process in which 'objective facts' are socially constructed (Kuhn 1962).

One of the reasons for the peripheral position of the hermeneutic perspective may be the confusion surrounding the many perspectives that are offered as alternatives to the positivistically-inclined mainstream, such as critical theory, discourse analysis, deconstruction, ethnography, narrative analysis, postcolonialism and symbolic interactionism (Prasad and Prasad 2002). The confusion may have to do with the fact that some of these approaches are what above was called methodologies, while others can better be characterised as methods. A methodology is a system of ontological and epistemological assumptions on which research is to be based; a research method is a particular strategy for collecting and analysing data (Llewellyn 1993). Adopting a hermeneutic perspective has ontological consequences, for in hermeneutics 'understanding is the original characteristic of the being of human life itself' (Gadamer 1999, p. 259), as well as epistemological ramifications, for a hermeneutician 'every "Thou" is an alter ego, i.e., it is understood in terms of the ego and, at the same, as detached from it and, like the ego itself, as independent' (Gadamer 1999, p. 250). Of course, a methodological position, such as hermeneutics, is also likely to have implications for the choice of a research method, but the two should not be confused.

In the first place, and most importantly, the hermeneutic perspective is associated with a different view of the nature of the subject of research in international business. This different view of the nature of the subject of research leads to different research questions. This is the type of implication I shall focus on in this chapter. In the second place, adopting a hermeneutic perspective may also have consequences for the choice of research methods. However, this is not usually a direct effect, but an indirect effect, working through the selection of research questions. Hermeneutics underdetermines the choice of method (Arnold and Fischer 1994). Nevertheless, I believe that hermeneutics does have something to say with regard to the process of doing research. This will also be discussed briefly in this chapter.

Below I shall first illustrate the applicability of a hermeneutic perspective to the field of international business. For this purpose I shall focus on international alliances, an increasingly popular organisational form, that however is plagued with high degrees of instability. In my view this is due to the fact that international alliances to an extreme degree face 'the challenges unique to international management' (Parkhe 1993, p. 243), because they require close interaction across organisational and national boundaries. Hence they form a particularly interesting phenomenon to look at from a hermeneutic point of view.

HERMENEUTICS AND INTERNATIONAL ALLIANCES

In this section I shall illustrate the application of hermeneutic methodology to international alliance research, drawing on a number of clinical studies reported in the literature. In all cases discussed, the cooperation between the two parent firms required intensive collaborative interaction, whether the alliance constitutes a separate unit (as in the case of a joint venture) or not. While none of the case studies described was performed from a deliberately hermeneutic perspective, the researchers show a remarkable sensitivity to the importance of the sensemaking processes within the alliances/joint ventures. I shall first focus on the influence of initial conditions and expectations, reflecting the prejudice on which understanding is unavoidably built. After that, cycles of joint sensemaking in international alliances are discussed, as an example of how practitioners go through the hermeneutic circle. Finally, I shall go into the process of interpretation by the researcher, and the relationship between this interpretive effort and other sources of information.

Initial Conditions and Expectations

Many authors have noted the importance of the initial structural conditions and partner expectations for unfolding processes within the international alliance (for example, Hagedoorn and Schakenraad 1994; Reuer and Miller 1997). This is also clearly reflected in case studies. But case studies also illustrate how expectations mould structural conditions, in the sense of contractual and other organisational arrangements, and the subjective nature of these expectations themselves. Hence, a mechanistic approach linking expected international alliance success to a set of objectively given environmental factors misses much of the action. Doz (1996) notes that the partners enter the collaboration with both a set of shared, explicit expectations, and privately harboured expectations. This complex amalgamate of expectations, partly explicit and shared, partly implicit and/or private, is the basis for the formal agreement underlying the venture. Salk and Shenkar (2001) studied a joint venture between a British and an Italian chemical firm from a social identity perspective. They conclude that the social identities of those involved, as established early in the venture, 'become a lens mediating the impact of contextual change on the enactment of the [international joint venture] setting and functioning by its members' (Salk and Shenkar 2001, p. 173). Changes in context and environment that these authors would expect to lead to a stronger identification of joint venture personnel with the joint venture did not in fact change the British–Italian divide initially established.

The initial expectations may be a powerful factor influencing further development of the international alliance. As remarked by Parkhe (1998a), anticipating business gains is a highly subjective process. Moreover, the partners initially have only a tentative understanding of each other's private motives (Doz 1996). They start from prejudice, so to say, in interpreting the behaviour of their counterpart. However, the initial expectations, explicit and implicit, will to a certain extent determine the contractual and organisational arrangements at the outset of the international alliance. These arrangements will subsequently influence the behaviour within and around the venture, which may create a self-fulfilling prophecy. Doz observes how the necessity to adapt to the other partner triggers 'defense mechanisms' which actually bolster existing tendencies towards inertia in organisations.

Cycles of Joint Sensemaking

Once the international alliance is under way, those involved (managers working directly for the alliance or joint venture as well as managers within the parent firms) will closely look for cues to 'validate, challenge or recast the initial expectations' (Doz 1996, p. 67). As a result, Doz notes, small early events may have very significant consequences for the further evolution of the alliance venture. A parent firm tries to interpret these small initial events; in other words, to read them as signs indicating the true motives, intentions and abilities of their partner. Subsequent actions will be based on these interpretations, which then are interpreted by the other firm, which will base its actions on this interpretation, and so on, in an ongoing process of mutual sensemaking. This process can lead to the gradual build-up and reinforcement of trust and cooperation within the international alliance (Parkhe 1998b). But it can also lead to a vicious cycle of suspicion and distrust. An initial tendency to believe in good faith may easily turn into its opposite, or, as Hamel (1991, p. 84) puts it: 'there may be a shift from "naiveté" to "paranoia"'.

The events and changes in circumstances met by the managers of alliances or joint ventures and their parent companies are often very real; it is not 'just' a matter of clashing interpretations. But at least as important is that at almost every junction the managers involved can indeed choose between divergent interpretations. Reluctance of one of the parties to give access to its distribution system for new product lines of the venture without renegotiation of the contract may be interpreted as a retreat from the original agreement, but it may also be seen as a normal reaction to an unforeseen change in the strategy of the alliance (Ariño and de la Torre 1998). The factors may be 'objective', but how they are interpreted by managers makes a lot of difference.

The cases also provide many examples of how organisational distance impedes the production of a shared meaning. In Doz's (1996, p. 67) description of an alliance the two partner firms 'projected onto the other, through the interface in the alliance, a set of organisational action routines borrowed from its own organisational context, that became baffling, disconcerting and ultimately aggravating to members of the other firm'.

Not only differences in organisational cultures, but also radically different technology bases make joint sensemaking difficult. In the case of an alliance between pharmaceutical firms, Doz (1996) notices that the respective technology bases were so different that one partner's technical personnel questioned the true potential of the other partner's technology. The interesting issue is that in Doz's rendering of the case it is not the objective characteristics of the technology *per se* that lead to this judgement, but rather the inability to communicate effectively. This discussion of technological learning (or the absence thereof) seems to bring us closer to the conventional predisposition of the alliance literature towards a learning perspective. However, the learning metaphor summons up a picture of a very deliberate, conscious cognitive process. The interpretation and sensemaking processes that are given a central position in this chapter, however, are of both a more fundamental and less deliberate nature. Thus, whereas Hamel (1991) treats 'learning' as a variable dependent on the intent of the partners, their transparency and their receptivity, sensemaking and interpretation are primary activities, and may even be seen as constituting human existence.

Incumbents' Meaning and 'Objective' Facts

In the hermeneutic view, the process of interpretation is not confined to the international alliance and its parents. The researcher studying international alliances is involved in a sensemaking process that is very much comparable to that of the subjects, or 'incumbents', of his or her study. This is what Giddens (1984, p. 284) calls the 'double hermeneutic'. A point that should be made, however, is that employing a hermeneutic approach does not mean that the researcher only tries to read the meaning ascribed to certain phenomena by the subjects of his or her study, and stops there.

In all the studies discussed, the researchers collect data on 'objective' external and internal events, as well as on the meanings ascribed to these events by incumbents. The goal of a hermeneutic analysis is not to take for granted the interpretations and meanings produced by incumbents (Gadamer 1999). Gadamer rejects the traditional hermeneutical rule that condemns interpretations that the writer or the (implied) reader could not have intended. In case studies of international alliances, data on 'objective' external and internal events are analysed, as are the incumbents' meanings ascribed to these events by incumbents. Doz (1996, p. 80) explicitly reflects on the need to do so in his statement that '[f]ocusing only on individuals would have led one to concentrate on interpersonal relationships and ignore, or not analyse in detail, the organisational and strategic contexts within which alliances unfolded; while focusing on strategic and organisational contexts would have led one to reify the organisation'. In other words, Doz pleads for paying attention to incumbents' meanings and the context in which they are produced. Hence the interpretation of the researcher is not meant to be a 'faithful' reflection of the practitioners' interpretations, as the latter are embedded into the worldview of the interpreter, which is also based on information not known to the practitioners studied, or interpreted differently by them.

External and internal events constitute the set of structural conditions within which actors operate (and which in turn may also be influenced by their actions, of course). How they operate, and which actions they perform, within the bandwidth of feasible options, depends very much on their subjective reading of these structures and events. The researcher looks at both the 'objective' structures and events and the 'subjective' meanings produced by practitioners within that context, and on the basis of these inputs tries to come to an understanding of the social phenomena studied. Thus the researcher does not have to take for granted the meanings produced by incumbents: 'the interpretation [by the researcher] of action can have a power of disclosure which transcends the limited horizons of the existential situation of the agent' (Rabinow and Sullivan, quoted in Llewellyn 1993, p. 238).

IMPLICATIONS FOR INTERNATIONAL BUSINESS RESEARCH

In this chapter, bridging distances is put forward as the essence of international business, and hermeneutics has been presented as a methodology in which the act of bridging distance has been given a central ontological and epistemological position. Taking this perspective seriously implies that (1) practitioners of international business are regarded as hermeneuticians, and (2) the researcher in this field is regarded as a hermeneutician. I shall discuss three key implications for international business research.

Managerial Perceptions are a Crucial Focus of Research

Like Molière's *Bourgeois gentilhomme* who has unwittingly spoken in prose all of his life, internationally operating managers are practising hermeneuticians without probably being aware of it. Studying the international manager as a practising hermeneutician implies a focus on organisational reality as interpreted by these managers, on the processes and activities that produce or influence their interpretations, and on the ways in which interpretations in turn mould organisational reality. A focus on the views of managers as a key factor in international business is in stark contrast to the preference for 'objective' data in more positivistically flavoured research. Milton Friedman has voiced the extreme position in this regard: 'answers given by businessmen to questions about the factors affecting their decisions [is] a procedure for testing economic theories that is about on par with testing theories of longevity by asking octogenarians how they account for their long life' (Friedman 1953, p. 85).

From a hermeneutic perspective, Friedman's position is untenable. It would deny any influence of the thoughts and feelings of key actors on the outcomes of international business activities. Although few scholars would nowadays subscribe to such an extreme view, the idea that 'objective' data form a more solid basis for conclusions than perceptions is widespread. In contrast, the position defended here is that identical 'objective facts' may be interpreted in radically different ways, and as a result of that also lead to different consequences. An example is international joint venture dissolution or duration. These 'objective facts' have often been used as indicators of the success or failure of the venture. But, as indicated by Gulati (1998), some alliances may be designed for limited duration, and the objective fact of termination combines timely and untimely deaths. But the two will be very differently interpreted by the managers involved, and these different interpretations are likely to have diverging consequences. This example illustrates that the perceptions of internationally operating managers are not only a legitimate, but even a crucial focus of research in international business. Research neglecting managerial perceptions runs the risk of remaining seriously incomplete.

Interaction Processes Influencing Perceptions Need to Be Studied

The second category of research issues suggested by hermeneutics consists of processes and activities that may be assumed to produce or influence managerial perceptions. If we take international alliances as an example again, there has in the literature been a notable lack of attention to process aspects (Doz 1996; Yan and Zeng 1999). From a hermeneutic point of view the interaction processes between managers involved in an international joint venture are of considerable interest, as it is through these processes that the distances between organisations and cultures are bridged, and interpretations are formed and adapted up to the point that there is a 'fusion of horizons'. Hence, it is important to study the relationship between characteristics of interaction processes and the formation and adaptation of interpretations. Analogous to the process dimensions studied in the context of trust building, researchers could focus on the duration, intensity and riskiness of interaction processes (Noorderhaven 1996). Duration is important because going through the hermeneutic circle is a time-consuming process. The intensity of the interaction process refers to the kind of communication (face to face rather than through an intermediary) and the degree of whole-person involvement (Dyer and Chu 2000). The more and more intensively managers involved in international collaboration communicate, the more likely a 'fusion of horizons' is. The riskiness of the interaction in the trust literature, finally, refers to the opportunity of one or both of the partners to defect. If he or she refrains from doing so, this is a powerful booster of trust (Coleman 1990; Noorderhaven 1996). In the context of interpretation and sensemaking, riskiness can best be interpreted as eventfulness. If, over time, more critical incidents take place, better sensemaking may be assumed to take place.

The consequences of the interpretations formed by internationally operating managers will very often be the phenomena international business research seeks to explain, for example, the longevity of international joint ventures, international control strategies, or expansion paths of multinational corporations. These variables also remain important if a hermeneutic perspective is adopted but, in contrast to the more conventional perspective, their explanation runs through managers' interpretations of organisational reality, as well as through the processes influencing these interpretations.

Dialogical Research Methods Are Important

Regarding the researcher as a hermeneutician means that attention is paid to the processes through which the researcher makes sense of the phenomena studied in an international business context, that is, self-reflexivity is important. If the researcher is to understand the interpretations formed by practitioners (the 'double hermeneutic'), a fusion of horizons is necessary here, too. A researcher, like his or her subjects of research, is placed in a historical and spatial context and understands within a finite horizon. However, the researcher should always try to expand this horizon, and, from this perspective, research methods that put the researcher in a veritable dialogue with the object of study (like personal interviews) are to be preferred over methods that prevent such a dialogue from taking place (like studying archival data).[4] After all, 'a horizon is not a rigid boundary but something that moves with one and invites one to advance further' (Gadamer 1999, p. 245).

Since in international business, research almost always implies the necessity to bridge cultural distances, the question of how this can be done deserves attention. The author is involved in a research project focusing on the attributes, antecedents and consequences of consensus decision-making at the Japanese–Dutch interface (for a first cut at the data, see Keizer et al. 2000). In the study, Japanese and Dutch managers were interviewed who worked side by side in either Japanese companies operating in the Netherlands, or Dutch companies in Japan. In order to gauge these managers' interpretations of consensus decision-making, open interviews were held organised around decision-making procedures, broadly defined. All the interviews were held by a team consisting of a Dutch and a Japanese researcher. The Dutch researcher had a basic knowledge of Japanese, and both were fluent in English. Language capabilities are extremely important from a hermeneutic point of view, as understanding across language barriers is particularly problematic. Learning a relevant foreign language is more than just an expedient for communication in international business research. To learn a language 'is to increase the extent of what one can learn' (Gadamer 1999, p. 442). In the (ongoing) process of interpreting the interview protocols, the diversity of cultural, linguistic and disciplinary backgrounds of the members of the research team is also fully utilised.

Whereas understanding the interpretations of internationally operating managers calls for research methods that promote a dialogue between researcher and practitioners, this is less true when studying the processes leading to interpretations. As indicated above, a number of interaction characteristics can be distinguished that are likely to influence the interpretation processes of international managers. These characteristics (duration, intensity and riskiness, or eventfulness) can be operationalised and measured in a relatively matter-of-fact and 'objective' way (for example, Krishnan and Noorderhaven 2001, 2002): a cooperative process has been going on for a certain number of years, the frequency of face-to-face interaction has a certain value, and particular events did or did not occur.

CONCLUSIONS

The primary aim of this chapter was to illustrate the usefulness of applying a hermeneutic perspective to the study of international business. Such an approach focuses on the interpretations of organisational phenomena of incumbent managers, on the interaction processes influencing these interpretations, and on their consequences. This focus does not constitute a radical breach with extant international business research, at least, not if we look at the more process-oriented research (for example, Brannen and Salk 2000; Doz 1996). The benefit of the hermeneutic perspective is that it gives coherence to a set of questions that, based on the findings of previous studies, have, over time, come to be seen as more and more crucial.

These questions might, perhaps, also have emerged from conventional wisdom or practitioners' insights. The fact remains that these questions have not yet become prominent in the international business literature. The assumption on which this chapter is based is that this has to do with the implicit logical empiricism on which most of the research is based. The application of the hermeneutic perspective, in contrast, puts these issues forward in a way which makes it impossible to avoid them. Hermeneutics is, thus, seen as especially important in determining the research agenda and the 'fore-understandings' guiding the research process (see Gadamer 1999, pp. 553, 560).

Another issue concerns the methodological implications of adopting a hermeneutic perspective. First of all, as stated before, hermeneutics, no more than any other perspective in the philosophy of science, dictates the research methods to be applied. These methods are determined by the research questions and the type of material studied. Questions pertaining to managerial interpretations favour the use of research methods able to gauge (changes in) the perceptions of key managers. Personal interviews appear to be more adequate here than mail surveys. But the influence of interaction process characteristics on the formation of interpretation can, at least in part, be studied using a cross-sectional design and a mailed survey. A fruitless either/ or opposition between interpretive and logical–empiricist methodological postures should be avoided (Llewellyn 1993). Gadamer is quite clear in this when he states that 'methodological considerations such as controllable procedure and falsifiability are taken to be self-evident' (1999, p. 551).

At the same time, the conventional hierarchy of research method stands in the way of the issues seen to be particularly important in a hermeneutic perspective holding a more central position. In particular, the rigorous division of labour (and the implied hierarchy) between qualitative and quantitative methods (and case studies/surveys, and subjective/objective methods) implied by logical empiricism needs to be reconsidered. If the objects of study are perceptions and interpretation processes, and the factors promoting and impeding these processes, qualitative case studies cannot remain relegated to the early stages of theory development. Very often, case studies will be needed in order to comprehend the findings of surveys. Qualitative studies have to be put into the context of justification; quantitative studies need to be taken out of the straitjacket of hypothesis testing and into the context of discovery.

The overall conclusion is that it does make a difference if international business research is informed by a hermeneutic methodology, even if it does not imply a wholesale change in research methods. What would change is researchers' awareness that what they try to understand and explain is a social system in which people who are partly different from, partly like themselves, trying to make sense of what they do and what is done to them. And that would make it more likely that the 'event' of understanding (Gadamer 1999, p. 309) also takes place for the researcher in the field of international business.

NOTES

1. Henry does not reveal the identity of the organisation in this paper. However, it can be deduced from a later publication in which his example is discussed (Dia 1996).
2. My translation from the French.
3. As this discussion indicates, philosophical hermeneutics is related to semiotics, that is, the study of signs. Ever since the linguist Ferdinand De Saussure developed his model of the sign, semiotics has strongly influenced philosophy. However, philosophers have taken Saussure's ideas about signs as existing of a 'signifier' (sign) and 'signified' (that to which the sign refers) as a basis for new ontologies and epistemologies. Hermeneutics in particular has developed in the direction of a philosophy of man as an 'interpreting animal'. For this philosophy to be possible, the insights of post-Saussurian semiotics are indispensable, for if there is identity of signifier and signified (or if their relationship is self-evident, or otherwise unproblematic), there is no need or scope for interpretation. So, semiotics is an important foundation for and building block of philosophical hermeneutics.
4. I believe this to be true even though hermeneutics originally was a method for interpreting texts. In philosophical hermeneutics, however, the concept of 'text' is taken as a metaphor for any product of the human mind that can be considered to bear meaning. In the case of a text, especially if it is a text from another historical period, the dialogue by necessity has to be with that text itself, as well as with other sources regarding the 'life-world' in which the text was created. However, in the case of organisational or management research, the 'text' consists of human (inter)actions. In principle, these can be studied using secondary sources. But I think that methods that allow a more direct dialogue between the researcher and the researched are to be preferred.

REFERENCES

Albert, H. (1988), 'Hermeneutics and economics: a criticism of hermeneutical thinking in the social sciences', *Kyklos*, **41**, 573–602.

Ariño, A. and J. de la Torre (1998), 'Learning from failure: towards an evolutionary model of collaborative ventures', *Organization Science*, **9**, 306–25.

Arnold, S.J. and E. Fischer (1994), 'Hermeneutics and consumer research', *Journal of Consumer Research*, **21**, 55–70.

Arrington, C.E. and J.R. Francis (1993), 'Giving economic accounts: accounting as cultural practice', *Accounting, Organizations and Society*, **18**, 107–24.

Barr, P.S. (1998), 'Adapting to unfamiliar environmental events: a look at the evolution of interpretation and its role in strategic change', *Organization Science*, **9**, 644–69.

Berger, P. and T. Luckmann (1966), *The Social Construction of Reality*, New York: Harper & Row.

Boland, R.J., R.V. Tenkasi and D. Te'eni (1994), 'Designing information technology to support distributed cognition', *Organization Science*, **5**, 456–75.

Brannen, M.Y. and J.E. Salk (2000), 'Partnering across borders: negotiating organizational culture in a German–Japanese joint venture', *Human Relations*, **4**, 451–87.

Butler, T. (1998), 'Towards a hermeneutic method for interpretive research in information systems', *Journal of Information Technology*, **13**, 285–300.

Caputo, J.D. (1989), 'Gadamer's closet essentialism: a Derridean critique', in D.P. Michelfelder and R.E. Palmer (eds), *Dialogue and Deconstruction: The Gadamer–Derrida Encounter*, Albany, NY: State University of New York Press, pp. 258–64.

Coleman, J.S. (1990), *Foundations of Social Theory*, Cambridge, MA: Harvard University Press.

Daft, R.L. and N.B. MacIntosh (1981), 'A tentative exploration into the amount and equivocality of information processing in organizational work units', *Administrative Science Quarterly*, **26**, 207–24.

Daft, R.L. and K.E. Weick (1984), 'Toward a model of organizations as interpretation systems', *Academy of Management Review*, **9**, 284–95.

Dia, M. (1996), *Africa's Management in the 1990s and Beyond: Reconciling Indigenous and Transplanted Institutions*, Washington, DC: World Bank.

Doz, Y.L. (1996), 'The evolution of cooperation in strategic alliances: initial conditions or learning processes?', *Strategic Management Journal*, **17**, 55–83.

Dyer, J.H. and W. Chu (2000), 'The determinants of trust in supplier–automaker relationships in the U.S., Japan, and Korea', *Journal of International Business Studies*, **31**, 259–86.

Ezzy, D. (1997), 'Subjectivity and the labour process: conceptualizing "good work"', *Sociology*, **31**, 427–44.

Feldman, M.S. and J.G. March (1981), 'Information in organizations as signal and symbol', *Administrative Science Quarterly*, **26**, 171–86.

Francis, J.R. (1994), 'Auditing, hermeneutics, and subjectivity', *Accounting, Organizations and Society*, **19**, 235–69.

Friedman, M. (1953), *Essays in Positive Economics*, Chicago, IL: University of Chicago Press.

Gadamer, H.-G. (1999), *Truth and Method*, 2nd revised edn, translation revised by J. Weinsheimer and D.G. Marshall, New York: Continuum.

Geertz, C. (1973), *The Interpretation of Cultures: Selected Essays*, New York: Basic Books.

Giddens, A. (1984), *The Constitution of Society*, Cambridge: Polity Press.

Grondin, J. (1994), *Introduction to Philosophical Hermeneutics*, translated by J. Weinsheimer, New Haven, CT: Yale University Press.

Gulati, R. (1998), 'Alliances and networks', *Strategic Management Journal*, **19**, 293–317.

Hagedoorn, J. and J. Schakenraad (1994), 'The effect of strategic technology alliances on company performance', *Strategic Management Journal*, **15**, 291–310.

Hamel, G. (1991), 'Competition for competence and inter-partner learning within international strategic alliances', *Strategic Management Journal*, **12**, 83–103.

Henry, A. (1991), 'Vers un modèle de management africain', *Cahiers d'Etudes Africaines*, **124**, 31–4, 447–73.

How, A. (1995), *The Habermas–Gadamer Debate and the Nature of the Social: Back to Bedrock*, Aldershot: Avebury.

Keizer, A., N.G. Noorderhaven, J. Benders and J. Stam (2000), 'Mirroring consensus: unity in diversity?', in J. Benders, N.G. Noorderhaven, A. Keizer, H. Kumon and J. Stam (eds), *Mirroring Consensus: Decision-Making in Japanese–Dutch Business*, Utrecht: Lemma, pp. 59–95.

Klein, H.K. and M.D. Myers (1999), 'A set of principles for conducting and evaluating interpretive field studies in information systems', *MIS Quarterly*, **23**, 67–93.

Krishnan, R. and N.G. Noorderhaven (2001), 'Alliance outcomes: the mediating effect of process', paper presented at the Academy of Management Conference, Washington DC, August.

―――― (2002), 'Effects of structural conditions and process characteristics on alliance outcome', paper presented at the European International Business Academy Conference, Athens, Greece, December.

Kuhn, T.S. (1962), *The Structure of Scientific Revolutions*, Chicago, IL: University of Chicago Press.

Lachmann, L.M. (1991), 'Austrian economics: a hermeneutic approach', in D. Lavoie (ed.), *Economics and Hermeneutics*, London: Routledge, pp. 134–46.

Lavoie, D. (1991), 'Introduction', in D. Lavoie (ed.), *Economics and Hermeneutics*, London: Routledge, pp. 1–15.

Llewellyn, S. (1993), 'Working in hermeneutic circles in management accounting research: some implications and applications', *Management Accounting Research*, **4**, 231–49.

Maurice, M., A. Sorge and M. Warner (1980), 'Societal differences in organizing manufacturing units: a comparison of France, West Germany, and Great Britain', *Organization Studies*, **1**, 59–86.

Maurice, M. and A. Sorge (eds) (2000), *Embedding Organizations: Societal Analysis of Actors, Organizations and Socio-Economic Context*, Amsterdam: John Benjamins.

Mercier, J. (1994), 'Looking at organizational culture, hermeneutically', *Administration & Society*, **26**, 28–47.

Myers, M.D. (1995), 'Dialectical hermeneutics: a theoretical framework for the implementation of information systems', *Informations Systems Journal*, **5**, 51–70.

Nnadozie, E. (2001), 'Managing African business culture', in F.M. Edoho (ed.), *Management Challenges for Africa in the Twenty-First Century*, Westport, CT: Praeger, pp. 51–62.

Noorderhaven, N.G. (1996), 'Opportunism and trust in transaction cost economics', in J. Groenewegen (ed.), *Transaction Cost Economics and Beyond*, Boston, MA: Kluwer Academic Press, pp. 105–28.

—— (2000), 'Positivist, hermeneutical and postmodern positions in the comparative management debate', in M. Maurice and A. Sorge (eds), *Embedding Organizations: Societal Analysis of Actors, Organizations and Socio-Economic Context*, Amsterdam: John Benjamins, pp. 117–37.

Parkhe, A. (1993), '"Messy" research, methodological predispositions, and theory development in international joint ventures', *Academy of Management Review*, **18**, 227–68.

—— (1998a), 'Understanding trust in international alliances', *Journal of World Business*, **33**, 219–40.

—— (1998b), 'Building trust in international alliances', *Journal of World Business*, **33**, 417–37.

Prasad, A. (2002), 'The contest over meaning: hermeneutics as an interpretive methodology for understanding texts', *Organizational Research Methods*, **5**, 12–33.

Prasad, A. and P. Prasad (2002), 'The coming of age of interpretive organizational research', *Organizational Research Methods*, **5**, 4–11.

Reuer, J.J. and K.D. Miller (1997), 'Agency costs and the performance implications of international joint venture internationalization', *Strategic Management Journal*, **18**, 425–38.

Ricoeur, P. (1991), 'The model of the text: meaningful action considered as a text', in P. Ricoeur (ed.), *From Text to Action; Essays in Hermeneutics*, II, translated by K. Blamey and J.B. Thompson, London: Athlone Press, pp. 144–67.

Salk, J.E. and O. Shenkar (2001), 'Social identities in an international joint venture: an exploratory case study', *Organization Science*, **12**, 161–78.

Sayer, A. (1992), *Method in Social Science: A Realist Approach*, 2nd edn, London: Routledge.

Sorge, A. (1991), 'Strategic fit and the societal effect: interpreting cross-national comparisons of technology, organization and human resources', *Organization Studies*, **12**, 161–90.

Sorge, A. and M. Warner (1986), *Comparative Factory Organisation: An Anglo–German Comparison of Manufacturing, Management and Manpower*, Aldershot, UK: Gower.

Thomas, J.B., S.M. Clark and D.A. Gioia (1993), 'Strategic sensemaking and organizational performance: linkages among scanning, interpretation, action, and outcomes', *Academy of Management Journal*, **36**, 239–70.

Thompson, P. (1993), 'Postmodernism: fatal distraction', in J. Hassard and M. Parker (eds), *Postmodernism and Organizations*, London: Sage, pp. 183–203.

Ugwuegbu, D.C.E. (2001), *The Psychology of Management in African Organizations*, Westport, CT: Quorum.

Weber, M. (1968), *Economy and Society*, Berkely, CA: University of California Press.

Weick, K.E. (1979), *The Social Psychology of Organizing*, 2nd edn, New York: Random House.

—— (1995), *Sensemaking in Organizations*, Thousand Oaks, CA: Sage.

—— (2001), *Making Sense of the Organization*, Oxford: Blackwell.

Yan, A., and M. Zeng (1999), 'International joint venture instability: a critique of previous research, a reconceptualization, and directions for future research', *Journal of International Business Studies*, **30**, 397–414.

PART II

Case Study Research

The Many Skills of the Case Researcher

Robert W. Scapens

> Case study research is remarkably hard, even though case studies have traditionally been considered to be 'soft' research. Paradoxically, the 'softer' a research technique, the harder it is to do. (Yin 1984, p. 26)

My experience in conducting case research certainly confirms Yin's view that case study research is remarkably hard. It is not just a matter of going to visit companies and writing up the results, as some critics seem to believe. Case study research requires clear research questions, a thorough understanding of the existing literature, a well-formulated research design with sound theoretical underpinnings, and above all excellent language skills. Whereas quantitative researchers need mathematical skills, language skills are essential for case study researchers. They must be able to synthesise large amounts of quite diverse data, such as interview notes and transcripts, documents, observations of meetings and so on, and from all these data produce theoretically informed and convincingly argued conclusions. Furthermore, they must be able to communicate with both the subjects of the research and the readers of their output.

It is important to be able to communicate with the subjects of the research, even if the different subjects are unable to communicate with each other. In one case study, I became a 'translator' for accountants and production personnel. Although these two groups were talking and, at a personal level, were well disposed towards each other, there was little effective communication between them. The accountants did not understand the concerns and standpoints of the production personnel and the production personnel did not understand the ways in which the accountants measured productive efficiency. For a number of years it had been accepted that production in this factory was less efficient than a sister factory in another country. However, the appointment of a new production manager led to various changes in production methods which, according to the production manager, were improving the factory's efficiency. However, despite these changes the accountants continued to report negative production variances. As a result, the production personnel did not trust the accountants and the accountants did not believe that effective actions were being taken in the factory.

When I started talking to the two groups they each criticised each other and suggested that I should pass on various comments and requests to the other group. This I did, but to communicate with each group and to help them to communicate with each other, it was necessary for me to understand their different standpoints. Simply taking their responses at face value would not have enabled me to understand fully what was happening in this organisation. Eventually, through my 'translations' they discovered a technical difference between the accounting system and the factory records which meant that a favourable production variance could never be reported. This difference had probably existed for many years, but nobody had recognised it – due to the lack of communication.

In this case, interviewing each group and recording their responses would simply have illustrated that accountants and production personnel do not understand each other – a not unusual situation. But by trying to get to the meaning behind the words, I was able to get a deeper understanding of the case. As this illustrates, my involvement led to a change in the relationship between the accountants and the production personnel. Hence, as a case researcher I was not neutral and independent of the case. However, I regard this as inevitable in all case studies, as the presence of a case researcher in an organisation is itself an intervention in the case. Communication is a two-way process, and interviewing people and asking questions can raise issues which had not previously been considered or discussed in the organisation.

REFERENCE

Yin, R.K. (1984), *Case Study Research: Design and Methods*, Beverly Hills, CA: Sage.

5. Designing and Conducting Case Studies in International Business Research

Pervez Ghauri

INTRODUCTION

A case study is not a methodological choice, but rather a choice of object to be studied. Case studies can be both quantitative and qualitative. In this chapter, I deal with the qualitative type of case study. I use the term 'case study' as it draws our attention to the question of what can be learned from a case. A case study is both the process of learning about the case and the product of our learning. The choice of case is made because it is expected to advance our understanding of the research phenomenon (Ghauri and Grønhaug 2002; Stake 1994). In this chapter, I emphasise designing the case study to optimise understanding of a particular situation or problem rather than generalisation.

In business studies, we normally study cases to provide insight into an issue, a management situation or new theory. In my own research I have used case studies to investigate many international business topics, such as international business negotiations, international joint ventures, market entry processes and headquarters–subsidiary relationships. A case study is a useful method when the area of research is relatively less known, and the researcher is engaged in theory-building types of research. This is perhaps the most frequently used approach for thesis and dissertation research in business studies generally, and international business research is no different. However, I shall argue that case studies are in fact a flexible research approach that are suited to a range of different types of research questions. Case studies have also been combined with a variety of different epistemological positions, from positivist to phenomenological. In this chapter, I avoid entering into such debates and instead maintain the stance that case studies can be used in both types of research.

Case studies involve data collection through multiple sources such as verbal reports, personal interviews, observation and written reports (for example, financial reports, archives, budget and operating statements including market and competition reports). The main feature is therefore the depth of and focus on the research object, whether it is an individual, group, organisation, culture, incident or situation. We need to have sufficient information to characterise and explain the unique features of the case, as well as to point out the characteristics that are common to several cases. Finally, this approach relies on the integrative powers of research: the ability to study an object with many dimensions and then to draw the various elements together in a cohesive interpretation (Selltiz et al. 1976).

This chapter deals with the stages of a case study project, the first being the decision to use the case study method, and the last concerning how to analyse data that has been collected through cases. Examples from my own case study research, published over the course of a twenty-year period, as well as from my experience as the editor of *International Business Review*, will be used to illustrate common dilemmas faced by the practising case study researcher. The hope is that this chapter will form a useful introduction for those embarking upon their first case study research project. Moreover, I aim at suggesting various ways in which case studies can be conducted in a more systematic way.

DECIDING TO USE A CASE STUDY

As Yin has famously said, case studies are a preferred approach when 'how' or 'why' questions are to be answered, when the researcher has little control over events and when the focus is on a current phenomenon in a real-life context (Yin 1994). Also influential in the development of case study research is Eisenhardt's (1989, pp. 548–9) argument that case studies are:

> Particularly well-suited to new research areas or research areas for which existing theory seems inadequate. This type of work is highly complementary to incremental theory building from normal science research. The former is useful in early stages of research on a topic or when a fresh perspective is needed, while the latter is useful in later stages of knowledge development.

However, this does not mean that case study research is only suited to exploratory and descriptive research. Case studies can in fact be used in all types of research: exploratory, descriptive or explanatory (Bonoma 1985; Ghauri and Grønhaug 2002; Yin 1994).

When to use which research approach ultimately depends upon the type of research questions being posed. When research questions concern only 'what' (for example, 'what are the most effective ways to operate an international joint venture?'), the objective of the study is to develop hypotheses or propositions for later testing. For such an exploratory study, a range of research strategies can be used. If the questions relate to 'how many?' or 'how much?', survey or archival strategies are favoured. For example, compiling a report on the population statistics or overview of a particular industry, that is, how many companies operate in the industry there, how many of these are domestic or foreign and what are their market shares and so on. But when 'how' and 'why' questions are asked, a case study method as a research strategy is recommended (Ghauri and Grønhaug 2002).

Over the years I have used case studies for a variety of 'what', 'how' and 'why' questions, covering a diverse range of topics in international business. For example: what measures of international competitiveness are relevant to the performance of small and medium-sized enterprises (SMEs) (Coviello et al. 1998)? How does a negotiation process in a domestic setting differ from a negotiation process in an international setting (Ghauri 1983)? How do international joint venture relationships develop over time (Hyder and Ghauri 1989, 2000)? How do headquarters–subsidiary relationships in the multi-national enterprise (MNE) change over time (Ghauri 1992)?

The case study method is particularly well suited to international business research, where data is collected from cross-border and cross-cultural settings. Surveys and/or experiments raise serious questions about equivalence and comparability of data collected from different countries. In spite of rather sophisticated methods of questionnaire translations and cross-translations, the understanding and interpretation of questions by respondents and of answers and findings by researchers are very difficult to compare and often lead to misleading conclusions. The case study method provides excellent opportunities for respondents and researchers to check their understanding and keep on asking questions until they obtain sufficient answers and interpretations. In-depth interviews are particularly suitable when a researcher wants to understand the behaviour of decision-makers in different cultures.

Case studies have the potential to deepen our understanding of the research phenomenon, first because they allow us to take a longitudinal approach. For example, in Hyder and Ghauri (1989, p. 26) we argued that joint ventures are best understood and studied as a 'historical process'. Moreover, we were able to extend the time period under study by later returning to the same joint ventures to conduct a follow-up study (Hyder and Ghauri 2000). As most case studies are done through a review of existing historical material and records plus interviews, the case study method is quite similar to historical review, but it is different in the sense that here we have the possibility of direct observation and interaction. The second strength of case studies is, as Yin (1994) has observed, their contextuality. In business studies, case study research is particularly useful when the phenomenon under investigation is difficult to study outside its natural setting – as typically occurs in international business research, since researchers are often studying the impact of different national contexts. This means that when we wished to understand the effect that the turbulent business environment in Eastern Europe had on foreign firms' entry strategies, case studies were an effective way of understanding the links between macro-environmental factors, industry-level relationships and firm decision-making (Ghauri and Holstius 1996). A third advantage of this method is that the level of depth with which each case is investigated allows for theory building, not just theory testing (for example, the model of international package deal negotiations that I developed in my 1983 study). Fourth, case studies are holistic, thus permitting the investigation of a phenomenon from a variety of viewpoints, covering a period of time, and crossing the boundaries between different factors (Ghauri 1983). Concepts and variables under study are often difficult to quantify since there are too many variables to be considered, which makes experiment or survey methods inappropriate to use (Bonoma 1985; Ghauri and Grønhaug 2002; Yin 1994).

To sum up, I would like to make it explicit that the case study method is not synonymous with qualitative research or methods. A case study may very well involve quantitative methods or even be entirely quantitative. Whether a case study is used as a research method depends upon the research question, objectives and the research setting/situation. Once this approach has been chosen, we need to think of the next steps such as how to select individual cases and to conduct and analyse them. The rest of the chapter will deal with these issues.

SELECTING CASES

How to select the cases is perhaps the most important issue in this type of research. As in other methods of data collection, it is important to decide the target population that is to be used for the investigation. It includes those firms, individuals, groups or elements that will be represented in the study. The next stage is to assess the accessible population, the population to which we can have access (Cooper 1984). Out of this accessible population we have to select one or a few cases, objects or firms, for study. This selection should be based on criteria that are consistent with the research problem. The cases should correspond to our theoretical framework and the variables we are studying. For example, if we are studying the behaviour of industrial buyers, we have to select firms that are dealing with industrial marketing and purchasing. Once we have selected a firm, the informant has to be a manager who is involved in the process of marketing and purchasing. An interview with the firm's public relations manager or an accountant may not provide us with the information we are looking for (Ghauri and Grønhaug 2002).

The time available for the study, financial resources for travelling, personal contacts and other practical issues are of great importance. For example, depending upon how much time we have to perform the study, the type of organisation or company we select might be different. Consequently, the researcher is likely to be required to mix theory with pragmatism when selecting cases. The most appropriate company in theoretical terms may be too far away, or may simply refuse access. The first meeting with the potential interviewee or company representative is likely to be decisive in terms of whether we are granted access or not. In my experience, the final decision about access is largely determined by our ability as researchers to impress the interviewee during the very first meeting. I have conducted case studies in many different countries and being a foreigner is not necessarily a disadvantage when negotiating access. Particularly when having to rely on a second language, expressions tend to be simpler and the overall communication tends to be more straightforward and direct.

Case selection should also take into account the type of organisation being studied. Based on my own experiences of conducting case studies in SMEs (Coviello et al. 1998) and multinational corporations (MNCs) (Ghauri 1992; Ghauri and Fang 2001), I would argue that research problems tend to be richer in MNCs, but it is likely to be harder to negotiate access and identify the right informants who have personally been involved in the phenomenon under study. In SMEs, on the other hand, the informants may be eager to learn and willing to participate in an academic study. It tends to be considerably easier to get in touch with people who have themselves participated in the issues being investigated. Hence, selecting the appropriate type of organisation is a balancing act between certain advantages and disadvantages.

To illustrate the case selection process, at the outset of my study on international package deal negotiations (Ghauri 1983) I had initial criteria for the selection of cases (for example, the seller must be a Swedish firm, but the buyer was to be an organisation from a developing country in one case, and from the domestic market of the MNC in the other, in order to contrast the influence of different environmental factors). These criteria were then modified by both pragmatic considerations (above all, the level of access that I could obtain with or without personal contacts of colleagues and friends) and by the emergent theory. Thus, when choosing the third and final case, a decision was made to focus on a buyer from a different part of the world than had been featured in the other two cases, namely Nigeria. However, important considerations in the selection process were not only differences but also similarities, with all the cases sharing some features that made them comparable (for example, size and value of the project).

How many cases should be included in a study? The answer to this question is very difficult as there is no upper or lower limit to the number of cases to be included in a study. Many times only one case is enough. As Mintzberg (1979, p. 583) says, 'What, for example, is wrong with a sample size of one? Why should researchers have to apologize for them? Should Piaget apologize for studying his own children, a physicist for splitting only one atom?'. It is the research problem and the research objectives that influence the number and choice of cases to be studied.

Single cases are appropriate when a particular case is critical and we want to use it to explain or question an established theory. It is a critical case because it meets all the conditions necessary to confirm, challenge or extend the theory. For example, in Marschan-Piekkari and Ghauri (1998) we studied regional control in headquarters–subsidiary and inter-subsidiary relationships in a single, Finnish multinational corporation. Given the limited number of earlier studies in the field, the aim was to extend existing theory on regional management in multinationals by examining in depth how control is exercised through regional centres. Another situation is when a single case is an extreme or a unique case; for example, particular organisations may be of interest because they represent 'outstanding successes' or 'notable failures' (Patton 1990, p. 169). Finally, a single-case design is appropriate when a case is revelatory. This means that we can observe and study a phenomenon which was previously not accessible and which can provide useful insights. We can also use single-case design in other situations, such as in a pilot study or an exploratory study that serves as a first step to a later, more comprehensive study (Ghauri and Grønhaug 2002; Yin 1994).

In *comparative or multiple case studies*, we ask or study the same questions in a number of organisations and compare them with each other to draw conclusions. The purpose of data collection in comparative case study method is to compare (replicate) the phenomenon (for example, strategy formation) in a systematic way, to explore different dimensions of our research issues or to examine different levels of research variables. In this approach we should be clear that every case has to serve a particular purpose in the study. In other words, the researcher has to justify the selection of each case. However, case study design is often flexible and can be changed, modified or revised during the study with proper justification. For example, in my study of international business negotiations (Ghauri 1983) I selected three cases of negotiation processes to investigate how international business negotiations in domestic environments differ from negotiation processes where parties come from different countries/cultures.

A related question is what is meant by 'a case'? For example, if we are trying to understand the process of decision-making in a firm, we may study multiple decisions on different issues, important/unimportant, novel/routine decisions and so on in the same organisation. This will provide variability along important factors (see, for example, Campbell 1975). Thus, in Ghauri and Fang (2001) we studied a single unit of an MNE (Ericsson in China), but in the context of this one unit we were able to analyse multiple instances of the phenomenon under study, namely international business negotiations.

The use of a particular case study method depends also upon the type of study we are doing, whether it is inductive or deductive, and also upon whether we are looking for specific or general explanations. In the situation of an inductive approach and specific explanations, we may use the single-case design. However, if we are looking for general explanations, we should use a multiple-case design. On the other hand, if we are doing a study with a deductive approach we can use the case study at an early stage to develop our hypotheses or propositions. A case study is a less recommended method if we are aiming at generalisations. I recommend that researchers using this method consult Yin (1994) and Ghauri and Grønhaug (2002) for further guidance.

CONDUCTING A CASE STUDY

Triangulation is one of the defining features of a case study. It refers to the collection of data through different methods or even different kind of data on the same phenomenon. The use of multi-methods or triangulation is not new and can be traced back to Campbell and Fiske (1959), who argued that to ensure validation one should use more than one method. The main advantage of triangulation, however, is that it can produce a more complete, holistic and contextual portrait of the object under study. In the case study method, it is particularly important as we need to check and validate the information we receive from various sources and examine it from different angles (Ghauri and Grønhaug 2002). For example, we can check the performance of a firm or a project, claimed by the interviewee, from annual accounts, archives or by interviewing another manager or company representative. In essence, we use triangulation to reduce the likelihood of misinterpretation. We employ various procedures to increase our understanding and explanation. It helps us clarify meaning by identifying different ways the phenomenon is seen (Denzin 1989; Flick 1992).

In my own research, I have tended to build up case data through interviews, written documentation and observation. When planning personal interviews, I have made a special effort to include multiple viewpoints in the data set by, for example, interviewing both joint venture partners and joint venture managers (Hyder and Ghauri 2000); internal company informants as well as external local authorities, officials and staff at foreign embassies (Ghauri and Holstius 1996). In my 1983 study on international package deal negotiations, interviews were conducted with both the buyer and the seller, so perspectives from both sides of a single negotiation were obtained. Moreover, for all but one firm it was possible to interview two employees, namely the negotiation leader and the project leader. To supplement these interviews, I was able to analyse company files related to each project. The number of files on each of the three cases ranged between 10 and 17, and incorporated such material as correspondence between the two firms, contract drafts as well as the final contract, technical specifications, and relevant government rules and regulations. It was therefore possible to compare data between interviewees within the same firm, between different firms, and in comparison with the written records of each company. Moreover, the comparison of archival and interview data is not the only option. As part of the case study reported in Ghauri and Fang (2001), I shadowed a top manager for a couple of years in the early 1990s. This method, which was very much built on trust and mutual respect between the top manager and myself, provided real insight into face-to-face situations and increased my own understanding of international negotiations. At the same time, the manager found it useful to jointly brainstorm and analyse various situations I had observed.

There are some problems with triangulation. Sometimes it can be difficult to judge the accuracy if the results from different methods and sources are not consistent. For example, the buyer may say he or she was responsible for initiating new products but suppliers indicate otherwise. A second problem arises when the different methods come up with contradictory results. For example, if a manager shows reports indicating no conflicts in the negotiation process while the archives demonstrate the existence of a number of conflicts, it is important to have this clarified during the interview with the manager by referring to the incidents mentioned in the archives. However, there is a general tendency that we need not evaluate interview responses or written documents as true or false reports on reality. 'Instead, we can treat such responses as displays of perspectives and moral forms' (Silverman 1993, p. 107). Moreover, it needs to be kept in mind that all research methods have advantages and disadvantages when it comes to different research problems. One conclusion is that triangulation or the usage of a multi-method approach on the same study object can be useful even if we do not get the same results. It can lead us to a better understanding or to new questions that can be answered by later research. Personally, I have found the study of documents tremendously useful. I have relied on them when preparing sharp and to-the-point interview questions. I have also used them when checking information mentioned in interviews. Hence, documents tend to be rich and have a lot to offer to the researcher both in pre-interview and post-interview situations.

ANALYSING CASE STUDIES

Interpreting and analysing qualitative data is perhaps the most difficult task while doing case study research. We cannot be satisfied merely with 'telling convincing stories', to use Silverman's (1989) phrase. In qualitative research 'authenticity' rather than reliability is the main issue. The idea is to present an 'authentic' understanding of people's experience. This means not just understanding the point of view of the individuals and groups being studied; in addition, data has to be interpreted against the background of the context in which they are produced (Hammersley and Atkinson 1983). But how can researchers ensure – and demonstrate – that they have produced an authentic interpretation rather than a misguided one? As put by Miles (1979, p. 591):

> The most serious and central difficulty in the use of qualitative data is that the method of data analysis is not well formulated … the analyst faced with a bank of data has very few guidelines for protection against self-delusion, let alone the presentation of unreliable or invalid conclusion to scientific or policy-making decisions. How can we be sure that an 'earthy', 'undeniable', 'serendipitous' finding is not, in fact, wrong?

Part of the answer lies in making sure that data analysis and collection are closely interconnected during the life cycle of the case study research. Many researchers put a lot of effort into data collection and keep on collecting data through case studies, hoping to do data analysis at the end of the process, sometimes months or years after the data collection. However, this will weaken both the analysis and the data collection processes. In case study research, interweaving data collection and data analysis right from the first case/interview is the best policy (Miles and Huberman 1994). This allows theory to develop alongside the growing volume of data, allowing the research problem to be formulated or even reformulated at the same time. This often leads to new questions and new data collection, and there is no definite phase of data analysis (Ghauri and Grønhaug 2002; Grønhaug 1985; Miles and Huberman 1994). Preferably, a second case study should not be started unless the data collected through the first one has been analysed. It will reveal the blind spots and deficiencies of data collected and the researcher can improve his/her data collection techniques in the subsequent cases. Moreover, early analysis reduces the risk that the researcher might simply drown in the sheer volume of data. It is often difficult for case study researchers to filter or discard irrelevant data before analysis commences.

While analysis may not form an isolated process, nevertheless it does involve some distinct stages. The first step of analysis is to construct a case description and explanation. This will help us understand 'how' things are developing and 'why' things occur the way they do. First we have to describe, that is, make complicated things understandable in their component parts, and explain, that is, show how their component parts fit together according to some rules (Bernard 1988). However, it is hard to describe and explain something satisfactorily unless you understand what this 'something' is. It is thus important to start with simple 'story telling' about a situation and progress in chronological order. Consequently, we can construct a map and locate different elements and variables. This will finally lead us to build a theory or a model, that is, how the variables are connected together and how they influence each other (Miles and Huberman 1994; Rein and Schon 1977). Step by step we can advance along the 'ladder of abstraction'. We start by trying to code and categorise text, then identify trends and establish findings. Finally, we integrate the data into an explanatory framework (Carney 1990; Gherardi and Turner 1987). These different techniques are summarised in Table 5.1.

Table 5.1   Case study analysis

Techniques for case study analysis	Explanation
Chronologies	Narratives of the events that took place, organised by date
Coding	Sorting data according to concepts and themes
Clustering	Categorising cases according to common characteristics
Matrices	Explaining the interrelationship between identified factors
Decision tree modelling	Grounding a description of real-world decisions and actions coherently by using multiple cases
Pattern matching	Comparison between a predicted and an empirically based pattern

The first stage of analysis, 'story-telling', can be done by writing chronologies or biographical histories of the organisation(s) or individual(s) under study. This is particularly important when the researcher is attempting to develop longitudinal explanations that track a phenomenon over time. For example, in my study of international package deals negotiations (Ghauri 1983), the first step in my analysis was to construct a simple narrative of each negotiation, from the first offer and informal meetings to the final negotiations and signing of the contract.

The second stage of analysis is also a sifting process. This means rearranging the data that has been collected, but into more conceptual rather than chronological categories. To analyse data we (often) have to code them so that they can be broken down, conceptualised, put together and presented in an understandable manner. Sorting the data in this fashion is typically done through coding, in other words, classifying the data. This coding and categorisation will help us to interpret the data and to relate the information to our questions and frameworks. This will also enable us to locate different categories when we are analysing data to find conclusions. As qualitative studies quite often help in building theories, coding requires extra care, and a balance between creativity, rigour and persistence has to be achieved.

There are several software programs available that can help researchers in coding, sorting and analysing qualitative data. However, we recommend that researchers should consult/visit these software packages before starting and planning data collection. Each software package might require specific data collection techniques/methods in order to be able to analyse the collected data. In other words, once you have collected that data, these software programs might be of little help. One such program is called NUD*IST and is available in several versions (for a discussion, see Lindsay, Chapter 24 this volume). Such software programs are particularly useful in rendering data analysis more systematic and providing counterarguments to those who claim that case study researchers are 'just telling stories'.

An important part of the sifting process is searching for common or conflicting themes in data, and looking for themes and trends related to our research questions. This will allow us to identify relationships between different themes and research questions. Moreover, it will enable us to detect gaps in our data and to write initial analytical reports. The requirement is that the pattern has to be sufficiently systematic. Many researchers suggest that case comparison can be done by forming types or clusters. This technique involves inspecting cases and trying to put them into groups or clusters that share similar patterns of configurations. These clusters can also be sorted according to some dimensions, for example, international versus domestic firms (Lofland and Lofland 1984; Morse and Bottorff 1992). Another way is to look for themes or variables that cut through cases. For example, Eisenhardt (1989) found evidence for the construct of 'power centralisation' by looking at data on CEO behaviour in 10 micro-computer firms: her matrix display included objectives describing decision style, quantitative measures and specific quoted examples (Miles and Huberman 1994).

Another possible step in the analytical process of answering our research questions is to test our propositions. This is done by cross-checking for commonality and integrating the data in one single framework through a meticulous case comparison. Developing a good case comparison in a multiple case study is essential but not very simple, as different cases might tell different stories and lead to different variables. It is also necessary to know/establish relevance and applicability of our findings to similar situations (Firestone and Harriott 1983). The most important reason, however, is to enhance our understanding and explanation, as this will help us explain under what circumstances/conditions our propositions/model work and under what conditions they do not. We can then conclude under what conditions the model is most likely to work (Glaser and Strauss 1970). In my capacity as the editor of *International Business Review*, I have noticed that case study researchers have considerable difficulties in drawing conclusions that clearly stem from the case data. In a number of manuscripts that I receive the connection between case analysis and the concluding section is very weak.

One way to draw conclusions from data collected through case study methods is to look for commonalities and differences, for example, in the case of multiple cases. As stated by Boyd et al. (1985, p. 51):

> In one study to improve the productivity of the sales force of a particular company, the investigator studied intensively two or three of the best sales representatives and two or three of the worst. Data was collected on the background and experience of each representative and then several days were spent making sales calls with them. As a result, a hypothesis was developed. It was that checking the stock of retailers and suggesting items on which they were low were the most important differences between the successful and the poor sales representatives.

As illustrated by the above example, we can find answers to our questions by comparing different cases. In some cases the best and worst comparisons are most suitable (Churchill 1991). In the same manner we could compare performance of several units/branches of a company by comparing them with each other.

Another approach is to use the strategy suggested by Miles and Huberman (1994, p. 176): 'stacking comparable cases'. According to this strategy, we can write up each of a series of cases, using more or less standard variables. Then we can use matrices and other displays to analyse each case in depth, and explore the interrelationship between different factors. Once each case is well understood, we can 'stack' the case-level display in a 'meta-matrix', which is then further condensed, permitting systematic comparison (for an example of a matrix display, see Figure 5.1). Eisenhardt (1989) called this strategy a 'replication strategy'. Gladwin (1989) suggested a further analytical approach, that of 'decision tree modelling', the starting point for which is to describe the factors in individual decision-making. Once a decision tree is constructed for each individual/case, one can do a composite tree. For more detail on these methods, I recommend that readers consult Miles and Huberman (1994, Chapters 7 and 8).

		Atmosphere		
		Cooperation and conflict	Distance	Power/ dependence	Expectation
	Offer				
	Informal meetings				
	Final offer				
Process	Planning for negotiations				
	Formal negotiations I				
	Internal meetings				
	Formal negotiations II				

Source: Ghauri (1983, p. 56).

Figure 5.1   An example of a matrix display in case study analysis

In case studies where data analysis leads to the development of propositions, the aim of the analysis should be a link between data and propositions. Campbell (1975) and Yin (1994) discuss 'pattern matching', where several pieces of information from one or several cases are related to a priori assumptions. If we can find a systematic or unsystematic pattern, we can accept or reject our propositions. In such studies, statistical tests are not necessary to establish a pattern and there are no precise ways of testing or setting criteria for interpreting these findings. The pattern has to be sufficiently systematic to accept certain propositions.

As case analysis is a difficult task, I recommend that researchers should use a mixture of the above-mentioned strategies: case comparison based on pattern seeking, clustering, matrices and other techniques displayed in Table 5.1. Most often, I start with a preliminary model or set of variables based on existing literature, then develop and refine a model as the analysis progresses. For example, my starting point in the 1983 study was the variables of an existing model, the so-called interaction model (Håkansson 1982). The interaction model explains the development of long-term relationships between firms, but its applicability to the short episode of a negotiation was not clear. During the course of the case study research, I was able to develop a model that could explain both the interplay between the different factors, and their temporal flow (Ghauri 1983).

The precise method of analysis will in addition depend on the type of study being undertaken. In descriptive research, the researcher has to work with specific research problems, propositions or hypotheses. While an exploratory study is characterised by flexibility (see, for example, Ghauri 1983), a descriptive study can be considered more rigid. It requires a clear specification of the who, what, why and how of the research problem. For further details into specific techniques for data analysis for descriptive studies, the reader should look into Churchill (1999) and Ghauri and Grønhaug (2002).

CONCLUSIONS

This chapter has dealt with case study research in international business studies. Based on my experiences of conducting case studies over a period of 20 years, it seems that case studies are becoming an increasingly accepted form of research. This can be observed, for example, at international academic conferences where conference papers demonstrate a high level of awareness of case studies. Moreover, in recent years a number of guide books have been published providing useful advice on how to conduct case studies. Several prominent scholars are also calling for case studies to provide us with a more in-depth understanding and insights into culturally embedded problems of our field. Yet we do not see case studies widely published in top class journals such as the *Journal of International Business Studies*, the *Journal of Marketing* or *Academy of Management Journal*. As a researcher and an editor, I would strongly encourage case study researchers to exercise a little self-criticism and move beyond 'just telling stories'. Moreover, we cannot keep on conducting 'theory development' studies in a particular discipline for several decades. Sooner or later we have to start testing the theories that have been developed and come up with somewhat generalisable results.

In this respect, I have been pleased to note that analysing qualitative data is becoming increasingly systematic, irrespective of the researcher's orientation. This chapter has thus treated the case study method in a manner that may permit some systematic analysis and enhance reviewers' confidence in findings (Miles and Huberman 1994). Although there are many methods available for collecting and analysing qualitative data, I have concentrated on case studies and analysing data collected through this method. I also want to re-emphasise that it is the research question that influence the choice of framework and methods, although initial data collection through cases may influence our conceptual framework. Finally, it is worth noting that the difference between qualitative and quantitative research is not that of quality!

REFERENCES

Bernard, H.R. (1988), *Research Methods in Cultural Anthropology*, Newbury Park, CA: Sage.

Bonoma, T.V. (1985), 'Case research in marketing: opportunities, problems, and a process', *Journal of Marketing Research*, **12**, 199–208.

Boyd, W.B., R. Wesfall and S.F. Stasch (1985), *Marketing Research: Text and Cases*, 6th edn, Homewood, IL: Irwin.

Campbell, D.T. (1975), 'Degrees of freedom and the case study', *Comparative Political Studies*, **8** (2), 173–93.

Campbell, D.T. and W. Fiske (1959), 'Convergent and discriminant validation by the multitrail–multimethod matrix', *Psychological Bulletin*, **56**, 81–105.

Carney, T.F. (1990), *Collaborative Inquiry Methodology*, Windsor, Ontario: University of Windsor, Division for Instructional Development.

Churchill, G.A. (1991), *Marketing Research: Methodological Foundations*, 5th edn, Chicago, IL: Dryden Press.

—— (1999), *Marketing Research: Methodological Foundations*, 7th edn, Fort Worth, TX: Dryden Press.

Cooper, H.M. (1984), *The Integrative Research Review: A Systematic Approach*, Beverly Hills, CA: Sage.

Coviello, N.E., P.N. Ghauri and K.A.-M. Martin (1998), 'International competitiveness: empirical findings from SME service firms', *Journal of International Marketing*, **6** (2), 8–27.

Denzin, N.K. (1989), *The Research Act*, 3rd edn, Englewood Cliffs, NJ: Prentice-Hall.

Eisenhardt, K.M. (1989), 'Building theories from case study research', *Academy of Management Review*, **14** (4), 532–50.

Firestone, W.A. and R.E. Harriott (1983), 'The formalization of qualitative research: an adaption of "soft" science to the policy world', *Evaluation Review*, **7**, 437–66.

Flick, U. (1992), 'Triangulation revisited: strategy of validation or alternative?', *Journal of the Theory of Social Behaviour*, **22**, 175–98.

Ghauri, P.N. (1983), *Negotiating International Package Deals: Swedish Firms in Developing Countries*, Stockholm: Almquist & Wiksell.

—— (1992), 'New structures in MNCs based in small countries: a network approach', *European Management Journal*, **10** (3), 357–64.

Ghauri, P. and T. Fang (2001), 'Negotiating with the Chinese: a socio-cultural analysis', *Journal of World Business*, **36** (3), 303–25.

Ghauri P. and K. Grønhaug (2002), *Research Methods in Business Studies: A Practical Guide*, Harlow, UK: Financial Times and Prentice-Hall.

Ghauri, P.N. and K. Holstius (1996), 'The role of matching in the foreign market entry process in the Baltic states', *European Journal of Marketing*, **30** (2), 75–88.

Gherardi, S. and B.A. Turner (1987), 'Real men don't collect soft data', *Quaderno*, **13**, Dipartimento di Politica Sociale, Università di Trento, 1–17.

Gladwin, C.H. (1989), *Ethnographic Decision Tree Modelling*, Newbury Park, CA: Sage.

Glaser, B.G. and A.L. Strauss (1970), 'Discovery of substantive theory', in W. Filstead (ed.), *Qualitative Methodology*, Chicago, IL: Rand-McNally, pp. 288–97.

Grønhaug, K. (1985), 'Problemer i empirisk forskning', in Norwegian School of Economics and Business Administration, *Metoder og Perspektiver i Økonomisk-Administrativ Forskning*, Oslo: Universitetsforlaget.

Håkansson, H. (1982), *International Marketing and Purchasing of Goods*, Chichester: Wiley.

Hammersley, M. and P. Atkinson (1983), *Ethnography: Principles in Practice*, London: Tavistock.

Hyder, S.A. and P.N. Ghauri (1989), 'Joint venture relationship between Swedish firms and developing countries: a longitudinal case study', *Journal of Global Marketing*, **2** (4), 25–47.

–––––– (2000), 'Managing international joint venture relationships: a longitudinal perspective', *Industrial Marketing Management*, **29**, 205–18.

Lofland, J. and L.H. Lofland (1984), *Analyzing Social Settings: A Guide to Qualitative Observational Research*, Belmont, CA: Wadsworth.

Marschan-Piekkari, R. and P.N. Ghauri (1998), 'Growing pains in multinationals: controlling subsidiaries through regional centers', Research Report 98B39, Research Institute Systems, Organisation and Management, University of Groningen, Netherlands.

Miles, M.B. (1979), 'Qualitative data as an attractive nuisance: the problem of analysis', *Administrative Science Quarterly*, **24**, 590–601.

Miles, M.B. and A.M. Huberman (1994*)*, *Qualitative Data Analysis*, 2nd edn, Thousand Oaks, CA: Sage.

Mintzberg, H. (1979), 'An emerging strategy of "direct" research', *Administrative Science Quarterly*, **24**, 582–589.

Morse, J.M. and J.L. Bottorff (1992), 'The emotional experience of breast expression', in J.M. Morse (ed.), *Qualitative Health Research*, Newbury Park, CA: Sage, pp. 319–32.

Patton, M.Q. (1990), *Qualitative Evaluation and Research Methods*, 2nd edn, Newbury Park, CA: Sage.

Rein, M. and D. Schon (1977), 'Problem setting in policy research', in C. Weiss (ed.), *Using Social Policy Research in Public Policy-Making*, Lexington, MA: D.C. Heath, pp. 235–51.

Selltiz, C., S. Wrightsman and S.W. Cook (1976), *Research Methods in Social Relations*, 3rd edn, New York: Wiley.

Silverman, D. (1989), 'The impossible dream of reformism and romanticism', in J.F. Gubrium and D. Silverman (eds), *The Politics of Field Research: Beyond Enlightenment*, Newbury Park, CA: Sage, pp. 30–48.

–––––– (1993), *Interpreting Qualitative Data: Methods for Analysing Talk, Text and Interaction*, London: Sage.

Stake, R.E. (1994), 'Case studies', in N.K. Denzin and Y.S. Lincoln (eds), *Handbook of Qualitative Research*, Thousand Oaks, CA: Sage, pp. 236–47.

Yin, R.K. (1994), *Case Study Research: Design and Methods*, 2nd edn, Thousand Oaks, CA: Sage.

6. The Architecture of Multiple Case Study Research in International Business

Pieter Pauwels and Paul Matthyssens

INTRODUCTION

Although many hot topics in the international business (IB) field require a qualitative research approach (Buckley 2002; Buckley and Chapman 1996), qualitative studies remain the exception in the better IB journal even today. Werner (2002) reports that over the last five years only 8.5 per cent of the empirical international management research published in 20 top journals applied a qualitative research strategy. Similarly, Andersen and Skaates (Chapter 23 this volume) conclude that approximately 10 per cent of all published international business research over the 1991–2002 period used a qualitative approach, with a notable last position taken by the *Journal of International Business Studies* with only 3 per cent qualitative studies over the same period. Explaining this poor representation, qualitative researchers typically refer to the inherent complexity and the time-consuming character of qualitative research, as well as to the apparent incompatibility between the fundamental premises of qualitative research and the epistemological foundations of established IB journals.

Notwithstanding these significant barriers, it is often claimed that the main impediment to getting qualitative research published is a lack of methodological rigour and an overdose of methodological vagueness (Dubois and Gadde 2002; Yeung 1995). Therefore, Yeung (1995, p. 314) argues that qualitative scholars have to take responsibility for what he calls '[h]ollowed [qualitative] methodology in international business research'. An important step to overcoming this 'hollowed methodology' criticism is the codification of methodologies and research techniques. Yet, in contrast to quantitative students, qualitative researchers seem to miss respected external reference points that serve as methodological anchors on which to fasten the methodological section of an empirical paper. Therefore, the aim of this chapter is to contribute to the codification of multiple (or comparative) case study research.

In the first part of this chapter, we present four pillars of multiple case study research – theoretical sampling, triangulation, pattern-matching logic and analytical generalisation – and cover possible architectures that span these pillars with a single superstructure or roof – validation through juxtaposition and iteration. Together they constitute a methodological framework for multiple case study research. The way they are conceived, these pillars and the roof allow for a flexible architecture of multiple case study research: strong and stable enough to withstand many of the current methodological criticisms fired at qualitative research, yet flexible enough to allow for a research design that meets the challenges of the actual research question, the phenomenon under investigation and the context of the study. Next, we translate this methodological foundation into a concrete architecture which illustrates how each pillar can be operationalised and interwoven with other pillars to support the structure as a whole, and how the roof covers all parts of the research design. We do this by presenting the methodology as applied in a recent multiple case study on international market withdrawal (Pauwels 2000; Pauwels and Matthyssens 2003).

MULTIPLE CASE STUDY RESEARCH

Within the current 'niche' of qualitative IB research, multiple case study methodology remains the most important research method by far (Andersen and Skaates, Chapter 23 this volume; Werner 2002). Hartley (1994, pp. 208–9) defines a case study as 'a detailed investigation, often with data collected over a period of time, of one or more organisations, or groups within organisations, with a view to providing an analysis of the context and processes involved in the phenomenon under study'. The ultimate aim of multiple case study research is the construction of explanatory middle-range theory (Frederickson 1983). In middle-range theory building, the researcher disaggregates complex contexts and situations into more discrete, carefully defined chunks, and then reintegrates these parts with an explicit analysis of their context (Bourgeois 1979; Peterson 1998). Unfortunately, multiple case study research in IB has been plagued by a lack of rigour and methodological vagueness. Too often case study 'research' aims at nothing more than a rich yet exploratory description of events or at providing partial support of a particular theory (theory testing) with an (implicit) inappropriate objective to generalise findings across a population (Easton 1995; Yin 1994). Although Eisenhardt (1989), Yin (1994) and Miles and Huberman (1994) among others have served as rare methodological anchors, more specific effort is needed to codify multiple case study research and, as such, create more specific methodological anchors for future IB research.

Our Epistemological Stance

Our epistemological stance is based on an ontological approach that departs from a time- and human-free objective reality towards a more context-bound intersubjective reality (Burrell and Morgan 1979; Kvale 1996; Morgan and Smircich 1980), in which the social world is to be understood from the point of view of the individuals who are directly involved in the events that are investigated. Not the isolated facts as such, but the perception and interpretation by agents of these facts, provide us with fundamental data. To summarise our epistemological stance, we briefly discuss objectivity, the event as the basic building block and causality in the context of multiple case study research hereafter.

At first sight, a context-bound intersubjective foundation of multiple case study research seems to be incompatible with the ultimate scientific aim of objectivity. However, this perception is false. A commitment to scientific objectivity does not imply a desire to 'objectify' the subject matter of the study by treating human beings as though they were no more than the features they may happen to have (Kirk and Miller 1986). In our perspective, multiple case study research aims at both the negative and positive moments of scientific objectivity as well as at intersubjectivity (Kvale 1996). In its negative moment, objectivity means free of bias and error, a study that is undistorted by the subjective influence of the researcher or of any irrelevant contextual factor. In its positive moment, objectivity means reflecting the nature of, and being true to, the object of the study. Multiple case study research aims at closing the gap between the objective of the study and the object of the study. In this respect, we explicitly aim at capturing the subjectivity that is embedded in the object. It is exactly this subjectivity we want to understand and explain. At the same time, we aim at reducing the researcher's subjective impact on the study to a minimum. Therefore, intersubjective testability and reproducibility of the study are characteristics of a scientifically sound qualitative study (Kvale 1996).

Within our ontological perspective, the event is a central building block of multiple case study research. We define an event as a discrete unit of information or meaning that can be linked to an interpretation process. Every event has some particular characteristics. It is unique, time bound, enacted and context-bound (Sztompka 1994). The notion of enactment allows for a proactive, a reactive or even a passive position of the agent in the event. A process is an event that in turn is made out of events. A process consists of sub-processes that occur in parallel. These intertwined processes often have their own momentum, pace and trajectory (Pettigrew 1997).

Whereas different kinds of relationships between events may exist, causality is the basic scientific relationship. Miles and Huberman (1994) discuss five critical features of causality in this perspective: local emphasis, causal complexity, temporality, retrospection and contextualisation. Local emphasis points to the fact that events hold a position, both in time and in space, and that causal factors can be arranged with respect to a certain focal point. Causal complexity implies that cause/effect relationships are arranged in networks. In these networks events can act as cause, effect or context in multiple relationships. Typically, effects may not result from unique causal paths (equifinality). Due to a strict (that is, unidirectional) temporality of events, feedback loops between causes and effects require additional plots. Assessing causality is essentially a retrospective matter. As such, explanation is retrodictive. Finally, contextualisation is a key characteristic of causal assessment in compliance with our ontological stance.

THE PRINCIPLES: FOUR PILLARS AND A ROOF

The architecture of an elaborate multiple case study design is built upon four pillars – theoretical sampling, triangulation, analytical pattern-matching logic, and analytical generalisation – and one roof – validation through juxtaposition and iteration. Together, they constitute the principles or rules of the game of multiple case study research. Totally ignoring one of these four pillars in the design of a multiple case study will make the architecture of the study unstable and, eventually, make the roof – the validation process – collapse. These four pillars and single roof emerged from our scrutiny of research designs of various notable multiple case studies (for example, Aharoni 1966; Burgelman 1994; Doz and Prahalad 1987; Drummond 1995; Ellis and Pecotich 2001, among others) as well as from a review of extant methodological anchors such as Eisenhardt (1989, 1991), Kvale (1989, 1996), Langley (1999), Miles and Huberman (1994), Van de Ven (1992) and Yin (1994) among others. Finally, we assessed the relevance and compatibility of each pillar in the context of IB research against our own experience in multiple case study research.

Although we claim that each of these pillars is needed to support sound multiple case study research design, we agree with Eisenhardt (1989) and Yeung (1995) that the operationalisation of these pillars into a particular architecture should remain a flexible process that allows for a tailor-made design. Therefore, we first present each of these pillars and the roof in isolation from any particular research context. In the second part of this chapter, we translate this methodological foundation into a concrete architecture by illustrating how each pillar can be operationalised and related to other pillars, and how the roof spans all parts of the research design and implementation.

Pillar 1: Theoretical Sampling

There seems to be a general belief that multiple case studies are preferred over single case studies. It is argued that more cases allow for more replication and eventually result in a more externally valid outcome (for example, Leonard-Barton 1990). However, this argumentation is false since it relies upon the inappropriate notion of the potential statistical significance of multiple case study research (Dubois and Gadde 2002). As such, the number of cases is not a quality criterion for (multiple) case study research (Eisenhardt 1991). The only argument to switch from single to multiple case study research (at the risk of losing depth) is to create more theory-driven variance and divergence in the data, not to create more of the same. Therefore, sampling should have a theoretical basis.

In theoretical sampling, the investigator deliberately selects both typical and atypical cases. Ideal-typical cases represent the empirical core of an emergent model. Cross-analysing these results in literal and theoretical replication of findings (Yin 1994) and the analysis of each additional ideal-typical case strengthens the emergent theory. Ideal-typical cases, however, are polar rather than identical cases, defined by an a priori typology. Investigators should also select atypical cases. The analysis of atypical cases produces contrasting results, however, for predictable reasons. Since it is the emergent theory that drives the sampling process, ideally sampling goes alongside data collection and analysis, as is discussed hereafter.

In many IB studies, theoretical sampling is complicated by its intrinsic multi-level character. Typically, not only multinational firms have to be sampled, but within these firms, business units, foreign subsidiaries and even individual managers have to be selected as well. It is crucial that the theoretical logic steers sampling at each level.

Pillar 2: Triangulation

Triangulation aims at the integration of multiple data sources in a multi-method design. The basic assumption of triangulation is that the weaknesses in each single data collection method/source are compensated by the counterbalancing strengths of another method/source (Jick 1979). Triangulation during data collection and analysis serves two goals. First, it is proposed as 'a near-talismanic method of confirming findings' (Miles and Huberman 1994, p. 266). In this perspective, data-source triangulation mainly reduces random measurement error (Kumar et al. 1993). Second, triangulation is useful in so far as different facets of the phenomenon are investigated through the most appropriate combination of method and sources (Yeung 1995). In this way, triangulation increases the internal validity of the study. In practice, triangulation can be accomplished in many ways. For instance, triangulation during data collection can be performed by interviewing various respondents on the same topic (synchronic primary data source triangulation), by interviewing the same respondent on a particular topic more than once (diachronic primary data source triangulation), as well as by the combination of primary and secondary data sources. Analytical triangulation can be performed by using dissimilar analytical methods (between-method triangulation) or by using variations within the same basic analytical technique (within-method triangulation).

Pillar 3: Pattern-matching Logic

Kaplan (1964) identifies the pattern model as a basic type of explanation in science. In a pattern model, events are explained when they are related to a set of other elements – that is, events and (sub)systems – in such a way that together they constitute a unified system. Pattern-matching logic is proposed as a general analytical strategy for multiple case study research (Miles and Huberman 1994; Yin 1994). Basically, with pattern-matching logic the analyst 'compares an empirical based pattern [of events] with a predicted one (or with several alternative predictions)' (Yin 1994, p. 106). As a result of this process, pattern models are described as chains of process propositions. These process propositions consist of hypothesised relationships between abstracted events. Pattern models that emerge from single cases (within-case analysis) are compared to each other (literal and theoretical replication across cases) and to pattern models described in the extant literature (that is, analytical generalisation, discussed hereafter). While pattern-matching logic is the analytical strategy, a limited number of analytical techniques within this strategy has been developed (notably inferential pattern coding in Miles and Huberman 1994).

Pillar 4: Analytical Generalisation

When a researcher arrives at a pattern model that consists of events and (causal) relationships between these events, then a legitimate question is whether these relationships hold outside the investigated sample. Two kinds of scientific generalisation predominate: statistical generalisation and analytical generalisation (Kvale 1996; Yin 1994). By definition, however, qualitative research is not suitable for statistical generalisation, since it does not rely on random sampling. Moreover, without an estimate of population variability in qualitative research, no basis for statistical inference exists. Through analytical generalisation an investigator aims at testing the validity of the research outcome (that is, a theory) against the theoretical network that surrounds the phenomenon and research questions (Yin 1994). The outcome of this analytical generalisation may indicate incompatibility with extant theories, which requires additional research, or overlap, which indicates that the 'new' mid-range theory is nothing more than a (partial) rephrasing of an existing theory.

The Roof: Validation by Juxtaposition and Iteration

While the four aforementioned pillars are the foundation of a methodological architecture for multiple case study research, validation is the roof that spans this architecture. A sound operationalisation of each pillar contributes to the balance within the architecture and, as a consequence, to the stability of the roof. Consequently, 'the emphasis on validation is moved from inspection at the end of the production line to quality control throughout the stages of knowledge production' (Kvale 1996, p. 236). Within our aforementioned ontological and epistemological perspective, validation is the ongoing deliberate creation and examination of possible sources of (in)validity. Sources of (in)validity may emerge from (1) juxtaposition of data, extant literature and the emergent theory, and (2) iteration between case selection, data collection, data analysis and comparison with extant theories (Dubois and Gadde 2002; Orton 1997). By juxtaposing data, analytical findings and the extant theory, the investigator creates internal and external reference points that allow for the falsification of the emergent explanatory logic (Orton 1997). A plethora of techniques may contribute to this validation through juxtaposition process, not least the aforementioned pillars. The researcher plays the devil's advocate by critically assessing the possible impact of sources of misfit or invalidity (Kvale 1989). While validation through iteration may look like a totally chaotic and unplanned process of jumping backwards and forwards between case selection, respondent selection, data collection, analysis and assessment against extant theories, it is a critical instrument to dynamically construct a valid theory-creating process (Orton 1997). For instance, new findings may upgrade the emergent theory, which in turn enhances the platform for further theoretical sampling. In sum, juxtaposition and iteration are two highly complementary validation strategies both aiming at the identification of possible sources of invalidity.

In this section, four methodological pillars were presented as the foundation of any multiple case study architecture. The omission of one of these pillars has a baleful influence on the methodological quality of the study and causes the roof – the ongoing validation process – to collapse. Yet, these pillars are only qualifiers: relying upon them is necessary though not sufficient. Each of the pillars should be operationalised and interwoven in a way that best fits the research questions and gives an optimal answer to the operational challenges of the study. In the remainder of this chapter, we build upon these four pillars and their superstructure by briefly discussing a concrete methodological architecture, which was applied in a study on international market withdrawal.

THE ARCHITECTURE IN CONSTRUCTION: A MULTIPLE CASE STUDY ON INTERNATIONAL MARKET WITHDRAWAL

The architecture presented hereafter was applied in a multiple case study on international market withdrawal (Pauwels 2000; Pauwels and Matthyssens 2003). International market withdrawal is a firm's decision to reduce its engagement in market-related activities in a foreign product/market combination. Although this phenomenon has been observed regularly, it seemed not to fit current theories of the internationalisation of the firm at first sight. At best, some exploratory studies (for example, Benito and Welch 1997) and compatible work in the organisational behaviour and strategy literature provided guiding foci and constructs (for example, Harrigan 1982). Therefore, the objective of this study was to unravel international market withdrawal and to explain the underlying organisational and strategy processes within the context of the ongoing internationalisation process of the firm. Clearly, the research question was a 'messy' problem (Wright et al. 1988). The empirical focus of the study was limited to a retrospective in-company (including foreign subsidiaries) analysis of antecedents, (sub-)processes – both decision-making and implementation – and consequences situated within an inner (for example, the corporate strategy of the firm) and outer (for example, foreign market dynamics) context of the decision to withdraw. The research question, as well as the conceptual and empirical context of this study, caused us to adopt multiple case study research as the dominant methodology. This study is particularly interesting since it harbours many complexities that challenge the intrinsic qualities and power of multiple case study research in IB.

In the present section, we discuss the methodological architecture of this study and present how case selection, data collection, analysis and generalisation were performed. Explicitly building upon one or more pillar(s) at each stage, we applied particular methodological techniques which took into account the complexities inherently related to the phenomenon under investigation, the research question and the IB character of the study. By examining each stage of the research process in turn, we show how the aforementioned principles of multiple case study research can contribute to the construction of a solid architecture.

Case Selection

Initially, we selected four polar cases of international market withdrawal in the context of medium-sized multinationals. Unfortunately, however, no process typology was found in the IB, strategy, organisation and marketing literature that could steer the initial sampling (Pillar 1). Therefore, we opted for a second-best solution: polarity at the level of the international venture. Three dimensions were selected from a broader international marketing perspective: (1) market entry strategy: active versus reactive export start; (2) the perceived strategic importance of this venture to the company (low versus high); and (3) the maximum profitability of the venture (poor versus strong). It was presumed that polarity at the level of the international venture would induce variance at the level of the emerging process model.

Identifying cases was another challenge. No accessible database was found that reported international market withdrawal at the firm level. Moreover, withdrawal remains a highly sensitive issue, typically not discussed in public documents. Within the organisation, many managers did not like to be reminded of this 'incident'. Eventually, the analysis across these four cases resulted in a tentative descriptive process model of international market withdrawal that was founded upon the four dimensions: organisational commitment, strategic flexibility, organisational stress and inertia (see Pauwels and Matthyssens 2003 for a further elaboration). By that time, it was clear how the emergent model could be further validated with additional ideal-typical cases (iteration). Nevertheless, additional sampling remained problematic.

Additional theoretical sampling (Pillar 1) on the basis of the emergent model required far more than a quick scan (that is, an exploratory interview) of potential cases. More than once this quick scan misled us. The emergent theory clearly indicated which polarity to look for but, unfortunately, less tacit proxies were required to circumvent the degree of abstractness in the emergent model and the aforementioned guiding constructs. For instance, one of these proxies was the ethnocentrism–polycentrism–regiocentrism–geocentrism (EPRG) model (Perlmutter 1969) through which we could identify the degree of geocentrism of the main players, using it as a proxy for the venture's degree of strategic flexibility with respect to changes in the foreign market environment. In this second sampling round, eight cases of international market withdrawal in the context of four large global firms were selected from a limited basket of about 30 potential cases. This basket was filled after an intense search for potential cases in firms that could be approached given the limits of project's budget (for example, travelling outside Europe was not possible) and the languages spoken by the researchers.

In sum, theoretical sampling was performed in two rounds. In the first round the theoretical basis was thin, which forced us to adopt a second-best solution. For the second round, the abstractness of the emergent process theory required developing more practical proxies. Nevertheless, the fundamental logic of theoretical sampling was respected. Moreover, relying on two sampling rounds contributed significantly to the validation process.

Data Collection

As difficult as it was to identify cases, it was easy to select the appropriate respondent: all protagonists who had played a significant role in an interviewee's story were eligible. Although not all respondents perceived all relevant roles, a converging snowball effect allowed for the identification of all relevant respondents per case. Yet data collection was hampered by the multinational character of the study. In the majority of the cases, interviews were performed at corporate top management level, at intermediate business management level, as well as at local sales management level. In practice, this required interviewing in different (sometimes loosely-coupled) organisational entities, which had separate strategic agendas as well as (organisational) cultures, and among which complex and dynamic relationships existed. For instance, sometimes critical information provided at top management level could not be revealed at the level of local subsidiaries. In total, over 35 decision-makers were interviewed at least twice. Interviews were performed in four different countries and three languages. Semi-structured interviewing was the dominant data collection method and interviews lasted between 1.5 and three hours. All interviews except for one were tape-recorded and transcribed verbatim.

Considering the aim for triangulation during data collection and analysis (Pillar 2), three data levels were identified (Kvale 1996): (1) factual, cognition-free information (for example, 'In 1989, we employed 15 Spanish workers'), (2) the reproduction of past interpretations (for example, 'At that moment, I thought everything was lost'), and (3) the interpretation of past events (for example, 'When I think about it now, leaving the market immediately would have been better'). It turned out that it was important to distinguish between these three data levels because each required a different interpretive and triangulation approach. When objective, value- and interpretation-free information was reported, we could easily check the information via alternative (preferably secondary) data sources. However, dealing with the respondent's reproduction of past interpretations was more problematic. At this level, apparently faulty information on actual facts was relevant to the analysis since these facts were perceived and interpreted as such by the respondent at the time of the actual process. In that case, the Thomas theorem – if people believe ideas are real, they are real in their consequences – complicated the triangulation of findings (Kvale 1996). Synchronic primary data source triangulation could not validate this information. Therefore, between-method and diachronic primary data source triangulation were valuable alternatives. Between-method triangulation was operationalised via a closed survey in which the respondent had to agree/disagree on seemingly 'theoretical' statements, which were drawn, however, from interviews with this particular person. In diachronic primary data source triangulation, the same issue was raised in a different context in a more structured follow-up interview, some weeks later.

Information at the third level – the current interpretation of past events – was the most complex to triangulate, analyse and validate. When a respondent was interpreting past events during the interview – that is, recreating past events – he/she might have had good reasons situated in the strategy process itself. Both the laddering technique (Reynolds and Gutman 1988) and synchronic primary data source triangulation with knowledgeable but neutral experts outside the firm were required to understand (1) why the respondent 're-created' past events, and (2) why he/she did this in that particular way.

In sum, data collection was mainly based upon interviews with all managers that played a relevant role in the international market withdrawal process. This primary stream of data input was complemented by several interviews with neutral experts. Although triangulation was the basic strategy, it was the character of the data that indicated which particular triangulation method was required. In the end, this data-driven application of the triangulation philosophy turned out to be a most effective instrument for the juxtaposition of data and analytical findings.

Within- and Across-case Analysis

Before anything else, reading the interviews was our prime means to achieve a valid interpretation of the data. In line with Kvale (1996, p. 223), four reading styles were explicitly adopted: (1) 'veridical reading': considering the respondent as a neutral informant, we read factual data; (2) 'experiential reading': considering the respondent as someone who experienced the phenomenon, we read his or her experience; (3) 'symptomatic reading': considering the respondent as a subjective person who makes sense of an experience, we read his or her reasoning; and (4) 'consequential reading': considering the respondent as a proactive agent in the phenomenon, we read the consequences of what her or she believes.

Within the context of pattern-matching logic as a general analytical strategy (Pillar 3), we applied inferential pattern coding (IPC) (Miles and Huberman 1994) to come to a middle-range process theory that is built upon a chain of process propositions, comprising the causal patterns embedded in the phenomenon. Situated within iteration logic (Orton 1997), IPC follows a process of literal and theoretical replication. For the implementation of IPC, we largely adopted the procedure as described in Miles and Huberman (1994). Next, we discuss the four fundamental analytical steps of IPC: (1)

pattern coding, (2) identification of within-case causal patterns, (3) identification of a causal meta-pattern across cases, and (4) the development of process propositions.

Step 1: pattern coding

On the basis of the research questions and the initial list of guiding constructs, a start list of codes was created. For instance, D/FLEX was the code used for events that related to strategic flexibility as a driver of organisational change. Next, simple, isolated coded events were integrated into a limited number of coded patterns. These coded patterns are abstracted representations of chains of events and attach meaning to emergent themes, scenarios, configurations and so on. During the coding process, the initial list of pattern codes was constantly upgraded, which required regular recoding of all data. Typically four types of pattern codes emerged: themes (for example, 'top management does not like to be troubled with problems in poorly performing subsidiaries'), causes/explanations (for example, 'a quick withdrawal is a successful withdrawal'), relationships among people (for example, 'you know, manager X acts like the CEO thinks'), and emergent constructs (for example, 'implicit bargaining among agents'). Convergence in the code list was the central criterion for stopping the process of coding and recoding. The outcome of Step 1 was an abstract map – in matrix and graphical format – of interrelated coded patterns of a particular case.

Step 2: within-case causal patterns

Within each case, a network of coded patterns started to emerge when all relevant patterns were integrated sequentially. Causal relationships in particular were highlighted and underpinned by additional findings in the literature. Non-causal patterns were linked to causal patterns in an effort to explicitly integrate the context of each causal pattern. Nevertheless, it turned out to be important to control for consistency and intra-network logic as some relationships between patterns turned out to be theoretically and/or logically non-complementary with others. In the end, we succeeded in delineating one chain of interrelated causal patterns, supported by many non-causal (that is, contextual) patterns per case.

Step 3: causal meta-patterns across cases

Through an ongoing iterative process of cross-case comparison, within-case re-analysis and the confrontation with relevant literature, we succeeded in constructing a complex causal meta-pattern across all 12 cases. This process led to an intermediate model after four cases and was validated and upgraded after the input of the causal patterns of the eight remaining cases. By means of step-by-step comparison of individual causal patterns, analysis converged towards a causal meta-pattern that accommodated all individual causal patterns. During this process, the conditions under which causal patterns held were further specified, for instance by further specifying related non-causal patterns. As expected, not every causal pattern was identified in all cases. However, unless they contradicted each other, all causal patterns were potential inputs to the cross-case model. When causal patterns seemed to contradict, we adopted three selection rules in the following order: (1) further limit conditionality via related non-causal patterns and include both, (2) include the causal pattern that is most supported in the literature, (3) exclude both.

While building this causal meta-pattern, the problem of causal complexity came up more than once. Typically, the model turned out to be regularly overspecified and parsimony had to be regained by means of permanent questioning of the relevance of each causal pattern and their interrelationships. A powerful tactic to regain parsimony was the (re-)isolation of (groups of) causal patterns. As such, we could delete meaningless or obsolete loops and identical trajectories.

Step 4: strategy process propositions
In this final step of IPC, the causal patterns that dominated the model created in Step 3 were translated into seven groups of non-overlapping process propositions. Together, these process propositions abstracted the international market withdrawal process as it was observed in the cases. Sometimes, additional literature input was required to translate the causal patterns into neutral yet theoretically sound propositions. As an example, proposition 2c ran thus: 'Rejection of tactical routine measures in reaction to decreasing performance induces the creation of alternative strategic options if and only if (1) sufficient, and (2) relevant market and business knowledge is (3) autonomously available in the venture's organisation' (Pauwels and Matthyssens 2003, pp. 141–2). As such, propositions accommodated both a causal pattern as well as non-causal yet conditioning patterns.

In sum, IPC is intrinsically built upon recurring comparison of data, analytical findings and theory (juxtaposition), and explicitly allows for feedback loops between, for instance, cross- and within-case analyses (iteration). Moreover, IPC is logically driven by a falsification logic and negative case analysis. In this way, IPC acted as a solid pivot for validation throughout our study. Nevertheless, we agree with Eisenhardt (1989, p. 539) that: '[a]nalysing data is at the heart of building theory from case studies, but it is both the most difficult and the least codified part of the process'. Even data 'analysis' software (in our case QSR NUD*IST 4), which really helped structure the data before and during every new analytical loop, was no substitute for the creative reasoning on the basis of recurring loops of reading, additional data collection, and consultation of additional literature.

Analytical Generalisation

Degrees of freedom analysis (DFA) was applied as an instrument for analytical generalisation (Pillar 4). Traditionally a quantitative technique, Campbell (1975) developed DFA in the context of qualitative theory creation. The heart of DFA is the development and testing of a prediction matrix. The statements in the prediction matrix are equivalent to hypotheses in the sense of traditional statistical hypotheses testing. In fact, DFA theoretically validates the middle-range process theory against established theories. A priori, we expected that our emergent theory would complement relevant extant theories. However, to be unique and theoretically viable, our process theory had to differ from these extant theories in its explanatory power over the central phenomenon. Assuming consistency between the fundamental assumptions of the competing theories, the ultimate ambition was to identify how and why our emergent theory did a better job in explaining the particularities of the cases and the underlying drivers than competing theories.

Operationalising DFA, we largely followed the procedure described and further developed by Campbell (1975), Wilson and Vlosky (1997) and Wilson and Woodside (1999) among others. The basic instrument of DFA is a prediction matrix that consists of parameters (Y-axis) and competing theories (X-axis). Each theory is represented by a bundle of 'scores' (or process propositions) on these parameters. Together these parameter scores encompass the full specificity of the process theories. Since all competing theories were (strategy) process theories, we adopted the six dimensions of strategy process research (Frederickson 1983) as the basic parameters. Next, each of the competing theories had to be translated into six parameter scores. Table 6.1 summarises these parameters and provides a short explanation for each parameter.

Our process theory of international market withdrawal was validated against two established process theories of organisational and strategic change: the punctuated equilibrium model of organisational change (for example, Gersick 1991; Romanelli and Tushman 1994) and Burgelman's (1994) strategy process theory of strategic business exit. More than other process theories, these two provided a theoretically competing explanation of our observations. In practice, DFA is a balancing effort. On the one hand, our model would not survive the comparison unless at least some process propositions (or parameter scores) matched the phenomenon better than the parameter scores of the competing theories. On the other hand, the more the models are complementary in their explanatory power, the more confident one is that the diagnosis is accurate and not subject to systematic bias. Practically, two arbitrary cut-off points were set: the models had to overlap on at least three parameters to be considered as competing and they had to be different in at least one parameter to be considered theoretically different. Eventually, our emergent explanatory theory turned out to be complementary to (that is, many similar parameter scores), though significantly different from, the two theoretical benchmarks. As an ultimate acid test, we were not able to restate our model in terms of one of the established theories.

Table 6.1 DFA parameters for the analytical generalisation of a process theory

Parameters	Analytical questions
Motive for initiation	Which stimuli cause a decision process to start or not to start?
	How and by whom is the decision process initiated?
	Where is the decision process initiated?
Concept of goals	What role do goals play in strategic decision processes?
	Do some goals have priority over others and why?
	Does executive decision-making attempt to achieve pre-established goals?
Relationship between means and ends	Does the organisation agree on ends before evaluating alternative means?
	How are ends affected by changes in available means?
	How are means adapted to comply with incompatible goals?
Concept of choice	Which underlying mechanism(s) drive(s) choice making?
Analytical comprehensiveness	How comprehensive do executives attempt to be during the decision-making process?
	Which mechanisms prevent an executive from being comprehensive and which mechanisms force him to be comprehensive?
Integrative comprehensiveness	Which mechanisms drive the integrative perspective on related sub-processes?
	To what extend do processes converge?

Source: Frederickson (1983).

Analytical generalisation is a crucial, yet mostly forgotten, step in multiple case study research. Juxtaposing the emergent theory of a particular study and competing theories from the extant literature allows assessing the viability and potential added value of the new theory beyond the original study.

Validation Throughout the Study

Throughout the previous sections attention was paid to the role of particular techniques for the validation of the study. It was illustrated that analysis and validation are closely related to, or even are a joint aim of, particular techniques. We believe that this parallel progression of analysis and validation comprises the core of sound qualitative research in two ways. First, techniques such as theoretical sampling, triangulation and inferential pattern coding do not just play a constructive role towards a new middle-range theory. At the same time they play an evaluative role by creating a controlled juxtaposition of different sources of information: raw data, initial findings, emergent models and existing theories. Second, a sound architecture of multiple case study research forces an investigator to build in feedback loops: across-case analysis may require new case selection, as well as additional within-case analysis. As a consequence, multiple case study research cannot be prescribed as a unidirectional process, yet is characterised by a continuous movement between different stages in the research design.

CONCLUSION

In this chapter, we aimed at the codification of multiple case study methodology in the context of international business research. Given that multiple case study research is a flexible research strategy, we do not dictate an ideal research design, simply because there is no such ideal design. Instead, we proposed four pillars: (1) theoretical sampling, (2) triangulation, (3) pattern-matching logic and (4) analytical generalisation. Together these pillars are the foundation of a multiple case study architecture that remains unique for every new research question. A balanced architecture props up a single superstructure: validation through juxtaposition and iteration. Removing one of these pillars destabilises any architecture and makes the roof vulnerable to collapse. In the second part, the design of a study on international market withdrawal was presented. While the discussion of this architecture was rather conventional (sampling, data collection, data analysis, validation), the reader was invited to dig deeper, in search of the four pillars of multiple case study research and their capacity to support the validity of the study. Future researchers are invited to apply, test and assess the present codification in the context of international business research. Stimulating discussion at the codification level significantly enhances both the standardisation and the quality of future multiple case study research.

ACKNOWLEDGEMENTS

The authors would like to thank Catherine Welch and Rebecca Marschan-Piekkari, the editors of this volume, for their very helpful comments and suggestions on earlier drafts of this chapter.

REFERENCES

Aharoni, Y. (1966), *The Foreign Investment Decision Process*, Boston, MA: Harvard University Press.

Benito, G.R.G. and L.S. Welch (1997), 'De-internationalization', *Management International Review*, **2** (special issue), 7–27.

Bourgeois, L.J. III (1979), 'Toward a method of middle range theorizing', *Academy of Management Review*, **4** (3), 443–7.

Buckley, P.J. (2002), 'Is the international business research agenda running out of steam?', *Journal of International Business Studies*, **33** (2), 365–73.

Buckley, P.J. and M. Chapman (1996), 'Theory and method in international business research', *International Business Review*, **5** (3), 233–45.

Burgelman, R.A. (1994), 'Fading memories: a process theory of strategic business exit in dynamic environments', *Administrative Science Quarterly*, **39**, 24–56.

Burrell, G. and G. Morgan (1979), *Sociological Paradigms and Organisational Analysis*, Aldershot, Hants: Gower.

Campbell, D.T. (1975), 'Degrees of freedom and the case study', *Comparative Political Studies*, **8**, 178–93.

Doz, Y.L. and C.K. Prahalad (1987), 'A process model of strategic redirection in large complex firms: the case of multinational corporations', in A.M. Pettigrew (ed.), *The Management of Strategic Change*, Cambridge, MA: Basil Blackwell, pp. 63–83.

Drummond, H. (1995), 'De-escalation in decision making: a case of a disastrous partnership', *Journal of Management Studies*, **32** (3), 265–81.

Dubois, A. and L.-E. Gadde (2002), 'Systematic combining: an abductive approach to case research', *Journal of Business Research*, **55**, 553–60.

Easton, G. (1995), 'Case research as a methodology for industrial networks: a realist apologia', *Proceedings from the 11th Industrial Marketing and Purchasing (IMP) Conference*, Manchester, UK: Manchester Federal School of Business and Management, pp. 368–91.

Eisenhardt, K.M. (1989), 'Building theories from case study research', *Academy of Management Review*, **14**, 532–50.

Eisenhardt, K.M. (1991), 'Better stories and better constructs: the case for rigor and comparative logic', *Academy of Management Review*, **16** (3), 620–27.

Ellis, P. and A. Pecotich (2001), 'Social factors influencing export initiation in small and medium-sized enterprises', *Journal of Marketing Research*, **38** (1), 119–30.

Frederickson, J.W. (1983), 'Strategic process research: questions and recommendations', *Academy of Management Review*, **8** (4), 565–75.

Gersick, C.J.G. (1991), 'Revolutionary change theories: a multilevel exploration of the punctuated equilibrium paradigm', *Academy of Management Review*, **16** (1), 10–36.

Harrigan, K.R. (1982), 'Exit decisions in mature industries', *Academy of Management Journal*, **25** (4), 707–32.

Hartley, J.F. (1994) 'Case studies in organisational research', in C. Cassell and G. Symon (eds), *Qualitative Methods in Organisational Research: A Practical Guide*, London: Sage, pp. 208–29.

Jick, T.D. (1979), 'Mixing qualitative and quantitative methods: triangulation in action', *Administrative Science Quarterly*, **24** (December), 602–11.

Kaplan, A. (1964), *The Conduct of Inquiry: Methodology for Behavioral Science*, San Francisco, CA: Chandler.

Kirk, J. and M.L. Miller (1986), *Reliability and Validity in Qualitative Research*, Sage University Paper Series on Qualitative Research Methods no. 2, Beverly Hills, CA: Sage.

Kumar, N., L.W. Stern and J.C. Anderson (1993), 'Conducting interorganisational research using key informants', *Academy of Management Journal*, **36** (6), 1633–51.

Kvale, S. (1989), 'To validate is to question', in S. Kvale (ed.), *Issues of Validity in Qualitative Research*, Lund, Sweden: Studentlitteratur, pp. 73–92.

Kvale, S. (1996), *InterViews: An Introduction to Qualitative Research Interviewing*, Thousand Oaks, CA: Sage.

Langley, A. (1999), 'Strategies for theorizing from process data', *Academy of Management Review*, **24** (4), 691–710.

Leonard-Barton, D. (1990), 'A dual methodology for case studies', *Organization Science*, **1** (3), 248–66.

Lincoln, Y.S. and E.G. Guba (1985), *Naturalistic Inquiry*, Beverly Hills, CA: Sage.

Miles, M.B. and A.M. Huberman (1994), *Qualitative Data Analysis*, 2nd edn, Thousand Oaks, CA: Sage.

Morgan, G. and L. Smircich (1980), 'The case for qualitative research', *Academy of Management Review*, **5** (4), 491–500.

Orton, J.D. (1997), 'From inductive to iterative grounded theory: zipping the gap between process theory and process data', *Scandinavian Journal of Management*, **13** (4), 419–38.

Pauwels, P. (2000), 'International market withdrawal: a strategy process study', PhD thesis, Diepenbeek: Limburgs Universitair Centrum.

Pauwels, P. and P. Matthyssens (2003), 'The dynamics of international market withdrawal', in S. Jain (ed.), *State of the Art of Research in International Marketing*, Cheltenham, UK and Northampton, MA, USA: Edward Elgar, forthcoming.

Perlmutter, H.V. (1969), 'The tortuous evolution of the multinational corporation', *Columbia Journal of World Business*, **9** (January–February), 9–18.

Peterson, M.F. (1998), 'Embedded organizational events: the units of process in organization science', *Organization Science*, **9** (1), 16–33.

Pettigrew, A.M. (1997), 'What is processual analysis?', *Scandinavian Journal of Management*, **13** (4), 337–48.

Reynolds, T.J. and J. Gutman (1988), 'Laddering theory, method, analysis and interpretation', *Journal of Advertising Research*, **28** (February–March), 11–31.

Romanelli, E. and M.L. Tushman (1994), 'Organisational transformation as punctuated equilibrium: an empirical test', *Academy of Management Journal*, **37** (5), 1141–66.

Sztompka, P. (1994), *The Sociology of Social Change*, Cambridge, MA: Basil Blackwell.

Van de Ven, A.H. (1992), 'Suggestions for studying strategy process: a research note', *Strategic Management Journal*, **13**, 169–88.

Werner, S. (2002), 'Recent developments in international management research: a review of 20 top management journals', *Journal of Management*, **28** (3), 277–305.

Wilson, E.J. and R.P. Vlosky (1997), 'Partnering relationship activities: building theory from case study research', *Journal of Business Research*, **39**, 59–70.

Wilson, E.J. and A.G. Woodside (1999), 'Degrees-of-freedom analysis of case data in business marketing research', *Industrial Marketing Management*, **28**, 215–29.

Wright, L.L., H.W. Lane and P.W. Beamish (1988), 'International management research: lessons from the field', *International Studies of Management and Organisation*, **18** (3), 55–71.

Yeung, H.W. (1995), 'Qualitative personal interviews in international business research: some lessons from a study of Hong Kong transnational corporations', *International Business Review*, **4** (3), 313–39.

Yin, R.K. (1994), *Case Study Research Design and Methods,* 2nd edn, Thousand Oaks, CA: Sage.

7. The Role of Negative Personal Experiences in Cross-cultural Case Study Research: Failure or Opportunity?

Karen Grisar-Kassé

INTRODUCTION

The particular strength of case studies lies in gaining contextual knowledge through the use of multiple sources of data. Yet a researcher's negative personal experiences[1] are rarely discussed as an avenue for the acquisition of such information. In general, negative personal experiences – likely to occur in different cultural settings – are not mentioned as potential data sources in the texts most often cited by management scholars (foremost among them Yin 1994). This omission bolsters the widespread conviction that negative personal experiences stand aloof from the actual research process and continue to be judged as unfortunate mishaps. As much as negative personal experiences are not discussed in textbooks, they are equally not mentioned in research reports of social scientists (with rare exceptions, see examples below). Instead, researchers tend to conceal shameful or embarrassing experiences.

However, the methodology of grounded theory offers researchers great flexibility in the choice of data. According to Strauss and Corbin (1990), contextual knowledge represents whatever the researcher (or research team) has read, heard, felt and experienced in the area of investigation. Contextual knowledge is of great relevance to the interpretation of data (see also Geertz 1973).

In this chapter, I attempt to show that *negative personal experiences* in cross-cultural case study research can provide a salient tool for data collection and interpretation. By telling a negative personal experience of my own (an encounter with local authorities in Senegal), I argue, together with proponents of grounded theory, that 'all is data'. Negative personal experiences in a culturally different and unfamiliar context can serve as a rich source of valid data, and also foster the researcher's comprehension of local values and viewpoints.

I shall first briefly sketch my research subject (an international mining enterprise), the ethnographic approach to the field (that is, arrival and living conditions), and the evolution of data collection. After narrating the key event, I shall point out some consequences and the insights I gained from the analysis of the negative experience. I shall, lastly, link the insights to my research focus and to the role they played in the subsequent research process.

THE CASE STUDY

The case study was carried out in the West African country Senegal. The Republic of Senegal today has been shaped by a long and eventful history of European invasion, occupation, slave trade and colonisation. Due to space limitations, only a few aspects can be mentioned here.[2] Islam was spread by Arabic traders and scholars from the tenth century on. Today, about 90 per cent of the population is Muslim. The first European invaders landed in the fifteenth century. From 1864 until political independence in 1960, Senegal was under French colonial administration. The French evolutionary model of societal development, placing the French on top and the Senegalese at the lower end of the hierarchy of civilisations, can best be studied in French assimilation, later association, policy (Crowder 1967). Senegal was in various ways an exemplary case of French colonial administration (Crowder 1967; Cruise O'Brien 1996; Harrisson 1988). The French constructed in Senegal a schooling system in which African history was absent and France was presented as a model nation and a great people. For the present study it is important to take into consideration that the ideology of French (or today also Western) supremacy and Senegalese inferiority is still evident in Senegalese thinking.

The Case Company

The focus of my research was a multinational corporation in Senegal – a phosphate mine with a strong export orientation.[3] The mine was founded in 1957 by French entrepreneurs, three years before Senegal's independence in 1960, in a rural area of small peasant villages near the coastline, some 60 miles north of the capital Dakar. The construction of houses for the freshly hired Senegalese miners near the mine's installations in 1962 and 1963 laid the basis for the mining town Mboro. Until 1980, the majority of the management was still French, whereas the workforce was practically all Senegalese. Through the process of Senegalisation after 1970 the French were systematically replaced by Senegalese senior executives and middle-level managers.

It seemed plausible to assume that Senegalese managers – accustomed to Senegalese cultural values – would be better able to handle their Senegalese subordinates. Interestingly, the opposite was the case. In 1983, three years after the shift from a majority of French to a majority of Senegalese managers had taken place, the workers went on a general strike for 24 days. In the following years the Senegalese managers progressively lost control over the work performance of their subordinates. Over a time span of ten years, the workforce mutated from a highly motivated and well-performing team with a strong corporate identity into listless and isolated workers waiting impatiently for retirement (see also Grisar 1997).

Between the years 1974 and 1990, the mine was, in terms of investment and turnover, one of the most successful enterprises in the country. It had an international reputation as an African model of successful industrialisation. Yet the dramatic social changes did not leave the economic performance of the enterprise untouched. From 1984 onwards productivity began to decline considerably and the old French-installed information system almost completely crumbled. As a consequence, the management was taken over and restructured by a neighbouring chemical company in September 1996. At that time, the firm had around 1400 employees under permanent contract.

Development of the Research Questions

While on an arduous search for evidence of my first research hypothesis,[4] I noticed that in conversations with workers, French expatriates were praised and their departure was widely regretted. Moreover, the mine's current social policy and management was relentlessly condemned. Before I started my research, I assumed Senegalese workers would feel relieved not to work under French management and control any more, because it certainly evoked in Senegalese minds bad memories of oppressive structures under colonial power. To my surprise, the relationship between the former French expatriates and their Senegalese subordinates in 'the old days' (referring mainly to the period of the enterprise's economic success) was glorified immensely. After a series of informal conversations, I suspected a link between the hidden loyalty of Senegalese workers to their departed French superiors and their dismay at Senegalese managers. Gradually over time, my research focus shifted from current to *past* behaviour, namely the much-vaunted French–Senegalese collaboration in the past, or better: the perception and reconstruction by both French and Senegalese of their particular relationship in retrospect.

My final research questions dealt with the reasons for and the characteristics of the French–Senegalese symbiosis and its impact on the new Senegalese superior–subordinate relationship.

Methodological Approach and Techniques

I conducted field research in the mining area from September 1995 until October 1996. The development of the research questions and the application and modification of methods for data collection was a dynamic process and a combination of personal research interests, coincidence, emerging opportunities, and empirical evidence.[5]

Taking a predominantly qualitative approach, I applied ethnography to the area under study. Since the focus of the study was not current, but past behaviour, the study is not an *ethnography* in the classical sense, which generally also includes the investigation of kinship genealogies, marriage patterns and rituals of distinct ethnic groups (Sanjek 1996). My aim was to integrate into the local mining community, to learn the local language, Wolof, and to share and observe – at least partly – the daily life of the local population. This integration served foremost to build trust and to facilitate an open communication between me and the local population. In addition, I wished to observe and understand the life of my host family, neighbours, friends, their behaviours, their motives and beliefs.

In my personal methodological conduct, I was much inspired by grounded theory which, today, is well known in the social sciences. The approach of ethno-psychoanalysis (Devereux 1967, 1978; Erdheim 1988; Morgenthaler et al. 1986), and more particularly the method of *self-reflexive encounters* developed by Maya Nadig (1986), was valuable for the analysis of negative personal experiences. In her field research with peasant women in Mexico, Nadig uses her own subjectivity, her feelings, her beliefs and assumptions in reaction to her informants as *the* important methodological tool to arrive at a deeper understanding of the underlying motives and convictions of her informants. In her research process the careful observation and analysis of her own *subjective irritations* about both the events and behaviour of her informants in the foreign context provide her with insight into their life worlds. Nadig suggests keeping the observations as a written text for later analytical work. For her 'the irritation is a reaction to two opposing positions – the one represented in the text and the other brought to the text – and a contradiction, a rupture in the manifest sense of the text' (my translation). According to Nadig, this is an entry to the latent dimension of the underlying subconscious meaning of the text (Nadig 1986).

I chose to conduct a case study, because it enables the researcher to illuminate a phenomenon from various perspectives through method triangulation. As Yin asserts '[w]ith triangulation, the potential problems of *construct validity* also can be addressed, because the multiple sources of evidence essentially provide multiple measures of the same phenomenon' (Yin 1994, p. 92; emphasis in original).

In the case research process I used multiple sources of data and various approaches and methods: trust building through social integration and local contacts; language acquisition (Wolof); explorative conversations; participation in daily life (participant observation) and field notes; focused interviews with focus groups (later abandoned); qualitative interviews with employees of all ranks; a survey for statistical and qualitative content analysis; collection of archived (official and unofficial) documents; two slide shows in order to discuss impressions with managers; two slide shows as a present for the local population.

Arriving and Living in the Senegalese Mining Community

On my first trip to Senegal in February 1994, I was 29 years old, a scholar from a German university, going on my first extended fieldwork. I got to know the chief ranger of the area, his three wives and nine children. After several meetings and lengthy conversations in the shade of his central compound tree, the ranger offered to host me during my period of field research, which I readily accepted.

I attended an intensive Wolof course in Dakar for six weeks before I returned in mid-September 1995 to the mining town. The ranger and his family warmly welcomed me, showing that the offer made 18 months previously was not an empty promise. Together with all family members and some friends, we negotiated which part of the compound would be best to lodge me.

The state-owned stone house was rather small and not sufficient for the entire family. The plot of land surrounding the house was, by contrast, relatively spacious and not fully used. Besides the house, the compound contained two straw huts. Two, or sometimes three, sons would spend the night in one of them, which was small but intact. The other larger straw hut was used to serve as a pantry and second kitchen, but the roof had rotted over time. The compound was completed by two enclosures which the family used to house a few goats and ducks.

It was decided to build a new straw hut for me, relatively central and adjacent to the goats' enclosure (this later resulted in considerable holes in my bedroom wall). An ailing little lemon tree was quickly removed to provide more construction territory. The new straw hut had two rooms. One was equipped with a bed and a little bedside table, the other larger one contained a little table (used as a desk) and a wooden chair, a large shelf for books and folders, two comfortable little armchairs and a coffee table made from palm leaves (a local handicraft). Stored in the corner of the living–work room was the obligatory clay *amphora* containing drinking water. The hut had two windows, one pointing to the family house and one pointing to the compound entrance and main road. The little zinc door pointed to the centre of the compound, giving a glimpse of the daily activities of the family in front of the house and of the other smaller straw hut. The compound territory was surrounded by a straw fence about 2 metres in height with an opening facing the main road in front. Another free-standing fence of the same height and about 2 metres in length was placed at a distance of about 2 metres behind the opening. It protected the compound from curious observers, but signalled enough openness for visitors to feel comfortable to enter and exit.

The ranger turned out to be an ideal host for me and my research interests. He was an open-minded, friendly man in his late fifties. Professionally and socially he was highly respected and well integrated in the rural and urban population in and around the mining town. Through his position as chief ranger, he was also a man of power. This turned out to be helpful for my integration within the local community, foremost because people could easily refer to me as *his guest*.

After three months of exploratory research, I summarised my first impressions in a slide presentation to the senior executives of the company. Not all of the senior executives had seen me before and so this was a perfect occasion to introduce myself and my research interests officially. My aim was to lay open my intentions to the top managers, to invite them to actively take part, if they wished, and to gain their full support for the study. The presentation focused on the poor living conditions of a relocated peasant village and on the current disastrous relationship and non-communication between workers and managers. The lecture was followed by a lively discussion among all participants. It was proposed that I include a survey within my methodological inventory in order to get even 'more valid and more precise' results. Although a survey was not my initial intention, I agreed to this suggestion, because it was an ideal occasion to demonstrate my willingness to cooperate. An empty office was given to me to assist with my further research.

Having heard so much about the mighty French, I assumed that this perception was an openly shared consensus. I planned to tape-record interviews with focus groups in various workshops of the enterprise. The focus group reaction unveiled the taboo character of the issue, because employees would not glorify the French in front of others. Instead, I turned to extended qualitative interviews (first only in French, later – as my language skills improved – also in Wolof), and created for each informant a confidential and anonymous situation in the office that had been assigned to me. Tape-recording the interviews was seen in a positive light as 'serious' research and therefore unproblematic.

I had access to various archives of the enterprise, so I collected internal company documents from the mine's foundation onwards until about 1986 (later documents were seldom accessible to me). An important source of data was also an archived company journal. It covered the years between 1970 and 1993. The purpose was to compare the employees' retrospective narration of events with the contemporary account given by the departed French, later Senegalese, management of those events.

A NEGATIVE PERSONAL EXPERIENCE AS A SOURCE OF DATA

It was mid-October. I was still fairly new in the area and not yet familiar with communication rules or hierarchy levels. I walked down from the hill, on which the living site for managers and students was located, to the mining town. I was on my way to the compound of my host family where I was expected for dinner. Midway a man suddenly addressed me, presenting himself as a plain-clothes police officer. He asked me to show him my passport and my green card (*carte de séjour*). I explained to him that my passport was in my apartment and that I was willing to get it if necessary. As for the green card, I told him, I had been informed that it was not needed in my case. He replied that he was not willing to let me get my passport and that he wanted to see my green card *at once*. I decided to go into detail, explaining to him exactly which different administrative offices had informed me. The police officer was about to lose his temper and yelled at me that he did not care about my explanation, but wanted to see my green card. His insistence and unwillingness to solve the problem evoked my suspicions about his intentions.

The conversation went back and forth without an end in sight. Finally, I got annoyed with his furious gestures in front of my face. I said, 'I know I don't need a green card and I find you very impolite!'. For a moment he looked at me as if in shock; he paused. Immediately, I sensed that I had violated some holy territory. After long uncomfortable seconds of his baleful stare he asked, 'What did you say?' – a rhetorical question of course. Yet the unreasonable and seditious part of me repeated the taboo words.

Furiously he instructed me that, whoever I was, I had no right whatsoever to say such a thing to him. Being in a state of total excitement myself, I was unable to analyse the situation or to reflect upon my conduct. All I knew was that I did not want to be an easy victim of corruption, even less wrongly accused on a matter about which I felt well informed. Anchored in the methodology of grounded theory, all I could think of at that moment was 'use him as an informant'. I asked him, 'Why don't I have the right to say what I think, if I feel my dignity is threatened by your aggressive way of talking, even more so as I know my rights and duties in this country?'. Unfortunately, his reply did not contain any useful analytical information. He abstained from any further explanation and shouted at me to follow him to the police station.

There we had to wait for the brigade commander to come back from some important mission. Once he had arrived, the police officer, still breathless and in great agitation, related the incident to him. To my surprise, the main issue in his account was not the missing green card, but my impudent and disobedient behaviour. When my turn came to say something, I already feared that explanations of my tediously collected information about the uselessness of a green card might be no more relevant. Nevertheless, I clung desperately to my version of the police officer's impolite behaviour. Obviously, this was not very smart, given that the brigade commander resembled a professional boxer and seemed to be unfamiliar with retorts of any sort. He approached me in a threatening pose and shouted at me: 'If you say another single word, I will put you in jail!'. Some eerie seconds passed while he was standing in front of me, slightly trembling, hands clenched, eyes flickering. For a second, I feared he would break my nose. This time, indeed, I preferred to shut up.

All that happened from then on was beyond my control. My host, the ranger, was called and arrived only a few minutes later (his compound was not far from the police station). While he was talking to the chief commander, I found his comportment, his gestures, even his tone of voice very odd. (I had never seen him like that before.) It was a behaviour of total submission and made me feel uneasy. He started to apologise for my behaviour and continued with praise for how good, sincere and decent I was. This was only interrupted with more excuses for my behaviour.

I understood that he did what had been expected of me before. Surprisingly, a short while later the personnel manager and an assistant of the phosphate mine arrived and talked to the chief commander in the same submissive manner. He vouched for my honourable intention and the importance of my scientific investigation to the phosphate enterprise. All this concerted energy was apparently needed to prevent my detention. At the same time it showed me the extent of my earlier transgression, whose effect I had underestimated. After about two hours of long discussions and excuses, the chief commander released us. Everybody agreed that I had to apply for a green card at the Ministry of Foreign Affairs in Dakar. I assumed that the matter was closed, but I was mistaken.

The following morning the personnel manager called me into his office to tell me I had to apologise officially for my defiance to the foreign police director in the department capital. I was shocked. I said to him, 'I can't do that. I think that's not fair!' and he replied, 'Yes, you will do so and you had better be very convincing with your excuse!'. After he had seen the bewilderment on my face, he said in a soft tone of voice, 'Look, I can imagine how you feel. I have lived long enough in France to know the European culture of open expression, but you are not in Europe. You now live in Senegal and you have to follow our rules. If you don't apologise, they will make you leave Senegal and we will all forget about your research project!'. After he had finished I had to take a deep breath, but he left no room for uncertainty about the issue.

I deeply loathed apologising to the police director and the local police officer a few days later. In fact, I had to prepare myself mentally to be convincingly remorseful. The collection of papers and documents to apply for a green card involved time and money, and consumed several weeks. This meant going back and forth between Dakar and Mboro, sitting around in administrative buildings, and waiting for authenticated documents from Germany. In the end, the efforts turned out to be useless, indeed. When I finally turned in all the documents required for the application, I got the official answer that a green card was not needed in my case!

The incident had both negative and positive consequences for me and my research. Negative were, of course, the extremely uncomfortable emotional states into which I was involuntarily driven. First, I was puzzled, because I did not know how to handle the police officer's reaction. I felt insecure not knowing how to behave correctly. Then I felt harassed and later threatened. The brigade commander's behaviour evoked in me anxiety and panic. When my advocates apologised for my behaviour I felt really ashamed, but also ridiculous. The subsequent encounter with the police director in the department capital was a daunting humiliation. Nevertheless, the gains by far prevailed over the losses. The perception of the local population about me had changed and my status and embeddedness within the local community was established. Furthermore, I had gained significant insights into hierarchies and power structures in Senegalese society.

Enhanced Personal Status as a Researcher

Before the incident, the locals seemed to wonder about the purpose of my presence in the town. Some speculated that I could be a government spy searching for illegal machinations in town. Another assumption was that I must be the fourth wife of the chief ranger, my host, and that some sort of sorcery must have influenced me. Apparently, it was difficult to understand why a young European woman would voluntarily live in a straw hut in the ranger's family compound. I had invested great effort in explaining to people who I was and what I wanted. But my explanation about doing research was certainly too abstract for the majority of people and, thus, my effort in this respect was not crowned with great success. People were often suspicious and not very forthcoming and as the only white woman in town, new in the area, I was closely observed.

However, after the incident the situation changed considerably. News of the event travelled quickly through the well-established informal information channels in town. My critical remarks regarding a police officer's behaviour had a positive effect. I became known as a stout-hearted woman and as somebody who would not readily accept arbitrary acts of the local authorities. All rumours and speculations of me being a government spy vanished.

The green card debate unveiled my stay as only temporary and not – as many had guessed – permanent. This proved that the chief ranger was just my host, not my husband. His behaviour in the situation had shown that he stood firmly by me and that, as my host, he felt entirely responsible for my acts. The personal manager's guarantee for me when I was facing prison revealed that the mining enterprise had a strong interest in my investigation. It showed that I had told the truth and that I indeed intended to do research. My scientific investigation was not just a pretext for hiding other secret motives. What I had attempted to clarify unsuccessfully before had all of a sudden turned into common knowledge: who I was, what I wanted, how long I intended to stay, where I lived and why. My transparency was rewarded with a deeper social acceptance and communal support for my study. My popularity in town soared, which was, of course, helpful in gaining the confidence of the local population. This certainly had an impact on the sincerity and frankness of my informants in conversations, interviews and surveys. I had suddenly mutated into a trustworthy person.

New Empirical Insights into Senegalese Power Structures and Hierarchies

Through my reading, I knew about the significance of hierarchical structures in Senegalese society. But up to the moment of the encounter with the brigade commander, I had no inkling of its true meaning for everyday life. Once in the situation myself I could feel how dangerous and threatening it was to challenge established hierarchies. As a foreigner I was still in relative safety (as I found out much later). The worst-case scenario was that I could face expulsion. The brigade commander successfully curbed a strong inclination to slap me; there was – I believe – an inhibition against punching a white European face. Being Senegalese in the same situation would quite certainly mean severe physical punishment, besides, of course, detention. This plain reality became clearer also through various other situations, which I observed or heard about without being personally involved.

In principle, all official and unofficial social institutions in Senegalese society are organised in strict hierarchies[6] and patron–client relationships.[7] Although asymmetrical, patron–client relations are based on reciprocity and mutual benefit (Mitchell 1996). In general, each interaction is shaped by the hierarchical ranks of the actors involved. Criteria for the hierarchical classification of a person depend also on the merit the person has gained through personal efforts in the social arena in which a given interaction takes place (such as the workplace, religious and political circles). More important for rank, however, are unalterable aspects: foremost age, gender and family background. Power holders can expect respect, obedience and loyalty. On the other hand, they are expected to take over social responsibility for others. This can mean providing financial or other material support (that is, food, clothing, shelter), but also giving advice and guidance to dependants. Responsibility for others will cement an already established power position and is considered a means to broaden one's social influence and control. Creating a net of social interdependencies is a general goal in Senegalese society. Open disagreement or disobedience elicits punishment, its severity depending on the circumstances and on the relationship of the actors involved. If both superior and inferior behave in tune with social norms and play their ascribed roles, then the contact will be very friendly and courteous. If the hierarchical position is challenged by an inferior (by disobedience for example), the superior will clearly show that his (rarely her) power can be threatening to the inferior's social integration and wellbeing. Usually, the inferior will try to avoid further negative consequences by repeated excuses and behaviour of clear devotion and submission. However, the social rehabilitation of an inferior depends heavily on his or her social allies and how powerful and important they are in the social arena (religious or political leaders for example).

I was rescued, because I had unwittingly built strong alliances with important power holders (personnel manager, chief ranger). In a conflict situation they became my advocates. Insightfully, my host father said to me, 'He [the brigade commander] too has to accept that you are not an isolated element, but that he has to expect strong counter-reactions, if he does you harm!'. Social interdependence with strong power holders is desired and sought. Social isolation has to be avoided at all costs in order to live in security in Senegal.

After my personal experience, I was sensitised to the dimension of social hierarchies, power affiliations and interdependence. I began to take another perspective on social interactions between Senegalese people. I was able to understand much better the Senegalese tendency to get close to powerful actors, taking now into consideration its significance for one's own protection.

The miners' enduring loyalty to their former French bosses was at first incomprehensible. Only after fieldwork, and through the analysis of my negative experience of power structures in Senegalese society, did I gradually understand that the powerful French expatriates were the perfect allies for the security and protection of their Senegalese employees. French expatriates and Senegalese employees had operated according to traditional patron–client relationship patterns.

The French managers of the mining enterprise had adopted an ideology of paternalism in collaboration with their Senegalese subordinates, which remained in the old order of the colonial 'mission to civilise' (*mission civilisatrice*). In their position as 'fathers', the French expatriates went far beyond their function as managers in an industrial complex. French top managers had established a system of competition among workshops and departments. Granting favours turned out to be a perfect means for French workshop leaders and department managers to evoke in their Senegalese subordinates extraordinary work efforts and total submission to the needs of the production process. Favours included a great variety of financial, material and moral support, but foremost salary advances and promotion. For French expatriates those various favours and services to Senegalese subordinates and their families served to keep the miners' minds on the work process. In the eyes of the Senegalese, however, French managers behaved as patrons and as protectors, giving them shelter and moral guidance. In a dire situation, subordinates would turn first to their French bosses for help, who perceived it also in a way as their moral duty. The French–Senegalese relationship in the mine was indeed based on reciprocity and mutual benefit (Kassé 2002).

The policy of granting salary advances without limits over many years gradually drew the Senegalese employees into serious debt. However, the full scale of the problem only became apparent after the Senegalese managers had taken over. While young Senegalese engineers and economists installed official limits on salary advances in order to solve the tremendous financial problem and struggled with older, overpromoted but underqualified workers, the French 'patrons' quietly departed one by one.

The reasons for Senegalese management failure are complex and multifaceted. However, the heritage of French management policy was a heavy burden for young and inexperienced Senegalese managers. Disappointed and embittered, the miners' loyalty and devotion remained attached to their former French 'patrons', their attention gradually shifted to other strong allies outside the company and away from the production process.

NEW METHODOLOGICAL INSIGHTS INTO CONTEXTUAL KNOWLEDGE

The field researcher as a sovereign objective observer has been widely demystified in the field of social anthropology.[8] Current textbooks on qualitative research methods, and more specifically ethnography, now widely include chapters on feelings and personal experiences within fieldwork (Hammersley and Atkinson 1995; Lofland and Lofland 1995; Neuman 1997). In some fields in the social sciences, in which qualitative approaches have gained considerable ground in recent years, there is an ongoing debate over whether there should be a fruitful integration of the researcher's subjectivity. Some social scientists (mostly anthropologists) have succeeded brilliantly in using negative personal experiences as an initial clue to decipher important cultural concepts of the groups studied. Yet in mainstream research in much of the social sciences, personal feelings and experiences of the researcher are still perceived as not relevant or even harmful to scientific objectivity and likely to bias the results.

Clifford Geertz (1973) explains in 'Deep Play' that he and his wife were ignored by the local population in a Balinese village until they coincidentally participated in an illegal cockfight. When suddenly a police officer appeared they ran like everybody else down the street to hide in a Balinese compound. On the following day, the Geertz couple were not only not ignored any more, but became the centre of attention in the community. This event allowed Geertz to study in depth the Balinese cockfight customs and their significance to male Balinese identity (Geertz 1973).

Jean Briggs (1970) spent 17 months with a family group of 20 to 35 Eskimos in an otherwise unpopulated and remote area. After several months of field research she lost her temper – 'very mildly as we ourselves would view it' – in an encounter with a white fisherman visiting the group; and 'as a result of my unseemly and frightening wrath at the fishermen I was ostracized, very subtly, for about three months' (Briggs 1970, p. 3). From this salient experience she draws the following analytical assumptions: 'Emotional control is highly valued among Eskimos; indeed, the maintenance of equanimity under trying circumstances is *the* essential sign of maturity, of adulthood. The handling of emotions is thus a problem that is of great importance also to the Utku [Eskimos] themselves' (emphasis in original). Briggs's ethnography, *Never in Anger*, shows that the use of negative personal experiences can be extremely insightful (see also Favret-Saada 1980).

The limited appreciation of negative personal experiences even among qualitative researchers may be due to the fear that they will be perceived as an indication of incompetence. The first few weeks in a culturally new environment are delicate, because the researcher is closely observed by the local population and, thus, defined by his or her inadequate behaviour, which may create a lasting image. This aspect cannot be underestimated when, in addition, the researcher's habits, manners and behaviour are equally unknown and *strange* to the local population, which represents after all the group of potential informants (see also Agar 1980; Nash 1963; Powdermaker 1966).

The researcher, at first unfamiliar with local customs, is constantly in danger of provoking negative reactions from the local people, on whose willingness to give information the researcher is highly dependent. The researcher also represents an ideal screen for the projection of all kinds of fears and expectations. In this first phase, the researcher may be in the stressful situation of having to adopt a culturally appropriate behaviour which he or she does not yet fully understand. In the event of a negative experience, the researcher may initially feel helpless. For a person who is accustomed to actively *lead* a research process, helplessness is in itself very uncomfortable and difficult to bear. In addition, he or she may feel puzzled or irritated by an unexpectedly harsh reaction. Other problematic feelings may emerge such as shame, humiliation, disappointment, desperation, outrage, contempt, anger, or even hate and wrath. Subjected to such emotional upheaval, having lost control, comprehension and perspective, the researcher might instinctively tend to misinterpret the event as a personal failure. He or she might accuse him- or herself of naivety, possibly of having paid insufficient attention to local values. Shame may emerge, a strong and agonising feeling. Still long after the event, a feeling of incompetence may prevail. Turning away from such an experience, physically and mentally, is a normal and legitimate human reaction. It would be absurd to proclaim that the researcher should immediately afterwards rise to analytical super-levels of sharp reflection. Of course, having survived the situation, we first have to recover from it. We take a break until we are able to take a different and more distant perspective.

We have subconsciously learned in a long process of socialisation and education to adapt and shape our behaviour to norms according to our own cultural environment. This enables us to avoid to a large extent negative personal experiences. In our own culture we are – consciously or subconsciously – familiar and accustomed to the social expectation of adequate behaviour. In a culturally foreign environment, we usually do not have all this information. Although we might be instructed theoretically about some important local conventions, we might not be able to apply this knowledge in a given unexpected situation. Naturally and subconsciously we react according to our own cultural norms.

Negative personal experiences are likely to occur when two different value systems meet. This particular difference should be, in fact, the analytical focus. For the analysis of a negative personal experience, reflections on the following questions could lead us to a deeper understanding: What kind of behaviour in a given situation was expected from us? For what reason was it expected? Who played which role in the situation? What was the role of the researcher?

In parallel, the researcher's subjectivity is to be analysed. What did the researcher truly expect of others in a given situation and which cultural assumptions lay behind his or her expectations? Nadig (1986) follows up her irritations by asking her informant confrontational questions. In my case, of course, I could not go back to the brigade commander and ask him confrontational questions. What I could do instead was to discuss the issue with Senegalese friends and host family members. Answering these questions, ideally abetted by other colleagues and local friends in discussions, may result in the clarification of local cultural perspectives and in the acquisition of further important contextual knowledge.

The concept of contextual knowledge is still very much limited to the methodology of grounded theory. But even within grounded theory, contextual knowledge is still poorly defined. Strauss (1987) dedicates only one paragraph to the term and refers to *experiential data* as 'experiences of various kinds' (p. 10) and mentions also personal experiences as 'potential gold' (p. 11). In a recent book, Glaser (2001, p. 145) adds:

> 'All is data' is a well known Glaser dictum. What does it mean? It means exactly what is going on in the research scene is the data, whatever the source, whether interview, observation, documents, in whatever combination. It is not only what is being told, how it is being told and the conditions of its being told, but also all the data surrounding what is being told. It means what is going on must be figured out exactly what it is to be used for, that is conceptualisation, not for accurate description. Data is always as good as far as it goes, and there is always more data to keep correcting the categories with more relevant properties.

In an early work within grounded theory, Glaser and Strauss (1967, p. 65) use the term 'slice of data' for '[d]ifferent kinds of data give the analyst different views or vantage points from which to understand a category and to develop its properties'. The term 'slice of data' is useful in conceptualising negative personal experiences, because it presents the slice as a unit with a start and a definite end. Although negative personal experiences may be enmeshed in ongoing processes, the hypothetical image of a 'slice of data' provides a fruitful analytical frame in regard to a methodological approach.

CONCLUSION AND OUTLOOK

In this chapter, I have dealt with the nature of negative personal experiences as one particular segment of contextual knowledge, and their potential for scientific insight. I chose to elaborate on this issue because I saw colleagues coming back from field research earlier than intended due to their negative personal experiences. In most cases, their early return did not endanger their research projects and written reports, but only reduced the amount of data. Perceived as private and extraneous to the research question, the negative experience was told only to intimate friends and family members.

And yet, I would argue, it is possible to prepare for such a situation at home. If we assume that a negative personal experience can provide valid data – which I attempted to show – then it should also be possible to elaborate a method to prepare for such events and to treat the subsequent written text about the event as data. One way of preparation can be the demystification of the sovereign researcher who is always in control of the research circumstances. If we assume that negative personal experiences are likely to occur in a culturally foreign environment, then qualitative researchers going abroad can be better prepared. Transparency about the issue may assist researchers in the field to treat negative personal experiences as an opportunity, instead of a personal failure that must be concealed. Among qualitative researchers it should become an issue for lively and insightful discussion. Negative personal experiences should therefore be integrated into training in qualitative methodology.

If we agree with Patton (1980, p. 9) that 'one of the cardinal principles of qualitative methods is the importance of background and context to the processes of understanding and interpreting data', we should also work on the various dimensions and the nature of contextual knowledge. It has not been my intention to develop a methodology of negative personal experiences here. But I hope I have encouraged further reflection on the issue.

NOTES

1. In this context, negative personal experience means the so-called *faux pas*, the unintentional breach of taboos. Threats to the researcher's life (such as attempted murder, rape, armed conflicts) are not discussed in this chapter.
2. For further readings, see Eades and Dilley (1994) and Gellar (1982).
3. The selection of the enterprise was pure coincidence. Interested in intercultural communication in African organisations, I met a French researcher who had grown up as the daughter of an expatriate engineer and his wife in the French community of the mine in the 1960s and 1970s. Through her contacts with the Senegalese management, I was able to make my first research contacts. The mining enterprise is the subject of previous studies (Fall Ndoye 1996; Founou-Tchuigoua 1976; Ndiaye 1992; Peroux and De Bernis 1963; Sow 1983).
4. As a consequence of regular relocations of villages because of further phosphate extraction, the peasants lose all agricultural land and therefore the base of their existence. My initial research interest focused on the massive impoverishment of the relocated peasant population in the area. I naturally assumed, in my Western views, a massive tension among conflicting interest groups within the area. In my perception, the phosphate mine embodied the post-colonial European invader and destroyer of a healthy African subsistence economy. Very soon, I had to realise, where I saw a huge problem the local peasant population did not!
5. Strauss and Corbin (1990, p. 23) assert 'one does not begin with a theory, then prove it. Rather, one begins with an area of study and what is relevant to that area is allowed to emerge'.
6. In addition, the complex system of traditional castes and classes interferes with social institutions like family, brotherhoods, workplace and state administration. The interested reader may turn to Abdoulaye Bara Diop (1981, 1985).
7. The persistence and constant reaffirmation of patron–client relationships in West-African states is seen as a strong predicament for democratisation (Chabal and Daloz 1999; Tetzlaff 1999).

8. Malinowski (1922), recognised as the founder of modern anthropological fieldwork, proclaimed the ideal image of the heroic ethnographer who carries out an experiment analogous to those in the natural sciences. In the demystification of the solely scientific and distanced field researcher, the publication of Malinowski's field diaries – revealing his own subjective standpoint and personal limits – played a salient role (Malinowski 1989).

REFERENCES

Agar, M. (1980), *The Professional Stranger*, London: Academic Press.

Briggs, J. (1970), *Never in Anger: Portrait of an Eskimo Family*, Cambridge, MA: Harvard University Press.

Chabal, P. and J.-P. Daloz (1999), *L'Afrique est parti! Du désordre comme instrument politique*, Paris: Economia.

Crowder, M. (1967), *Senegal: A Study of French Assimilation Policy*, London: Methuen.

Cruise O'Brien, D.B. (1996), 'The Senegalese exception', *Africa*, **66** (3), 458–64.

Devereux, G. (1967), *From Anxiety and Method in the Behavioral Sciences*, The Hague: Mouton.

—— (1978), *Ethnopsychoanalyse: Die komplementaristische Methode in den Wissenschaften vom Menschen* (Ethnopsychoanalyse complémentariste, German), Frankfurt a. M.: Suhrkamp.

Diop, A.B. (1981), *La société Wolof*, Dakar: Karthala.

—— (1985), *La famille Wolof*, Dakar: Karthala.

Eades, J. and R. Dilley (1994), *Senegal* (World Bibliographical Series, No. 166), Oxford: Clio.

Erdheim, M. (1988), *Psychoanalyse und Unbewußtheit in der Kultur: Aufsätze 1980– 1987*, Frankfurt a. M.: Suhrkamp.

Fall Ndoye, F. (1996), 'Evaluation des Conditions de Travail et de l'Etat de Santé des Conducteurs d'Engins Lourdes dans une Compagnie Minière de Phosphates du Sénégal', PhD thesis, Dakar: University Cheikh Anta Diop.

Favret-Saada, J. (1980), *Deadly Words: Witchcraft in the Bocage*, Cambridge: Cambridge University Press.

Founou-Tchuigoua, B. (1976), *The Impact of Multinational Firms on Employment and Incomes: A Case Study of Phosphates in Senegal*, Geneva: International Labor Office.

Geertz, C. (1973), 'Deep play: notes on the Balinese cockfight', *Daedalus*, **101**, 1–37.

Gellar, S. (1982), *Senegal: An African Nation between Islam and the West*, Boulder, CO: Westview Press.

Glaser, B. (2001), *The Grounded Theory Perspective: Conceptualisation Contrasted with Description*, Mill Valley, CA: Sociology Press.

Glaser, B.G. and A.L. Strauss (1967), *The Discovery of Grounded Theory: Strategies for Qualitative Research*, Chicago, IL: Aldine.

Grisar, K. (1997), 'Globalization of work culture: African and European industrial cooperation in Senegal', *Research in the Sociology of Work*, **6**, 223–46.

Hammersley, M. and P. Atkinson (1995), *Ethnography: Principles in Practice*, 2nd edn, London: Routledge.

Harrisson, C. (1988), *France and Islam in West Africa 1860–1960*, Cambridge:

Cambridge University Press.

Kassé, K. (2002), 'Paternalism as interactive management in Africa: a case study of ethnic staff division of Senegal', in C. Alsop Kraft (ed.), *Grenzgängerin – Bridges between Disciplines: Eine Festschrift für Irmingard Staeuble*, Kroening: Ansanger Verlag, pp. 154–72.

Lofland, J. and L.H. Lofland (1995), *Analyzing Social Settings: A Guide to Qualitative Observation and Analysis*, 3rd edn, Belmont, CA: Wadsworth.

Malinowski, B. (1922), *Argonauts of the Western Pacific*, London: Routledge.

———— (1989), *A Diary in the Strict Sense of the Term*, 2nd edn, London: Athlone Press.

Mitchell, J.P. (1996), 'Patrons and clients', in A. Barnard and J. Spencer (eds), *Encyclopedia of Social and Cultural Anthropology*, London: Routledge, pp. 416–17.

Morgenthaler, F., F. Weiss and M. Morgenthaler (1986), *Gespräche am sterbenden Fluß: Ethnopsychoanalyse bei den Iatmul in Papua Neuguinea*, Frankfurt a. M.: Fischer-Taschenbuch-Verlag.

Nadig, M. (1986), *Die verborgene Kultur der Frau: Ethnopsychoanalytische Gespräche mit Bäuerinnen in Mexiko*, Frankfurt a. M.: Fischer Taschenbuch Verlag.

Nash, D. (1963), 'The ethnologist as stranger', *Southwestern Journal of Anthropology*, **19**, 149–67.

Ndiaye, A.I. (1992), 'Crise économique prolongée et formes de reponses des travailleurs: étude de la résistance du salairie sénégalais', PhD thesis, Dakar: University Cheikh Anta Diop.

Neuman, William L. (1997), *Social Research Methods: Qualitative and Quantitative Approaches*, 3rd edn, Boston, MA: Allyn & Bacon.

Patton, M.Q. (1980), *Qualitative Evaluation Methods*, Beverly Hills, CA: Sage.

Peroux, F. and G. De Bernis (1963), *Etude d'une firme dans une jeune nation insuffisamment developée*, Dakar: Institut de Science Economique Appliquée.

Powdermaker, H. (1966), *Stranger and Friend*, New York: W.W. Norton.

Sanjek, R. (1996), 'Ethnography', in A. Barnard and J. Spencer (eds), *Encyclopedia of Social and Cultural Anthropology*, London: Routledge, pp. 193–8.

Sow, M. (1983), 'Exploitation minière et vie regionale: exemple des phosphates au Sénégal', PhD thesis, Dakar: University Cheikh Anta Diop.

Strauss, A.L. (1987), *Qualitative Analysis for Social Scientists*, Cambridge: Cambridge University Press.

Strauss, A.L. and J. Corbin (1990), *Basics of Qualitative Research*, Newbury Park, CA: Sage.

Tetzlaff, R. (1999), 'Der Wegfall effektiver Staatsgewalt in den Staaten Afrikas', *Friedenswarte – Journal of International Peace and Organisation*, **74** (3), 307–30.

Yin, R.K. (1994), *Case Study Research: Design and Method*, 2nd edn, Thousand Oaks, CA: Sage.

8.   First the Sugar, Then the Eggs... Or the Other Way Round? Mixing Methods in International Business Research

Leila Hurmerinta-Peltomäki and Niina Nummela

INTRODUCTION

Methodology is always a controversial topic among researchers, and in particular the idea that various methods might be combined has provoked a rather lively debate. Those with a background in qualitative methods have been the prime initiators of the discussion, which is not completely neutral, however, because the roles of qualitative and quantitative methods seem quite fixed (see Tashakkori and Teddlie 1998). It is commonly assumed that if methods are mixed, the main one is quantitative and the qualitative results are supplementary and somehow subordinate. Given this underlying assumption, it is not surprising that the qualitative part of the study is sometimes not reported at all, as it is considered mainly a source of pre-understanding (for example, Birkinshaw, Chapter 28 this volume). Nevertheless, a growing number of studies in the field of international business confirm that there are alternative ways of using mixed methods.

The aim of this chapter is to familiarise the reader with methodological pluralism and its philosophical background. Alternative ways of mixing qualitative and quantitative methods are also introduced, and some examples are given. The examples all comprise case study research, which is the dominant qualitative method in international business research (Andersen and Skaates, Chapter 23 this volume). The chapter ends with a discussion about and conclusions on the potential of mixed methods in international business research.

The title of this chapter compares the researcher to the baker because, in our opinion, the choice to mix methods could apply to both. Certain traditional, unwritten and almost compulsory norms exist in the culinary field and in academic research. However, an increasing number of actors in both are seeking variation and argue that deviation from strict rules and novel, even bold experiments would open up interesting new arenas.

BACKGROUND FOR MIXED METHODS – TO MIX OR NOT TO MIX?

The methodological background of international business (IB) research lies in other sciences, particularly in the social sciences. Researchers in these fields have been actively discussing the use of mixed methodology, and diverse schools of thought have emerged. Opinions vary considerably, the opposite ends of the continuum being the 'purists' and the 'pragmatists' (Creswell 1994; Tashakkori and Teddlie 1998). A similar type of division exists in the culinary arts between distinguished and experienced bakers who stick to the well-known recipes and newcomers who rebel against contemporary traditions and norms.

The distinguishing characteristics of these schools are both philosophical and methodological (Patton 1990). According to the strictest purists, methodological decisions are not made in isolation, but are always related to the researcher's assumptions of the phenomenon itself (ontology), the basis of the knowledge (epistemology), and the relationship between human beings and their environment (compare Burrell and Morgan 1979). Thus, a researcher with a positivist/objective approach emphasises the methods and values of research in the natural sciences and is bound to adopt quantitative methods. On the other hand, a researcher with a constructivist/subjectivist orientation attempts to get as close as possible to the phenomenon in question in order to acquire a more hermeneutic understanding (for more on hermeneutic research design, see, for example, Gummesson 1991). This, in turn, requires the use of qualitative methods (for example, Burrell and Morgan 1979; Lee 1989). Consequently, purists also argue that compatibility between quantitative and qualitative methods is impossible because of the underlying different paradigms (Tashakkori and Teddlie 1998).

A few scientists have made even higher demands, arguing that methods must be consistent with the epistemological presumptions of the researcher, the theory and the research problem (Arbnor and Bjerke 1997; Brannen 1992). However, some of them do admit that the philosophical assumptions of the researcher seldom determine the choice of method, and acknowledge that this is usually affected by several practical limitations (Brannen 1992). This concession brings us closer to the other end of the continuum, the pragmatists.

Pragmatists argue that researchers should use both paradigms effectively in order to increase their understanding of the phenomenon in question (compare Creswell 1994). For them, the starting point in the method selection is the research problem. In other words, the method – either a single one or a combination – should be selected based on its theoretical relevance (compare Denzin 1978). Additionally, the selection of mixed methods should be based on the fact that important elements of the research problem would remain unresolved if only one method were used (Bryman 1992). Thus, the aim of mixing methods is to capture a complete, holistic picture of the subject matter, presumably with a view to uncovering something that might have been missed with a simpler research design (Jick 1979). Furthermore, according to the pragmatists, mixing methods encourages the researcher to find innovative solutions. It may, for example, open his or her eyes to alternative, unexpected interpretations of reality. Different perspectives are likely to produce some elements that do not fit a theory, a model or previous understanding, and divergent results promote deeper, more complex and less evident explanations (Jick 1979; Patton 1990). It has also been argued that different methods complement each other and thus increase the validity of the findings (Bryman 1992; Denzin 1978; Eisenhardt 1989; Jick 1979; Lincoln and Guba 1985; Patton 1990). However, the effectiveness depends on how well the weakness of one method is compensated by the strength of another (Creswell 1994; Denzin 1978; Jick 1979).

For pragmatists, then, the end justifies the means: that is to say, purity of method is less important than dedication to relevant and useful information (Patton 1990). At the moment, it seems that the number of pragmatists has been growing among social scientists (Tashakkori and Teddlie 1998). In the field of international business, the interest of researchers often lies in very complex and multi-faceted phenomena. Therefore, in our opinion, particularly in this field, researchers should take advantage of the possibilities of mixed methods in order to increase their understanding of the subject matter. In other words, the use of innovative recipes and combinations of ingredients would often be more than welcome.

TRIANGULATION – THE CORE CONCEPT IN MIXING METHODS

A dear child has many names, they say. In the social sciences, the combination of diverse methodological approaches has been discussed in various terms, such as multiple methods, mixed methods, multi-method research and methodological mix (Tashakkori and Teddlie 1998). What is probably the most common concept, however, is triangulation. The terms 'triangulation' and 'mixed methods' are used synonymously in this chapter, given that mixed methods represent one form of triangulation.

Denzin (1978) classified the concept of triangulation into four basic types, according to the focus: (1) data, (2) investigator, (3) theory and (4) methodological triangulation. He further divides methodological triangulation into within-method and between- or across-method triangulation, the first referring to the use of multiple research strategies within one methodological approach (for example, participant observation and interviews). This study concentrates particularly on across-method triangulation, which refers to the use of two or more methods in a single piece of research (for example, survey and cases).

Researchers in the social sciences (for example, Denzin 1978) and organisational research (for example, Jick 1979) often refer to the seminal works of Campbell and Fiske (1959) and Webb et al. (1966) when defining triangulation. A generally accepted definition is the one put forward by Denzin (1978), which states that it refers to the use of multiple methods in the study of the *same object* (for example, a company). Jick (1979) applied this definition to organisational research, and argues that it means the use of multiple methods in a study, but with a view to examining the *same dimension of a research problem*, that is, the same subject (for example, internationalisation). Even though Jick's definition resembles Denzin's, there is a clear difference in focus. In our opinion, triangulation in IB research may be applied both in studies in which the subject or object is the same, and in those with different subjects and objects. This issue is discussed in detail later in this chapter.

HOW SHOULD WE MIX QUALITATIVE AND QUANTITATIVE METHODS?

Researchers who decide to apply mixed methods in their studies should address a few elementary questions before proceeding to the actual data collection. These relate to the order, role and purpose (Figure 8.1[1]). In terms of our baking metaphor, it is sometimes very important to add the ingredients in the correct *order*, as this determines the end result. Sometimes it is sensible to use a sequential mode: the different methods follow each other in the research process, and the researcher first collects qualitative, then quantitative data, or vice versa (Hirsjärvi and Hurme 2001; Tashakkori and Teddlie 1998).

Further, the *role* of different ingredients in the dough, or in the method, may vary. The study may be a balanced aggregate, in which all methods are equal in importance, or one method may play a bigger role, that is, it has a dominant versus a less dominant method design (compare Creswell 1994). In this situation, the data collected using the dominant method is the main source of information. On the other hand, the researcher may obtain valuable additional information using the less dominant method. For example, he or she may decide to conduct a qualitative expert interview early on in order to acquire pre-understanding for a quantitative survey. Both balanced and biased solutions may serve well in a mixed-method study.

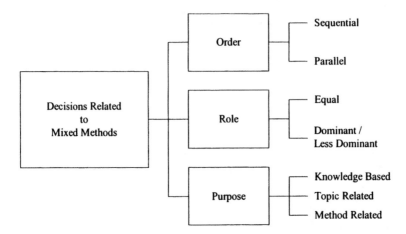

Figure 8.1   Key decisions in studies using mixed methods

Finally, an experienced baker is aware of the effect of each ingredient and thus may be able to modify the original recipe slightly in order to improve the end result. Using mixed methods in research also requires methodological knowledge because all methods usually serve their own *purpose*. The purposes for using mixed methods can be classified as knowledge based, topic related and method related. Each of these has its roots either in the theory or in the empirical phenomenon under study. When the study focuses on a subject on which considerable theoretical research has been conducted, the purpose is knowledge based and closely related to prior theory, such as hypothesis testing (compare our example 4 below). On the other hand, empirical evidence sometimes exists, but no specific theory about it has yet been developed. In this case, too, the purpose is knowledge based (compare the quantitative part of our example 2). In both of the cases mentioned, the purpose is to build on an existing knowledge base, which has been created by systematic theoretical or empirical research.

Topic-related purposes can be identified in situations where some information – either theoretical or empirical – is available but is insufficient or scattered. While no researcher starts with a *tabula rasa*, there may be little existing knowledge to draw on. Consequently, topic-related purposes reflect the researcher's need to become acquainted with a phenomenon that is either very new or as yet rather unexplored. The study may apply existing theories to a novel context (for example, innovation theories in internationalisation, compare the qualitative part of our example 2), or it may be exploratory. A typical example of the latter is an inductive case study, which aims at acquiring pre-understanding.

The purpose of triangulation may also be method related. The use of mixed methods may be obligatory for technical reasons, such as when the population of potential study objects is unknown. A quantitative survey may be the only way to identify theoretically interesting cases, as in our example 1. However, in that study – as in many others – the data collected using the less-dominant method also facilitated and inspired the interpretation of the findings and improved the theoretical discussion.

To conclude, regardless of their purpose, all studies using mixed methods aim at a similar end result: to validate the research results, to complement each other, to inspire the research process and/or to facilitate interpretation of the results (compare Hirsjärvi and Hurme 2001). Examples from existing empirical studies are presented in the following sections in order to demonstrate the variety of purposes in mixed methods.

MOVING BACK AND FORTH BETWEEN METHODS

In this section we briefly introduce to the reader four empirical studies in international business in which mixed methods have been applied. In selecting the examples we deliberately decided to focus on doctoral dissertations (Hurmerinta-Peltomäki 2001; Lindqvist 1991; Nummela 2000; Ridderstråle 1996) because the description of the methods used is often rather short and superficial in other types of publications, mainly due to space limitations. Additionally, the authors' own dissertations offered the opportunity to reflect on their personal experiences in the text. The other two dissertations were included in order to illustrate the variety and innovativeness of research design. As stated earlier, most qualitative research in the field of international business has involved case studies, and it seemed natural to restrict our examples to this type of investigation. As the focus of this article is on methods, the emphasis is on methodological solutions, not on empirical results.

Example 1: From a Quantitative Pilot Study to In-depth Cases

The objective of Nummela's study (2000) was to promote deeper understanding of small and medium-sized enterprise (SME) commitment to export cooperation. The empirical part was a mixture of a quantitative pilot study and a qualitative case study based on two in-depth cases. The pilot study was supplementary, offering a broad overview of SME export cooperation, and particularly creating a pre-understanding of partners' commitment to it. This pre-understanding helped in selecting meaningful and interesting cases for the qualitative study, as well as in facilitating the interpretation of the results. The dominant data-collection method was the case method.

The empirical data for both the pilot study and the cases was collected from Finnish export circles, which are cooperative arrangements organised and governed by a semi-public organisation, FINPRO. The pilot study included all firms that had participated in the export circles during the years 1993–97, and that met certain criteria, resulting in a total of 326 companies. They were all contacted by telephone and the respondents were asked to participate in a structured telephone interview. The majority agreed, and the response rate was 87 per cent.

On the basis of the findings of the pilot study, the firms were divided into three groups according to their level of commitment: high, moderate or low. In line with previous research on inter-firm cooperation, commitment and satisfaction turned out to be key elements of export cooperation, although the association between them is much more complicated. Thus, these two concepts were used as key criteria in the case selection.

The data collected in the pilot study were reviewed in the first case-selection phase, and the respondents who had described their export network as excellent or weak were separated from the others in order to find extreme cases of export cooperation. These firms were then analysed in more detail, and were divided into two groups in the second phase: satisfied and not satisfied. The next screening phases focused on firms from export circles with more than one satisfied partner, since this group appeared to offer more fertile research material. Two cases were then selected in the final screening phase. They offered good grounds for comparison, since in the first one the partners were quite unanimous, whereas in the second their satisfaction with the cooperation varied.

A closer look at the two export circles and at the partners' commitment to export cooperation confirmed the selection. In case A, the level of satisfaction varied, but the level of commitment was relatively similar. On the other hand, all of the partners in case B were quite satisfied, but their commitment varied noticeably. In sum, the selected cases appeared to offer two different but interesting perspectives on commitment to export cooperation. Consequently, representatives of each partner firm in both networks were interviewed. The researcher also had the opportunity to discuss issues related to export cooperation with the personnel of FINPRO, which was responsible for the governance and financial support of export circles. The interview data was complemented with documentary material from the archives of FINPRO and the companies concerned.

To conclude, two methods were combined in order to study the same object, companies that had participated in FINPRO export circles. The *order* was sequential and the *role* of the qualitative approach was dominant, as the face-to-face interviews with the key informants in both case networks clearly dominated the acquisition of information. However, each method had a slightly different *purpose*. The qualitative method embraced the research problem as a whole, that is, it had a topic-related purpose, whereas the quantitative part, in particular, facilitated the case selection: thus it had a method-related purpose.

Example 2: From a Survey-tested Hypothesis to In-depth Cases

The objective of Hurmerinta-Peltomäki's study (2001) was to investigate the export–adoption lag[2] in the internationalisation process of industrial small businesses by emphasising the time-related approach. Accordingly, the sub-objectives were to identify, describe and understand the existence and appearance of the shortened export–adoption lag, and to describe and understand the influence of the individual's and/or the organisational past (as antecedents of a shortened adoption lag) on the export–adoption process.

The study was longitudinal and it was divided into two phases, a quantitative phase (mail survey and telephone interviews) combined with a qualitative case study of six SMEs (two rounds of interviews, the second four years after the first). Each stage was intended to provide knowledge and give a reason for further research. Pre-understanding, that is, insight into the problem area, was acquired by familiarisation with the theory and with previous studies on the subject. As a result, *the first research question* was refined as follows: how should the phenomenon of a shortened export–adoption lag be understood in industrial small business internationalisation? At this phase, the focus was on the export–adoption construct.

The empirical part of the study started with testing the hypothesis: 'The export–adoption lag has been shortened' among small and medium-sized industrial firms in south-western Finland. The basic data for the study was collected through a mail survey in 1989 and it was based on the responses of 556 firms. The response rate exceeded 21 per cent. The study rested on two variables – the year of establishment and the year of export start – both of which had to be provided by the respondents. Excluding the incomplete questionnaires, the final number was 133. The findings of the survey indicated that the hypothesis was supported, that is, at the organisational level the export–adoption lag was shortened.

However, the majority of studies on the export–adoption lag had been confined to the organisational level. This may have led to rather superficial analysis, because in a small firm the individual, that is, the owner–manager, has a decisive role. Deeper analysis of the phenomenon of the shortened export–adoption lag was required, particularly from an individual perspective, and therefore more inductive research was called for. This was achieved through case interviews (first round) on the assumption that the true length and content of the export–adoption lag in a small firm may be different than was revealed in the findings of the survey.

A round of telephone interviews preceded the first round of interviews in the case companies. This was an important part of the research process because it facilitated the completion of unanswered questions in the survey, the updating of the company data and, most importantly, the selection of the cases. A total of six cases were selected based on theoretical usability and availability.

The first round of interviews gave a deeper insight into the time of export adoption. They showed how important it was to look at the individual or organisational past rather than only the present. They also increased understanding of the original hypothesis, and raised some further questions about the influence of the individual and/or organisational histories on the internationalisation process. As a result, *the second research question* was thus refined as: 'What is the influence of the individual and/or organisational past on a firm's export–adoption process?'. Another round of interviews was subsequently conducted four years later in the same case firms, focusing on the export–adoption lag on both the organisational and individual levels. This time, the emphasis was on the internationalisation process. This second round of interviews strengthened the observations made after the first round. The case analysis also indicated that the nature of the experience of the owner–manager dictates how quickly and how far along the export–adoption process the firm is able to go.

Thus, triangulation was ensured in this study by using a combination of research methods. The initial findings, and also the methods, inspired the process. The contributions of the sources of information and methods to each objective were partly overlapping. The *order* of applying the different methods could be described as sequential. The research process was not originally planned in several stages, but the need to expand it arose during the process. Thus, in terms of *role*, the quantitative part gave way to the qualitative part. In other words, the objectives for each stage were finalised only at the end of the study.

The *purpose* of the mail survey (quantitative part 1) was knowledge based, that is, to test the hypothesis and to verify the basis for further studies, while that of the telephone calls after the survey (quantitative part 2) was to validate the results from the survey and to find cases for the qualitative study, thus it was method related. As the qualitative part aimed at understanding export–adoption lag at the individual level – a phenomenon yet unexplored – its purpose was topic related. The first round of interviews helped in the interpretation of the results of the survey, thereby clarifying the theoretical construct of the export–adoption lag, as the obvious explanations were not immediately acceptable. The interviews also raised questions for further research. The second round had its own research objective in addition to validating the results of the first interviews. Altogether, the qualitative part of the study furthered the research objectives in that investigation of the same subject and object resulted in a deeper understanding of the phenomenon in question.

Example 3: Cases and Survey Intertwined

The objective of Ridderstråle's study (1996) was to describe and analyse how multinational companies organise and manage international innovation projects (IIPs). This was divided into two sub-objectives: to describe different modes of organisation and managing international innovation projects and to find patterns in the effects of the various forms, particularly in terms of the critical problems faced by project managers and members.

The study combines a qualitative multiple-case study and a quantitative survey. The research process started with a literature review that gave the study a preliminary purpose. The next step was the multiple-case study, the cases being innovation projects at two multinational corporations (MNCs). The selection of cases was based on theoretical sampling. Two MNCs, ABB and Electrolux, were selected in order to compare the key elements in different administrative structures. On the other hand, it was advantageous to have more than one project in a firm in order to be able to identify different types of requirements and approaches to coordination within the same organisation. The innovation projects selected were mid-range, that is, neither slow, incremental innovations nor revolutionary breakthroughs. Potential market novelty was also used as a selection criterion: the researcher searched for heterogeneous cases in this respect. The projects selected were followed in real time, using a longitudinal research approach.

The primary case study data were collected through interviews and observation. Given the research problem, it was critical to talk to a variety of people in different positions representing different countries and functions in order to obtain multiple viewpoints. The researcher conducted a considerable number of semi-structured interviews (62 in ABB, 21 in Electrolux) in many countries. The interviewees were selected using the snowball technique. Additionally, secondary data was obtained from documentation and archival records. The empirical data collection in the first case project functioned as a pilot study, and the interview questions were subsequently refined and improved.

Next, the researcher decided to supplement the cases with a quantitative survey in order to obtain additional data and further develop the interpretations and ideas in the light of a larger sample. The aims of the survey could be summarised as follows: to describe the characteristics of IIPs, to identify the problems perceived to be most important and most difficult to solve, and the perceived advantages and disadvantages, and to assess perceived success. For the quantitative survey, 20 MNCs were contacted and usable responses were received from 11, with data on 32 IIPs in total. The data from the survey were used mainly for descriptive purposes.

Mixed methods were not an obvious solution in this study. On the contrary, the researcher initially considered starting with a more quantitative approach. However, because the knowledge of the innovation process was rich but fragmented, the creation of an integrated set of testable and meaningful hypotheses would have been difficult. A combination of methods was used instead, and quantitative data complemented the case-based interpretations.

The researcher points out that the use of multiple sources of evidence increased the validity of the study. It is also possible that the use of mixed methods led him to choose a less common reporting structure for his dissertation. Instead of the traditional theoretical start, followed by empirical observations and analysis, the phases of the innovation process were used as the primary structuration principle.

In conclusion, the *order* of qualitative and quantitative methods was parallel. The value of this emerged in the analysis as both quantitative and qualitative data complemented each other. However, the qualitative method had the dominant *role*, as the case studies were the main source of information. Both methods were used to study the same subject, but within this broad subject matter they had specific, topic-related *purposes* (see also Birkinshaw, Chapter 28 this volume for a similar type of design). Methodologically, the object of the study was different in the qualitative and quantitative parts, as the case companies ABB and Electrolux were not included in the survey.

Example 4: From Case-based Hypotheses to Testing by Survey

Lindqvist's (1991) study started with a literature review showing that there had been few studies on the combined effect of a limited firm size and technology intensity on internationalisation behaviour. Thus, the main purpose was twofold: to describe the international behaviour of young technology-based Swedish firms in terms of speed of internationalisation, pattern of market selection and choice of foreign-entry form, and to analyse variations in internationalisation behaviour in an attempt to understand the factors that might explain them. The firms included in the study were selected according to four criteria: size, age, share of R&D and exports, and independence.

The study was divided into two empirical phases: qualitative case studies and a quantitative survey. In order to develop a basic understanding of the process, personal interviews were first conducted with managers of 15 small, technology-based firms. The researcher decided after 15 interviews that further ones would add only a limited amount of information, and therefore the number of cases was not extended. The data collection was based on several different types of data sources, consisting of primary (interviews and written material produced for both internal and external use) and secondary material, although on a very limited scale. By conducting the personal interviews it was possible to explore the relatively complex process of internationalisation and the influence of firm and industry characteristics over time.

The first case could be regarded as a pilot study, since a more extended case description was developed after the interviews, which were conducted with representatives of the firm and of some of its foreign distributors. The remaining 14 interviews were carried out in order to develop illustrative mini-cases. They revealed that the process was influenced by a number of factors other than size and technology, such as ownership structure, previous experience and industry structure. In order to further explore the possible effects of industry structure, two of the mini-cases were expanded into industry studies, comprising interviews, in person or by telephone, with competitors and industry experts. Overall, these case studies gave an initial understanding of the process of internationalisation and they were used during the development of the questionnaire.

In the second phase, a mail survey was sent to a larger number of small, technology-based firms. A response rate of 66 per cent was achieved and the final sample comprised 144 firms. The purpose of the mail survey was twofold. The first, which was based on previous research and empirical observations from the exploratory phase of the study, was to develop and test a number of hypotheses concerning the possible effects of internal firm characteristics and industry structure on international behaviour. The second aim was to describe the process of internationalisation in a more systematic way, thereby complementing the mini-cases and the industry studies. This increased the generalisability of the results.

A number of possible explanations for the rapid speed of internationalisation was identified during the case analysis. Since internationalisation is a longitudinal and iterative process, a cross-sectional survey was perceived to capture only certain aspects of it. To overcome some of the methodological shortcomings of a mail survey, the researcher returned to the case studies, which brought her closer to process-oriented research (compare example 2 earlier). In her view, the case studies facilitated the interpretation of the findings of the mail survey and, by combining the strengths of each method, gave a more complete picture of the internationalisation process.

In sum, the *order* of methods in this study was sequential: first the qualitative pilot study and the in-depth case studies and then the quantitative survey. The sequence was clear, and the *role* of the approaches could be described as equal. The qualitative part of this study had versatile topic-related *purposes*. First, it had an important role in the hypothesis formulation; it explored the research field and the cases assisted in the creation of the questionnaire. On the other hand, the interpretation of the survey results emerged from the mini-cases. The research project could be described as a cycle in which the explanation and further understanding of the survey results followed from the case studies (compare example 2). The hypotheses were tested with the quantitative survey, thus this method mainly served a knowledge-based purpose.

To conclude, the four examples illustrate diverse alternatives in the use of mixed methods in IB research. The main decisions concerning the use of mixed methods – order, role and purpose – are summarised in Table 8.1. As the table indicates, all the examples were studies in which the role of the qualitative method was either dominant over or equal to that of the quantitative method. This is slightly contradictory to the majority of studies using mixed methods, in which the quantitative part is often dominant. However, as our aim was to illustrate the potential of mixed methods from the viewpoint of qualitative research, it seemed appropriate to use examples with a qualitative emphasis.

Table 8.1   Order, role and purpose of methods in the examples

Example	Order of data collection	Role of methods	Main purpose of each method	
1	Sequential	Qualitative dominant	QUANT:	Method related
			QUAL:	Topic related
2	Sequential	Qualitative dominant	QUANT 1:	Knowledge based
			QUANT 2:	Method related
			QUAL:	Topic related
3	Parallel	Qualitative dominant	QUAL:	Topic related
			QUANT:	Topic related
4	Sequential	Equal	QUAL:	Topic related
			QUANT:	Knowledge based

Table 8.1 also points out the linkage between the order, role and purpose of methods and the research question. From the perspective of the researcher, the use of mixed methods may be an interesting alternative but also sometimes a 'must'. Without triangulation, the research problem could not

have been solved, or at least the information acquired would probably have been biased, insufficient or even misleading. The level of understanding we finally reach is affected by the method that we choose to use. The use of method is influenced by method-specific characteristics as well as the purpose (knowledge based, topic related or method related). The purpose has its roots in the research question and the level of understanding, and none of these three key constructs may be treated separately from the others.

The choice of type of triangulation also depends on what kind of understanding is aimed at. First, if the objective is to arrive at a pre-understanding, we could study the same subject matter in different empirical objects. In this case, the qualitative part would typically come first. A case in point is example 4 above. Second, if the researcher is aiming at a deep understanding of the phenomenon, he/she probably studies the same subject and object by combining various methods. Example 2 illustrates this well, and also shows that quantitative data may be collected first. Third, if the aim is to give a broad, holistic picture, we could focus on one study object but analyse it from diverse perspectives. For example, if we would like to study the growth of a geographically dispersed multinational company from a long-term perspective, we should consider diverse viewpoints and use various methods. A similar approach might be applicable in analyses of cross-cultural phenomena, which often offer rich material from several theoretical perspectives, and multiple methods. Because of time constraints, this would perhaps require the parallel use of different methods.

THE CHALLENGES OF MIXING METHODS

Our examples pointed out the strengths and potential advantages of mixed methods, but also demonstrated some of the critical challenges. Mixing methods is by no means easy. First, triangulation should only be used if it helps in solving the research problem. This requires the researcher to have sufficient conceptual and theoretical knowledge of the phenomenon under scrutiny (Jick 1979).

Second, several researchers have pointed out that intertwining findings from multiple methods is a complicated process (for example, Bryman 1992; Creswell 1994; Jick 1979). One of the problems is that the results do not necessarily converge. What should the researcher do, then? No general guidelines exist on how different types of data should be weighted, for example. This in the end becomes a matter for the researcher's own judgement, although any evaluation should not be subjective, but rather based on the researcher's first-hand knowledge of the field.

We agree with the quite common argument that quantitative and qualitative approaches produce different types of data, and would like to add that the two often complement each other. Whereas generalisable findings often arise from quantitative research, they still may remain superficial, even deceptive. For instance, in our example 1, the use of multiple methods revealed that the informants interpreted the theoretical constructs used, particularly the key concept of commitment, differently. This created unexpected variation in the quantitative findings, and the qualitative phase was necessary in order to understand the phenomenon and interpret the findings of the quantitative part. In sum, it is quite understandable that studies of mixed methods produce qualitative findings that are often quite significant when the conclusions are drawn.

Furthermore, there are no rules determining the end of a research process. If each stage leads to new questions, when should the research stop? As our examples 2 and 3 showed, the researcher does not often intend to use multiple methods, but as the study progresses, it becomes the most sensible option. However, following new leads may end in a lengthy research process, which is not always practicable. Thus, the use of mixed methods is often limited by practical considerations, such as limited resources (both time and money), access to suitable units of observation, and disciplinary and political contexts (Brannen 1992; Denzin 1978; Jick 1979; Patton 1990). For instance, Maria Lindqvist (example 4) considered additional interviews among the firms in the case companies' network. She tried this in the pilot study, but it turned out to require too many resources and was therefore excluded from the study.

The research process may also be full of surprises; for example, when you start you may not even know all the purposes for which the method will be used. Denzin (1978) wrote about the demand for researcher flexibility and readiness to alter courses of action, change methods, reconceptualise problems and even start over if necessary. Sometimes the research question itself needs to be amended, or in extreme cases abandoned altogether. Researchers must continually evaluate their methods, assess the quality of incoming data and note the relevance of the data to the theory. This refers to the various possibilities of methodological pluralism, and highlights the importance of methodological flexibility. Thus, when mixed methods are used, the research process is closer to the qualitative than to the quantitative.

The use of multiple methods involves several critical turning points at which significant methodological decisions are made. The initial research design is usually tentative, and the order, role and purpose of different methods are determined. This is only a plan, however, which often changes along the way. The findings of the pilot study may become more meaningful, and new interpretations may emerge when evaluated in the light of the qualitative information. Jick (1979, p. 609) describes this quite well when he states that 'qualitative data and analysis function as the glue that cements the interpretation of multimethod results'.

CONCLUSIONS – WHAT DID WE LEARN ABOUT IT ALL?

The aim of this chapter was to demonstrate to the reader the potential of mixed methods in IB research. Various alternatives for combining qualitative and quantitative methods were introduced and described in terms of the key decisions made. Such decisions concerning the order, role and purpose of each method were discussed in the context of four illustrative examples, and were found to be related to the research question, and particularly to the level of understanding the researcher aims at. Additionally, we would like to stress that international business as a research field also has its own specific characteristics, which affect the use of mixed methods.

Individual IB researchers often operate internationally. The study objects may be spread worldwide and the phenomenon under scrutiny may cross all kinds of boundaries, particularly geographical ones. In practice, therefore, research in this field is very resource demanding, and the related financial costs are considerable. Finding suitable and rich material also involves risk, which is bound to affect decisions concerning methodological order. In other words, IB researchers frequently use the less risky sequential approach rather than the parallel approach. After all, what if it turns out during the data collection that the research question is irrelevant, or that the key concepts have been misinterpreted by informants because of cultural differences?

IB research typically involves cross-country comparison and cooperation with international research teams. This kind of study usually emerges from ideas or research findings in one country or research team, and it spreads among other interested parties. The sequential order in this case is self-evident, as the purpose of the first research team is merely to inspire international research, and the ones who join later concentrate on validating and complementing the results. Sometimes the first findings are applied repeatedly in later studies as well, because of their triggering effect.

The use of mixed methods is also supported by the multi-disciplinary nature of the IB research area. As a relatively new field, it typically requires some kind of pre-understanding before a more extensive study is carried out. For example, at the time of the introduction of the 'global start-up'[3] concept by Mamis, in 1989, rapidly internationalising small firms were first perceived as rare exceptions to the rule. Researchers tried to catch this phenomenon by identifying firms fulfilling the same criterion identified by Mamis – aiming at a basic understanding of the phenomenon through qualitative case studies. This gradually led to the need for more in-depth understanding. Simultaneously, hypothesis-testing survey studies also gained ground along the path towards more general, theoretical understanding. Recently the expanding number of these companies has gradually led to an increase in studies aiming at a broader understanding of rapidly internationalising SMEs, and applying mixed methods.

To conclude, mixed methods offer IB researchers the possibility to acquire rich empirical data as well as a more comprehensive understanding of the phenomenon under study. In spite of these advantages, methodological pluralism is not very common. Why is this? It is obvious that triangulation as a research strategy is not new. It is very probable that in the field of international business, too, this approach is embedded in many doctoral theses, but when the findings are refined for publication as articles, the authors tend to highlight only the quantitative methods they have used (see Birkinshaw, Chapter 28 this volume), possibly because researchers do not value triangulation as a research strategy. Jick (1979) argued in the late 1970s that journals tended to specialise in terms of methodology, thus encouraging purity of method. Birkinshaw repeats this observation; in other words, nothing has changed in a couple of decades. This may be one reason, added to the fact that space limitations in journals often prevent the presentation of mixed methods. Birkinshaw also quite aptly describes the prejudices of reviewers towards qualitative research, and it is very probable that the barriers against accepting boundary-breaking solutions, such as mixed methods, are even higher.

In our opinion, this situation is bound to change, particularly in the field of international business. The globalising world and quickening pace of international business operations will create more complex and multi-dimensional phenomena that deserve the attention of researchers. Traditional research tools offer very little in this context, and more innovative approaches are needed. Mixed methods offer one alternative, and, in principle, baking a cake is not difficult. After all, it is just a question of using old ingredients in new recipes!

ACKNOWLEDGEMENTS

The authors thank the editors of the book for their valuable and constructive comments on earlier versions of this article. They are also grateful to Maria Lindqvist DSc (Econ.) and Jonas Ridderstråle DSc (Econ.) for their cooperation and support in its preparation.

NOTES

1. Our diagram was inspired by Creswell's (1994) models of combined designs and the classifications of Hirsjärvi and Hurme (2001) and Tashakkori and Teddlie (1998).
2. The export–adoption lag is defined as the delay between the year of a firm's establishment and the year of export adoption, that is, the year of its first export entry.
3. The terms 'born globals' and 'international new ventures' have also been used to describe

this phenomenon.

REFERENCES

Arbnor, I. and B. Bjerke (1997), *Methodology for Creating Business Knowledge*, Thousand Oaks, CA: Sage.

Brannen, J. (1992), 'Combining qualitative and quantitative approaches: an overview', in J. Brannen (ed.), *Mixing Methods: Qualitative and Quantitative Research*, Aldershot: Avebury, pp. 3–37.

Bryman, A. (1992), 'Quantitative and qualitative research: further reflections on their integration', in J. Brannen (ed.), *Mixing Methods: Qualitative and Quantitative Research*, Aldershot: Avebury, pp. 57–78.

Burrell, G. and G. Morgan (1979), *Sociological Paradigms and Organizational Analysis: Elements of the Sociology of Corporate Life*, Aldershot: Gower.

Campbell, D.T. and D.W. Fiske (1959), 'Convergent and discriminant validation by the multitrait-multimethod matrix', *Psychological Bulletin*, 56, 81–105.

Creswell, J.W. (1994), *Research Design: Qualitative and Quantitative Approaches*, Thousand Oaks, CA: Sage.

Denzin, N.K. (1978), *The Research Act: A Theoretical Introduction to Sociological Methods*, New York: McGraw-Hill.

Eisenhardt, K.M. (1989), 'Building theories from case study research', *Academy of Management Review*, 14 (4), 532–50.

Gummesson, E. (1991), *Qualitative Methods in Management Research*, Newbury Park, CA: Sage.

Hirsjärvi, S. and H. Hurme (2001), *Tutkimushaastattelu* (Research interview), Helsinki: Yliopistopaino.

Hurmerinta-Peltomäki, L. (2001), *Time and Internationalisation: The Shortened Adoption Lag in Small Business Internationalisation*, Turku: Turku School of Economics and Business Administration, Series A-7.

Jick, T.D. (1979), 'Mixing qualitative and quantitative methods: triangulation in action', *Administrative Science Quarterly*, 24 (4), 602–11.

Lee, A.S. (1989), 'Case studies as natural experiments', *Human Relations*, 42 (2), 117–37.

Lincoln, Y.S. and E.G. Guba (1985), *Naturalistic Inquiry*, Thousand Oaks, CA: Sage.

Lindqvist, M (1991), *Infant Multinationals: The Internationalization of Young, Technology-based Swedish Firms*, Stockholm: Stockholm School of Economics, Institute of International Business.

Mamis, R.A. (1989), 'Global start-up', *Inc.*, August, 38–47.

Nummela, N. (2000), *SME Commitment to Export Co-operation*, Turku: Turku School of Economics and Business Administration, Series A-6.

Patton, M.Q. (1990), *Qualitative Evaluation and Research Methods*, Newbury Park, CA: Sage.

Ridderstråle, J. (1996), *Global Innovation: Managing International Innovation Projects at ABB and Electrolux*, Stockholm: Stockholm School of Economics, Institute of International Business.

Tashakkori, A. and C. Teddlie (1998), *Mixed Methodology: Combining Qualitative and Quantitative Approaches*, Thousand Oaks, CA: Sage.

Webb, E.J., D.T. Campbell, R.D. Schwartz and L. Sechrest (1966), *Unobtrusive Measures: Non-Reactive Research in the Social Sciences*, Chicago, IL: Rand-McNally.

PART III

Interviewing in International Business Research

Getting the Ear of the Minister

Henry Wai-chung Yeung

Qualitative research in international business (IB) studies often involves face-to-face contacts with informants who are powerful figures in business and government. This is particularly the case for qualitative research in developing countries where business and politics can be highly entangled. Approaching these powerful elites requires what I call 'procedural credibility' – defined as the *perceived* credibility of the researcher based on the process through which the contact is made. Once established, procedural credibility may allow an IB researcher access to the unthinkable in very unexpected circumstances. Let me offer an anecdote from my own experience of researching into Hong Kong firms operating in Indonesia.

Still a graduate student in June 1994, I was conducting personal interviews with top executives and government officials in Indonesia as part of my doctoral research on Hong Kong firms in Southeast Asia. I obtained the names of these executives and officials from business directories and official publications by the Capital Investment Coordinating Board (BKPM) of Indonesia. From my research base in Singapore, I then faxed a letter to these elites to explain the purpose of my study and to request an interview and access to other relevant materials. Before I left Singapore for fieldwork in Indonesia, I received very few responses from over 30 faxes I had sent. I was worried, to say the least. After settling into my relative's home in Jakarta, I made many phone calls to establish contacts with the offices of those top executives and government officials. One day, I got hold of a lady in the BKPM and explained to her that I had faxed Mr Subianto (a pseudonym) about my research. I had previously found Mr Subianto's name and designation as a 'corresponding person' in the BKPM publication on foreign investment in Indonesia. She immediately said that Mr Subianto was expecting me and quickly arranged an interview for me in two days' time.

I promptly went to the BKPM office two days later, thinking that I would be speaking to a corresponding person. I was even prepared for the worst scenario whereby this person might not know much of what was going on with foreign investment in Indonesia, let alone specific issues related to Hong Kong firms. The lady I had previously spoken to showed me into Mr

Subianto's meeting room, which was adjacent to his office with a private door connecting the two rooms. The meeting room was huge by any corporate standard and was lavishly decorated with all sorts of ornaments, sculptures and paintings. It crossed my mind that Mr Subianto was doing very well indeed. After a brief wait, I managed to speak to him in person for almost an hour. He was very forthcoming and dealt confidently with my questions and queries. I was very impressed. Towards the end of the interview, he even asked the Head of the Data Processing Unit of the BKPM to come into the meeting room and to generate as detailed Hong Kong foreign direct investment (FDI) data as I required. Three days later, the Head did present me with a very detailed set of data on Hong Kong FDI in Indonesia by industry, investment amount and assets from 1980 to 1994. He also gave me a complete list of over 150 Hong Kong firms operating in Indonesia with their full addresses, investment amount and contact persons. All these data were generated, with additional programming work, within three days of my interview with Mr Subianto, not bad at all for a developing country like Indonesia. Best of all, the data were free of charge!

By the time I got out of the meeting room, I was a very happy researcher who apparently had a great interview and the promise of a solid set of unpublished FDI data. While I was waiting for my cousin to pick me up, I had a look at the 1993 annual report of the BKPM and found Mr Subianto's name on the inside cover. The real shock came when I saw his official designation as the Investment Coordinating Minister of the Indonesian Government! Had I known this fact much earlier, I probably wouldn't quite have dared to ask for an interview with him. Or if I had, I might not have conducted the interview with the same confidence and curiosity. With hindsight, I am pretty sure that the official fax I sent him earlier must have established my credibility as a foreign researcher worthy of his extremely valuable time (considering Indonesia was attracting a lot of FDI in the early 1990s). I doubt I could have got hold of Mr Subianto without the fax that enabled him to *perceive* me as a credible researcher. Ever since then, this personal experience of getting the ear of the Indonesian minister tells me that procedural credibility may just work very well in many developing countries where formality and status do matter a great deal. My subsequent experience in conducting interviews in China, Malaysia and Thailand has undoubtedly confirmed the significance of procedural credibility.

9. Interview Studies in International Business Research

John D. Daniels and Mark V. Cannice

INTRODUCTION

We focus this chapter on the preparation, conduct and analysis of interview-based international business (IB) research. Beyond the issues common to interview data collection and analysis in a domestic context, we specifically concentrate on those elements unique to IB research (cultural context and technological and financial issues). We rely on our own experiences (about a dozen interview studies in nearly 300 companies in ten countries, plus many case development projects), as well as those of other authors who have published IB interview-based studies. We also rely on our own and others' experiences in non-interview IB studies so as to compare the appropriateness of one type of study versus another. Because few published interview studies provide the reader with an extensive guide to the schedule and conduct of the research, we hope our recollections and recommendations will provide appropriate and valuable insight for future interview-based studies in international business.

We define an interview study as one where the data and findings are based on direct researcher-to-respondent conversations (in person or by phone). In IB studies, these conversations may or may not be in a foreign country for either the interviewer or the informant. However, an IB interview study must include issues concerning international business. Concomitantly, interview studies may be combined with other types of data collection. For example, Reitsperger (1986) collected comparative performance data for domestic and foreign-owned television manufacturers in the United Kingdom by examining production output records; however, he sought to discover reasons for variances through interviews. We do not mean to imply from this example that interview studies are used only for qualitative (explanations by inference rather than by statistical analysis) purposes. In fact, they may yield substantial quantitative data and cover a significant portion of a population, especially when the population is small.

The authors' experiences include both domestic and foreign interviews, as well as interviews in both locales with both home-country nationals and expatriates. In the following we explore the arena of IB interview-based research by first discussing the motivation for and against it. We then discuss the challenges to this type of research, review our own experiences (both positive and negative), and offer normative recommendations.

MOTIVATION AND APPROPRIATENESS OF INTERVIEW-BASED INTERNATIONAL BUSINESS RESEARCH

Before laying out the conduct and analysis of IB interview-based studies, we explore the motivation for them. Simply, when are interview-based studies appropriate for IB research? We offer three situations where interview-based research may be appropriate for business research in general and, thus, for IB research as well. We follow this by discussing situations specific to international business, where interview research is advantageous.

First, interview-based research studies are particularly well suited for *exploratory* and *theory building studies*; that is, when researchers study an issue with little or no pre-existing theoretical bias (Eisenhardt 1989; Parkhe 1993), or when there is too much to learn for a survey questionnaire to do justice. In these cases, interviews allow the researcher to discover new relationships or situations not previously conceived. These may lead to theories, which researchers test later. For example, Daniels (1971) theorised from headquarters interviews in five countries that companies move incrementally internationally, from similar to dissimilar environments and from low to high commitments therein. Many researchers, such as Johanson and Vahlne (1977), have since tested these relationships in what is called Internationalisation or Nordic School Theory. In other cases, interview data may serve to illustrate a variety of company responses to a given situation so that practitioners and academics may consider different alternatives that companies may undertake. For example, Teigland et al. (2000) made such comparisons among three companies' approaches to international knowledge dissemination. Finally, interview studies may result in cases, which professors use primarily for teaching.

Second, interview-based research may be optimal when there is a *small population of possible respondents*. In this case, researchers must focus on the depth of collected data when the breadth is simply not attainable. Of course, a researcher should not seek depth just to overcome the problem of a small population; rather, interviews offer an opportunity to acquire a richness of information from each respondent. For example, Garcia (1996) examined technology transfers between old and new automobile plants in Mexico. Few companies had both types of plants, so he spent considerable time at each paired plant and interviewed multiple informants on several occasions in each. Nevertheless, when collecting primary data, researchers need to consider a variety of factors when deciding between interviews and questionnaires. They should consider what information they want, from whom they need to receive information, and how many responses they need to obtain representative answers. Usually, if the target population is individuals rather than companies, researchers need more responses. Finally, researchers must take into account how many interviews they can feasibly undertake. For example, Hofstede (1984) needed a very large sample base to collect statistically significant data to compare employees' work related values in 50 countries. Had he collected his over 100 000 responses through interviews rather than questionnaires, at two interviews per work day (a very ambitious schedule), he would have taken over 200 years to complete his data collection.

Nevertheless, whether researchers use interviews or mail questionnaires, they encounter grey areas in terms of how many responses are optimal. For example, national governments face this dilemma when deciding whether to conduct a census through sampling or through visits or questionnaires to virtually every residence. In one study, given our definitional parameters, we determined there was a total population of only 42 companies. We considered this population to be of a size favouring visits to as many companies as would be willing to participate, and 40 of the companies did participate. As a result, we had rich data from nearly the total population; however, a few academicians criticised the 'overkill' of responses by saying we could have achieved similar results with fewer participants. Ultimately, a researcher must make a subjective judgement when considering whether to use questionnaires or interviews because of small population sizes.

Third, interviews may allow researchers to *develop a deeper rapport with informants* than is possible through written questionnaires. This may be necessary to gain honest and accurate responses and to add insights that lay the groundwork for larger or follow-up studies. The researcher can also overcome the possibility that someone other than the target informant supplies the information. Further, an interviewer may leverage a trusting relationship to gain cooperation when needing information or undertaking follow-up studies. Our experience is that once an interviewer develops rapport with informants, the informants will seek out accurate information and facilitate cooperation with other managers (superiors, subordinates and counterparts – both within and outside their own companies), who may contribute to the study. Thus, by properly managing interview studies, researchers can develop a network of new data, insights and referrals. Although this is important for IB interview research undertaken domestically (for example, Cannice 1997), it may be even more important when seeking information from respondents in a foreign country. For example, Richards

(1995) found no directory of US expatriates and realised that building a mailing list to compare the cultural adaptation of those in Thailand with those in the United Kingdom would be cumbersome. She would first need to contact company headquarters to get expatriates' names and addresses. Then she would need to contact the expatriates to seek participation. Given the need to contact managers at two levels, she knew she had a slim chance of receiving sufficient responses. Thus, she interviewed at a small number of US headquarters, where she obtained background information, explained the purpose of her research, and solicited expatriate names and cooperation. With a few names in hand, she visited Thailand and the United Kingdom, where she networked interviewees to expand the number of expatriates participating in her study.

The above three reasons for collecting data through interviews apply both to domestic and international research projects. In addition, our experience as US academic researchers is that we get better interview responses for requests to interview abroad than to interview domestically. This may be partially due to the higher status given to academicians in some countries than in the United States, such as in Germany. Further, headquarters managers at US companies have become so deluged with academic research requests that many now routinely respond with non-customised information packets, references to their Web pages, or standard letters saying they no longer participate in academic studies. While this practice of non-participation is higher for larger than for smaller US companies, many research projects need substantial responses from larger, more internationally experienced companies, in order to draw relevant conclusions. So far, companies outside the United States, including subsidiaries of US companies, have been less inundated with academic research requests. However, this situation is obviously changing rapidly in some countries. Thus, researchers may now receive a better reception to their requests outside the United States only *if* they approach potential participants effectively.

Whether researching inside or outside the United States, we have found that people are more prone to throw out a questionnaire than to deny an interview request after a researcher has sent them letters in advance and persisted to schedule an appointment. This is undoubtedly due in part to people's reluctance to say 'no' orally and in part to their appreciation that a researcher is making the effort to come to see them, especially if the researcher is coming from a foreign country. For example, it is hard to turn down a request such as: 'My letter of ____ detailed my research project, and I'm phoning from Chicago. I'd like to visit you for about an hour at your office in Madrid during the week of ____ at your convenience'.

Three other factors favour interviews over mail questionnaires sent internationally. First, a researcher can facilitate domestic responses by including stamped, self-addressed envelopes with the questionnaires, but different postal systems preclude this internationally. (We know a US researcher who tried to overcome this problem by arranging for stamped response envelopes to go to a local hotel in the Netherlands; however, because he did not speak Dutch, he included '76 rooms with bath' as the return address.) Second, many countries have unreliable postal services. For example, Peruvian services have been sporadically poor, thus companies in Peru hire couriers to deliver letters for which respondents must sign. In such a situation, getting delivery and response even for locally mailed questionnaires is challenging. Third, in some cultures, executives are neither accustomed to responding to questionnaires nor convinced that their responses will remain anonymous. The development of rapport through interviews is very important when informants are suspicious of how information may be used.

Often, a combination of all three factors makes mail questionnaires problematic. For example, McCalman (1997) sent a large number of questionnaires to companies in three countries. His response rates for the United States and the United Kingdom were 18 per cent and 23 per cent, respectively. However, his response rate for Mexico was only 1 per cent, despite having his cover letter and questionnaire professionally translated and tested, and including a supporting letter from a Mexican trade association with his mailing. Nevertheless, we, along with many other IB researchers, have successfully gathered information in Peru and Mexico through interviews.

EXTENT AND LIMITATIONS OF INTERVIEW-BASED INTERNATIONAL BUSINESS RESEARCH

In spite of the advantages we have discussed about IB interview studies, we certainly do not mean to imply that interviews are always the best means of collecting data. In fact, we have illustrated that time constraints preclude using interviews for large samples. In addition, researchers' objectives and the existence of reliable databases may negate the need to gain the type of information that interviews would yield. Finally, interviews, particularly those in foreign countries, may not be for everyone because they require certain interpersonal skills in addition to traditional research skills. For example, a high face-to-face or voice-to-voice rejection rate may be harder to take than simply not having a questionnaire returned. Further, researchers must have the ability to interact with high-level executives whose incomes and status are often much higher than those of the researcher. Nevertheless, we believe that too many researchers are shying away from interview research, perhaps for the wrong reasons.

Our own experience is that publishing interview studies is neither easier nor harder than publishing research using other methodologies for data collection, thus, researchers should pick a methodology based on the quality of information that methodology is likely to yield. Unfortunately, we have data neither on the longitudinal popularity of conducting interview studies nor on journals' acceptance rates of interview studies versus studies using other methodologies. The best we can do is compare how many interview studies appeared in journals over time. We examined the *Journal of International Business Studies* (*JIBS*) and *Management International Review* (*MIR*) for the years 1991, 1996 and 2001, and found a number of papers in both journals that relied on interview data in whole or in part. For example, Tsang (*MIR*, 2001) conducted semi-structured interviews with managers of manufacturing companies in Singapore, and with the managers of 18 of their Chinese subsidiaries, to study managerial learning in international joint ventures (IJVs), while Wong and Ellis (*JIBS*, 2001) conducted in-depth case analysis interviews of 18 Sino-Hong Kong international joint ventures in their study of IJV partner identification. Table 9.1 indicates each journal's number of papers that used interview data over the total number of papers published in that journal for each year we reviewed.

Table 9.1   Publication frequency of interview-based IB research

Year of journal examined	*MIR* (Papers with interview data/total papers)	*JIBS* (Papers with interview data/total papers)
1991	2/18	3/29
1996	4/17	5/36
2001	3/16	3/42

It appears from this review of three years of journal publications, that while *MIR* publishes a greater proportion of papers that use interview data than *JIBS* (approximately 20 per cent for *MIR* versus 10 per cent for *JIBS*), the relative proportion of interview studies has remained more or less constant for both journals. Therefore, it appears that well-constructed and relevant IB interview-based research continues to find a home in leading IB journals.

Buckley (2002) has questioned why so little theory is now being developed in international business. One possible explanation is that the IB field has matured. The 1960s and early 1970s were a period of infancy for international business research – a period in which scholars visited companies to ask such a basic question as 'What does the term multinational company mean?' (Ogram 1969). As academicians, we often knew too little to devise questionnaires, thus, we had to leave our 'ivory towers' to explore. However, the field now has both sufficient databases and theoretical foundations so that we can pinpoint inquiries in a questionnaire or analyse data that someone else has collected.

Another possible explanation is that scholars – at least in the USA – have become more reluctant to participate in international interview studies due to changes in the academic competitive environment. First, the time in rank before being promoted has increased. Second, the number of publications needed for promotion and tenure has increased. Third, promotion and tenure decision-makers have become more prone to evaluate on the basis of numbers and places of publications rather than on the contributions that studies have made. As a result, junior scholars, who are typically the most prolific researchers, are pressured to turn out refereed articles quickly. Thus, it is understandable that many prefer to analyse existing databases rather than take the two-staged approach of collecting primary data that they must subsequently analyse. Many also prefer, because of expediency, to test existing theories on different populations rather than to develop new ones. However, we have found that the viability and efficiency of IB interview data can be quite good if planned well. For example, we can report that various portions of a case/interview data set we collected for a recent large study of ours was eventually used in four scholarly journal articles, one scholarly book chapter, and several conference presentations and proceedings.

Nevertheless, there are some prevailing opinions that we think are myths: that international interviews require expensive and time-consuming travel, that qualitative research is more difficult to publish, and that cultural obstacles are too formidable for interviews in a foreign country. We shall address these 'myths' as we review our own experiences and offer recommendations.

PLANNING AND CONDUCTING THE INTERVIEW PROJECT

Regardless of where researchers conduct interviews, they must decide what information they want, develop interview instruments to obtain that information, determine their target informants, persuade the target informants to participate, plan and carry out the logistics for a meeting, conduct the interviews, and analyse the interview data. Although the process usually follows this order, different steps may be interrelated. For example, location may influence the choice of individuals to interview. We shall discuss each of these steps, giving emphasis to nuances in the international context.

Setting Information Objectives

The information needed depends on the studies' purposes and whether researchers are approaching the topic area without a preconceived theory (for example, Eisenhardt 1989), or are trying to modify or validate an existing theoretical premise (for example, Yin 1994). Starting without a preconceived theory would tend to lead towards more open-ended discussion with only a broad topical area to guide interviews. Essentially, this approach assumes that broad discussions on a general topic with experts will lead to new insights and eventually new theory. However, when researchers begin projects to validate or modify a theoretical premise, they should focus their questions much more. In either case, whether conducting the study domestically or abroad, interviewers should thoroughly familiarise themselves with related studies so that they can converse intelligently about the subject with the respondent.

Interview Instruments

The beginning premise (theory discovery or theory validation) should direct the interview instrument's development. Although it is useful to examine instruments that others have developed in successful studies, published articles based on interview studies seldom include a copy of their interview instruments. Nevertheless, we have found other researchers quite willing to share their interview instruments with us, and we have found that dissertations based on interviews usually include appendices showing the instruments. We have always used semi-structured interview guides. An interview guide is essentially a check list for the researcher to follow to help ensure that all topic areas are covered during the interview. Having an interview guide helps ensure that no information needs are overlooked in the meeting. Although responses will, in large part, be open ended, the interviewer can use the interview guide to direct the conversation so that it stays on course. This is important because informants may allocate limited time to spend on the interview, and the interviewer may be unaware of how limited that time is. Thus, if informants spend too much time on points not related to the study, the interview may end without covering some important point. An interview guide also serves as a framework to compare responses. Even though different informants may supply information in different sequences, the researcher can compare responses more easily by keeping them in archives that correspond to the order in the interview guide.

We have included one of our interview guides in the appendix. That interview guide was used to help structure interviews with senior executives in 36 Silicon Valley technology firms. In these interviews, we attempted to develop new insights into the foreign investment decision process and technology management strategies of US high-technology companies entering the Asia Pacific Rim. We have used interview guides for both theory development and theory validation. We have also combined interviews with other methods of data collection. For instance, in one study we interviewed corporate personnel in the United States along with heads of their subsidiaries in three foreign countries. In addition, we also administered questionnaires to local managers in each of the foreign countries.

Choosing Informants

Having developed an interview guide, who should be interviewed? This is tricky domestically, but even trickier internationally. The decision is two-tiered if researchers use companies as their population to study. They first need to determine which companies to include. Then they must determine whom to interview within those companies. Let us start with the first tier, which is easier. Researchers may rely on directories or databases to identify companies, such as those with some minimal annual sales or those located in some specific geographic area. However, directories and databases are often inaccurate; in some developing countries they may not even exist. When directories and databases are inadequate, we have found trade associations and chambers of commerce or industry to be helpful in supplying vital company information. We have also contacted local members of academic associations, such as the Academy of International Business (AIB) and the Business Association of Latin American Studies (BALAS), to get more information on companies in their locales.

When interviewing people, especially abroad, accurate identification of companies, individuals and addresses is very important because a miscue may lead to non-participation. Further, a mistake abroad can be more costly than a mistake domestically. For example, if you drive to a local interview that does not materialise, you lose no more than a few hours' time and minimal transportation costs. However, you may lose much more with non-materialisation abroad. We once sent a letter explaining our study to a company in Winnipeg, which we had identified in a US government directory as a Canadian company with foreign direct investments in the United States. We later phoned the company, explained our study further, made an interview appointment, and flew from Detroit to Winnipeg. On arrival at the company, the CEO indicated that the company had no investments in the United States. The mix-up cost three days, a round trip ticket, and two nights in a hotel.

When initially contacting a company, it is always best to write to a specific person. Sometimes a researcher can identify appropriate people through their titles in companies' annual reports or Web pages. For example, in a study dealing with expatriate managers in US companies, we identified vice-presidents of human resources. In another study dealing with European regional headquarters of US companies, we identified vice-presidents whose titles indicated they had European regional responsibility. In several studies, we identified vice-presidents in charge of international operations, because the companies had international divisions – something that most companies do not have. However, many companies' public documents do not show the functional or area responsibility for their executives. In addition, companies seldom show the names of subsidiary managers in their public documents. Without having the name of a target, a researcher must get in touch with someone at headquarters to find out who has responsibility over the area that is being studied. Sometimes, a few phone calls will uncover this information. In other situations, the researcher may write to someone requesting that the letter be passed to the appropriate person. One alternative is to contact the CEO. Another is to contact someone at a level below who may be less hounded by research requests. We have done both with no discernible difference in results.

If the research requires interviews abroad at foreign companies, researchers need to determine what titles mean before they write to executives. For example, we once wrote to the president of a company in the UK, thinking that the title meant the same as in the United States. We received a scathing letter in return, explaining that president in the UK is an honorary title for a retired managing director. Fortunately, we were able to resend a letter to someone else in the company.

Assuming that the first letter is positively received, the researcher must then determine if the person who received it is sufficiently knowledgeable about the situation in question. Given the amount of management mobility (internal and external), the people with current responsibility for an area may have little first-hand knowledge about events that occurred even recently. A researcher can usually determine that with a short phone call and be redirected, if necessary, to the right person. This is important so that there are no information gaps, so that responses reflect actual occurrences rather than myths that have developed around them, and so that there is external acceptance of results. On this latter point, the work of the noted anthropologist, Margaret Mead, has come under criticism because she interviewed missionaries about Samoans rather than interviewing the Samoans themselves (Brunton 2001).

Persuading Potential Informants to Participate

We have discussed the need to write letters soliciting participation in the study. The question then is how to design these letters so that recipients will respond positively. We suggest sending a formal request on university letterhead to show the legitimacy of the study. This request might also include a letter or letters of support from university officials, heads of trade associations, or government officials. These letters should be from sources that would be familiar to potential respondents. For instance, we received a letter of support from a textile trade association in Peru for a study of Peruvian textile companies and a letter from the Dean of the University of San Francisco School of Business for a study of companies in California's Silicon Valley. Getting these supporting letters will usually require some additional face-to-face discussions about the purpose and importance of the research.

To help increase the likelihood of cooperation, we suggest calling each letter's recipient about a week after the letter's estimated delivery. At this time, determine whether the recipient is the proper person to interview. If so, confirm a date and time to meet. You will almost always speak first with his or her assistant. This conversation is very important. A favourably impressed executive assistant will tentatively put the researcher into the boss's schedule, after which the boss will almost certainly participate in an interview.

If you reach a recording rather than a person when you phone, try to avoid using voice mail. Voice mail is too easy to ignore for a busy executive or executive assistant. However, do not be surprised if you get the boss directly when you call. After sending a letter to the executive vice-president of a Fortune 100 company, we phoned the company's general number to ask for this executive's office. Without even asking our name or affiliation, the company operator connected us directly to the executive. We had expected to go through several layers of secretaries. In another case, the CEO and founder of a large French company phoned us directly to schedule an interview as soon as he received our letter. So, be prepared to explain any aspect of the study and your scheduling needs when you phone the company. Also, keep notes handy for any unexpected incoming calls.

We find the most common reasons executives will grant an interview are that the topic is of interest to them and that they may learn something about other executives participating in the study. Further, assuring anonymity is normally expected and will put the respondent more at ease. However, some respondents do not mind being quoted; in fact, some like to see their names in print. Thus, the first contact letter should promise anonymity if the respondent wants that. This promise should be reiterated at the beginning of the interview. Promising a copy of the final report is also helpful. We do not know to what extent the professor's prestige or academic affiliation makes a difference in gaining participation. However, we have found a favourable reception when we happened to contact someone who studied at the institution shown on the letterhead of our correspondence.

While abroad, the choice of hotel is important. First, you need one that has a good phone service, including message-taking. We have found that one of the first questions we have been asked when scheduling an interview is where we shall be staying. This question is purportedly asked to provide directions or to arrange transportation. (Many companies abroad send company drivers to fetch visitors at the hotel.) However, we suspect that the hotel's prestige influences whether an appointment is granted and the level of the person granting an interview.

The Logistics

Interviews, especially ones abroad, present some travel challenges. Given that most academic research has tight budgets, a researcher can reduce travel expenses by narrowing visits to a few locales. In so doing, the cost of interviewing should not be significantly higher than the cost of collecting primary data from a large sample by using mail questionnaires. Nor should the time to collect data through interviews be any longer. For IB research undertaken domestically, researchers may limit interviews to a few nearby locations. For example, in one study, we limited interviews only to companies in California's Silicon Valley. In another, we limited interviews only to companies headquartered in Pennsylvania. However, this strategy has the disadvantage of disregarding some out-of-the-way companies whose managers have some real insight.

In some countries, such as the United Kingdom and France, most large internationally active companies are in or near the capital. This is also true of many developing countries, where almost all activity is in the capital or a few major cities. In other countries, such as Canada and Germany, the internationally active companies are quite dispersed. When a researcher visits companies quite apart from each other, the cost per visit is quite high because transportation cannot be amortised over several visits.

Although a researcher may schedule interviews very close in time to each other to minimise time and cost, there is a danger in doing this. Allow for some slack time. Interviews sometimes do not start on time and may take longer than anticipated. (Remember that informants are doing you a favour, so you cannot be too aggressive in holding them to an agreed-upon timetable.) Further, our experience abroad is that companies often schedule lunches and company tours for researchers, even though they do not mention this when agreeing to an interview that you have told them should 'take about an hour'. There are also unforeseen occurrences, such as bad weather or political events that may cause last-minute rescheduling. For example, during one study abroad, a general strike caused cancellation of our incoming flight and caused us to arrive one day late. However, this actually worked to our advantage. Since companies were closed, executives conducted interviews in their homes, where they had much more time to answer questions. Of course, in planning interviews abroad, researchers must consider both official and unofficial holidays. An example of the latter is the whole month of August in

Paris, when vacations bring company operations close to a standstill.

To reduce travel costs, researchers might consider relying on phone interviews. Our own experience is limited inasmuch as we have never devised a study to collect information this way. However, we have conducted a few phone interviews because of respondents' requests. For example, when we called to schedule one meeting, the respondent said he would be travelling extensively over the next few months but could immediately answer our questions over the phone. A further advantage of phone interviews is that they allow the researcher to take extensive notes during the conversation without appearing impolite to the respondent. Although our few phone interviews have elicited good information, we feel uneasy about doing an entire study this way. We simply believe that face-to-face interviews are ideal for gaining in-depth responses. In fact, the need for face-to-face communication may help to explain the high incidence of business travel, especially internationally, in spite of advances in communications.

Collaborative research with academicians in other locales is another means to reduce transportation costs. Although collaboration is common for questionnaire studies, such as asking a colleague at another university to administer questionnaires to students there, such collaboration is relatively rare for interview studies. Although team interviewing provides some advantages – for example, having one interviewer focus on taking notes and ensuring all items from the interview guide are covered – teamwork on interviewing may also be difficult because of individual differences in personalities and interpretations of responses. Thus, any collaboration should involve all researchers going together for some pilot interviews so that they agree on consistency in what and how they learn from informants. Simply, any deviation from the agreed-upon interview norm may distort findings. To help ensure consistency for the collection of comparative interview data in Peru, we went to Peru and conducted six pilot interviews with a Peruvian colleague. Confident that his interviewing and interpretation would approximate ours, we then returned to the United States. However, after conducting three interviews on his own, he phoned to say he was not getting as complete information as he did when we conducted the interviews jointly. We discovered that his academic institution, which was paying part of the research cost, had asked him to try to sell space in its executive programmes during his visits. Therefore, the respondents thought his real purpose in visiting was to sell, so they were reluctant to provide information. Fortunately, we quickly rectified that problem as he reverted to the original interview methods. A probable lesson from this is that there should be clear-cut agreement on what to do based on preliminary work. Further, there should be frequent communication among researchers to ensure that the data collection does not go astray.

A problem in interviewing headquarters managers with international responsibilities is that they tend to travel a great deal. In fact, many are gone some days every week, thus when they are in the office, they are catching up on what they have missed while away and planning for the next trip. Thus, scheduling interviews with them is difficult. Further, whereas they can fill out a questionnaire while on a flight, they cannot conduct an interview that way.

Conducting the Interview

Researchers should be so familiar with the interview guide that they do not have to refer to it during the interview. In other words, while listening and remembering what the informant is saying, the researcher needs to mentally check off questions that have been answered and remember the ones that still need to be covered. Although some researchers successfully tape-record interviews, our experience is that informants are more guarded when being taped. In fact, the knack of a good interviewer is to get respondents to become so interested in the subject and their recollections that they stop thinking about being interviewed. Likewise we have found that even when we take notes, the informants begin talking less freely and stopping until we finish entering our notes. Thus, concentration and a good memory are essential for gaining good information in interviews. Admittedly, we have not tried interviewing with and without simultaneous note taking in different cultures, thus we cannot say whether there are cultural differences in responses to note taking. Simply, we have found that our undivided attention to respondents seems to work well, and we have not wanted to jeopardise success by experimenting with other techniques.

At the beginning of an interview, after exchanging business cards, we have found that spending a few minutes to talk about things not related to the study (for example, the weather, functionality or beauty of the building, the trip to make the visit, recent newspaper accounts about the company) helps put the informant at ease. (Although we have conducted interviews in both high-context and low-context cultures, we have not noted national differences in how quickly respondents want to get to the subject of the interview. Their schedules for the particular day seem to be more important in this respect than national cultural differences.) Then, we briefly explain the study again and why we are undertaking it. Finally, we once again reassure the informant of the confidentiality of his/her responses, mention how many companies or individuals we are interviewing, and offer to provide a copy of the final report. Once we enter the core of the interview, we let the respondent talk about topics that interest him/her, but we are careful to control the interview's direction.

Thus far, we have given the impression that we interview one person at a time. This is not necessarily the case. We have had occasions (with no advanced notice) in which several people are present for the interview. Simply, the contact persons were sufficiently interested in the subject that they brought together a group who could reply with information that is perhaps unknown by the others. At times, these respondents have discussed among themselves some point until they are all in agreement. When we have had multiple respondents in the room, we have been careful to get cards from all of them and to direct our questions to the group as a whole. Nevertheless, we have maintained our major focus on our contact person. We have also had situations in which a single respondent has been unable to answer a question and has then contacted a colleague for us to see in order to fill in gaps. When writing a thank-you letter, we have directed this letter to our contact person, but we have mentioned the names of the other people and have asked the contact person to express our appreciation to them.

The researcher needs to consider cultural differences. Morrison et al. (1994) provide a good guide to understanding business etiquette issues across a range of cultures. Initial contact, type of greeting, meeting formality, and follow-up etiquette are all influenced by the cultural norms of the host country in which the interview is taking place. These norms may also exist for local subsidiaries of foreign companies or even among non-domestic staff of local firms. Nevertheless, we have found that upper-level managers with international responsibilities, regardless of nationality, behave very similarly in an interview situation, that is, there seems to be a cosmopolitan cultural norm to which they generally adhere. Further, we have not known the nationality of participants until we arrived for an interview. For example, in one study on European regional headquarters of US companies, our respondents included home-country, host-country and third-country nationals. In addition, some of the third-country nationals were not even from the region, such as a Peruvian in charge of the European headquarters office of a US company in London. Thus, we have involved local scholars only in a small minority of our interview studies, that is, those where we were dealing with local companies. (Given the nature of our research subjects, our interviews have always been with fairly senior managers, both at home and abroad. Thus, we may not be able to generalise our experiences to interviews of people at other organisational levels.) Although there may be expectations that academicians from the United States are somewhat informal, we believe it is better to err on the side of being too formal than too informal. Thus, we dress in conservative suits and do not address people by their first names unless they first address us that way.

When ambiguity arises, we seek clarification quickly to avoid losing precious time with the respondent. Language also plays a role in the pacing of the interview. While English is the accepted language of business across most of the industrialised world, respondents' working facility of English is far from uniformly excellent. In writing a questionnaire, one can reverse translate to ensure that the meaning has not changed, but this is impossible for a direct interview. Nevertheless, an interview affords the possibility of asking clarifying questions, such as what the respondent means exactly by 'graduate studies' or 'reporting relationships'. Regardless of whether the interviewer is speaking in English with people whose first language is English or not, the researcher should avoid jargon, use common words, speak slowly, and clarify responses by asking additional questions and paraphrasing what has been said. We have always asked if we can conduct interviews in English or whether we need to arrange for an interpreter. In only one case (in Germany) did we have to use an interpreter, and the company provided one. However, the interpretation was sequential rather than simultaneous, so the interview took twice as long.

Before leaving the respondent, we have tried to facilitate future contact if needed. We have also sought referrals to other executives who may provide useful input to the study and have asked permission to use respondents' names when contacting other executives to solicit their participation in the study. We also think it is important to thank informants at the end of the interview and by letter afterwards. We also thank any secretaries who helped schedule appointments.

Analysis

After the interview, we write down notes and recollections as soon as possible, often in the car before leaving the parking lot. We put responses in the same order as the interview guide so that we can organise and compare responses more easily. We use spreadsheets (either from computer programs or simply ones created by hand) to compare responses to different questions we have asked. We also include not only the discussion points but also our impressions and analysis. At this point, we occasionally see a need for clarification or to fill in gaps, and we call respondents to complete our information needs. We include each new interview in a case database (Yin 1994), which includes the interview transcript and analysis, as well as any other public or private documentation we have collected on the company or individual.

We try where possible to triangulate separate sources of data to validate answers and impressions on the interview script. For example, we compare our open-ended interview script questions with Likert-type questions (1–5 scale) covering the same topics with semantically differentiated questions to help ensure the internal consistency of responses. When we are able to interview several respondents from the same company, we check for internal consistency of respondents from that company, taking into account each respondent's responsibilities and level in the organisation. We also compare our interview data with public company reports and press releases, internal company documents (when available), and other articles written about the company and its operations. When more than one researcher is working on a project, we also check for inter-rater reliability to ensure that our coding of each case agrees. Where it does not, we discuss the discrepancies, seek confirming information, or revert to the informants to clarify our joint interpretation.

We also look for trends in the cross-case analyses and, if the sample is large enough, attempt some quantitative analysis of the qualitative data (frequencies, correlations and so on). On the very few occasions we have encountered inconsistencies, we have communicated with our respondents to rectify the situation. Subsequently, we have been confident about the accuracy of the information we have received.

In our interviews and subsequent transcription and coding, we have often found unexpected information that did not quite fit into the outline of the interview guide. To accommodate this unexpected information, we reserve a row in our coding spreadsheet for 'new insights' or 'unexpected findings'. In fact, it is this serendipity and flexibility in interviewing that makes this a strong methodology for theory building. If these new insights do not support theory development, they can often be incorporated into a final paper as either anecdotes or suggestions for future research.

In analysing interview data, there is always a question of whether to request respondents to examine drafts before writing articles or before submitting articles for publication. We have always done this for cases because, even if we disguise the company's name and certain information about it, readers are apt to identify the company. In fact, one company refused to let us publish a case because its managers concluded it was impossible to conceal its name and proprietary information. Respondent feedback on case studies has otherwise been very useful, not so much for correcting information about business decisions, rather about technical industry-specific data. In one interview study, we helped validate the data through participating executives' feedback and critique at a review seminar we organised, a technique suggested by Henderson and Clark (1990). We found general agreement from the participating executives. We also mailed a draft of our findings to all participating executives, along with a request for critique and feedback. However, we have generally found that executives have little time to read drafts and tend not to respond at this point.

In combining information from different companies, we have found it useful to code responses so that we can see tendencies, such as what percentage considers a certain factor to be important. We have never used software to do content analysis of interviews. The types of studies and collection methods we have employed do not lend themselves to this.

However, for interviewers doing focused group interviews that they record, content analysis may certainly be warranted.

There are some excellent treatises on the analysis of interview data. Eisenhardt (1989) and Parkhe (1993) cover interviews as theory-building research. Yin (1994) provides a guide for qualitative methods on theory validation. Cavusgil and Das (1997) provide a comprehensive literature review of methodological issues in cross-cultural research, while Easterby-Smith and Malina (1999) and Teagarden et al. (1995) give unique descriptions of some of the challenges of planning and coordinating qualitative research teams. We recommend that researchers examine these treatises before embarking on interview studies. Again, the objectives of the research (theory development or theory validation) will direct the type of analysis. Theory development (Eisenhardt 1989) will normally rely on the identification of trends across company cases to allow new insights to emerge from the data. Theory validation (Yin 1994) directs the researcher to compare each case to a predetermined theoretical template to assess the fit of each new case data point to the template theory. Consistent fit on ensuing case data implies the goodness of the theoretical template and thus its validation.

CONCLUSION

While interview studies are not suited to all research studies, or to all researchers, they provide a unique vehicle for theory development and the best means of collecting primary data for theory development and theory validation in some countries. Although many researchers shy away from interview studies, we hope we have dispelled some of the negative myths about them, such as cost, cultural barriers and excessive time to complete a study. Further, our subjective evaluation of IB research through the years is that many of the most significant and enduring pieces of research have come from interviews. Finally, a cursory examination of research by Fellows of the Academy of International Business indicates that most have conducted interview studies at some points in their careers.

Nevertheless, interview studies, like studies using other forms of data collection, need to be logically conceived and rigorously conducted. We have elaborated on our experiences in developing subjects to study, deciding to use interviews rather than other forms of data collection, getting potential respondents to participate, collecting the information and analysing results. However, our experiences, although extensive, are certainly not totally encompassing. Given the types of research questions we have studied, we have restricted our interviews to high-level managers who tend to be cosmopolitan and English-speaking, and we have dealt with international (operations cutting across national boundaries) rather than comparative (activities in one country versus another) data. If researchers focus on other organisation levels or other research questions, they may need to be more culturally sensitive when building their research designs. For example, focus group interviews to compare worker attitudes or consumer preferences from one country to another would logically require collaboration among researchers in different countries and a great deal of planning to ensure that results are truly comparable.

While statistical analysis techniques continue to advance, we expect that relevant and well-organised IB interview studies will continue to provide valuable contributions to the development and validation of IB theory. Further, improving telecommunication technologies (video conferencing, broadband internet and so on) may facilitate future IB interview data collection across a range of new topics and environments.

REFERENCES

Brunton, R. (2001), 'Cultural wars', *Review – Institute of Public Affairs*, **53** (3), 14–15.

Buckley, P.J. (2002), 'Is the international business research agenda running out of steam?', *Journal of International Business Studies*, **33** (2), 365–73.

Cannice, M.V. (1997), 'Linking foreign operating mode decisions to performance: a theoretical integration and comparative case analysis of U.S. "high-tech" ventures in China and other Asia/Pacific Rim countries', PhD thesis, Bloomington, IN: Indiana University.

Cavusgil, S.T. and A. Das (1997), 'Methodological issues in empirical cross-cultural research: a survey of the management literature and a framework', *Management International Review*, **38** (1), 71–96.

Daniels, J.D. (1971), *Recent Foreign Direct Manufacturing Investment in the United States: An Interview Study of the Decision Process*, New York: Praeger.

Easterby-Smith, M. and D. Malina (1999), 'Cross-cultural collaborative research: toward reflexivity', *Academy of Management Journal*, **42** (1), 76–86.

Eisenhardt, K.M. (1989), 'Building theories from case study research', *Academy of Management Review*, **14**, 532–50.

Garcia, R. (1996), 'Learning and competitiveness in Mexico's automotive industry: the relationship between traditional and world class plants in multinational firm subsidiaries', PhD thesis, Ann Arbor, MI: University of Michigan.

Henderson, R. and K. Clark (1990), 'Architectural innovation: the reconfiguration of existing product technologies and the failure of established firms', *Administrative Science Quarterly*, **35**, 9–30.

Hofstede, G. (1984), *Culture's Consequences: International Differences in Work-related Values*, Beverly Hills, CA: Sage.

Johanson, J. and J.E. Vahlne (1977), 'The internationalization process of the firm: a model of knowledge development and increasing market commitments', *Journal of International Business Studies*, **8**, 23–32.

McCalman, D. (1997), 'When in Rome: recipient country effects on strategy and technology in manufacturing foreign direct investment', PhD thesis, Bloomington, IN: Indiana University.

Morrison, T., W.A. Conaway and G.A. Borden (1994), *Kiss, Bow, or Shake Hands*, Holbrook, MA: Adams Media Corporation.

Ogram, E.W. Jr. (1969), *The Emerging Pattern of the Multinational Corporation*, Atlanta, GA: Georgia State University Bureau of Business Research.

Parkhe, A. (1993), 'Messy research, methodological predisposition, and theory development in international joint ventures', *Academy of Management Review*, **18**, 227–68.

Reitsperger, W. (1986), 'British employees: responding to Japanese management philosophies', *Journal of Management Studies*, **23** (5), 563–86.

Richards, M. (1995), 'The impact of culture on the overseas operations of U.S. multinationals in the United Kingdom and Thailand', PhD thesis, Bloomington, IN: Indiana University.

Teagarden, M.B., M.A. von Glinow, D.L. Bowen, C.A. Frayne, S. Nason, Y.P. Huo, J. Milliman, M.E. Arias, M.C. Butler, J.M. Geringer, N.H. Kim, H. Scullion, K.B. Lowe and E.A. Drost (1995), 'Toward a theory of comparative management research: an idiographic case study of the best in international human resources management project', *Academy of Management Journal*, **38** (5), 1261–87.

Teigland, R., C.F. Fay and J. Birkinshaw (2000), 'Knowledge dissemination in global R&D operations: an empirical study of multinationals in the high technology electronics industry', *Management International Review*, **40** (1), 49–77.

Tsang, E.W.K. (2001), 'Managerial learning in foreign-invested enterprises of China', *Management International Review*, **41** (1), 29–51.

Wong, P.L.-K. and P. Ellis (2001), 'Social ties and partner identification in Sino-Hong Kong international joint ventures', *Journal of International Business Studies*, **33** (2), 267–89.

Yin, R.K. (1994), *Case Study Research: Design and Method*, 2nd edn, Thousand Oaks, CA: Sage.

APPENDIX

The interview guide below was used in the gathering of interview/case data for the Cannice (1997) dissertation study (John Daniels and Paul Marer, Co-chairman) on the Foreign Investment Decision Process of US High Technology Companies.

Interview Guide

I. Lead-in
Thank you
Describe study I am examining the foreign <u>investment decision</u> for firms participating in the Asia/Pacific Rim. I am trying to link the factors considered and the entry choice to the performance of the venture.
Implications Certain entry modes may be <u>higher performing</u> given certain conditions as perceived by the firm.
Why Important Develop <u>road map</u> for corporate decision makers to more quickly and effectively choose the appropriate entry vehicle for a specific market and the current perceived conditions.
Appreciate By soliciting <u>executive insight</u> into this process from specific experiences, hope to develop a better and more useful model. Will analyse recurring themes between firms and aggregate some empirical data. Should develop significant analytical tools and help develop international management theory.
Show knowledge of company based on background reading.
Your responses are confidential.

II. Today's agenda
   (1)   Ask you to *reflect on a specific foreign entry mode decision* in which you were involved and *describe* the process, from determination of the objective to contingency planning, major challenges, how overcame, significant learning or insights gained during the process.
   (2)   Will ask you about *10 open-ended questions* about specific strategy and technology not covered in your discussion.
   (3)   Will administer a *short survey* with rating scales on specific factors and performance perceptions.
Part I Please describe a specific foreign entry decision process in which you were involved in a Pacific Rim nation. Describe the process from need recognition, the process involved, major factors considered. Then the implementation: major obstacles, surprises, expectations, learning, satisfaction, performance.

Part II

(1)   Type entry mode? Country of venture? Type technology transferred?
(2)   Primary objectives for venture?
(3)   Primary factors considered?
(4)   Most important factor, why?
(5)   Decision process?
(6)   Major obstacles during planning?
(7)   Major obstacles/challenges during implementation?
(8)   How overcame challenges?
(9)   How judge performance?
(10) Typical of most entry decision's and operations?
(11) Describe firm's overall corporate strategy for international market participation?
(12) What role do you see China playing in long-term corporate strategy?
(13) Do you anticipate increased level of commitment in China (sales office, joint venture, manufacture)? When?
(14) What have been some of the most important things you have learned in your experience in beginning foreign operations?

Part III   Administer survey

Part IV   Closing

Any further documentation? Referrals to other executives in your firm or from other firms?

Thank you.

10. Improvisation and Adaptation in International Business Research Interviews

Ian Wilkinson and Louise Young

Chance favours the prepared mind (Louis Pasteur)

INTRODUCTION

The research process is often depicted as a sequence of planned stages in which research design precedes information gathering, followed by analysis and report writing. While these are the key elements of the research process, this neat, logical progression does not accurately portray the process of good qualitative research. Instead, researchers are likely to find themselves cycling back and forth between stages as they learn and adapt to new and unexpected circumstances, opportunities, problems and findings. This is exacerbated in international settings, where the researcher is dealing not only with the inherent uncertainties of research but also with unfamiliar cultures, customs, opportunities and problems.

Research is an emergent process. At the outset we do not know what we will find out or the problems we might encounter, and we must be prepared to be led by and to adapt to the knowledge and insights and chance events we encounter along the way. Improvisation and adaptation are an intrinsic part of a research process in which you are trying to find out things you do not already know from sources you are unfamiliar with. This focus on the emergent nature of research and interviews is in keeping with recent work on the role of chance discovery and opportunity recognition in the innovation and knowledge development (Ohsawa 2002; Shane 2000). It also fits with the growing recognition of the importance of improvisation and adaptation in a world of ever more rapid change, international interconnectedness and 'surprisefulness' (Chelariu et al. 2002).

We are not advocating a rule-less research process in which anything goes. But we are counselling against a mechanical following of 'rules' of interviewing no matter what. The chapter is designed to help researchers, particularly researchers new to interviewing, be better prepared to take advantage of unexpected opportunities, deal with unexpected problems of interviewing and better utilise these in their research. This involves being aware of their potential role and importance, having the right equipment and resources available and developing certain skills and sensitivities.

To describe this process we bring our experience of many years of teaching qualitative research methods and in conducting interviews in a wide range of settings and countries. This includes over ten years spent supervising research teams of senior students, both undergraduate and graduate, to conduct interviews in local and international markets as part of international and domestic business research projects undertaken for Australian-based firms and government organisations.

The chapter is organised as follows. First, we examine the kinds of interviews that are likely in international business research. Second, we consider the ways in which researchers can best prepare themselves for the various kinds of opportunities and problems that may arise. We conclude with discussion of the emergent nature of the interview process and strategies for managing this serendipity.

THE NATURE OF THE INTERNATIONAL QUALITATIVE INTERVIEW

International business research is carried out for many purposes. Here, in line with the student projects we have supervised, we shall assume that the goal of the research is to analyse the nature of a potential market or markets for a particular type of product or service. Such research is not about conducting an informal poll of the opinions of different types of people in business, government and elsewhere about the likely prospects for a particular product. Instead its aim is to assemble a comprehensive assortment of information that enables us (1) to understand the factors affecting a product's success in the relevant market, (2) to determine the characteristics of those factors and how they are likely to change, and (3) to provide some checks on the reliability and validity of the information gathered.

We find it productive to think of the task as the collection and assembly of pieces of a knowledge jigsaw puzzle; one in which you do not know the shape or nature of the final picture. The problem for the researcher is to seek varying information 'assortments' that different types of potential informants may be willing and able to provide. Interview targets are defined in terms of what they are likely to know and include those not directly involved in the business or market of interest, such as academics working in the area, reporters and editors who cover relevant business issues. Interviews may share some common questions but each is unique so as to shape and develop the unique 'puzzle piece' that is needed.

Two kinds of knowledge are sought through this type of interview: knowledge that contributes pieces of the knowledge jigsaw puzzle and knowledge of how to discover and know. Knowing how to know is concerned with finding out how information may be collected in a given environment. This is an important and neglected aspect of the interview process and is particularly relevant in international business. Local informants are embedded in personal and business networks and have all sorts of information, including knowledge of who the key organisations and people are in the relevant marketing system. Even when informants cannot provide the information you seek, they may have useful ideas about where to look, what to look for, who might have the information or who may know who has such information. For example, in researching the market for fibre cement products in Turkey, it was difficult to identify potential customers. Instead, interviews were conducted with cement suppliers because they were likely to have our targets in their networks. These firms proved most cooperative in identifying the informants we needed and making introductions on our behalf.

This is an example of snowball sampling, in which initial interviews help define later interviews. They are useful in identifying interview targets and information sources. It may take only one interview to start a snowball sampling process going, but the 'right' informant(s) to identify follow-up contacts is critical. Not only are the informants' personal and professional networks relevant, the networks of the researchers and interpreters may also be useful. In research in Asia with senior university students, their networks and those of local interpreters provided unexpected sources of introduction – sometimes to informants themselves, other times to those who connect us to the people with whom we wished to speak.

INTERVIEW PREPARATION

As Pasteur said, chance favours the prepared mind. And to be prepared for unexpected opportunities and problems a researcher needs to have the necessary resources and equipment available and to make some prior arrangements and contingency plans. In interviews we can find out things we had not expected and we can also fail to find things out because of unexpected events or situations. Many an interview has had to be cut short, cancelled or severely compromised by a failure to be fully prepared. There are three types of preparation we have identified: preparation to do with logistics, advance management of the physical context and properties of the interview situation, and mental preparation.

Logistics preparation is concerned with planning that will get you to the right place at the right time for your interview. This requires much more thinking and organisation in international settings than when conducting research at home. Needed are a map, good directions and any and all information about local conditions, including how long it will take to get there. This can vary enormously by country, day and time. Our experience has included being stuck in traffic jams for hours in Bangkok, being delayed by flood waters in New Delhi, becoming enmeshed in mass demonstrations in Seoul and we have come across closed and non-existent roads and bridges in various countries. Assuming the worst does happen, having a mobile phone to let the informant know what is happening is both comforting to you and polite.

It is important to get briefed about local transport, including availability, quality, reliability and security. Some sources of information will be more reliable than others – your hotel versus the word of say, taxi drivers, who tend to claim they know where they are going so as to get a fare. In some places security is an issue and hotels may have their own or approved taxis. The hotel can also communicate your destinations to the driver and can provide directions written down in the local language. It is also useful to note the meaning of such instructions in your own language on the same paper if you do not speak or read the local language.

Preparation of physical properties of the interview includes organisation of the venue, appropriate dress, business cards, props and recording. The interview venue is not always under the control of the interviewer. The informant's convenience and availability will usually dictate the site. Often, interviews take place at the informant's workplace. However, if available, options away from the workplace including a meeting room at the interviewer's hotel, a business centre or a restaurant can remove inhibitions of informants, remove them from distractions and interruptions, and facilitate the flow of communication. In our experience, a more formal meeting place is usually desirable to start the interview, with the possibility of it continuing over lunch, dinner or a coffee later.

Dress appropriately, as clothing is an important form of non-verbal communication. Researchers need to be comfortable, but aware of and conforming to the local norms and professional in appearance. Business cards are usually required for professional introductions and are an important part of the introductory ritual in some countries. Cards need to be carefully translated to ensure that they are equivalent to the original – as one of us discovered to their cost in Japan when their academic title had been translated into something rather junior! Business cards should be carried in a good quality holder to ensure you can find them easily and that the cards remain in good condition. In some countries it would be an actual insult to offer a bedraggled looking card. Materials such as brochures and samples (appropriately translated if possible) facilitate communication during the interview, especially with regard to technical matters. If sophisticated video or computer demonstrations are required, make sure you have stand-alone capabilities and/or appropriate connectors – and do not forget an extension lead!

Recording devices should be taken, even though you may not always be able to use them. Many times we have been assured beforehand that taping of interviews is never allowed, only to find that this was not the case. Carry a small and high-quality recorder with you at all times – it is also useful for you to make notes. Record a few opening words before an interview to indicate its nature and purpose, date and location – otherwise confusion later is almost inevitable. Use high-quality tapes, as background noise in poor-quality tapes can more than double the time it takes to transcribe them. Spare tapes and batteries are also good to have. Also take a small camera, which can be used, with permission, to record the interview situation and people, as well as other relevant material. In a project on computer-based design facilities, our photographs of the offices ended up the most valuable source of information.

Mental preparation is concerned with getting ready to facilitate the flow of information and deciding – as much as it is possible – how you will manage the interview process.

An interview guide is essential as it helps to direct the interview process. This may be a one-page list of the main topics and some sample questions in a logical order. Or you may wish to incorporate more detailed instructions to yourself, including speculating upon/articulating alternative modes of questions depending on how the interview unfolds, and reminders of observations you wish to make about the informant's state of mind, interest level and apparent knowledge level. Whatever the form, the interview guide should allow you to quickly review topics before and during the interview, to ensure no important topics have been omitted and to prioritise. This guide can and should be added to as more interviews are completed.

Informants do not always have enough time to answer all questions and it may be necessary to decide very quickly which topics to cover. Again you may want to explicate some contingencies in advance. Interviews using interpreters are much slower and this needs to be borne in mind when developing the interview guide and estimating the length of the interview. For every question and response the time is roughly doubled.

Mental preparation is also concerned with making decisions about how the interview will be managed. If more than one member of the research team is to be present at the interview, it is necessary to work out in advance the roles each is to play and ways to coordinate and control each other. It is best that this is not an emergent process. Someone needs to take the lead in introductions and in questioning. Others can act more as scribes, key listeners or observers, and check the timing and coverage of topics. Deciding who will (if possible) determine and direct the seating positions of those in the interview is important. The layout of the room is relevant and the main interviewer should try to sit close to or opposite the informant, with any interpreter by their side. Once you sit down it is difficult to rearrange things.

Recording the interview is a topic that needs handling with care. There is usually no need to raise the topic until some time after your opening research description. The atmosphere of the meeting needs to be assessed, as well as the rapport with the informant. Often, the longer you can leave asking permission to tape the greater the likelihood that informants will agree, as it gives informants time to get your measure. Prior to an interview in Turkey we were assured that taping would not be allowed. After some time, when a good rapport had been established with the informant, the issue of taping was raised in a tactful way. The informant immediately agreed as they were now comfortable with the interview and were aware that no sensitive, confidential material was being requested. Even if you do record the interview also take some notes during and after the interview – informants sometimes change their minds about recording and tapes can get lost and damaged.

Effective communication requires a common language. This includes technical language, especially for industrial products and services. In order to understand how a new type of material might be used and how it compares to competition, it may be necessary to research the background of an industry. For example, to understand aspects of the production process and to be able to speak the technical language of the informant background reading or interviews may be necessary. Informants in such cases might include an engineer, technician and/or scientist.

To facilitate communication interpreters are often used by both sides. Professional interviewers are a valuable part of the interview process when they are needed, and it is thus a false economy to try to minimise these costs by using less experienced interpreters or relying on the respondent to provide someone. Good interpreters become your eyes and ears. They help with translation and interpretation of both verbal and non-verbal communication and they are a guide in terms of cultural sensitivity issues. You want an interpreter you can trust and who is fully briefed about the research so that they can become an integral member of the interview team. They need to be conversant with any technical terms and issues that may arise and be on your side. Typically, this will not be someone working for the respondent. You should try to get to know them and their background and establish rapport. They need to get used to your accent and to the phrases you use and the speed of your speech. They may also be sources themselves of relevant information because of their past experience and connections.

COMMUNICATING AND QUESTIONING

The above discussion deals with creating a framework for an interview that will enable the researchers to maximise the value that will flow from it. Within this framework there is then the potential for effective questioning and also for more serendipitous communication, the impossible-to-anticipate areas of discussion that will enrich your research.

The process of communication begins before the interview. From the time you approach the place of interview, things that the research team do and say can, and often are reported to your informant. You do not know whom you are interviewing or who works for them. Unfortunate comments made in the elevator or in a reception area can quickly travel back to the informant and compromise the interview. So be careful about side conversations or comments you might make to your colleagues. This includes comments about what you did last night, how you feel, your last interview, the travel experience you just had, as well as the state of local architecture and amenities and the nature and purpose of the interview. Interviews usually begin with some kind of introductions and exchange of business cards. The exchange of business cards is a formal ritual in some countries. The researcher wants to get to know who the informant(s) is (are) and the nature of their position and relative status.

It is not always obvious who is senior and you should not jump to conclusions too quickly. Sometimes more senior people will take a back seat and let their juniors handle the interview, occasionally making a contribution. One story we have been told is of a trade mission visiting China in the early days of its opening up. During their many interviews and meetings held at a trade show in China, the same old man inevitably served tea. Later, when permission was granted to meet the senior official involved in making trade decisions, who should this official turn out to be but the aforementioned tea man!

Some polite talk may precede the interview proper and this is useful for gauging the participants and the atmosphere of the interview and for putting each other at ease. The opening informal talk is *not* the time to recall the problems you faced getting to the interview and for launching into a critique of the transport system and the weather. This may give offence rather than lighten the mood of the interview. Cultural sensitivity requires that the interviewer has taken the time to develop a sense of what topics are appropriate for such informal chats and what is taboo. It is also important to be aware of more general social taboos. For example, blowing your nose in public is inappropriate in Japan particularly with a handkerchief. Sniffing is preferable and tissues are used for such purposes.

If an interpreter is used they need to sit next to the main interviewer and in such a position that they can hear the responses clearly. They will usually need to make notes to help their interpretation so space is needed for this. The interpreter can be briefed to make the opening introductions and to explain the purpose of the interview in order to make better use of time. It may be appropriate for the interpreter to have a copy of the interview guide before them, in addition to the researcher, but this can become a problem if the interpreter begins to orchestrate the interview and not the researcher.

The opening question needs to be well chosen to put the interviewer at ease, yet be a meaningful question for the researcher to make a good first impression. A question about the organisation or the role the informants play can be a good opening but the researcher should have done his/her homework so as not to waste time on gathering information that is easily obtained elsewhere. The first questions should reflect this. You want to convey to the informant that you are well-prepared and making good use of their time.

Questioning, Listening and Responding

In personal interviews the interviewer is the research instrument and the interview is an opportunity to enter the mind of another and to see the world as they see it (McCracken 1988). To facilitate this, questions need to be framed using terms the respondent understands, be about things they can meaningfully respond to and be asked in ways to which they can respond (Briggs 1986). It is a waste of time to ask respondents about topics of which they have no real knowledge and it is probably misleading as they will most likely attempt to answer the questions anyway, possibly misdirecting you. Sometimes informants are asked to perform feats of mental gymnastics and analysis that would defy Einstein. This is the case, for example, when people are expected to remember details of distant past events, to make generalisations, characterise trends and central tendencies about highly variable phenomena, or draw conclusions about the impact of global forces and complex factors on specific outcomes. Examples are questions such as 'What kinds of effects do you think the Asian crisis will have on the computer industry?' or 'What is the most effective distribution system for this product?'. Informants do not know the answers to your research questions'. But they can contribute relevant parts of the jigsaw puzzle that it is then up to you to assemble.

Question phrasing needs to be sensitive to the needs of interpreters as well as informants. Long sentences with many qualifying clauses are to be avoided. Bite-size pieces are required so the interpreter can keep the sense of the question clear and the informant can understand and remember the full question. A common mistake is trying to be over-polite and using many English phrases that show sensitivity, but which just tend to confuse the issue and the interpreter. For example, compare 'If you would be so kind, could you please tell me, if it would not be too much trouble, how the decisions to buy X are made, in general, in this firm?' with 'How are decisions made to buy X in this firm?'. The interpreter can be briefed to put it in the necessary local polite form.

There is a tendency to look at the interpreter rather than the respondent during the interview and this is both impolite and can have a negative effect on the respondent, who will begin to feel ignored. So pay attention and acknowledge the informant when answers are being given, even in a language that you do not understand. The body language may be informative and the rapport you can establish this way is invaluable. Also, do not forget that they may understand and speak your language! For similar reasons side conversations or gazing out of the window are to be avoided during the time questions or answers are being translated. These are moments to think about the last answer and the way to proceed with the interview, and for taking some notes. Do not turn off the tape recorder during such times as later you and the interpreter will be able to go over the questions actually asked and the answers more fully and get more out of the interview.

The informant's knowledge base and the meaning he/she attaches to particular terms need to be checked. Failure to do so can result in inadvertent leading questions and questions with hidden assumptions that go unchecked – such as that the informant is familiar with a particular product or process or firm. Leading questions are those that constrain and direct the response of the informant. Thus in trying to confirm a piece of information the question should not assume it is true, as in 'We believe that X is the case, don't you agree?' versus 'What is your opinion about X?'. We have observed keen interviewers seeking to verify information and virtually defying the respondent to disagree and have observed interviewers trying to be too helpful and suggesting answers that the respondent is too polite to disagree with.

It is sometimes useful to appear to be more on the naive side or slightly dim, though interested at various points of an interview (McCracken 1988). For example, in identifying those in another culture involved in home renovations it is helpful to have people provide a detailed account of a recent personal example, including all the processes involved in getting permissions, raising funds, designing, agreeing, locating builders and so on. A fuller articulation, particularly early in an interview, can help to guard against hidden assumptions that may arise because interviewers assume situations or contexts are similar to those they are familiar with.

Various props may be used to help recover and reconstruct the memory of a respondent or to help the respondent to articulate his/her answer. These include various forms of visual aids, the use of specific examples, and encouraging respondents to draw diagrams or help complete or comment on proposed diagrams of channel and industry structures. To summarise such things only in words is not easy and can lead to things being omitted.

In addition to their personal experiences and knowledge, informants may have valuable opinions and beliefs about more general aspects of an international market. In seeking such information it is better to go *from the particular to the general*, that is, to ground questions first in the particular of the informant's experience and then to try to generalise. Having asked people about the specifics of their own situation they are in a better position to compare themselves with others in the same industry or market and to point to differences and similarities.

Serendipity and Insight

While there is a need to ask questions in the informant's knowledge domain, we cannot emphasise too strongly the value of information that emerges by chance in interviews (see also Knapp 1997). This occurs because neither the informant nor we always know what there is to know. For example, while interviewing architects in Italy about who was involved in decisions and planning for house renovations, attention turned to a catalogue from an annual trade fair that involved everyone from the building industry. The informant had a copy of the most recent catalogue and this was a useful source of information. But we also asked how you could obtain copies of this or other catalogues like it. The informant was interested in discovering this too and an inspection of the catalogue plus subsequent phone calls revealed that it was only the publisher of the catalogue that kept copies to show prospective clients. The publisher was not part of the building industry but was a key source of information.

Such unexpected insights only emerge if the researcher is prepared to listen and ask the right kinds of questions. Sometimes simple questions of the type 'If you were looking for this type of information, where would you start or go?' have led to valuable subsequent interviews as well as to other data sources that otherwise would be extremely difficult to identify. Follow-up questions and probing are an essential part of a qualitative interview and this requires listening and responding to what the respondent has said, not just asking questions. There is no way to anticipate all the kinds of responses that may arise and the interviewer needs to seek clarification and further elaboration as appropriate. This can involve rethinking the direction of questioning during the interview as the interviewer becomes aware that this informant has different pieces of the knowledge puzzle than was anticipated. While some contingency planning can and should be undertaken, the interviewer may be forced to think fast and move to unexpected lines of enquiry.

The fictional character Rumpole of the Bailey once said that barristers should never ask a question in court that they did not already know the answer to. It is just the opposite in qualitative interviewing. We want to permit ourselves to be surprised – to allow the respondent to provide answers or contribute information we never thought of asking for. It is a waste of time asking informants for information about things you already know or for information you can obtain easily elsewhere. Hence the interview needs to include some freeform questions that give the respondent the opportunity to respond on his/her own terms. Examples are questions such as 'What do you think are the main problems or issues confronting this industry/your firm at this time?' or 'Why do you think this firm is doing this?'.

We tend to assume that the information we require is stored in the respondent's head somehow and can be accessed through appropriate questioning. This may be so for more concrete or objective types of information about the frequency of behaviour and economic values, but in other cases the knowledge may not pre-exist and is co-created through the interactions taking place in the interview. This point is stressed in a number of writings about interpretive, ethnographic interviews (for example, Creswell 1998; Holstein and Gubrium 1995; Schwandt 2000; Spradley 1979). Questions are stimuli that elicit responses that would not otherwise have occurred. For example, in attitude surveys it may be argued that people's attitudes are formed only in response to the questions asked, rather than reflecting any pre-existing predispositions. In a broader sense, this is what happens when an interviewer and respondent work together to develop a picture of a person's theories in use, how decisions are made or information is acquired and responded too. Knowledge is co-created, which did not exist before.

Interviews develop a rhythm that the interviewer in part creates. Rhythm includes easy transitions between topic areas using linking sentences like: 'Now I would like to ask you some questions about ...' Interviewers should work to create and, when necessary, alter the interview rhythm. Allowing respondents to ask questions or asking them if they have any questions or issues they would like to raise is another way of facilitating the flow of communication. Putting informants more at ease creates further opportunities for unexpected insights.

Interview Culture and Interview Relationships

Lack of direction and structure and/or too much familiarity and informality can prove counterproductive because the interviewer is not taken seriously – what McCracken (1988) refers to as 'over rapport'. But this must be balanced with the need to sometimes introduce more informal topics into the process to help establish rapport and to increase informant motivation. This must be assessed on a case-by-case basis. For example, during an interview in Istanbul the director of an industry association left to attend to another meeting and was replaced by his deputy. It became evident that this person was uncomfortable with the interview and guarded in her responses. Informal topics were raised including whether she had ever visited our home country of Australia. It turned out she had applied twice unsuccessfully to emigrate. This interlude allowed the interviewers to understand the respondent's attitude better and led to a productive interview with important follow-up introductions and interviews.

The many issues of questioning we have been discussing are mediated by culture, especially in international interviews between people from different cultural backgrounds. This is a vast topic beyond the scope of this chapter. Here we mention only a few issues we have found to have a significant effect on the productivity and serendipity of an interview. There are obvious issues of translation from one language and culture to another and the problems of communication that can occur (Deutscher 1968). Sex and age differences between the researchers and informant can be important in some cultures and have a major effect on the extent and form of communication. For example, we have been in interviews where the senior and lead interviewer is female but all responses are directed to the males present. Other issues are the form in which questions may be put and the kinds of topics that are taboo.

'Face' is important in many cultures and questions should not lead informants to lose face by, for example, asking them to criticise their organisation, boss, or government. Where possible, the interviewer should try to enhance the respondent's face by suitable characterisations of their organisation and its behaviour. Again the appropriate balance between gaining relevant information, keeping the cooperation of the respondent and not avoiding important topics is emergent on an interview-by-interview basis. If you do not ask you will not find out and you will not offend, if you do ask about sensitive topic areas you may offend. The way a question is put can be critical and an interpreter may play a valuable role. For example, rather than focusing on the reasons for firm's poor performance it is easier to focus on ways a firm can increase its performance. Many of the reasons for previous poor performance will emerge from such a focus.

Cultural sensitivity is also necessary in understanding and interpreting answers to questions. In a number of Asian cultures and elsewhere, people avoid disagreements and seek harmony. This can lead to easy apparent agreement with the interviewer if they are directive and leading in their questions. The word for 'Yes' in many cultures is often used as a simple acknowledgement of having heard a person. It does not necessarily mean 'yes' in the sense of 'I agree with you' or 'I will do what you ask'.

As we have seen there are a variety of relations to be managed during the interview process: the interviewer–respondent relationship, relations among the interview team members, relations among different respondents, interviewer–interpreter relations and respondent–interpreter relations. There may also be the issues of interpreter–interpreter relations when both sides use their own. All of these require attention and cultural sensitivity. Each can be both a source of potential problems and opportunities.

For example, we have had success using bilingual senior university students from well-regarded local business or technical programmes as our interpreters. This is because they can, often, quickly understand the nature of the subject matter. But there are dangers too. First, they are young and, in some countries, may be totally lacking in practical/industry experience and unable to talk to senior people in business or government. Also, local cultural norms may lead to them being poorly regarded by informants. Their motives may also conflict with yours. They may be more interested in not giving offence and impressing the respondent, to the point of not asking your questions correctly and/or being too easily satisfied with any answers given. They may even be job hunting!

Other issues of cultural sensitivity and personal characteristics arise in selecting interpreters. Age and gender issues are relevant in the same way they are for the interviewer. Another issue is that local speakers may have important accent differences that may signal relative status in a culture. The social distance between the interpreter and the respondent, including both inferior and superior status, can inhibit an interview (Welch et al. 2002). A related issue is that of emigrants returning to their country of origin. They may not be familiar with current language styles and customs and may be regarded with suspicion or even distrust. For example, problems can arise in conducting interviews in Vietnam using interpreters from your home country who were once refugees.

Interpreters may also play other roles in an interview, apart from facilitating the communication process. Respondents may not be confident with their English ability or whatever the language of the interviewer is. Hence they use an interpreter but yet may well understand most of what is going on. We have been in a number of interviews where the respondent corrected the interpretation of the interpreter and later even began to answer the questions directly. Another reason for using interpreters by respondents is that it gives them more time to compose their answers and to observe the interviewers more carefully.

What this all means is that various types of social interactions can be taking place among the parties involved, all of which can have an impact on the way an interview develops. An interview is not always a simple dyadic interaction between an interviewer and a respondent.

ENDING AND AFTERMATH

Time management is an area that can lead to problems in interviews. Inexperienced interviewers tend to stick rigidly to their interview guide, which can sometimes be at the expense of greater insight. Avoid a machine gun approach to questioning with consequential superficial answers, just so that you get through all the questions you intended to ask. Be aware of how much time is available and manage the questioning to focus on what emerge as the key issues. Following serendipitous leads can reveal new topics that deserve follow-up, which means straying from your interview guide. When time pressures arise, do not mechanically rush through all the remaining issues. It is generally best to explore a few issues in more depth. Often judgements as to what *not* to ask about will have to be made on the spot. Follow-up interviews and requests for further information are a possible way of filling in the gaps – so long as a good rapport has been established.

Time management also involves knowing when to bring an interview to a close. Interviewers need to read body language, as well as what is said, to ensure they do not overstay their welcome. Some time near the appointed finish time it is useful to ask how much more time the respondent has available. This is an opportunity for the respondent to signal that the interview can run over, which helps the interviewer better plan his/her questioning, or to indicate how much time is left.

Often, interesting information will come out as the interview is winding up. Informants seem to get a 'second wind' when the end has been signalled and will sometimes bring up new topics or will expand on a previous topic. This is especially so once a tape recorder has been switched off. So be prepared to note such information. People tend to relax and even to comment on earlier responses, signalling issues that were too sensitive to bring up when the interview was being recorded. A useful closing question to ask informants that encourages further discussion is: 'Is there anything else that we have not discussed that you think is important?'. This allows a respondent to tell you what you have missed. There is an opportunity to clarify various matters: to ask if you can contact informants again, in order to follow up any issues you do not fully understand, and to make sure you are sent the names, contacts, reports or referrals that were promised during the interview.

Depending on the rapport established, interviews can often extend beyond their allotted time and even move on to a meal or drink, where further, more informal, exchange of information can take place and personal bonds can be developed. This 'after-interview' is a tremendous opportunity. It can contribute to the productivity of the interview and the ability to follow up.

Recording the Process: Post Interview Write-up and Analysis

Once away from the interview it is a good idea to *immediately* write down or record first impressions and comments on the interview that would not be obvious in the recording, including different points of view that may exist among the research team. Preliminary assessment of the mix of anticipated and serendipitous information and the questioning styles that were the most effective for eliciting responses should be noted. If the interview was not recorded, now is the time to reconstruct as much as you can from your notes and make sure they are readable. These notes need to be as detailed as possible and contain quotes.

Now is not the time for major interpretation and decisions as to what is relevant or not. If an interpreter has been used this is an opportunity to get the extra detail that the interpreter could not convey during the interview and to get his/her view of what went on. People forget much of the detail and nuances of the interview in the first few hours after it is completed. Some writers (for example, Glesne 1999) recommend that a reflective field journal be kept containing all of this, as well as more general reflections as they occur to you. Plane trips, long drives to interviews and other times when the mind is not actively engaged are good times for such activity.

When the research trip is completed, a short note of thanks to each respondent and the interpreters is advisable as this helps maintain the relationship and opens the door for subsequent questioning. If a summary of the interview is to be provided, this should be included.

It is beyond the scope of this chapter to consider the analysis of interviews in detail. This is covered elsewhere. Most qualitative writers would agree with us that analysis is an ongoing emergent process itself. It should be done in conjunction with interviewing, rather than after it (for example, Coffey and Atkinson 1996; Patton 1990). This allows you to shape and focus the research as it occurs, to take advantage of serendipity, to respond to problems and events and to contribute meaningfully to the overall emergent research process.

A picture of the international market you are investigating, or the answers to other research questions, is gradually built from assembling the key pieces and insights of the various interviews into an overall coherent interpretation(s). The process switches between 'intra-interview' and 'inter-interview' analysis, and between theory and data, in an abductive way (Gadde and Dubois 2002). We go back and forth between the data and our generalisations and theory to seek the general in the particular. This requires creativity and disciplined thinking, not an easy combination, as well as an awareness and appreciation of different theoretical perspectives. It also requires that you make clear to yourself and any client what is speculation, interpretation and hypothesising – as distinct from description (Patton 1990).

CONCLUSIONS

We have provided an overview of some of the main issues that arise in conducting qualitative interviews in international business research. Our focus has been on interviewing and research as an emergent process in which chance events and unexpected opportunities and problems arise that shape the final outcome in important ways. The researcher need not be at the mercy of these events but, with appropriate preparation, sensitivity and skill, can respond to them in ways that maximise the value of the interview. It is part art and part science, using and developing both explicit and tacit knowledge learned from experience. These tacit aspects of interviewing are usually learned in practice, working with more experienced researchers; in much the same way a young artist learns from a master (Nonaka and Takeuchi 1995).

Good research requires a clear sense of the research questions and the types of information needed to answer them. The process of gathering information is always imperfect and constrained by issues of incompleteness, reliability and validity. In order to deal with these issues the researcher needs to be aware of the various types of errors that may occur and to minimise them as much as possible. But the research process is also *enabled* by the unexpected, the unplanned and unknowable in advance. Throughout our discussion we have shown how the prepared mind of the researcher can seek out and benefit from adjusting the research to such unanticipated sources of knowledge. It is not just a matter of 'muddling through', but also an active process of *looking for the overlooked* and improvising and adapting accordingly. In this way the pieces of the knowledge jigsaw puzzle are identified and assembled into a meaningful whole, with a clear underlying analytical or theoretical framework that generates the value and provides potential answers to the research questions.

REFERENCES

Briggs C.L. (1986), *Learning How to Ask*, New York: Cambridge University Press.
Chelariu, C., W.J. Johnston and L. Young (2002), 'Learning to improvise, improvising to learn: a process of responding to complex environments', *Journal of Business Research*, **55** (February), 141–8.
Coffey, A. and P. Atkinson (1996), *Making Sense of Qualitative Data*, Thousand Oaks, CA: Sage.
Creswell, J.W. (1998), *Qualitative Inquiry and Research Design: Choosing Among Five Traditions*, Thousand Oaks, CA: Sage.
Deutscher, I. (1968), 'Asking questions cross-culturally: some problems of linguistic

comparability', in H.S. Becker (ed.), *Institutions and the Person*, Chicago, IL: Aldine, pp. 318–41.

Gadde, L.-E. and A. Dubois (2002), 'Systematic combining: an abductive approach to case research', *Journal of Business Research*, **55** (July), 553–60.

Glesne, C. (1999), *Becoming Qualitative Researchers: An Introduction*, 2nd edn, New York: Longman.

Holstein, J.A. and J.F. Gubrium (1995), *The Active Interview*, Thousand Oaks, CA: Sage.

Knapp, N.F. (1997), 'Interviewing Joshua: on the importance of leaving room for serendipity', *Qualitative Inquiry*, **3** (3), 326–43.

McCracken, G. (1988), *The Long Interview*, Newbury Park, CA: Sage.

Nonaka, I. and H. Takeuchi (1995), *The Knowledge-Creating Company*, New York: Oxford University Press.

Ohsawa, Y. (2002), 'Introduction to chance discovery', *Journal of Contingencies and Crisis Management*, **10** (2 and 3) (special issues on chance discovery), 61–2, 117–18.

Patton, M.Q. (1990), *Qualitative Analysis and Research Methods*, 2nd edn, Newbury Park, CA: Sage.

Schwandt, T.A. (2000), 'Three epistemological stances for qualitative inquiry', in N. Denzin and Y.S. Lincoln (eds), *Handbook of Qualitative Research*, Thousand Oaks, CA: Sage, pp. 189–213.

Shane, S. (2000), 'Prior knowledge and the discovery of entrepreneurial opportunities', *Organization Science*, **11** (July–August), 448–69.

Spradley J.P. (1979), *The Ethnographic Interview*, New York: Holt, Rhinehart & Winston.

Welch, C., R. Marschan-Piekkari, H. Penttinen and M. Tahvanainen (2002), 'Corporate elites as informants in qualitative international business research', *International Business Review*, **11**, 611–28.

11. Language and Languages in Cross-cultural Interviewing

Rebecca Marschan-Piekkari and Cristina Reis

INTRODUCTION

Cross-cultural interviews are very context specific as acts of communication, involving data collection in different national, cultural and linguistic environments (Ryen 2002). The choice and use of language, as well as the researcher's and the interviewee's language skills, affect the dynamics in various ways. As Wright (1996, p. 73) argues, 'cross-cultural studies should not be carried out in a unilingual English language fashion'. The collection of valid and trustworthy data from non-English contexts is likely to require a multilingual approach. Moreover, neglecting or misusing foreign languages may be interpreted as unprofessionalism – as if the researcher has completely ignored the interviewee. Therefore, becoming aware of the role played by language, and considering various ways of dealing with it, belongs to methodological contextualisation (Marschan-Piekkari and Welch, Chapter 1 this volume; Michailova, Chapter 18 this volume; Punnett and Shenkar 1994). In this chapter, methodological contextualisation means the act of aligning language considerations with situational conditions, and thus ensuring fit.

The challenges posed by diverse languages are by no means new to methodology literature pertaining to international business. Scholars have suggested various ways of translating survey instruments from the original language into a number of foreign languages. Techniques such as back translation[1] have been proposed to maintain as accurately as possible the original meaning of questionnaires (Birbili 2000; Brislin 1970; Hatim 1990). Field researchers have also teamed up with local researchers who have been delegated the task of translating the original survey instrument into the local language for replication (Harzing et al. 2002). In such projects, researchers are confronted with language differences primarily in the early phases of the study when the questionnaire is being designed and tested. Once it has been finalised and the data collection has commenced in different countries, the language issue is considered 'solved' and its implications tend to be forgotten.

In qualitative research – particularly in studies drawing on cross-cultural interviews – language challenges keep re-emerging throughout the life-cycle of the project. The researcher's ability to develop trust and rapport, and to establish relationships with interviewees, is of utmost importance for gaining access, and for collecting and analysing data (Ryen 2002). The process is an outcome of communication and language skills, and the challenge is exacerbated in cross-cultural interviews in which the researcher and the interviewee may have a different mother tongue. However, this whole issue may be invisible to an English-speaking researcher who conducts cross-cultural interviews in English and contributes to international business as a field of study.

Language may also affect the research process at the pre-interview stage, even without the researcher being fully aware of it. As Chapman et al. (Chapter 14 this volume) argue, the selection of appropriate research phenomena and questions is likely to be determined, at least partly, by the researcher's language skills. Access to potential informants and the nature of the relationship with them are very much influenced by the shared language between the researcher and the interviewee. In terms of the interview situation itself, the first challenge is to find a common language which may be a second language for both the researcher and the local informant. Consequently, the exchange between the two may suffer from misunderstanding, interviewer and response biases, and neglect of important cues such as non-verbal communication (Punnett and Shenkar 1994; Ryen 2002). An interpreter may be used, but as Usunier (1998, p. 92) points out, the introduction of this third party 'produces noise, artificiality and an absence of tempo', thus damaging the intimacy and the natural rhythm of the interviewing process. At the very final stage of the research project, cross-cultural interview data need to be carefully translated into the language of publication. Maintaining original nuances and subtleties in terms of what the interviewee actually meant is a considerable challenge for any qualitative researcher (Macdonald and Hellgren, Chapter 13 this volume).

Despite the fact that crossing language boundaries is an inherent part of international business research, language is often taken for granted and its methodological implications are seldom problematised. As Chapman et al. (Chapter 14 this volume) argue, our field is very much an English-language domain in which our research objects – internationally operating firms – and research outlets – top academic journals – promote the use of English (see also Martin and Collinson 2002). Yet if we start reflecting upon this issue, a number of questions start emerging: for example, what if the researcher conducts some of the cross-cultural interviews in the same research project in a native language, while conducting the rest in a second language? How open and cooperative is the interviewee who has to operate in a second language? Are the two sets of interviews even comparable and how is the overall quality of the data affected? These questions are equally important for English-speaking researchers as well as those using English as a second (or third) language.

The purpose of this chapter is thus to examine how language skills influence cross-cultural interviewing across the life cycle of a qualitative research project. We acknowledge that a number of factors other than language affect cross-cultural interviewing, including age, gender, social class and the researcher's institutional affiliation. However, our aim is to separate the language effect on the interview process in a cross-cultural setting even though it operates in conjunction with a number of other factors. We examine the researcher's and the interviewee's ability to operate in the interview language, diverse native and non-native accents, the use of idiomatic expressions and translation challenges. We argue that language is not merely a technical problem (see also Michailova, Chapter 18 this volume) that can be solved by 'correct' translation. Rather, it is a factor shaping our research processes in both subtle and noticeable ways. Instead of a unilingual, English-dominated approach to cross-cultural interviewing we propose a multilingual approach. We draw on our own experiences of conducting two single-case studies, along with the experiences of our colleagues.

The rest of the chapter is organised as follows. We first introduce our case studies and explain why and how language is an important methodological issue to consider. Thereafter, we examine multinational corporations, the context of our research projects, as multilingual organisations (Barner-Rasmussen and Björkman 2003) and analyse the language diversity inside them. We then turn to various types of interviews and discuss the importance of the interviewee's/researcher's language skills in different interview situations. The body of the chapter is devoted to analysing the effect of language in the pre-interview, interview and post-interview stages of a qualitative research project. Finally, we draw some conclusions based on the analysis.

OUR COLLECTIVE EXPERIENCES AND PERSONAL BACKGROUNDS

In examining the role and effect of language on cross-cultural interviewing, we shall be reflecting upon our own PhD projects. The first one, which is henceforth referred to as the Finnish study, examined a multinational engineering corporation headquartered in Finland (Marschan 1996). The second one, which we have called the German study, investigated a large conglomerate operating worldwide but headquartered in Germany (Reis 2002).

The Finnish study investigated internal communication flows within the multinational corporation. The data was primarily collected through 110 personal interviews with top and middle managers as well as operatives. These interviews were conducted by the researcher in English (67 per cent), Spanish (19 per cent), Finnish (13 per cent) and Swedish (1 per cent) although the common corporate language was English. The researcher was Finnish by nationality and native speaker of Finnish, Swedish and Russian. Moreover, she spoke fluent English, and was competent in Spanish and French.

The German study focused on examining how international managers working and living in Germany, England and Portugal dealt with their professional and private lives. A total of 64 male managers were personally interviewed for the study: 19 in Germany, 18 in England and 27 in Portugal. The researcher conducted the interviews in German, English and Portuguese although the common corporate language was German. She was Portuguese, by nationality, but she had lived and studied in the USA and Canada (Ottawa). The promotion of bilingualism and multiculturalism is particularly important in Canada. Before embarking upon her PhD programme in the UK, she had worked as a management trainer, which allowed her to become fluent in the professional language of managers.

Table 11.1 summarises the cross-cultural interviews across the Finnish and German projects. We use the terms 'linguistic equality', 'linguistic advantage' (both for the researcher and the interviewee), and 'mutual linguistic challenge' to depict different weightings that language may have in cross-cultural interviews and to categorise our interviews accordingly. We consider language a factor of power affecting the dynamics of the interview situation.

As Table 11.1 shows, the first category, linguistic equality, refers to a situation, in which both the researcher and the interviewee speak their mother tongues and the parties are thus on equal terms. In the Finnish study, 14 per cent of the interviews were of this type, while in the German study the corresponding figure was 42 per cent. In the second category, either the researcher or the interviewee may possess a linguistic advantage, meaning that one of the parties is able to use their mother tongue. In both of our case studies, it was always the interviewee who was granted linguistic advantage, never the researcher. Unlike in the Finnish study, all of the interviewees participating in the German study had the opportunity to respond in their mother tongue. This gave them a linguistic advantage, as the researcher was operating in a second or third language in 58 per cent of the interviews. Coupled with the interviewees' elite status (see Odendahl and Shaw 2002; Welch et al. 2002) this affected the power balance in the interview. We use the final category, mutual linguistic challenge, to describe interview situations in which both parties operate in a second or third language. Language fluency varies considerably in this category. For example, if an interview is carried out between two non-native speakers of English, one of them may be very competent, almost 90 per cent fluent in the interview language, while the other one may feel highly uncomfortable responding in English. Moreover, an interviewee may master the professional jargon and 'company speak' very well in a second language, but as soon as the interview moves outside this field, he/she may find it challenging to communicate. In the Finnish study, the majority of the interviews (59 per cent) were conducted in a second or third language for both parties. As in the situation of linguistic equality, the researcher and the interviewee face an equal language challenge, but this time the equality could be experienced as negative. There is evidence suggesting, however, that non-native speakers frequently prefer to communicate with other non-natives rather than with natives due to the use of more simple expressions, fewer subtleties and more direct dialogue (Bartlett and Johnson 1998). Compared to the other interview categories, linguistic mutual challenge is perhaps more characterised by awareness of language issues. The researcher and the interviewee are likely to make special efforts to facilitate the exchange in a second or third language.

Table 11.1   The power of language in cross-cultural interviews

Research project	Linguistic equality	Linguistic advantage	Mutual linguistic challenge
Finnish project	14% (Finnish, Swedish)	Researcher's advantage 0% Interviewee's advantage 27% (Spanish, English)	59%
German project	42% (Portuguese)	Researcher's advantage 0% Interviewee's advantage 58% (German, English)	—

Clearly, we attempted to develop a broad framework for understanding linguistic considerations in cross-cultural interviewing. However, following our field experiences, some of our interviewees were hard to categorise due to their highly international personal backgrounds. They had lived most of their lives outside their home countries, had studied abroad and married local partners, which gave them a linguistic advantage in several idioms. In fact, they seemed to have multiple mother tongues. During the course of one interview, it was possible for the balance between the researcher and the interviewee to change, or even switch between linguistic equality to linguistic advantage. We return to this later in the chapter.

LANGUAGE DIVERSITY IN MULTINATIONAL CORPORATIONS

The multinational corporation has been widely studied in international business. One of the distinguishing features is its multilingual nature (Barner-Rasmussen with Björkman 2003), frequently manifest in a common corporate language, a parent country language and subsidiary languages (Marschan-Piekkari et al. 1999). Many multinationals introduce a common corporate language to facilitate internal communication flows between headquarters and foreign subsidiaries as well as directly between foreign units. Yet regardless of the degree of internationalisation, the multinational still has a country of origin and thus a parent country language.[2] It may coincide with the common corporate language or it may be different, which tends to be the case for many European multinationals originating from non-English-speaking countries such as Finland and Germany (Welch et al. 2001). In the Finnish case company, the common corporate language was English, while in the German company it was German.

From the researcher's perspective, it may be a relief to find out that the multinational corporation has adopted one common corporate language for internal information exchanges. Yet this is likely to apply primarily to formal communication, leaving personal, informal exchanges outside its influence. Moreover, prior research has shown that there may be a considerable time lag between top management's decision to introduce a common corporate language and its implementation in each and every foreign subsidiary located in various parts of the world (Laine-Sveiby 1991). This is particularly evident in multinationals that expand through foreign acquisitions and thus constantly face the challenge of integrating new members with diverse language skills into the corporation. In addition, top management at headquarters and foreign subsidiaries may be relatively comfortable in using the common corporate language but as soon as personnel at middle-management and lower organisational levels are involved in the research project, the language challenge may become more visible (Marschan-Piekkari et al. 1999). We would argue that one feature that separates corporate elites from non-elites is the ability to effectively operate in the dominant language of the corporation. In the Finnish study, it was English, the lingua franca of international business, while in the German study it was German. Clearly, then, language is a tool for exercising power within the multinational corporation as well as in the interview situation. We return to this issue later in our chapter.

Despite the fact that many multinationals have adopted English as their common corporate language, the type of English used in these companies may differ from the researcher's expectations. Many researchers, who are non-native speakers of English, have been trained in Oxford or BBC English (see also *The Economist* 2002). However, given a large number of foreign subsidiary languages the researcher is likely to encounter a 'world of Englishes': these may include various native accents in varieties of American, Australian and Canadian English, as well as non-native accents such as those of French, Spanish and German speakers (see also Charles and Marschan-Piekkari 2002). Multinationals may also have developed their own 'company speak' reflecting the professional language of the industry or sector.

The following illustrates the language diversity in the largest division of the Finnish multinational. English is used as the common corporate language although only 35 per cent of the total international workforce speaks it as their native tongue. The parent country language is Finnish, and not surprisingly, employees describe the corporate language as 'Finglish', a specific version of pidgin English (Bartlett and Johnson 1998). Such business language is seldom grammatically correct. It could probably more accurately be described as 'bad English',[3] but it fulfils the main purpose of a business language, namely to get the message across. The major subsidiary languages within this multinational are French (12 per cent), German (11 per cent) and Italian (10 per cent). Given the language diversity within the firm, inter-subsidiary exchanges are carried out in any available shared language, while English is used particularly in formal communication between headquarters and foreign subsidiaries.

FORMS OF INTERVIEWING

Before examining the specific impact of language on various stages of the cross-cultural interview we need to distinguish between different forms of interviewing. The importance of the researcher's and the interviewee's language skills is likely to vary depending on the form of interview.

Gubrium and Holstein (2002, pp. 57–8) identify five ways of using interviews as vehicles for tapping into people's knowledge and experiences: survey-based, qualitative, in-depth, life-story and focus group interviews. The effect of the interview on the exchange between the researcher and the interviewee is perhaps most evident when survey-based interviews (that is, structured interviews via a standard instrument) are compared with qualitative interviews, which also reflects the underlying neopositivistic and romantic epistemologies, respectively (Alvesson 2003). In survey-based interviews, the discussion has a predefined purpose and the roles and behaviours in the interview situation tend to be very clear. The researcher uses the interview as 'a pipeline for transmitting knowledge' (Holstein and Gubrium 1997, p. 113), aiming at 'objectivity', 'neutrality' and 'standardisation' of responses. The problem with this kind of interviewing, however, is that the respondents may produce only superficial and cautious responses (Alvesson 2003, p. 16).

Various types of qualitative or unstructured (Patton 1990) interviewing, on the other hand, tend to be more flexible and open. The interviewer sees the exchange relationship as open-ended, primarily designed for collecting information on the meanings and qualities of the interviewee's experiences (Gubrium and Holstein 2002, p. 57). In a similar vein, Alvesson (2003, p. 13) defines qualitative interviews as 'relatively loosely structured and open to what the interviewee feels is relevant and important to talk about, given the interest of the research project'. In such interview situations, the participants are no longer limited by the structured questionnaire or the interview guide. Consequently, language skills start playing a more prominent role in the interview dynamics and are seen as resources rather than sources of bias. In qualitative interviews, the researcher uses relevant language skills in order to be flexible and responsive to unexpected and emerging themes in the interview situation (see also Wilkinson and Young, Chapter 10 this volume). Similarly, the respondent needs to be able to develop and elaborate on underlying meanings and explanations. The interviews we undertook in our studies were qualitative in nature.

LANGUAGE SKILLS IN CROSS-CULTURAL INTERVIEWING

The following section examines the impact of language skills across pre-interview, interview and post-interview stages. We share our own experiences of having used multiple languages when interacting with key informants, and also refer to the stories of our colleagues.

Pre-interview Stage

In international business research, the selection of research objects and questions tends to be based on pragmatic considerations. As Chapman et al.

(Chapter 14 this volume) point out, 'our research opportunities, and even what we are able to discover, are language-determined'. Our own experiences largely confirm this observation. Given the resource intensity of any cross-cultural interview project *per se*, it seems that we seldom learn another foreign language for research purposes. From this perspective, Grisar-Kassé's (Chapter 7 this volume) efforts to study a Senegalese multinational corporation and learn the Wolof language are exceptional.

In the process of trying to arrange interviews with and gain access to individual informants, language is likely to play a role in building up a rapport and gaining trust. In the German study of managers' private lives, the mother tongue of the potential informants was used when approaching them by phone and working the way through the various gatekeepers of the German multinational firm. The choice of using the managers' mother tongue rather than the common corporate language when calling them personally was to emphasise the personal and confidential purpose of the study, which was to investigate the private lives of male managers in relation to their managerial practices.

If one moves below the management level to foreign subsidiaries, where subsidiary languages often differ from the common corporate language, access is likely to become even more language-dependent. The Finnish study involved interviews in Spain and Mexico where English is not widely spoken. The researcher's skills in Spanish allowed her to conduct interviews also with people who were not comfortable using English. Relying only on English in carrying out cross-cultural interviews would have meant far more restricted access, as some respondents would have withdrawn from the study. The choice of interview language may be crucial even in the pre-interview stage, as we may effectively exclude key informants from the research process. Wright (1996) takes this further by arguing that due to the dominance of English in cross-cultural studies we may end up accessing a group of respondents who are fluent in English but may also differ in attitudes and behaviour from non-English informants. This raises concerns about validity.

Another important consideration in the pre-interview stage is the wording of interview questions in a linguistically correct and culturally sensitive way. This can be achieved by carrying out pilot interviews, for example. Expatriates tend to represent a highly multilingual group often mastering the common corporate language, the parent country language and the host country language (at least by the time they have been repatriated!). We have sometimes asked pilot interviewees the same question in several languages and have also used a supporting interview guide translated into multiple languages. This enables dubious words or expressions to be adjusted based on the feedback. For example, subsidiary staff in Asia were interviewed as part of the Finnish study. Rather than focusing on 'perceived problems in communication with other subsidiary units', it was considered better to focus on 'suggestions to improve inter-subsidiary communication'. In the German study, the question, 'what qualities does your wife have?' could not be literally translated into German, as the word '*Qualität*' is used for a machine with commercial value. Instead, the word was replaced by '*Vorzug*', meaning quality and merit. Hence the appropriate term was found by comparing corresponding expressions in the different languages at hand, and agreeing upon the most appropriate word with the interviewee. This 'negotiated' terminology was then employed in subsequent interviews throughout the study. Scrutinising semantics is thus crucial at the data collection stage of both qualitative and quantitative studies.

The Interview

Researchers, who take a unilingual, English-dominated approach to cross-cultural interviewing, often assume that employees of international companies are fluent in English regardless of their nationality. The role of English as the corporate language of many multinationals is frequently used as justification for the language choice. For example, Daniels and Cannice (Chapter 9 this volume), two American researchers, did not encounter major language challenges in their cross-cultural interviews because they restricted them 'to high-level managers who tend to be cosmopolitan and English-speaking'. Based on our experiences, however, it seems that the fluency of the English is associated with the organisational level the respondents represent. Our experiences of interviewing both top and middle managers confirm that the lower one goes in the organisation, the poorer the language skills become. For example, a Malaysian middle manager commented on frequent staff transfers in the Finnish unit, 'Last time we used to have Mr X. He was very approachable, but apparently he was relocated to Hong Kong. Then after that we communicate [*sic*] with Mr Y. I hear not very sure [*sic*] that he has also been relocated' (English in the original). However, in the interview situation the researcher may ask a clarifying follow-up question.

In reality, as previously mentioned, different 'Englishes' may exist within a unilingual approach, posing a distinct set of challenges. The researcher is likely to encounter a variety of English accents and dialects used in different parts of the world during cross-cultural interviewing. As non-native speakers of English, we have had to struggle with various native accents as well as with an entire repertoire of Asian and European accents. As two Australian managers said in a broad local accent:

> If they've got some problems I can generally help them so that they don't feel that here is another fat cat, expat ... whose housing is paid for and all of the other

things. (English in the original)

The movement to go and see other people's operations and what they are up to and get that sort of help and sort of support from them has always been very strong. And that has always been sort of kind of positively encouraged. (English in the original)

An Italian top manager used an expression in Italian in his commentary:

I think the most important example of the capacity to decentralise in our group was to move the headquarters from Helsinki to Brussels. They have understood that Brussels was in the centre of the most important activity of the group and they had the courage to move the heart out of Finland, *la casa madre*, you know. (our emphasis, English in the original)

In the German study, interviewees used multiple languages in their responses. One German top manager, who had been on several foreign assignments during his career, replied using German, English and Portuguese:

I am going to tell you in German [that] it is a good *Besitzstand* and that is a thing I can't live without in many senses. Not in the sense of a *Wirtschaftlichkeit* but in the sense that work gives a lot to my life in terms of self-confidence and to see what I can do with my skills, *Begabung, Kompetenz*, this is how can I use my competence ... *I did the 'Abitur'*, vamos dizer o sonho sempre foi de ser chefe de pessoal ou de recursos humanos numa certa área desde o primeiro momento e baseou-se num pensamento ja na juventude. Eu trabalhei na *Evangelist Jugend*, que se chamava *Jugendleiter* ... (our emphasis, multiple languages in the original)

The researcher always had the themes of her interview guide in three languages, English, Portuguese and German, allowing her to comfortably switch languages as the respondent wished during the course of the same interview. Such a 'cocktail of languages', however, does pose problems when transcribing and analysing data in the post-interview stage.

Yet, by no means all of the interviewees were as comfortable using foreign languages as the German top managers. Many felt uncomfortable using a foreign language in an interview situation, their responses were short and superficial and the entire rapport between the researcher and the interviewee sometimes suffered due to language problems. For example, as a Chinese operative employee in Hong Kong replied to a question posed in English about the organisational structure of the Finnish company, 'I think the most important is the communication. Because in Asia, our order guys, they did not ... how should I say this in English ...' (English in the original).

It is also worth considering that interviewees may provide slightly different answers depending on the language in which the questions are asked (Wright 1996; Wright et al. 1988). We think differently depending on which language we are using, since we tend to accommodate the cultural values of a particular language and subconsciously acquire cultural attitudes and values associated with it. Harzing et al. (2002) investigated the use of English and native-language questionnaires. Their findings show that the language of the questionnaire does affect the way respondents answer the same questions. Many questionnaire items are not seemingly 'neutral' but contain an element of culture, and hence the 'use of English-language questionnaires might obscure important differences between countries' (Harzing et al. 2002, p. 17). Harzing et al. therefore advise cross-cultural researchers to adopt a multilingual approach and to respond to language differences by translating their questionnaires into local idiomatic languages. As far as the cross-cultural interview is concerned, a multilingual approach involves the researcher conducting interviews in different languages, often alongside English, as we have done, or using interpreters to assist in the conversation. Moreover, utilising a second language may have its advantages. As Ghauri (Chapter 5 this volume) argues, expressions tend to be simpler and the overall communication is likely to be more straightforward and direct when a second language is employed.

Far too often, however, a multilingual approach to cross-cultural research is seen as a 'liability of foreignness' (for example, Zaheer 1995), an additional barrier for the researcher to overcome. In their discussion of language issues in cross-cultural surveys, Harzing et al. (2002, p. 17) note, that 'researchers seem to have little choice but to accept the cost and inconvenience of questionnaire translation'. Their article focuses on one of the problems in cross-cultural surveys, namely respondents with different native languages.

There is another aspect of cross-cultural interviewing, however. Unlike surveys, in which the researcher and the respondent may not meet, an interview effectively offers an opportunity to acquire additional cross-cultural information by clarifying potential misunderstandings and discussing language related problems. As Chapman et al. (Chapter 14 this volume) suggest, the use of multiple languages may, in fact, be a gateway into the very cross-cultural differences the researcher is trying to explore (see also Hearn and Parkin 1995). These issues may otherwise go unnoticed when English is used as the only interview language. For example, in the Finnish study, there was a concern to find out about personal, informal communication relationships within the multinational corporation. For this purpose, a German subsidiary manager was interviewed in English. When asked about informal contacts, he became defensive because he interpreted the term as referring to his involvement in something against top management's stipulations. Instead of the term 'informal' he used the term 'unofficial' contacts in his response, which was clarified during our conversation by switching between English, German and Swedish. In fact, the language barrier provided additional insights into the hierarchy of the local subsidiary unit. A similar need to clarify a key concept arose in the Italian subsidiary, where the use of the term 'personal relationships' had connotations of very intimate contact with a colleague.

Differences in language skills between the researcher and the interviewee may place them in a superior–inferior relationship, further enhancing (or alternatively undermining) the relationship between a powerful corporate elite person and a lower-status student. Language competence is often considered part of professionalism, and unfortunately, poor language skills may sometimes be equated with a low IQ (Yoshihara 2001). In the Finnish study, the 110 interviewees were distributed across organisational levels as follows: top managers (22 per cent), middle managers (52 per cent) and operatives (26 per cent), while the interviews in the German study covered both top managers (53 per cent) and middle managers (47 per cent). As Welch et al. (2002, p. 613) suggest, many of them could be characterised as corporate elites occupying a top or middle management position; having functional responsibility in an area that enjoys high status within the corporation; possessing long industry experience and frequently also long tenure with the firm; having broad networks of personal relationships and considerable international exposure. In the Finnish study, most of the interviews were conducted in a mutual second language, thus balancing the power differences between the researcher and the interviewee. In the German study, on the other hand, the interviewees were always granted a linguistic advantage over the researcher, further enhancing their elite status.

The power of language in the interviewees' responses was demonstrated in the German study, in which some managers switched between the business language – German – and the language of their private life (English or Portuguese) during the course of the same interview. These multilingual respondents might describe work-related matters at the beginning of the interview, and then comfortably proceed in another language describing their family situation and the relationship with their private/business life. One could argue that through their choice of the language these managers invited the researcher to enter their private world.

Interpreters may be used to facilitate communication and cross-cultural understanding when no common language between the researcher and the interviewee exists. They may even be used on both sides. As Wilkinson and Young (Chapter 10 this volume) argue, selecting culturally suitable interpreters, briefing them and simulating the interview situation beforehand are essential elements in managing the sensitive dynamics in the actual interview situation. At best, '[g]ood interpreters become your eyes and ears' (Wilkinson and Young, Chapter 10 this volume). Interpreters may even be a valuable resource for locating appropriate interviewees at the pre-interview stage, as well as in the post-interview stage for interpreting what went on in the interview. We did not use interpreters ourselves, but we recognise that many cross-cultural researchers do and the implications of this need to be carefully considered (see Wilkinson and Young, Chapter 10 this volume).

Post-interview Stage

We encountered different types of language challenges in the post-interview stage, depending on whether the interview language was the same or different from the publishing language, which in both studies was English. The challenges we experienced in our respective projects are examined separately below.

From English to English

Some of our interviews were conducted in English with native and non-native speakers. The proportion of English-language interviews in the German study was 28 per cent, and in the Finnish study 67 per cent. American, Australian and British native speakers often interspersed their talk with sport analogies, which was challenging for an English-as-a-second-language researcher. As one Australian manager said:

> I've seen it so many times in my long career in this business that when things are not going all that well, that people tend to hide rather than you know as they say in baseball, step up to the plate and you know at least try to *hit the pitcher out of the ball park*. (our emphasis, English in the original)

We also encountered expressions of 'company speak', which required a fair knowledge of the jargon used within the case company. For example, one interviewee commented, 'I think there will be a strong push back toward *row 80 issues* for each of the local companies' (our emphasis, English in the original).

Both of us transcribed the interviewees' accounts literally, including the grammatical and lexical mistakes. We asked foreign colleagues, who were native speakers of the various accents, to interpret the meaning of idiomatic expressions such as sport analogies. One of us worked with a British modern linguist in order to increase the fluency and readability of the verbatim accounts.

From mother tongue/second/third language to English

A careful translation process was required when the interview language was different from the reporting and publishing language. In the German study, 72 per cent of the interviews were in German or Portuguese, while in the Finnish study, 33 per cent were in Finnish, Swedish or Spanish. These non-

English interviews were of two different kinds. Some of them involved translating from our mother tongues (Portuguese, Finnish and Swedish, respectively) into English. Others were conducted in a second or third language (German and Spanish, respectively), and these were also translated into English, as both our PhD theses were published in English.

In the German study, the researcher translated the transcripts from Portuguese, her mother tongue, into English in collaboration with the British linguist. Some of the Portuguese transcripts were translated in full into English, while in some cases, only the parts used in the analysis were translated. In a similar vein, in the Finnish study, the researcher transcribed the Finnish and Swedish interviews in full and translated the relevant parts into English. During the writing-up phase, the quotations were discussed with the supervisor, who was a native speaker of English. The final draft of the thesis was also language-checked.

Transcribing and translating from a second or third language into English was clearly the most challenging phase. In the German study, this concerned the interviews conducted in German, as neither German nor English was the mother tongue of the researcher. The researcher collaborated closely with a German native speaker who had previously studied English as a second language, and who was also from the same town in which the interviews took place. This was an important factor as some German managers spoke the local dialect. The German translator was also the daughter of an international manager working for another German multinational corporation, which gave her valuable contextual information. These interview transcripts that had been translated from German into English were later discussed with the British linguist. Thus the process involved two native speakers representing the source and the target languages of the translation as well as a multilingual researcher. In the Finnish study, the interview tapes in Spanish were translated directly into English. They were discussed with a Finnish university lecturer in Business Spanish. Again, the selected quotations used in the final publication were scrutinised together with native speakers of English. An unintended consequence of the English translation, however, was that the researcher lost valuable data. For example, in the German study, once the German and Portuguese transcripts had been translated into English, interesting data about how multilingual interviewees switched languages during the course of the same interview were very difficult to find.

We used a meaning-based approach to translating interviewee accounts into English in the form of a decentring technique (Campbell and Werner 1970; Eckhardt, Chapter 20 this volume). Unlike direct translation and back translation, such an approach implies that the original meaning of the interviewee is revealed through paraphrasing and interpretation of the local context. As a technique, it takes us from an instrumental perspective on translation (Steyaert and Janssens 1997) to a cultural perspective, drawing on close collaboration and consultation with native speakers of the languages in question (see also Eckhardt, Chapter 20 this volume; Napier et al., Chapter 19 this volume). Despite the insights gained during the lengthy and intensive translation process, we found the differences between the interview language and the publishing language to be a major challenge for cross-cultural researchers.

Language Issues in Data Verification

The final issue that has language implications is data verification. In the Finnish study, the interview transcripts were sent to all interviewees for data verification. The researcher was hoping that, in addition to checking the factual data, the interviewees, who were less fluent in spoken English during the interview itself would be more comfortable with written English and thus able to correct the text. In most cases, however, the interview transcripts that were returned were from those fluent in English, and therefore their revisions of language were of rather minor importance. The Spanish and the Mexican interviewees received translated English transcripts instead of the original version in Spanish. Depending on their level of English, some of them did not recognise the discussion from the translation and it was beyond their language ability to verify the contents. Thus, very few of these transcripts were returned to the researcher.

One Italian interview transcript is worth mentioning. The interview had been conducted in English with an Italian top manager. To the researcher's surprise, his secretary, who had a good command of English but who was not present in the actual interview, had reinterpreted the transcript, as she explained in her accompanying letter: 'I am sending you your interview with [Mr X's] corrections and my interpretation of the same. He has read it and agrees with the clarifications I have made' (English in the original). This 'reinterpretation' was not very helpful in terms of the original interview content but is most interesting as a tale from the field.

During the process of returning the interview transcripts, some of the interviewees, particularly top managers, wished to make changes and engaged in a process of post-rationalisation. Given the large number of cross-cultural interviews in our case studies, considerable time had unavoidably elapsed between the date of the interview and the receipt of the transcribed text. As an Austrian top manager wrote in his letter to the researcher: 'I discovered a lot of repetitions and useless words, beside the fact that some single negative experiences during the very last time have led me to [be] a bit pessimistic ... in several passages' (English in the original).

In the Finnish study, summaries of local interviews in each foreign subsidiary were also submitted to a limited number of key persons at headquarters and in the foreign unit. These brief executive summaries contained the researcher's observations and preliminary findings. The following is from a letter written by an Italian subsidiary top manager in response to the interview summary:

> We have received your preliminary comments on the interviews you collected at the end of March in [our company], and we appreciate your ability to catch – not without a certain critical spirit – elements that characterize our situation. This was certainly not a simple task, especially if you consider small amount of time available, and the fact that you are studying the more subtle elements of our organization. We are grateful for the opportunity that your letter of 18 April gives us to make some comments before you make your final draft of the report ...
>
> Your point 3, paragraph 2 – As for the problem in the relationship between [the units], we feel that rather than a 'barrier' we could define it as a situation of stances that represent differing but legitimate points of view, easily kept under control and which could be considered positive, if coupled with a constructive spirit and competitive professionalism, as usually happens. (*sic*, English in the original)

The data verification stage provided some additional insights into language and the issues under investigation. However, it also introduced some new challenges in terms of how to manage relationships with key company informants.

CONCLUSIONS

The purpose of this chapter was to examine how language skills influence cross-cultural interviewing, and to increase awareness of language implications among international business researchers who frequently see fieldwork through lenses coloured by the English language. On a general level, one may question whether it is at all possible to carry out research into 'others' with whom the researcher does not have immediate points of identification through a common language (Fawcett and Hearn 2004). On a practical level, one may claim that, due to globalisation, the world is becoming more homogeneous, thus erasing cross-cultural differences between interviewees. Our experiences suggest that it is indeed possible to study 'others' by operating in a second or third language, but it is more challenging. We believe that globalisation may actually produce a growing assertion of heterogeneity and diversity (Ryen 2002), rendering a unilingual, English-dominated approach to cross-cultural interviewing problematic.

Here we make a case for a multilingual approach to cross-cultural interviewing, and show how the researcher's and the interviewee's language skills affect the balance of power in the interview situation. We identify situations of linguistic equality, linguistic advantage and linguistic mutual challenge between the interview parties and show how the openness and collaborativeness of the interviewee and the overall richness and quality of data are affected by language considerations. Our experiences stem from the simplest form of cross-cultural interviews, namely a set-up between one researcher and one interviewee. Obviously, when cross-cultural interviews are conducted by a team of researchers and involve multiple interpreters, language implications become even more complex.

Our chapter focuses on the language skills of corporate informants in the context of multinational corporations (Marschan-Piekkari et al., Chapter 12 this volume). In addition to examining language fluency, and native and non-native accents, we also touch upon issues such as a common corporate language, subsidiary language and 'company speak'. These contextual factors introduce an additional dimension to the analysis. We argue that, as a multilingual organisation (Barner-Rasmussen and Björkman 2003), the multinational corporation is tremendously rich and diverse in terms of language. Future research could compare the use and forms of language such as technical speak across organisational levels and functional boundaries.

We have made an effort here to focus on the effects of language on cross-cultural interviewing. Obviously, a number of other factors such as age, gender and nationality, are likely to intervene in the act of communication. We do acknowledge the difficulty of disentangling language effects from the broader social interaction between researcher and interviewee. Therefore, we regard this chapter as a first attempt to proceed along this research path.

ACKNOWLEDGEMENTS

We are very grateful to Catherine Welch for the original suggestion of writing this chapter, and to Jeff Hearn for introducing us to each other. We also wish to express our gratitude to Jeff Hearn, Catherine Welch, Denice Welch and Lawrence Welch who generously provided us with helpful comments and suggestions. Finally, we are indebted to Joan Nordlund who did the language-check.

NOTES

1. Back translation is a technique used to check whether any 'losses in translation' have occurred.
2. The Finnish case company had two parent country languages, Swedish and Finnish, as Finland has two official languages. However, Finnish was the dominant one.
3. The CEO of Electrolux, the Swedish whitegoods corporation, is reported to have said that the common corporate language was 'bad English allowing every employee and manager to feel comfortable speaking a non-native language' (*Appliance* 1995).

REFERENCES

Alvesson, M. (2003), 'Beyond neopositivists, romantics, and localists: a reflexive approach to interviews in organizational research', *Academy of Management Review*, **28** (1), 13–33.

Appliance (1995), Electrolux in-house magazine, interview with Leif Johansson, CEO, E-26.

Barner-Rasmussen, W. with I. Björkman (2003), 'The impact of language and interaction ties on interunit social capital in the MNC', in W. Barner-Rasmussen, 'Knowledge sharing in multinational corporations: a social capital perspective', PhD thesis, Helsinki: Swedish School of Economics and Business Administration Press, pp. 97–118.

Bartlett, C. and C. Johnson (1998), 'Is business English a pidgin?', *Language and Intercultural Training*, **16** (1), 4–6.

Birbili, M. (2000), 'Translating from one language to another', *Social Research Update*, **31** (Winter), unpaginated.

Brislin, R.W. (1970), 'Back-translation for cross-cultural research', *Journal of Cross-Cultural Psychology*, **1** (3), 185–215.

Campbell, D.T. and O. Werner (1970), 'Translating, working through interpreters and the problem of decentring', in R. Naroll and R. Cohen (eds), *A Handbook of Method in Cultural Anthropology*, New York: The Natural History Press, pp. 398–420.

Charles, M. and R. Marschan-Piekkari (2002), 'Language training for enhanced horizontal communication: a challenge for MNCs', *Business Communication Quarterly*, **65** (2), 9–29.

Economist, The (2002), 'We want to talk proper', 7 December, 57.

Fawcett, B. and J. Hearn (2004), 'Researching others: epistemology, experience, standpoints and participation', *International Journal of Social Research Methodology*, **7**, forthcoming.

Gubrium, J.F. and J.A. Holstein (2002), *Handbook of Interview Research: Context and Method*, Thousand Oaks, CA: Sage.

Harzing, A.-W., M. Maznevski, I.F. Yaconi, C.L. Wittenberg, K.B. Myloni, J.C.K. Low, F.B. Castro, L. Zander and A. Feely (2002), 'The interaction between language and culture: a test of the cultural accommodation hypothesis in seven countries', *Language and Intercultural Communication*, **2**, 1–20.

Hatim, B. (1990), *Discourse and the Translator*, London: Longman.

Hearn, J. and W. Parkin (1995), *'Sex' at 'Work'*, New York: St. Martin's Press.

Holstein, J.A. and J.F. Gubrium (1997), 'Active interviewing', in D. Silverman (ed.), *Qualitative Research*, Thousand Oaks, CA, Sage, pp. 113–29.

Laine-Sveiby, K. (1991), 'Företag i kulturmöten: tre finländska företag och deras svenska dotterbolag – en ethnologisk studie', PhD thesis, Stockholm: Akademitryck AB, University of Stockholm.

Marschan, R. (1996), 'New structural forms and inter-unit communication in multinationals: the case of Kone Elevators', PhD thesis, Helsinki: Helsinki School of Economics Press.

Marschan-Piekkari, R., D. Welch and L. Welch (1999), 'In the shadow: the impact of language on structure, power and communication in the multinational', *International Business Review*, **8**, 421–40.

Martin, P. and D. Collinson (2002), 'Over the pond and across the water: developing the field of 'gendered organizations', *Gender, Work and Organization*, **9** (3), 244–65.

Odendahl, T. and A.M. Shaw (2002), 'Interviewing elites', in J.F. Gubrium and J.A. Holstein (eds), *Handbook of Interview Research: Context and Method*, Thousand Oaks, CA: Sage, pp. 299–316.

Patton, M.Q. (1990), *Qualitative Evaluation and Research Methods*, Newbury Park, CA: Sage.

Punnett, B.J. and O. Shenkar (1994), 'International management research: toward a contingency approach', in S.B. Prasad (ed.), *Advances in International Comparative Management*, **9**, Greenwich, CT: JAI Press, pp. 39–55.

Reis, C. (2002), 'The private and public lives of men managers in a European multinational company: a feminist cross-cultural analysis of England, Germany and Portugal', PhD thesis, London: University of London.

Ryen, A. (2002), 'Cross-cultural interviewing', in J.F. Gubrium and J.A. Holstein (eds), *Handbook of Interview Research: Context and Method*, Thousand Oaks, CA: Sage, pp. 335–53.

Steyaert, C. and M. Janssens (1997), 'Language and translation in an international business context: beyond an instrumental approach', *Target*, **9** (1), 131–54.

Usunier, J.-C. (1998), *International and Cross-Cultural Management Research*, London: Sage.

Welch, C., R. Marschan-Piekkari, H. Penttinen and M. Tahvanainen (2002), 'Corporate elites as informants in qualitative international business research', *International Business Review*, **11** (5), 611–28.

Welch, D., L. Welch and R. Marschan-Piekkari (2001), 'The persistent impact of language on global operations', *Prometheus*, **19** (3), 193–209.

Wright, L.L. (1996), 'Qualitative international management research', in B.J. Punnett and O. Shenkar (eds), *Handbook for International Management Research*, Cambridge, MA: Blackwell, pp. 63–81.

Wright, L.L., W.L. Henry and P.W. Beamish (1988), 'International management research: lessons from the field', *International Studies of Management and Organization*, **18** (3), 55–71.

Yoshihara, H. (2001), 'Global operations managed by Japanese and in Japanese', in J.H. Taggart, M. Berry and M. McDermott (eds), *Multinationals in a New Era*, Chippenham: Palgrave, pp.153–77.

Zaheer, S. (1995), 'Overcoming the liability of foreignness', *Academy of Management Journal*, **18**, 439–64.

12. Interviewing in the Multinational Corporation: Challenges of the Organisational Context

Rebecca Marschan-Piekkari, Catherine Welch, Heli Penttinen and Marja Tahvanainen

INTRODUCTION

It is widely acknowledged that qualitative research is well suited to capturing contextual factors. In fact, qualitative research is so closely associated with the study of phenomena in their 'natural setting' or 'local context' that this is regarded as one of the key distinctions between qualitative and quantitative research (for example, Dubois and Gadde 2002; Lincoln and Guba 1985; Miles and Huberman 1994; Yin 1994). To conduct qualitative research therefore entails coming to terms with context.

Doing 'in-context' research presents both theoretical and methodological challenges. The former involves the researcher incorporating contextual processes and phenomena into theoretical explanations. The latter concerns adapting to and recognising the impact of context on the research process itself. These methodological implications of context form the focus of our chapter. The effect of context is, we argue, far from a peripheral issue, and raises fundamental validity and reliability concerns. The dynamic relationship between research and the context in which it is being conducted is an important consideration for both methodological 'credibility' and theory development.

It could be said that in the field of international business (IB), context is usually equated with the cultural or national environment. The effects of variations in national culture on research design, instruments and analysis have generated a long tradition of methodological debate, with notable contributions from Adler (1984), Roberts (1970), Redding (1994) and Schaffer and Riordan (2003). However, in this chapter we explore another type of context that we argue also has a considerable impact on the research process, namely the organisational context of research. Much (although by no means all) IB research is conducted in and on a specific type of organisation – the multinational corporation (MNC) – yet the constraints and possibilities posed by such an organisation are seldom aired. We are therefore seeking to understand how the unique features of the MNC as a research site affect the stages of the research 'cycle' and where appropriate, compare it with small and medium-sized enterprises (SMEs). We recognise that the implications of organisational context are important for both qualitative and quantitative researchers, but we concentrate on the qualitative IB researcher and the in-depth research interview, since there are likely to be variations in how context affects different research methods.

Thus, the purpose of this chapter is to problematise the organisational context of the research interview in IB. We first explain the different dimensions of context, including organisational context. Given this organisational focus, we briefly review existing literature on qualitative approaches to organisational and management research. Our review suggests that while organisational research generally is becoming more sensitive to the need for contextualisation, this has not been reflected in discussions on using qualitative methods for organisational research. We then consider the specific organisational context of the MNC. Drawing on research into the MNC, we pinpoint the unique characteristics of this type of organisation and show how they may impact on the process of collecting and analysing interview data. Drawing on our own field experiences, we show how the MNC has methodological as well as theoretical implications, and seek to make a case for the contextualisation of IB research. We also provide recommendations on how to contextualise IB research.

WHAT IS CONTEXT?

Context has been specified as 'the surroundings associated with phenomena which help to illustrate that [sic] phenomena' (Cappelli and Sherer 1991, p. 56), often at a different level of analysis than the focus of the study (see also Johns 2001). Researchers, however, need to consider the context of the research process, not just the context of the phenomenon they are studying. We would therefore go further, and define context as both the environment of the phenomenon under study and the setting within which research is conducted. Our conceptualisation of context therefore explicitly includes the contextualisation of the research process, not just the object being researched. Context is a rather broad concept, so attempts have been made to delineate its meaning more clearly. One potential source of confusion is that context is a relative term, since the context of a phenomenon depends on the unit of analysis under study: in one study, if the unit of analysis is the individual, the organisation may form the context; while in another case, the external environment may constitute the context of the organisation being studied. As well as the unit of analysis, other factors come into play. Johns (2001) distinguishes between methodological and substantive context: substantive context being derived from the organisational conditions and constraints that affect the research process; while the methodological context concerns the conditions associated with the particular research method selected. Rousseau and Fried (2001) make a somewhat different distinction, analysing geographic, temporal and cultural dimensions of context.

In order to clarify the concept of context, it might be useful to consider context as four interdependent levels: individual context, interview context, organisational context and external context (see Figure 12.1). The individual context refers to the context of both the interviewer and interviewee in terms of external influences such as professional culture and education, social networks, organisational affiliation and countries in which the individual has lived or worked. The degree to which the individual context of the interviewer differs from that of the interviewee plays a role in the dynamics of the interview. Self-reflexivity on the part of the researcher is needed to increase the awareness of how such individual factors can subtly affect interview data (Prasad 2002; see also Michailova, Chapter 18 this volume).

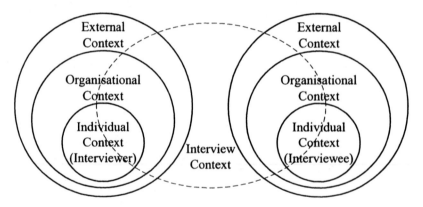

Figure 12.1   Four contextual levels of the research interview in IB

The interview context consists of situational factors such as the mood the interviewee/er is in, the setting in which the interview takes place, the time pressures on the interviewee, the number of interruptions and so on. In the course of the interview, the interviewer and interviewee generate a shared context for the exchange of experiences, ideas and meaning. This 'intersubjective' character of interviews has been noted by Kvale (1996), and distinguishes the interview from other research methods. Moreover, the interview context is very much contingent on the time and space in which it occurs. For example, an interviewer who conducts repeat interviews at different points in time with the same informant may have a very different experience on each occasion. Considerations of space, or the physical location in which the interview is conducted, are equally significant. Typically, the interview is conducted at the premises of the informant, thus requiring the researcher to adapt to, even blend in with, the office environment. However, the interviewer and interviewee may not always be located in the same physical space, particularly in view of the availability of modern communications that create 'virtual' interview spaces.

The type of organisation under study – its size, structure, strategy, culture, history and so on – forms the organisational context of the interview, although it is also affected by the researcher's organisational context, that is, the academic institution. The organisational context also includes units and divisions of the organisation, such as a functional or product division. Even if the research question under study is not directly related to one of these organisational characteristics, researchers are likely to find that they shape the research process. Pettigrew (1985) dubs this the 'inner context', to distinguish it from the 'outer', or external, context. The external context encompasses the (supra-)national cultural, political, economic and industry/competitive environments in which organisations are embedded. Pettigrew (1985, p. 243) strongly argues that organisational theory that does not account for the external context is likely to end up as nothing more than 'misdirected' and 'impotent managerialism'. In addition, it is important that researchers consider the impact of the external environment on each stage of the research process, in order to avoid false assumptions of universalism. Figure 12.1 depicts the dual external contexts that are a feature of the IB interview.

In the case of IB, the influence of national context has been widely analysed, with cross-cultural and comparative management research paying particular attention to the research implications of operating in different national environments (for example, Punnett and Shenkar 1994). For example, Michailova (Chapter 18 this volume) and Eckhardt (Chapter 20 this volume) address the degree to which research designs need to be adapted or even changed in order to conduct trustworthy and credible qualitative research outside the developed world. They argue that the research findings cannot be separated from the context in which data collection and analysis take place (see also Devereux and Hoddinott 1993).

While it is the organisational context that is the focus of our chapter, the four contextual levels are closely interwoven and influence one another. The way in which these levels simultaneously interact to affect the interview therefore needs to be taken into consideration. Just as organisational researchers are increasingly advocating a 'multi-level' or 'meso' approach to theory (for example, Goodman 2000), so too is there scope to consider the different but simultaneous effects of different contextual levels on the process of interviewing.

While the focus of this section has been on the theoretical and methodological implications of context, it should also be noted that contextualisation is affected by the ontological and epistemological stance adopted by the researcher. While a purely objective science holds that research objects can and must be 'abstracted from their context' in order to be accurately measured (Morgan and Smircich 1980), more subjective approaches are likely to adopt the position that the meaning of a phenomenon cannot be understood in isolation from the social processes through which that meaning is constructed and enacted. 'Contextualism' has in fact been identified as a distinct research paradigm, with Morgan and Smircich placing it mid-way in the continuum between objective and subjective approaches to the social sciences. The hallmark of contextualism is a holistic ontology, based on the assumptions that reality is inherently situational and that a research object cannot be divorced from its 'wider background' (Morgan and Smircich 1980, p. 496; see also Pettigrew 1985). However, even if researchers do not adopt a contextualist approach, they inevitably make decisions about contextualisation on the basis of their (often implicit) assumptions about the nature of social reality and knowledge production.

CONTEXT IN ORGANISATIONAL RESEARCH

Since our concern in this chapter is the organisational context of the IB interview, we turn now to research on organisations. Organisational research in general has been criticised for failing to explicitly incorporate contextual factors (for example, Pettigrew 1985). The lack of detail provided in journal publications about the organisations under study means that only a 'small tip of a large iceberg of obscurity' concerning research sites is revealed (Johns 2001, p. 36). One possible reason for this lack of attention to context lies in the perception that 'context-free' research is more generalisable and therefore more scientific (Blair and Hunt 1986; Pettigrew 1985; Rousseau and Fried 2001). Another reason may be found in the influence on organisational behaviour (OB) of psychology, which focuses on individual cognition and behaviour at the expense of factors external to the individual (Cappelli and Sherer 1991). A third reason has been put forward by Rousseau and Fried (2001), who point out that contextual factors are very often taken for granted and their influence overlooked. Taken-for-grantedness can in fact occur on the part of both the interviewer, who often does not consider organisational influences on the findings, and the interviewee, whose accounts often personalise events and exclude organisational effects.

There is, however, a growing recognition among organisational theorists that context needs to be taken into consideration, both in conceptual as well as methodological terms (Rousseau and Fried 2001). Decontextualised research is in danger of oversimplification and even misinterpretation. Contextualised research, by contrast, has the advantage of linking individual behaviour to situational factors, incorporating multiple levels of analysis, and producing more robust explanations and models of organisational behaviour (Johns 2001; Rousseau and Fried 2001). In addition, it has the potential to increase the managerial relevance of research findings (Johns 2001; Pettigrew 1985). Cassell and Symon (1994, p. 5) go further to argue that context is especially 'paramount' to research on organisations, since to study an organisation is to study one type of context for human behaviour and endeavour: 'the field itself is defined by the context of organisational life'.

Just as organisational theory has traditionally been 'context-poor', so too is the debate on the application of qualitative methods to organisational research. Discussion of qualitative research methods in organisational and management research was galvanised by a special issue of *Administrative Science Quarterly*, edited by John van Maanen in 1979. Since this time, numerous books on the topic of qualitative methods for organisational research have been published (for example, Cassell and Symon 1994; Gummesson 1991; Lee 1999; Symon and Cassell 1998). Many such texts (for example, Cassell and Symon 1994; Symon and Cassell 1998) take a very broad approach to the topic. Cassell and Symon (1994, p. 11) acknowledge that 'issues' may 'arise' from the work context which researchers are studying, but do not elaborate on what these issues are. Their book provides a general introduction to various qualitative research methods rather than seeking to problematise the organisational context in which research is being conducted. One exception to this very general approach is Gummesson (1991), who displays a lively recognition of the challenges that are faced when trying to treat organisations as research sites.

More recently, postmodern, critical and interpretive approaches to organisational and management research have provided new perspectives on the research process itself. One example of how new theoretical developments can spark a rethinking of methodological practices is the 'critical' research of Alvesson and Deetz (2000). The methodological implications of this approach are that 'local grounding' of research is essential to achieve critical awareness (p. 126). Organisational researchers need to be aware of, and take into account, the historical situatedness of the organisation. Organisations are imprinted by their historical, cultural and economic contexts. They are also sites of power and ideology. In order to undertake critical research, researchers need to be sensitive towards the political interests of informants, and of discourses of power that will be reflected in the responses they hear from organisational members. While researchers need to have a thorough understanding of the organisational context, at the same time they also need to maintain a critical distance from their object of study. The 'hostage syndrome' (Macdonald and Hellgren, Chapter 13 this volume) and the trap of 'going native' (Chapman et al., Chapter 14 this volume) have been identified as potential dangers of getting too close to the organisation under study.

Despite these recent trends, the literature on doing research in organisations is still largely silent on the question of how different organisational types affect the research process. One way to differentiate among organisations is by industry or sector (Blair and Hunt 1986), or between domestic and international companies. Accordingly, we now turn to the MNC, to understand how this organisational type may impact on the process of collecting and analysing interview data.

THE MNC AS AN ORGANISATIONAL CONTEXT

The criticisms made about the decontextualised nature of the literature on organisational research methods in general could also be applied to IB research in particular. Because much IB research is conducted in a distinctive type of organisation, namely the MNC, we suggest that this organisational context poses some unique challenges for the researchers studying them. It can be argued that the international dimension of IB research, and the spanning of national borders, makes contextualisation both more complex and more critical.

Empirical research from the 1980s onwards has shed light on many facets of the MNC, and highlighted the distinctiveness of this type of organisation. In this section, our aim is not to provide a comprehensive overview of the literature on MNCs, but rather to identify the unique aspects of this particular form of organisation, and show how changing theoretical conceptualisations of MNCs also have implications for how the MNC is researched. The most obvious difference between MNCs and domestic organisations is the MNC's operations are by definition geographically scattered. The ways in which MNCs coordinate and integrate their far-flung units are an enduring theme of MNC research.

In the early stages of researching the MNC, much of the discussion concerning integration within the MNC was viewed through the lens of headquarters–subsidiary relationships. Particularly in Europe, subsidiaries were very autonomous and connected to headquarters through one-way vertical flows. In recent years, research on headquarters–subsidiary relationships has been complemented by an increasing number of studies into subsidiaries as the unit of analysis (Birkinshaw and Hood 1998; Holm and

Pedersen 2000). In this stream of research, there has been a tendency to deconstruct the headquarters–subsidiary dyad and depict the MNC as a multi-centred organisation (Forsgren 1990). Consequently, the concept of integration has expanded to encompass direct horizontal flows between subsidiary units. In addition to internal linkages, research on knowledge and communication flows within the MNC has also included external relationships (that is, with customers, suppliers, government authorities and so on) in the analysis of the degree of integration within the MNC (for example, Andersson et al. 2001). An underlying, dominant conceptualisation of the MNC here is the global standardisation–national responsiveness grid by Doz and Prahalad (1987). Thus, an emerging picture when reviewing MNC literature is that of a networked organisation embedded in different national environments. Far-flung subsidiaries occupy various roles and responsibilities within the MNC, which has resulted in the need to tailor, for example, control and coordination mechanisms to meet the requirements stemming from each subsidiary's specific situation (Gupta and Govindarajan 1991). Over time, the unit of analysis has changed from the headquarters–subsidiary relationship to the subsidiary and the individuals inside them. Compared to OB, where research has been criticised for its neglect of levels of analysis beyond the individual (Cappelli and Sherer 1991), IB as a field has followed a different path. The individual as a central unit of analysis has been rediscovered fairly recently for better understanding, for instance, of the creation of social capital in MNCs (Kostova and Roth 2002).

While the literature on MNCs has multiplied in recent years, the implications of these contexts for the research process have not formed part of the research agenda. We seem to know more about our research object – the MNC – than we do about how to research it.

INTERVIEWING IN THE MNC: ONE COMPANY, MULTIPLE UNITS

In the following, we discuss our own experiences concerning the methodological implications of the MNC context, as well as observations from prior research. We show how characteristics of the MNC, such as its multilocational nature and its degree of integration, have very tangible effects on the interview process.

Negotiating and Renegotiating Access with Multiple Units

As is the case with any organisation, access is a major challenge, and research in organisations is constrained by the fact that it is always done 'by permission' (Buckley and Chapman 1996, p. 239). Access to the MNC can be even more of a challenge, since the researcher is often seeking access to multiple units in different locations, and access to one unit does not guarantee access to all. Yeung (1995) found that a 'top-down' approach, that is, establishing a personal relationship with top executives, facilitated the process of gaining access to subsidiaries. However, researchers gaining access to the organisation in this manner may also risk being seen as a 'headquarter[s] spy' (Welch et al. 2002).

The researcher needs to consider more than just access to the headquarters of the MNC under study. The practical question facing many IB researchers is how to gain access at multiple levels, that is, corporate, subsidiary, horizontal (for example, alliance partners) and the individual informant. For example, in one of our studies, the researcher was given general access to the organisation at a corporate level, but was denied access to particular subsidiary units because of a recent acquisition and closure of a manufacturing facility. It might sometimes be easier to get access to a more distant subsidiary location by escaping the control of headquarters. Thus, sampling becomes a multi-staged process in which the researcher needs to select not just the organisation(s), but also the number and types of units to include.

In order to gain access, researchers require the stamp of organisational legitimacy for their research. Organisational legitimacy can be initially established through a letter signed by a senior manager in the organisational hierarchy – something that, in itself, is not always easy to obtain. The openness of the corporate culture is likely to have a very direct impact on the company's receptiveness to a research project. Some companies have a well-established tradition of involving outside researchers and students in their activities, and welcome new ideas and innovation. Companies in a dynamic and fast-growing environment may be so busy that researchers find it difficult to successfully negotiate access and do not find staff responsive to their questions. On the other hand, companies experiencing a downturn may react with suspicion when approached by a researcher, and react highly sensitively to research findings. Industry conditions may, of course, change rapidly, with a company being open one year but becoming more hostile at a later date. The degree of openness is also affected by national traditions, with Nordic firms typified as having a relatively close association with academic institutions (Björkman and Forsgren 2000).

However, legitimacy cannot be established through a single letter; rather it is a process that needs to be consolidated and reaffirmed throughout the course of the research project. The researcher needs to be able to develop a two-way relationship in which the organisation can be seen to be receiving something in exchange for their time and trust. An article published in an academic journal – the ultimate legitimisation in the researcher's own organisational context – is not likely to be considered to be a sufficient return on the MNC's investment in the research. The relationship a researcher develops will often be a personal one, involving key supporters in the organisation. Access is therefore an ongoing process, and the modern organisation seldom grants the researcher unconditional entry. Rather, the degree of access is something that is renegotiated over time, requiring the researcher to invest considerable time and effort into communicating with key organisational members, tailor the presentation of the expected findings to the specific needs of the organisation, emphasise future implications rather than retrospective analysis, and be prepared to brainstorm key research ideas with organisational members. This trend is accentuated in those situations in which the organisation is directly funding the research being undertaken.

Given the complexity of the large MNC, it would seem obvious that the SME would be a less challenging object for research. The researcher can more easily understand the organisational structure and access decision-makers, many of whom are based in an export or international department in the home country. Given the small number of decision-makers in the company, it is relatively easy to get to know key players on a personal basis, and to be introduced to them, often even on the first visit to the company. Compared to MNCs, smaller companies, particularly with family ownership, tend to have strong organisational memories, due to the continuity of key staff, and have a tradition of 'storytelling' about the company's founding and subsequent development. These oral traditions can provide a rich source of data for research. However, this intimacy can prove to be a barrier, in that SME informants may be more demanding of the researcher. For example, the researcher may be asked to provide unpaid consultancy services to the company, or act as a 'therapist' or counsellor, when interviewing key staff members (Welch et al. 2002).

The complexities of access to the MNC can be illustrated by the following example from our own research. One of us was interested in carrying out a study of a strategic alliance between an MNC and its foreign partner. After successfully negotiating access with the main architect of the alliance, an executive vice president at corporate headquarters, the research proposal was forwarded to a local manager on the ground who was responsible for the relationship with the foreign alliance partner on a daily basis. The local manager, however, found the research topic irrelevant and uninteresting. After several months of negotiations, reassurance and preparation by the researcher, the local manager agreed to collaborate. The confidentiality agreement was about to be signed and the date of the field trip had been set, but access to individual interviewees was still restricted. In addition to interviews with his own staff, the local manager was willing to arrange only one interviewee with a representative of the foreign alliance partner. Through her own networks of contacts, the researcher was able to directly negotiate access with a top manager in the foreign alliance company. The local manager interpreted this as a breach of trust, even though the researcher had openly communicated her intentions. When withdrawing from the research project and cancelling the interviews that had already been set, the local manager explained that he expected the researcher to follow 'the very simple principle of not by-passing him or the case company by contacting the foreign partner directly'. The researcher's 'misconduct' gave the local manager a perfect excuse not to participate in the study. This example illustrates a range of pressures the researcher may face: a clash of views between units of the MNC; the uneasy status of strategic alliances which are both inside and outside the organisation; attempts by (parts of) the organisation to control the study; and the power imbalance between organisational members and the researcher (see Welch et al. 2002).

Collecting Data in Headquarters and Subsidiary Units

Depending on the research question and the history of the organisation, it may be necessary to collect data from multiple units of the MNC, such as corporate/divisional/regional headquarters and foreign subsidiaries, in order to be able to contrast and compare several viewpoints. The history of the organisation's internationalisation path is likely to affect the process of data collection: for example, whether one or all of the company's product divisions have internationalised, or whether the company has established units with regional and not just national responsibilities.

Yeung (1995) criticises research into Asian MNCs for its 'methodological separatism'; in other words, the tendency to study either headquarters or subsidiary units, but not both. Such 'methodological separatism' may obscure an understanding of the complexity of the MNC as a research site. Mezias et al. (1999) advise researchers to include multiple units in the research design, as headquarters cannot be assumed to be the ultimate source of truth about organisational developments. In fact, headquarters staff may be ignorant or mistaken about the 'reality on the ground', an observation also supported by Holm et al.'s (1995) study. This may require researchers to triangulate the responses from headquarters with, for example, subsidiary views. The very multilocational character of the MNC leads us to suggest a new type of triangulation, that is, 'unit triangulation', in addition to the established ones such as data triangulation, method triangulation and investigator triangulation (Denzin 1989; Patton 1990).

Potentially, the number of units included in a study might be affected by the degree of integration of the MNC itself. In tightly integrated MNCs, subsidiary behaviours might be expected to be fairly uniform and from this viewpoint more predictable. This may mean that the researcher encounters less variation than in decentralised, less integrated MNCs where foreign subsidiaries are likely to act in highly autonomous and diverse ways. For example, when one of us was interviewing a Finnish-owned subsidiary in Australia, it became clear that subsidiary staff saw their unit as being 'at the end of the tail of the dog'; in other words, so far removed from the European core of the company's operations that this isolation gave them more freedom from corporate directives than subsidiaries in Europe. Its geographical location, accompanied by the then fairly decentralised management approach, resulted in a low level of integration. From the researcher's perspective, it became important to understand the particular contextual factors of the Australian subsidiary to better explain and interpret the research findings.

When headquarters as well as foreign subsidiaries are both included in the research design, thus avoiding methodological separatism (Yeung 1995), the researcher may be more exposed to involvement in internal power plays of the organisation. The recent trend towards regional management responsibilities adds another dimension to the balance of power within the MNC. During the course of the research, the researcher may be used as a 'channel' or 'conduit' to influence headquarters or subsidiary management (Laine-Sveiby 1991). This may have the result of complicating the feedback process, with different parts of the organisation attempting to use research findings for internal political purposes. It may reduce the researcher's independence and result in parts of the organisation attempting to influence findings. This is particularly evident where the researcher is seeking to make recommendations for future company action and is likely to take a side in internal divisions over future developments.

During the course of the study, foreign units may have a different perception of the researcher to that held by headquarters. If the researcher is from the same country as company headquarters, he/she may be perceived as more important and powerful by the foreign units than tends to be the case in the home operations. Personnel in the foreign unit(s) may even react eagerly to the opportunity of channelling information via the researcher back to headquarters. As a visitor or guest to the foreign unit, the researcher may also be received with 'VIP' treatment, being taken to lunch or dinner, given an office during his/her stay, and having various practicalities organised by the 'hosts'. Since foreign units are also typically smaller than domestic operations, the researcher's visit is often well broadcast through informal channels so the researcher becomes known quite quickly, and often has the chance to schedule additional interviews and discussions. This may result in the researcher gaining very different sorts of data sets in subsidiaries than at headquarters, making the two difficult to compare.

Given that a company may have multiple divisions and many geographical units, generalising about the company as a whole becomes very difficult. In writing up findings, the researcher may take characteristics from a particular part of the organisation to reflect the rest of the company. We have ourselves committed the fallacy of referring to our case companies as 'Kone' or 'Nokia' without reflecting that in fact our data have been collected from only a limited number of units or divisions. Generalising from several subsidiaries to the entire organisation involves, however, similar challenges as generalising from one organisation to many.

Qualitative research projects in particular are likely to involve a lengthy period of time, during which extensive organisational transformations in headquarters–subsidiary and inter-subsidiary relationships may occur. When tracing, for example, evolutionary patterns of MNC subsidiaries over time (see, for example, Birkinshaw and Hood 1998), research findings may need to be altered or reinterpreted, and access restricted. Dubois and Gadde (2002) report that when a company they were studying changed its strategy, they as researchers were forced to reorient their study both in terms of focus and phenomenon under study. For example, in one of our studies, a fraud was discovered within a subsidiary unit that one of us had visited only months before the fraud was publicly exposed. This episode raised new questions for research, cast doubt on existing findings and obviously strained the relationship between the subsidiary under study and headquarters. It also complicated communication between the researcher and the contact person at headquarters.

Locating Appropriate Interviewees in MNCs

Locating the right informants for a particular research question can be difficult in any organisation, but even more so for an MNC with multiple centres. For example, a particular function of the organisation, such as marketing, may be controlled by a subsidiary with global or regional responsibilities. Depending on the research question, the best informants about the activities within the organisation may sometimes be found outside the organisation itself. These informants can be industry consultants, customers, suppliers, competitors, alliance partners and government officials. The importance of outsiders may be accentuated firstly by the increasingly blurred boundaries of the organisation due to the wide range of collaborative relationships that MNCs forge during their internationalisation. Second, rapid turnover of staff means that former employees of the organisation may be a rich source of data. However, compared to existing MNC employees they can be harder to identify and locate.

As is the case in any organisation, interviews in the MNC are likely to vary depending on the experience and organisational position held by the interviewee. Access to a clear diagram showing the organisational hierarchy, reporting lines and business units often facilitates locating appropriate informants for the study. However, in some organisations, such as Nokia until recently, the organisational structure is in such flux that the company did not even produce a formal organisational structure. Frequent relocation and even retrenchment of key informants pose additional challenges when trying to keep track of current and potential interviewees.

Welch et al. (2002) make the distinction between 'elite' and 'non-elite' interviewees who can be based in both headquarters as well as subsidiary units. There seems to be a tendency in IB research to focus on elite interviewees. For example, Ghoshal et al. (1994) and Gupta and Govindarajan (1991) conducted case studies drawing primarily on interviews with senior managers in headquarters and subsidiary units. While they incorporated the perspectives of multiple units into the research design, the exclusive focus on senior management may suggest that some rich contextual data was not captured. Senior managers tend to share a transnational elite culture which transcends national and cultural boundaries and, therefore, they are more likely to provide fairly convergent views compared to interviewees at other organisational levels, or even informants outside the MNC (Welch et al. 2002).

One special category of elites in the MNC consists of the expatriate specialist or manager. Expatriates, when compared to other employees, often possess large informal networks spanning different countries and units, and can answer questions from the viewpoint of both headquarters and subsidiary. The value of the expatriate as informant therefore goes beyond research projects on expatriate management or international human resource management. Our experience has been that many expatriates are able, within the course of an interview, to switch from wearing their 'HQ' hat to putting on their 'local' hat. However, it may not be appropriate to assume that an expatriate's perspective coincides with that of, or represents, the local viewpoint. The researcher may come across very divergent views, depending on whether he or she is interviewing an expatriate or local. Consequently, if the researcher is interested in portraying both viewpoints, it is insufficient to interview solely one or the other.

A question related to locating appropriate interviewees is the researcher's and potential interviewees' skills in different interview languages (see Marschan-Piekkari and Reis, Chapter 11 this volume). Despite the fact that MNCs tend to adopt a common corporate language, often English, with the purpose of facilitating internal communication (Marschan-Piekkari et al. 1999), individual interviewees may prefer to operate in another language. There is often a lengthy time lag between the corporate decision to introduce a common language and its widespread adoption by different levels and geographical units within the company (Laine-Sveiby 1991). For example, when one of us was interviewing subsidiary staff in a company that had used English as the corporate language since the early 1970s, she nevertheless found that many staff were uncomfortable using English in the interview situation. This needs to be taken into account when trying to locate appropriate interviewees, particularly below top management level. Moreover, the issue of language shows how multiple levels of context – the organisational, the interview and the personal – are interrelated (see Figure 12.1).

Distance as a Practical Problem

The 'multilocational' nature of the MNC causes practical problems for researchers, who are faced with high travel budgets in order to collect data in a variety of locations. Geographical distance often places limits on the number of locations in which data can be collected. It may also affect other parts of the data collection process: for example, access may be more challenging in a location that is foreign to the researcher and in which he or she does not have any existing contacts (see also Wilson, Chapter 21 this volume). Moreover, secondary data on foreign units may not be as readily available as general information about operations in the home country. The researcher may also need to cope with interview 'overload', having to schedule far too many interviews per day.

The problems in obtaining sufficient funding to support the travel required for overseas interviews often leads researchers to look for alternatives. A common alternative is to form cross-border research teams or consortia. In the European Union (EU), one option is funding under research framework programmes. While such programmes might lead to sufficient funding, other complications arise. Identifying research partners in other EU countries and negotiating the substance of an application is in itself time-consuming. The criteria imposed by the EU often mean establishing new research links with unknown partners who do not share a common history of collaboration. Once the funding has been granted, it can then be a struggle to collaborate with such partners, and establish the necessary level of trust and interpersonal chemistry.

Another practical problem to be found in firms with international operations is that potential informants often spend a large amount of time travelling across borders. The researcher may even arrive in the foreign location just to find out at the outset of the interview that the interviewee has other demands on his/her schedule. The international nature of their activities is the very reason that makes them difficult to access for an interview. For example, one of us finally managed to have an interview with a manager who had spent ten months of that year overseas. The peripatetic lives of many global managers means that interviewers may not be able to access the informants best suited to the study in terms of expertise and role.

RECOMMENDATIONS FOR CONTEXTUALISATION

Our starting point for this chapter was the recognition that qualitative research methods are powerful techniques for gaining in-depth understanding of contextual factors. Consequently, an obvious question to raise here is how to enhance contextualisation in academic publications. This is not just an issue for the individual researcher, but rather is a challenge for the community of IB scholars as a whole, in terms of the generally accepted criteria used for evaluating the quality of IB research contributions.

Rousseau and Fried (2001) advise researchers to provide rich descriptions of the organisation under study, the different research sites and the process of gaining access. Of course, the challenge lies in the brevity of most journal articles which renders this recommendation almost a 'mission impossible'. Already in the planning of the research design, various data collection methods such as direct observation and examination of archival data (Welch 2000) could be included to improve contextual understanding. Researchers should also make an attempt to analyse the direct impact of contextual factors on the research setting. Rousseau and Fried (2001) suggest comparative studies as an effective way of illuminating context.

Given that our research object, the MNC, is such a complex beast, one can speculate whether a sole researcher, based in one location and with limited resources, is capable of capturing its essence. Cross-border research teams are often advocated as a means of capturing different external contexts (for example, Boyacigiller and Adler 1991; Steers et al. 1992; Usunier 1998), and can also be used to span different units of the MNC. Such teams may consist of members from different countries, institutions and disciplines. Consequently, the team members are likely to have distinct mindsets and different epistemological and ontological assumptions, which brings considerable complexity to the simplified model of contextual levels presented in Figure 12.1. It follows that collaborative teams are not a 'quick fix', but rather require a negotiated solution to the potential 'clash' of different contexts.

Time is often recommended as a surrogate of context (Johns 2001; Rousseau and Fried 2001). As researchers, we may not always be aware of the impact of timing on the way in which the research project unfolds and the final outcomes of the study. Not surprisingly, it seems that particularly research on transition economics has captured this aspect of contextualisation in a powerful manner (Michailova, Chapter 18 this volume; Napier et al., Chapter 19 this volume). Contextualisation of research findings should therefore consider this temporal dimension.

Since senior managers tend to label much of the information they provide to academic researchers as 'confidential', it can be difficult to publish research findings under the company name. Needless to say, naming the organisation is likely to provide the reader with a considerable amount of contextual data necessary for interpreting the study in an appropriate way. The researcher may therefore need to be careful in balancing the need for anonymity with that for contextualisation.

CONCLUSIONS

This chapter has taken as its theme the interrelationship between the MNC as a research site and the process of interviewing. In IB research, context is often equated with national environments and we seem to know relatively little about the influence of the organisational context on the research process. In this chapter, we identified the unique aspects of the multinational corporation and suggested their implications for how the MNC has been and can be researched. In light of recent theoretical conceptualisations, we portrayed the MNC as a differentiated network with blurred boundaries and multiple units embedded in various national environments. Accordingly, we argued that important characteristics of the MNC to consider when conducting research include its multiple locations, the relationship between different units and degree of integration, organisational hierarchy, internationalisation process, corporate language and role of expatriates. We also provided recommendations on how to contextualise IB research.

Organisational context is often experienced by researchers as a direct, pragmatic concern, particularly at the stages of gaining access to the organisation and obtaining permission for the publication of a study's results. However, we have argued that the implications of the organisational context are much wider. The nature of the MNC affects sampling (for example, the number of units to be included, and whether both local and expatriate managers should be interviewed); data collection (in particular, how the researcher manages the potential clash of contexts between interviewer and interviewee); and data interpretation and analysis (crucially, the transferability and generalisability of findings across MNC units). Even the research topic and questions may be the result of a compromise between the researcher and the key contact person and an outcome of a lengthy process of negotiation and renegotiation. Moreover, the very concept of reliability becomes problematic once the context-bound nature of the interview is considered. Given that contextual factors are unlikely to remain constant, strict replication of a study is impossible: for example, a researcher from the same country as MNC headquarters may obtain different data and conclusions from interviews in a foreign subsidiary than a researcher from a third country. While some have responded to this dilemma by arguing that traditional concepts of reliability are not applicable to qualitative research, others argue that reliability can be addressed by the researcher carefully and reflexively considering relevant contextual factors when reporting the results of a study (see, for example, Seale 1999). However, practices of 'reflexive accounting' and reporting sit uneasily with the traditions of decontextualised research that arguably are still the dominant approach in IB.

The MNC is an organisational form experiencing rapid change, and it may well be that researching the MNC is becoming more challenging. Not only is the organisational context becoming increasingly complex, but so too is the external environment in which the organisation operates. MNCs are increasingly coming under pressure and scrutiny from global capital markets, thus compelling them to seek concrete payoffs and performance requirements from researchers. The traditionally long timeframe for academic research does not sit comfortably with the immediate results-driven management outlook dominating many MNCs today. Another external change relates to new national laws concerning intellectual property rights, which traditionally were settled between the organisations and academic institutions involved in the research project, often on a case-by-case basis. In this very dynamic environment, the influence of context can therefore hardly be overstated.

ACKNOWLEDGEMENTS

The thoughtful comments by Jeff Hearn are gratefully acknowledged. The authors also wish to thank audiences at the Swedish School of Economics and Business Administration for their suggestions, as well as participants at the European Academy of Management Conference in Milan (2003), where an earlier version of this chapter was presented.

REFERENCES

Adler, N. (1984), 'Understanding the ways of understanding: cross-cultural management methodology reviewed', *Advances in International Comparative Management*, **1**, 31–67.
Alvesson, M. and S. Deetz (2000), *Doing Critical Management Research*, London: Sage.
Andersson, U., M. Forsgren and U. Holm (2001), 'Subsidiary embeddedness and competence development in MNCs – a multi-level analysis', *Organization Studies*, **22** (6), 1013–34.
Birkinshaw, J. and N. Hood (1998), *Multinational Corporate Evolution and Subsidiary Development*, London: Macmillan.
Björkman, I. and M. Forsgren (2000), 'Nordic international business research: a review of its development', *International Studies of Management and Organization*, **30** (1), 6–26.
Blair, J.D. and J.G. Hunt (1986), 'Getting inside the head of the management

researcher one more time: context-free and context-specific orientations in research', *Journal of Management*, 12 (2), 147–66.

Boyacigiller, N.A. and N.J. Adler (1991), 'The parochial dinosaur: organizational science in a global context', *Academy of Management Review*, 16 (2), 262–90.

Buckley, P.J. and M. Chapman (1996), 'Theory and method in international business research', *International Business Review*, 5 (3), 233–45.

Cappelli, P. and P.D. Sherer (1991), 'The missing role of context in OB: the need for a meso-level approach', *Research in Organizational Behavior*, 13, 55–110.

Cassell, C. and G. Symon (1994), *Qualitative Methods in Organizational Research*, London: Sage.

Denzin, N.K. (1989), *The Research Act: A Theoretical Introduction to Sociological Methods*, 3rd edn, Englewood Cliffs, NJ: Prentice-Hall.

Devereux, J. and J. Hoddinott (1993), 'The context of fieldwork', in J. Devereux and J. Hoddinott (eds), *Fieldwork in Developing Countries*, Boulder, CO: Lynne Rienner, pp. 1–24.

Doz, Y. and C. Prahalad (1987), *The Multinational Mission*, New York: Free Press.

Dubois, A. and L.-E. Gadde (2002), 'Systematic combining: an abductive approach to case research', *Journal of Business Research*, 55, 553–60.

Forsgren, M. (1990), 'Managing the international multi-centre firm: case studies from Sweden', *European Management Journal*, 8 (2), 261–7.

Ghoshal, S., H. Szulanski and G. Korine (1994), 'Inter-unit communication in multinational corporations', *Management Science*, 40 (1), 96–110.

Goodman, P.S. (2000), *Missing Organizational Linkages: Tools for Cross-Level Research*, Thousand Oaks, CA: Sage.

Gummesson, E. (1991), *Qualitative Methods in Management Research*, Newbury Park, CA: Sage, 1991.

Gupta, A. and V. Govindarajan (1991), 'Knowledge flows and the structure of control within multinational corporations', *Academy of Management Review*, 16 (4), 768–92.

Holm, U., J. Johanson and P. Thilenius (1995), 'Headquarter knowledge of subsidiary contexts in the multinational corporation', *International Studies of Management and Organization*, 25 (1–2), 97–119.

Holm, U. and T. Pedersen (2000), *The Emergence and Impact of MNC Centres of Excellence: A Subsidiary Perspective*, London: Macmillan.

Johns, G. (2001), 'In praise of context', *Journal of Organizational Behavior*, 22, 31–42.

Kostova, T. and K. Roth (2002), 'Adoption of an organizational practice by subsidiaries of multinational corporations: institutional and relational effects', *Academy of Management Journal*, 45 (1), 215–33.

Kvale, S. (1996), *InterViews: An Introduction to Qualitative Research Interviewing*, Thousand Oaks, CA: Sage.

Laine-Sveiby, K. (1991), 'Företag i kulturmöten: Tre finländska företag och deras svenska dotterbolag: En etnologisk studie', PhD thesis, Stockholm: University of Stockholm: Akademitryck AB.

Lee, T.W. (1999), *Using Qualitative Methods in Organizational Research*, Thousand Oaks, CA: Sage.

Lincoln, Y.S. and E.G. Guba (1985), *Naturalistic Inquiry*, Beverly Hills, CA: Sage.

Marschan-Piekkari, R., D. Welch and L. Welch (1999), 'Adopting a common corporate language: IHRM implications', *International Journal of Human Resource Management*, **10** (3), 377–90.

Mezias, S.J., Y.-R. Chen and P. Murphy (1999), 'Toto, I don't think we're in Kansas anymore: some footnotes to cross-cultural research', *Journal of Management Inquiry*, **8** (3), 323–33.

Miles, M. and M. Huberman (1994), *Qualitative Data Analysis: An Expanded Sourcebook*, 2nd edn, Beverly Hills, CA: Sage.

Morgan, G. and L. Smircich (1980), 'The case for qualitative research', *Academy of Management Review*, **5** (4), 491–500.

Patton, M.Q. (1990), *Qualitative Evaluation and Research Methods*, 2nd edn, Newbury Park, CA: Sage.

Pettigrew, A. (1985), 'Contextualist research: a natural way to link theory and practice', in E.E. Lawler (ed.), *Doing Research that is Useful for Theory and Practice*, San Francisco, CA: Jossey-Bass, pp. 222–48.

Prasad, A. (2002), 'The contest over meaning: hermeneutics as an interpretive methodology for understanding texts', *Organizational Research Methods*, **5** (1), 12–33.

Punnett, B.J. and O. Shenkar (1994), 'International management research: toward a contingency approach', *Advances in International Comparative Management*, **9**, 39–55.

Redding, G. (1994), 'Comparative management theory: jungle, zoo or fossil bed?', *Organization Studies*, **5** (3), 323–59.

Roberts, K. (1970), 'On looking at an elephant: an evaluation of cross-cultural research related to organisations', *Psychological Bulletin*, **74**, 327–50.

Rousseau, D.M. and Y. Fried (2001), 'Location, location, location: contextualizing organizational research', *Journal of Organizational Behavior*, **22**, 1–13.

Schaffer, B.S. and C.M. Riordan (2003), 'A review of cross-cultural methodologies for organisational research: a best-practices approach', *Organizational Research Methods*, **6** (2), 169–215.

Seale, C. (1999), *The Quality of Qualitative Research*, London: Sage.

Steers, R.M., S.J. Bischoff and L.H. Higgins (1992), 'Cross-cultural management research: the fish and the fisherman', *Journal of Management Inquiry*, **1** (4), 321–30.

Symon, G. and C. Cassell (eds) (1998), *Qualitative Methods and Analysis in Organizational Research: A Practical Guide*, London: Sage.

Usunier, J.-C. (1998), *International and Cross-Cultural Management Research*, London: Sage.

Welch, C. (2000), 'The archaeology of business networks: the use of archival records in case study research', *Journal of Strategic Marketing*, **8** (2), pp. 1–12.

Welch, C., R. Marschan-Piekkari, H. Penttinen and M. Tahvanainen (2002), 'Corporate elites as informants in qualitative international business research', *International Business Review*, **11**, 611–28.

Yeung, H.W. (1995), 'Qualitative personal interviews in international business research: some lessons from a study of Hong Kong transnational corporations', *International Business Review*, **4** (3), 313–39.

Yin, R. (1994), *Case Study Research: Design and Methods*, 2nd edn, Thousand Oaks, CA: Sage.

13. The Interview in International Business Research: Problems We Would Rather Not Talk About

Stuart Macdonald and Bo Hellgren

INTRODUCTION

Despite some appreciation that empirical research is complex, the reasons presented for undertaking it are commonly simple in the extreme. Empirical research is supposed to capture reality (Sciberras 1986). Empirical research, and particularly interviewing, is the 'going and seeing' which both balances and complements the 'sitting and thinking' (Emmet 1991, p. 14). As Pettigrew (1985) has observed, it is naive to see empirical research as merely a technical exercise, a rational response to an obvious research problem. Empirical research is also a social process, a matter which is often neglected by those who teach research techniques (Hyman 1967). We take empirical research to be research based on observation, distinguished from theoretical research by the efforts of the researcher to gather information in and about the world he/she is studying. The interview is a subset of empirical research and entails talking – usually face to face – with those knowledgeable about what is being studied.

Just how essential to business research, and international business research in particular, is the interview? How much does it really contribute? Perhaps its importance lies not in the gathering of information, but in other functions altogether. In particular, we wonder why the difficulties inherent in exploiting information from interviews have not been more widely acknowledged. The chapter explores some of these difficulties, indicates why they might have been overlooked, and offers some suggestions about how they might be overcome. The chapter argues that the greater the researcher's attempts to exploit the wealth of interview data, the greater the problems that arise. We intend drawing heavily on personal experience and that of our colleagues. Italicised quotations throughout the chapter come from interviews with managers, an incestuously improper method in which the interview is recruited to study the interview.

THE RESEARCHER'S HIDDEN AGENDA IN INTERVIEWING

Those who interview are commonly keen to talk to the most senior people in the organisation, and are commonly triumphant when they succeed. In much international business research, top managers are key informants (Welch et al. 2002). Academics explain that the more senior the individual, the more that individual will know about the organisation. But this justification assumes that the organisational hierarchy is also an information hierarchy. It is not. Both experience and theory suggest that top management may not know most about what is going on in the organisation, that middle management is likely to be much better informed, and that junior managers may be most knowledgeable of all on specific matters (Johanson and Mattsson 1988, 1992). In the words of one manager we interviewed, '*I'm Head of TV Sales, but I don't have a direct line management to the executives, and this is what is so wrong. This is what is killing this place over the last four years ... I'm an appendage on the side*'.

It may be that researchers prefer interviewing senior managers because their research is more concerned with the making of decisions than with the operations of the organisation. Or perhaps researchers are less interested in the acquisition of information than in the acquisition of an authority for their findings that would not be bestowed by more junior managers. It is not unknown for management researchers to measure the success of an interview not in terms of the information procured, but rather in terms of the organisational importance of the individual interviewed and the time he/she has spared.

It is always naive to assume that the value of information is unrelated to its source, but in business research value may also be related to the means by which information is acquired. While theoretical information gains in authority the more it has been used – the more second-hand it is – just the opposite seems to hold for empirical information. Value attaches to empirical information not having been disclosed before, to its virginal status, which may be why business studies boasts so few publications that test theory by trying to replicate the empirical findings of others (Hubbard and Lindsay 1995). Just why should empirical information that is second-hand be considered second-rate? It may be that the information is less valued for its meaning than as proof that the researcher knows the organisation and therefore what he/she is talking about? Similarly, desire for credibility might be a partial explanation for the popularity of case studies in international business studies. That they are often thin and meagre representations of reality suggests that the information they reveal about the organisation may be of secondary importance.

When business researchers are not explicit about how many managers they have interviewed, the cynic is tempted to imagine that very few have been disturbed (Kumar et al. 1993). In other cases, researchers are proud to claim that they have interviewed a great many managers:

> In excess of 359 recorded interviews, conducted at all levels of the firm and sector involved over a three-year period, indicate the scale and intensity of the research. (Pettigrew and Whipp 1991, p. 36)

> We interviewed 236 managers in the nine companies, both at their corporate headquarters and in a number of national subsidiaries ... (Bartlett and Ghoshal 1989, p. 217)

These researchers tend to be less explicit about the problems of information overload, problems with which the senior managers they interview are likely to be all too familiar. It cannot be the case that more information is always preferable to less. Diminishing returns must set in somewhere.

Pettigrew (1990) suggests that it is reasonable for a full-time researcher to conduct about 50 in-depth interviews per 'case' and that four to six cases are appropriate over a three-year period. This means between 200 and 300 interviews for each researcher – one or two interviews a week – even in projects in which interviewing is but a small part of the methodology. But time spent interviewing is only the tip of the iceberg; the researcher must prepare to meet his/her manager, must journey to the interview, and must transcribe notes or tapes afterwards. An hour of interview requires about ten hours of transcription. In short, one or two interviews can easily occupy the whole of a working week. And if international communication and travel are involved, the time required obviously increases. Because interviewing is extremely resource-intensive for both the researcher and the organisation (Mintzberg et al. 1976), it is important to appreciate just when returns do begin to diminish. Yet this is not an obvious concern of business researchers: their attitude – perhaps derived from survey methodology – seems to be that the more interviews conducted the better the research (see, for example, Ghoshal and Westney 1991; Marcus 1988; Simsons 1991).

Despite extensive resort to interviews in business studies (and international business is no exception), researchers seem less than comfortable with the methodology (for example, Miller and Friesen 1977). Perhaps this is because business journalists also interview and academics are anxious that their work be seen as more thoughtful and substantial. Academics seem to be much more comfortable relying on theory rather than on interview material to support their arguments. Information from interviews, it would seem, may decorate a paper, but serious scholars are not supposed to rely on such information to support serious argument. So, despite consensus that the interview can provide a wealth of first-hand information about what is really going on in the organisation, there is precious little interest in using this information. This may be because there are constraints on the use of this information, constraints that, serious though they be, are seldom acknowledged. This chapter seeks to make good the deficiency.

ACCESS TO THE ORGANISATION

Interviewing requires access to the organisation being studied. Even where the organisation is not funding the research directly, it is contributing resources in terms of expensive management time, and access may not be granted lightly. In practice, the need for access may make the researcher more subject to organisational constraints than any direct funding. It is possible, of course, to talk to a few individuals within the organisation without official sanction: it is not feasible to interview large numbers of senior managers about the organisation without the organisation's formal approval. A research project with such an interviewing base must be a research project deemed important by organisational criteria. Failure to meet organisational, not academic, criteria means no access and no interviews.

> Academic researchers rarely seek or receive open access to organizations; hence, how can they discover what is really going on? Most of us do not even get a five-minute tour through the executive suite. Instead, we dip our rusty fishing hooks in backwater streams and hope to get a nibble. (Greiner 1985, p. 251)

Yet, some management researchers do gain not only access, but access to the executive suite. How? Pettigrew describes the process as networking, insinuation into an organisation so that access to one individual leads on to access to another:

> [I]n Britain the game that's played is essentially a networking game. They allow access in a small node or corner of the network, and then you get tested out on that node. And if you are deemed acceptable on whatever criteria, then you pass on to the next part of the node and then the next part. (Pettigrew 1985, p. 264)

Our own experiences of interviewing in Sweden and Britain suggest that the process by which access is gained to British companies is much more formal, complex and lengthy than that required to enter Swedish organisations of the same size. In Britain, after having entered the organisation through the executive suite, the researcher has to re-negotiate separate access to each level lower down the organisation. In contrast, once access has been granted by senior management in Sweden, the doors are open at all levels. What, though, are the criteria by which acceptability is judged? It is conceivable (though only just) that managers may find outspoken academics with radical views delightfully refreshing and may welcome them with open arms. However, the academic whose outlook on the world matches that of managers may be more acceptable (see Hultman and Klasson 1994). British managers often seem to be less comfortable than Swedish ones when confronted with a very different view of reality.

Globalisation is making access increasingly difficult to arrange. For example, when the corporate headquarters of a Swedish multinational was transferred from Sweden to London, our research team in Sweden suddenly found itself on the organisational periphery. In negotiating with the new corporate headquarters, our team had to navigate its way past several layers of gatekeepers. When Swedish firms are acquired by, or merged with, foreign corporations, their traditionally open and receptive attitude towards research is likely to change. This may eventually transform the research climate in the Nordic countries, increasing the distance between the academic and the business world. As qualitative methods and interpretive analyses based on interviews and company material have tended to dominate Nordic research on mergers and acquisitions (Hellgren and Schriber 2003), research methods may have to change. There may be fewer longitudinal case studies, which require excellent access and trust, and much more survey-based research.

THE HOSTAGE SYNDROME

If hostages, no matter how badly they are treated, begin to identify with their captors, it is hardly surprising that researchers may identify with the organisation in which they are interviewing. The organisation's interests become the researcher's interests. Most academics have never been in anything but the most minor of management positions: interviewing puts them in direct contact with those responsible for decisions that affect thousands, with those who allocate vast resources, with those who are powerful in another world altogether and who exercise skills utterly different from their own. Moreover, unlike academics, who have only title and reputation to parade their status, senior managers are surrounded by all the structure and trappings of power. Nearly always, these are the surroundings in which interviews take place, the surroundings in which objectivity can easily turn to deference, impartiality to common cause, disinterest to rapture and capture. It is interesting to speculate whether the information garnered from interviews, and the questions asked for that matter, would be very different were interviews conducted in universities. We might also speculate to what extent the cult of the chief executive as hero in the process of organisational change is inspired by researchers experiencing him/her holding court in full regalia (see Hellgren et al. 1993). Would academic deference be quite as marked were chief executives interviewed digging the garden?

Just as hostages, their fate in the hands of their captors, may identify with those who have very different interests, so interviewers may surrender objectivity by aligning themselves with the interests of senior managers in the organisations they are studying (Fletcher 2002). They must continue to please powerful people to retain access. Failure to please may be punished with expulsion. The more interviews the researcher completes in the organisation, the greater his/her investment and the greater his/her desperation to please. We have already considered the relationship between the satisfaction of powerful people in the organisation and gaining access to other powerful people, but on this same satisfaction also depend access to other organisations, and – to some, often considerable, extent – offers of consultancy work and appointments to advisory positions, prospects of further funding, and hopes of academic advancement. The academic may be putting at stake a great deal when he/she sets off interviewing (Nilan 2002). All these considerations are, of course, quite irrelevant to the immediate purpose of the interview, and would certainly be beyond the purview of any text on empirical research, but it is not inconceivable that they may influence the manner in which the interview is conducted. It is also possible that they may influence research findings.

> We have cooperated with you in the past in what we believe has been a constructive relationship but this latest paper is both inaccurate and wholly unacceptable and will undoubtedly destroy that relationship ... (letter from senior manager concerning a draft paper based on interview material, June 1993)

ACADEMIC VERSUS BUSINESS WORLD

Empirical research places researchers within the environment of the organisation. Much can be learned simply by walking into a factory, without necessarily talking to anybody. Interviewing is much more intimate. The more involved researchers become with the environment of the organisations they are studying, the more they risk being enveloped by it. Business culture is radically different from academic culture, although traditionally – as already noted – the Nordic countries have been characterised by a close, almost symbiotic relationship with the business world. The former is hierarchical and tightly structured, especially in large organisations: the latter – at least traditionally – is just about the opposite and especially in research, where the findings of the famous may be challenged publicly by the unknown. For the academic researcher, peer review and membership of a community of scholars are important. Senior managers do not always appreciate this importance: '*They tell me you academics write two or three papers a year.*

How many thousand words is that? I must write that much in a week'.

Researchers may find themselves forced to defend their values, to preserve their culture, in a hostile environment. This can be difficult: it is hard to question closely a manager who is not accustomed to being questioned at all. For example, in our interviews with top managers on cross-border mergers and acquisitions, we found it difficult to go beyond the publicly legitimate view of the deal created by media. We were surprised to find how unanimous top managers were despite the fact that they represented different organisations in two different countries. We would argue that the public media creates an official view of the merger and the negotiation process which top managers are likely to accept. Obviously, it is much easier for the researcher simply to accept what is said, to accede to the culture of the organisation, to go native. It is easier still, and much more conducive to reaping the benefits that flow from the satisfaction of those interviewed, to ask the questions managers wish to answer, and to ask them in ways managers will find immediately acceptable. Thus, for example, a question on the role the manager has played in corporate success is much more acceptable than a question about his/her role in corporate failure (see Major and Zucker 1989). It matters not that there may be more to learn from failure than from success; business studies produce a great many accounts of corporate success and remarkably few accounts of corporate failure:

> *I'm now trying to re-establish myself here. It's amazing because if you are unsuccessful at something, people just forget all your successes in what you have done beforehand. I learnt a lot from that. Not a very nice experience ... Lesley used to work for me at one time, and now – see what I mean, how things change when you go to a disaster job.*

In the wake of the dot.com, Enron, Marconi and many other corporate catastrophes, questions are being asked about managerial competence and especially about rewards for failure. A chasm has opened between popular understanding and managerial perceptions of failure. If the chasm is ever to be closed, those who try to understand managers will have to rely less on what they have to say about themselves, and for themselves.

MAKING SENSE OF INTERVIEW DATA

Interviews yield so much, and such diverse, information that even simple aggregation presents problems. Contradictory information is often the rule rather than the exception (Myrdal 1970). Consider a single sentence from one senior manager, interspersed with comments (in italics) from other senior managers in the same organisation:

[T]he non-executive directors recognised that there was the need for another leader to come and cause change to happen in [the company] ...

That's why he was brought in; he was brought in by the non-executive directors of [the company] to make a radical change, but this is definitely not for attribution.

... and one of the great things that [the new CEO] has brought to [the company] is not only the creation of the mission statement ...

Our strategy mission statement here is motherhood.

... but the rigidity with which we have applied it to our businesses since.

Does there have to be synergy? ... I know that the main board have often thought of becoming a holding company ... I mean that might bring into question then [the CEO's] quest for [the sort of] company that since I have known him he has started to say less about looking for. He has just expressed frustration that it didn't happen.

The survey approach – where '77 per cent of managers think that ...' – overcomes the problem of aggregating, but at the unacceptable cost of masking the variety and individuality of interpretation that interviews reveal. The same survey approach to interviewing seems to suggest that interviews will produce better information if they are as structured as possible, if interviewing is made to resemble a laboratory experiment. This seems to ignore two factors: that the interview demands a personal and individual relationship between interviewer and interviewee, and that interviewees resent being used as guinea pigs. Despite the ingenuity underlying recommended interviewing techniques (for example, Brewer 2002), interviewing is not a scientific process, and trying to make it one is probably a mistake (Cawthorne 2001; compare Partington 2000). Indeed, interviewing is probably the most irrefutable reminder of all that research in the social sciences is inevitably value-laden.

Managers often choose to confide in the interviewer, but then insist that their most interesting information not be used: '*I think at the present time it's the Minister that opposes it. As I understand (and I hope you fillet out this part), he is extremely paranoid about it*'. Sometimes matters about which managers feel most strongly, matters that may be important to academic argument, are expressed with an emotion that is difficult to capture in the prose of academic publication, and that is quite unsuitable for quotation:

[The parent company] can go to bloody hell. They make zilch contribution here ... I look upon [the parent company] as a bank. It provides no more than finance.

Managerially and in social terms, [the manager] was a buffoon. He's got no political savvy at all, and has behaved in a way which is frequently very insensitive to the rest of his colleagues.

I have the impression that [the company] feels – quite rightly – that it has to manage change, it has to become much more cost effective. And the senior management – many of whom I know, we go back a long way – who are doing this are people who have never in their lives so much as run a corner shop.

I'm fascinated by someone who is so incompetent, as far as I can see, in understanding any kind of management theory, and doesn't seem to have any insight into where this business is going, but can nevertheless manage to make money in private industry. If anything has convinced me that it must be a bloody pushover out there, it's watching [the manager] in action.

Quotation is excellent for capturing the nuances and subtleties of a situation, but these may be lost when the quotation is translated into another language. One of us is supervising a Swedish doctoral thesis on the mergers and acquisitions in China of a large Swedish corporation. The Swedish student speaks Chinese and is competent to conduct interviews in Chinese. However, the student must translate the interviews into Swedish in order to communicate with her supervisor and then into English for her thesis. It seems unlikely that the richness of quotation can survive multiple translation, yet this problem is rarely raised (see Marschan-Piekkari and Reis, Chapter 11 this volume).

As has already been noted, interviewing is almost guaranteed to provide a mass of detail, but using this detail in the presentation of findings creates problems for the academic. Detail is messy; often confusing and contradictory – not characteristics that editors generally welcome in the papers they publish:

It is a collection of thoughts and public statements made by executives in various firms ... I do not see a systematic thought emerging from this collection of statements (which is considered as empirical evidence by the authors – I don't think that is a correct claim). (referee's comment on paper based on interviews)

I still have doubts about the included quotes. Can we learn anything from such anecdotes? How do we know that these quotes are representative or were merely selected to fit the points that the author wants to make? (referee's comment on paper based on interviews)

Similarly, business school students are taught about organisations through rendering the chaos and confusion of reality neat and ordered (Mangham 1990), and business studies – desperate to be science rather than art – searches for laws to explain the behaviour and characteristics of the organisation when both are inherently unruly (Numagami 1998). Consider the following sterile attempt to squeeze all irregularity from the study of organisation; there is clearly no role here for information from interviews:

> Beckhard defines five phases in the organizational development process: diagnosis, strategy planning, education, consulting and training, and evaluation. In their more general model of the planned change process, Lippitt, Watson, and Westley also define five phases: development of a need for change, establishment of a change relationship, working toward change, generalization and stabilization of change, and achieving a terminal relationship. Lawrence and Lorsch see four stages: diagnosis, planning action, implementing action, and evaluation. Schein's approach to process consulting has seven stages: initial contact with the client, defining the relationship, selecting a setting and a method of work, data gathering and diagnosis, intervention, reducing involvement, and termination. In the consultation model presented below, we have incorporated the major points in these models ... (Kolb and Frohman 1970, p. 52)

In practice, then, there are powerful pressures to deny the complexity of reality that interviews can reveal. It may be enough that the interviewer has been exposed to this reality without having to wallow in it. Researchers may even perceive a public duty to protect their audience from similar exposure: 'It is from this mix of opinion and fact, of detailed descriptions and broad impressions, that we have developed our conclusions ... Our hundreds of pages of interview notes are full of stories, anecdotes and quotes' (Goold and Campbell 1987, p. 7).

The interview is far from being the only means available to the empirical researcher of gaining information about the organisation. Much information may be in the public domain and may be obtained without the consent of the organisation's managers. For instance, there are the organisation's own publications, unpublished archives in public collections, articles in the media, academic publications directly concerned with the organisation (such as case studies), publications from other organisations (such as government departments and trade associations), and a whole host of peripheral publications (such as business and trade magazines) (see Hellgren et al. 2002 for a study based on media texts).

The researcher encounters major problems integrating information gained from interviews with this other information. Among these is the problem of reconciling the manager's view of reality with other views, particularly those from outside the organisation (see Chen et al. 1993). Some managers value their own view of reality well above views from the world outside. Consequently, researchers may be tempted to simplify these external views, to unify so that the focus of attention remains on the empirical information they have unearthed at such cost. Resources being finite, and interviews exceedingly resource consuming, there may be few to spare to treat external views as exhaustively as internal. So, researchers may find themselves prisoner of their own methodology, condemned to look inwards, deprived of the context external views of reality provide.

The problem becomes acute when the mixing of public information with that from interviews reveals more – often much more – than managers intend. For example, the use of public information may reveal the identity of a company promised anonymity by the researcher. With a huge investment in interviews, the researcher may prefer to sacrifice other information in preference to interview material. Consider the following information which, because it was given in confidence, severely restricted the use that could be made of public information about the event. In this case – and this case is not at all uncommon – the interviewee severely restricted the information that could be revealed about the organisation:

> *In a nutshell, there was a cabal, almost a secret society within [the subsidiary] of a few individuals – not that many. We were trying to collect debts, we were sending in the heavies, sending in the heavies to take back [property] in lieu of debt, all that type of thing. I'm not too sure whether money was actually being laundered. Certain of the individuals are going to be, and are being, prosecuted ... [The responsible director] did not know what was going on at all.*

No study can rely on empirical information alone, no matter how rich the information. Empirical information must also be integrated with theory and this is often no easy task (see Flanders 1965), particularly with interview data. Empirical work is generally accepted as complementing theory, but how well do the two really fit? Does not a mite of the empirical sometimes merely decorate a muckle of the theoretical? Does not theory sometimes merely lend a spurious respectability to the interpretation of reality? How often are empirical findings presented which are at variance with the theory that accompanies them? Not often. Most practising managers are not familiar with the latest developments in management theory, or are acquainted only with the bowdlerisations of those who popularise management theory. Unless managers are unacceptably led by the interviewer, they cannot be expected to provide their information in a form that is compatible with theory. This, of course, is where the researcher's skill should come into play, but the skills required to extract information are not necessarily the skills required for integration. There may be evidence of this in the tendency of academic publications in business studies for empirical information to be presented quite separately from theoretical information. This makes starkly evident that empirical research has been performed while minimising the problems of integration.

ORGANISATIONAL CONTROL OF RESEARCH

Wherever the organisation being studied is also funding the investigation, doubt should be cast on the objectivity of the findings. Even where there is no direct funding and the organisation attaches no conditions to the nature of the findings or to the form and timing of their presentation, or the audience to which they will be released, there may still be an expectation that nothing will be said of which the organisation would disapprove. Implicit expectation, because it is boundless, can be more inhibiting than explicit restriction.

All empirical research gives the organisation under investigation an influence over the results of the research. When an organisation completes a survey form or gives access to documents, it can obviously control its input to research. But there cannot be quite the same level of control over the information given by individuals in interview. Good research practice demands that those who are interviewed approve the use of their information in the context in which the researcher has placed it. The huge effort required to do this for a paper reliant on interviews may explain why the convention is not always observed in business or international business studies, and why so many papers in the field emphasise the theoretical (Ormerod 1996). Even complying with standard agreements to ensure that information published is accurate and not confidential can pose problems. Individual managers do not relish this responsibility and there is no obvious institutional office to accept it. That part of the organisation dealing with public relations may well be left to handle the task – with predictable results. From the perspective of public affairs, publication about the company should be publication that will make a favourable impression on the public:

> You asked various of my colleagues to comment on your draft ... Some confusion has arisen because it is our normal – and preferred – practice to have drafts of this kind sent to the Department of Public Affairs ... (letter to author from a director of public affairs, July 1993)

> The first paragraph of page 20, which may be an accurate quotation, is not something we would wish to have included within a published document. (letter to author from a human resources director, September 1993)

The latter observation seems quite unexceptional, but in this case the objection was to a quotation from a manager in another company altogether. Similarly, one Swedish company demanded not only that the answers its managers had given be changed in the draft paper it was sent, but also that the questions be altered (Melin and Strategier 1977).

Good research practice is to define precisely what control the organisation will have over results before the empirical work begins, but neither side can know in advance precisely what results the research will produce. No matter how carefully framed, agreements cannot be dynamic: much may change in the organisation during the years between the beginning of empirical work and academic publication. Managers, and their expectations of the research, may change several times over. Particularly catastrophic is the replacement of the manager who championed the research with another who realises that his/her predecessor will take whatever credit attaches to the research. To the successor goes only the blame.

The organisation may insist on scrutinising output. Sometimes, the researcher may find this a helpful exercise: sometimes less helpful. The interview may open up the organisation for the inspection of the researcher, but – much more than any other form of empirical research – it condemns his/her findings to being laid bare for the dissection of the organisation. Objections to the revelation of even minor details can often preclude the use of more significant information, and can undermine major arguments. In consequence, the researcher has some considerable incentive to avoid detail – the very detail that the interview is supposed to reveal – or at least to avoid making any substantive use of it:

> The factual information given by [the author] about [the company] has no obvious errors. I have not had the chance to check the accuracy of the scores of references … [The author] expresses a number of unsubstantiated and potentially damaging opinions … [The author] liberally laces the document with quotations, many of which are injurious, many of which are unattributed. A continually damaging theme is thereby built, without enabling the reader to judge the reliability of that theme. (comment from senior manager on draft paper based on interview material, January 1991)

Because managers are not always familiar with academic culture (even in the Nordic countries), problems can arise in using information gained from interviews. Managers may not be sympathetic to the demands of academic rigour; for example, the requirement that what they say must be checked against information from other sources. There was a time when managers were less guarded than they are now over what they said to researchers and what researchers made of it. This was when virtually the only outlet for academic publication on such matters as cross-border mergers and acquisitions was academic journals, largely unread by managers themselves. But the same pressures that have forced academic research to become more obviously useful (and more empirical) have also encouraged academics to disseminate their findings more widely, especially through the media. What is said about the firm in the media concerns managers greatly. Much care is taken to cultivate media relations in order to discourage the appearance of information which may influence share price. The point is a small one, but it encapsulates nicely many of the problems of the interview as a means of acquiring information in international business studies. It is incontrovertible that the interview can provide invaluable information about the organisation, but the greater the attempts to exploit this wealth of information, the greater the problems that arise (Miles 1979). In practice, there is every incentive for researchers to claim for their research the benefits that interviews bestow, while avoiding the costs by actually making very little use of the information they can provide: 'We are told that over 400 people were interviewed to secure a variety of perspectives; few make their appearances in these pages and we learn little directly of what they had to say' (Mangham 1993, p. 27).

CONCLUDING THOUGHTS

What, then, might be done to solve these seemingly intractable problems? We cannot share the apparent pessimism of the report of the Economic and Social Research Council in the UK into the quality of management research, though it does address our concern that rigour may be seen as less important for research quality than relevance (see Carroll 1994): 'Research can and does contribute to today's problems, but it has a greater contribution to make: it should also contribute to tomorrow's problems' (Commission on Management Research 1994, p. 27).

At several points we have hinted that a shortage of resources is a basic problem. Empirical research is extremely resource-intensive, and an extensive interviewing programme particularly so. This may mean that insufficient resources are available not so much for talking with managers, for that need is obvious, but to process their information, gather other information, to aggregate, integrate, and use the information acquired. The more interviews conducted, the more resources – not the fewer – are required for non-interview research. Miserly funding and thus further dependence on the largesse of the organisations being studied are not conducive to reputable research.

The examples provided here of management research in the Nordic countries suggest that a different model is possible, one in which firms are more open to academic research than they are in most parts of the world. Such a model allows an academic contribution to business that is not necessarily either immediate or direct. It allows academics to give more to managers than lessons on how to manage. When organisations are open and welcoming to the academic and do not demand immediate payback, many of the problems associated with interviewing as a research method diminish and even disappear. For example, if access is easy, the concessions the academic must make to acquire and maintain access are no longer needed. Other problems will remain, of course. For instance, the limited resources of the academic mean that the interview will always be a difficult method for the study of the global firm.

But the dogma of the times is that academic research must be useful. It is hard to quarrel with this, but useful to whom? Little academic research can even aspire to be useful to everybody, and none can be equally useful. So, academic research is expected to find its market. For international business studies, this is seen to be managers themselves, those who make policy that will affect organisations, and others who study organisations. Of the three, managers themselves are reckoned by far the most important market, the reasoning being that their use of research not only satisfies one market, but also validates the research for other markets. Interviews play an important part in this crude legitimation process.

But is it really satisfactory to regard managers as the primary customers of research in business studies? Two assumptions would seem to be critical to the assumption. The first is that managers know what research will be of most use to them – in the medium or long term, as well as the short term. The second is that the research that is of most use to managers must be the research that is of most use to the economy and to society as a whole. Neither assumption is justified (DeNisi 1994). It is questionable whether managers have ever learned much from academic publication, or ever will. Managers do not typically keep up with the latest academic literature, and it is naive to think that academic research has much to teach managers directly. That, in part, is the self-appointed task of management gurus, who – unlike academics – are often held in high esteem by managers. The popularity of their folksy analogies and simplistic prescriptions is an exemplar to those researchers who value successful dissemination, and perhaps the rewards of dissemination, over successful research. The role of the academic is surely to understand and explain, not to prescribe, and certainly not to confuse (see Stewart 1996).

The more modern thinking about empowerment as autonomy actually fits [this company] very, very well ... I mean you just can't manage that matrix other than at the local level. The principle by which we try to manage our business was the notion of global localisation. Or was it local globalisation?

The key to successful management is the Three Cs, and the first of these is Change. What were the other two, Ian?

This does not mean that managers cannot learn from academic research, but perhaps they can learn most indirectly. It is disingenuous to insist that research *on* the organisation, research *in* the organisation, even research *for* the organisation, should have a direct impact on the organisation. Such insistence assumes that no research findings, and no impact of research findings, can reach the organisation from suppliers, competitors or customers, from government departments, from industry and trade associations, from business magazines, from the media, from consultants, or from the personal contacts and networks of individual managers (von Hippel 1988). It also assumes that academic research has nothing to offer the manager beyond lessons on how to manage, that there is no demand from managers for wider knowledge, even intellectual stimulation.

In some academic disciplines, it is unclear just who the customer is. This is not the case in business studies. The obvious customer is the manager and his/her organisation. Consequently, there is every incentive for the researcher to undertake the sort of research that managers judge to be appropriate to their interests. Equally, there is every incentive to adopt a method that demonstrates how central to the research are the views of the organisation's managers. Empirical research in general, and the interview in particular, have thus become increasingly important components of research in international business studies. Academics in business studies have been quick to seize the advantages offered by empirical research and by interviewing. Though they must surely have come to appreciate as much as we do the disadvantages, they have been reluctant to acknowledge them. As a means of acquiring information about what really goes on in the organisation, interviewing has no equal, but it poses problems for international business studies. Interviewing, perhaps appropriately enough, asks fundamental questions about the nature and purpose of research in international business studies, questions to which there are no ready answers, and which many in international business studies would probably prefer to leave unanswered.

ACKNOWLEDGEMENTS

Versions of this chapter have been published as Macdonald and Hellgren (1998, 1999). The authors are grateful to a number of colleagues who have been generous in sharing their experiences of empirical research, and especially to Chris Bennett. They acknowledge the patience and very helpful comments of the editors of this volume, Rebecca Marschan-Piekkari and Catherine Welch. They are also grateful to the many managers who, over the years, have permitted the authors to interview them.

REFERENCES

Bartlett, C. and S. Ghoshal (1989), *Managing Across Borders: The Transnational Solution*, Boston, MA: Harvard Business School Press.

Brewer, D. (2002), 'Supplementary interviewing techniques to maximise output in free listing tasks', *Field Methods*, **14** (1), 108–18.

Carroll, A. (1994), 'Social issues in management research', *Business and Society*, **33**, (1), 5–29.

Cawthorne, P. (2001), 'Identity, values and method: taking interview research seriously in political economy', *Qualitative Research*, **1** (1), 65–90.

Chen, M-J., J.-L. Farh and I. Macmillan (1993), 'An exploration of the expertness of outside informants', *Academy of Management Journal*, **36** (6), 1614–32.

Commission on Management Research (1994), *Building Partnerships: Enhancing the Quality of Management Research*, Swindon: Economic and Social Research Council.

DeNisi, A. (1994), 'Is relevant research irrelevant? On evaluating the contribution of research to management practice', *Journal of Management Issues*, **6** (2), 145–59.

Emmet, E. (1991), *Learning to Philosophize*, London: Penguin.

Flanders, A. (1965), *Industrial Relations: What is Wrong with the System?*, London: Faber & Faber.

Fletcher, D. (2002), '"In the company of men": a reflexive tale of cultural organizing in a small organization', *Gender, Work and Organization*, **9** (4), 398–419.

Ghoshal, S. and D.E. Westney (1991), 'Organizing competitor analysis systems', *Strategic Management Journal*, **12**, 17–31.

Goold, M. and A. Campbell (1987), *Strategies and Styles: The Role of the Centre in Managing Diversified Corporations*, Oxford: Blackwell.

Greiner, L. (1985), 'Response and commentary', in E. Lawler et al. (eds), *Doing Research that is Useful for Theory and Practice*, San Francisco, CA: Jossey-Bass, pp. 249–74.

Hellgren, B., J. Löwstedt, L. Puttonen, J. Tienari, E. Vaara and A. Werr (2002), 'How issues become (re)constructed in the media: discursive practices in the AstraZeneca merger', *British Journal of Management*, **13**, 123–40.

Hellgren, B., L. Melin and A. Pettersson (1993), 'Structure and change: the industrial field approach', *Advances in International Marketing*, **5**, 87–106.

Hellgren, B. and S. Schriber (2003), 'Nordic research on mergers and acquisitions: doctoral dissertations between 1990–1999', *Nordiske Organisasjonsstudier*, **5** (1), 102–11.

Hubbard, R. and M. Lindsay (1995), 'Caveat emptor applies to the consumption of published empirical research results, too', *Management Research News*, **18** (10–11), 49–55.

Hultman, G. and A. Klasson (1994) 'Learning from change? A note on interactive action research', paper presented to the Conference on Learning and Research in Working Life, Lund, June.

Hyman, H. (1967), *Interviewing in Social Research*, Chicago, IL: University of Chicago Press.

Johanson, J. and L.-G. Mattsson (1988), 'Internationalization in industrial systems', in N. Hood and J.-E. Vahlne (eds), *Strategies in Global Competition*, London: Croom Helm, pp. 287–314.

——— (1992), 'Network positions and strategic action: an analytical framework', in B. Axelsson and G. Easton (eds), *Industrial Networks*, London: Routledge, pp. 205–17.

Kolb, D. and A. Frohman (1970), 'An organization development approach to consulting', *Sloan Management Review*, Fall, **12**, 51–65.

Kumar, N., L. Stern and J. Anderson (1993), 'Conducting interorganizational research using key informants', *Academy of Management Journal*, **36** (6), 1633–51.

Macdonald, S. and B. Hellgren (1998), 'The interview in management research', *Iconoclastic Papers*, **1** (2), www.solent.ac.uk/sbs/iconoclastic/index.htm.

——— (1999), 'Supping with a short spoon: suppression inherent in research methodology', *Accountability in Research*, **6**, 227–43.

Major, M. and L. Zucker (1989), *Permanently Failing Organizations*, London: Sage.

Mangham, I. (1990), 'Managing as a performing art', *British Journal of Management*, **1**, 105–15.

——— (1993), 'Judgement and book covers', review of A. Pettigrew, E. Ferlie, L. McKee, *Shaping Strategic Change: Making Change in Large Organisations: The Case of the National Health Service*, *Times Higher Education Supplement*, 26 November, 27.

Marcus, A. (1988), 'Responses to externally induced innovations: their effects on organizational performance', *Strategic Management Journal*, **9**, 387–402.

Melin, L. (1977), *Strategisk inköpsverksamhet: organisation och interaction*, Linköping Studies in Management and Economics, Linköping University.

Miles, M. (1979), 'Qualitative data as an attractive nuisance: the problem of analysis', *Administrative Science Quarterly*, **24**, 590–601.

Miller, D. and P. Friesen (1977), 'Strategy-making in context: ten empirical archetypes', *Journal of Business Studies*, **14**, 253–80.

Mintzberg, H., D. Raisinghani and A. Theoret (1976), 'The structure of "unstructured" decision processes', *Administrative Science Quarterly*, **21**, 246–75.

Myrdal, G. (1970), *Objectivity in Social Research*, London: Gerald Duckworth.

Nilan, P. (2002), '"Dangerous fieldwork" re-examined: the question of researcher subject position', *Qualitative Research*, **2** (3), 363–86.

Numagami, T. (1998), 'The infeasibility of invariant laws in management studies: a reflective dialogue in defense of case studies', *Organization Science*, **9** (1), 2–15.

Ormerod, R. (1996), 'Combining management consultancy and research', *Omega*, **24** (1), 1–12.

Partington, D. (2000), 'Building grounded theories of management action', *British Journal of Management*, **11**, 91–102.

Pettigrew, A. (1985), 'Contextualist research: a natural way to link theory and practice', in E. Lawler et al. (eds), *Doing Research that is Useful for Theory and Practice*, San Francisco, CA: Jossey-Bass, pp. 224–74.

——— (1990), 'Longitudinal field research on change: theory and practice', *Organization Science*, **1** (3), 267–92.

Pettigrew, A. and R. Whipp (1991), *Managing Change for Competitive Success*, Oxford: Blackwell.

Sciberras, E. (1986), 'Indicators of technical intensity and international competitiveness: a case for supplementing quantitative data with qualitative studies in research', *R&D Management*, **16** (1), 1–14.

Simsons, R. (1991), 'Strategic orientation and top management attention to control systems', *Strategic Management Journal*, **12**, 49–62.

Stewart, J. (1996), 'Management', *Qantas Club*, September, 29–33.

von Hippel, E. (1988), *The Sources of Innovation*, New York: Oxford University Press.

Welch, C., R. Marschan-Piekkari, H. Penttinen and M. Tahvanainen (2002), 'Corporate elites as informants in qualitative international business research', *International Business Review*, **11**, 611–28.

PART IV

Alternative Methods and Methodologies

Seeing and Experiencing Culture

Mary Yoko Brannen

Out of the nine expatriate managers at TSP Papers, a Japanese subsidiary paper plant in New England, came several distinct patterns of naming. The president, Takahiro Wagatsuma, liked to be called 'Tak'. His right-arm man, Hirosuke Fujiya, the Vice-President of Finance, went by 'Hiro'. The Vice-President of Corporate Planning, Shinichi Matsumoto, dubbed himself 'Barracuda' and invented a logo drawing of the creature to personalise his signature. Makoto Ariga went by 'Mac'. Shu Ozawa went by 'Shu'. Kennichi Otake went by 'Ken'. Michihiro Murakami went by 'Mitch'. Akihito Nomizu went by 'Aki'. But, Hirosuke Katsu the Plant Manager, preferred that everyone call him 'Katsusan' in a more traditional fashion. (Brannen 2004)

One of the most obvious ways in which work organisations are changing is in the internationalisation of the workforce and the growing global context for doing business. Cross-cultural consultants, when asked how to address Japanese business associates, will generally answer that a conservative, traditional response is best – last name with a title, such as '-san' – Mr, Ms and so on. Yet as this anecdote from a real-life organisational setting suggests, there are many exceptions to this rule. Without alternative data collection methods such as ethnography involving fieldwork and participant observation, we simply cannot begin to understand the complex embeddedness of work culture in internationalised contexts. The only way to understand the interaction between the various layers of culture from national culture and organisational culture, all the way down to multicultural, bicultural, and idiosyncratic family-of-origin issues that are salient and pronounced in today's complex cultural work environments is to actually see and experience the complexity.

Fieldwork helps to uncover linkages between abstract theoretical concepts such as 'organisational learning' or 'organisational culture' and the everyday work reality of the individuals enacting them. Such concepts are rather reified. In fact, organisational behaviour itself is a reified concept. Organisations themselves don't behave! They are enacted by individuals. To be able to understand the links between the learning that individuals do and how it is translated into 'organisational learning', or the complexity of cultural orientations that people bring with them to the workplace and how this is translated into 'organisational culture', one has to study the individual in action and observe how the organisation somehow institutionalises the learning, experience and complexity of the individual.

REFERENCE

Brannen, M.Y. (2004), *Global Meeting Grounds: Negotiating Complex Cultural Contexts Across Organizations*, New York: Oxford University Press.

14. The Ethnographic International Business Researcher: Misfit or Trailblazer?

Malcolm Chapman, Hanna Gajewska-De Mattos and Christos Antoniou

INTRODUCTION

There is very little ethnographic work within international business (IB) research. This chapter asks why this might be, and explores some possible answers. The academic discipline which has invented and fostered ethnographic method has been social anthropology. All three co-authors of this chapter have some close relationship with social anthropology. The chapter therefore begins with a section looking at the relationship (and absence of relationship) between social anthropology and business studies. It then goes on to discuss a range of specific but interlinked problem areas, where ethnographic methods and international business research meet.

SOCIAL ANTHROPOLOGY AND BUSINESS STUDIES: THE INSTITUTIONAL DIMENSION

Social anthropology and business studies are different in their intellectual history, character and style. One of the authors of this chapter, Malcolm Chapman, has a research training in social anthropology,[1] and has taken the rather unusual step of moving into business studies. Malcolm Chapman has supervised the doctoral work of the two other co-authors of the chapter – Christos Antoniou (2002) and Hanna Gajewska-De Mattos (2002). He has clearly influenced their choice of research method and intellectual inspiration, in that the work of both shows strong evidence of influences from social anthropology. It is this mixture of business studies and social anthropology, embodied in the authors, that has given rise to this chapter.

The differences between social anthropology and business studies are many. Social anthropology as a subject is in many ways defined by its research method – long-term participant observation fieldwork. Anthropologists expect to spend at least a year in the field, and consider it a matter of pride (naive and misguided pride, perhaps, sometimes) to learn and use the 'native' languages.[2] Social anthropologists have usually tried to study a single society (tribe, village, island ...), and study it in a holistic manner. The study of 'meaning' has for long been central to anthropological work; anthropologists have asked what experiences 'mean' to the people who live and create them. Social anthropologists have made a virtue out of trying to see social realities from the perspective of those who live in them, rather than trying to impose would-be objective frameworks. And so on.

The philosophical terrain here is familiar enough. If we invoke standard dichotomies:

positivist	interpretive
quantitative	qualitative
numbers	words
reductive	holistic
measurement	meaning
objective	subjective

then we could say that social anthropology has tended to inhabit the far right-hand tendency of these dichotomies. This is extreme shorthand, of course, for complex arguments. We do not necessarily mean to suggest that all of these dichotomies represent the 'same' opposition (although there are certainly overlapping family resemblances); nor do we mean to suggest that the dichotomies are all unproblematic as expressions of the difference that we are trying to invoke. On the contrary, they are, as oppositions, all of them rather tired in many ways. They recur, however, through human argument about humans, in such a way that leads one to fear that the dilemmas they represent are inescapable – part, perhaps, of the problems faced by an entity that is both conscious and material, studying itself in a world made up both of consciousness and materiality.

If social anthropology is the far right-hand tendency in the list above, then of course business studies makes things simple for us by leaning towards the far left. Business academia has tended to take a positivist, numerical and objective approach to research and knowledge, in emulation of the natural sciences. In this it has followed the social sciences to which it is most nearly indebted – economics and social psychology (with perhaps a large supporting role for sociology in its positivist guise).

There is endless debate about the relative nature and merits of scientific positivism and humanistic interpretation (see, for discussions, Buckley and Chapman 1996a, 1996b). Business studies, young in science, has probably been naive in its embrace, expecting and even proclaiming results. The appeal to science and scientific method, within business schools in the postwar period, was ambitious and far-reaching. All aspects of business and management were included. The technical and statistical management of production posed, within this appeal, the same kinds of problem as the design and management of efficient organisations – theory, hypothesis, data-gathering, the accumulation of scientific evidence, the advance towards prediction and certainty (Mulligan 1987; Pierson 1959).

This is still the (often undiscussed) prevailing ethos of the early twenty-first-century business school – despite the fact that some areas of management studies (organisation studies and consumer behaviour, for example) have developed rich non-positivist agendas. International business, as a sub-domain, has by contrast remained dominated by the scientific agenda – as the *Journal of International Business Studies* (*JIBS*) attests. This would not matter if the drive to science had produced the science which was its ambition. Opinions may vary on this. We think that it has not.

An anthropologist in a business school is, therefore, obliged to re-engage in a philosophical debate which, within social anthropology, had already seemed settled. It has been suggested elsewhere that there is almost a generation of lag between the formulation of these arguments within social anthropology, and their subsequent emergence within business studies (Chapman 1996–97). Or say, arguments that were flourishing within anthropology in the 1960s or early 1970s, were finding echoes within business studies in the 1990s. Postmodernism has emerged in the intervening period, to provide a partial language for expressing the problems, and muddling the historiographies further.

There is still room for debate about which direction the argument is taking, in the medium term. The Oxford social anthropologists of the 1970s were in no doubt that the tide was running against positivism, and in favour of more humanistic approaches. Within international business, as a specific sub-domain of business studies, the characteristic conference contribution is still the multiple regression, but qualitative voices are increasingly heard. One could argue that the reason for this is a (somewhat half-formed) dissatisfaction with the chronic failure of the positivist agenda to deliver the science that it promised, particularly in areas relating to people and organisations.

The process by which *fieldwork* becomes *field notes*, and by which *field notes* become written and published output, has been much agonised over by social anthropologists in recent years. The process is open-ended, lacking in clear rules and protocols, and problematic in many respects. It is not surprising that positivist researchers find it an epistemological nightmare. One interesting result of this is that ethnographic research, where the ethnographer usually really knows what he or she is talking about, is often dismissed within business studies as being 'anecdotal' or of suspect 'validity'; questionnaire research, by contrast, often of the most trivial kind, is objectified into statistics without the same philosophical qualms. This is not because ethnographic research is conceptually more questionable than number-based questionnaire research, but rather because, in ethnographic research, the problems stand up to be seen – the informant, the researcher, the reader.

There are, therefore, good reasons why qualitative work should have found it relatively difficult to find encouragement and tolerance within business studies academia. These reasons all play, *a fortiori*, in the more specific domain of *international* business studies, where the shadow of economics looms dark.

CHALLENGES OF CONDUCTING ETHNOGRAPHIC IB RESEARCH

The preceding arguments address an academic–institutional issue. Academic disciplines tend to construct themselves according to criteria of definition and exclusion, and IB studies has been defined in such a way that qualitative work is not central to its self-image or its characteristic practices. This provides an explanation for the relative scarcity of qualitative work within IB studies.

We could imagine that things were otherwise, and that IB academia had grown out of social anthropology. In that case, qualitative work would be centre-stage. But perhaps the problem is not institutional–academic. Perhaps it is absolute in some way. Perhaps qualitative work within international business is simply more difficult to 'do' than quantitative work? It is difficult to conceive of absolute constraints, in the absence of the institutional and conceptual configurations provided by the existing academic disciplines. Part of 'being difficult to do' surely stems from these configurations.

But what if there are other problems, that will not be defined or thought away, however much we reconfigure the academic domains? The rest of this chapter explores a variety of issues where problems seem to arise, and asks whether these problems are open to solution, or are always and unavoidably present. The problems that we look at all relate, in different ways, to the relationship between the individual researcher, the company under research, and the research community to which the researcher belongs. The problems are discussed in something like chronological order, in the sense in which a researcher experiences them during a hypothetical research project. The different problems are illustrated both through general discussion, and through specific examples drawn from the experiences of the authors. We start by looking at problems of access, then move on to look at the nature of the relationship that the researcher can come to have with those under research. This is followed by a discussion of language use in IB research, and a contrast is drawn between attitudes to multiple language use in business studies and in social anthropology. After this, we look at issues relating to disclosure – how much can the researcher tell, and what are the ethical and practical issues that will arise. Lastly, we have a section called 'The Black Hole'. This dramatic subheading is a metaphor, and we think a justified one. Black holes, in an astronomical sense, draw matter into them, and let nothing back out. Are companies like black holes? Is that why we see so little reported ethnographic research into organisations involved in international business?

Access – Being Allowed In

There was once an anthropologist who parachuted into the Amazon rainforest, to find a people that had not previously had contact with Western civilisation. This really happened. The anthropologist did not ask whether he could come or not. He just dropped in. Usually the act of self-invitation was a little more circumspect, but traditionally self-invitation was the norm. In situations of colonial rule, and particularly in situations of colonial rule amidst political unrest, anthropologists were accustomed to comply with constraints to their freedom of action. In many cases, however, anthropologists chose where to go, and went there. Bronislaw Malinowski went to the Trobriand Islands, A.R. Radcliffe-Brown to the Andaman Islands, Lawrence Wiley to the village in the Vaucluse, Juliet du Boulay to the Greek mountain village, without feeling the need to ask whether the people would mind being studied.

This habit of mind has changed slightly, as anthropologists (among others) have become increasingly aware of the need to accord dignity and integrity to those whom they study. Nevertheless, anthropologists still readily contemplate going somewhere to 'do' fieldwork, without necessarily bothering to ask the unwitting objects of their attention whether they want to be 'done'. There was also a question of time. In many traditional societies, and indeed in some parts of all societies, there are people with time on their hands. Talking to an anthropologist might be quite fun, a valuable addition to a day's activities.

Business corporations are not such easy meat. Their secrets are worth money. Time is money within them, for management especially. They have receptionists and secretaries to get in the way. They have highly protected and specialised meeting places within them, where only the known and the privileged may gather. The inquisitive anthropologist, with solar topi, cleft stick and khaki shorts,[3] is rapidly noticed, and not welcomed.

Arranging access to business corporations for interviews is difficult and time-consuming. Arranging access to business corporations for participant observation at managerial level is almost unknown. Reports of research in an ethnographic style within organisations, tend to be based upon public sector organisations (hospitals, schools and the like) – organisations which share some intellectual and moral affinity with sociologically-minded researchers. Managerial-level participant observation studies of multinational business enterprises are rare (for some attempts in this direction, see d'Iribarne et al. 1998; Salk 1996–97). Antoniou (2002), in his summary of work in this domain, divides his discussion into a section headed 'those who have talked about it', which is rich in references (including references to Chapman), and 'those who have done it', which is rather short.

Access – Who are You?

The first section of this chapter discussed some different philosophical possibilities in the constitution of the social sciences, and of business studies within these. We contrasted two ideas: one, the positivist version, where the world is available for inspection to all, if only they look carefully enough; and two, the non-positivist version, where the researcher and the researched are necessarily involved in the process by which knowledge is created and consumed. Most of us live our lives between the two extremes, and both positions have merit. Nonetheless, anthropologists have tended to the latter. This means that *who* and *what* you are as an anthropologist, matters to what you are readily able to discover and to understand.

For the authors of this chapter, opportunities for discovery and understanding have been strongly shaped by age, by ethnicity and nationality, by sex – by the indivisible package that is an individual – Malcolm Chapman, Christos Antoniou, Hanna Gajewska-De Mattos.

Chapman's perception of these issues is strongly coloured by language learning in bilingual environments (Gaelic/English and Breton/French, particularly). In situations where dual language use is structured along age and gender lines, then there are social limitations to learning which are insuperable. As Chapman put it:

> No matter what an anthropologist does, he cannot become a woman if he is a man, or a man if she is a woman. He cannot, by the same token, be old if he is young, or young if he is old. In Plouhinec, today, to be a socially normal Breton user, you must be over forty years old. When I began fieldwork there I was 28, and a fresh-faced 28 at that, and Breton was not appropriate for me, as I was often explicitly told. (Chapman 1992a, p. 46)

There were also crucial and interesting nationality issues, based upon two different discourses of belonging – a local discourse of nation-statehood (English, French, the Second World War, the Bosch, the Resistance), and a more urban and intellectual discourse of Celtic nationality (Breton, Welsh, Cornish). Being 'English' was a different experience, within these different discourses (see Chapman 1992b; McDonald 1989).

For Antoniou, being Greek was a basic condition of working for, and so having access to, the internationalising Greek family firm on which his PhD was based. Being a man in Greek society and Greek business gave him certain kinds of freedom of movement, and certain kinds of opportunity, that would not have been available to a woman. Being of mixed Greek and German parentage gave him insights into the world beyond Greek business, which were both social and linguistic. Being young gave him an enthusiasm that age might well have blighted, and gave him the energy to pull off the difficult task of having a full-time job and writing a PhD at the same time. It might well be arguable that the combination of sex, bilingual and binational background, education and age, provided the particular conditions within which somebody both *wanted* to do a PhD on this subject, in terms of intellectual curiosity and ambition, and was *able* to do so, in terms of access and opportunity. Change the conditions only a little, and the PhD does not get conceived, or carried through, or finished. The company continues its trajectory through time, but we as researchers know nothing of it. It is probably through detailed considerations of issues of this kind that we can begin to understand the striking *lack* of ethnographic studies of IB activities. And of course Antoniou came to have a doctoral supervisor who was a social anthropologist. That part of the jigsaw also had to fit.

For Gajewska-De Mattos, issues of sex and nationality also shaped the research outcomes. She is Polish, researching business interactions between Polish and German companies, and Polish and English companies. The three-country focus was determined by a complex mixture of opportunity and theoretical interest. Part of the opportunity was that she spoke Polish as a native language, had a very good command of English, and a respectable knowledge of spoken and written German.

The relationship between Poland and Germany is 'close and intense' (Gajewska-De Mattos 2002), in contrast to the more distant relationship between Poland and England. Gajewska-De Mattos was interested in how the Germans viewed the Poles, and how the Poles viewed the Germans. Speaking about this to Poles, she was speaking to people that understood her, and knew the common ground. The material was rich and eloquent. Speaking about this to Germans, she was speaking to people that had every reason to be highly sensitive about the legitimacy of their opinions, and guarded and cautious rather than candid. Germany has spent much of the period since 1945 apologising for itself, and Poland is among the most prominent of subjects for which it owes the world an apology.

Gajewska-De Mattos was also a young woman, and younger-looking perhaps than her years. Business is serious. Was she old enough, serious enough, to share information with? One interesting methodological feature of this was that the German executives were unhappy with participating in interviews which were not structured through the use of a questionnaire, preferably one which they had seen in advance. Gajewska-De Mattos had intended to carry out only semi-structured interviews, which would allow the interviewees to develop and pursue their own ideas and experiences. The German executives were reluctant to play this game, however. They queried the absence of a questionnaire. They asked for the questions in advance. This might of course be related to the perceived sensitivity of the issues. It might be related to certain kinds of procedural caution in German business life. More probably it was a combination of these influences. The outcome was that the information from German executives was less rich than that from other sources.

So, Hanna was young, female, Polish, and attempting to carry out semi-structured interviews about a particularly sensitive issue related to Polish–German relations. There is every reason to suppose that had she been middle-aged, male and German, with a structured questionnaire, the interviews would have grown into free and frank exchanges of information and confidence once the structured questionnaire had been administered. But you cannot be what you are not. In retrospect, we should probably have anticipated these problems, and played a different hand.

Insiders, Outsiders and 'Going Native'

If you have sent a postal questionnaire to a thousand potential informants, and been sent some back, the strength of your social relationship to your informant is negligible. If you have worked alongside a small group of people for several years, doing participant observation, then you have probably developed social relationships with the people that you are studying, which are as intimate and rich as any that you will have in life. Major life events can bind you to the social context which you have chosen to enter -- friendship, enmity, love, marriage, birth, death. The social context which you have chosen to enter may not want to let you go, and you may not wish to leave it.

You might start as an outsider, but part of your research ambition is to become an insider, in as full a sense as possible. *Real* insiders, however, do not stop after three years to go somewhere else and write a PhD. *Real* insiders typically stay where they are, and live all the options of life. By trying to be a real insider, but at the same time privately harbouring the intention of not staying, you are tampering with some very important rules and conventions.

Colonial authorities, and social anthropologists after them, used the metaphor of 'going native' to express some of the problems here. Among an older generation of British anthropologists, those whose ethnographic experience was in the one-time colonies of the British Empire, the phrase 'going native' was in common use, to describe a particular range of temptations and dangers. It has a longer history still in the experience of colonial administrators, for whom 'going native' tended to be regarded as a moral weakness (perhaps associated with taking a 'native' wife). Favret-Saada (1985) reports similar attitudes to 'going native' in the French anthropological research context. In a somewhat similar vein, Adler and Adler (1987) write of 'going native' as a problem, rather than as a desirable option. It is worth noting that 'going native' is commonly used to describe expatriate managers who have come to identify too strongly with the local personnel, and who neglect headquarters interests as a result (Dowling et al. 1999, p. 127). 'Going native', in all these formulations, is undesirable.

On the other hand, anthropologists since Malinowski have made a virtue of closeness to, and participation in, 'native' culture, as a guarantor of their understanding (and Malinowski himself clearly struggled with some of the moral and intellectual problems involved; see 1989). As we have already noted, there are moral and ethical problems arising from seeking close intimacy for research purposes, and abandoning that intimacy without scruple when the research purposes are served. There are problems with closeness and distance. Closeness allows the researcher to understand from a 'native' perspective. By contrast, there is a virtue to distance as well; the analyst looking from a distance sees patterns that may be invisible or unconscious to the native. Some alternation between the virtues of closeness and distance is necessary. The anthropologist coming from outside finds distance easy, and closeness difficult to achieve. The truly 'native' ethnographer has the opposite problem. On the whole, the problem of the truly 'native' ethnographer is probably more easily resolved. The ethno-methodologists would tend to urge researchers to become full members of the communities they observe, and to take methodological pride in this membership; they would regard any empirical evidence not generated in this way as incomplete (Adler and Adler 1987). There is no final answer on whether it is good or bad to study your own culture (Bernard 1995), with costs and benefits, virtues and vices, from both perspectives.

It is perhaps worth adding that one's relationships to people encountered during fieldwork will inevitably be heterogeneous. It is generally felt that researchers should not conceal their research intent (see, for example, Adler and Adler 1987, in their review of the Chicago School sociologists), although concealment has certainly been attempted by some (see, for example, Rapport 1993). Not admitting to the research dimensions of social participation imposes unhappy constraints upon the researcher, as well as arguably amounting to an abuse of the other social actors involved. It is almost inevitable, however, in complex social environments, that however open you are about your research intent, some people will know more about you, and understand more about you, than others. Antoniou, for example, in his participation, disclosed his intentions fully to the group closest to him, not only in professional terms, but also in amity and informality. Outside this group was a larger number who knew, but did not understand much about it and did not care. And there was a still larger group that was not told. There were two reasons for this. One, because the social encounter with them was too brief and distant to need the information. And two (and this is related to the previous one), there were those who, in the researcher's assessment, would not understand the research motive, and would feel suspicious in their potential encounters with the researcher, thus unnecessarily making data collection more difficult. We must remember that Antoniou was first and foremost a practising manager. He did not need those he was managing to be suspicious of his ordinary actions as a manager. And second, we are typically talking here about quite brief interactions (an annual visit of one hour, say, rather than sharing an office), in order to achieve the business purpose. Explaining the nature and intent of a business school participant observation PhD would not have been possible in the time, or within the context of that social interaction.

Language in IB Research and Social Anthropology

The previous section discusses constraints and opportunities which present themselves because of unchangeable demographic features of the researchers concerned. We have discussed, among other things, age, sex and nationality. Another major feature (implicated of course in these others) is language competence.

There is an enormous difference between attitudes to dual and multiple language use in IB research, and in social anthropology (Chapman and Rae 1995). In social anthropology, linguistic expertise is regarded as a necessary element of cultural expertise. Anthropologists, as already noted, take pride in a language well-learned. Ever since Malinowski, working in local languages has been an ambition, often successfully realised. Translators were to be avoided. Not all of this linguistic ambition made sense, and expertise was perhaps sometimes claimed when it was not present. But social anthropologists had a keen interest in language, accompanied by a keen interest in the conceptual structures that accompanied language, and that differed from one culture to another (Ardener 1989, ch. 1 provides the best discussion; see also 1968). Anthropologists had a tendency to boast, tacitly perhaps, about how good their linguistic skills were; and also to conceal, equally tacitly, how poor they were.

In IB research, the picture is totally different. Such research is very largely an English-language domain. The subject has emerged into prominence largely since the time that English became the *de facto* lingua franca of the world scientific and academic community. The subject is still strongly tied to its roots in the Anglophone USA. International business, for the first several decades after 1945, was dominated by US companies, and by emerging US multinationals, and international business as a research domain still reflects this in many ways. The most prestigious research outlets are all English-language journals.

In consequence, the prevailing attitude to language(s) in IB research, is to accept a stress upon proficiency in the English language. Native speakers of English have this proficiency without effort, and accept without question the struggle on the part of everybody else to achieve an equivalent proficiency. Scholars and researchers whose first languages are from South America, India, China, Russia, nevertheless report their research in English. Frequently their research has in any case been conceived and carried out with English-speaking co-researchers and co-authors. Because proficiency in English is the first and overriding aim, those who are not proficient in English wish to be so, and tend to regard their own linguistic background as a disadvantage to be overcome, rather than a resource to be exploited. People who speak ancient languages, of grandeur and beauty, give no hint of this, but blush instead for their mistakes in English.

This different attitude to language, as between social anthropology and IB research, is congruent with more general differences in epistemological approach. Social anthropologists tend to regard a particular language as part of the specific socially constructed conceptual world to which the language is appropriate. From this perspective, differences between languages are of the keenest importance, and conceptual mismatches between one language and another are a resource, an opportunity, a focus of interest, and a pleasure. IB scholars, by contrast, tend to share a positivist world view, in which the world is there to be observed, documented, and above all counted, in an objective sense. A hundred washing machines are a hundred washing machines, whatever language you use. Words are labels for realities. Problems of translation between one language and another are then typically experienced, by people for whom English is a second language, as failures of expertise in English – failures which should be apologised for, rectified, or covered up. The same problems, for an anthropologist, might be doorways into the very cultural differences that the subject is keen to explore.

So we have an IB research scene where language use, multiple language use, and languages in general, are underthought, and underplayed. The authors of this chapter have complex individual experiences of language use and language learning, with many competing lessons to be learned. Perhaps the point that most needs stressing here is that language ability is not very malleable, in anything like the short term. Language ability has something in common with sex and age, in that it defines the researcher, and that you have to make do with what you have got. To be sure, we learn new languages, but the great majority of IB researchers have made careers out of using the languages that their parents gave them, and supplementing this with English if necessary.

We are not, therefore, as IB researchers, encouraged to think that our research opportunities, and even what we are able to discover, are language-determined. But we know that they are. Chinese students study China. Portuguese speakers study Brazil. Of course they do. But as an academic community we pretend that this does not matter, that the issue is merely a technical one, one that could be solved with translators if the native speakers were not available. We need to think about this problem much more deeply.

Gajewska-De Mattos had Polish as a gift from her mother and father, Russian as a gift from the USSR, and German as a gift from her schooling. English she acquired in the post-cold-war enthusiasm for turning westward, that was so strong in Poland and other central European countries. The choice of Anglo-Polish and German–Polish business relationships, as a focus of study for her PhD, was determined by these greater biographical and political influences. Gajewska-De Mattos carried out interview research in Poland, England and Germany. In Poland she spoke Polish, a first language both for her and her interviewees. As mentioned previously, the results were full and rich. In England she spoke English, a first language for her interviewees, and a second language for her. That worked.

In Germany she tried her German out, but found that it was not as good as the English that her German informants spoke. So the interviews were carried out in English, a second language for both parties to the conversation. We have already referred to the social and political obstacles that her German interviews encountered, and there can be no doubt that the use of a mutual second language as the medium of communication compounded all of these. She had intended to use open-ended unstructured interviews to encourage a stream of anecdote, reminiscence and reflection, as people pursued their ideas and experiences. This flow would need to be encouraged, perhaps, but would have its own momentum. When people are talking in their native language, this momentum is often present (see Chapman 2001). When they are talking in a second language, however, then the driving narrative of necessity encounters a constant friction, caused by problems of translation and expression. The friction stops the narrative. It is our opinion that in addition to social and political difficulties this was another element in the relative difficulty that Gajewska-De Mattos encountered in her German interviews. Again, the solution might be to accept the ineluctable. We need a native German speaker if we are going to pursue this subject further.

The problem of language use and learning in IB research is also compounded by the expectations placed upon the typical doctoral student. In business schools today, there are many pressures which lead doctoral students to try to finish their doctorates within three to four years. For social anthropologists of a previous generation, this was not the case. Language learning takes a long time, and the academic community was tolerant of doctorates that took a long time in their formation (Chapman, for example, registered for a doctorate in 1977, and finished it in 1986). For doctoral students in IB studies, there is no time within this three- or four-year framework, even by the most enthusiastic estimation, for any real attempt at the necessarily leisurely process of learning a new language in any meaningful sense.

This academic–institutional constraint effectively means that if detailed qualitative work is to be done within companies, it will tend to be done by native speakers of the languages relevant to the company. This was the case for Antoniou, whose native Greek, particularly, was essential to the research that he carried out. And it is a language that not many people learn. How many international business scholars have learned Greek in order to carry out research in Greece? None?

Disclosure

The traditional attitude of social anthropologists to disclosure of information, was that it did not matter. You studied illiterate people on one side of the world, and came back to the other side of the world to publish a monograph about them for a small academic audience. You no more expected the subjects of your monograph to read it, than did an entomologist or primatologist. You could publish black and white photographs of the naked natives, without any sense that privacy was perhaps being violated.

When Chapman began studying in what was then the Oxford Institute for Social Anthropology, the great Africanist E.E. Evans-Pritchard was still alive, and still an active presence in the Institute. Students of his were also by then his colleagues, and senior figures themselves – Africanists like Godfrey Lienhardt, Edwin Ardener, and Wendy James. Evans-Pritchard had published some classic and groundbreaking monographs – *Witchcraft, Oracles and Magic among the Azande* (1937), *The Nuer* (1941), *Nuer Religion* (1956). His students and colleagues had by then published their own monographs, a generation later. By the early 1970s, there were Nuer and Dinka from southern Sudan, studying in the Institute. There was some amusement, and also some concern, among them, looking in the monographs for black and white photographs of their naked ancestors. The issue of disclosure had emerged. An information loop had closed, a circuit had been made. Consequently, anthropologists have become increasingly concerned about disclosure, and about the ethics of doing research and publishing the results (the Association of Social Anthropologists website currently carries a long and laudably anxious document about these problems, which if enacted according to the strictest interpretation might well make participant social research virtually impossible).

For multinational corporations, the issue of disclosure has never been other than problematic. The multinational corporation is information hungry. It monitors the world for information relevant to its activities. You cannot publish an academic article in which the secrets of a multinational company are revealed, without the full expectation that the multinational company will discover the revelation. Disclosure is a major issue. Secrets are commercial secrets. Knowledge is intellectual property. Litigation looms. The disclosure issue is related to access problems. Because multinational companies do not wish disclosure to be made, they have every reason for limiting access in the first place.

Antoniou's work is interestingly placed in relation to these issues. He was faced with the problem that, although he had explicitly told the main informants of the nature of his research, he knew that they did not fully comprehend the *depth* of the research undertaken 'under their nose' (see McDonald 1989, for a similar example). He always excused himself for this on the grounds that the relevant people did not much care about the research which might be produced in what was, to their eyes, a remote British academic institution. We have still to find out whether this excuse was a good one.

Another difficult aspect of disclosure is that ethnographic research, by its very nature, intrudes into sensitive areas. If the researcher is to report on these sensitive areas, then he or she must decide what position to adopt concerning the identities of people, like managers and employees, and legal entities, like companies and organisations. The researcher at this stage has to make a choice: in-depth research will inevitably reveal some negative qualities of some people in the organisation, and will note events which the participants might prefer to forget.

Gummesson (1991, p. 101) says that the researcher is 'confronted with the problem of choosing between a presentation of anonymous cases where [he] can be frank, or case studies where names are given but unpleasant aspects are excluded'. This choice is perhaps valid up to a point. In the case of much business research, however, the researcher is even more compromised than Gummesson suggests. The travel industry in Greece, despite being the biggest sector in the economy, is of no great size, and the facts related in Antoniou's PhD, even when rendered anonymous, would allow any only moderately informed outsider to work out which companies and individuals were being described.

The Black Hole

We have looked at problems that an IB researcher might have in getting *in* to a company. Even more intriguing, perhaps, are the problems that he or she might have in getting *out*. Chapman (2001, 2003) has explored these issues by using the metaphor of the 'black hole' from which no information comes. It was suggested that truly deep qualitative study of a company, of an anthropological kind, would involve the research worker in the company to such an extent that he (or she) would be more valuable to the company (as a vehicle of company-specific knowledge) than to academia (as a purveyor of only one case study among thousands). As such, the knowledge that they had acquired would remain undisclosed, part of the intellectual property which gave the company the advantages of ownership, location and internalisation (OLI) (see Dunning 1993):

> If an anthropologist succeeded in doing a long term of participant observation in a single company, he or she would probably, as a result, be in a position to start operating as a consultant in various domains. Such people would stop being anthropologists, and become something else, too busy to go to conferences or to write learned articles, because the opportunity costs would be so high. (Chapman 2001, p. 32)

This is a real problem, and one which has not previously been discussed in the research literature. It represents a profound and significant exemplification of the idea that knowledge is something that we make and use, specific to particular social realities. The generation, revelation and consumption of knowledge of business organisations are structured by the value of that knowledge. It is obvious enough to any business with ownership and internalisation advantages to protect, or to any business with unique resources. To social scientific researchers that have tried to think of their subject as an emulation of the natural sciences, the idea is difficult to admit. The company is not there to be studied, like a fossil ammonite. It moves away, wriggles, hides, confuses, lies, prevaricates, entraps.

One scenario where the researcher *can* escape, after intimate experience of a major business organisation, is where the encounter was bruising, unsatisfactory and terminated. It is interesting that one of the few social anthropologists that has written about experience inside a business organisation, is writing from precisely this position (see Ouroussoff 1993, 2001).

CONCLUSION

There are good reasons why there is a scarcity of ethnographic research on companies involved in international business. We have discussed these as being broadly of two types: (1) due to the arbitrary configuration of the academic disciplines that we work within (and we have particularly drawn a contrast between business studies and social anthropology); and (2) real objective difficulties which would be there however the academic domains were configured. Some of our discussion is based upon our own particular experience of widely acknowledged problems. Some of our discussion, however, has real novelty in the IB context; we think this to be particularly true of the issues related to the characteristics of the researcher, language competence and value of researcher's information. Can we solve any of the problems that we have talked about?

From an academic–institutional perspective, we can perhaps ask that more effort be made to make business studies into an environment congenial to qualitative research. One of the authors of this chapter was recently a member of the panel of evaluators at the doctoral session at the Academy of International Business (UK Chapter) annual conference. A doctoral candidate was proposing to carry out qualitative research. Her research outline was intriguing, interesting and innovative. There were three evaluators. One of them told this PhD hopeful that if she wanted a career in academia, she should approach her subject in a quantitative way, otherwise it would never get published. The message was that simple, and delivered not in a spirit of criticism, but as a helpful reminder of prevailing realities. Until we can sort this out, then we can hardly expect ethnographic research to flourish. *JIBS* is the leading journal in IB studies, and does not regularly, either from habit or policy, publish the results of qualitative work. Unless that changes, we are going nowhere. And, more to the point, we are taking PhD students nowhere, and that is a grim prospect.

After that, we move on to problems that we have still less control over. The issues that we have discussed relating to the characteristics of researchers, to access and disclosure, to language use, and to the value of information, are not going to change much in their configuration. As an interlocking structure of difficulties, they have a degree of inevitability, and are in some measure intractable. Any solution to them is bound to be highly personal.

The academic–institutional difficulties undoubtedly compound the problem. If qualitative ethnographic work were properly encouraged within business studies, more people would think of doing it, and so more people would be able to exploit the individual set of advantages that they carry (advantages in relation to access, ambition, experience, language competence and so on). If business studies had a less myopic picture of what counts as 'scientific knowledge', then researchers with profound experiential knowledge of single examples would be credited with the intellectual credibility that is now denied them. If words and not numbers were the medium of the expression and manipulation of academically-sanctioned truth, then qualitative researchers would know that their access to knowledge was as good as that of their quantitative colleagues (or perhaps better, or perhaps just different). If single-company ethnographic research were intellectually encouraged and rewarded, then more researchers would try harder to persuade more companies to let them try it. The black hole might still hold them in; but perhaps some would escape back to academia to tell the tale. If multiple language competence were regarded as an intellectual resource within IB studies, then a whole domain of discourse would open up, within which qualitative research and qualitative reporting would flourish. If ethnographic research were highly considered and rewarded, then young researchers would feel able to take the bet that a single research project, in a single company, carried out perhaps over several years, was a viable option. Such projects take a large part of life. Like a heavyweight boxer, you only have a limited number of fights in you; most social anthropologists engage with only a very limited number of fieldwork exercises in their lives. Investing your life in a research project of this kind is dangerous, if the rewards are not assured.

We also perhaps need to consider the relationships that we encourage between business academia and business practice. The relationship between business schools and the businesses operating around them, is often thinner than it should be. It is easier for businesses to ignore business academia than it is for them to engage with active researchers. It is easier for business school academics to teach and read and send out questionnaires to addresses from a database than it is to engage in the personalised realities of complex business issues in a real business environment. As business academia matures, perhaps we can look forward to a real strengthening of the relationship between business and business academia – one in which the attitude of businesses to researchers would be one of welcome and trust, not one of impatience and incipient paranoia.

We have floundered into theory building without paying sufficient attention to our knowledge of the empirical realities. We have built theories and hypotheses on dubious conceptual bases, and acquired questionnaire data that is thin, trivial and dubious. We have analysed these using statistical analysis that is at once rigorous and meaningless. We need real basic well-founded knowledge about what companies do, and why they do it. Ethnographic research is one sure way of providing good detailed information. Let's try it.

NOTES

1. Chapman studied social anthropology at Oxford University, gaining a first degree in Human Sciences, a Diploma in Social Anthropology, and a B.Litt and a D.Phil degree by research. He subsequently gained an MBA at the University of Bradford Management Centre. He was

particularly influenced by his friend, teacher and supervisor, Mr Edwin Ardener, of St John's College, who died in 1987.

2. The language of expression of these issues is evidence of the early-modern colonial origins of social anthropology. Social anthropologists go to a 'field' to do research, as if they were going out of doors to study wildlife. The languages that they learn to do their research are 'native' languages. Does this mean that the 'natives' are a kind of 'wildlife'? For the nineteenth-century colonial powers, the answer to this was yes, along multiple dimensions of metaphor. The idea now feels more than a little awkward. Nevertheless, the terms 'field' and 'native' are still in normal usage. 'Field' has been generalised into other areas of academia, as a term delimiting an area of study. 'Fieldwork', for the social sciences, often seems to include any kind of research where the researcher gets out of the library or office. It also tends to connote qualitative as opposed to quantitative methods of research and analysis. 'Native' at least has its etymology to rescue it from pejorative or primitivist intent.

3. In the summer months Jane Chapman, Malcolm Chapman's wife, wears khaki shorts that she inherited from Malcolm's doctoral supervisor, the late Edwin Ardener. She has numerous pairs, all made for a tour of fieldwork in Cameroon in the early 1960s. Edwin Ardener was slight of frame, and they fit her well. Anthropologists really did wear khaki shorts.

REFERENCES

Adler, P. and P. Adler (1987), *Membership Roles in Field Research*, Beverly Hills, CA: Sage.

Antoniou, C. (2002), 'Everything under the sun: the study of a Greek business organisation', PhD Thesis, Bradford: University of Bradford.

Ardener, E. (1968), *Documentary and Linguistic Evidence for the Rise of the Trading Polities between Rio del Rey and Cameroos, 1500–1650*, London: Tavistock.

———— (1989), 'Social anthropology and language', in M. Chapman (ed.), *The Voice of Prophecy and Other Essays*, Oxford: Basil Blackwell, pp. 134–54.

Bernard, R.H. (1995), *Research Methods in Anthropology: Qualitative and Quantitative Approaches*, 2nd edn, London: Sage.

Buckley, P.J. and M. Chapman (1996a), 'Economics and social anthropology: reconciling differences', *Human Relations*, **49** (9), 1123–50.

———— (1996b), 'Theory and method in international business research', *International Business Review*, **5** (3), 233–45.

Chapman, M. (1992a), 'Fieldwork, language and locality in Europe, from the North', in J. Pina-Cabral and J. Campbell (eds), *Europe Observed*, London: Macmillan, pp. 39–55.

———— (1992b), *The Celts: The Construction of a Myth*, New York: St. Martin's Press.

———— (1996–97), 'Preface: social anthropology, business studies, and cultural issues', *International Studies of Management and Organization*, **26** (4), 3–29.

———— (2001), 'Social anthropology and business studies: some considerations of method', in *Inside Organizations: Anthropologists at Work*, Oxford: Berg, pp. 19–33.

———— (2003), 'Transaction cost economics and the emerging "science of organization": how the trick is played, for analysts and practitioners', competitive paper presented at the Academy of International Business Annual Conference, Monterey, California, 5–8, July.

Chapman, M. and H. Rae (1995), 'Languages and learning in international business', workshop paper presented at the Academy of International Business (UK Chapter) Annual Conference, University of Bradford Management Centre, April.

D'Iribarne, P., J.-P. Segal, S. Chevrier and T. Globokar (1998), *Cultures et Mondialisation: Gérer par-delà les frontières*, Paris: Seuil.

Dowling, P.J., D.E. Welch and R.S. Schuler (1999), *International Human Resource Management: Managing People in a Multinational Context*, 3rd edn, Cincinnati, OH: South-Western.

Dunning, J.H. (1993), *Multinational Enterprises and the Global Economy*, Wokingham: Addison-Wesley.

Evans-Pritchard, E. (1937), *Witchcraft, Oracles and Magic among the Azande*, Oxford: Clarendon.

—— (1941), *The Nuer*, Oxford: Clarendon.

—— (1956), *Nuer Religion*, Oxford: Clarendon.

Favret-Saada, J. (1985), *Les mots, la mort, les sorts*, Paris: Gallimard.

Gajewska-De Mattos, H. (2002), 'Mergers and acquisitions in Poland: a comparison of general management perceptions from Germany, the United Kingdom and Poland', PhD thesis, Leeds: University of Leeds.

Gummesson, E. (1991), *Qualitative Methods in Management Research*, Newbury Park, CA; London: Sage.

Malinowski, B. (1989), *A Diary in the Strict Sense of the Term*, Stanford, CA: Stanford University Press.

McDonald, M. (1989), *We are not French! Language, Culture and Identity in Brittany*, London: Routledge.

Mulligan, T. (1987), 'The two cultures in business education', *Academy of Management Review*, **12** (4), 593–9.

Ouroussoff, A. (1993), 'Illusions of rationality: false premises of the liberal tradition', *Man*, **28**, 281–98.

—— (2001), 'What is an ethnographic study?', in D.N. Gellner and E. Hirsch (eds), *Inside Organizations: Anthropologists at Work*, Oxford: Berg, pp. 35–58.

Pierson, F.C. (1959), *The Education of American Businessmen*, New York: McGraw-Hill.

Rapport, N. (1993), *Diverse World-Views in an English Village*, Edinburgh: Edinburgh University Press.

Salk, J. (1996–97), 'Partners and other strangers: cultural boundaries and cross-cultural encounters in international joint venture teams', *International Studies of Management and Organization*, **26** (4), 48–72.

15. The Relevance of Ethnography to International Business Research

Diana Rosemary Sharpe

BACKGROUND

Published research, particularly in international business (IB) journals, has only occasionally been based on ethnographic approaches. It could be argued that the kinds of questions that have been asked in the field, and the underlying assumptions about organisations, have discouraged the adoption of ethnographic approaches. Taking, for example, dominant approaches to the study of internationalisation and multinational firms, much research has been shaped by an 'economic view of the world' that includes assumptions of rationality, goal-directed action and the determinant nature of market processes. Research has tended to leave unexamined or unproblematic a huge part of the social life of firms and multinationals in favour of model building based on assumptions of rationality and efficient market mechanisms (Morgan 2001a).

This chapter argues for the relevance of ethnographic research approaches to the understanding of social processes within the field of IB. The understanding of social processes within firms recognises the social embeddedness of rationality, that is, that rationality is always context-dependent. Such an approach seeks to examine actual existing differences between firms by understanding differences in social institutions and practices. This approach (see, for example, Morgan 2001a, 2001b) considers multinationals not as rational, goal-directed economic actors but as forms of transnational communities, and therefore offers a different starting position to that of much of the IB literature. This starting position also provides a reference point for the framing of research questions that acknowledge the social basis of firms such as the multinational, and the 'precarious and conflictual nature of the social order' (Morgan 2001a, p. 12) that develops within them. It also opens up questions concerning the connections between local-level processes and the more global dimensions of local changes.

This chapter focuses on the conduct of ethnographic studies in the field of

IB and draws on my own experience (Sharpe 1998) of conducting ethnographic research for a doctoral thesis. Ethnographic research approaches are discussed that may be premised on a critical realist underlabourer philosophy or a social constructivist, hermeneutic position. Having examined the kinds of research questions that may be framed in ethnographic research, the chapter focuses specifically on the potential contribution of ethnographic research to IB. The second part of the chapter addresses the implementation of the research, including managing the process of entry into the field, working in the field and leaving the field. The chapter ends by turning attention to global ethnography and its potential to contribute to IB research.

INTRODUCTION TO ETHNOGRAPHY

The ethnographic approach is based on what may be termed 'naturalistic modes of inquiry' (Gill and Johnson 1997, p. 96) involving participant observation, often in an inductivist framework. Such an approach is based on the belief that the social world cannot be understood by studying artificial simulations of it in experiments or interviews. The use of such methods only shows how people behave in those artificial situations. Ethnographers' commitment to naturalism leads them to argue that, in order to explain the actions of people working in organisations, it is necessary to arrive at an understanding of the various cultures and subcultures in the setting. They argue that action is embedded in and rational within specific systems of meaning, beliefs and values (Hammersley and Atkinson 1995).

Ethnography can be described as a longitudinal research method that is often associated with participant observation, but can also draw on other research approaches such as contextual and historical analysis of secondary data published by or on the group being studied. Participant observation is the principal method of data collection involved in an ethnographic study. The literature on ethnographic research often refers to the issue of participant versus non-participant observation in research, and the possible social or 'field' roles that a researcher may assume, ranging from complete participant to complete observer (Junker 1960). These roles relate to the extent to which the researcher participates in the research setting being studied (see Hammersley and Atkinson 1995 for an in-depth discussion of field roles).

However, Van Maanen (1979) argues that ethnographic research is more than a single method and can be distinguished from participant observation in that it has a broader aim of achieving an analytical description of a culture. In an organisational setting the researcher faces the essential ethnographic question of what it is to be, rather than to see, a member of the organisation. This approach, according to Van Maanen, allows the researcher to use the culture of the setting (the socially acquired and shared knowledge available to the members of the setting) to account for the observed patterns of human activity.

The ethnographic approach to developing an in-depth understanding of people's behaviour makes it well suited to studying organisations. Ethnography is geared towards a process-based understanding of organisational life, as noted by Rosen (1991, pp. 12–13): 'at its best ethnography is a method of "seeing" the components of social structure and the processes through which they interact'. Classic workplace ethnographies such as of those of Roy (1952) and Lupton (1963) highlight the potential contribution of ethnography to organisations: 'by attempting to observe and explain events within the context in which they occurred, they generate an understanding of behavior which was premised upon the cultural perspectives of the people being studied' (Lupton 1963, p. 29).

The adoption of an ethnographic approach can also be based on the rejection of the belief that social processes can be studied as artefacts of consciousness, accessible through questionnaire surveys (for example, Braverman 1974). From an ethnographic perspective, such methods are seen as superficial, remote and mechanistic in attempting to understand such issues as alienation, status and stratification. In contrast, participant observation enables researchers to immerse themselves in the social processes being studied. The following section examines the two main contrasting philosophies on which ethnographic studies tend to be premised.

FORMS OF ETHNOGRAPHY

Hermeneutic ethnographies may be distinguished from critical realist ethnographies in terms of the ontological and epistemological premises that guide them. Ethnographic studies in the hermeneutic tradition tend to follow the thesis of Winch (1958), that a set of behaviours can be termed an action if they are given or could be given a meaning by those carrying out the action. Meaningful behaviour is explicated as governed by rules. In this way the analysis of reasons, purposes and rules is more appropriate to the study of social processes than cause, effect and law, thereby requiring a study of the culture in which these are embedded.

While ethnographic studies in the hermeneutic tradition work with an ontology encouraging focus on agents' conceptualisations, there is a relatively smaller number of ethnographic studies in the field of business and IB premised on a critical realist ontology (see, for example, Porter 1993; Reed 2001; Sharpe 2001). A critical realist ontology would support the view of Porter (1993, p. 596) that 'exclusive concentration on, and uncritical acceptance of, subjects' own accounts is the Achilles' heel of phenomenological ethnography'. Realist ontologies therefore go beyond agents' conceptualisations of events and seek to look at social structures. Critical realism can help inform social research in the field of IB by providing a philosophy of the nature of the social world. This includes both an ontology of how we conceptualise the social world and an epistemology which informs how we can study the social world and make knowledge claims. As noted by Bhaskar (1975, 1979), critical realism can act as a 'sensitising tool' and means of conceptualising the phenomenon studied (see also Archer et al. 1998; Layder 1993; Porter 1993; Sayer 1993, 2000; Tsoukas 1989).

Within a realist ontology social phenomena are seen as the result of a plurality of structures. Human action is conceived as both enabled and constrained by social structures, but this action in turn reproduces or transforms those structures (Bhaskar 1979). Ethnographic investigation within this context can be used to explore the relationship between agency and structure. A realist approach to ethnography aims not only to describe events but also to explain them, by identifying the influence of structural factors on human agency. Explanation also focuses on how agency maintains or transforms these structures. This focus on 'structures' as well as agents' conceptualisations distinguishes critical realist ethnographies from ethnographies in the hermeneutic tradition. Critical realist ethnography provides a means of examining and theorising about the connections between micro-practices and macro-structures, and between changes in micro-practices and changes in macro-institutional structures. In this way critical realism provides the means for a theoretical hoist out of the micro-level of agents' conceptualisations to the macro-level structures in which those actors are participating.

Drawing on a critical realist ethnography (Sharpe 1997a, 1997b, 1998, 2001), my own research focused on changing forms of managerial control on the shop floor within a Japanese subsidiary in the UK. An important area of interest was examining how new managerial control systems were changing workers' *informal activities* on the shop floor, including their opportunities for informal resistance. Such questions could not be addressed through 'remote' interviews with managers detached from the shop-floor cultures. In line with the critical realist approach, the manager, trainer, associate and internal relations in the Japanese work organisation can be seen to form a social structure. As this social structure is (re)produced, the particular combination of individuals that is formed modifies their power in fundamental ways (Sayer 1993). Thus social structures have powers irreducible to those of individuals. In this way, explanation of the actions of individuals in the research required supplementing of agents' conceptualisations with a 'macro-regress' to the social structures in which they are located.

Idiographic explanatory case studies carried out under a critical realist ontology shed light on the specific contingent conditions under which generative mechanisms (underlying social structures) may combine and operate (Tsoukas 1989). Similarities in the units of analysis are explained by the generative mechanisms and the similar types of contingencies that have been responsible for the mechanisms' activation. Differences may be due to the operation of different generative mechanisms or different contingencies across units within which similar generative mechanisms were operating.

In my own comparative ethnographic research, six comparative 'cases' were studied. Each case was a work 'team', and the comparative analysis focused on the outcomes of social interaction in the teams and the influence of underlying structures and controls on the teams' behaviour. The comparative analysis across cases sensitised the study to how managerial control systems were sustained in different contexts and with what outcomes. The following section will discuss the link between the micro and the macro in the context of my own study in IB.

ETHNOGRAPHY AND INTERNATIONAL BUSINESS

As discussed in the opening paragraphs, in the field of IB the study of the internationalisation of firms and the functioning of multinationals has often been premised on notions of the economic rationality of the firm, as opposed to what may be conceptualised as the contextual rationality of the firm (Morgan 2001a). The notion of contextual rationality provides a link into the internal functioning of the multinational firm as a set of social processes of coordination and control, disorganisation and resistance (Morgan 2001a) – once this link is made, the role of ethnography in studying and explaining these processes can be seen (Sharpe 2002).

In examining the role of ethnography in understanding global issues, Burawoy et al. (1991, 2000) begin by asking the question of how can ethnography be global? How can it be anything but micro and ahistorical? How can the study of everyday life grasp lofty processes that transcend national boundaries? I would like to take the side of Burawoy et al. who respond that there is a place for ethnography in understanding and explaining comparative processes of change and inertia within organisations in a global context.

A challenge facing any IB researcher lies in making theoretical linkages between the micro level and the macro level, between the local and the global. Burawoy et al. (2000) argue that the connection between micro-practices and macro-structures tends to remain under-theorised. For example, while those focusing on the analysis of institutions do not deny the diversity between forms of democracy, they leave ethnographers who work from the ground upwards without theoretical tools to delve into the connections between micro-practices and macro-structures. In this way Burawoy argues that ethnographers appeared to have no theoretical hoist out of the local. However, global ethnographers cannot be outside the global processes they study. In this way global ethnographers have to rethink the meaning of fieldwork, from being bound to a single place and time.

The notion of contextual rationality provides a path into the multinational and a theoretical hoist by providing a view of the multinational as a complex social system or transnational community. In research conducted on Japanese and Korean expatriate managers as members of transnational communities (Morgan et al. 2003) the expatriate managers provided a window into the complex set of social relationships that existed between head office and subsidiary, and the ways in which this transnational social space was a field where the interplay of rival groups took place. The groups in turn drew on resources embedded in local, national and supranational institutional contexts such as capital, skills and knowledge, networks, access to scarce resources and political influence (Morgan 2001a). In-depth interviews and participant observation enabled the researchers to gain insights into the meaning of the expatriate assignment for the expatriates, and the ways in which those expatriates perceived themselves as part of social structures that cut across the boundaries of the firm and nation.

AN ETHNOGRAPHIC STUDY OF THE TRANSFER OF MANAGEMENT PRACTICES WITHIN A JAPANESE MULTINATIONAL

The methodology for this research built upon an exploratory study that was carried out within the UK subsidiaries of a Japanese multinational in which a cross-section of managers was interviewed regarding the implementation of the existing management system. It was felt that the interviews were only able to tap the surface characteristics of the shop-floor practices and control systems operating in the day-to-day social relations on the factory shop floors. Managers tended to refer to the systems and procedures they had introduced, but to say little about the social processes surrounding them. What happens when you try to introduce lean production to UK shop-floor workers, for example? How do workers react? How do expatriate managers work with local managers in seeking to introduce change? What are the informal ways in which workers may resist, as well as the more formal patterns of resistance? It was very difficult to explore in any detail the social processes that emerged in such settings, by relying on the accounts of the managers (Scott 1994). Ethnographic approaches to the study of workplace relations can help explain the complexity of social change. Through ethnography, an understanding of the ways in which members of the work setting conceptualised the work situation can contribute to an understanding of social processes and outcomes on the shop floor of the subsidiary, while at the same time placing an understanding of these social processes in a study of the underlying structures.

The comparative ethnography completed in my doctoral research on the transfer of management practices within a Japanese multinational involved comparative analysis across shop-floor work teams spanning two UK factory locations. Participant observation took place over a 15-month period in which I spent six months working at one site and nine months at the second site. The time spent in each work team depended on good fortune as much as any systematic plan. It was influenced by fluctuations in workloads across sections. Over time I realised that I needed less time within a work group to understand some social processes as I became more familiar with the shop floor. I tried and was fortunate to be able to spend at least six weeks in most work groups. The two UK factories had themselves very different histories. One factory was established as a greenfield site (being built from scratch) by the Japanese parent company. The second factory had a long history under local ownership before being purchased by the Japanese parent company. The comparative ethnography across sites therefore enabled a study of how the local context mediated the ways in which management practices – including total quality management and teamworking – were introduced, sustained and resisted. By living close to each factory, I was able to immerse myself in the local labour market and community and learn more about the orientation to work of the shop-floor workers in both communities. By working on the shop floor I was also able to study the day-to-day relations between the workers and their immediate managers, and between the expatriate engineers on the shop floor and the local employees.

There were interesting differences across sites. Workers at the greenfield site tended to come from rural areas and have little previous experience of traditional UK manufacturing environments. There was heavy foreign direct investment in the area and some workers had prior experience working for Japanese companies. This significantly influenced their expectations and orientations to the work practices. Compared to these greenfield site workers, workers in the second factory came from a heavily unionised industrial area and many had worked for the company under the prior ownership for many years. The study examined how their prior experiences and expectations influenced their responses to the planned management changes. The comparative analysis also examined the management of the UK subsidiaries over time. For example, the Japanese company began by taking an arm's-length approach on the brownfield site that had a long history. Only when the business was doing poorly did it inject expatriates into many of the senior positions to manage change in the organisation. The study explores the communications between local managers and expatriate managers, drawing on the social, cultural and institutional influences on their approaches to management. The study highlights the unintended consequences of introducing systems across cultures. A good example of this was the emergence of subcultures on an assembly line in response to the social controls being introduced. By being a participant observer on the assembly line I was able to study these group processes as they unfolded.

The comparative analysis enabled the study of how social processes within the teams were shaped by the nature of the technology, the workers' orientations and the control processes. In this way the underlying generative mechanisms of technology and control systems were compared across teams and the ways in which these were activated was studied through participation in the teams.

The comparative study of shop-floor practices within the UK subsidiaries of a Japanese multinational sensitised me to the need to look at the role of national and supranational institutions in influencing change within the firm and the need to adopt a longitudinal, historical perspective to explain change over time. It also sensitised me to look at contingent factors, such as the nature of the local labour market, influencing outcomes in specific situations by utilising in-depth comparative longitudinal case studies.

I also believed it was important to capture workers' experiences of the shop-floor work and their day-to-day actions in influencing change and stability on the shop floor. It was important to ask about the implications of change and stability in the management systems within the subsidiary for the experience of work, and how workers make sense of and respond to the situations they face. In this way I wanted to stress the importance of maintaining a level of analysis that secured a voice for the worker.

In working at the level of abstraction of social structures there is no language to capture agency and the implications of change for, and influence on change by, the individual. I wanted to know how workers experienced the control systems being adopted in the subsidiaries, how they made sense of it, how they responded and how it impacted on them as individuals, not at the level of the collective. In this way the critical realist ethnography can be described as 'critical' in that it was arguing a role and a space for human agency in influencing change in social systems (Harre 1979, 1986) and in helping shape the rules of the game (Kristensen 1997). As noted by Sayer (2000), social actors are always likely to respond to their structural contexts and material conditions in creative ways, which may lead to innovation and change to existing organisational forms and their future developments.

The following sections focus on the management of the research process in doing ethnographic research and includes discussion of entering the field, managing in the field and leaving the field. While any participant observer will have to face important decisions on how to manage issues in the field, this discussion is focused particularly on the concerns of doing ethnographic IB research, which may involve working within multinational organisations or comparing organisations across national borders.

ENTERING THE FIELD

As discussed by Hammersley and Atkinson (1995), research design for ethnographic fieldwork is a reflexive process which operates throughout every stage of the project. The researcher usually embarks on a study with 'foreshadowed problems' (Malinowski 1922, pp. 8–9), that is, sets of issues or questions that they want to study. The aim in the pre-fieldwork phase and in the early stages of fieldwork is to turn the foreshadowed problems into sets of questions for the research. In my doctoral study on Japanese multinationals in the UK the research questions became more refined and precise as I spent time in the field. They began with the broad concern to understand shop-floor processes under new forms of work organisation. This remained the broad concern throughout the ethnographic fieldwork and this was refined into finer specific questions on an ongoing basis as I learned more from the field and was able to formulate questions relating to the specific contexts I was working in.

Gaining access to the research setting is a significant part of doing ethnographic research and often continues on an ongoing basis as the researcher seeks to access new social groups during the research. The actual entry into a setting involves decisions on how to approach 'gatekeepers', how to introduce oneself into the field and what to say. Negotiating access can take a significant amount of time and energy and in IB research this can often be accentuated. Research in the subsidiary of a multinational requires initial investigation of who the appropriate gatekeepers may be. This may vary across organisations depending on the parent company culture, organisational structure and control systems. In the Japanese organisations I have researched, for example, gatekeepers tended to be at head office in Japan and informal social networks became very important in gaining access. In another research project on Japanese multinationals (Morgan et al. 2003), access to subsidiaries was obtained with the assistance of a research assistant who, while American, spoke fluent Japanese, had lived for many years in Japan and had himself networks into the same alumni and social organisations as the head office managers. This builds on the arguments of Hoffman (cited in Hammersley and Atkinson 1995) concerning the role of personal networks, which for IB researchers may be particularly important in those contexts where the culture emphasises the notion of insiders and outsiders.

In my ethnographic study of a Japanese subsidiary in the UK, access came from a local human resources director who, along with the subsidiary Japanese managing director, shared in all strategic decisions of the subsidiary. My access to do participant observation came after a series of initial meetings with the two directors in which I introduced myself as a doctoral student and my research on Japanese manufacturing organisations. I began the initial meeting with an interview with the two directors. At the end of the interview, gauging the interest of the directors in my research, I approached them with the proposal to work as a shop-floor worker in the subsidiary. This surprised them and, fortunately for me, impressed them that I would actually wish to work on the shop floor as a way of advancing my learning. They agreed, with the condition that I be taken on under the same terms as anyone else and not be given any special treatment, terms which I was very happy with.

For many ethnographers the possibility of becoming a member of the group being studied, and of participating in its activities, is central to developing an understanding of the culture of the group and the meanings of events for them (Diamond 1993; Emerson et al. 1995; Goffmann 1989). This consideration therefore is uppermost in the mind of ethnographers working in the field of IB. The ethnographer therefore often needs also to have some specific competences or skills that can be brought to the role of participant observer in the IB context. In my own research I was able to enter as a shop-floor trainee, where the requirement was a positive attitude to learn on the job. For Mir (2001), in his ethnography of an American multinational in India, it was the credentials of prior management experience that facilitated his participation in company projects in his study of knowledge transfer within the multinational.

As already discussed, participant or non-participant observation is often accompanied by other forms of data collection. In my own shop-floor study my participation in work groups was supplemented by interviews with supervisors, managers and directors, and various collections of secondary data. The level of access provided is an important factor in shaping the kinds of research questions and issues that can be addressed. In the course of my research, my participation as a shop-floor worker allowed me to join shop-floor groups on the same terms as other members. However, while opening up some avenues for research it also necessarily constrained others. I was not, for example, able to 'interview' team leaders or stop work to follow up on something in another section.

Reflexivity in carrying out ethnographic research is important (Geertz 1983), and this is highlighted when considering ethical issues in the conduct of research. It can be argued that the researcher has a responsibility to reflect on the ethical issues raised in any social research, and that the particular characteristics of ethnography give them a distinctive quality. Ethical issues are raised in areas including consent, privacy, harm, exploitation and the consequences for future research (Hammersley and Atkinson 1995; Rosen 1991).

In IB research, reflection on ethical issues may require additional consideration of, for instance, how host cultures perceive ethical practice in the context of power and authority relations within organisations. For example, in the Japanese organisations studied it was considered inappropriate to question the decision of a senior manager in front of colleagues or to attempt to speed up decision-making within a management team before a consensus was built. Moreover, a multinational organisation typically receives continual requests from researchers for access. Ethnographic research is asking for a substantial level of trust from the organisation in accepting a person into the organisation for a significant amount of time. The consequences of a researcher's actions for future access is an important factor to consider.

LIVING IN THE FIELD

In my own research on the shop floor of a Japanese subsidiary in the UK, the first step was to introduce myself in the field to the people I was to work with. As with any organisation, social groupings existed which tend to have insiders and outsiders. On the shop floor this was something I had to learn in each section that I moved to. These social groupings were often along the lines of age and gender, as well as job tasks on the shop floor. In this way, for example, the men and the women in one factory tended to have their own informal groupings and rest areas which restricted the possibilities for me to enter into the male informal groups. I found that only after I had learned the rules, norms and conventions of a social group was I able to start proactively asking questions. My transition into shop-floor life was also helped by starting out with a female-dominated group on the assembly lines rather than the male-dominated work stations.

A great deal of time was first spent just being in informal groups and listening, trying to understand how people in the group interpreted and made sense of their behaviour and the behaviour of others. There were usually choices I had to make about which groups I was going to get to know better, as once a person had settled into an informal social grouping it was difficult to move out. To manage such processes in the field the researcher therefore needs to be actively reflecting on the research objectives and the choices that are available as they unfold on a continual basis. My prior interviews with the directors before beginning the participant observation gave me some background and sensitised me to areas I wanted to study in more depth from a shop-floor perspective.

In researching a Japanese manufacturing company it was interesting to see how the social spaces which I could move into were actually enhanced to some degree by the open-plan, single-status ethos where shop-floor workers shared the same facilities as office workers and managers. However, the English shop-floor workers still remained very much within their own informal social groupings, as did the expatriate Japanese managers, making it difficult for me to move between groups informally. I was able to talk to expatriate engineers and managers in the dining room and also when I was moved to work with an engineering group who were based in the office.

Participant observation is by its nature also demanding in terms of the need to meet the job requirements and carry out the role expected of you as a formal participant – in my case as a shop-floor worker – while at the same time thinking through the research issues and trying to make sense of what is going on around you. In my own research the greatest frustrations came from being put on jobs where 'nothing was happening', having really interesting dialogues that I could not keep notes on (I did not formally take notes on the shop floor as this would have made workers uneasy and set me apart from the other members of my work team), being encouraged by workers to do things that 'distracted me' from research issues (for example, not being able to walk around or read the noticeboards in the breaks without comments from other workers). I was taken on in the company in a temporary work experience role, being introduced to the shop floor as a university student interested in learning more about how the factory worked. This did raise a few comments from shop-floor workers about me only being there for a while and then leaving, but what I learned was that the most important concern for people was that everyone pulled their weight and had no special treatment. This fitted in well with my concern to be treated on the same terms as other workers.

During the fieldwork there was a need to continually keep on top of field notes and this took up most of my spare time when I was not working. I found it particularly helpful to try to reflect at the end of each week on my field notes and bring out the key issues and points of analysis. I systematically typed up field notes after work each day and this became very helpful for my later analysis.

As researchers we enter the field with our own individual makeup such as age, gender, ethnicity and so on. Such characteristics can shape how we are received into different groups in the field and also influence the ways in which we can develop social relationships in the field. Being English and not Japanese was in itself a challenge in developing social relations with the expatriate Japanese on the shop floor, whose informal social banter tended to turn to things back home in Japan. However, part of an ethnographer's work is exactly the desire to understand and see another culture from the shoes of those being studied. In this sense entering into informal social groups with the Japanese expatriates raised many of the same questions as entering other social groups on the shop floor. How people in this group make sense of and interpret their actions and those of others on the shop floor, for example, was a central question in all groups studied. Being a woman also provided an obstacle to me being readily assimilated, for example, into the informal 'male' shop-floor poker groups and the informal Japanese expatriate male coffee lounge groups. Nevertheless, I was able to capture the meaning of such concepts as *kaizen* and teamworking for the expatriates as my formal work role enabled me to interact with them in training sessions and meetings where they discussed the meaning of practices to me, and I was able to see how they translated this into the day-to-day work practices expected on the shop floor.

In earlier sections of this chapter I introduced critical realist ethnography as an approach that seeks to link the micro-level ethnographic insights with the underlying structures and mechanisms that sustain social systems or introduce change in social systems. In the study of the expatriate managers, for example, I contextualised my shop-floor insights of their discussions and implementation of a 'Japanese management system' and the ways they sought to maintain it or adjust it, with a macro-regress to the ways in which the Japanese management system had evolved and been contested in Japan, as well as to the historical evolution of the specific Japanese company, its location in a *keiretsu* and the strategic thinking of the company. In this way I was able to examine the differences in culture between the local and the expatriate managers by supplementing the ethnography with a study of the institutional structures and labour market, economic, social and political contexts in which the management systems had evolved and were sustained.

The issue of 'going native' is extensively discussed in ethnography (Agar 1980; Gans 1994; Van Maanen 1988). Towards the end of my research I realised that I was taking much more for granted and found that I was finding it more difficult to stand back and detach myself from the culture to ask questions of what was going on around me. Social interaction that would have seemed interesting for me earlier went unnoticed, or was just registered as insignificant. I also started to feel increasingly alienated or estranged from the life of the business school where I was doing my PhD. Going back there felt very strange as I saw middle-class students dressed in suits, chatting on mobile phones, sipping cappuccinos, talking of their weekend break to Europe. I found it difficult to adjust from the regimented shop-floor life and I felt somehow marginal to both groups. This stress of being a 'marginal native', 'professional stranger' 'self-reliant loner' or 'self-denying emissary' has been reported in many ethnographic studies (see, for example, Agar 1980; Burgess 1994; Gans 1994; Sanday 1979; Van Maanen 1988). At this point, as throughout my fieldwork, a supervisor or mentor is really helpful. I continued to send weekly reports to my supervisor from the field. These helped me to develop some degree of detachment and develop my focus. They also forced me to reflect on my field notes and start to organise them under themes and issues.

I coped with the demands of the work on the shop floor in an idiosyncratic way which was shaped by my background. I knew I was only there for a while, whereas for many on the shop floor they saw few alternatives within their reach. Sometimes I 'bought into' the continuous improvement culture of the Japanese expatriates as a way of trying to cope and make sense of what I was doing on the shop floor. Other times I felt a naive sense of frustration at the shop-floor workers for not collectively resisting the intensification of work. One of my research questions became why resistance remained at the individual level and mainly passive.

LEAVING THE FIELD

In carrying out a study of what became six different teams spread across two factory sites I experienced the process of 'leaving' a social group many times during the research. This was in itself emotionally demanding as it involved leaving a group that I had worked with intensively (typically for a two-month period or more) and beginning with another group. As I spent more time in one factory it did become easier to make the adjustment across groups and I found I was able to manage the transition in terms of picking up on the social rules and norms of the group a little more quickly once I had spent some time in a shop-floor environment. Leaving the field for the final time was also emotionally demanding. I felt a huge sense of privilege that I could just 'walk away' from shop-floor life, but the task of telling the workers' stories remained. In the literature on the transfer of management practices within multinational organisations and the changing nature of work organisation, the experience of work under changing forms of managerial control was rarely researched from an ethnographic perspective. I reflected on the works of other ethnographers in the area throughout my research, including Delbridge (1998), Graham (1995), Kunda (1992) and Watson (1994), and in considering the writing up of my research. Having made weekly reports from my field notes I was now able to go back to them and the themes I had been looking at.

As noted by Hammersely and Atkinson (1995, p. 239), writing is at the heart of the ethnographic enterprise: 'given the reflexivity of social inquiry, it is vital to recognize that ethnographers construct the accounts of the social world to be found in ethnographic texts, rather than those accounts simply mirroring reality. And those accounts are constructed on the basis of particular purposes and presuppositions'. Van Maanen (1988) provides an important examination of alternative writing styles including realist, confessional, impressionist, and also styles informed by critical, formal, literary and 'jointly told' approaches. While a discussion of writing styles is outside the scope of this chapter, the reader is encouraged to explore texts that address writing styles at an early stage of the research (see also Burawoy et al. 2000; Emerson et al. 1995).

In my own 'writing up' of the fieldwork I found it helpful to work on writing up individual cases (one case for each section of the shop floors that I worked on) sequentially. Some cases were written up in draft form and presented at conferences while I was still completing the fieldwork. For example, a study of subcultures on one assembly line was built on the narrative of the field data and tried to capture the day-to-day social interaction on one assembly line. Still being in the field was in some ways an advantage in this kind of 'realist tale', as I was still a marginal native in the culture I was writing about. The writing up of the comparative analysis across cases was more difficult to do while I was still in the field and this was done once I left the factory and was able to gain more distance from the actual shop floor.

My own writing style was that of critical realism. By that I mean I was looking to present events in a way that could also provide the basis for reflection on the social conditions that I was reporting. In this way I felt that my writing was representing the concerns of the workers whose voices are not usually heard in standard accounts of practices in organisations. I would argue that in the field of IB research there is an increasing need to understand the reality of work practices and social processes, and to move away from a 'black box' understanding of economic rationality to a more processual and contextualised understanding of organisational life.

CONCLUSION

The field of IB has in the past arguably been dominated by mainly positivistic economic paradigms. Research questions have been framed in a way that tended to be decontextualised, ahistorical and insensitive to process. The study of 'globalisation', for example, has often been framed through approaches which seek statistics to demonstrate the flows of trade and people and ideas around the world. I would like to end this chapter by making a case for the role of ethnography in addressing important research questions in IB. To continue the example, traditional studies of globalisation could be balanced by studies that are grounded, that study 'globalisation' as it looks from the position of those who are experiencing its forces, from the 'black holes' of human marginality (Castells 1998) in a study of globalisation from below.

Ethnographic studies are able to delve into the ways in which people experience globalisation, be they shop-floor workers in a multinational, executive directors of these organisations or local communities that interface with and are affected by the foreign subsidiaries' activities. In my own research following my doctoral thesis I have been able to continue research on the comparative study of multinational organisations with colleagues working from a variety of methodological (primarily qualitative) perspectives. From my membership of such groups, I strongly believe there are complementarities that can be gained from collaborations of scholars who seek to use a variety of research methods to study IB from a standpoint of the organisation as socially embedded and contextually rational (Morgan et al. 2001). This chapter has discussed how ethnographic research that is placed into a historical context, and that links micro-level analysis to a macro-level analysis of institutional structures, can contribute to such research programmes in the field of IB.

REFERENCES

Agar, M.H. (1980), *The Professional Stranger*, London: Academic Press.

Archer, M., R. Bhaskar, A. Collier, T. Lawson and A. Norrie (eds) (1998), *Critical Realism: Essential Readings*, London: Routledge.

Bhaskar, R. (1975), *A Realist Theory of Science*, London: Verso.

────── (1979), *The Possibility of Naturalism: A Philosophical Critique of the Contemporary Human Sciences*, Brighton: Harvester.

Braverman, H. (1974), *Labor and Monopoly Capital: The Degradation of Work in the Twentieth Century*, London: Monthly Review Press.

Burawoy, M., J.A. Blum, S. George, Z. Gille, T. Gowan, L. Haney, M. Klawiter, S.H. Lopez, S. Riain and M. Thayer (2000), *Global Ethnography: Forces, Connections and Imaginations in a Post Modern World*, London: University of California Press.

Burawoy, M, A. Burton, A.A. Ferguson, K.J. Fox, J. Gamson, N. Gartrell, L. Hurst, C. Kurzman, L. Salzinger, J. Schiffman and U. Shiori (1991), *Ethnography Unbound: Power and Resistance in the Modern Metropolis*, London: University of California Press.

Burgess, R.G. (1994), *Field Research: A Sourcebook and Field Manual*, London: Routledge.

Castells, M. (1998), *End of Millennium*, Volume 3: The Information Age, Oxford: Blackwell.

Delbridge, R. (1998), *Life on the Line in Contemporary Manufacturing*, Oxford: Oxford University Press.

Diamond, T. (1993), *Making Grey Gold: Narratives of Nursing Home Care*, Chicago, IL: University of Chicago Press.

Emerson, R., R.I. Fretz and L.L. Shaw (1995), *Writing Ethnographic Fieldnotes*, London: University of Chicago Press.

Gans, H.J. (1994), 'The participant observer as a human being: observations on the personal aspects of fieldwork', in R. Burgess (ed.), *Field Research: A Sourcebook and Field Manual*, London: Routledge, pp. 53–61.

Geertz , C. (1983), *The Interpretation of Cultures*, New York: Basic Books.

Gill, J. and P. Johnson (1997), *Research Methods for Managers*, London: Paul Chapman.

Goffmann, E. (1989), 'On fieldwork', *Journal of Contemporary Ethnography*, **18**, 123–32.

Graham, L. (1995), *On the Line at Subaru-Isuzu*, Ithaca, NY: ILR Press, Cornell University.

Hammersley, M. and P. Atkinson (1995), *Ethnography: Principles in Practice*, London: Routledge.

Harre, R. (1979), *Social Being*, Oxford: Oxford University Press.

———— (1986), *Varieties of Realism*, Oxford: Blackwell.

Junker, B. (1960), *Field Work*, Chicago, IL: University of Chicago Press.

Kristensen, P.H. (1997), 'National systems of governance and managerial prerogatives in the evolution of work systems', in R. Whitley and P.H. Kristensen (eds), *Governance at Work: The Social Regulation of Economic Relations*, Oxford: Oxford University Press, pp. 3–46.

Kunda, G. (1992), *Engineering Culture: Control and Commitment in a High Tech Corporation*, Philadelphia, PA: Temple University Press.

Layder, D. (1993), *New Strategies in Social Research*, Cambridge: Polity Press.

Lupton, T. (1963), *On the Shop Floor*, Oxford: Pergamon Press.

Malinowski, B. (1922), *Argonauts of the Western Pacific*, London: Routledge & Kegan Paul.

Mir, R. (2001), 'Migrating ideas: an empirical study of intra-organizational knowledge transfer', PhD thesis, Amherst: University of Massachusetts.

Morgan, G. (2001a), 'The multinational firm: organizing across institutional and national divides', in G. Morgan, P.H. Kristensen and R. Whitley (eds), *The Multinational Firm: Organizing Across Institutional and National Divides*, Oxford: Oxford University Press, pp. 1–26.

———— (2001b), 'Transnational communities and business systems', *Global Networks*, **1** (2), 113–30.

Morgan, G., B. Kelly, D. Sharpe and R. Whitley (2003), 'Global managers and Japanese multinationals: internationalization and management in Japanese financial institutions', *International Journal of Human Resource Management*, **14** (3), 1–19.

Morgan, G., P.H. Kristensen and R. Whitley (eds) (2001), *The Multinational Firm: Organizing Across Institutional and National Divides*, Oxford: Oxford University Press.

Porter, S. (1993), 'Critical realist ethnography: the case of racism and professionalism in a medical setting', *Sociology*, **27** (4), 591–609.

Reed, M.I. (2001), 'Organization, trust and control: a realist analysis', *Organization Studies*, **22** (2), 201–28.

Rosen, M. (1991), 'Coming to terms with the field: understanding and doing organizational ethnography', *Journal of Management Studies*, **28** (1), 1–24.

Roy, D. (1952), 'Efficiency and the fix: informal inter-group relations in a piecework machine shop', *American Journal of Sociology*, **57**, 427–42.

Sanday, P.R. (1979), 'The ethnographic paradigm(s)', *Administrative Science Quarterly*, **24** (December), 527–38.

Sayer, A. (1993), *Method in Social Science*, London: Routledge.

———— (2000), *Realism and Social Science*, London: Sage.

Scott, A. (1994), *Willing Slaves: British Workers Under Human Resource Management*, Cambridge: Cambridge University Press.

Sharpe, D.R. (1997a), 'Managerial control strategies and sub-cultural processes', in S.A. Sackmann (ed.), *Cultural Complexity in Organizations*, London, Sage, pp. 228–49.

——— (1997b), 'Compromise solutions: a Japanese multinational comes to the UK', in R. Whitley and P.H. Kristensen (eds), *Governance at Work: The Social Regulation of Economic Relations*, Oxford: Oxford University Press, pp. 171–89.

——— (1998), 'Shop floor practices under changing forms of managerial control: a comparative ethnographic study', PhD thesis, Manchester: University of Manchester.

——— (2001), 'Globalization and change', in G. Morgan, P.H. Kristensen and R. Whitley (eds), *The Multinational Firm: Organizing across Institutional and National Divides*, Oxford: Oxford University Press, pp. 196–221.

——— (2002), 'Taking stock: theoretical and methodological issues in the comparative study of organizations', paper presented at the European Group for Organization Studies Conference, Standing Working Group on the Comparative Study of Organizations, Barcelona, July.

Tsoukas, H. (1989), 'The validity of idiographic research explanations', *Academy of Management Review*, **14** (4), 551–61.

Van Maanen, J. (1979), 'The fact of fiction in organizational ethnography', *Administrative Science Quarterly*, **24**, 539–49.

——— (1988), *Tales of the Field: On Writing Ethnography*, London: University of Chicago Press.

Watson, T.J. (1994), *In Search of Management*, London: International Thompson Business Press.

Winch, P. (1958), *The Idea of a Social Science*, London: Routledge.

16. Interpreting the International Firm: Going Beyond Interviews

Hans De Geer, Tommy Borglund and Magnus Frostenson

INTRODUCTION

How can we get under the surface of a new organisation? How can we make credible interpretations that go beyond the answers we obtain from interviews? We think one way is to work with multiple qualitative methods, using a hermeneutic approach, including interpretation and reinterpretation over time in a longitudinal study, then presenting our results in an impressionistic way. We are inspired by ethnography even though we are not conducting a full-scale traditional ethnographic study. To get to a deeper structure it is important to use a variety of methods for data collection. It is equally important to have a consistent philosophical and methodological approach underlying a diversity of methods. In our case we build upon hermeneutics and ethnography.

We hope to demonstrate how the use of observations and document analysis can be built into the traditional routine of an interview-based study. There are a number of reasons why it is important to move beyond an over-reliance on interview data. First, when studying processes of change as researchers, we are confronted with a variety of opinions expressed by persons involved in the organisation. Balancing data from interviews with other sources of information gives us a chance to see the ironical and contradictory – something we shall come back to later in our discussion. Second, by using multiple methods for collecting information we can build well-grounded interpretations that are more credible to readers. Third, we can gain an understanding of the shared values and meanings that organisations live by as a result of studying a pattern emerging from both observations and documents as well as interviews. Fourth, using a range of methods helps us study changes over time. Documents written some years ago allow us to travel back in time and make comparisons with narratives from interviews about situations in the past.

In this chapter we shall reflect on data from a project aimed at defining and analysing how the core values of Swedish corporations change as they turn international through mergers or acquisitions. Core values signify both a system of values and a system of norms that organise and interpret thinking and action in the organisation. We hope our way of working can be used in other areas of international business as well, such as when studying behavioural aspects of change processes affecting organisation, strategy or culture. In particular, it is suitable to work in this way when studying phenomena where one, like we do, needs to penetrate a deeper structure to answer the research questions. It can be used when a researcher feels the need to gain a deeper understanding of a complex and contradictory phenomenon that might not be easy to measure or to study just by using a single method of gathering information.

OUR APPROACH

Hermeneutics as a Starting Point

We see hermeneutics as the natural starting point for our research. Like qualitative research in general, hermeneutics is characterised by interpretation and an emphasis on understanding rather than explanation. The hermeneutic researcher wants to understand the meaning of the whole. Following Gadamer (1960), a holistic understanding can be constructed without reducing what is being studied to a mere 'object' in the strictest sense. Accordingly, the aspect of 'dialogue' between the researcher and the object of study has a special place in hermeneutics. Alvesson and Sköldberg (1994) mention the tradition of 'empathy' within hermeneutics, that is, the ability of the researcher to adopt the role of the actor that is being studied in order to understand his or her thoughts and intentions better, sometimes even better than the actor him/herself. You could say that within hermeneutics there is a constant process of understanding both the 'object' of study in all its aspects and your own (pre-)understanding. This way of reasoning comes close to the hermeneutic circle described by, for example, Heidegger (1972). In order to gain a holistic understanding we have to consider the parts and in order to grasp the parts we must have a concept of the whole.

This approach challenges positivism, one of the problems of which is that it oversimplifies the role of the researcher, who is assumed to be able to expunge any interests and pre-understandings that may bias the research. The relationship between the subject and the object – that is, the role of interpretation – is seldom problematised. A hermeneutic approach pays attention to the role of the researcher in the study, showing that a researcher's own pre-understanding influences – and even enables – the interpretations made, and that these interpretations develop over time in a 'dialogue' with the object under study (Figure 16.1).

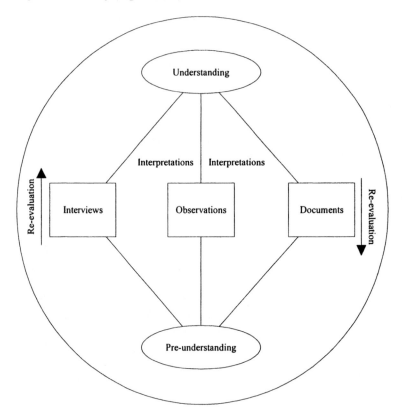

Figure 16.1   A hermeneutic circle

Pre-understanding

Even though our work is exploratory, we do have a pre-understanding coloured by the recent debate in Sweden on mergers and acquisitions between Swedish and foreign firms. They are frequently described as being turbulent for the organisation and as having negative consequences for the employees. It is important for us to examine how our own pre-understanding affects the process of data collection and interpretation. There is a risk that we might look at the acquisition of Swedish companies as more dramatic and more threatening to people's integrity than researchers of other nationalities. Also, being Swedish might make us pay heed to Swedish respondents more than to respondents from other countries, since we share the same language and presumably the same values. There is a risk that we construct interpretations from a national perspective instead of considering alternatives. For example, it could be that changes in the organisation are mainly due to a large company taking over a small company, rather than a foreign company taking over a Swedish one. The same type of changes might also have occurred if a large Swedish company had bought a small Swedish company. Thus, we must reflect on other possible interpretations as well.

Ethnography

To some extent we are inspired by the ethnographer's way of working. To Fetterman (1989), ethnography is the art and science of how to describe a group or a culture. Marcus and Fischer (1986) describe an ethnographer as a researcher who observes, takes notes and takes part in the everyday life of a culture, then presents his/her findings in descriptive details. Atkinson and Hammersley (1994) point to the advantages of ethnography when it comes to exploring the nature of a particular social phenomenon rather than setting out to test hypotheses about it. Ethnography allows us to understand the 'life' of the organisations we are studying.

Ethnography (or at least, some traditions of ethnography) is linked to hermeneutics in the sense that it ascribes an important role to interpretation and that it rarely claims to deliver any absolute truths. It provides us with situations that can be interpreted and given meaning. Ethnography functions as our inspiration, in particular, as Alvesson and Sköldberg (1994) describe, when it comes to its emphasis on the ideas, thoughts, symbols and hidden meanings of the organisation. As Smircich (1985, p. 66) describes it when discussing cultural analysis of organisational life: 'organisations are symbolically constituted worlds, like novels or poems; they can be known through acts of critical reading and interpretation'. The use and analysis of metaphors is important in ethnography, and can also be found within hermeneutics. Ricoeur, for example, uses text metaphors, claiming that human actions leave traces that can be understood as documents to be analysed with hermeneutic methods (Sellstedt 2002).

Ethnography is by definition a longitudinal method with a process-based understanding of organisational life (Rosen 1991). It is important to focus on the flows and interrelationships of behaviour and action, and not only use data to obtain a snapshot view. We do not conduct participant observations, nor do we live as natives inside the organisation for a longer period of time. But we do follow the organisations in a longitudinal study for a year or two by returning to the organisations for follow-up studies. We then conduct additional interviews with new people in the organisation and sometimes re-interview people we met on previous occasions. The ethnographic approach seems to be of use even though it is not possible to devote our research object a full-time commitment for a year or two, as a full-scale ethnographic study would demand.

MIXING QUALITATIVE METHODS

Almost anything can be empirical material for an ethnographer, but especially important in ethnography are observations and interviews (Kaijser and Öhlander 1999). In this study, we follow the ethnographic tradition of mixing data sources by using observation, interviews and documents. We use a form of triangulation with a variety of sources in the study as an attempt to secure an in-depth understanding of the phenomenon (Denzin and Lincoln 2000). According to a traditional view of triangulation, the use of multiple methods allows us to check for controversial results: for example, if something an interviewee says does not really seem to fit with the observations made (Yin 1994). However, our view of triangulation is a little different, since our ambition is to look for the ironical. Irony to Sköldberg (1990) is dialectical, paradoxical and contradictory. Irony sheds light on irrationality and ambiguity in situations. It also contains scepticism and doubt (Alvesson and Köping 1993). When trying to capture irony, the use of multiple sources is invaluable. This reduces the likelihood of misinterpretations and oversimplifications by using multiple perceptions to problematise and not just clarify meaning, thus identifying different ways the phenomenon is seen (Stake 2000). Consistent with our view on the importance of irony, we do not expect that different sources can or should be reconciled in order to achieve a single, harmonious, convergent explanation about the phenomenon under study. Rather, we wish to reflect and represent the contradictions that we encounter in the field. We are getting close to the concept of 'crystallisation' (Richardson 1994, p. 522), implying the use of multiple methods that reflect the complex, multidimensional and fragmented nature of phenomena. However, we are not prepared to adopt this postmodern idea in full, since we believe that we in fact are interpreting phenomena of a distinct although subjectively understood nature.

Interviews as Storytelling

From a social constructivist perspective, interviews can be seen as constructed by the interviewee and interviewer (Berger and Luckmann 1966). Reality is not independent from the interview situation, but is created by it. The role of the interviewer should be to allow the interviewee to construct his/her meaning, and to be sensitive to this meaning when analysing the interview data. Interviews are good micro-sites for producing narratives (Czarniawska 2000). By asking for stories in the interview situation we obtain rich narratives to be used in the presentation and analysis of our research work. These stories commonly concern 'critical incidents' that illustrate subjects people are sometimes reluctant to discuss or do not even have a notion of, such as values and virtues of the organisation (Fisscher 2002). By asking for stories of such incidents, we encourage the respondent to talk about subjects that might otherwise be too abstract or too sensitive. These narratives are, as Pentland (1999, p. 715) argues, 'a window onto the values of a cultural group'.

We designed semi-structured interviews that would allow time for storytelling by interviewees, as well as responses to specific questions. Using a model suggested by Kylén and Vestlund (1980), we went from a shorter list of open questions to more detailed follow-up questions, giving the respondents plenty of time to develop their own stories. Building on their model we prepared questions divided into different sections (Figure 16.2). We started with general questions in a warming-up phase, for example about the respondent's position and background. Second, we switched over to a 'free description' phase where the respondent answers very broad questions, talking about whatever subject the respondent chooses. We stimulated storytelling in the 'free description' part of the interview, even though narratives tended to crop up on the initiative of the respondent in other phases of the interview as well. In the next phase, the focus phase, we posed precise questions about subjects important to us, such as conflicts connected to the merger. In the ensuing control phase we checked answers by asking the same questions again in a slightly different way. Towards the end of the interview, in the final phase, we asked about more general subjects, moving away from sensitive issues to round things off. These might for example be about developments in the industry as a whole, rather than in the company itself.

We interviewed 'rank-and-file' employees in the organisation and not just managers. In our case this could, for example, be a secretary, a worker in the transport unit or a technician testing product quality. Interviewees may not be used to talking about abstract concepts like culture or values, or might feel suspicious about the study. Thus, it is important to make the respondent feel at ease with this situation and to cope with a person who might be reluctant to give away information. In addition, the respondent may want to manipulate the interviewer, leaving out some information or adjusting answers to expectations (Kaijser and Öhlander 1999). Data from interviews are interpreted and connected to other information, and, according to the traditional view of the interview, this enables the researcher to check the extent to which a respondent hides some aspects and highlights others. But more importantly – and going beyond an evaluation of the 'truthfulness' of interviewees' statements – we see the information obtained in interviews as the respondents' construction of reality, so we are looking for clues to understand their worldviews. This perspective implies that the phenomenon studied must be understood according to the meaning that individuals (including ourselves as researchers) ascribe to it, not in terms of external measures of 'truth' or 'distortion' (Silverman 1993). Merged and acquired companies are not isolated phenomena but are a result of our understanding and apprehension, which, in turn, are shaped by our experiences and underlying norms and values.

| Warming Up | Free Description | Focus | Control | Final |

Figure 16.2   Phases of the interview

For example, interviews gave us the following clues as to which values govern the organisation in one of the companies we have studied, a Swedish company that was bought by an American company. It is a medium-sized firm with about 200 employees, manufacturing electrical appliances. This is an excerpt from the focus phase of the interview (see Figure 16.2):

'What is the same in the two companies?'
'You can just look at such a simple thing as how they dress. They are rather casual, just as we are ... There are no dark suits or such things. Then there is a rather strong engineering culture within the companies.'
'What is not the same?'
'There's probably a more direct culture in their company ... They are more direct during meetings and much more prompt to say that they don't agree ... Or they can even shout that this is bloody wrong. Here we are much more indirect.'
'How should you behave as an individual to be appreciated in their world?'
'That is a good question. They are more direct, but at the same time you are supposed to be nice. You should not have too much attitude; you should not be too pushy. But you should have a strong drive and be result-oriented.'
'To what extent has this changed compared to how it was before?'
'I have personally become more direct, I think. They put greater pressure on you.'
'How?'
'They follow up things much harder and demand better results.'
'To what extent are these demands accepted?'
'Right now people want to do the best they can. We want to show that we can achieve things so that we obtain a good position and get respect. What will happen in the long run I do not know, but I think that we are stretched out about as much as the organisation can take.'

This is how one of the employees describes the engineering culture in the same company, prior to the merger:

'We try to analyse and work with facts in an objective way. The result is more

important than the process, the result has to be good, and we have to make good stuff. You want to make the products a little cool; you try to improve them, trying to make the wheel a little rounder.'
'What personal talents are important to fit in here?'
'At the management level you are supposed to be outspoken and serious and used to taking decisions. You should have a feeling for details and a good knowledge of the market, but not necessarily of handling people. At the lower levels you should be an engineer, technically oriented but not necessarily innovative.'

A preliminary interpretation of these interviews is that people in the Swedish organisation are goal-oriented, value high quality and have an interest in advanced technical solutions. There is a casual atmosphere and indirect communication style among the co-workers in the organisation.

Observations

A second tool that is crucial for us is observation studies. That is, to observe objects and situations in the workplace and look for symbols of culture, norms, virtues and values. We use these observations as an additional source of information in our interpretation, and they also give us a chance to make the presentation more colourful and hence give the reader a better understanding of the changes in everyday life. For practical reasons, our observation studies will be of a basic form: just being in the environment for shorter periods of time, observing and taking notes. We try in a discreet way to make just a few notes during our visits, typing them out later. People could get suspicious if we took extensive notes during a tour, making it harder for us to talk to them.

We focus on observations that can be crucial for interpreting value systems. We look for symbols of, for example, organisational culture, power structure and identity. This makes some aspects of the environment more interesting to observe than others. Even so, we consider our observations to be open since we are not working with distinct hypotheses. You can separate an open observation from a focused observation, in that the focused is used when trying to test a hypothesis and the open is used when working without a hypothesis to test (Kaijser and Öhlander 1999). There are also different forms of observations with different levels of involvement: observation, participant observation and cooperation (Kaijser and Öhlander 1999). The forms refer to the extent to which you are working inside the firm, living close to the people you are observing. We do what Yin (1994) calls a 'direct observation' and we follow Yin's advice in terms of making the observation more reliable by being two observers in the field. Of course it does not protect the study from the fact that the researcher always influences the environment studied. Often we have a guide with us when doing tours of the facilities and to some degree we are prevented from seeing all that we would like to see. Very rarely does the guide try to hide things from us, but of course we expect to be shown the facilities that the company is most proud of and not other more troubled sites.

Observations give us impressions that cannot easily be obtained through interviews and documents. How the company furnishes its premises or what co-workers put on the walls can, for example, be symbols of the company's values or leadership style. Consider this observation we made at the same company as the one above, the Swedish firm that merged with an American firm:

> The reception has recently been renovated. The tiled floor makes an impression, as does the aquarium in the corner. The receptionist answers the phone using the new name of the company. The reception is decorated in wood with rather plainly styled furniture, covered with grey textiles and a cushion on every chair. The pictures on the walls show the products of the firm. We see vessels and oil tankers with company equipment on board. The environmental policy of the firm can also be seen on the walls, as can its quality policy. The framed texts are in both Swedish and English. On the wall there is also a picture of a big group of employees. The doors to the production departments are open. The firm's activities here are assembly and testing. The broad concrete stairs in one of the corners lead to the other floors. Security means a lot. Photography is forbidden, according to a sign, and we read that we are on private property. People wear rather simple clothes, although they don't look shabby – lots of sweaters and trousers, but few suits and ties. A person with an expensive coat and a scarf breaks the pattern. Around fifteen people are sitting in a coffee room in the corner of the production department. We see them through glass windows where they are drinking coffee. There is a relaxed atmosphere with people laughing and talking. Most of those working here are men. Many of them say hello to our guide who is a rather young girl, an engineer who is telling us about the machines and the products very enthusiastically. They seem to be fond of our guide although she does not seem to be one of them, at least not if we consider she is a university-trained graduate engineer. Only first names, no surnames, are used.

An interpretation of this extract is that the style in the organisation is casual, that people in the organisation are informal, using colleagues' first names, and that product quality and environmental issues are regarded as important. Together with the interview excerpt in the previous section, which highlights a casual and indirect communication style, you could say that the different impressions add up to a picture of a rational, goal-oriented organisation with a rather strong engineering culture honouring egalitarian values. This could be said to conform to popular stereotypes of a Swedish organisation, but also perhaps reflects the company's industry and professional culture.

Study of Documents

Another source of information is written documents of different kinds. Texts provide us with complementary information along with the interviews and observations. But, as is the case with all sources, they must be treated with a critical eye. This brings us into the field of historical methodology (Jarrick and Söderberg 1993). What appears in the files of the companies as texts can be used as sources of knowledge in two different capacities. They could be regarded as remnants of earlier processes in the organisation: the documents as such bear witness to activities in the past. Take for example the minutes of a board meeting found in the archives. They tell us, when identified as such, about the activity of the board. The minutes are a remnant from the board meeting proceedings. The researcher has to make a correct identification and verify the authenticity of the document. That done, the document can be used without further hesitation in the research process, if we are interested in board meetings, board decisions and the like. Here the document can be regarded merely as an artefact, a leftover, just like the pen that was used when writing the text, or the gavel the chairman used to confirm the decision.

However, the minutes of the board meetings can also be important in another capacity. As texts they can tell us a story. They tell a story of what happened in the board room, they might tell small stories presented by board members to underpin their respective standpoints, and in the attachments of the minutes we might find numerous stories about situations, processes and attitudes within the organisation. But these stories cannot be used without critical scrutiny. In addition to the test of identification and authenticity, we must add an assessment of the relationship between the narrator and the object and focus of the narration. Was the narrator close enough in time and space to witness what he/she is saying, or did the story pass a number of links in a chain of communication before reaching our informant? Would the informant have any interest in changing the story in his/her own favour, or in order to suit other interests that he/she made his/her own?

The written documents that we use include internal and external material issued by the companies, such as ethical codes and policy documents. These allow us to compare evidence from the merged companies. Also, it gives us the opportunity to stretch the time perspective and see developments before and after the mergers. Thus we may identify differences and changes in contents, focus and language and, from a longitudinal perspective, follow the transformation of the organisation over time.

It is important to identify the source of the documents. Ethical codes, for instance, often express the official values of the companies, and do not necessarily reflect everyday work ethics as experienced and expressed by the employees. Agle and Caldwell (1999) illustrate this in their framework of value research, in which they classify values into distinct types: individual, organisational and societal values. In this case, when we are talking about organisational values expressed in documents, there may be a sharp contrast to actually held individual values. Our longitudinal research, covering different sources of information, makes it possible for us not only to identify values on different levels but also to investigate the role they actually play in the organisation.

The study of documents forms part of the qualitative study that we pursue. We do not perform any quantitative content analysis counting words connected to certain subjects and so on, but symbols and metaphors used in the documents are important clues for us. They contribute to our analysis of the self-descriptions and self-images of the examined firms. We have studied internal documents that reflect the values of the two companies, both American and Swedish. The documents were produced inside the two companies before the purchase was made. Looking at the list of values for the Swedish company (Table 16.1), we see the value of cooperation fitting together with the informal style and forming a picture of a strong emphasis on teamwork. That is a value also present in the American organisation. The value of a winning attitude and courage can be said to be connected to the picture of the organisation as result-oriented and committed to reaching its goals. That is also something to be found in the American organisation, expressed in terms of the 'achievement' value. The value of cost awareness might be said to be a part of the engineering culture marked by a quest for high quality and efficiency. These documents also show that there actually are some similarities between the two organisations, since both organisations independently have formulated similar values.

Table 16.1   Comparison of case companies on the basis of documentary evidence

Values of the American company	Values of the Swedish company
Continuous improvement	Winning attitude
Honesty	Courage
Achievement	Customer focus
Recognition	Cooperation
Respect	Future orientation
Teamwork	Cost awareness

UNDERSTANDING AND PRESENTATION

The Challenge of Interpretation

Interpretation is central to our hermeneutic approach. But of course, interpretive processes always risk bias, and coping with the hermeneutic circle is not always easy. How do we actually know that our interpretation is true? Alvesson and Sköldberg (1994) claim that to hermeneutics this question is based on a misunderstanding, since it assumes the correspondence between a statement and reality. Within hermeneutics, the traditional correspondence theory of truth is brought into question. In some senses, this has to do with the situation we find ourselves in when studying something. We are not trying to establish a mathematical truth, or something close to it. Instead we want to understand a hermeneutic situation (which we are part of ourselves) by means of interpretation, a situation that is in constant flux. What we can hope for are well-founded interpretations with no claims of representing objective truth since other interpretations are possible. The dividing line between good and bad interpretations should rather be internal coherence and consistency. This means that our interpretations should have value in a pragmatic and contextual sense.

We have to carry out the interpretation at several levels and not be satisfied only with our first impression. We use three levels of interpretation (Alvesson and Köping 1993; Alvesson and Sköldberg 1994). At the first discursive level we describe what we see and learn without problematising the information more closely. At the imaginative level we look for the meanings of different actions and languages. At the level of action and relationships we look for the patterns and structures that the different actions form. We have to interpret our material – interviews, observations and documents – on all three levels to gain a high level of understanding of the phenomena through which we can find what the fundamental values of internationalised firms are. At the discursive level we can expect to find concrete expressions, words, actions and opinions, while at the imaginative level we look for symbols and metaphors constructing meaning. At the level of action and relationships it will be possible for us to draw conclusions about the structural and social framework in which fundamental values are formed. The meanings of different actions and answers will be knitted together to form a pattern from which we can expect to abstract a picture of a culture in change.

Impressionism

It is important to let each reader have a chance to follow our process of interpretation. Credibility increases if we create a chain of evidence from the research questions asked, to the information obtained and to the conclusions. It increases the quality of the study if the readers can follow our interpretations and study the data they are based on. One way of doing this is to write in such a way so that anyone can follow life in the organisation and allow the reader to see how the researcher has constructed his or her interpretations. We can do that by telling stories, akin to painting pictures of everyday life in the organisation. Following van Maanen (1988) we use the 'impressionist' method of ethnographic descriptions. Narration, according to the impressionist method, consists of creating a picture, map or image by using small separate impressions of reality. In isolation these impressions may not say very much but together they provide us with enough material to create a picture of 'reality'. Using the language of art, it is possible to say that we will use the different impressions to paint an image that constitutes a totality. Impressionist writing tries to keep both the subject and object in constant view. An impressionist tale describes both the culture(s) in the organisation and the researcher's knowledge of it, so that the reader can examine both.

The use of impressionism and narratives increases the credibility of the study. As Geertz (1988, p. 16) points out, ethnographers need to convince the readers that they actually have 'been there'. This implies that had the readers themselves been there they would have made the same observations and interpretations as the ethnographers: 'that had we been there we should have seen what they saw, felt what they felt, concluded what they concluded', as Geertz writes. By using impressionism, we prove to the readers that we have 'been there' and give them a chance to follow our conclusions.

Golden-Biddle and Locke (1993) point to the fact that ethnographic texts should be convincing for the readers. In relation to this, they discuss three dimensions: authenticity, plausibility and criticality. Authenticity means that the researcher has grasped the world of the organisation's co-workers according to their own constructions of it. Plausibility is the ability to connect the reader's world with the studied world so that the story makes sense to the readers. Criticality addresses the question of whether the text activates readers to re-examine their assumptions after reading. We think that our longitudinal approach and the use of multiple sources for gathering data give us an authentic view of the everyday life in the organisation as constructed by its co-workers. In addition, we hope that our impressionistic way of presenting the results will show the multiple perspectives we have encountered, as well as make readers reflect on their own experiences of mergers and processes of change.

We shall now show how impressionism works in practice. By giving glimpses of life in the organisation coming from interviews, observations and documents we produce an impressionistic painting. For example, in the impressions of the Swedish company bought by an American competitor, we saw signs of the Swedish organisation as goal-oriented with a strong engineering culture and honouring egalitarian values. It was an organisation with an informal style, colleagues using each other's first names. Product quality and high technical competence were important, together with the ability to reach stated results. While interviews uncovered a sense that there were significant differences between the cultures of the two merged companies, and observational data suggested the company presented itself as typically Swedish, the documentary analysis showed that there were in fact similar underlying values shared by the American and Swedish companies.

Moreover, both shared values derived from a professional culture, if not a national one. One interpretation of this partly contradictory finding could be that what co-workers initially experienced, amidst the shock and turmoil of change, as differences between the companies, actually could be resting on a base of similar values. This is something that becomes evident only when the organisation is investigated more thoroughly, and also something that can be a valuable insight for the managers coping with cultural conflicts in the merger process. We can see how the use of multiple sources deepens the interpretations and helps us to give the reader a more finely grained view of the life in the organisation.

We have another example from one of our other cases. It is an Internet company in Stockholm that was bought by a German competitor. We visited the company during the days of the Internet boom. These are the thoughts of a project manager we interviewed:

> You not only work in the office, it is also a meeting place. You meet and plan the weekend. There are toys, like computer games, here, so you can stay in the office instead of going home. The work also gives you a chance to do what you are interested in. You plan your work as you choose, some do other things during the day and work in the evening. People can stay until ten or eleven.

This is how another employee described the life in the organisation:

> You were supposed to try to do any project, even though you did not know how to do it. You had to work it out in some way. Sometimes you managed just by chance to come up with solutions late in the project and by working many nights, which made things more expensive. You should be working until the early hours of the morning to make the project fun, someone told me. It is cool to work late.

Now, compare these interviews with this observation from the workplace:

> The kitchen on the first floor has a modern design in wood. Close to an espresso machine there are several young people standing in line, chatting while waiting for coffee. They do not seem to be in a hurry. There are no clean coffee cups so we have to take some from a pile of dirty cups close to the dishwasher and wash them ourselves. Close to the kitchen there is a big open dining room with several round tables. There is room there for about 30 people. Here the company offers breakfast to the employees every day. It is served until ten in the morning. The purpose is to get people to come on time in the morning.

Then, add the impression from this letter from management to the employees when it was time to go on summer holiday in June 2000:

> Friends. Soon time for holidays. It has been an intense spring with hard work and not very much peace and quiet. Together you have all done an amazing job. You have won the most important pitches ahead of our competitors, worked on an innumerable number of successful projects and new web projects. You have

started two new business areas at the same time as two new offices are being built.

PS. We will start the autumn with an 'after summer party' on the 25th of August for our Nordic business and all the other nice people we know. In the beginning of September we will also have the postponed introduction days for all those who have been employed during spring and summer 2000.

These impressions give us a picture of an entrepreneurial organisation where you have your best friends as colleagues. Social talent is required and having fun at work is an important driving force. You are expected to have a pushy attitude, be flexible, enthusiastic and possess a go-ahead spirit. However, we can also detect a darker side to the organisation: there are almost inhuman demands on the staff that lead to considerable stress. This can be especially difficult for individuals not sharing the same entrepreneurial enthusiasm as the founders of the company, for example persons newly recruited from other firms used to a better balance between work and spare time.

Metaphors

Both in the process of interpretation and in impressionistic presentation, metaphors are crucial. Metaphors are important clues to how people think. They are symbols of how people construct their world. Metaphors help us paint the impressionistic painting and give readers a deeper understanding of the organisation we are describing by stimulating readers' imagination. Alvesson and Köping (1993) suggest that we should distinguish between 'field metaphors' and 'theoretical metaphors'. The former are those that we observe being used in the field by the people that we interview. They use them as images to describe their own situation. Theoretical metaphors, on the other hand, are those used by the researcher as parables to describe what he or she sees. We used both types of metaphors, even though we have a special interest in field metaphors since they tell us a lot about the self-image of the interviewee and his or her company. For example, we found the 'family' field metaphor in the Internet company we studied. Some respondents compared the organisation to a family, before it was taken over:

> It has always been safe to have the culture we had from the beginning, which is family like, consisting of the little company and its soul … It is like a family, where it is not very hierarchical, where you can take initiatives and where you have friends at work. This has now changed to something bigger.

In our research we use another metaphor, the 'guardian angel'. It is a theoretical metaphor founded on our interpretation of the German company being seen as a 'guardian angel' who brings a stronger financial situation, better administrative systems and a more mature management; a 'guardian angel' who helped the company to survive when the stock prices of Internet firms fell and customers became more reluctant to hire Internet consulting firms, rescuing the employees from disorder and the company from bankruptcy. Consider this interview with a project manager in the firm:

> People felt it was a comfort having them as owners. Had we been on our own it would probably have been chaos, so we were lucky to have them there. A lot of people felt it was good not to have been bought by a Swedish firm. They were not doing so well at the time. We could always tell our customers that our company was doing well in Germany.

The use of metaphors fits our approach since we are influenced by the symbolist's view on culture. Symbolists like Smircich and Alvesson regard culture as a process in constant change. According to them we should not have a static conception of culture, but rather see it as something that emerges out of interaction between actors. If this is true we should regard the process of internationalisation and globalisation as an ongoing activity, in which actors with different perspectives come together creating something new. Metaphors are a clue to this process of sensemaking and production of meaning.

CONCLUSIONS

We have argued for the importance of using multiple sources in qualitative research in an international environment. Observations and document analysis can be used to enrich a traditional interview approach to data, giving us a chance to study the multiple natures of organisational behaviour and ethical thinking by adding new dimensions and triangulating data. Combining data from several sources also makes it possible to perform a longitudinal study going back in time by studying documents and narratives. In addition, it furnishes us with the possibility of studying changes to various parts of the organisation, such as comparing reactions of co-workers from different countries and divisions. While we used different methods for collecting data, our research design and implementation followed a consistent philosophical and methodological approach based on hermeneutics and ethnography. Other researchers in the field of international business, we hope, can find this way of working beneficial as well. It is especially important for a researcher who needs to gain more of a holistic understanding of change processes and for someone who recognises the role of the researcher him/herself as integral to the interpretations made. By taking such an approach, researchers may be able to construct new perspectives on the internationalisation process of firms, and incorporate dimensions not revealed in the short space of an interview or the truncated comments of survey responses.

REFERENCES

Agle, B.R. and C.B. Caldwell (1999), 'Understanding research on values in business', *Business and Society*, **38** (3), 326–87.

Alvesson, M. and A. Köping (1993), *Med känslan som ledstjärna – En studie av reklamarbete och reklambyråer*, Lund: Studentlitteratur.

Alvesson, M. and K. Sköldberg (1994), *Tolkning och reflektion – Vetenskapsfilosofi och kvalitativ metod*, Lund: Studentlitteratur.

Atkinson, P. and M. Hammersley (1994), 'Ethnography and participant observation', in N. Denzin and Y. Lincoln (eds), *Handbook of Qualitative Research*, Thousand Oaks, CA: Sage, pp. 248–61.

Berger, P. and T. Luckmann (1966), *The Social Construction of Reality*, Harmondsworth: Penguin.

Czarniawska, B. (2000), *The Use of Narrative in Organization Research*, Gothenburg Research Institute (GRI) Report 2000:5, Handelshögskolan vid Göteborgs Universitet.

Denzin, N. and Y. Lincoln (eds) (2000), *Handbook of Qualitative Research*, Thousand Oaks, CA: Sage.

Fetterman, D.M. (1989), *Ethnography: Step by Step*, Newbury Park, CA: Sage.

Fisscher, O. (2002), 'Qualitative methods in business ethics research', lecture given at the European Business Ethics Network (EBEN) doctoral conference, Brussels, August.

Gadamer, H.-G. (1960), *Wahrheit und Methode: Grundzüge einer philosophischen Hermeneutik*, Tübingen: Mohr.

Geertz, C. (1988), *Works and Lives: The Anthropologist as Author*, Stanford, CA: Stanford University Press.

Golden-Biddle, K. and K. Locke (1993), 'Appealing work: an investigation of how ethnographic texts convince', *Organization Science*, **4** (4), 595–616.

Heidegger, M. (1972), *Sein und Zeit*, Tübingen: M. Niemeyer.

Jarrick, A. and J. Söderberg (1993), *Praktisk historieteori*, Stockholm: Almqvist & Wiksell Förlag.

Kaijser, L. and M. Öhlander (1999), *Etnologiskt fältarbete*, Lund: Studentlitteratur.

Kylén, J.-A. and N. Vestlund (1980), *Intervju*, Stockholm: Utbildningskonsulter AB.

Marcus, G. and M. Fischer (1986), *Anthropology as Cultural Critique*, Chicago, IL: University of Chicago Press.

Pentland, B. (1999), 'Building process theory with narrative: from description to explanation', *Academy of Management Review*, **24** (4), 711–24.

Richardson, L. (1994), 'Writing: a method of inquiry', in N.K. Denzin and Y.S. Lincoln (eds), *Handbook of Qualitative Research*, Thousand Oaks, CA: Sage, pp. 516–29.

Rosen, M. (1991), 'Coming to terms with the field: understanding and doing organizational ethnography', *Journal of Management Studies*, **28** (1), 1–24.

Sellstedt, B. (2002), *Metodologi för företagsekonomer – Ett försök till positionsbestämning*, Stockholm: Stockholm School of Economics/Ekonomiska Forskningsinstitutet (EFI) Working Paper Series in Business Administration no. 7.

Silverman, S. (1993), *Interpreting Qualitative Data: Methods for Analysing Talk, Text and Interaction*, London: Sage.

Sköldberg, K. (1990), *Administrationens poetiska logik – stilar och stilförändringar i konsten att organisera*, Lund: Studentlitteratur.

Smircich, L. (1985), 'Is the concept of culture a paradigm for understanding organisations and ourselves?', in P. Frost (ed.), *Organisational Culture*, London: Sage, pp. 55–72.

Stake, R. (2000), 'Case studies', in N.K. Denzin and Y.S. Lincoln (eds), *Handbook of Qualitative Research*, London: Sage, pp. 435–54.

Van Maanen, J. (1988), *Tales of the Field: On Writing Ethnography*, London: University of Chicago Press.

Yin, R. (1994), *Case Study Research: Design and Methods*, 2nd edn, London: Sage.

17. Critical Discourse Analysis as a Methodology for International Business Studies

Eero Vaara and Janne Tienari

INTRODUCTION

Scholars of international business (IB) have typically not been interested in the broader social and societal dimensions of internationalisation and globalisation. They have all but avoided taking up critical views and methodologies. They have allowed sociologists and philosophers to ponder upon the potentially more problematic aspects of international business, managing and organising. Such a division of labour is problematic, however. In terms of IB research, it seems to lead to a lack of understanding of the fundamental social forces and counter forces in internationalisation and globalisation, and thereby to sustain simplified, ideal-type decision-making models in a complex 'postmodern' business landscape. It also appears to lead to a paradoxical inability of international business as a discipline to contribute to broader theoretical discussions of internationalisation and globalisation in social studies.

As part of this artificial division of labour, the bulk of IB studies have been characterised by positivistic methodological traditions. This has provided few tools for more in-depth critical analysis. Consequently, even those people in the IB field who have aspired to conduct different kinds of analyses have found it extremely difficult and time-consuming. In this sense, research time and effort have been misallocated.

We argue that, in order to conduct more critical analyses of various topics related to international business, scholars should consider making use of methods that have proved to be useful tools in humanist and social studies more generally. In this chapter, we present a version of critical discourse analysis (CDA) as a methodology that could benefit IB scholars and students interested in the social and discursive construction of internationalisation and globalisation.

Although we maintain that there are several ways of conducting CDA, we outline a model that may help in structuring research efforts, especially in international business. By drawing on our own experiences in conducting empirical studies on international consolidation through cross-border mergers and acquisitions, we illustrate what such analysis may include. We discuss what kinds of methodological and practical challenges are inherent in CDA, and show what kinds of results and theoretical insights may be achieved through such analysis. In particular, we concentrate on a media text – an editorial – that at a first glance appears to discuss recent (and future) cross-border mergers and acquisitions in the financial services sector in a 'neutral' and 'factual' manner. We go on to illustrate how such texts involve a myriad of discursive practices used to legitimate and naturalise international consolidation and its problematic consequences.

CRITICAL DISCOURSE ANALYSIS AS A METHODOLOGY

In brief, discourse analysis is a cross-disciplinary methodology[1] that has been linked to the analysis of text and talk in almost all of the humanities and social sciences during the last few decades (see, for example, van Dijk 1997). Discourse analysis is also often closely connected to postmodern and post-structuralist philosophy (see, for example, Foucault 1980). The definition of and meanings ascribed to the terms 'discourse' and 'discourse analysis' are, however, varied and far from unambiguous. Linguists appear to understand discourse as language use, psychologists as cognition, and sociologists as social interaction (see van Dijk 1997). Potter and Wetherell (1987) have famously claimed that there may be two textbooks on discourse analysis with practically no overlap. There are also different levels and units of analysis, extending from utterances to meta-discourses, and different methods ranging from detailed textual or symbolic analyses to the broader delineation of general socio-cultural discourses (see Alvesson and Kärreman 2000).[2]

We see discourses as one important area of social practice. Whether written or spoken, they are constitutive in a variety of ways. Discourses, in fact, (re)produce knowledge, culture, identities, subjectivities and power relationships in social and societal settings. At the same time, specific social actors are very much constrained and even disciplined by the available discursive resources and practices – of which they are often unaware. Discourses and specific discursive practices are also intertwined with other social practices, to the extent that an adequate understanding of discursive acts and processes usually requires contextual knowledge of the specific social and societal conditions in question.

Critical discourse analysis is a methodology that allows us to consider the constitutive role that discourses play in contemporary society (for a comprehensive introduction to CDA, see Wodak and Meyer 2002). There are two distinctive traditions in critical discourse analysis. The approach developed by Norman Fairclough (1989, 1992, 1995, 1997) focuses on three elements in specific texts. According to him, discourses should be analysed simultaneously on three levels: textual (micro-level textual elements), discursive practices (the production and interpretation of texts) and social practice (the situational and institutional context).[3] The discourse–historical method of Ruth Wodak (1996; Wodak et al. 1999), in turn, emphasises the importance of the historical dimension in such analysis by maintaining that the emergence of specific discourses always takes place in a particular historical context.[4]

What, then, are the general characteristics of CDA? The following four features, at least, are essential (see, for example, Titscher et al. 2002; Wodak and Meyer 2002). First, CDA aims at revealing taken-for-granted assumptions in social, societal, political and economic spheres, and at examining power relationships between various kinds of actors. Of specific concern are usually social problems and inequalities in the contemporary world. In a sense, CDA attempts to make visible such things which often pass unnoticed.

Second, from this follows an understanding that the researcher is not a 'neutral observer', but that his/her role is to acknowledge a particular kind of (critical) perspective. At the same time, he or she should be fully aware of the implications of this position. For example, being interested in a critical analysis of globalisation may imply a focus on the discourses and discursive practices that legitimate and naturalise the phenomenon. In this, as in any endeavour, the researcher should be acutely aware of the dangers in only looking for texts that confirm his or her own presuppositions.

Third, contextuality is a crucial issue in CDA. Consequently, the ability to place specific texts in their contexts is essential. On the one hand, this means taking the social, cultural and institutional settings seriously. For example, in studies of globalisation, the social practices that push the concept forward, as well as their problematic consequences, should be analysed carefully. Likewise, one should pay specific attention to practices that marginalise specific actors or silence particular voices. On the other hand, the historical dimension is especially important here. One cannot understand specific texts and discourses without considering the historical processes that have led to the current situation. Studies of globalisation in a particular context should therefore specifically focus on the historical events and historically produced conceptions that are relevant in shaping the contemporary discourses. This is particularly important given the fact that such historical understandings are often 'underlying', or have to be 'read between the lines' in the specific texts.

The final key issue in CDA, which is closely related to contextuality, is intertextuality – the linkages between different discourses and texts. In brief, one cannot fully understand specific texts or discursive acts without linking them with other texts and discursive acts. If, for example, one studies specific phenomena related to globalisation and analyses a particular newspaper column, one should focus on the general characteristics and dynamics of the media coverage, and place the specific discursive elements and practices in the text in question in this wider context.

As a methodology, CDA allows for the use of different kinds of methods in specific research projects. However, this kind of research in particular demands the ability to make sense of the linkages between specific textual characteristics and particular discourses on the one hand, and between the discourses and the relevant socio-cultural practices and historical developments on the other. This means that research of this type generally tends to favour in-depth scrutiny of and reflection on specific texts rather than more formal methods such as content analysis relying on quantitative measures. This is not to say that content analysis or other similar methods are not valuable tools in CDA, rather that, on their own, they are usually insufficient for 'digging deep' into the relationships between the text, discourse and socio-cultural practice.

What, then, are suitable empirical materials for CDA? Basically, any kind of textual material (media texts, archival material, interview transcriptions) is open to more critical inquiry. However, we focus on media texts in the following. We do this for three main reasons. First, the value of media texts has seldom been recognised in IB studies, in which interview material tends to strongly dominate qualitative analyses. It is thus a potentially novel form of inquiry for the audience of this volume. Second, media texts are readily available to the eager researcher. Texts in the printed press are increasingly available in electronic form on the Internet, which makes them practical and relatively easily accessible sources of evidence. This is especially important in critical studies for which it is frequently extremely difficult to gain access to specific companies – for obvious reasons. Third, media texts are public material. This means that, from the researcher's viewpoint, the often problematic question of confidentiality has already been 'solved'.

APPLYING CDA TO INTERNATIONAL BUSINESS STUDIES

As outlined above, CDA is a methodology that one can make use of in various ways. Through our own trial-and-error process, we have come to appreciate a specific approach, which we put forward in the following as a pragmatic model for IB scholars interested in discourse analysis. Our starting point is that we emphasise the importance of placing individual texts in larger contexts. Therefore, we stress that closer reading of specific texts – the core of CDA – is only one, albeit crucial, part of the analysis. It should also be noted that, due to the dominance of more traditional methods, critical discourse analysis is likely to raise more questions concerning 'sampling' and 'generalisability' in fields such as IB than among people who are used to it.

In brief, our model consists of the following steps: (1) defining/refining the research questions/interests; (2) overall analysis of the textual material; (3) close reading of specific texts; and (4) refining the findings and generalisations (see Figure 17.1).

Step 1: Defining/Refining the Research Questions/Interests

As in all kinds of research, it is extremely important to define the specific research questions of the study as carefully as possible before plunging into textual material. Although our version of CDA is inductive by its very nature – as most discourse analysis is – this should not mislead people into thinking that the texts could 'speak for themselves' without being seen through a specific kind of lens (research question). At the same time, due to the inductive nature of this kind of analysis, it often happens that these research questions and interests have to be modified and even radically changed. In fact, it is only at the later stages of the analysis that it is possible to tell whether the original themes of interest are to be found in the material at all and, consequently, whether the research questions should be modified and refined.

In our example to follow, we focus on the legitimation and naturalisation of cross-border mergers and acquisitions. In this case, the research question could more specifically be formulated as follows: 'Through what kinds of discursive practices do the Finnish media legitimate and naturalise international consolidation in the financial services sector?'.

Step 2: Overall Analysis of the Textual Material

A crucial question in this kind of critical discourse analysis is the selection of the textual material. This selection should obviously be guided by the research questions. In practice, it is important to cover a sufficiently wide range of material to be able to understand the themes and discursive practices that are typical, and which are exceptions. In our experience, handling more than around 100 media texts is difficult without a clear understanding of what one is looking for. In practice, it is easier in any case first to look for an abundance of material and then to narrow down the selection, rather than vice versa. This initial selection should not be confused with a more focused reading of specific texts at the next stage, however. Regardless of the initial selection, one usually has to make choices later regarding which texts or parts of texts to analyse more closely and which to present as illustrations in research reports or articles.

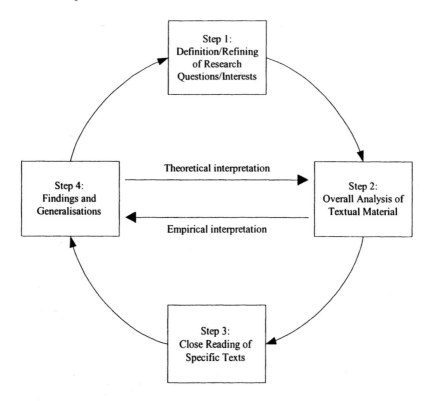

Figure 17.1 Critical discourse analysis as an inductive process

This stage provides the basis for contextual and intertextual understanding, and it is now that one is also required to gather all kinds of other material around the focal textual material. This may mean looking at previous studies, extending the selected material for specific reasons, for example, in order to understand the historical roots of specific issues or the emergence of specific public debates, or to conduct supplementary analyses such as target interviews. As a general guideline, at this stage one should be able to understand how the texts are linked with the historical events and conceptions that one is studying and the role of the selected material in the wider inter-discursive context.

In our view, this overall textual analysis could be best described as an attempt to grasp or 'take control' of the totality of the chosen textual material. This is an iterative process involving scanning, reading and interpretation.

What is most important here is that one is able to read 'between' and 'across' the lines and texts in order to understand the potential linkages between different themes. It is also important to pay attention to the 'unsaid', in other words to elements that, for one reason or another, are not given explicit attention in the texts in question. Early reflections on the 'unsaid' help in understanding, at the next stage of analysis, what are taken-for-granted assumptions in the discourse in question, what issues are not legitimate to be openly addressed, what concerns are not raised at all or given very little attention, and which voices are not heard.

Although methods may vary, it is possible to structure this stage of the analysis thematically. What themes are to be found in the textual material obviously depends on what one is looking for. This sounds like a truism, but it is important to bear it in mind in this kind of analysis. First, textual materials – especially if they are carefully examined by applying in-depth methods that focus on micro-elements, things said 'between the lines', and what is marginalised or not said at all – are extremely rich. Consequently, one finds a myriad of themes or issues even in short pieces of text. If one deals with wider social and organisational phenomena illustrated (and constructed) in media texts, the number of potentially interesting issues and questions is usually extremely large. Second, the methods used also guide the researcher to a great extent. For example, what words or ideas are taken to represent specific themes is a question of fundamental importance when one scans through the material.[5] Moreover, what passes as interesting in a more impressionistic reading is not random, but depends on what one already knows and what one is more or less consciously expecting to find.

For our example that follows, we were in a privileged position in the sense that we had gathered extensive material concerning the restructuring of the Finnish financial services sector in our previous studies (Kuronen et al. 2000; Vaara and Tienari 2002; Vaara et al. 2003; Risberg et al. 2003; Tienari et al. 2003; Kuronen et al. forthcoming). In brief, we had already concluded that a 'rationalistic' discourse drawing on the discourse and ideology of 'global capitalism' (see Fairclough 2000) appeared to dominate the public discussion. However, a 'nationalistic' discourse, in particular, at times seems to challenge this rationalistic discourse by drawing on context-specific nationalistic ideas and ideologies. This is the case especially in the context of the threat of a foreign takeover.

Conducting CDA implies a critical perspective. We wish to make it clear that this does not automatically imply condemning all international mergers and acquisitions, or the decisions taken by the managers in the companies in question. What CDA does imply, however, is a special emphasis on the alternatives to and problematic consequences of these restructurings, which are otherwise often paid little attention. Consequently, we wish to stress that these deals often have significant consequences for individual people who may lose their jobs or be forced to comply with all kinds of imposed changes, for individual shareholders having to convert their shares to those of foreign companies, for specific organisations and institutions whose governance and structures, not to speak of objectives and practices, change, and for the national control of specific sectors, which is bound to diminish dramatically when multinationals assume control of specific operations. It is therefore appropriate to focus on specific – often 'invisible' – legitimating and naturalising practices.

Step 3: Close Reading of Specific Texts

The close reading of specific texts is creative work that is difficult to describe in a short methodology chapter. This is not to say that one should not try to proceed in a structured and rigorous manner here, guided by the research interests/questions and the observations concerning the overall textual material, and making use of the existing work by others. What is important in this analysis, in any case, is the ability to identify and describe distinctive ways of making sense of the world that are linked with textual representations, specific socio-cultural practices and particular ideologies. This close reading requires focus, so in the following we analyse the exemplary text by moving from more general observations concerning the genre, the historical context and the interdiscursive context to a more detailed analysis of specific legitimation practices.

The following text was an editorial in the leading Finnish newspaper *Helsingin Sanomat*. We selected this particular text for close reading because it is in our experience a typical example of how the journalists writing for this newspaper – among many others – argue for and legitimate cross-border mergers and acquisitions in the Nordic financial services sector. It focuses on a rumoured cross-border merger between the Finnish–Swedish Merita-Nordbanken and the Danish Unidanmark (which took place in March 2000), but also refers to the planned acquisition of the Norwegian Kreditkassen by the same group (which eventually took place in October 2000). We shall show how this superficially 'neutral' and 'factual' editorial legitimates international consolidation through a variety of discursive practices that easily pass unnoticed. The point is thus not to focus on the justifications of these particular deals, but to look at how this text portrays international consolidation and the associated ideas of global capitalism as 'inevitable'.

HELSINGIN SANOMAT EDITORIAL 16 SEPTEMBER 1999

THE CONSOLIDATION OF BANKING CONTINUES IN THE NORDIC COUNTRIES
If it takes place, the merger between Merita-Nordbanken and the Danish

Unidanmark would be a logical step on the path that the management of Merita-Nordbanken announced would be followed when it was established two years ago. Merita-Nordbanken is seeking strong partners in other Nordic countries.

The Nordic banking markets are evolving in ever-greater units. Following the Merita-Nordbanken merger, Handelsbanken in Sweden bought the mortgage bank Stadshypotek, Sparbanken has taken over Föreningsbanken, SE Banken has bought the insurance company Trygg-Hansa, and the Danish Den Danske Bank has bought Östgöta Bank. In Denmark, Unidanmark has swallowed the insurance company Tryg-Baltica, SE Banken has bought Codan Bank, and Föreningsparbanken has made an offer for FIH Bank. Meanwhile, in Norway, the Danish Den Danske has been acquiring Fokus Bank, and the Norwegian Den Norske Bank and Postbanken are merging; and in Finland, Postipankki and Vientiluotto have merged to form Leonia, the OP group has been reorganised, and the Swedish FöreningsSparbanken has become a strong minority owner of Aktia.

Experts following the banking industry expect the consolidation to continue. Aside from the negotiations between Merita-Nordbanken and Unidanmark, there is interest in what the Norwegians, the Wallenberg family and the Finnish state are doing. The Norwegians are at this moment engaged in an internal discussion on whether cross-border banking mergers make sense, or whether to strengthen the sector through domestic consolidation. Nationalism is still strong in Norway, where mergers are distrusted because the Norwegians do not achieve a dominant position in the arrangements. There is also speculation about whether the Wallenberg family is interested in maintaining SE Banken as a general bank. One alternative would be to sell its general banking operations and for SE Banken to concentrate on corporate, investment and private banking: the general banking network would then fit in with Den Danske, which is looking for acquisition targets in Sweden. In Finland, people are anxious to see what the Finnish government will do with Leonia.

The focus apparently continues to be on general banking and treasury operations, in which size is an advantage. The concentration of activities and large volumes create efficiency in general banking, and technological development only accelerates this process.

The merger of Merita and Nordbanken has aroused special interest in the banking world because it is the first European merger of equals across national borders. The various difficulties and strengths that emerged have been closely watched. Hans Dalborg, the group CEO, clearly has a firm grip on the bank. This may sit badly with the Finns for national reasons, but for the success of the banking merger it is an advantage that the bank has strong management.

If Merita-Nordbanken now succeeds in getting a third party to join the alliance, the constellation will become even more complicated; after this the business cultures of these countries will have to be moulded into one banking culture. From the Finnish perspective, there is a danger that the Swedes and the Danes will form an alliance and leave the Finns out. In the longer run, there is the more philosophical question to be addressed: what is banking? Technological change is demolishing not only national but also industrial borders. Banks will face new competitors from surprising quarters.

Genre

In order to understand the specific text in question, it is important to examine its genre – a particular kind of institutionalised use of language (see Fairclough 1995, pp. 13–15). The text in the focus of our analysis is an *editorial* from *Helsingin Sanomat*. Such editorials are usually characterised by carefully written commentaries on specifically important contemporary phenomena. *Helsingin Sanomat* is a particularly widely read and influential newspaper in Finland, and it is fair to say that its editorials provide major forums for shaping public opinion. These kinds of columns that construct the 'inevitability' of specific social or economic trends could, in fact, be seen as particularly influential discursive acts in the public discussion around specific phenomena such as international consolidation.

Setting the text in historical context

We now turn to specifically important contextual information for analysing the editorial. Although it is easy to see the financial services sector as one industry among others, it is important to note that banking and insurance are an inherent part of national economic and financial systems, and thus of particular national and societal importance. Hence, consolidation across borders is a phenomenon that involves many nationally significant issues and tends to raise all kinds of questions concerning the ability to control international banking groups and to retain services in specific areas, for example. In this sense, Norway, Finland and Sweden are especially interesting cases because the banks experienced severe, although somewhat different, crises in each of these countries in the early 1990s. The state had to rescue the banking sector by instituting extremely costly financial operations. In all three countries, the crisis also provoked heavy rationalisation, which was often linked with domestic mergers and acquisitions. This has made many people suspicious of the longer-term consequences of mergers and acquisitions. Denmark is somewhat different in the Nordic context in these respects.

The merger between Merita (Finland) and Nordbanken (Sweden), announced in October 1997, could be seen as a pioneering cross-border 'merger of equals' in the European financial services industry. This case was followed by a further cross-border merger uniting Merita-Nordbanken and the Danish Unidanmark (in March 2000), and by the acquisition of the Norwegian Kreditkassen (October 2000). The two cases on which our analysis concentrates are (at this point) the last steps in the creation of the pan-Nordic financial services group now called Nordea. This group is thus a forerunner in the consolidation of the Nordic financial services sector and in the internationalisation/globalisation of this industry in the respective countries.

Intertextual observations

It is also very important to place the specific texts in their intertextual context, that is, to outline their position in the overall public discussion in this case. The merger between Merita and Nordbanken triggered a great deal of public discussion in Finland. In these commentaries, two discourse types were particularly prominent: the 'rationalistic' and the 'nationalistic' (Risberg et al. 2003; Vaara and Tienari 2002). In brief, 'rationalistic' discourse draws on the discourse/ideology of global capitalism (Fairclough 2000). Characteristic of this discourse is an abstract and objectified tone, and a focus on industries and companies, without singling out specific social actors. The 'inevitability' of industrial restructuring, as well as considerations surrounding the need to improve 'competitiveness', to create 'synergy' and to 'rationalise', seem to be essential elements of this discourse.

Nationalistic discourse, in turn, tends to look at international consolidation from the perspective of particular 'nationalist interests'. This type of discourse was frequently employed by Finnish journalists in the context of the Merita-Nordbanken merger. The texts were accordingly often based on 'us versus them' settings in which the theme of international 'confrontation' was dominant. In contrast to 'neutral' rationalistic discourse, the rhetoric of nationalistic discourse is often emotional, appealing to taken-for-granted, although often ambiguous, collective national sentiments (see Billig 1995; De Cillia et al. 1999).

Interestingly, when the focus shifted to the Merita-Nordbanken-Unidanmark merger and the acquisition of Kreditkassen, the strength of this nationalistic discourse appeared to decrease in the Finnish media. In fact, most of the articles on these cases tended to be 'rationalistic' in tone, as in the case of our text, although there were exceptions. There are two explanations for this. First, as people get used to domestic and cross-border mergers and acquisitions, industrial consolidation tends to become naturalised. Second, when it is a question of multinationals with no one home country, such as Merita-Nordbanken, nationalistic framing is more difficult than with purely national companies. This decreasing role of nationalistic discourse is, in any case, an interesting observation as it implies that new and ever-larger deals are apparently not as easily criticised from a nationalistic perspective as the steps leading up to them.

Legitimation practices

What happens in the studied editorial is that the future international consolidation is more or less consciously legitimated and naturalised through the use of different discursive practices. We shall now take a closer look at these practices. In our analysis, we make use of the model developed by Van Leeuwen and Wodak (1999) in which they distinguish authorisation, rationalisation, moral evaluation (we call it ideological evaluation) and mythopeosis (dramatisation) as typical legitimating practices.

Authorisation One of the means of legitimating international consolidation is to refer to authorities. 'Experts following the banking industry' is the most obvious example in this text. In other articles, 'markets' often serve as a powerful authority deeming the success of the project in question, but almost never questioning the need to proceed with consolidation across borders. In our text, the numerous references to other companies also serve as powerful examples of a general pattern to be followed. Note that the editorial appeared during a period of economic boom during which a large number of merger and acquisition plans were developed. After this hype, several of the projects referred to have proven to be less successful, or have even been abandoned. The text does not refer to companies following alternative strategies: for example, apparently profitable local banks are not mentioned.

Rationalisation What is the rationale behind international consolidation? Texts echo the typical argument that international consolidation is based on economies of scale. 'Size is an advantage' coins the idea that growing is the best thing to do. Although the argument is specified in the sense that size effects are associated mostly with general banking and the treasury, the reader does get the impression that these benefits are readily available. It is noteworthy that the text does not really discuss the problems that are often associated with creating such benefits, related to the costs of setting up a new infrastructure to benefit from the 'technological development', or the practical difficulties in planning for and enforcing the organisational changes required to reap the synergies, for example. However, specific integration problems are later touched upon twice in the text. The first time it is done by referring to 'difficulties and strengths', but this serves more to say that people have learned their lessons from the Merita-Nordbanken merger rather than to highlight the problems of integration. Second, it is stated later that 'the constellation will become even more complicated' with a third party, and that 'the business cultures of these countries will have to be moulded into one banking culture'. Here, the difficulties are not really portrayed as obstacles to the merger, but are rather set out as inevitable challenges – to be overcome.

The particular merger between Merita-Nordbanken and Unidanmark is specifically justified by a more complete structure, although the last paragraph does suggest that this may also make things more 'complicated'. Thus the reader does not get an overly positive picture. However, what is crucial for this analysis is that, despite the reservations about this particular merger, the basic rationale for international consolidation is never questioned.

Ideological evaluation On the whole, rationalisation discussed above is 'instrumental' in the sense that the ultimate objectives of international consolidation are not explicitly reflected upon. The reader is, in fact, supposed to share the basic ideology of global capitalism, according to which banks, like other corporations, are supposed to compete in global markets and to primarily create profits for their shareholders. This has, of course, not been the case historically, as many of the banks operating in the Nordic countries were built to serve 'national needs', or particular customer groups on a cooperative basis. 'Nationalism', an alternative ideology, is nevertheless explicitly de-legitimated in the first part of the text. This is done through claims such as 'Nationalism is still strong in Norway'. In a sense, Norwegians are portrayed here as 'old-fashioned' compared to the Finns, who have apparently already been wise enough to accept the logic of global capitalism. Ironically, nationalism was at times very strong in the Finnish media in the context of the Merita-Nordbanken merger carried out some time earlier.

The last two paragraphs of the text could actually be seen as a reflection that is directly linked to the nationalistic concerns that Finns may have about the Merita-Nordbanken merger. The fact that the Swede Hans Dalborg now has 'a firm grip on the bank' is explicitly portrayed as positive for the management of the multinational. In this context, it is acknowledged that 'this may sit badly with the Finns for national reasons'. The national reasons refer to the wide public debate in Finland concerning the previous cross-border merger between Merita and Nordbanken, when issues such as the distribution of ownership, the balance of power at the board and top managerial levels, the choice of location for the corporate headquarters, and the choice of the corporate language created strong reactions. Here, however, such concerns are treated as side issues that should be seen as unfortunate but inevitable in the wider context of multinational corporations.

Nevertheless, at the end, the question is raised as to what would happen if the Swedes and Danes were to form an alliance and leave the Finns outside. This is apparently a legitimate nationalistic question given the importance of the deal. However, like the concerns related to 'complexity' and developing a unified 'banking culture', this could be seen more as a challenge for the Finns in the new bank than a consideration that should prevent the merger from taking place.

What escapes attention, however, are the consequences for the employees and the customers. This would require some kind of a 'humanistic' discursive frame. As far as the employees are concerned, and especially during the Nordic banking crises, banking sector mergers and acquisitions have already led to massive layoffs, and have created all kinds of problems for employees struggling with continuous changes and the need to be competent enough to remain employed. One reason for this lack of reflection in this text is that cross-border mergers and acquisitions apparently involve fewer overlapping operations and therefore fewer immediate rationalisation needs than domestic deals. However, if one believes in the arguably inevitable technological development and in the need to improve efficiency while growing in size, this would obviously lead to consideration of the workforce at some point of time.

From the customer perspective, consolidation and rationalisation trends have usually led to the closing down of branch offices and to poorer service, especially for those who live in more rural areas and who may not be used to dealing with Internet banking, or who are not considered the most profitable. It would be legitimate to criticise the consolidation trend in this context, but this text, like almost all others, keeps silent about such potentially negative concerns.

Dramatisation   The text also uses age-old dramaturgical practices – mainly the construction of storylines – to legitimate international consolidation in financial services. As such, the references to the other banks and insurance companies are likely to make most readers think about the specific stories related to their merger, acquisition or alliance projects. From this perspective, the examples trigger a sense of drama and the expectation of seeing or hearing about new projects, such as the one being discussed. Such international consolidation projects thus become naturalised.

There are also more direct examples of dramatisation in the text. The title already implies that 'consolidation continues'. In the first sentence, the new merger is portrayed as the 'logical step on the path' that the company has to follow after it was 'established' in the Merita-Nordbanken merger. The second paragraph starts with a reference to 'evolving' Nordic banking markets. In the last two sentences of the text, 'technological change is demolishing not only national but also industrial borders' and '[b]anks will face new competitors'. Here the reader is left with the feeling that this international consolidation, resembling a natural force, is inevitable, and that it is probably better to be actively involved than to remain a bystander.

Step 4: Findings and Generalisations

Note that our example is not a 'complete' study in its own right, but rather an example from our long-term research project on international consolidation. However, as we are able to contrast this editorial with other materials that we have examined, we can draw some tentative conclusions. This text, which is in many ways a typical one, does illustrate how international consolidation is constructed by the media as an inevitable trend, and how this is done primarily by mobilising the 'rationalistic' discourse linked with the ideology of 'global capitalism'. It also illustrates how the legitimation of international consolidation involves discursive practices such as authorisation, rationalisation, ideological evaluation and dramatisation.

There is clearly a case for going further in specifying the findings and their generalisability in this case. As far as the overall textual analysis (step 2) is concerned, refining and categorising texts according to discourse types and showing, for example, tables summarising the frequencies of specific discourses or discursive practices would add to the accuracy of claims concerning the dominance of specific discourse types and make them more convincing. Such overall analysis could also involve comparisons across genres and publication outlets, as well as international comparisons. In our case it would be interesting to contrast the Finnish material with Swedish, Danish and Norwegian texts. As mentioned above, such overall analysis is demanding, and extending the scope usually brings with it a variety of theoretical and practical challenges.

Another option would be to compare specific discursive practices in different newspapers (broadsheets, tabloids and the business press), for example, both domestically and internationally. Historical comparisons are particularly interesting. In our case, we could follow up and examine the differences in media coverage over time. As discussed above, discourses and discursive practices apparently change when people become used to cross-border mergers and acquisitions. To better understand the dynamics of discourse formation, one could also examine the rare texts that do criticise this consolidation trend, and analyse the discursive resources and practices employed in these criticisms.

As should be clear by now, critical discourse analysis continuously forces the analyst to take a stand on issues, more so than in conventional analyses. This should not be misinterpreted as a licence to produce any kind of critical comment based on one's convictions or general observations, however. On the contrary, precisely because one is usually dealing with complex issues that allow one to express multiple and contradictory points of view, it is necessary to make sure that one's own interpretations are backed up by textual evidence and logical chains of argumentation. Structuring one's analysis into different steps, as suggested here, is likely to help in this difficult endeavour.

Finally, it is important in this context to note two practical questions that international business scholars are confronted with: the insider/outsider role and the translation of textual material. As far as the insider/outsider role is concerned, it is very clear that a native of a particular country is in a privileged position in terms of being able to place specific texts in their historical and intertextual contexts. This is one of the reasons why we recommend working in cross-national teams when comparing discourses in different countries (for example, Risberg et al. 2003). The translation issue is another matter: it is by no means straightforward to translate original texts and analyses from one language into another. For most IB researchers, like us, it would appear to be most meaningful to conduct the actual analysis in the original language, in this case Finnish, and then to translate the findings into the publication language, in this case English. However, here researchers should be aware of the fact that specific texts lose and gain meaning as an inevitable result of the translation process.

CONCLUDING REMARKS

Our starting point in this chapter was that there is a great need for critical IB studies. While there are various approaches to conducting critical research, we have been particularly inspired by critical discourse analysis. We have therefore presented our approach as an alternative that helps to guide the efforts of people conducting discourse analysis, and thereby to open up significant questions and develop theoretically and empirically grounded arguments on internationalisation and globalisation.

We have focused on the analysis of media texts, but critical discourse analysis can obviously be applied to other types of texts as well. Interviews, all kinds of company reports and memos, personal notes and diaries, Internet discussions and various other forms of communication are suitable targets for analogous analysis. Although a tricky endeavour, the existing academic literature on various international business topics would itself also provide interesting material for critical scrutiny. Nor should one discard visual representations as part of texts, although their in-depth analysis requires specific knowledge and skills. Moreover, this methodology could obviously also complement other research efforts. For example, studying the social construction of specific phenomena in international business could very well involve combinations of ethnographic methods and critical discourse analysis, as long as the researcher does not attempt to do too much and is aware of the underlying assumptions behind the specific methodologies in question.

The step-wise model outlined here is based on the idea of proceeding from relatively large sets of textual material to the close reading of carefully selected texts. The approach calls for specific abilities to distinguish linkages between texts and contexts, skills in terms of reading between the lines and reflecting upon the unsaid, as well as creativity in terms of being able to distinguish different discourse types and analyse their ideological underpinnings and implications. There are also specific challenges coming from the restricted amount of space available (such as in an academic article or a book chapter), and/or from a potentially ignorant audience such as hegemonic positivistic scholars in international business. It is thus a demanding methodology. However, if and when we wish to develop a better understanding of the social and discursive construction of key phenomena in international business, something like this is probably a prerequisite.

ACKNOWLEDGEMENTS

We are very grateful to Marja-Liisa Kuronen, Anne-Marie Søderberg and the editors for their insightful comments on this chapter.

NOTES

1. We wish to call discourse analysis and critical discourse analysis *methodologies* in order to emphasise the fact that such approaches may include various types of *methods*, in other words, specific ways of analysing empirical material.
2. See, for example, van Dijk (1997), Titscher et al. (2002) or Joergensen and Phillips (2002) for comprehensive reviews of different approaches to discourse analysis. For organisation and management scholars, Phillips and Hardy (2002) provide a particularly useful methodological reflection.
3. While all three levels of analysis – textual, discursive and socio-cultural – are important in CDA, it is also good to acknowledge that specific studies cannot focus on everything at the same time. Therefore, it is to be recommended that social scientists in general, and management researchers in particular, think carefully about how deeply they will delve into the linguistic analyses of specific textual structures, processes and functions. At the risk of being misinterpreted, we would in the end emphasise that it is even more important for people such as IB scholars to focus on the linkages between discourses and socio-cultural practices than to examine micro-level textual and linguistic questions.
4. Going more deeply into the ontological and epistemological underpinnings of these or other approaches to critical discourse analysis is beyond the scope of this chapter, but those interested in these questions are advised to read Titscher et al. (2002), Wodak and Meyer (2002), Fairclough and Wodak (1997), or any of the other books referred to above.
5. Contemporary information technology allows for carrying out relatively formal, 'quantitative-like' content analysis of texts. Software tools such as NVivo and NUD*IST may be of great assistance in such analysis. These tools assist in structuring textual material. It is useful to bear in mind, however, that (subjective) interpretation can never be avoided in analysing social texts from the perspective of CDA. In our view, the above-mentioned quantitative content analysis can never be a substitute for interpretive inquiry, in which the researcher also reflects on his/her own contextual knowledge and position as a subjective interpreter of particular texts. For the applied critical discourse analysis advocated in this chapter, quantitative content analysis would at best provide a crude overall picture of the material under study, with indications of the frequencies of key terms.

REFERENCES

Alvesson, M. and D. Kärreman (2000), 'Varieties of discourse: on the study of organisations through discourse analysis', *Human Relations*, **53**, 1125–49.
Billig, M. (1995), *Banal Nationalism*, London: Sage.
De Cillia, R., M. Reisigl and R. Wodak (1999), 'The discursive construction of national identities', *Discourse and Society*, **10**, 149–73.
Fairclough, N. (1989), *Language and Power*, London: Longman.

—— (1992), *Discourse and Social Change*, Cambridge: Polity.

—— (1995), *Media Discourse*, London: Arnold.

—— (1997), *Critical Discourse Analysis: The Critical Study of Language*, London: Longman.

—— (2000), 'Guest editorial: language and neo-liberalism', *Discourse and Society*, **11** (2), 147–8.

Fairclough, N. and R. Wodak (1997), 'Critical discourse analysis: an overview', in T. van Dijk (ed.), *Discourse and Interaction*, London: Sage, pp. 67–97.

Foucault, M. (1980), *Power/Knowledge*, Brighton: Harvester.

Joergensen, M.W. and L.J. Phillips (2002), *Discourse Analysis as Theory and Method*, London: Sage.

Kuronen, M.-L., J. Tienari and E. Vaara (2000), '"Päättyykö Meritan viidakkoretki?" Kielitieteilijän ja organisaatiotutkijan tulkintaa muutoksen sosiaalisesta rakentumisesta', *Virittäjä*, **104** (4), 518–41.

—— (forthcoming), 'The merger storm recognises no borders – an analysis of media rhetoric on a business manouver', *Organization*.

Phillips, N. and C. Hardy (2002), *Discourse Analysis: Investigating Processes of Social Construction*, London: Sage.

Potter, J. and M. Wetherell (1987), *Discourse and Social Psychology – Beyond Attitudes and Behaviour*, London: Sage.

Risberg, A., J. Tienari and E. Vaara (2003), 'Making sense of a transnational merger: media texts and the (re)construction of power relations', *Culture and Organisation*, **9** (2), 121–37.

Tienari, J., E. Vaara and I. Björkman (2003), 'Global capitalism meets national spirit: discourses in media texts on a cross-border acquisition', *Journal of Management Inquiry*, **12** (4), 377-93.

Titscher, S., M. Meyer, R. Wodak and E. Vetter (2002), *Methods of Text and Discourse Analysis*, London: Sage.

Vaara, E. and J. Tienari (2002), 'Justification, legitimization and naturalization of mergers and acquisitions: a critical discourse analysis of media texts', *Organization*, **9** (2), 275–303.

Vaara, E., J. Tienari and R. Säntti (2003), 'The international match: metaphors as vehicles of social identity building in cross-border mergers', *Human Relations*, **56** (4), 419–51.

Van Dijk, T.A. (1997), *Discourse as Structure and Process*, Vols 1 and 2, London: Sage.

Van Leeuwen, T. and R. Wodak (1999), 'Legitimizing immigration control: a discourse-historical analysis', *Discourse Studies*, **1** (1), 83–118.

Wodak, R. (1996), *Disorders of Discourse*, London: Longman.

Wodak, R., R. de Cillia, M. Reisigl and K. Liebhart (1999), *The Discursive Construction of National Identity*, Edinburgh: Edinburgh University Press.

Wodak, R. and M. Meyer (2002), *Methods of Critical Discourse Analysis*, London: Sage.

PART V

Researching Outside the Triad

Eating Alone and Other Experiences

Russell Belk

Soon after arriving in Romania several new acquaintances invited my wife and I for dinner at their home. But on two such occasions we ended up eating alone. It was shortly after the 1989 revolution and food was still hard to find in the Romanian city where we were living for a year. So we were as grateful for the food as we were for the companionship and for the opportunities to begin my research into the effects of economic transition on Romanian consumers. We arrived at the apartments of our new friends near the appointed times, only to be told over drinks that they had already eaten but that we should please eat while they sat and chatted with us. We thought these requests somewhat odd, but nevertheless we complied. Our hosts were professionals and business people so we thought that perhaps a late business luncheon had necessitated that they eat earlier. It was only after two such occurrences and a little more time in Romania that we realised that our friends had sacrificed their own meals in order to have enough to feed us. These incidents are now a vivid reminder of both how generous research informants can be and how naive we could be before a more prolonged immersion in this initially unfamiliar culture.

More recently at the end of the 1990s, my wife and I were fortunate to be able to spend a year in Zimbabwe. This time my research project involved the consumption patterns of the new black elite of the country and I decided to pursue a more collaborative type of research. I was teaching MBAs at a new private university and my students were themselves well on their way to becoming members of the economic elite. As part of a research course and an international marketing course in which they were students, I had them observe and interview doctors, lawyers, politicians and business people. The MBAs used video and sound equipment I had brought to record this data. They also helped me secure further informants and acted as my film crew while I interviewed and observed *nouveaux riches*. Two joint videos and several written papers came of this collaboration. This not only proved to be a very effective way to gather data, but the rapport, insights and enthusiasm that the MBAs brought to the project provided far richer and more valuable information than I would have been able to gather without them.

Besides these year-long projects, I have also conducted a number of shorter qualitative studies in such non-Triad locales as India, Thailand, China, Turkey, Hong Kong, Aboriginal Australia, Ghana and Nepal. I was only able to do this thanks to partnerships with local researchers. In most of these cases language alone (both verbal and non-verbal) would have otherwise precluded me from carrying out the research. Without partnerships, even a year in a new culture is only enough to gain a tentative understanding of local practices and beliefs.

But I have also learned that unfamiliarity sometimes can be an advantage. Without our taken-for-granted knowledge of a familiar culture, we can see things more freshly, 'with the eyes of a child' for whom everything is new and wondrous. Roland Barthes (*Empire of Signs*) even analysed Japanese semiotics, despite his lack of familiarity with the language and culture. Although there is a very real danger of Edward Said's Orientalism with such an extreme approach, researching very different cultures has a further benefit. It helps to de-familiarise us with our own cultures, so that we can begin to see them afresh. In an age of globalism we must pursue both the local and the global in order to understand either one. The global supermarket of consumer lifestyles means that we can eat alone no longer. *Bon appétit*!

18. Contextualising Fieldwork: Reflections on Conducting Research in Eastern Europe

Snejina Michailova

INTRODUCTION

The central theme of this chapter is methodological contextualisation. My underlying assumption is that fieldwork goes far beyond the 'sterile exercise of data-gathering' (Devereux and Hoddinott 1992b, p. 18) and that accuracy of the data could be compromised by ignoring or not taking seriously methodological contextualisation. The latter is defined by Johns (1991, 2001) as the information about how research access was achieved, why certain research decisions were made, and the practical costs and benefits of any intervention. Methodological contextualisation includes both contextualising the process of conducting fieldwork and contextualising the outcome in terms of generated data. In this chapter I focus particularly on the contextualisation of fieldwork. I illustrate some of my thoughts with examples from my own fieldwork in Eastern Europe.

My views on contextualising fieldwork have been shaped by a few sources. The first is recognition of the fact that the vast majority of books and articles on methodology are written by Westerners and most of the examples given in the methodological literature are based on Western organisations. Although I absolutely recognise their legitimacy and usefulness, there are a number of important methodological issues with which one has to deal differently from the way suggested in these writings when investigating non-Western or not entirely Western organisational settings.

The second source for shaping my views on contextualisation is my own accumulated experiences in conducting qualitative studies primarily in Eastern Europe. The organisational settings I shall explore here to discuss fieldwork contextualisation are of two kinds: Russian- and Bulgarian-owned companies and Russian companies with Western participation. My fieldwork in these settings provides evidence that some methodological issues need to be approached differently from the way suggested in the well-known methodological writings. As I shall explain later, an example is the identification of the field and the negotiation of access to it. Other issues, such as collecting empirical data in organisations in which suspicion and secrecy dominate, or meeting respondents who are not at all interested in receiving feedback from the researcher, are, to my knowledge, not discussed in detail in the methodological literature.

The third source of inspiration that motivates this chapter is a more general one and comes from my work as European editor of the *Journal of World Business*. In this role I am exposed to a large number of manuscripts, as well as to the correspondence between authors and reviewers. The editorial work, as well as my review work for other academic journals, equips me continually with evidence that methodological contextualisation in general and contextualisation of fieldwork in particular is largely ignored, or in the best case underdeveloped, in the majority of manuscripts. Situational influences become underplayed and universal claims tend to dominate. This is a sad fact, bearing in mind that as the subsequent review rounds take place and the revision process unfolds, in many cases it becomes obvious that authors do possess the required information to make the manuscripts much more contextualised. But only if shared with the readers, of course. My experience from a number of academic conferences and workshops on transition in Eastern Europe which I attended over the last ten years goes in the same direction: we as researchers in this field are preoccupied with sharing results and findings, but often tend to underestimate the importance of sharing how precisely we collect our empirical data. The latter tends usually to be limited to a few sentences indicating facts we cannot avoid mentioning, such as, for instance, the country where the study was conducted, the number of companies and respondents. A Western research team reporting that their conclusions regarding identities of Hungarian managers are based on 20 interviews in private Hungarian companies in the 1998–2000 period is, however, far from satisfactory. A Polish researcher assuming that there is no need to explain how she accessed the particular Polish case companies and conducted her observations there suffers from similar shortcomings. These are issues we hardly discuss and often quietly ignore. However, they define to a great extent not only the reliability and the validity of the research we conduct, but constitute the very content of the understandings and interpretations we offer. I am convinced that accurate and detailed contextualisation needs to be given voice and discussed explicitly.

Yet another source for shaping my views on the theme I explore in this chapter is my own background and orientation. In opposition to the claim that researchers must guard against imposing their own cultural perspective on the research design, data collection, interpretation and analysis (Adler 1983), I tend to argue that it is important to be aware – and make the reader aware –

of one's own conditioning and background, since they serve as the starting point of the research process. According to Hofstede (1993, p. 82), 'management scientists, theorists, and writers are human too: they grew up in a particular society in a particular period, and their ideas cannot but reflect the constraints of their environment'. Hofstede asserts that theories, models and practices are developed in particular countries and are infused with the distinctive characteristics of that culture. Boyacigiller and Adler (1991) point out that one of a researcher's responsibilities is to specify clearly the cultural boundaries of their work. I am a 37-year-old Bulgarian, born in Bulgaria and have lived in the country for 27 years. I hold a PhD degree in organisation studies from Copenhagen Business School in Denmark, where I have been studying and working for the last eight years. I have been conducting qualitative fieldwork, primarily in Bulgaria and Russia, for the last ten years. My observations and reflections are drawn mostly from case study research. Although most of my academic writings are in English, I have been conducting my fieldwork in Bulgarian, Russian, German, Danish or English depending on the particular situation in the field. I have always been interested in issues related to qualitative methodology, however, I do not regard myself as a specialist in methodology. There are many more questions that remain intriguing for me than those I believe I have found answers to.

IMPORTANCE OF CONTEXTUALISATION

Action and its local interpretation are always embedded within the social world of the actors themselves (Morrow and Brown 1994). Following Devereux and Hoddinott (1992a, p. xi), 'the context within which fieldwork is conducted is absolutely integral to the research process. "Contextual" and "methodological" considerations should be considered jointly, not as two distinct categories in which the first obstructs the pursuit of the second'. I go a step further and argue that transforming contextualisation into a methodological issue in its own right is more fruitful and rewarding than assuming implicitly that context is inherent in fieldwork. Such a view implies that context is not an external construct *within* which fieldwork takes place; it is internalised and constitutes the very nature of fieldwork. One immediate implication of such an approach is that subjectivity is not something to be criticised and avoided, excused or overcome, but instead taken seriously, valued and learned from. Following Gadamer (1975), our interpretive skills are grounded in, and only become possible through, our experiences and prejudices; denying or suppressing them can only distort the communication process and our ability to interpret. Viewing contextualisation as an integral highlight inseparable from fieldwork means that the researcher consciously and responsibly accepts contextualisation as one of his/her core responsibilities.

Viewing context and contextualisation in their own right is not to be confused with approaching them for their own sake. The meaning of a particular research approach is determined by the context of its system of epistemological beliefs. 'Methods do not operate independently of the system of inquiry adopted by the researcher, but rather they take their validity and reliability from their participation in this particular system of inquiry' (Polkinghorne 1983, p. 6).[1] Rousseau and Fried (2001) also advocate an appreciation of the integral links between context, well-specified theory and research design. In the same vein, Johns (2001) points out that the means for fostering context have to be used in a way that adds explanatory value to the conducted research. He suggests that the best question one can ask oneself in this respect is: does the inclusion of this information or the use of this design feature explain the constraints on, or the opportunities for, the phenomenon I am studying?

Having said this, I shall now move to a discussion of two particular ways one can let context and contextualisation be issues in their own right. One is associated with the need to discuss the specificity of the field where the researcher generates data. The other way to make fieldwork more context sensitive is to bring in seriously a discussion of the researcher as not merely an outsider to the field, but as a complex individual engaged in playing a variety of roles while being in the field as well as when entering and exiting the field. The rest of this chapter unfolds by following these two routes, taking into account my own experiences in conducting qualitative fieldwork in Eastern Europe.

CONTEXTUALISING THE FIELD IN EASTERN EUROPE

Fieldwork is not conducted in some ideal setting, but rather takes place in a certain set of organisational arrangements. In that sense it is always contextualised. My purpose in this section is to show how the particular context of Eastern Europe affects the different stages of fieldwork.

Identification of the Field and Negotiating Access

A number of authors have reflected upon different types of difficulties regarding access to the studied organisation and to individual informants (Andersen et al. 1995; Brown et al. 1976; Buchanan et al. 1988). Gummesson (1991) refers to this phase as *the* problem in qualitative research. The reasons for the difficulties are, however, of a different nature in Eastern European organisations as compared to Western ones. Getting access to the field is an issue which in my experience is rather divergent from what is described in the methodological literature. Buchanan et al. (1988) maintain that negotiating access is a game of chance, not of skill. My consistent experience, as well as that of numerous colleagues of mine who have been engaged for years in collecting field data in Eastern Europe, shows that fieldwork there is not the art of the possible, the art is to make it possible (Michailova and Liuhto 2000, p. 20).

One particular feature of the Bulgarian and Russian contexts in this respect that can be used for getting access to the field is recognition of the importance of personal networking. The researcher's informal networks usually constitute parents, friends, friends of friends, parents' friends, former high school and university mates and so on. Activating personal contacts and connections for identifying the field and getting access is often the only option in both Bulgaria and Russia since there is still a lack of systematically collected and filed information that is needed and helpful for identifying the potential organisation(s) to be studied. There are no reliable databases, files, registers or archives that may provide the preliminary information the researcher needs at the identification and pre-access phase (Michailova and Liuhto 2000). The main disadvantage of using personal connections for determining the field is that the researcher may in this way be forced to conduct a study in an organisation that may not be the most appropriate one for investigating the particular research issues he/she intends to deal with. Relying on informal networking, however, also has a number of advantages. First, the probability of getting access is rather high. In a cross-cultural Chinese–UK collaborative study (see Easterby-Smith and Malina 1999), it has been observed that access to UK companies proved much more difficult than to Chinese organisations. In China, as well as in Eastern European countries, strong personal links and well-functioning personal networks allow researchers to avoid dependence on official gatekeepers. Second, one may expect that if access to the field is secured by personal connections, the latter will also be employed for arranging interviews, getting access to meetings and other arrangements in the field, receiving more information in an informal manner and so on.

Another specific feature related to using personal networking is the reciprocity of exchanging favours associated with it. Reciprocity is a vitally important feature of personal networking. One is viewed as untrustworthy in Russia if one refuses to return a favour and does not follow the reciprocity rule. Helping friends through connections is regarded as a pleasure by many Russians (Wilson and Donaldson 1996), and the picture is similar in Bulgaria; both countries are particularistic societies.[2]

I shall now provide an example that illustrates the importance of such exchanges in the Bulgarian context and how they can be used for negotiating access to the research field. In 1996 I spent more than a month trying to get access to a company. I was making telephone calls and attending meetings one after the other explaining the purpose of the study, its design, the potential benefits for the company and so on. It simply did not work until I realised in an informal chat with a company worker that the company's CEO had a daughter who wanted to continue her studies at a foreign university. I immediately knew that the conversation with this worker gave me a card that could probably open the company door for me. It was now important to play this card carefully. Two days later there was an appropriate occasion and I managed to mention in passing, while the CEO was there, that because of the nature of my work, I had access to information regarding the conditions and requirements for obtaining a place at foreign universities. The CEO was impressed and very interested in receiving this information. He gave me permission to conduct my study during this very conversation and I provided him with the reliable information his daughter needed.

Preparations are Needed, but Surprises Await

One of the issues I have continually encountered during my fieldwork in Bulgaria and Russia is the discrepancy between the efforts I invested in planning and organising the field visits and how they really turned out. In both countries I have experienced again and again the following situation: there is intensive e-mail communication and fax exchanges, usually between the CEO and me, centred around the exact arrival time, days to be spent in the company, meetings to be attended, respondents to be interviewed and so on. In most cases, however, my appearance, which exactly followed the arrangements that had been confirmed several times, almost always turned out to be a surprise to people in the company, including the very insiders involved in organising the visit. The planned respondents were not even informed that they should act as respondents, the meetings were rescheduled without me being informed and so on. I attribute this to the fact that people in Bulgarian and Russian companies define themselves as 'very flexible': they continually interrupt each other, are suddenly called for meetings, and are used to situations where they are suddenly asked to involve themselves in an activity completely different from the one they were occupied with. Giving an interview would be such an activity, for instance.

Although my arrival in the company tended in most cases to be a surprise for the people in it, I was always immediately relaxed by them with the words: 'You shouldn't worry. Just tell us whom you want to talk to and we will organise it immediately'. Which they always did. I was given the opportunity to interview those people I wanted, and often more, and I was also brought to meetings, although none of the meeting's participants knew about that in advance.

No History of Cooperation with Researchers

In Eastern Europe, the very appearance of researchers on the company stage is still perceived by the majority of organisational members as 'very strange'. Managers and employees in socialist organisations were not at all used to encountering, and even less, working with, people from academia (Michailova and Liuhto 2000). There is no tradition of the academic community working closely with the business community, a picture that differs especially from the Nordic countries where these relationships have existed for a long time (Björkman and Forsgren 1997). The vast majority of people in Eastern European organisations are highly suspicious and resistant towards strangers from universities and business schools. They are highly insecure about the real aim of the data collection and the ways it will be used later on. In addition, they are uncertain about their own role in the process of data generation, mainly because they do not possess any previous knowledge related to this. Is it only they who are asked to be respondents? Who else has been interviewed? What did the others say? Does the CEO actually know we are asked to be interviewees? These are valid questions potential respondents struggle with. In addition, most of them act as respondents for the first time ever in their lives and there is a great deal of sensitivity and effort needed to make them providers of information.

One possible way to reduce the barriers provided by the climate of suspicion and insecurity is to have the CEO as the first interviewee. Having conducted an interview with the particular CEO, the introduction to the following interviewees could explicitly point out that (1) the CEO knows of the researcher's presence and data collection in the organisation; (2) the CEO has allocated time to give an interview. These details usually carry weight and informants tend to feel more secure. I applied this approach where possible. 'If the chief has agreed to give her an interview, it can't be totally wrong if I agree, too.' This approach eliminates the key obstacle, namely, the danger of acting as a respondent, which is usually deeply embedded in many organisational members' minds. Otherwise respondents remain in doubt about whether the researcher really has approval for conducting the fieldwork in their company. An assurance from the researcher's side that he/she is allowed access is not enough, but an interview already given by the CEO is proof. I have not really experienced that the initial reluctance then spills over to affect the behaviour of the respondent in the actual interview. Some respondents are, of course, more careful in revealing information and providing their interpretations, but this is not a feature specific to the Eastern European context.

When the data collection takes place in Eastern European organisations but the data is analysed and presented/published in a Western context and primarily for a Western audience, it helps if the researcher clearly communicates this fact to the Eastern European respondents. This eliminates much of their anxiety (Michailova and Liuhto 2000). In one of the Bulgarian companies several interviewees made this point explicit:

> Denmark is far away and you will be writing in English. Even if we make mistakes and tell you something wrong [in the sense that it does not fit with what is expected or officially approved by the company], nobody here will know about it. None of us speaks English, so it does not really matter.

Use of Tape Recorders

There is a host of issues related to using a tape recorder when conducting interviews in East European organisations and a number of those issues are discussed by Michailova and Liuhto (2000). Whereas a tape recorder is viewed as the accepted technology (Buchanan et al. 1988) for collecting data in the Western context, it poses a serious dilemma to the researcher in the Eastern European context. What should he/she opt for: ask for permission to tape-record the interview and, as a rule, get a refusal, or tape-record in a visible way without explicitly asking for permission and get the richness of the interview data? In all cases I opted for the latter although I did not feel comfortable about the approach. I was, however, sure this was the right thing to do if I wanted reliable data. Typically I asked: 'You don't mind if I tape-record the interview, do you?', and never 'Do you mind if I tape-record the interview?'. This makes a big difference in the Bulgarian language and I used this in order to avoid refusal.

The difficulties with using a tape recorder increase the importance of taking field notes. Field notes are an ongoing stream-of-consciousness commentary about what is happening in the research (Van Maanen 1988). Eisenhardt (1989, p. 539) suggests that the researcher should write down whatever impressions occur 'because it is often difficult to know what will and will not be useful in the future'. Taking field notes concerning the various conditions, circumstances, specific events and so on during fieldwork – besides those that reproduce the studied members' interpretations – is highly relevant. It is normal and very common that Bulgarian or Russian respondents conduct several telephone conversations during an interview, or interviews are interrupted by people coming into the respondent's office with several issues or questions that need to be solved, as they believe, here and now. There are disadvantages to being interrupted on a regular basis when conducting interviews. However, precisely these interruptions may provide the researcher with an excellent opportunity for gathering data.

Lack of Interest in Receiving Feedback

Another specificity of conducting fieldwork in Eastern European organisations is that company insiders are not interested in receiving the researcher's feedback. In Michailova and Liuhto (2000) I offer two probable explanations for this. First, I have speculated several times about whether managers in these companies intentionally did not want an outsider's feedback in terms of how he/she understands and interprets their organisational reality. Second – and I am tempted to opt rather for this one – as already mentioned, there is a general lack of experience of having researchers (especially in the field of social sciences) conducting empirical work in companies. From the various studies I have conducted, I can mention only one single case in which a middle manager agreed with me that 'it would actually be interesting to see the results of the analytical work'. Organisational members usually perceive providing an interview as a personal favour to the researcher. In general, organisational members do not approach the study as a mutual process from which they too might learn and benefit. They are in general not aware of what they may gain from this process.

The lack of feedback from the field respondents poses a challenge in terms of verifying research findings. Realising that respondents, including top managers, did not hit upon the idea of requesting feedback in any manner, I offered different options, such as a seminar at which I could present some of the findings, a written executive summary, or a later meeting with the CEO. This was always turned down politely and excused with the words: 'You don't need to worry about this', or 'We don't really have the time for this'. This confirms my earlier observation that providing the researcher with the possibility of collecting data is approached as merely doing the researcher a personal favour. In addition, this lack of interest in the researcher's feedback is another strong argument for making sure that interviews are tape-recorded in terms of assuring the exactness of the information. An additional technique to cope with the issue is to make a serious attempt to triangulate both research methods and data collected.

CONTEXTUALISING THE RESEARCHER

As introduced in the beginning of the chapter, one way to contextualise fieldwork is to discuss the variety of roles in which the researcher engages in the process of collecting empirical data. Situations in the field are never the same and they often unfold differently from the pre-planned, prepared or imagined manner. Attributes such as the researcher's age, nationality and language skills play a different role in the field and lead to different fieldwork decisions. In addition, these attributes are often perceived differently by the different participants in the field. As I shall illustrate in this section, Eastern European and Western managers in the same organisation have a very different – sometimes opposing – understanding of the researcher's roles and tasks, and consequently they develop different and sometimes contrary expectations towards the researcher's work and the desired outcomes of the study. In such a context the way the researcher plays the various roles, the way he/she combines them and prioritises them in the different situations and his/her ability to shift between multiple identities is not just important, but can largely determine the success or failure of fieldwork. I shall now explore the above-mentioned attributes on the basis of my experiences in the Eastern European context and, where appropriate, I will contrast this with my fieldwork experiences in Denmark.

Age

Let me start by pointing out that the terms 'young(er)' and 'old(er)' are culturally embedded, and people in different societies have different associations with and mental maps of what they mean when they use these notions. In Bulgaria, it is largely assumed that younger people are those below 35. This has for many years been associated with the fact that one could become a member of the Bulgarian Communist Party if one was below 35. By contrast, when the Danish Research Council calls for applications for research grants, 'younger researchers' are usually defined as being 'not older than 46'.

I was 24 years old when I conducted my first empirical study in Bulgaria. The more serious and ambitious ones I began at the age of 29. My first data collection in Denmark took place when I was 33. In the minds of my respondents, age was closely related to experience. The way I was perceived by the majority of my older respondents was as a not very experienced person, whom they would tell 'how things are' in their company. I knew about this perception and did not feel uncomfortable with it. Instead, I fuelled it by, for instance, referring myself to my age, either explicitly or implicitly. Bearing in mind both the length and the depth of the interviews I conducted, as well as the insights my older respondents shared with me, I can claim that the age difference was not a barrier – neither in Bulgaria and Russia, nor in Denmark. On the contrary, it had a number of positive sides. First, attributes such as status, power and very high expectations towards me and my work were not significant issues to speculate about. Being a younger researcher exposed to experienced and highly positioned respondents immediately implies a high level of inequality in terms of status, power and influence (Welch et al. 2002). The power asymmetry I have continuously experienced was so unambiguous that none of the parties, neither the interviewee nor I, considered status, power and influence as something to think of or speculate about – the situation was rather straightforward. Therefore, I could fully concentrate on the very interview or observation. Second, being younger, or much younger, than my respondents gave me the possibility of asking more provocative or more naive (at least at first glance) questions. The answers to those tended to be highly important for my analytical work, both while being in the field and in the subsequent stages of the research process. Respondents tended to clearly associate the directness and provocativeness of the questions I posed with my age. In both Russia and Bulgaria, however, I found it more problematic to talk to people around my age. This was probably because the comparison and competition in career development was immediately an issue, although hidden. This I have not experienced in Denmark.

Nationality and Cultural Background

Being Bulgarian helps tremendously when generating data in Bulgaria. Mastering the language is one important factor to consider in this respect and I shall discuss this in a section below. I am not certain whether I would be able to access the companies I do had I not substantial knowledge about what people there, as Bulgarians, find important or less important and what they view as appropriate behaviour. This applies not merely to securing access to the field, but also to conducting the entire fieldwork. This is not to say that a Westerner who masters Bulgarian would be less successful in such field settings. The costs in contextualising fieldwork with respect to national background would, however, be different. Whereas a Bulgarian grows up with Bulgarian values, attitudes and norms, and learns those through socialisation processes from a very early age, a Westerner needs to invest much more serious, conscious efforts in becoming familiar with various cultural dimensions.

This is not to say that a Bulgarian researcher is safe in conducting fieldwork in Bulgarian organisations just because nationality does not seem to be a critical issue in such a setting. As a matter of fact, collecting data in a culturally familiar environment can be disadvantageous precisely because the researcher assumes he/she is safe on these dimensions and he/she tends to take for granted much more than he/she actually should. The temporal dimension, that is, the specific point in time at which the research is done, can, for instance, be of greater importance than anything else, including national cultural familiarity with the research setting. The following example illustrates what I have in mind.

In 1994 I was collecting data in a famous large Bulgarian industrial company. I was at the stage of conducting interviews and searching for and studying archival documents. In relation to the latter, a company insider accidentally found and provided me with a number of photographs taken in the company back in the socialist years. I thanked the insider and took the pictures back to the Marketing Department office, which was assigned to be my base camp while in the company. The marketing people, most of them appointed by the company after 1992, looked at the pictures and found them 'funny' – on some of them we could see the present CEO and other top managers with their hands raised, obviously voting for a particular Party decision taken in the 1970s. An immediate spontaneous reaction in 1994 looking at this would clearly be: 'a totalitarian picture!'. This, at first glance, innocent, photo-episode came very close to costing me continued access to the company after some old-timers heard that I had these pictures. Why? Because 1994 was still a year when CEOs were appointed thanks to their political affiliation rather than professional capabilities; because employees were still insecure and afraid of losing their job if they sympathised with the (former) Communist Party; because company insiders at that time believed that locking up old pictures, reports, minutes of meetings, and other documents in lockers or burning them would help distance themselves faster from the socialist past when they had been heroes and key actors. And because I, the company outsider, although a Bulgarian, got access to something that was locked up and I did not hide it carefully.

I have experienced a number of advantages being Bulgarian and collecting qualitative empirical data in Russia. What mattered to my Russian respondents was not the fact that I was a researcher based in Denmark but that I was Bulgarian. In relation to this, it is important to point out that, compared to the other former socialist countries, Bulgaria has been the closest to Russia for centuries. This is rooted in old cultural traditions and in a series of *ad hoc* historical conditions and political explanations. Russians and Bulgarians used to call each other 'brothers', 'brother nations', 'common souls' and they still do. I was always exposed to expressions by the Russian respondents, such as 'You are Bulgarian? That's great, you are a Slavic soul!', 'You are Bulgarian, so you understand what I mean', 'Your parents live in Bulgaria, so you know what I am talking about'. To be sure, the respondents did not completely ignore that fact that I was now based in the West, but they, with my help, certainly valued my nationality more highly and as something much more stable and important than the, maybe temporary, fact that I happened to be based in the West. Whenever possible and appropriate, I encouraged my respondents' way of ranking the two attributes. My experiences and reflections are very similar to those of George and Clegg (1997, p. 1021), who elaborated on the process of organisational research in Sri Lanka being conducted by a researcher of the same nationality:

The commonality of personal experience proved crucial. After establishing this fact, the research was able to proceed – not because we established research, university or supervisory legitimacy, but because the respondent 'knew' and could vouch for an important and shared datum in the biography of the researcher. Particularism and personalism counted for far more than either the universalism of science or the objectification of the university as an institution.

The first set of my observations above related to my experiences as a Bulgarian doing fieldwork in Bulgarian companies and the second one to a Bulgarian conducting fieldwork in Russian organisations. I shall now briefly discuss some of the challenges I was exposed to in my fieldwork in mixed organisational settings where my respondents were both Russians and Westerners from the same companies. Besides Russians and Westerners treating the above-mentioned attributes rather differently, having different motivations for participating in the study and different expectations about the outcome of the fieldwork, there are additional challenges the researcher can be confronted with. I shall again employ some examples in order to illustrate my points.

In 1996, I was asked to write a case description of a Russian–Western company. The case was supposed to be used in a high-profile Western leadership executive training programme conducted in Russia by both Western corporations and Western business schools. One of these corporations was a partner in a Russian–Western joint venture and one of the Westerners working there offered this joint venture as the case company. My access to it was negotiated with this Western expatriate, together with the mediation of another highly placed executive who was among the initiators of the programme. Let me also mention that my meeting with the expatriate took place in Denmark right after a seminar which a number of top executives from all Western corporations involved in the programme were attending while I was representing the Western business schools involved in it.

Soon after the meeting I was invited to conduct my fieldwork in the company in Russia and collect the data I needed for developing the case description. When I arrived in the company, another Westerner, the deputy general manager of the joint venture, assured me that I could interview all five Western expatriates whenever it was convenient for me. He also gave me a list containing the names of 14 Russians I could interview. The list was accompanied with a schedule, according to which I had 30 minutes available for each interview. My immediate reaction was that I needed at least one hour per interview. The answer to that was: 'But the Russians in this organisation don't talk. We know them by now, we have been here for two years. It would actually be a success if you can make them talk to you for 30 minutes'. To the Western expatriates, I was clearly the researcher from a Western business school.

But there were more attributes I played with. To the Russian respondents, I was the Bulgarian, and not really the researcher from Copenhagen. And mainly because of this, combined with the fact that the interviews were in their language, I did not have a single interview that took less than one-and-a-half hours. Already after the first day of interviews, the Western expatriates became extremely interested in receiving at least part of the information I gained during the interviews with the Russian managers and employees. I had to resolve a dilemma. On the one hand, the Western expatriates provided me with the access to the company that would have been impossible without them. They also made sure that respondents were available and took care of all practicalities surrounding my stay in Russia. On the other hand, I did not want to reveal the insights the Russian respondents shared with me, and only with me. They trusted me and I got to know things which, I am sure, their Western colleagues will never get to know. In two interviews, the respondents, men over 50 years of age, cried when sharing their frustration about what they were experiencing in the company. The way I responded to this ethical dilemma was to avoid revealing the specific insights from the interviews, but rather stick to some more general observations. I also opted for taking up the issues that appeared as really critical in the interviews and referring to other researchers' findings on similar topics in similar organisational settings. I also referred to the case description as the only agreed outcome of the data collection in the company, and clearly refused to be treated as a short-term consultant for the Western expatriates. It was frustrating to realise the Russians and the Westerners were misinterpreting each other deeply and continuously, most often without being aware of it. Although this was brilliant empirical data to exploit for research purposes, it was painful to see, being placed between the two subgroups, some of the negative (and very expensive!) practical consequences of such mutual misunderstanding.

I have experienced the considerable advantages of conducting studies in a team with another researcher from a different national and cultural background. This was especially helpful in terms of avoiding being trapped in one's own culturally embedded assumptions. A colleague who is not so familiar with the culture where the studied setting is situated has the advantage of wondering about and asking questions about things a cultural insider takes for granted. Having a different angle offered by a co-researcher of a different nationality is also a great source of inspiration in the phase of analysing the generated data. Over the last four years I have conducted a number of field trips to Russia with a Danish colleague. There was not a single interview at which I have not been surprised by either questions asked or comments made by the Danish co-researcher, in the sense of believing that the answers to those would be so obvious that one does not need to ask. And every time I was surprised how wrong such an assumption can be.

Both in Russia and in Denmark, I have also conducted a number of interviews of Danish male respondents jointly with a Danish male researcher. I have repeatedly experienced situations that I found far from pleasant: a number of interviewees avoided eye contact with me and explicitly addressed my colleague when answering questions formulated by me. My thoughts, when speculating about the reasons for such behaviour, go in a few different directions: this might be due to my nationality, it might be due to age, probably due to gender, and most likely due to the combination of age, gender and nationality.

Language

The languages we master influence our research, including ourselves, the researched field, and the ways in which we collect data and address issues (Usunier 1998). Language is not merely a technical issue, it shapes both our individual views and the ideas we share with those who speak the languages we speak. People's understandings are not uniform, and concepts and terms are not used in a vacuum. They involve different associations in different cultural environments. In that sense, concepts themselves might be viewed as cultural artefacts and language as a means of communication in a particular culture rather than a universal means of communication. Therefore, mastering the language of the field is of critical importance. Otherwise it is enormously difficult and often impossible for the researcher to capture irony, humour, idiomatic expressions or sayings coming from the folklore of the respondent's culture. These are very powerful nuances in the process of interpreting qualitative data.

In a context where different cultures interact, language is a guide for classifying reality into perceptual units that make a difference for people in the culture (Terpstra and David 1991; Whorf 1956). In organisations where different languages are used and the parties do not speak 'the other' language, one encounters frequent reports of confusion and misunderstanding, unless two interpreters are used – one to carry out the translation, and the other one to monitor and provide feedback about the extent to which the intended meaning has been conveyed (Michailova 2000). During my fieldwork I experienced several cases of misinterpretation. In a Russian company with Western participation, for instance, in eight of the interviews with Russians our interviewing team of two researchers used the company's interpreter, although I spoke Russian and the interpreter knew that. Had one of us not understood Russian, we would not have been aware of the fact that on a number of occasions the interpreter completely modified the meaning of the questions or the respondent's answers. As I have concluded earlier (Michailova 2000), there are serious consequences of misinterpretation for organisational everyday life: the interpreter we engaged in the interviews was interpreting in the daily operations of the company and nothing can prevent me from assuming that if misinterpretations occur several times within a few hours in an interview, they also happen on a continual basis in the everyday communication in the company. In this particular case I would associate the misinterpretation by the translator with lack of concentration and failure to catch and/or reproduce the nuances contained in the respondent's answers.

I was, however, exposed to something much more interesting from a research viewpoint, but dangerous from a company's perspective. During one of my field visits in a Russian company with Western owners and managers, I happened to be at the office of the Western human resources manager when he conducted a meeting with seven Russian middle managers. The Westerner did not really master Russian and none of the Russians understood English, so the entire communication at the meeting was basically conducted with the help of the Western manager's assistant who was translating both ways. By the end of the meeting the Western manager outlined a few tasks that needed to be accomplished before the next meeting. The Russian interpreter translated those and, to my big surprise, added some more assignments, just by herself and without even informing her boss. He remained unaware of the situation. I can without major hesitation assume that this was not the first time the interpreter allowed herself to play with the power given her by the fact that she was the only one speaking both languages. Certainly, by mastering the languages too, I was privileged in my ability to spot all these situations while being in the field as well as access contextually embedded meanings.

CONCLUSIONS

In this chapter I argued that fieldwork contextualisation, integrated with a particular system of inquiry, constitutes to a great extent the very content of the understandings and interpretations we offer on the basis of the data we collect. I advocated the need to discuss explicitly and in a detailed manner why and how we contextualise our fieldwork. Not as an exercise for the sake of contextualisation itself, but as an important component of striving for meaningful knowledge.

The discussion in this chapter unfolded along two routes which presented distinct ways of letting context and contextualisation be issues in their own right. The first is associated with the need to discuss the specificity of the field where the researcher generates data. I illustrated my thoughts and arguments in this direction on the basis of the Eastern European organisational context and looked into a few particular challenges. These were extensive use of personal networks in order to identify the field and negotiate access to it, investing time and effort in preparing field visits jointly with company insiders and still being met with complete surprise from their side when appearing at the agreed time and place, dealing with insiders' suspicion mainly because it is new for them to have researchers around, the host of issues related to using a tape recorder, and the need to find alternative ways for verifying findings since people in the field are not interested in the researcher's feedback. The second road for contextualising fieldwork was centred around the need for the researcher to play a number of different roles in the field depending on the particular situation. Staying with my own fieldwork in Eastern Europe as an example, I discussed roles centred around attributes such as the researcher's age, his/her national cultural background and his/her language abilities.

Each field is unique in exposing the researcher to a number of challenges and contextualising fieldwork is not an easy and straightforward adventure. There are learning costs associated with becoming familiar with the context as well as remaining context sensitive. At the same time, the more you know and learn about a context, the more likely it is that you start taking it for granted, and thus there is a danger of becoming less context sensitive. In both cases, the learning costs are usually high. This is an additional argument, besides the ones I have already put forward in this chapter, as to why it is a good idea to share our experiences with our readers, both in terms of the joy and happy moments of success, and the mistakes we make and the frustrations we go through in the different stages of conducting our fieldwork. In other words, we need to extend the moments of reflexivity in terms of gaining insights into ourselves rather than into the object, process or phenomenon under investigation. Related to this, we need the skills and courage to make reflection much more explicit. Consider the following observations provided by Karl Weick in the 1999 *Academy of Management Review* special issue on theorising:

> There seem to be growing pressures on theorists to prolong and deepen those moments [of reflexivity] so that they will then see just how situated and constructed their universals are and how few voices their situated assertions incorporate. In Thorngate's language, there is pressure to move toward greater accuracy in explanations, but it is directed at the explainer rather than the objects being explained. (Weick 1999, p. 802)

Making such a move is a responsibility we need to take seriously.

NOTES

1. According to Mitroff (1973, p. 255), '*what* we know about a problem is not independent of *how* we have obtained that knowledge or information, and in this sense, it is not independent

of the particular system we have adopted for inquiry' (emphasis in original). For more on 'systems of inquiry', see Churchman (1971).

2. According to Hampden-Turner and Trompenaars (2000), particularism refers to the claim that a certain event is outside the scope of any rules and is unique. Particularistic cultures focus on the exceptionality of present circumstances. Rules are not as important as personal relations; individuals are not managers or representatives of remote institutions, but friends, brothers, sons, or persons of unique personal importance with special claims on emotional involvement. Members of particularistic societies such as Russia and China have a strong tendency to divide people into two categories: those they know and can trust and those who are strangers and who could be dangerous. In-group network relationships are very intimate, whereas trust towards strangers is typically very low. However, if fated to work with strangers, particularists are compelled to attempt to form personalised relationships with them (see also Michailova and Worm 2003).

REFERENCES

Adler, N.J. (1983), 'Cross-cultural management: issues to be faced', *International Studies of Management and Organization*, **13** (1–2), 7–45.

Andersen, I., F. Borum, P.H. Kristensen and P. Karnøe (1995), *On the Art of Doing Field Studies: An Experience-based Research Methodology*, Copenhagen: Copenhagen Business School Press.

Björkman, I. and M. Forsgren (1997), *The Nature of the International Firm: Nordic Contributions to International Business Research*, Copenhagen: Copenhagen Business School Press.

Boyacigiller, N. and N.J. Adler (1991), 'The parochial dinosaur: organizational science in a global context', *Academy of Management Review*, **16** (2), 262–90.

Brown, C., P.G. De Monthoux and A.E. McCullough (eds) (1976), *The Access Casebook*, Stockholm: THS.

Buchanan, D., D. Boddy and J. McCalman (1988), 'Getting in, getting on, getting out, and getting back', in A. Bryman (ed.), *Doing Research in Organizations*, London: Routledge, pp. 53–67.

Churchman, C.W. (1971), *The Design of Inquiring Systems*, New York: Basic Books.

Devereux, S. and J. Hoddinott (1992a), 'Introduction', in S. Devereux and J. Hoddinott (eds), *Fieldwork in Developing Countries*, New York: Harvester Wheatsheaf, pp. xi–xiii.

——— (1992b), 'The context of fieldwork', in S. Devereux and J. Hoddinott (eds), *Fieldwork in Developing Countries*, New York: Harvester Wheatsheaf, pp. 3–24.

Easterby-Smith, M. and D. Malina (1999), 'Cross-cultural collaborative research: toward reflexivity', *Academy of Management Journal*, **42** (1), 76–86.

Eisenhardt, K. (1989), 'Building theories from case study research', *Academy of Management Review*, **14** (4), 532–50.

Gadamer, H.-G. (1975), *Truth and Method*, edited by G. Barden and translated by J. Cumming, New York: Seabury.

George, R. and S.R. Clegg (1997), 'An inside story: tales from the field: doing organizational research in a state of insecurity', *Organization Studies*, **18** (6), 1015–23.

Gummesson, E. (1991), *Qualitative Methods in Management Research*, London: Sage.

Hampden-Turner, C. and F. Trompenaars (2000), *Building Cross-Cultural*

Competence, Chichester: John Wiley & Sons.

Hofstede, G. (1993), 'Cultural constraints in management theories', *Academy of Management Executive*, **7**, 81–94.

Johns, G. (1991), 'Substantive and methodological constraints on behavior and attitudes in organisational research', *Organisational Behavior and Human Decision Processes*, **49**, 80–104.

——— (2001), 'In praise of context: commentary', *Journal of Organisational Behavior*, **22**, 31–42.

Michailova, S. (2000), 'Contrasts in culture: Russian and Western perspectives on organisational change', *The Academy of Management Executive*, **14** (4), 99–112.

Michailova, S. and K. Liuhto (2000), 'Organisation and management research in transition economies: towards improved research methodologies', *Journal of East-West Business*, **6** (3), 7–46.

Michailova, S. and V. Worm (2003), 'Personal networking in Russia and China: Blat and guanxi', *European Management Journal*, **21** (4), 509–19.

Mitroff, I.I. (1973), 'Systems, inquiry, and the meaning of falsification', *Philosophy of Science*, **40** (2), 255–76.

Morrow, R.A. and D.D. Brown (1994), *Critical Theory and Methodology*, Thousand Oaks, CA: Sage.

Polkinghorne, D. (1983), *Methodology for the Human Sciences: Systems of Inquiry*, Albany, NY: State University of New York.

Rousseau, D.M. and Y. Fried (2001), 'Location, location, location: contextualizing organisational research. Editorial', *Journal of Organisational Behavior*, **22**, 1–13.

Terpstra, V. and K. David (1991), *The Cultural Environment of International Business*, 3rd edn, Cincinnati, OH: South-Western Publishing.

Usunier, J.-C. (1998), *International and Cross-Cultural Management Research*, London: Sage.

Van Maanen, J. (1988), *Tales of the Field: On Writing Ethnography*, Chicago, IL: University of Chicago Press.

Weick, K.E. (1999), 'Theory construction as disciplined reflexivity: tradeoffs in the 90s', *Academy of Management Review*, **24** (4), 797–806.

Welch, C., R. Marschan-Piekkari, H. Penttinen and M. Tahvanainen (2002), 'Corporate elites as informants in qualitative international business research', *International Business Review*, **11** (5), 611–28.

Whorf, B. (1956), *Language, Thought, and Reality*, New York: Wiley.

Wilson, D. and L. Donaldson (1996), *Russian Etiquette and Ethics in Business*, Chicago, IL: NTC Business Books.

19. Conducting Qualitative Research in Vietnam: Ethnography, Grounded Theory and Case Study Research

Nancy K. Napier, Suzanne Hosley and Thang Van Nguyen

INTRODUCTION

This chapter draws on the experiences of three researchers to examine the similarities and differences of doing qualitative research projects in Vietnam. Because of this book's emphasis on methodology and due to space limitations, we shall not discuss our projects' contents but rather shall focus on the research process and approaches used. In particular, we focus on our experiences with qualitative methods in a country going through economic transition and one where research has had a very different meaning from traditional approaches in developed countries. We follow somewhat the template of another contributor – Snejina Michailova (Chapter 18 this volume) – on doing research in Eastern Europe, because the contexts of transition affect both areas.

The rest of the chapter proceeds as follows. First, we begin with the practical realities of doing research in Vietnam, the difficulties these raised for us, and why we nonetheless persevered in doing our research. The section closes with a brief description of each of our projects. The next three sections examine the main tasks of research as well as the problems and opportunities we encountered in designing, conducting and disseminating results of our research. We close with a summary of lessons learned.

RESEARCH REALITIES IN VIETNAM

'Research' as a word takes on different meanings in different parts of the world. In Vietnam, and perhaps in other transition economies, scholars approach research in ways quite different from those of scholars in developed economies. This means that academic research in Vietnam has not traditionally conformed to 'international standard research' – in other words, research that is publishable in international refereed journals. In this first section, we discuss the nature and perceived value of research in Vietnam to organisations that seek it and to scholars that produce it.

The Nature and Perceived Value of Academic Research

In Vietnam, university lecturers and professors have traditionally viewed research as solution-oriented work, with little reference to or development and testing of theory. It is done for universities, ministries or other national government offices and it addresses issues specified by the research sponsor. The value of the research then depends upon the organisation sponsoring it: research sponsored by ministries or national organisations carries much greater weight and is perceived as having higher value than university-sponsored projects, for example. To be invited to conduct research for a ministry, scholars must be well known (that is, have a strong network within university and ministry organisations) and have seniority. The tradition of university scholars selecting their own topics, choosing their own research colleagues and team, and pursuing research using methods they choose does not exist. Instead, projects are selectively staffed with senior professors (whose names appear first) and junior lecturers (who usually do the work and whose names appear last). The nature of the research, as mentioned, tends to be more solution-oriented or responsive to specific questions than theory building or testing. In part, this stems from the educational grounding of Vietnamese scholars. Fundamental practices of international standard research such as recording or taking notes during interviews, reliability and validity, or using sampling techniques, which are covered in graduate courses in Australia, North America or Europe, are either considered unimportant or not considered at all in Vietnamese graduate education.

Another contributing factor to the challenges researchers face in following international standard research practices is Vietnamese culture. For example, interviewees will not talk with strangers and researchers must have an 'introduction' to be able to speak (somewhat freely) with interviewees. By their very nature, such interviews are convenience samples rather than random samples. Likewise, written mail surveys are rarely used because (1) the mail system is unreliable; (2) there is a lack of sampling frames; (3) subjects would not readily complete surveys received from a stranger; (4) the concept of surveys is unfamiliar to most people; and (5) if they did complete a survey, participants would expect payment.

Payment expectations arise elsewhere, as well. A major difference between Vietnamese research practices and those in developed countries is that faculty members in Vietnam expect to be paid for doing research. Because faculty members receive compensation for each activity performed in the university (for example, teaching classes, grading papers, attending meetings, conducting training programmes), the notion of doing research solely to build one's (or one's university's) reputation is not common. Moreover, there is limited funding available for research projects. In the past, scholars have rarely taken on research projects unless their superiors required it and/or they received payment for doing it.

But a change in attitude has begun. Some Vietnamese scholars are indeed initiating and participating in research that is being published in international refereed journals (for example, *Journal of International Business Studies, Organization Studies*) on their own or with foreign partners. When they do this, they are less likely to expect payment, since the opportunity to attend international conferences is in itself an incentive to do the work.

Publishing in journals is also valued differently in Vietnam from elsewhere. Sponsored research results, if published at all, appear in Vietnamese language journals, and the articles are often no more than four pages in length. Articles published by a single author contribute 100 per cent to the benefit of the scholar whereas the value of co-authored pieces is distributed proportionately based on the number of authors. Thus, a three-page Vietnamese language journal article published by a single author has more value in the traditional Vietnamese university context than does a 30-page article published by two or more authors in an international journal such as the *Academy of Management Journal* or the *Journal of International Business Studies*. In addition, it usually takes just one to two months for a solution-oriented article to get published in Vietnam compared to months or years for an article based on original research for an international journal. It is thus easy to see why local scholars doubt the benefit of doing international standard research.

The implication of such practices has been that international standard research in Vietnam has been performed by two groups: Vietnamese scholars trained abroad and foreign scholars with an interest in Vietnam. Until recently, it has been hard for such Vietnamese scholars to find colleagues with whom to share or discuss their work and/or domestic conferences at which they could present their work. This too is changing: as increasing numbers of Vietnamese scholars receive doctorates from abroad, they are developing networks with each other and with foreign scholars, and as foreign scholars initiate international standard research with Vietnamese partners, opportunities for Vietnamese scholars to present such research results at international conferences and/or publish in international journals are growing (for example, Litvack and Rondinelli 1999; Napier and Vu 1998; Ralston et al. 1999; Scheela and Dinh 2001).

Three Qualitative Approaches

This section briefly describes the three approaches we used in our research. Because of some of the limitations and constraints described above and summarised below, qualitative research is well suited to the Vietnamese context. Conducting surveys (telephone, e-mail or mail) is difficult: few people in Vietnam have telephones, fewer still have computers or e-mail and mail service is spotty. As stated previously, people are neither familiar nor comfortable with the idea of responding to mail surveys. Giving information to strangers is not done in a country where relationships dominate all aspects of life. Lack of familiarity with surveys is also a reflection of the political situation – while consumer surveys, for example, were used as a commercial tool in South Vietnam prior to 1975, this practice ceased once the country was reunified.

Thang is Vietnamese, grew up in a rural area of the northern part of Vietnam, has received his doctorate from an American university, and has been a lecturer at his Vietnamese institution for over five years. His project on the dynamics of inter-firm networks in Vietnam used a case study approach, following Yin's (1994) case study method and focusing on a private manufacturing firm in Vietnam. Thang spent two months shadowing senior managers, taking notes from formal and informal interviews with managers and employees of the firm, reviewing documents, and visiting and interviewing managers working for the firm's business partners.

Suzanne's project used a grounded theory approach (Strauss and Corbin 1998) to develop theory about how individuals learn and organisations change in capacity development projects in Vietnam. She conducted semi-structured interviews with over 60 people, observed behaviour in dozens of meetings and analysed over 100 project documents in three projects in the northern part of Vietnam over a period of one year. She then used coding and memo writing on her ongoing reflections with the help of NVivo software to develop and test theory from patterns emerging from the resulting data. Suzanne, a Canadian who has worked in Hanoi since 1990 and lived there for seven years, had rudimentary Vietnamese language skills: she did not speak much, but she could understand the basics. Her length of stay there and her relationship with a number of Vietnamese colleagues and friends gave her some insights into Vietnamese culture. Both Suzanne and Thang conducted their research projects as part of their doctoral programmes. Thus the design and conduct of the research was very systematic, thorough, and lengthy.

Nancy's research developed out of her work as a project adviser, rather than beginning as a research project from the start (Lynton 1998). She used an ethnographic approach, collecting data while living and working in Vietnam for a year and continued her data collection during the following three years as she commuted between the USA and Vietnam (spending 50–60 per cent of her time in Vietnam). She used participant observation and document analysis, using field notes, e-mails, documents and news reports, to track changes in a newly forming business school over the period. She then used an ethnographic software package for content analysis of key terms and changes. As she conducted the analysis and wrote up the research – discussed more below – she positioned parts of the project for different audiences and used the research as a spin off for subsequent projects as well. Nancy is American, with a background in international management research and experience in Europe and Asia, and has worked in Vietnam for nearly nine years. Suzanne and Nancy speak little Vietnamese and worked in settings where most of the Vietnamese were trying to conduct work in English.

In the following three sections (Design, Doing the Research, Disseminating the Results), we condense our observations, experiences and lessons learned. Using examples and illustrations from all three projects, we identify commonalities in terms of challenges and opportunities.

DESIGN

Designing the research projects included two main questions, discussed below: (1) determining what we could (or could not) study or investigate and (2) gaining access to the organisations we wanted to examine.

What to Study?

In designing the research, two of us let the research topics 'emerge' while the third (Thang) approached it more from a traditional theory-driven standpoint. Thang began with an existing theoretical base for explaining inter-firm networks (for example, Ring and Van de Ven's (1992) extension of transaction cost economics). He then argued that these existing theories were developed with an assumption that firms operate under strong market institutions and thus that these theories may not be readily generalised to firms operating in transition economies. To explore this issue, he used the case study method for data collection and analysis.

With her goal of building theory to understand and explain how people, processes and contexts interact to influence the individual learning and organisational change required for successful capacity development, Suzanne started with a literature review on aid effectiveness and capacity development that identified the limitations of previous research on the topic and helped to set the interview protocol. With no preconceived theory or hypotheses to start with, she let the theory develop from patterns emerging from analysing the field data. Nancy likewise moved back and forth between drawing upon field data and existing research on change in transition economies and change management (for example, Greenwood and Hinings 1996; Newman 2000; Newman and Nollen 1998) to create her broad research questions.

In all three situations, we discovered that the environment played a significant role in what we could investigate and/or report on. Some of those limits were unique to Vietnam; others are common to research anywhere. As is common in Vietnam and China, discussions about politics, the single party system, and criticism about government were generally off limits for discussion. In addition, government representatives and members of the Communist Party within the organisations we examined were sensitive about discussing personnel issues. We found we could not openly discuss strengths and weaknesses of individuals, that we had to be careful not to link events or situations to individuals and that, not surprisingly, we could not disclose confidential business information. In the private firm, for example, the manager limited Thang's involvement with and reporting on any meetings with customers or discussions about pricing. Even so, there were plenty of topics of value to research and consider. In the research on capacity development projects, Suzanne had to disguise the identity of the people providing comments and quotes so that they would not be recognised. While some of the constraints (such as specific political or personnel topics) were sensitive because of the context, many of the restrictions we faced are common in many settings (for example, not disclosing confidential information, disguising identities).

Gaining Access

In each case, we had to gain the trust, agreement and involvement of the groups we wanted to study. Personal introductions and/or direct involvement were critical. Sometimes access was quite difficult; other times less so – similar to qualitative research in many settings. Before gaining access to the private firm, for example, Thang expected problems because he was a scholar. Business managers in Vietnam typically see university faculty members as too far removed to understand business or to have anything useful to contribute to them: they do not understand or value the concept of research. Thus he anticipated resistance to the idea of him (as a scholar) being allowed to do a case study. Moreover, he expected that permission to 'shadow' managers would be hard to obtain because some business activities might be too sensitive for an outsider to observe (for example, dealing with government officials). He received an introduction to a firm through a third party and, contrary to what he had anticipated, he discovered that his impending doctoral degree from a US university enhanced his stature and increased the willingness of organisational members to meet and talk with him. Once 'in' the company, he spent informal time (for example, drinking beer, eating lunch) with the employees and managers, gained trust from them, and found access and openness to be no problem.

In the ethnography case, Nancy had two years of experience working within the organisation before she decided to study more systematically the process of change that the business school and its members faced. Only at that time did she begin to conduct more formal interviews, keep consistent field notes, and collect relevant documents. She had built trust and credibility through joint teaching and management training programmes with faculty members, working with office staff on mundane tasks, doing smaller research projects with faculty members, and consistently providing support to the university and business school administrators on the project she worked on. She also drew upon experience from a team-taught course on Management of Change, which fed directly into the research.

Suzanne's long involvement managing a development project in Hanoi had given her many contacts in donor agencies and other projects in the country. Using those contacts provided her access to three projects for intensive interviews, document review and observation. In all three cases, she obtained permission from the donor and the recipient organisation to conduct the research. Both parties in the three organisations were eager to participate in exchange for a written copy of the case study to help them analyse and assess their projects and to improve the possibility of success in future projects.

Given our backgrounds, time spent working in Vietnam, contributions and efforts to support the programmes we were involved with, we had earned some degree of local credibility and respect prior to starting up each of our projects. That in-country credibility, in the eyes of both the organisations where we worked and the broader group of organisations we contacted, made access more viable, allowing us to talk to people who otherwise might not have been willing to meet with 'strangers'. In most cases we were not strangers and when we were, the credibility and introductions by non-strangers helped the process.

Building and maintaining trust were critical in each situation, as they are in most research projects. Because of the general wariness of Vietnamese towards foreigners, trust took time to develop, resulting in the research being more sensitive to certain issues and constrained in certain areas. As we mentioned, the interviewees or organisation leaders sometimes placed restrictions on the areas we could discuss (for example, personnel, customers). Yet, in all of our cases, the organisational members had no obligation or requirement to participate in the research. Given the views about research and general scepticism of outsiders, we were surprised that they did so openly and willingly. Recognising that access was a special privilege, we made a point of building and maintaining trust in several ways. We tried to show respect towards participants and interviewees, we respected restrictions on areas/topics that could not be broached, we followed suggestions as to protocol, we maintained the privacy and confidentiality of interviewee and institutional names, and we provided non-research-related benefits or support to the organisation. For example, the general manager whom Thang shadowed had a daughter interested in studying in the USA. He introduced mother and daughter to Nancy, who discussed her university, gathered information for the daughter and offered to help support the application process.

DOING THE RESEARCH

Once we had access to the organisations or projects for research, we realised yet another difficult task was about to begin. Doing the research itself raised some challenges across the three methods that we used. Below, we discuss two issues: (1) acquiring accurate information and (2) data collection and analysis.

Getting Accurate Information

As with any qualitative project, gaining information that is timely and accurate challenged us. In this section, we discuss several issues and how we dealt with them.

In each case, we either spoke Vietnamese (Thang) or worked with colleagues who did (Suzanne and Nancy). Whereas Thang was able to understand the language and its verbal and non-verbal cues, Nancy and Suzanne had to learn over time (or asked others) how to interpret actions and words. For example, when a situation arose where the concepts of 'face' or 'risk taking' seemed contradictory to what she thought she understood, Nancy questioned some of her Vietnamese colleagues to understand the ideas in more depth.

Both Suzanne and Nancy gravitated towards people who were willing and able to play 'cultural interpreter'. Such people tended to be broad thinkers, with much exposure to foreigners and their mode of thinking, and could help interpret actions or decisions in a Vietnamese context for Nancy or Suzanne to understand. For example, Vietnamese sometimes take risks in their working lives, although the general assumption is that risk taking is uncommon. When questioned in more depth, colleagues explained that taking a risk in a generally unpredictable and chaotic environment provided an odd sense of 'control' over a small part of the environment. For all of us, this role of 'interpreter' was fundamental and essential to help decipher meanings behind the data we gathered. Some of the 'interpreters' were Vietnamese, others were foreigners who had lived and worked in Vietnam for several years.

Thang had several 'interpreters' within the private firm he investigated. The manager often explained to external parties that Thang was the company's and her 'trusted friend who is conducting some theoretical research for his doctoral thesis'. She also always emphasised that Thang was an 'insider' (*nguoi nha*) and his presence should not interfere with the conversation in any way. The manager he shadowed was clearly the most involved, and he used her as a first stop for reviewing what he saw and heard. On one occasion, Thang observed a cheerful conversation between the manager and her business partner. The manager wanted to subcontract some business to the partner, and the partner happily promised to 'consider and call back'. After the conversation, Thang probed the manager by reminding her that she perhaps had found a subcontractor. The manager, contrary to Thang's assumption, said, 'No. He said that just to be polite. He did not ask for specific issues, such as price or specification. That means he is not interested. We cannot sit and wait for him to call back! If a potential partner is not your close friend, he/she never says "No" directly to you'. On another occasion, two officials visited the manager. There were three people – Thang, the manager and a technician – in the office. One of the officials commented: 'Ah! There are many people here today'. The technician then asked Thang to help carry some product samples out of the office and told him, once they were both outside: 'The official suggested that they wanted to work with Mrs M. [the manager] alone'. These subtle meanings are hard to recognise for an observer, and thus both the original observations/language and the interpretations became part of Thang's data.

In two of Suzanne's cases, most interviewees did not speak English and she therefore used a language interpreter to translate her questions and respondents' answers. The interviewer selected was familiar with one of the projects (he had acted as a consultant to it) and with the 'language' of the second project (it was in a field that he was an expert in). In addition to translating questions and responses therefore, this interpreter also acted as a 'cultural interpreter' by commenting on the answers, after an interview or observation, and assessing participants' openness and meanings. He was also able to provide background information that put some of the answers in perspective: for example, who had been part of which power struggle, who had come out on top, and what the consequences were in terms of feelings and reactions to some of her questions. In the third case, she knew the people quite well, having worked with them for over seven years, and could 'interpret' their reactions and responses herself, yet she still required the use of language interpreters to interview some people who did not speak English. In this third case, it was important to select an interviewer who was not associated with the project to ensure that the interviewees felt free to discuss sensitive issues such as past decisions and impacts of these decisions.

Nancy found four Vietnamese colleagues who became 'cultural interpreters'. As fellow teachers, researchers, trainers and general colleagues, these individuals became her sounding board. She bounced ideas off them about what she was seeing and hearing, tested out her explanations with them, asked them how to interpret ideas she could not understand, and discussed with them which topics were reasonable and appropriate to pursue. In some cases, she had to back off from some inappropriate avenues of inquiry. One colleague finally said, after much discussion and patient joint analysis of some sensitive information she had heard, 'Be careful what you ask and whom you ask'. As mentioned above, certain issues like personnel decisions, promotions, or transfers were typically off limits for open discussion; unlike in the USA where such moves could be interpreted positively as a signal of organisational change and are not regarded as sensitive. Also, as ethnographers recommend, Nancy disguised names of her interviewees and informants and has continued to do so where necessary in presentations and publications.

In all of our projects, we found the use of a variety of 'cultural interpreters' and other interpreters critical to gaining insights into and adding depth to the observations we made. Recognising weaknesses in language limitations (Suzanne and Nancy) or business knowledge (Thang) forced us to find others who had more acumen in those areas and who, we think, helped to strengthen the results.

Data Collection and Analysis

We used a variety of data collection methods – several that were similar, but some that were not. Each of us used documents, interviews and observation. Nancy's university ethnography and Thang's case study used participant observation, since each of them either worked, or spent major portions of time, in their organisations. We discuss briefly our use of these basic methods in Vietnam.

Documents

Many secondary sources, especially statistics, are notoriously unreliable in Vietnam and yet because there is little else formally published, we used a number of these sources to help understand the context. Each of us used newspaper articles and magazines (for example, *Vietnam Investment Review, Vietnam News, Vietnam Economic Times, Statistical Yearbook*) and research reports published by donor organisations (for example, the Mekong Project Development Fund) as sources of information about the general political, economic, social and cultural environments, as well as for background on industries, organisations or donor organisations. We recognised that

Vietnamese publications were often biased and verified the information obtained with that available from international publications (for example, *The Economist*, the *Far Eastern Economic Review* or the *Asian Wall Street Journal*), to arrive at some 'unbiased' estimate of the true situation. In addition, Thang used directories of organisations (for example, lists of small and medium-sized enterprises (SMEs), donors) and statistics on economic and industry growth or aid donations as background information. Suzanne used articles and publications from donor organisations as well as from the Vietnamese government, as they offered differing views of the same situation. Reconciling different views often meant asking several people for their perspectives and building a clearer or more consistent case.

Further, all three of us examined documentation available from the organisations themselves, notably university publications, donor newsletters, company annual reports, project documentation, contracts with business partners, donors and consultants. For Nancy and Thang, the internal documents were not always extensive (or perhaps accurate) so we sometimes had to change the nature of the research data collection to 'fit' the limits of the data. For example, Thang wanted to study the nature of the contracts that the firm had with subcontractors. Because those contracts were often hard to get or lacked detail, he changed his inquiry from examining the nature of the contracts to the more fundamental question of whether they existed or not. In her research, Suzanne was given open access to substantial documentation such as government-to-government agreements, project proposals, terms of reference, contracts, progress reports, evaluations and so on, as well as internal correspondence. It was, however, important to acquire documents from donors, consultants and recipients, as different sides sometimes reflected different views of events and results.

We each sat in and observed meetings, reviewed e-mails and memos, and read relevant reports. In two cases (the grounded theory and ethnographic projects), the reports were written by foreigners involved with the activities (for example, consultants) as well as local participants. Thus part of the challenge was to overcome language difficulties: expressions were sometimes stilted if reports were written by non-native English speakers, Vietnamese reports had to be translated and misunderstandings occurred frequently in e-mails due to language barriers.

Interestingly, e-mails provided an unobtrusive measure of technological progress and adaptation to such in the ethnography project. Before 1996, e-mail was unavailable in Vietnam. After that, it was available to a privileged few that had computers and access to the Internet. By the late 1990s, the school had its own account and Vietnamese faculty members were able to access it easily but until 2000, few used it regularly. In fact, one Vietnamese faculty member noted that Asians tend to build relationships face to face, whereas North Americans (even more than Europeans) tended to be comfortable building relationships via e-mail, telephone or fax. As a result, he feared that the Vietnamese would lag behind others in their ability to generate and do business long term. By 2001, however, even some of the most resistant faculty members were using e-mail regularly – although of course that use brought a new set of problems and misunderstandings because of the lack of cultural and non-verbal cues available. This study of e-mail usage thus provided a type of unobtrusive measure of change within the business school.

Interviews

All of us held interviews with numerous people within each organisation. Some were formal interviews, in which we used the same/similar protocol; often we had informal discussions. During the formal interviews, Nancy and Suzanne always took notes. We always asked the interviewee if he or she was comfortable with note taking and all interviewees agreed, as long as the interviews were confidential and would be read/used only by the interviewer. Suzanne offered to provide interviewees with the interview transcripts so that they could assess the accuracy and completeness of the notes and make any corrections if required. Only one interviewee asked to read the interview transcript.

Suzanne recorded each interview on tape, a necessary step so as to provide additional verification of the interview translations (tapes were given to a second translator who translated the Vietnamese into English and this was then checked against the original taped translation for accuracy). There was only one case where an interviewee – a government representative – asked not to be recorded. In all other cases, interviewees were indifferent to the taping of the interviews. Thang faced the opposite reaction: he discovered that people were often reluctant to talk if he had a tape recorder. Perhaps the difference was that while Thang's interviewees were less familiar with the idea of recording interviews, Suzanne's (many of whom were foreigners) were more comfortable with the practice. Most of Thang's interviewees were managers of small Vietnamese firms, were not used to being interviewed, and often felt insecure about having their comments being recorded. Consequently, he had to rely solely on interview notes with lots of abbreviations, that he rewrote after the interviews, and transcribed at the end of the day. Suzanne was able to use her notes and the tapes together to transcribe interviews, which increased the accuracy of the transcripts, as the tapes were often difficult to hear given the background noise so often present in Vietnamese offices.

For the formal interviews, we all used semi-structured, open-ended questions as we were all seeking to understand why situations or events occurred and to gain insights into participants' reactions. Since we were all using qualitative approaches, we needed to let thoughts and topics emerge and we needed to elicit opinions and reactions to emerging patterns and to partially formulated frameworks. Finally, since little work has been done on organisations in transition economies, particularly in Vietnam, we did not want to limit the scope of people's responses, so we used questions that were as broad as possible.

Informal interviews or discussions took place in any setting where we had contact with members of the organisations we studied. We had discussions over beer, travelling together, before other meetings, and at parties. In such situations, we tried to note the bulk of the information as soon as possible afterwards. In all three cases, we recorded the content of informal discussions in field notes after the event.

Two other elements arose – one that can be common in any setting and another that may be more common in transition economy and developing countries than it is in developed ones. First, the interviewing process tended to be unpredictable, in terms of the amount of time needed and the conditions under which the interviews occurred. Thang frequently found that an interview he expected to be one hour could be double in length because of interruptions (from employees, from the phone, from the need to repeat the question, start over with the topic). Suzanne had no problem with interview time *per se*, as the schedules were all set in advance, but the travel time to interview sites added hours to the process. In two of her cases, people interviewed lived in different villages and communes in mountainous areas and many hours were involved in travelling by car and on foot to the locations.

The second issue relates to infrastructure and support. Often in Vietnam, the power goes out (for unpredictable amounts of time), which may make the research site uncomfortable (very hot, cold, dark) and difficult to concentrate in (for both researcher and interviewee). Conditions during Suzanne's interviews were often difficult, both in terms of recording information and in terms of managing the discussion. Many interviews were done in collective rural housing where entire families surrounded the interview team and noise from the fields, animals and household activities often interfered. All three of us conducted interviews in offices that had no windows but were close to busy motorways or parking lots, so the noise of truck motors and horns often drowned out the interviewee and/or the interviewer. Yet all of us found that the ability to put up with hot, uncomfortable and less than salubrious conditions alongside the interviewees and fellow workers helped build respect and credibility.

Forms of observation

For each of our projects, observing the organisational members, the means of interaction and understanding how things 'worked' was critical. Thus, we each used a form of field notes. For instance, Nancy recorded field notes – often several pages – every night for the year she lived in Hanoi and then continued to do so when in Vietnam over the following three years. She also maintained records of relevant e-mails for four years. The e-mails were from colleagues within the Vietnamese university or in her home institution, to and from others who were involved in the project (for example, visiting professors).

Thang's approach, for his case study of a single firm, was somewhat different. He shadowed the manager for two months, sitting in on meetings (except those with customers), visiting partners and suppliers, watching and listening (to the manager's side) in phone conversations. After such meetings, he debriefed the manager to gain more insights into the underlying meaning or objective of the discussions. As he sat in on meetings and was debriefed later, he also began to learn how to look at and 'read' the body language of the manager and stakeholders. He learned, for instance, to understand what was *not* asked about in meetings and why that was important. During or after those meetings, he recorded both the verbal and non-verbal content. He noted expressions, tone of voice and body language, for instance, and knew through his own familiarity with the culture how to interpret these, or discussed with and learned from the manager about the nuances.

Suzanne observed verbal and non-verbal interactions among actors before and after interviews, during informal discussions and during project meetings that she was asked to participate in. Note taking was done as soon as possible thereafter. Behaviour and body language were also noted during all interviews and notes about these were incorporated in the interview transcripts.

Whatever the method of data collection, finding culturally appropriate ways to thank participants – formally and informally – became critical as the projects got underway. Thang's motto was 'small gift, big impact' – the act of giving is more important than the gift itself. He found that providing pens or T-shirts with his US university logo went a long way in showing appreciation and opening up doors for more in-depth discussion. He also offered to help the manager and members of the firm in ways that he could. Nancy continued to bring gifts to the office staff and key administrative members, as well as faculty members, over the course of her involvement with the university in Hanoi. Interestingly, some of the recipients made comments after a couple of years that she did not need to bring gifts all the time, that they knew she appreciated their help without doing so. Suzanne did not use gifts *per se*. The *quid pro quo* used in her research was access to the results of the research on completion, which all organisations and most interviewees were keen to have. The most interested were the donor organisation and project management members, who could imagine conducting similar projects in the future.

In this section we have mentioned some of the realities we faced working in Vietnam. We have discussed the issues that arose during the course of the design and data collection of our three projects. Some of our experiences reconfirmed the problems identified in our initial discussion, others were new.

DISSEMINATION OF RESEARCH

While the idea of a report is useful to the organisations themselves (and Suzanne's organisations desire such reports), to reach broader audiences, all three of us seek to publish results or present them at conferences. In pursuing that goal, we found some twists and a few obstacles along the way to publication that we had not anticipated. These included: (1) a lack of interest by organisations in receiving or reviewing results; (2) a lack of understanding among the organisational members (and some colleagues) regarding the process of dissemination, in particular the lengthy time required; and (3) as is common in many research projects, negative reviewer reactions.

While organisations that are the focus of research often welcome (or even request) copies of the results from a project in North America, Australia or Europe, that was not always the case in Vietnam. In Thang's case, the offer of 'results' was not an incentive for the case study manager at all, whereas Suzanne's interviewees were all interested in receiving a copy of the results, in the form of a report to the organisations and, eventually, published articles. The difference seems to stem from the perception of how useful the results would be to the organisations being examined.

Although Thang was able to review and correct observations during data collection, his informants were not interested in reviewing the results following the study. In this aspect, Suzanne's experience was different again: all the project managers have expressed interest in seeing the finished product and are anxiously awaiting the results for review. In fact, many are expressing impatience at the length of time it is taking to come up with a final product.

The reaction of organisation members to review results – apathy in Thang's case and impatience in Suzanne's case – perhaps relates to the general lack of understanding about how the 'dissemination' process works. Organisational members anywhere tend to be surprised at the elaborate and lengthy process of publication. Often the process can take up to two years to submit a manuscript, revise once or more, wait for reviews and acceptances, and finally receive the finished publication. When organisational members hear about such a process, they may think that there is little point to the research since it will perhaps be out of date by the time the publication appears.

Related to this is the review process from the scholar's perspective, of course. Assessing research in a transition country, as well as qualitative research, sometimes means challenges for researchers and journal reviewers alike. Reviewers who may be unfamiliar with either component (transition country challenges or the nature of qualitative research) can be harsh and unforgiving. Thang found that one set of reviewers for an international journal was adamant in saying he should have included reaction and interviews with customers. While he agreed it would have made his study stronger, this was a condition of the manager of the case study – that he not be involved in meetings, discussions or calls on customers. Thus, his research limitations frustrated him as well as reviewers. Since he cannot change his research conditions, he must find other outlets for his research.

Despite the challenges, however, we have managed to publish or present pieces of our specific research, as well as other research done in Vietnam. Nancy intended to publish a full ethnography of the creation of the school and the change process it went through. She was unable to attract a book publisher interested in the Vietnamese experience, since most felt audience appeal would be too narrow. Instead, she is in the process of completing a book on transition economy management, of which working in Vietnam is a part. Further, she has completed several papers and articles relating to that project – ranging from challenges facing a start-up business school, to bi-cultural team teaching, to investigating paradoxes in the USA and in Vietnam, to conceptual and empirical examination of human resource practices in developing countries generally and Vietnam in particular.

Thang's research has also led to spin-offs of papers and publications that build on his case study and related research – on uncertainty in SMEs, on cultural differences between managers working in the northern and southern parts of Vietnam. In addition, he is writing a case study for class discussion as well as two manuscripts based directly on the case data he collected.

Suzanne's research is yet to be completed, but preliminary results of her research have been presented at two refereed conferences and are now being put together for submission to journals. Further, she expects that, because qualitative research is more supported in Australia (where she is receiving her degree), she will seek and be able to find non-US journals more open to her research.

SUMMARY AND CONCLUSIONS

Writing this chapter has allowed us to review our experiences conducting research in Vietnam. Our observations, we hope, are useful on several levels, primarily because we have each had extensive experience in Vietnam, we have tried to conduct systematic investigations (and have worked with each other on these and other efforts), and tend to be analysts of our activities no matter what. Further, conducting qualitative research in Vietnam or other transition economies may continue to be challenging but has been among the most fascinating experiences we have had as scholars.

Nevertheless, any researcher seeking to work in a country like Vietnam must recognise and decide how to deal with the challenges in such settings. In this chapter, we discussed challenges in four areas: (1) understanding the realities of research in Vietnam, including determining what is feasible to study; (2) designing research, including gaining access to organisations through networking and building personal trust; (3) conducting research, which includes acknowledging and working within conditions that are hard to understand and control, using 'cultural interpreters', language interpreters and local partners, and being ready and able to find alternative approaches when needed; and (4) disseminating research, which may require creative approaches to packaging the research output or to finding appropriate outlets.

As we have mentioned, however, we did adjust our research strategies somewhat because of the Vietnamese context. The questions we asked were somewhat limited because of political and other sensitivities. We realised that gaining trust and building credibility came from recognition by our informants of our long-term interest in, concern about and attempts to understand Vietnam's situation. And finally, we recognised that publishing would likely be (and has been) more challenging because of the research limitations than it might be had we done similar research in a developed country. Despite the obstacles, however, we would do it all again – maybe smarter but we would do it again!

REFERENCES

Greenwood, R. and C.R. Hinings (1996), 'Understanding radical organizational change: bringing together the old and the new institutionalism', *Academy of Management Review*, **21** (4), 1022–54.

Litvack, J.I. and D.A. Rondinelli (1999), *Market Reform in Vietnam*, Westport, CT: Quorum.

Lynton, R.P. (1998), *Social Science in Actual Practice: Themes on My Blue Guitar*, New Delhi: Sage.

Napier, N.K. and V.T. Vu (1998), 'International human resource management in developing and transitional economy countries: a breed apart?', *Human Resource Management Review*, **8**, (1), 39–77.

Newman, K.L. (2000), 'Organizational transformation during institutional upheaval', *Academy of Management Review*, **25** (3), 602–19.

Newman, K.L. and S.D. Nollen (1998), *Managing Radical Organizational Change*, Thousand Oaks, CA: Sage.

Ralston, D., T.V. Nguyen and N.K. Napier (1999), 'A comparative study of the work values of north and south Vietnamese managers', *Journal of International Business Studies*, **30** (4), 655–72.

Ring, P.S. and A.H. Van de Ven (1992), 'Structuring cooperative relationships between organizations', *Strategic Management Journal*, **13**, 483–98.

Scheela, W. and N.V. Dinh (2001), 'Opportunities and challenges of doing business in Vietnam', *Thunderbird International Business Review*, **43** (5), 669–87.

Strauss, A. and J. Corbin (1998), *Basics of Qualitative Research*, Thousand Oaks, CA: Sage.

Yin, R.K. (1994), *Case Study Research: Design and Method*, 2nd edn, Thousand Oaks, CA: Sage.

20. The Role of Culture in Conducting Trustworthy and Credible Qualitative Business Research in China

Giana M. Eckhardt

Your name or your person,
Which is dearer?
Your person or your goods,
Which is worth more?
Gain or loss,
Which is a greater bane?
That is why excessive meanness
Is sure to lead to great expense;
Too much store
Is sure to end in immense loss.
Know contentment
And you will suffer no disgrace;
Know when to stop
And you will meet with no danger.
You can then endure.

(Lao Tzu, *Tao De Ching*, 5 BC)

INTRODUCTION

Lao Tzu, in the above quote, advises not to constantly strive for more than one currently has, but rather to seek contentment with one's lot in life, in terms of one's acquisition of material goods and place in the social hierarchy. This is a fundamental tenet of Taoism (and similar ideals are prominent in Buddhist beliefs), yet this sentiment does not necessarily align with many motivational theories that have been used in marketing or management research, or even with the basic tenets of capitalism. This is illustrative of the following point: engaging in qualitative business research in China has many challenges, with one of the most prominent being gaining a thorough cultural grounding in the lived experience of the people under investigation, whether it is managers, entrepreneurs, retailers, distributors, CEOs or consumers. To do this, a general understanding of some of the nuances of Chinese culture and psychology is needed. Most of the qualitative business research that is conducted in China is done either by Western researchers or by indigenous researchers educated in Western methods, both of whom typically do not make many methodological modifications to account for what are sometimes profound differences in the psychology of those under investigation to those in the West, for whom the methods were typically developed. This issue is especially relevant when using qualitative methods, as the epistemological goal is often to understand those people under study in an experience-near fashion, or from an emic perspective. An emic perspective is the actor's understanding of the situation he/she is in, as opposed to the etic view, which discerns patterns from the conceptualisation of the analyst (Geertz 1975).

Often it is difficult to undertake trustworthy and credible empirical qualitative research without this understanding, with trustworthiness and credibility being two of the most important criteria in evaluating qualitative research (Stewart 1998; Wallendorf and Belk 1989). This is due to a variety of factors, ranging from not giving respondents the appropriate situation in which to express themselves to not interpreting results with a proper cultural understanding. This chapter outlines some of the most important cultural issues to be aware of in China. How these cultural issues affect a variety of data collection topics is explicated in detail. These range from designing a study properly, to collecting data in the most appropriate manner, to implementing modifications in methodologies, unit of analysis issues, appropriate analytical techniques, and issues of foreign/local research collaboration. It is argued that in many cases if substantial modifications from typical qualitative research guidelines are not put in place with regard to the above issues, especially in relation to psychological tendencies and responses of informants, credible qualitative research cannot take place in a Chinese context.

The analyses and recommendations offered are supported by a variety of studies that I undertook in the People's Republic of China using a range of methodologies, as well as literature in cultural anthropology, psychology and cross-cultural marketing and business. The methodologies that will be discussed include ethnographic observation, individual in-depth interviews, group interviews, scenario completion and experience sampling. In contrast to other chapters in this volume, these studies encompass consumer research, rather than managerial or firm research, and thus this chapter complements the discussions of qualitative methods in other chapters, which focus on managers, workers and firms.

While other authors in this volume (for example, Michailova, Chapter 18 and Napier et al., Chapter 19) explore aspects of society, such as politics and economics, that impact on the research process, this chapter focuses on aspects of the people who will be researched, with an emphasis on psychology as it interacts with culture. There are as many if not more differences within China as between China and the West, making it problematic to generalise about cultural tendencies. There are also tremendous differences within varying Chinese contexts, for example between Taiwanese and Chinese in Singapore. However, this chapter focuses on cultural traits that emerge from Buddhist, Taoist and Confucian traditions, which are common to many Chinese contexts. Several key aspects of Chinese culture and psychology will be discussed along with their implications for qualitative research design, data collection and data analysis. The two areas focused on will be social hierarchy and interdependence, two constructs that are closely related in that they both reflect the interrelatedness of society in China and its immense influence on behaviour, but also distinct in that social hierarchy reflects external determinants of behaviour whereas interdependence reflects internal, psychological determinants of behaviour.

THE INFLUENCE OF SOCIAL HIERARCHY ON QUALITATIVE BUSINESS RESEARCH

China is characterised by having, among many other cultural traits, Buddhist, Taoist and Confucian traditions. All three traditions emphasise the importance of social hierarchy to interpersonal interactions. For example, in Bond and Hwang's (1986) discussion of Confucianism, they outline three essential aspects that shape the Chinese psychological makeup: (1) man exists through, and is defined by, his relationships to others; (2) these relationships are structured hierarchically and are immovable; and (3) social order is assured through each party honouring the requirements in the role relationship. From this, we can see the emphasis on harmony in relationships. Society emphasises not trying to move up in the social hierarchy, but rather accepting one's place in it. A person's place in a hierarchy is of utmost importance to societal harmony, and a good citizen should not strive to break out of his/her place in the hierarchy but rather learn the expectations of that place in the hierarchy and adhere to them as much as possible. This creates a stable and harmonious society.

In contrast to the Confucian ethic of social responsibility and hierarchy, Taoist philosophy teaches solitude and introspection. To illustrate, the last two lines of a Chinese folk song with Taoist overtones read, 'The power of the ruler cannot influence me, I follow the rule of nature' (Bond and Hwang 1986, p. 223). Taoist followers do not believe in societal interactions, obligations or sanctions. Taoist followers do believe, however, that humans are fundamentally linked with nature, and that people should give up striving towards goals that make them materially better off and rather should accept their place in nature (Lao Tzu 1963). Confucianism has been the major influence on modern Chinese thought and politics, but Taoism still exerts a major influence on the daily life of the Chinese (Bond and Hwang 1986).

Both Taoism and Confucianism encourage one not to rely on inner attributes or ego-related characteristics to interact with others, but rather to see everyone equally as a part of the collective, each contributing proportionately regardless of particular characteristics or social standing. These cultural characteristics have many implications for how consumers and managers view the world around them, make decisions, and interact with others in the workplace and marketplace. For example, although materialism is becoming much more common in China, it is not a value that is necessarily advocated within society. Wong and Ahuvia (1995) suggest that in the West, materialistic behaviours reflect internally held materialistic values, but in a Chinese context, materialistic behaviours reflect face-attaining and -saving strategies rather than a personal value system. Ross (1991) and Eckhardt and Houston (2001) go further by suggesting that what is considered a material possession at all is qualitatively different for the Chinese than what has been reported in the materialism literature for Westerners. These authors suggest that the concept of material possessions be expanded to include non-material objects such as identity, personality, beliefs, ideologies and important others, to encompass results obtained with Tibetan Buddhists and urban Chinese residents. Thus an understanding of Chinese culture by the business researcher is needed to understand the construct of materialism from an emic perspective.

Social Hierarchy Influences on Responses

These cultural traditions have important implications for qualitative business research. First, when respondents are being interviewed, they will often first think about what someone in their place in the hierarchy should say or do before responding. In my experience, this often takes the form of subordinates not wanting to say anything negative about management, even when assured that their responses will be confidential. Also, younger people typically will not contradict older people and, although this is changing, you will still see females responding to questions in a way they feel is appropriate to their position in relation to males in many cases. How the respondent rates his/her place in the social hierarchy compared to the interviewer is also of crucial importance. In China, Westerners are often seen as high in the social hierarchy simply by virtue of being from the West, even by business elites. Because of the rigid nature of hierarchies, participant immersion in a fieldsite often does not overcome this barrier. I have found that having an indigenous researcher conduct interviews is the best way to address this issue. The interviewer must be intimately familiar with the goals and epistemology of the study, and the researcher has less control over steering the interview in the direction that he/she wants (especially when the questions are quite open ended and thus the direction of the interview is far from predetermined). However, it is worth the time and effort to develop research relationships with indigenous researchers rather than trying to break down the rigid social hierarchy barriers.

The Group as the Unit of Analysis

It should be clear from the above characterisation of Confucian, Taoist and Buddhist outlooks that the importance of others is one of the largest influences on behaviour. This has implications for choosing the unit of analysis when designing a qualitative research study. In most Chinese contexts the appropriate unit of analysis is typically the group not the individual, as almost all internally-held beliefs, attitudes and values are the product of important ingroup interactions (Markus and Kitayama 1991). This applies to managers or anyone in an organisational context as well as to consumers, as these psychological tendencies are not exclusive to consumer behaviour. This means that especially when conducting interviews, this should be done in groups not individually (see Eckhardt and Houston 2001, 2002 for a further discussion of this). Guangzhou and Shanghai consumers, whom I interviewed, for example, felt much more comfortable opening up when they were in a group setting rather than alone. Especially if the research goal is to solicit deep, rich verbal data on a particular subject, it is very difficult to achieve this when speaking with respondents individually. The interviews that took place in Eckhardt and Houston (2001, 2002) took place in groups, and the data garnered from these were far richer than the informal, individual interviews that also took place as part of the accompanying ethnographic fieldwork. Even the key informants in some fieldwork I engaged in, with whom I developed close relationships, were more comfortable expressing themselves in group rather than individual settings with me. From the characterisation of Confucian, Taoist and Buddhist outlooks described here, it is easy to see that manifestations of psychological processes, such as interpretations, evaluations and attitudes, are done collectively rather than individually, and thus it is not only a matter of being able to solicit the richest data possible, but to solicit meaningful data. If a respondent is forced to answer questions individually, this will not be an indication of what he/she would think/feel in more natural circumstances.

After choosing the group rather than the individual as the unit of analysis, to be able to capture important elements of social hierarchy and interpersonal interactions in a Confucian/Taoist/Buddhist society, the membership of the group needs to be decided. The group under investigation should be an appropriate peer group, not a randomly formed one. Because there are so many social aspects of interaction that are so integral to expressing oneself, the group needs to consist of people that enable the respondents to be the least constricted in their responses. In Eckhardt and Houston (2002), our scenario completion respondents were divided into three groups based on age. In China, younger respondents feel social pressure to agree with older respondents as a sign of respect, for example, stemming from the Confucian value of filial piety. Thus, putting them in their own age group enables them to have the most natural social interaction. Depending on the topic, creating groups based on gender is sometimes important. If interviewing managers within the workplace, hierarchy is of the utmost importance.[1] Creating groups based on place in the hierarchy is key in getting respondents to open up in the most natural way. The importance of the composition of the group in data collection is congruent with elements of a Confucian society, as the nature of the interpersonal relationships between the respondents is of utmost importance in creating and expressing opinions.

THE INFLUENCE OF PSYCHOLOGICAL INTERDEPENDENCE ON QUALITATIVE BUSINESS RESEARCH

While not all interactions are influenced by hierarchical concerns, they are all influenced by interdependence between people. Indeed, one of the most important cultural markers to be aware of is that the Chinese psyche is typically very interdependent. Being interdependent implies that one will behave and have thoughts, feelings and actions only in relation to the context one is in rather than in relation to internally-held values, attitudes or beliefs. Many Chinese do not necessarily think of themselves as distinct from others, do not necessarily construe themselves as having unique internal attributes (that is, abilities, traits, motives and values) and do not necessarily behave as a consequence of internal attributes (Geertz 1975; Shweder and LeVine 1984). The interdependent person is a relational being connected to others and belonging to groups, constituted as a member of society by virtue of this participation in a web of relationships and roles which people devote their lives to creating, sustaining and enhancing (Fiske et al. 1998). 'From this perspective, an assertive, autonomous, self-centered person is immature and uncultivated' (Fiske et al. 1998, p. 937). For people with an interdependent orientation, positive feelings about the self come from fitting in with others, engaging in appropriate behaviour, promoting other people's goals, and maintaining harmony (Markus and Kitayama 1991). For example, with regard to attitude research, as described by Fiske et al. (1998), for cultures that emphasise interdependence, it may be regarded as selfish, immature or disloyal to act in accord with personal attitudes – or even to express such attitudes – if they conflict with the maintenance of a smooth social equilibrium. Indeed, Fiske et al. suggest that people with an interdependent psychology need not hold one attitude about an issue at all. It is the norm to have a different attitude about the same object or issue depending on the social situation.

This interdependence has implications for a variety of constructs of interest to the international business (IB) researcher. Having an interdependent psychology will have consequences for cognition (Cousins 1989; Shweder 1990), emotion (Lutz 1988; Soloman 1984), motivation (Bond 1986; Murray 1938), the role and construal of the self (Fiske 1995; Triandis et al. 1990), attribution (Miller 1984; Morris and Peng 1994), rationality (Peng and Nisbett 1997), morality (Gilligan 1982; Miller 1994), the biological system (Gaines 1992; Jenkins 1994), self-esteem (Stevenson and Stigler 1992; Triandis 1989), interpersonal relationships (Moghaddam et al. 1993; Smith and Bond 1993), conflict management (Lebra 1984), and interpersonal communications (Smith and Bond 1993; Wertsch 1991).

Theoretical Constructs to Focus on

This psychological interdependence has implications for the qualitative research design process as well. When first setting out to investigate the business construct of interest, the theoretical constructs concentrated on might not necessarily be the ones that have been focused on in Western research settings. External rather than internal variables are typically much more predictive and explanatory of behaviour than internal variables in interdependent China, for example. As suggested by Geertz (1973) and Miller (1984), what is important in understanding behaviour is not an individual's attitudes, values, choices, desires, needs and motives, but instead roles, rules, social expectations and interpersonal relationships. Thus, in many cases in China, it is problematic to conceptualise the same link between attitudes and behaviour that is done non-problematically in the West. Thus, focusing an investigation on the nature of manager or consumer values, attitudes or beliefs – all internal psychological variables – may be inappropriate, and external, social variables such as ingroup and outgroup distinctions, face (Hu 1944) and status should be focused on instead.

When I was interested in investigating the nature of brand meaning in urban eastern China, most of the research with regard to this topic had focused on relating brand meaning construction to internal aspects of an individual, such as cognitions, memory and attitudes (for example, Aaker 2000; Briley et al. 2000; Schmitt and Zhang 1998). When I was designing my study, I instead opted to investigate the nature of interpersonal relationships in different consumption contexts in determining brand meaning (Eckhardt and Houston 2002). This had emerged as the most important determinant of brand meaning in ethnographic fieldwork I had engaged in prior to designing this study, and is consistent with an interdependent psychology. While culturally appropriate, it was more difficult to design the study as I could not follow the guidelines established in the literature for this sort of inquiry (developed in the West). The richness of the results, along with the fact I triangulated the results of this study with ethnographic fieldwork, ultimately led to meaningful, trustworthy, credible and novel results directly related to cultural effects.

The Importance of Context

An interdependent orientation also leads to cognitions being created and held in relation to important others rather than in a general, acontextual manner. An implication of this is when designing a study that will include interviews or self-reports by respondents, all questions should be couched in a specific context. It is extremely difficult for respondents with an interdependent orientation to respond to issues acontextually, as most opinions and beliefs are held only with respect to particular aspects of a situation. In the past, Chinese respondents have sometimes been characterised as unreliable because when asked about their views on certain topics, their answers change based on the aspects of the situation (Markus and Kitayama 1991). This reflects the malleability of internal constructs. In practice, this means that one cannot ask respondents acontextual questions such as 'How do you think the organisational structure in your company is run?' or 'How would you describe this brand?'. It will be extremely difficult for respondents to come up with acontextual answers, and more importantly even if they did, because they felt an obligation to respond, the answers would most likely not represent anything meaningful. Couching questions in terms of specifics is much more appropriate and will lead to meaningful, interpretable results. For example, asking 'Under the leadership of the current CEO, how do you think the organisational structure has benefited or not benefited you and your co-workers in your immediate unit?' or 'When you encounter this brand when you are out shopping at a mall on the weekends with your friends from university, how would you describe its image?'.

Eckhardt and Houston (2002) used three scenarios in a scenario completion task to capture a range of contexts. In one of the scenarios, in which the respondents had to give their impressions of the McDonald's brand, the scenario first said, 'Imagine you are out on a date'. During the pilot study using the scenario, the Chinese respondents all said, 'Which date is it?'. Whether they were out on their first, second, or fifth date made a big difference as to how they interpreted the brand. In the end we decided to say fourth date, as the social connotations surrounding being on the fourth date were closest to what we were looking for. We also used two other scenarios that described vastly different situations (being at lunch alone and in a hurry, and being out at a party with extended family) to compare brand interpretations based on context. If one was interested in brand interpretations in general, one would have to gather a variety of interpretations based on different, relevant scenarios and try and pull common themes from them rather than either asking acontextually or couching questions in one context only. In sum, seemingly meaningless contextual aspects of a question or situation can have considerable effects on responses.

Flexibility of Interview Protocols

Interdependence also implies a less linear way of thinking about and responding to constructs, as cognitions and responses will be formed and expressed in response to relationships and context. Flexibility needs to be included in the research design, as well as many open-ended questions in any interviewing technique, to accommodate this. While these are common features of many qualitative research designs, most Chinese respondents reply in more abstract ways to direct questioning than many Western respondents, and a more circuitous route towards finding the essence of what they mean is often needed. China is characterised by holistic thinking (Morris 1994), meaning that respondents do not typically speak in the straightforward, 'logical' manner many researchers are used to. Thus, being flexible in terms of implementation of an interview protocol, for example, becomes quite important. For instance, when asking consumers in urban China about their brand interpretations of global brands, consumers would sometimes have opposite opinions on brand image for the same brand, as these interpretations were based mainly on contextual variables rather than internally-held beliefs (Eckhardt and Houston 2002). Having inconsistent cognitions was not experienced as dissonant by any of the respondents, in line with the holistic nature of thought patterns. Having the flexibility to alter interview questions in the field and allow respondents to contribute their views in a totally open-ended fashion is what enabled these sorts of findings to emerge, and what allowed me to interpret this holistic nature of brand interpretation in a meaningful manner.

In sum, interdependence is one of the most important cultural traits for qualitative IB researchers to understand. Interdependence (as a cultural trait) manifests itself in a variety of ways, individually and organisationally, and knowing the basic tenets of an interdependent mindset will help guide the research process, and make it more trustworthy and credible. Even if one is not directly investigating cultural effects, but rather, say, the intricacies of joint venture set-ups or advertising campaign creation, having the cultural awareness described in this section allows the data collection effort to be designed and analysed to maximise the findings, to be able to put the findings in their proper cultural context, and to be able to interpret what may seem like deviations from well-accepted psychological and organisational theories.

The Necessity for Triangulation

The group centredness that comes with an interdependent orientation has some important implications for data collection. First, when planning the research effort, the qualitative IB researcher has a toolbox of methods to choose from. Many times the methods chosen will not include observation. However, in many Chinese contexts, there is a heightened need for observational fieldwork to accompany verbal self-report research techniques (that is, depth interviews, focus groups).[2] While it is not always possible to engage in observational fieldwork, using it as a form of triangulation is one of the most powerful ways to establish credibility and trustworthiness in the data. This is because it is discouraged in Chinese culture for people to speak out on their true inner thoughts and feelings (Fiske et al. 1998), so it is very difficult if not impossible to get the level of disclosure that can be achieved in interviews in a Western context. It is not encouraged in the educational system as people are growing up to develop individual opinions and be able to express them in a complex and well-developed manner. No matter how well designed the interview questions are, how comfortable the respondent is with the interviewer, how informal and/or unstructured the discussion between the respondent and researcher is, it is typical to receive one- and two-sentence answers to most questions.

For example, when I was asking urban Chinese consumers about their most prized possessions, as part of an extended study on how consumers attach meanings to products, interviews would typically last 20 minutes, whereas the same interviews would last 40 minutes in the USA (Eckhardt and Houston 2001). This was utilising a research assistant who was of the same peer group as the respondents conducting the interviews, and she was even a close friend of some of the respondents. For example, some of the respondents described their most important possession as their family, or their love of family. When prompted to expand on this, such as what about your family makes it so important, or what aspects of your love for your family are most important to you, they were dumbfounded that anyone would even ask that sort of question. They would typically respond by saying simply that nothing is more important than family or love of family and could not expand on it any further. The meaning and importance of these concepts is so widely shared by society, and more importantly by their ingroup, it is not necessary for people to explain themselves. Because meanings and thoughts and feelings are shared, and in fact jointly developed, people are not used to explaining individual feelings, preferences and reasonings.

Thus, using observation not only to triangulate self-report results but also to add to their richness greatly enhances the usability of the data. For example, as described in Eckhardt and Houston (2001), most key informants said in their verbal reports that motorcycles symbolised foreignness, decadence and danger. Many respondents related this product category to non-traditional Chinese values, and implied that people who rode motorcycles were embracing Western values. However, extended observation of one of the neighbourhoods under study revealed that motorcycles actually reinforce many traditional Confucian values, such as enhancing close bonds with neighbourhood ingroup members, by virtue of the way motorcycles are stored (communally in the street, held together by a chain, run by local women). This aspect of the meaning of motorcycles was not verbalised, yet was important in understanding the verbal data that had been collected and enriched the analysis process.

The Importance of Insider/Outsider Teams

A group orientation also implies that if one is a member of an outgroup (as foreigners typically are, even after extended time periods of living in a community – it is notoriously difficult, if not impossible, to break into the strictly defined ingroups in China), behaviour and responses from participants in a study will be qualitatively different from when a member of an ingroup is collecting the data. Collaborating with Chinese colleagues, and having them actually collect the data, improves the trustworthiness of the data collection dramatically, primarily due to these demand effects. Ideally, working in insider/outsider teams is recommended (Greenfield 1997). This is when at least one member of the research team is from the culture under study and at least one member is from an outside culture. This helps to ensure both culturally relevant data collection design and analysis, as well as an outsider's input that might uncover insights unrecognisable to one from the culture under study (Ratner 1997). During actual data collection, it also means that there will be a degree of comfort and familiarity (for the respondents) if the researcher from the culture under study collects the data. I have found dramatic differences in the richness of the data gathered when I am present during interviews compared to when I am not present, even after developing relationships with respondents. When it has not been possible for me to collaborate with an academic researcher from the culture under study, I have hired a professional qualitative market researcher to assist me. The time and effort spent educating the researchers as to the intricate nature of the research project and data collection exercise is more than made up for by the increased level of richness in the data, by virtue of the respondents feeling much more comfortable with someone from their local area.

The ideal situation is for the interviewer to be not only from the culture under study but also to be of the actual ingroup of those under study. In Eckhardt and Houston (2001) we used a local research partner to help us collect the data, and she organised group interviews with members of her peer ingroups from her university. While it is not always possible to be able to do this, anything that can be done in the data collection process to make the respondents feel comfortable with the researcher will increase the credibility and trustworthiness of the data, from a psychological standpoint.

There are significant issues to be dealt with when using insider/outsider teams. Ideally the local research partner will be fluent in English as well as the local language, and also a qualitative methods specialist. This helps to ensure that communication between the two partners is as transparent as possible, and to minimise misunderstandings. Using academics and paid professional researchers each has its pros and cons. For example, using an academic as a local partner usually means he/she will be familiar with the theories of interest in a study, and also that he/she will be able to analyse data in a very insightful manner. There are fewer questions as to whether the interpretation of data is credible. However, a professional qualitative researcher typically is more familiar with current methodological best practices, and has a wealth and variety of experiences to guide the research design process that a local academic may not have. In practice, the choice of which local partner to use often comes down to convenience: when going to a country where one has connections with local academics it is often easiest to use them, and hiring a local researcher is often quite expensive, so this is only possible when the budget permits.

Using a cultural insider to assist with the interpretation of the data will lead to the most meaningful understanding of the data. For example, when I was conducting group interviews in Shanghai, I had the interviews videotaped. When analysing the data, I was trying to determine how the nature of the interpersonal relationships in the groups affected the results (Eckhardt and Houston 2002). By showing the videotapes to my Chinese research partner, she was able to interpret the non-verbal communication and interaction that was occurring in a much richer manner than I was, as I had not conducted an ethnography of my respondents, and thus was not intimately familiar with their forms of expression. The respondents were aware they were being videotaped, of course, but the camera was unobtrusive, situated in the corner of the room out of the sightline of interviewers and interviewees, and did not appear to have any negative effects on the interviews. Indeed, being able to analyse the ingroup interactions later greatly enhanced the quality of the analysis of the transcripts. Using a local research partner for this sort of analysis implies a high level of trust in terms of verifying the interpretations. It is not recommended if you are not intimately familiar with the cultural expertise of the local research partner.

Finally, the issue of language comes up when using insider/outsider teams. I have found that using this type of team allows for a meaning-based approach to translation issues, as advocated by cultural anthropologists. This typically takes the form of a decentring approach to translation (Campbell and Werner 1970). A decentring approach involves not favouring the source language (that is, not making the translations fit the cultural categories created by the English language in this case), but rather using such variables as paraphrasing and context to come up with phrasings that will reflect local understandings of concepts. A decentred approach to translation implies that there is no one correct way to translate a phrase into another language, but rather seeks to make the two versions coordinated in different languages. This approach has been characterised, compared to direct translation and back translation, as the most highly regarded translation technique when engaging in cultural business research (Green and White 1976). Specific procedures used include coming up with alternate interpretations of metaphoric and idiomatic expressions and synonyms for phrases, then deciding which were most appropriate for representing what the original speaker was trying to get across. This type of collaborative translation technique – as it is usually done in close consultation between the insider and outsider research partners – is the method I use most often, and has also recently been used by other business researchers such as Joy (2001).

CONCLUSION AND RECOMMENDATIONS

When conducting qualitative business research in China, it is imperative to understand the underlying cultural dimensions and how they will affect the processes of data design, collection and analysis. In many cases cultural considerations make modifications to qualitative techniques mandatory, and they also help to dictate which particular methods should be used in the first place. There are significant cultural effects in the research design process, the data collection process, and the analysis process. The above analysis points towards some generally applicable conclusions beyond the specific Chinese cultural context.

Many IB qualitative research methods are not appropriate to analyse the cultural nature of a phenomenon. As Ratner (1997, p. 129) points out, 'qualitative methodologists have traditionally focused on personal experience. They have neglected its cultural organization'. Choosing from the toolbox of qualitative analysis approaches to find an appropriate one for understanding the effects of culture on business phenomena entails evaluating which methods encompass contextual effects into the analysis, not just the text itself. If the purpose of the IB research being engaged in is to analyse the effects of culture on business phenomena, as is quite common for research in China, hermeneutics is typically the appropriate analysis technique to use. Hermeneutic analysis is a process by which parts of the data are analysed in conjunction with the emerging understanding of all of the data. In this part-to-whole analysis, referred to as the hermeneutic circle, interpretations of parts of the data change as a deepened understanding of the whole emerges and vice versa (Thompson 1997). For example, in Eckhardt and Houston (2001) we first understood responses such as 'dead grandfather's spirit' to questions about prized possessions to be an indication of the strength of family ties, even beyond the grave. As it emerged that there is a decidedly non-tangible aspect to the notion of possession – later demonstrated by responses such as a computer as a prized possession when the computer was not actually owned by the participant – the interpretation of dead ancestors' spirits as possessions took on additional meanings in the light of this overall trend. Hermeneutics is especially appropriate for capturing cultural effects, as it emphasises the cultural formation of experience (Arnold and Fischer 1994). In contrast, phenomenology, symbolic interactionism and structuralism reject the inherent tie between culture and behavioural phenomena, rendering their analytical use inappropriate (Ratner 1997).

In addition, being as culturally aware as possible is the first step towards meaningful data interpretation. This can be achieved through a variety of methods. First and foremost, data should not be collected from a distant locale, with the researcher knowing next to nothing about the culture under study. Going to your data collection site and supervising the data collection is highly recommended. Talking informally with contacts in your area of interest is also highly recommended, to gain a grounded understanding of the realities of their positions. Reading extensively on the culture and psychology of your data collection site also adds valuable insights. Knowing that the Chinese construe materialism in a fundamentally different way from the way it is construed in the West, for example, enabled me to make sense of responses that were identifying 'love for family' as one's most important possession, and understand those responses in relation to cultural traditions rather than thinking the respondent had not understood the question properly, or writing off a response like that as an outlier in the study. This particular example relates to translation issues: I was able to recognise what I had initially thought to be a translation error by having an understanding of the way the construct of interest was conceptualised in that culture, and realise that the responses I was getting, although unexpected, were appropriate from a cultural perspective.

Making the sort of methodological modifications recommended in this chapter brings up an obvious issue of cross-cultural comparability. If an IB researcher is involved in a qualitative study of materialism in 20 countries, for example, and has to use different questions, different techniques for responding, and a different unit of analysis when collecting data in China, how will one compare the data at the end of the process, and attempt to ensure equivalency? When conducting comparative research, the methods used might need to be non-comparable to achieve comparability in constructs. To gain meaning equivalence, comparability can occur at the construct level not necessarily the implementation level. If the researcher can get the most meaningful data on materialism from culturally variable populations by invoking different techniques for eliciting responses, this is the equivalence that should be strived for, not an implementation-level equivalence that ensures the same methods are used but that meaning is lost in the process. (See Singelis (2000) for a summary of a recent special issue of *Journal of Cross-Cultural Psychology* which details the above argument in depth.) Qualitative IB researchers should more readily embrace this concept than quantitative researchers, as qualitative researchers are typically striving for a more experience-near, meaning-based approach in general.

One of the major benefits of engaging in the research design, data collection, and data interpretation processes in China in a culturally appropriate manner, beyond being able to achieve trustworthy and credible results, is the opportunity to add to the IB literature from an indigenous perspective. This is when theories, constructs and methods come from non-Western thought patterns, philosophies and traditions, thus truly globalising IB research, rather than always having Western theories, constructs and methods used to universally explain business phenomenon. Kim et al. (2000) describe this as indigenisation from within, which is when theories, concepts and methods are developed from a truly emic approach, not from what is typically termed a universalist approach but what is really an imposed etic approach. An example of this approach would be the Chinese Cultural Connection's (1987) discovery of the value 'filial piety' in China as an important motivator for behaviour, which was then measured and used to explain behaviour in cultures other than China. We have not seen this approach widely applied in IB research, yet it has the potential to truly globalise such research.

Some of the more important recommendations offered in this chapter include the following. Try not to rely on verbal methods as the sole representation of the data. Triangulation including observation greatly increases the credibility and trustworthiness of the conclusions, as there is a myriad of cultural influences which make verbal disclosure not as straightforward as typically thought of in IB research. In fact, if respondents can be given the opportunity to write down their thoughts/feeling/opinions as well as relate them verbally, that also leads to enhanced validity. The questions asked must be situated in a particular context of interest to the researcher, however; acontextual questions are to be avoided. Also, an understanding that most decision-making and behaviour is typically group related rather than individual in China is of paramount importance so the correct unit of analysis is achieved, and the data collected is meaningful. The psychology of the Chinese has been described as being interdependent, not independent. Thus many of the constructs that are typically used in IB research – such as attitudes, beliefs, values and norms – are going to be collectively created and held, not individually, and consequently the unit of analysis associated with the data collection, as well as the data collection itself, will have to reflect this interdependent orientation. Indeed, even using these variables as theoretical constructs of interest needs to be rethought, as many behaviours are more directly related to social norms. Using insider/outsider teams during the data collection and translation processes is also recommended, as is situating any questions or scenarios put to respondents in specific contexts. In sum, culture affects the qualitative business research process in many ways, and must be accounted for in many ways throughout the research process, such as in terms of the method of qualitative analysis used and when establishing cross-cultural construct equivalence. Most importantly, strive to see the world through the eyes of your respondents when analysing your data, and let your research output reflect their cultural experiences.

NOTES

1. For example, a prominent theme that has emerged from fieldwork data I have collected in urban China from 1997 to 2000 is that employees in firms will only wear the brand of clothing that is suited to their level in the workplace hierarchy. The general manager of the firm is expected to wear an expensive, Western brand (for example, Ralph Lauren), the next level of management will wear a less expensive brand of Western clothing, and so on down the hierarchy until lower management is wearing an affordable Chinese brand, such as Baleno. One does not see aspirational consumption, such as middle management wearing upper management brands, as this would be an affront to workmates and to upper management. Similarly, it is a serious *faux pas* for upper management to wear a cheaper brand of clothing, as then everyone under them will have to find an even cheaper brand to wear to work.
2. This does not have to be participant observation, but that would be the ideal.

REFERENCES

Aaker, J.L. (2000), 'The influence of culture on persuasion processes and attitudes: diagnosticity or accessibility?', *Journal of Consumer Research*, **26** (4), 340–57.
Arnold, S.J. and E. Fischer (1994), 'Hermeneutics and consumer research', *Journal of Consumer Research*, **21** (1), 55–70.

Bond, M.H. (ed.) (1986), *The Psychology of the Chinese People*, Hong Kong: Oxford University Press.

Bond, M.H. and K.K. Hwang (1986), 'The social psychology of the Chinese people', in M.H. Bond (ed.), *The Psychology of the Chinese People*, Hong Kong: Oxford University Press, pp. 213–66.

Briley, D., M. Morris and I. Simonson (2000), 'Reasons as carriers of culture: dynamic versus dispositional models of cultural influence on decision making', *Journal of Consumer Research*, **27** (2), 157–78.

Campbell, D.T. and O. Werner (1970), 'Translating, working through interpreters and the problem of decentering', in R. Naroll and R. Cohen (eds), *A Handbook of Method in Cultural Anthropology*, New York: Natural History Press, pp. 398–420.

Chinese Culture Connection (1987), 'Chinese values and the search for culture-free dimensions of culture', *Journal of Cross-Cultural Psychology*, **18** (2), 143–67.

Cousins, S.D. (1989), 'Culture and self-perception in Japan and the United States', *Journal of Personality and Social Psychology*, **56** (1), 124–31.

Eckhardt, G.M. and M.J. Houston (2001), 'To own your grandfather's spirit: the nature of possessions and their meaning in China', in P. Tidwell and T. Muller (eds), *Asia Pacific Advances in Consumer Research*, **4**, Valdosta, GA: Association for Consumer Research, pp. 251–7.

——— (2002), 'Cultural paradoxes reflected in brand meaning: McDonald's in Shanghai, China', *Journal of International Marketing*, **10** (2), 68–82.

Fiske, A.P. (1995), 'Culture', in A.S.R. Manstead and M. Hewstone (eds), *The Blackwell Encyclopedia of Social Psychology*, Cambridge: Blackwell, pp. 161–3.

Fiske, A.P., S. Kitayama, H.R. Markus and R.E. Nisbett (1998), 'The cultural matrix of social psychology', in D. Gilbert, S. Fiske and G. Lindzey (eds), *Handbook of Social Psychology*, 4th edn, Vol. II, New York: Random House, pp. 915–81.

Gaines, A.D. (1992), 'Medical/psychiatric knowledge in France and the United States: culture and sickness in history and biology', in A.D. Gaines (ed.), *Ethnopsychiatry*, New York: State University of New York Press, pp. 171–89.

Geertz, C. (1973), *The Interpretation of Cultures*, New York: Basic Books.

——— (1975), 'On the nature of anthropological understanding', *American Scientist*, **63** (1), 47–53.

Gilligan, K.C. (1982), *In a Different Voice: Psychological Theory and Women's Development*, Cambridge, MA: Harvard University Press.

Green, R.T. and P.D. White (1976), 'Methodological considerations in cross-national consumer research', *Journal of International Business Studies*, **7** (2), 81–7.

Greenfield, P.A. (1997), 'Culture as process: empirical methods for cultural psychology', in J.W. Berry, Y.H. Poortinga and J. Pandey (eds), *Handbook of Cross-Cultural Psychology. Volume 1: Theory and Method*, 2nd edn, Boston, MA: Allyn & Bacon, pp. 301–46.

Hu, H.C. (1944), 'The Chinese concepts of face', *American Anthropologist*, **46** (1), 45–64.

Jenkins, J.H. (1994), 'Culture, emotion and psychopathology', in S. Kitayama and H.R. Markus (eds), *Emotion and Culture: Empirical Studies of Mutual Influence*, Washington, DC: American Psychological Association Press, pp. 307–35.

Joy, A. (2001), 'Gift giving in Hong Kong and the continuum of social ties', *Journal of Consumer Research*, **28** (2), 239–56.

Kim, U., Y. Park and D. Park (2000), 'The challenge of cross cultural psychology: the role of indigenous psychologies', *Journal of Cross-Cultural Psychology*, **31** (1),

63–75.

Lao Tzu (1963), *Tao De Ching*, translated by D.C. Lau, New York: Penguin.

Lebra, T.S. (1984), 'Nonconfrontational strategies for management of interpersonal conflicts', in E.S. Krauss, T.P. Rohlen and P.G. Stenhoff (eds), *Conflict in Japan*, Honolulu: University of Hawaii Press, pp. 41–60.

Lutz, C. (1988), *Unnatural Emotions: Everyday Sentiments on a Micronesian Atoll and their Challenge to Western Theory*, Chicago, IL: University of Chicago Press.

Markus, H.R. and S. Kitayama (1991), 'Culture and self: implications for cognition, emotion and motivation', *Psychological Review*, **98** (2), 224–54.

Miller, J.G. (1984), 'Culture and the development of everyday social explanation', *Journal of Personality and Social Psychology*, **46** (5), 961–78.

———— (1994), 'Cultural psychology: bridging disciplinary boundaries in understanding the cultural grounding of self', in P.K. Bock (ed.), *Handbook of Psychological Anthropology*, Westport, CT: Greenwood, pp. 139–70.

Moghaddam, F.M., D.M. Taylor and S.C. Wright (1993), *Social Psychology in Cross-Cultural Perspective*, New York: Freeman.

Morris, B. (1994), *Anthropology of the Self: The Individual in Cultural Perspective*, Boulder, CO: Pluto Press.

Morris, M.W. and K. Peng (1994), 'Culture and cause: American and Chinese attributions for social and physical events', *Journal of Personality and Social Psychology*, **67** (6), 949–71.

Murray, H.A. (1938), *Explorations in Personality*, New York: Oxford University Press.

Peng, K. and R.E. Nisbett (1997), 'Cross-cultural similarities and differences in the understanding of physical causality', in M. Shield (ed.), *Proceedings of Conference on Culture and Science*, Bowling Green, KY: Kentucky State University Press, pp. 10–21.

Ratner, C. (1997), *Cultural Psychology and Qualitative Methodology: Theoretical and Empirical Considerations*, New York: Plenum Press.

Ross, S.A. (1991), 'Freedom from possession: a Tibetan Buddhist view', *Journal of Social Behavior and Personality*, **6** (6), 415–26.

Schmitt, B. and S. Zhang (1998), 'Language structure and categorization: a study of classifiers in consumer cognition, judgement and choice', *Journal of Consumer Research*, **25** (2), 108–22.

Shweder, R.A. (1990), 'Cultural psychology: what is it?', in J.W. Stigler, R.A. Shweder and G. Herdt (eds), *Cultural Psychology: Essays on Comparative Human Development*, Cambridge: Cambridge University Press, pp. 1–46.

Shweder, R.A. and R.A. LeVine (1984), *Culture Theory: Essays on Mind, Self and Emotion*, Cambridge: Cambridge University Press.

Singelis, T.M. (2000), 'Some thoughts on the future of cross-cultural social psychology', *Journal of Cross-Cultural Psychology*, **31** (1), 76–91.

Smith, P.B. and M.H. Bond (1993), *Social Psychology across Cultures: Analysis and Perspectives*, New York: Harvester Wheatsheaf.

Soloman, R.C. (1984), 'Getting angry: the Jamesian theory of emotion in anthropology', in R.A. Shweder and R.A. LeVine (eds), *Culture Theory: Essays on Mind, Self and Emotion*, Cambridge: Cambridge University Press, pp. 238–54.

Stevenson, H.W. and J.W. Stigler (1992), *The Learning Gap: Why our Schools are Failing and What We Can Learn from Japanese and Chinese Education*, New York: Summit Books.

Stewart, A. (1998), *The Ethnographer's Method*, Qualitative Research Methods, Vol. 46, Thousand Oaks, CA: Sage.

Thompson, C.J. (1997), 'Interpreting consumers: a hermeneutical framework for deriving marketing insights from the texts of consumers' consumption stories', *Journal of Marketing Research*, **34** (4), 438–56.

Triandis, H.C. (1989), 'The self and social behavior in differing cultural contexts', *Psychological Review*, **93** (3), 506–20.

Triandis, H.C., C. McCusker and C.H. Hui (1990), 'Multimethod probes of individualism and collectivism', *Journal of Personality and Social Psychology*, **59** (5), 1006–20.

Wallendorf, M. and R. Belk (1989), 'Assessing trustworthiness in naturalistic consumer research', in E. Hirschman (ed.), *Interpretive Consumer Research*, Provo, UT: Association for Consumer Research, pp. 69–84.

Wertsch, J.V. (1991), *Voices of the Mind: A Sociocultural Approach to Mediated Action*, Cambridge, MA: Harvard University Press.

Wong, N. and A. Ahuvia (1995), 'Self-concepts and materialism: a cross-cultural approach', in D. Stewart and N. Vilcaddim (eds), *Marketing Theories and Applications*, Vol. 6, Chicago, IL: American Marketing Association, pp. 112–19.

21. An Outsider in India

Elisabeth M. Wilson

INTRODUCTION

This chapter discusses the challenges of conducting qualitative research as a foreigner in India. The position of an outsider is often seen as disadvantageous, a 'liability of foreignness' (for example, Zaheer 1995), which is difficult to overcome. Just as companies encounter a liability in terms of their lack of knowledge of foreign markets, so do we as researchers. Yet, as my experiences demonstrate, this very liability can also be turned into an advantage.

In the following sections, I shall examine the life cycle of my research project from the perspective of a foreign researcher in India. It aimed at investigating gender and difference (the principal one of which is caste) in formal Indian organisations. Four case studies were undertaken, principally in South Indian City:[1] Indeng, an engineering company, in 1998, and local offices of India Post and two non-governmental organisations (NGOs) in 2001. I shall explain how I reviewed indigenous Indian literature; how I gained access to these organisations; my principal methods to assemble and validate empirical material; and my own identity (re)construction as a researcher. I also discuss a range of practical considerations and suggest lessons for the future.

During the course of the project my epistemological stance changed to an approach that could be described as critically reflexive (Alvesson and Deetz 2000), hence where appropriate sections are written in the first person. This change was not directly related to the project, reflecting a growing interest in critical management studies in a broad rather than narrow sense. An increasing curiosity about postcolonialism (see Westwood, Chapter 3 this volume) led to further self-examination and reflection, which informs some of the discussion in the chapter.

LITERATURE REVIEW

I had already encountered the first challenge of being a foreign researcher before entering the field when I attempted to undertake a sufficiently comprehensive literature review, not only using US and UK sources, but also material generated in India. There were several important but disparate elements. First, use was made of available management electronic databases via my university library. This elicited a certain amount of material written by indigenous and expatriate Indian authors, and Western collaborators, such as Sahay and Walsham (1997). Second, I perused bookshops and the bookshelves of Indian acquaintances for helpful publications, in particular literature that elucidated Indian culture from a sociological or social anthropological point of view (Nabar 1995; Srinivas 1996). Third, a search was made of Indian management literature to find out what work had been undertaken already in this area, as there is an established network of business schools in India, many publishing their own journals. I negotiated access to a well-known business school, and used their library catalogue. I was fortunate to be directed towards an Indian database, Institute for Studies in Industrial Development (ISID), containing material relating to research in education, management, social services and politics. This indicated publications, most of which I was able to locate in the Indian business school library, or from my own university.

The literature search indicated the existence of two parallel literatures within what might be termed the West and India. While some publications referred to the other literature, a majority did not. This meant that Western published authors were writing without knowledge of recent research and thought in India, and vice versa. Within Indian business and management writing I found a growing body of research about women in management, but this was generally within the gender-as-variable paradigm, and therefore not situated within the broader field of gender and organisation with its consideration of power issues. Perhaps more significant was the lack of overlap between the management and sociological literature in India. Considerable contributions have been made by Indian academics in the fields of postcolonialism and gender (Dube 1996; Seth and Gandhi 1998), but these were not evident in management publications. The epistemological implications of all this are considerable, and I had to survey, review and incorporate sufficient of these parallel literatures to formulate an intellectually and empirically coherent literature review.

The timing of the searches had some bearing on the substantive project. The initial searches were undertaken simultaneously with the first case study, which limited my understanding of some cultural nuances. In retrospect a literature review is essential preparation for a foreign researcher prior to entering the field. However, for logistical and financial reasons it would have been difficult to undertake a comprehensive review of material written in India before the first study. The bulk of the search and a substantial part of the review were undertaken after the first case study, and before the others. The challenge therefore was to survey sufficient material, and to persist in not relying solely on Western sources. A key role of the foreign researcher may therefore be to act as a bridge between indigenous and foreign literatures.

ACCESS

Access posed challenges at two levels, organisational and individual. Gaining access to organisations is often problematic, and this was compounded by the physical distance between India and my country of abode, England. Contacts and networks often play a role in facilitating entry to case study organisations, and this seemed doubly important in India. Access to the first organisation, the engineering company 'Indeng', was serendipitous. While undertaking research in a British organisation, I discovered in promotional literature that they had a joint venture with a company in South Indian City, which I already knew as a tourist, and they arranged access to Indeng. Seeking a public sector organisation, I used an alumni list from my Institute, which led me to India Post, where the successor to the identified alumnus expressed his interest in my research. I have no doubt that my institutional connection with his predecessor assured him of my bona fides. For the third organisation I targeted the NGO sector, and asked acquaintances to recommend one in good standing in South Indian City. Thus I approached RCNGO directly. I gave each organisation a summary of my research protocols in writing, supplemented with verbal explanations of my intentions. Imagine my concern therefore, when on my last visit to South Indian City, the director of RCNGO indicated that he would severely curtail my access. One Indian acquaintance suggested that I had been too honest about time requirements, and another considered that there was a gender issue. I was, however, permitted to interview four people formally and one informally. On a later visit specifically arranged to undertake a short interview with the director, the gatekeeper told me he had gone out for the day, and subsequent phone calls were not returned. As soon as these problems became evident with RCNGO, I had mobilised acquaintances, and was fortunate in being directed to a smaller organisation, SecNGO. The director was willing to allow me access, subject to confirmation of my status. Fortunately the empirical material available from SecNGO more than supplemented that from RCNGO. Thus three organisations were accessed via contacts or networking *in situ*; the only one that was approached directly restricted access shortly after entry. Adaptation to the challenge of access was only possible because of my pre-existing social capital within South Indian City.

Access to the organisation in principle is only the first stage, however. I wished to access individuals from a cross-section of people in administrative and managerial jobs. In the UK, where I had conducted the same study, female employees had been selected, and then matched to male employees in similar grades. But this was not feasible in the Indian organisations to the same extent, because of gendered employment patterns. In each organisation I requested and was allocated a principal contact person to assist with the selection of suitable interviewees. In most cases this worked well, but only because I was prepared to be available at short notice for interviews. In the UK, where I conducted my previous research, I had generally been given pre-booked appointments, or more usually a list of telephone numbers for potential interviewees, with whom I could deal directly. In India visits were usually arranged less than 24 hours before they took place, even at one hour's notice. A mobile phone was invaluable in this situation. It was common to arrive at a predetermined time, and be allocated to someone there and then. The look of surprise on the faces of some of the interviewees at Indeng indicated that they had no prior knowledge of my visit. My understanding of this way of arranging interview access to individuals lies in attitudes towards time, synchronic rather than monochronic in India (Kluckhohn and Strodtbeck 1961), and to a lesser extent issues of status and authority (Sahay and Walsham 1997). Differing attitudes towards time were also evident in the fact that prearranged appointments could often be delayed. This was more likely to happen when I had arranged to meet top managers of organisations. It appeared to relate to attitudes towards clock time (Trompenaars and Hampden-Turner 1997), rather than indicating any lack of welcome. Adaptation was enabled both through modern technology, and also by adjusting my temporal attitude.

CHOICE OF METHODS

The initial choice was guided by an intention to elicit empirical material that could be compared cross-culturally with UK organisations in the public and private sectors. The focus of the research was similar but not identical. In outlining methods I shall concentrate on aspects that required adaptation. For epistemological reasons I had a preference for taking an 'insider' approach, aiming to understand life within each particular organisation (Sackmann 1991). The methods used have already been fully discussed elsewhere (Wilson 1997), and the sections below on the repertory grid technique, workshops and organisational documents draw upon this previous work.

Interviews: General Aspects

Interviewing within the Indian cultural context is far from the 'objective' performance traditionally suggested, and much nearer to the paradigm suggested by feminist writers (Oakley 1990), which necessitates being prepared to reveal the self and engage with the interviewee. This meant that as well as the usual preliminaries explaining the purpose of my research and the role I wished the interviewee to play, it was also important to establish my personal as well as professional credentials. In terms of basic politeness, and for rapport, it was necessary to be prepared to answer personal questions, particularly about my spouse and children. For instance, I was frequently asked whether I was looking for a husband for my 26-year-old daughter. The importance of establishing a personal aspect to the research relationship could be understood intellectually as the difference between diffuse and specific cultures (Trompenaars and Hampden-Turner 1997). I prefer however to view it as an aspect of being human. I was similarly prepared to talk about my personal circumstances when undertaking research in the UK, although it occurred less frequently. Additionally, in both countries I was asked for advice based on my research experience about issues of concern to interviewees, with which I complied. Adaptation required me to understand personal questions not as intrusive, but as friendly.

Another difference in the Indian context was that my assumptions of exclusivity in relation to time and space during interviews were not shared by all respondents. It was common for others to be present for part (and in one case all) of the interview. The most bizarre example of this was when I was interviewing a female clerk in an Indian sub-post office. We were placed in a central room that acted as a passageway for most of the rest of the building. In addition to passers-by, one colleague hovered, standing up. I asked the interviewee if she would prefer to talk to me without his presence, but she indicated she wanted him to be there. During the interview an English woman came in looking for the sub-postmaster, and the easiest way to curtail the interruption was to direct her to his office. On another occasion I was talking to a senior manager while some maintenance work was taking place in relation to the information technology facilities in his room. He talked quite frankly and did not seem to feel the need to temper his opinions in the presence of junior colleagues. Whereas I would interpret the first incident as probably related to the interviewee's anxiety (other aspects of the interview indicated this), on the second occasion I felt that the subordinates were simply not regarded as important enough to consider. However the most common reason for the interruption of interviews, particularly in Indeng and India Post, was the arrival of *peons*. The word *peon* can be translated as messenger or attendant. *Peons* run errands all day long, and deliver mail between offices on an *ad hoc* basis. It was a frequent experience for a *peon* to enter the room, place a letter or report in front of the interviewee, who then perused it, signed it, and returned it to the *peon* for onward transmission, all without comment. This reflects patterns of hierarchy (Sahay and Walsham 1997), and schemes of delegation within Indian workplaces.

Most of the people interviewed had had an English-medium university education, and so conducted the bulk of the interviews directly. Standard English as spoken in India and the UK are not identical, and over time I became acquainted with subtle differences of meaning (Ashcroft and Griffiths 1995). In particular, the word 'sincere' was used to indicate someone who accepted responsibility. It was not a question of their spoken English being incorrect, as Ashcroft and Griffiths state that we should think in terms of 'englishes' rather than English. However, sometimes it was necessary to rephrase questions or explain my point, but it has to be acknowledged that that had also happened in the UK occasionally.

Three interviews and one group discussion were assisted by interpreters. I could probably have interviewed two respondents myself, but the presence of the interpreter helped clarify some points. For the third interview and the group discussion the interviewees were not sufficiently confident to express themselves in English. For all use of interpreters I explained their presence and qualifications, and reiterated assurances about confidentiality. However, both were Indian academics with specialist literature/language knowledge rather than trained interpreters, and I was aware of tendencies to summarise replies.

I had anticipated that the topics of gender and difference would be sensitive areas for interviewees, as they touch on basic assumptions about self and Other (see Westwood, Chapter 3 this volume), in-groups and out-groups. This was based on my experience of how these topics are socially constructed in Europe and North America. The principal components of diversity in the Indian context are socio-economic status, ethnic background (which includes caste), linguistic composition, and gender (Monappa 1997; Sivaramayya 1996).[2] Caste is a hierarchical social system, determined by birth, and distinguished principally by endogamy (marriage within one's one caste or subcaste) and rules about physical and social contact with other castes (Dube 1996). Despite attempts to change differential outcomes for those of lower caste in educational, social and economic life, its salience persists. Women have a persistently low status in India, and despite progress, a gender gap remains in relation to female education, employment and per capita income (Hindu 2000). Social change has led to changes in attitude towards the educated women, and the prejudice against working outside the home is disappearing in urban centres (Ghosh and Roy 1997). However, there are a number of significant problems still faced by women workers.

Before I embarked on the first case study in 1998, I was very diffident about introducing the topic of caste, and felt that it was something I would never understand. On reading the edited volume by Srinivas (1996) I was considerably reassured. I learned that even in-depth studies of villages by

Indian sociologists and social anthropologists fail to achieve agreed descriptions of *varna*, the hierarchical relationships between castes (Shah 1996). In relation to gender, I felt on somewhat firmer ground, but still had some anxieties about dealing with a potentially sensitive issue. However, from the first case study it became evident that my concerns, although appropriate, would not prevent my collection of empirical material. Although gender and ethnicity are important and intimately involved with power relations, the lack of a regime of political correctness meant that many respondents did not appear constrained in speaking their minds. People in India talk quite straightforwardly about 'a lower-caste fellow', 'slum children' and 'sex workers'. Although the essentialising this implies might be deplored, as a researcher I actually found it quite refreshing. This open expression included respondents from disadvantaged groups, both women and lower-caste members, who felt their position keenly and expressed this bitterly.

Contrary to my assumptions about caste and gender as sensitive issues, I found that there were strong cultural taboos against discussing individual managerial failings. This appeared to be related to cultural assumptions about hierarchy, and respect for older people derived from the social hierarchy of caste and familial expectations, respectively (Sahay and Walsham 1997). This indicated that I was extrapolating the location of cultural sensitivities from my own cultural origins, and had not sufficiently anticipated the likely effect of Indian cultural patterns upon interviewees. As discussed below, this posed a challenge to my use of repertory grid.

The Repertory Grid Technique

It seemed likely that any interview format that relied on eliciting a direct answer on issues of gender and difference might be unreliable, because of the tendency for interviewees to give socially pleasing answers. I had found repertory grids a helpful technique during the UK investigations (Wilson 1997), and saw no reason not to replicate it in Indian organisations. Readers unfamiliar with this method are referred to Stewart et al. (1980) and Easterby-Smith and Thorpe (1996). I focused on two topic areas: first, what underlies selection and promotion processes; and second, individuals' concept of a good manager.

First of all, 'elements' must be selected as the raw material for discussion, in this case people likely to have the range of properties that I wished to explore. The initial set of elements was drawn from interviewees' colleagues: three people who had done well or who were recognised as potential high flyers; three who were making steady progress and might expect one or two more promotions; and three who were low achievers without prospects. The aim of selecting these elements was to find out those constructs individuals associated with success. The second set of elements were drawn from managers perceived respectively as good, sometimes competent and sometimes not, and the third group poor or bad. These elements were selected to find out what respondents associated with managerial competence. In each case I encouraged respondents to select a mixture of men and women.

Choosing elements in UK organisations had been unproblematic, but I encountered difficulties in relation to the second set of elements in India. One manager in India Post told me that all managers within the organisation were indistinguishably good. He point-blank refused to undertake the second repertory group exercise. A female clerk stated that she was not qualified to comment on the managerial capacities of her superiors, and therefore chose elements from employees from similar grades. Meeting a similar problem in RCNGO, I rephrased my request as good, better and best managers. At one point the interviewee concerned slipped up and referred to a colleague as a poor manager, then quickly corrected herself, so this appeared an effective adaptation.

The next stage in the repertory grid is construct elicitation, usually comparing triads (Stewart et al. 1980). The interviewee is asked in what way two have something in common not shared by the third (Stewart et al. 1980). Constructs can be explored in greater depth by 'laddering up' – asking why a particular set of constructs is important – and 'laddering down' – asking the interviewee to give an example or explanation (Easterby-Smith and Thorpe 1996; Stewart et al. 1980).

From a cross-cultural perspective, the fact that repertory grid allowed the interviewee to elicit and explore his or her own constructs made it a more sensitive instrument than using a priori categories (Alvesson and Deetz 2000) within a semi-structured interview, for example. It was through this that the construct 'sincere' appeared, for instance. However, one of the main advantages that I found using repertory grid was the openings that it gave for more open-ended discussion, on topics that neither of us might have thought of exploring. This was as true in the Indian context as in the UK one.

There are also disadvantages to using repertory grid, principally the nature of the constructs elicited (Gammack and Stephens 1994), and these problems were apparent in the Indian context, as they had been in the UK. However, this did not invalidate the method. My experience in both the UK and India is that there are always one or two people who are unable to understand what is required, and find the whole process difficult or trying. They tend to generate only small numbers of constructs. Nevertheless, overall as an interview technique I was pleased with the success of replicating repertory grid in another cultural context.

Semi-structured Interviews

There were some interviews, both planned and unplanned, that did not follow the repertory grid format. In most cases these were the initial meetings with the top manager in the facility concerned, or additional meetings with my named contact for clarification of issues. There were, however, two people who did not engage with the repertory grid technique, and with whom I undertook impromptu and unprepared semi-structured interviews. The first of these was a senior manager, who specially made time to see me in her busy schedule, and the second was an NGO project manager with whom I started to talk while awaiting the arrival of scheduled interviewees. Both were people who talked volubly with very little prompting. In the first instance issues of access and power in relation to the elite skewed the conduct of the interview (Welch et al. 2002), as I was left in no doubt by colleagues that I was seeing a very important person. My indecision as to whether to embark upon repertory grid was exacerbated by the fact that it was never clear how much time was available. In retrospect, time uncertainty was more salient than power differences, and indeed some of the power differences were diminished by a strong personal and ideological identification between us, as we were both middle-class women with feminist sympathies. I was also tapping a very rich vein of empirical material – the view of someone at the higher echelons of the Indian civil service – and pragmatically it made sense to carry on.

In the second impromptu interview I attempted to engage the project manager using repertory grid, but he immediately backed off, to re-engage once I resumed a less formal approach. This pattern of behaviour has been noted by others (Roper 1994). However, I was able by prompting to cover similar ground to other interviews. In both cases I extrapolated all identifiable constructs from my notes and used them in the thematic analysis.

Workshops

The second main method for assembling empirical material was a workshop/discussion group, also discussed in Wilson (1997), and based on Schein (1992).

As I assumed that the impact of gender relations was likely to be as strong in the Indian as in the UK context, I intended that the workshops would be held with women and men separately. There is evidence that women in mixed groups contribute differently quantitatively (Alimo-Metcalfe 1993) and qualitatively (Blanksby 1988). Unfortunately, separate workshops only happened at Indeng. There were some logistical difficulties or misunderstanding about arranging workshops at India Post, and consequently a joint workshop was held. Significantly the three men and three women sat in two separate groups, but this gender differentiation did not prevent two of the three women present being very vocal. It was impossible to arrange a workshop in RCNGO, and I was only able to have a discussion with two employees of SecNGO on my very last day in India, nevertheless covering a lot of ground.

Despite these difficulties, the workshop method transferred surprisingly well to India, and as in the UK, I discovered that a considerable amount of empirical material could be generated within two to three hours. I used a similar format, choosing topics in areas where I wished to confirm or disconfirm preliminary findings from the interview data. As in the UK I also started with less sensitive topics such as dress codes or modes of address, proceeded through topics such as promotion and discipline, and finished by asking about gender and other differences. In every case I left enough time to recapitulate at the end, identifying jointly with the group espoused values and underlying assumptions (Schein 1992). The group meetings were recorded on flip chart sheets, and subsequently transcribed. Groups in India were as receptive as groups in the UK to Schein's model of culture as a framework for discussion and analysis, and equally forthcoming.

I adapted to the difficulties I experienced by being prepared to conduct a workshop-based discussion with as little as two people. Extrapolating from the 'just in time' approach to arranging interviews, I think the logistical difficulties related both to attitudes to clock time, previously discussed, and limited understanding of the purpose of the workshops.

Organisational Documents

The third method of generating empirical material was to peruse relevant organisational documents (Forster 1994; Schein 1992), such as personnel procedures, and application and appraisal forms. The existence, accessibility and usefulness of these varied between organisations, which replicated my experience in the UK. There were well-developed written human resource policies in Indeng, although significantly no equal opportunities policy. India Post had a highly bureaucratic appraisal system, encompassing reservation, but for general personnel policies I was directed to Swami's Guide (Muthuswamy 2002), a commercial publication that summarises Government of India rules. I was unable to obtain any written material from RCNGO, and there was very little available at SecNGO, although verbal inquiries indicated well-developed human resource policies at both. A web-based search of India Post undertaken shortly after completion of the study yielded additional information. Forster (1994) suggests that company documentation should never be taken at face value as it is context specific, and so written material, and information about policies was evaluated against other material. In total, my experience differed little from the UK in terms of the variable accessibility, quantity, and quality of documentary material.

ANALYSIS AND INTERPRETATION

The key question here was how I as a foreign researcher ensured that my interpretation was credible and true to the experiences of those under study (see Noorderhaven, Chapter 4 this volume). To a certain extent this is always a problem, even when researching in one's own country. Philosophically I was partly wedded to an interpretive approach, with a social constructionist view of reality. This implies trying to understand from a 'native' point of view. Conversely, from a critical perspective I reserved the right to make my own interpretation.

As each case study progressed I had discussions with interviewees and other informants to check out my perceptions. In some cases I could use my initial contact, for instance in Indeng, and in other cases I tested out ideas on later interviewees after my ideas had started to form, for instance in India Post. Lastly I made casual observations and reflected on my own reaction to the organisation. I also collected material opportunistically, for instance observing while waiting for appointments.

Janesick (2000) suggests that qualitative researchers should jettison ideals of validity, which are tied to positivist approaches, and instead strive for credibility. Accordingly, I had discussions with informants in all organisations in order to check both 'facts' and perceptions. Additionally the principal manager in each organisation was sent a consultancy style report, summarising constructs elicited by both repertory grid exercises, and adding additional sections on gender, diversity, organisational culture and organisationally specific issues. Each organisation was also offered a presentation of the findings, although only one took place. A video presentation was sent to Indeng, a live presentation was made to India Post on a return visit, but a planned presentation to SecNGO was cancelled because riots made travelling to South Indian City inadvisable. Substantive feedback was only forthcoming from India Post, although I heard informally that the Indeng CEO had been very pleased with my report, and I also received an e-mail thanking me profusely from SecNGO. Providing and receiving feedback was more difficult than when researching in the UK because of the distance between the UK and India. This is a real problem for a foreign researcher, as by the time transcription and interpretation has taken place, one is likely to be back home.

It will be evident from the discussion above that I commenced the project with certain a priori categories to investigate: gender, caste, other differences in the workplace, management style, organisational culture and national culture. At the same time I remained alert to other categories that emerged. Thus in Indeng I found that there were a number of references to being 'aggressive' that on exploration did not relate to behaviour within the company, but rather in relation to other companies. In India Post it became evident that time orientation was a significant diagnostic tool in relation to the organisation's readiness to develop less educated employees, which was significantly at odds with the organisation's avowed public service and entrepreneurial aspirations. This was not mentioned specifically by any interviewee, but became evident to me on re-reading my field notes.

Thematic and interpretive exploration of the data was supported by QSR NUD*IST (see Lindsay, Chapter 24 this volume). This was used to enable multiple access to material and assist categorisation, rather than to construct theories. I used it iteratively to help me integrate not only interviewees' constructs, but also to develop those that emerged from my own reflections.

I also used more mundane methods of analysis. All the repertory grid constructs were written on one side of file cards, with my notes of the interview on the back. These were manually sorted into categories relating to managerial skills and behaviour, prior life and career opportunities and choices, personal characteristics, and primary identifiers of difference such as gender and caste. This kind of categorisation, particularly when expressed in quantifiable form, can never be completely accurate, but certainly indicates broad trends and differences, and enabled comparison with the UK material.

Through the selection of interviewees I was able to give voice to those who felt oppressed by their lower social status by using feedback mechanisms. This conflicted with, in some cases, bland assumptions about the equity of organisational procedures. However, in conclusion I think interpretation may always be more difficult when researching in a foreign culture. First, there is the gap in background knowledge; second, even with excellent language skills there may be subtle misunderstandings; and last, feedback is logistically less likely.

IDENTITY (RE)CONSTRUCTION OF THE RESEARCHER

During the course of my project there were multiple role expectations placed upon me, and shifting constructions of identity in interactions with Indian informants. As this chapter has a reflexive thread to it, it is appropriate that I examine this process of identity (re)construction, and the impact that it had on the collection of data.

I already had some familiarity with South Indian City as a repeated tourist, and had a series of acquaintances ranging from academics and local worthies to small-business people, male and female. This experience at least ensured appropriate dress. It is seemly in South India for adult females to cover their legs and the tops of their arms. At the same time a *saree*, formal dress for Indian women, exposes the midriff and a modest *décolleté*. Most of the time I wore Western tailored trousers and short-sleeved, button-up blouses, and on several occasions I also wore *shalwar kameez*, also known as Punjabi suits. In addition, for the feedback presentation at India Post I wore a *saree*, which was greatly appreciated. Through my dress I hoped to convey myself as a *respectful visitor*.

Echoes of the British Raj were evident to some extent in my relations with educated Indians who sometimes treated me as a *foreign expert*. Although most top managers I met had travelled abroad, for postgraduate training or business, there was an assumption, sometimes voiced and sometimes referred to obliquely, that my expertise would be superior to that of an indigenous researcher. When I suggested to the manager at India Post that I might work with an Indian collaborator, he said he thought I would be more objective. This was not the occasion for discussion about epistemology, and my views about objectivity and subjectivity. I merely concurred with his wishes. I felt there were aspects of postcolonialism in this type of encounter (see Westwood, Chapter 3 this volume), which reflects widespread underlying assumptions in Indian management education, valorising work by Western authors or based on Western models. Alternatively, it might also be understood as greater willingness to talk to someone without local networks (see also Welch et al. 2002).

By contrast, my research protocol was denigrated by the director of RCNGO, who asserted 'they will all say the same [thing]'. I countered politely that this was not my experience elsewhere. My encounter at RCNGO started oddly. I arrived at the appointed time and was told the director was in a meeting, not in itself unusual. I was perfectly used to waiting for important people in India and generally took a book. What was different on this occasion was that he came out of the meeting room and swept by without acknowledgement. I had to ask again at the reception desk and was then directed to his room. The disappointing conversation about access to personnel took place at this juncture. From this point on I felt cast in the role of *grateful supplicant* (see also Welch et al. 2002). I felt that there were power and gender issues in this encounter, but as these were also evident to some extent in interviewees' accounts, it did not seem specific to me. It may be this was a more authentic Indian experience for someone in a subordinate position.

Having tiptoed around the topic of caste in Indeng and found that respondents were not offended by my inquiries as I had anticipated, I decided to be more direct in other organisations. The role of *naive stranger* was one that I deliberately adopted in order to encourage interviewees to expand on comments, particularly about caste. I asked quite straightforwardly if they could enlighten me, as it was something I did not understand. This put my respondent in the role of expert, and they were then usually happy to oblige. The wide range of opinions expressed appeared to indicate that they were generally frank.

I was often treated as an *honoured guest*. For instance when I told the gatekeeper at one India Post facility that I had come to see 'madam', he positively twinkled; I had status by association. India Post officials also gave me a small gift as a thank you for my research. On another occasion the manager at Indeng invited me and my husband to his home for an evening meal with friends. He also offered me a soft drink on each visit to the factory before introducing me to the next interviewee. By contrast I was treated as an ordinary visitor at SecNGO, and on more than one occasion generously invited to share the midday meal offered to all employees.

My gender was generally not problematic, but this was because the lower-status associations of being a woman were compensated in three ways. The first was my professional background. Status is generally ascribed in India (Trompenaars and Hampden-Turner 1997) so my professional title of doctor was probably additionally advantageous. Second, I am clearly not a young woman, and age is respected in India. Third, there was my higher status as a foreigner.

PRACTICAL CONSIDERATIONS

Last I come to some of the nuts and bolts that are generally ignored within methodology texts.

On each occasion I travelled to South Indian City on my own by plane and then train. I have already alluded to the fact that I was familiar with South Indian City as a tourist, and had built up a small network of acquaintances, which expanded thanks to personal and academic networks. Through these contacts I found relatively modest accommodation. Household management was not easy, however. Indian middle-class housewives rely on domestic help rather than domestic appliances, and although the former was readily available I ran into language problems. I was able to eat out in restaurants cheaply, but for various reasons still had a heavier domestic burden than at home.

Most of my travel was in and around South Indian City, and I generally took auto-rickshaws (motorbike taxis). I frequently had to argue in order to pay the regulated fare. One of the Indeng facilities was out of town, but as they had cars regularly running in and out, I was able to arrange to travel with these. For the later case studies I bought a local mobile phone, which made a great deal of difference. I never felt unsafe travelling around South Indian City on my own. However, returning from a visit to a rural NGO project by hire car, I was considerably discomfited when the interpreter said that we were travelling through bandit country in the dark; our departure had been delayed by the late arrival of interviewees.

Because of the British tax system, I had to produce receipts for most purchases, and found my own receipt book invaluable. Some people were suspicious of this, but usually concurred when I said it was for my boss. I tried to save some time by using a typing service, but found local ones unreliable and unsatisfactory. On my second and third trips my research grant covered Dragon software, so that I could dictate my field notes.

CONCLUSION

This chapter has examined the challenges and opportunities of being a foreign researcher in India through the life cycle of a qualitative project. In fact, the first logistical dilemma had already been encountered in the pre-field stage when attempting to conduct a literature review incorporating indigenous Indian literature. Yet it was worth the effort. Access to research undertaken by indigenous academics was extremely helpful. I was fortunate to have access to organised library resources within India, which might be more difficult in other countries. Additionally these resources were written in English. There are probably many countries where there are no relevant or accessible databases or library catalogues to help, but I would urge persistence in avoiding over-reliance on Western sources, and including non-academic sources such as newspapers. My position meant that I was able to act as a research bridge between the different literatures, Western and Indian.

In the light of my own experiences, I would reiterate the need for acculturation, including thorough prior reading. Ideally one should have some sort of exposure to a country before undertaking research. However, my own experience was that being a tourist was woefully inadequate preparation. On a personal note, I have decided to use an indigenous collaborator in future to combine the elements of surprise (Schein 1992) and familiarity with the culture, both of which have advantages.

In terms of access to Indian organisations and key informants, there were some tactical benefits in being a foreign researcher, as I was perceived as a foreign expert. There were, however, more substantive advantages. I think that for some respondents, the fact that I was not part of local kinship or social networks enhanced the degree of openness and trust possible. Being a foreigner exacerbates distance (see Noorderhaven, Chapter 4 this volume), but can highlight issues that are often taken for granted, and I think this helped my interpretation of the material. By the same token, the obvious disadvantage was the potential gulf of cultural understanding between myself and the interviewees. In addition there were logistical problems in giving feedback to interviewees at an appropriate time, or at all.

It was clearly advantageous to use personal networks to access organisations. There was, however, difficulty in accessing organisations that were sufficiently similar cross-culturally to allow for comparative work between India and the UK. However, access via social networks could have caused bias in selecting organisations that were more positive towards difference, but the alternative might have been no access.

In my choice of methods the value of qualitative research was reinforced, as the material generated was open to interpretation in a number of ways. For instance, the paper on India Post (Wilson 2002) tapped a rich vein of material for theoretical examination. The use of repertory grid to explore respondents' own constructs was more useful than semi-structured interviewing for this particular project. Other advantages were the tendency of the technique to engage interviewees, and to root discussion in their day-to-day material experience. The methods used proved helpful for exploring politically, and potentially personally, sensitive issues. In summary my methods enabled me both to generate new findings, and also to propose new theories. I think, however, that where the data collection technique is unfamiliar, such as workshops, purpose and content may have to be clearly explained. As an engaged researcher, I think it is important to be open personally and intellectually, and prepared to be flexible in terms of the opportunities presented and methods used.

The last area concerns ethical dimensions. It could be suggested that the project *per se* was a postcolonial endeavour (see Westwood, Chapter 3 this volume), taking information from a former British colony for my own use. I would counter this by pointing to the opportunity it gave to people at lower echelons of the organisation to express their voice, on a topic largely unexplored by Indian researchers. Postcolonialism leads to the consideration of where and how to publish in a way which is accessible to Indian researchers, if 'data rape' is to be avoided. I define this as the extraction and use of data in a way that assists the foreign researcher, and gives nothing in return. Too often Western researchers utilise material from overseas contexts to boost their own standing as 'international' researchers; this is exacerbated by national research scoring systems such as the Research Assessment Exercise in the UK. To counter this, as previously discussed, I offered written and verbal feedback to each organisation. This was undertaken as a means of being courteous to the organisation, in addition to acknowledging ethical considerations about not merely extracting information in an exploitative way. At the time of writing one paper has been published in conference proceedings in India, and a freely accessible working paper has been publicised on my departmental web site. In addition, parallel but not identical versions of the main papers (with due acknowledgement) are planned for Western and Indian management journals.

Writing and editing this chapter has allowed, indeed encouraged, me to engage reflexively with the process as opposed to the content of my research in India. As well as highlighting the advantages and disadvantages, and amendments to methods necessitated by my encounter as a foreign researcher, on a personal basis it has reawakened the intense feelings I had at the time. Some of these were negative in terms of frustration, boredom when waiting around, uncertainty and self-doubt. These were outweighed, however, by the privilege and sheer intellectual interest of becoming absorbed in another culture, and engaging with concerns of organisational members. I hope readers of this chapter can build upon my experience and venture forth.

ACKNOWLEDGEMENT

This research was supported by the British Academy.

NOTES

1. Pseudonyms are used for the private and NGO sector organisations, to prevent identification of individuals. Permission was given to identify India Post.
2. Some of the material in this section is taken from Wilson (2003).

REFERENCES

Alimo-Metcalfe, B. (1993), 'Women in management: organizational socialization and assessment practices that prevent career advancement', *International Journal of Selection and Assessment*, **1** (2) 68–83.

Alvesson, M. and S. Deetz (2000), *Doing Critical Management Research*, London: Sage.

Ashcroft, B. and G. Griffiths (1995), 'Hybridity', in H. Triffin (ed.), *The Post-Colonial Studies Reader*, London and New York: Routledge, pp. 183–4.

Blanksby, M. (1988), 'In their own words: the clues to how to develop women managers', *Women in Management Review*, **3** (2), 71–7.

Dube, L. (1996), 'Caste and women', in M.N. Srinivas (ed.), *Caste: Its Twentieth Century Avatar*, New Delhi: Penguin Books India, pp. 1–27.

Easterby-Smith, M. and R. Thorpe (1996), 'Using repertory grids in management', *Journal of European Industrial Training*, **20** (3), 2–30.

Forster, N. (1994), 'The analysis of company documentation', in C. Cassell and G. Symon (eds), *Qualitative Methods in Organizational Research*, London: Sage, pp. 147–66.

Gammack, J.G. and R. Stephens (1994), 'Repertory grid technique in constructive interaction', in C. Cassell and G. Symon (eds), *Qualitative Methods in Organizational Research*, London: Sage, pp. 72–90.

Ghosh, R.N. and K.C. Roy (1997), 'The changing status of women in India: impact of urbanization and development', *International Journal of Social Economics*, **24** (7–9), 902–17.

Hindu (2000), 'EC concern over rise of case-based parties', 27 December.

Janesick, V. (2000), 'The choreography of qualitative research design: minuets, improvisations, and crystallization', in N.K. Denzin and Y.S Lincoln (eds), *Handbook of Qualitative Research*, 2nd edn, Thousand Oaks, CA: Sage, pp. 379–400.

Kluckhohn, F. and F. Strodtbeck (1961), *Variations in Value Orientations*, Elmsford, NY: Row, Peterson & Co.

Monappa, A. (1997), *Managing Human Resources*, New Delhi: Macmillan India.

Muthuswamy (2002), *Swamy's Handbook*, India: Swamy.

Nabar, V. (1995), *Caste as Women*, New Delhi: Penguin India.

Oakley, A. (1990), 'Interviewing women: a contradiction in terms', in H. Roberts (ed.), *Doing Feminist Research*, London: Routledge, pp. 30–61.

Roper, M. (1994), *Masculinity and the British Organisation Man since 1945*, Oxford: Oxford University Press.

Sackmann, S.A. (1991), 'Uncovering culture in organizations', *Journal of Applied Behavioral Science*, **27** (3), 295–317.

Sahay, S. and G. Walsham (1997), 'Social structure and managerial agency in India', *Organization Studies*, **18** (3), 415–44.

Schein, E. (1992), *Organizational Culture and Leadership*, San Francisco, CA: Jossey-Bass.

Seth, S. and L. Gandhi (1998), 'Postcolonial studies: a beginning', *Postcolonial Studies*, **1** (1), 7–11.

Shah, A.N. (1996), 'The judicial and sociological view of other backward classes', in M.N. Srinivas (ed.), *Caste: Its Twentieth Century Avatar*, New Delhi: Penguin Books India, pp. 174–94.

Sivaramayya, B. (1996), 'The mandal judgement: a brief description and critique', in M.N. Srinivas (ed.), *Caste: Its Twentieth Century Avatar*, New Delhi: Penguin Books India, pp. 221–43.

Srinivas, M.N. (ed.) (1996), *Caste: Its Twentieth Century Avatar*, New Delhi: Penguin Books India.

Stewart, V., A. Stewart and N. Fonda (1980), *Business Applications of Repertory Grid*, London: McGraw-Hill.

Trompenaars, F. and C. Hampden-Turner (1997), *Riding the Waves of Culture: Understanding Cultural Diversity in Business*, London: Nicholas Brealey.

Welch, C., R. Marschan-Piekkari, H. Penttinen and M. Tahvanainen (2002), 'Corporate elites as informants in qualitative international business research', *International Business Review*, **11**, 611–28.

Wilson, E. (1997), 'Exploring gendered cultures', *Hallinnon Tutkimus/Administrative Studies (Finland)*, **4**, 289–303.

Wilson, E.M. (2002), 'Time orientation as a diagnostic tool: the case of India Post', in U. Pareek, A. Osman-Ghani, S. Ramnarayan and T.V. Rao (eds), *Human Resource Development in Asia: Trends and Challenges*, New Delhi and Kolkota: Oxford and IBH Publishing, pp. 709–16.

——— (2003), 'Gender and caste issues in organisations in India', in M. Davidson and S. Fielden (eds), *Diversity and Gender in Organisations*, Chichester: John Wiley, pp. 149-69.

Zaheer, S. (1995), 'Overcoming the liability of foreignness', *Academy of Management Journal*, **18**, 439–64.

22. The Rhythms of Latin America: A Context and Guide for Qualitative Research

Victoria Jones

INTRODUCTION AND OVERVIEW

She was far from her home in Brazil, in a French village where she was conducting interviews. The older couples she visited always insisted that she take more sugar in her coffee. 'Help yourself to more.' 'You have not had enough.' 'We have plenty to share.' Every interview included the same refrain, almost a ritual. 'Please have more sugar.'

The Brazilian sociologist was intrigued. Her work was about housing and land use, but she raised the subject of sugar with her French colleagues.

'It's simple', they explained. 'During the war years sugar was extremely scarce. It is still highly valued among those who were forced to live without it.'

And suddenly the Brazilian saw what her colleagues had been too close to understand. The sugar was not just valued by these French villagers as a luxury food, it was a powerful 'core symbol' (Hall and Noguchi 1993). By understanding the meaning of sugar, one could immediately grasp the context that shaped the values of these people, the deprivations of war, the reversal from scarcity to security. Further, the offering itself was symbolic. They were demonstrating to the researcher that they accepted her. It was not enough to open their doors, they showed their generosity by opening their sugar bowls to her.

The Brazilian sociologist Marina Heck later returned to Brazil where she researched and wrote an original and moving book based on the food memories of immigrants, *Cozinha dos Imigrantes: Memórias e Receitas* (The Immigrant's Kitchen: Memories and Recipes) (Heck and Belluzzo 1998). Sugar was only a beginning as her subjects shared their deep associations with Portuguese king's cake, Italian minestrone soup, Japanese sushi, and Lebanese candied almonds. The rich culinary memories reveal the complex identities of immigrants, what it means to be foreign as well as what it means to be Brazilian.

Sugar-as-symbol was revealed when a foreigner looked at the culture with naive, attuned and observant sensitivity. But without the local interpretation, the sugar ritual would have remained a quaint oddity, 'thin' as opposed to 'thick' description (Geertz 1973). Through qualitative research and multicultural perspectives, Dr Heck discovered the descriptive and interpretive power of culinary memories.

Because the intersection of different cultural perspectives holds tremendous potential for breakthroughs in qualitative research, this chapter is designed to encourage and facilitate cross-cultural qualitative research about Latin America. Though it is written for foreigners working in Latin America, it will also be helpful for Latin Americans interested in comparative work. It addresses key issues of culture and context. How are we different and how are we similar? What practical and interpretive adaptations should we consider? How can we work together successfully?

I am myself North American (the term South Americans use for people from the USA since we are all Americans). My PhD is in intercultural communication, which applies social psychology to human interactions across cultures. In my case, the applications are primarily in organisational behaviour and marketing. I began to focus my studies on Latin America about ten years go and have lived in Brazil for the past four years. My students and friends like to tell me I am 'almost Brazilian' and I sometimes use 'we', to include myself, when referring to Latin Americans. The material presented here is based on my own research experience as well as those of my Latin American colleagues, some of whom I interviewed especially for this chapter and others with whom I have enjoyed long conversations over late dinners. Many Latin Americans have been trained in research methods developed in Europe and the USA. The possibilities and limitations of qualitative research are being debated and discussed here as in other parts of the world (Fleury et al. 1997). The references I use about the region are both local material in Spanish and Portuguese and material written for foreigners in English. What is presented in this chapter is necessarily a simplified version of the region's complexities, but it represents some of the 'common knowledge' that is generally agreed upon by Latin American scholars today.

This chapter begins by describing the broad socio-political context of Latin American fieldwork and then explores some of the behavioural characteristics of Latin American cultures. Applications and implications for qualitative research are offered throughout the chapter focusing on issues of problem definition, sampling, data collection and appropriate analysis. Since Latin America is a huge and diverse region, what is presented here will only touch on a small part of the beauty, variety and challenge of this region. On the other hand, every effort has been made to provide rich descriptions that can guide not only research methods but analyses that are appropriate to the complexities of the region.

SOCIO-POLITICAL LATIN AMERICA

Latin America is defined geographically, but it can also be defined culturally, by the shared values and behaviours of a people. Geographic Latin America covers everything from Mexico to Argentina and includes the islands between the continents such as Cuba and Puerto Rico. The Caribbean is generally considered a separate but related region. A new perspective considers the US population of Latin American descent to be a vital part of Latin America through cultural rather than geographic proximity. The world's fourth largest Latin market is the Latino/Hispanic market in the USA (Robles et al. 2003). This group shares many behavioural traits with other Latin Americans (Tharp 2001).

The population of Latin America is about 508 million people (Robles et al. 2003). The fast growth in this region, along with trends towards economic and political stability, has made it an increasingly important business focus. Mexico and Brazil are the two most impressive individual countries based on the size of their populations and economies. Brazil alone represents half of the South American population with some 175 million people.

One of the things that often surprises foreigners who visit Latin America is how much we talk about politics and economics. Conversations in cafes, beauty salons and at bus stops swing easily to the World Bank, currency exchanges and tax reform. These are not mere philosophical musings. People feel that politics and trade affect them personally and immediately. They have felt the effects of military dictatorships and hyperinflation on their daily purchases of fresh bread. To understand Latin America for analysis and for research design, one must first come to terms with the macro issues. This section will discuss regional diversity, class differences, infrastructure development and resource accessibility, and international relations.

Latin American Diversity

Behind the round figures, Latin Americans are a diverse mix. The size and economic power of the countries vary tremendously. The population includes indigenous peoples who have been present for thousands of years, whites who came first as colonisers or immigrants, and blacks who were originally brought as slaves (mostly to the eastern countries). About 150 languages are spoken in Mexico alone (Condon 1985). Racial mixing has been a common practice, producing a blend of appearances as well as cultures (Degler 1971).

On the other hand, there are distinct differences within the region. The indigenous roots are more evident in Mexico and Peru, for example, while many southern Brazilians have the blonde straight hair of their German immigrant ancestors. Another area where distinct differences are evident is in the social hierarchy. Although each country is composed of a mix of peoples, the elites continue to be mostly white. Racial and ethnic diversity do not cross class and hierarchical levels (Fleury 2001).

This broad diversity makes decisions about the unit of analysis very important. While some values and experiences are commonly shared, the practice and meaning can vary widely between regions and social classes. For practical reasons that sometimes lead to oversimplification, many companies develop strategies for Latin America as a bloc, and single-country research may be titled 'Latin American'. Especially with the smaller sample sizes of qualitative research and the logistical complexity of multi-country data collection, it is important that researchers choose research samples that fit the desired level of analysis.

The social profile of respondents must also be carefully considered and will be described in more detail in the sections that follow. When studying organisations, the experience and perceptions of salaried employees and managers are likely to be quite different from those of manual or day workers. For consumer research also, it is important to closely match sample characteristics with the population to which the results will be applied. While it may seem efficient to include all social classes in a consumer sample, most products sold in Latin America are priced, packaged and distributed so that only the upper or lower classes would buy any single brand.

Extreme Class Differences

One of the hardest things to find in Latin America is a middle class. The extremes of wealthy and poor are characteristic of the region. There are a variety of statistics that illustrate this dichotomy. All reveal the same trend. And they change little from year to year.

The wealthiest 5 per cent of Latin Americans account for 25 per cent of total income. As a comparison, the wealthiest 20 per cent of North Americans (US) control less than 50 per cent (Robles et al. 2003). Some of the figures presented at a meeting of ex-presidents of Latin American countries included these: 30 per cent of Latin American workers earn only 8 per cent of labour income. The upper end of the salary scale is 32 times the lower end, while the differences in the USA are 10–12 times. Some 210 million people, or about one-third of the entire population, are poor and of those almost half are destitute. When considered as a whole, the Gini Index for the region is 0.58 compared to 0.40 for the whole world (Pizano 2001).

Social class is an important reference group identification and the structure of the system is rarely questioned. Instead of blaming self-replicating inequities in the socio-political infrastructure, the poor often explain their own misery as a matter of fate, or God's will, or by simply saying they were born 'unlucky'. While the rich and poor are in frequent contact through the demand for and delivery of services, the two groups are virtually isolated from one another in all other respects. The life experiences and daily realities of the rich and poor have very little in common.

When designing research in Latin America, one of the first questions researchers must consequently ask themselves is whose problem shall I address? The same general issues of leadership, compensation, budgets, brands and media habits will be defined and understood differently by the wealthy and the poor. Problem definition, as with most of life, is subject to class divisions. Will your target market be the wealthy class A or the bigger and much less affluent middle class C? The lower classes D and E rarely enter consumer studies since they are largely excluded from the formal economy except for the simplest trades of rice, beans and fat-based soaps. Class differences are also critical in organisation studies. Besides the different benefits and conditions that lead to job satisfaction for managers and assemblers, they are likely to understand the concept itself in very different ways. Organisational hierarchies are rich areas for qualitative explorations, but the distinctions must be respected and different groups should not be collapsed without good reason.

Infrastructure Issues

The infrastructure of Latin America reveals two divisions. One is an internal division, primarily between urban and rural areas. The other is the division between this region and the more industrialised regions of the globe. The first division is important to researchers because it affects access to research subjects and appropriate frames for analysis. The second division is important because foreign researchers will probably find very different conditions here than they may be used to in their home countries. Both divisions and their implications are discussed in this section.

At the start of the new millennium, Internet penetration in Rio de Janeiro and São Paulo was growing exponentially. At the same time, the federal government announced that it had accomplished its goal of opening a post office in every city in the country. These sorts of extreme differences have led Brazilians to jokingly call their country 'Belindia' – a cross between Belgium and India. This contrast is a result of both the rich–poor divide and the unequal physical infrastructure of rural and urban areas. The pattern is repeated throughout Latin America.

Much of Latin American land is still wilderness – dense jungle, vast wetlands and broad stretches of grassy plains. However, most of the population lives in dense urban sprawl. Mexico City and São Paulo are two of the world's largest cities. Hundreds of thousands of people live in shanty towns without basic services. Indigenous peoples living in wilderness areas survive with the skills passed through generations, but there are also small collectives and villages with few resources and almost no way to access the social services that could help them.

Foreign researchers should also be aware of the differences between the infrastructure and resources available in Latin America and more industrialised parts of the world. A North American colleague who works in Mexico calls it 'molasses land' because progress is so slow there. A ratio of paved miles to square miles of territory is illustrative of the infrastructure differences between regions. Germany's ratio is 4:1. The US ratio is 1:1. Argentina is 1:20 while Paraguay is 1:75. Telecommunications resources also vary greatly between Latin America and other regions. OECD (Organization for Economic Cooperation and Development) countries have 561 phone lines for each 1000 people, 332 mobile phones for each 1000 and 64.1 people of every 1000 have Internet access. In Latin America there are 139 phone lines for every 1000 people, 66 mobile phones for each 1000 and 1.5 people of every 1000 have Internet access (1999 findings reported by Pyramid Research Group, cited in Rich 2002). Large areas are considered 'technologically excluded regions' including southern Mexico, parts of tropical Central America, some Andean countries, and most of tropical Brazil (Rich 2002).

This urban–rural divide is critical for understanding and researching in Latin America because the experiences and accessibility of the two groups are extremely different. With 70 per cent of Latin American buying power concentrated in ten metropolitan areas, most businesses simply ignore the smaller population centres. International marketers in Latin America have traditionally limited their activities to the cities because it is easier to distribute products efficiently to large numbers of consumers. However, due to increasing saturation and competition in the cities, the areas for future expansion are in smaller urban centres (Robles et al. 2003). Research into consumer and organisational behaviour should reflect this shift.

As with the wealthy and poor, the urban and rural are distinct contexts and should be considered as such for both sampling and analysis. Additionally, the infrastructure issues pose serious problems for data collection. Secondary data sources are scarce and often contradictory. Official government estimates for things like population and income distribution can vary dramatically from the numbers reported by private and foreign sources. This is not due to corruption or information control but to the difficulties of collecting accurate data. All sources must rely on some form of estimate to overcome obstacles in the infrastructure.

And, even when information is collected, the distribution is limited and may be poorly referenced. A business school library of only 60 000 titles is a relatively extensive collection. The publishing industry in Latin America is robust but poorly archived and documented. Many Latin American journal titles are published for both academic and executive audiences, but the content is not indexed so researchers must physically open issues one by one to find relevant material. Wealthier schools subscribe to US and European indexing services for international journals. Scholars must buy articles they want for relatively high prices and then wait days or weeks for the article to arrive by mail. It can be a challenge to build a thorough literature review and theoretical base for academic studies.

Much of the information sharing that takes place among Latin America scholars happens through conferences rather than publications. BALAS (Business Association for Latin America Studies), CLADEA (Consejo Latinoamericano de Escuelas de Administración/Latin American Council of Business Schools), the Iberomerican Academy of Management and ENANPAD (Encontro Nacional da Associação Nacional dos Programas de Pós-Graduação em Administração/National Meeting of the National Association of Graduate Programmes in Administration) are some of the bigger conferences devoted to administration in Latin America. Industry trade fairs and executive seminars are also common places for information sharing.

International Relations

For many decades, the struggles within Latin American countries have been more dramatic than those between Latin American countries. Relationships are friendly with significant trade, however, there has been little success in establishing meaningful regional blocs that could negotiate and compete with other regions. There is a trade agreement between Andean countries and Mercosur is expected to gather strength in the coming years. However, the countries of the region, and especially those of South America, tend to operate very independently of one another.

Latin America, especially South America, leans most heavily towards Europe for its cultural influences (Wagley 1995). The common Latin roots of language and culture can be seen through similarities in the arts and politics of Spain, Portugal, Italy, France and Latin America. Although Latin America has developed its own distinctive styles such as magic surrealism and tango and samba in music, the early models for art, government, law and public education came from Europe. On the other hand, as colonies, Latin American countries had a lesser status than European countries and a persistent sense of inferiority marks Latin American–European relations from the Latin American side (Condon 1985).

Relations with the USA are far more complex for Latin Americans than are relations with Europe. Feelings about the north are a mix of respect and resentment. Perhaps the best comparison is to the successful older brother who is better at sports, earns the best grades and dates the prettiest girls. While Latin American countries are eager to learn and apply US technologies and management techniques, they also resent the vast advantages leveraged by the USA and its intervention in Latin American politics (Burns 1993). Latin Americans often contrast their passion, warmth and spirituality with stereotypes of the US love for money, commerce and materialism. The high US divorce statistics and geographically-dispersed families are evidence to Latin Americans that people in the USA do not value family or relationships as much as they themselves do.

Research in Latin America is also more strongly linked to Latin–European rather than Anglo-Saxon traditions. Academics here tend to prefer studies drawn from the humanities rather than the social sciences. Criticism and reflection are more appreciated here while statistics and scientific controls are less valued than in the USA. However, the US academy does exert an influence since many of the region's business schools were founded by or with the assistance of US business schools.

Latin America has weaker links to Asia than to Europe and the USA though there are pockets of influence such as Chile's strong trade with Japan and the São Paulo Japanese community which comprises the largest number of Japanese outside of Japan. Relations with Africa are historically significant, primarily due to the slave trade, but are currently weak.

One's country of origin is important to Latin Americans and foreigners may find that their national identity evokes some strong stereotypes and generalisations. For instance, my research on race in Brazilian advertising is often met with comments about how race is a violent issue in the USA but is not a legitimate topic for research in Brazil, which is a 'racial democracy'. I was at first frustrated by these generalisations because they implied that my work had no relevance in Brazil, although I developed the line of research specifically because of its national importance. Some 47 per cent of Brazil's population is non-white while only 3 per cent of the people in advertisements are non-white. When faced with these comments now, I acknowledge that the USA has many racial problems. This admission puts us on common ground. I then explain that my research is about learning from Brazilians. This usually quells the fear that I am trying to create a US-style civil rights movement in Brazil. It also focuses on learning rather than judging.

North American and European researchers are respected and even a bit envied for their rigorous training and resources. On the other hand, they are 'outsiders' and must earn trust through relationships not credentials. Latin Americans generally find more affinity with the humanities and critical-studies orientation of European scholars than they do with the quantitative and statistical focus of North Americans. In Latin America, understanding is generally more valued than counting. In-depth interviews are more respected than short questionnaires. New discoveries are more interesting than refining old theories. Qualitative methods and objectives are welcomed and respected here.

LATIN AMERICAN BEHAVIOUR AND SOCIAL NORMS

In any research endeavour, we must know enough about our subject not only to ask questions, but to understand the answers. In cross-cultural qualitative research, this depth of understanding is particularly critical, especially when compared to cross-cultural quantitative research. In quantitative research, the scholar wrestles most with cultural differences in the design stage: translation and back-translation of surveys, appropriate measures for the same construct in different cultures, scale validity and reliability among different samples and so on (Craig and Douglas 2000). Once the data are collected and the statistics run, it is difficult to search for further explanations without another study, a new design.

Qualitative research, on the other hand, requires an integrated process of data collection and interpretation. Design is certainly critical and must be appropriate to the cultures being studied, but the analysis also requires great sensitivity to cultural differences. Nuances of language, subtleties of gesture, ways of organising material, what is assumed or ignored as much as what is made explicit – these are the data from which the qualitative researcher must find answers to his/her questions. And the process is further complicated by the interaction of the data with the researcher's own culture (Strathern 1995). In this section I shall look at some Latin American behavioural tendencies including interpersonal orientation, power and hierarchy, time orientation, passion versus planning, and conversation patterns.

Interpersonal Orientation

In etic terms, Latin Americans are collectivist as opposed to individualist, paying careful attention to group norms, social duties and familial obligations (Hofstede 1980). However, this simple categorisation cannot account for some apparent contradictions in Latin American behaviour. The richer emic characterisation is that Latin Americans manage their lives based on a web of overlapping social circles.

Simpatía is highly valued and people are generally open, warm and expressive. It is important to maintain harmonious relationships, to avoid criticism and not offend (Albert 1996). Relationships are more important than task outcomes and are often the way tasks are accomplished. For example, jobs often come through family and social connections (Harrison 1995). The poor who live in *favelas* pool their resources. Co-workers in corporations pull together even after hours to 'put out fires'. Cooperation organises life within one's social circle rather than competition or individual effort. In one graduate programme, the forced-curve grading system was applied until it was discovered that students negotiated among themselves to decide who would work hard on an exam or submit a substandard project so that the lower and higher grades were evenly distributed each semester. Classmates are members of a common social circle as are work colleagues, family members, close neighbours, members of professional associations, sports clubs and so on.

Collectivism is not, however, universal. It applies in the limited context of one's own family, friends and associates. For those inside the circle, there is almost no limit to how much one will help the others both personally and professionally. However, those outside this limited sphere are not considered relevant to the collective and are often ignored. Thus issues of poverty are not common social concerns; they belong to the government and to the poor. Throwing candy wrappers on the street does not litter our property; the streets belong to no one. I can cut off another driver when I am anonymous in my car, but I could not disagree with my boss face to face. One's own membership group is treated differently from other groups (Tajfel and Turner 1979). Equitable exchange is different for in-groups and out-groups (Gudykunst and Kim 1997). Particularism applies in Latin America. Behaviours are chosen according to the social relationships between the actors. They are not based on universal principles (Trompenaars and Hampden-Turner 1997). There is a Brazilian expression that illustrates this nicely: 'For my friends, everything. For my enemies, the law'.

Access to research subjects will come more easily from relationships than from credentials. A personal introduction will be necessary in almost all cases. Before committing to anything, people here will often ask, 'Who referred you to me?'. A professor and editor of an academic journal in Brazil taught me a useful strategy. He makes a list of all the subjects he wants to interview. Then he makes a second list of all the people he knows who have a relationship with his subjects. Instead of calling the subjects himself, he calls the people on his second list and asks them to make the first call and introduction.

How can a foreigner make personal contacts? Local academic partners are good starting points for this. Attend the Latin American conferences and visit over coffee. Expect to meet personally several times and visit more than once before any formal research is begun. Trust and not mutual interest form the basis for relationships. This takes longer to establish than more goal-oriented sorts of exchanges – think weeks of accumulated contact hours instead of hours of meetings. Also, the more demanding your need, the closer the relationship has to be in order to reach your objectives. In other words, short interviews on non-sensitive subjects may be granted with a phone call explaining that your friend provided the contact. Participant observation in a workplace will be granted as a special favour based on a long-term relationship – either yours or that of your friend who is making the request on your behalf.

Government agencies and business associations such as consulates and chambers of commerce are prepared to provide introductions to foreigners. However, these organisations exist to stimulate commerce and may or may not recognise the value of academic research. Their members want business contacts and opportunities for trade. Most business executives are interested in immediate results and do not recognise the benefits of academic research for their particular business challenges. Establishing reciprocity will be discussed in the next section.

Building relationships in some countries is based on an exchange of information, but in Latin America it is based on mutual trust. Latin Americans are dialogue-oriented while some other cultures are data-oriented (Oliveira 2001). Joining a social circle is an act of becoming that extends to one's identity. It is not merely a transaction, though transaction relationships can also be established and will be discussed in the next section.

Power and Hierarchy

Latin American countries score relatively high on power distance scales (Hofstede 1980). The social hierarchy is maintained peacefully through interdependence among the classes. Those more powerful extend favours to those less powerful and expect loyalty and availability in return (Roett 1995). 'Leaders' practise paternalism through a concentration of power in formal relationships and through personal favours in informal relationships. The 'led' practise flexibility through taking on a spectator role in formal relationships and avoiding conflict in informal relationships (Prates and Barros 1997). The hierarchy itself and one's vertical position are rarely questioned. People in each group manage their relationships according to the resources available to them. One researcher told me the story of contacting a company manager for an interview. The manager said he would need permission from his boss. Additionally the researcher's boss would need to phone the manager's boss in order to ask permission. The hierarchy was carefully maintained.

As a foreigner with academic credentials, you start at a middle-upper level on the hierarchy. Good manners, courtesy, intelligence and affinity will be appreciated. What matters is not displays of wealth but displays of common courtesy and appreciation. Use formal titles and forms of address until you are invited to move to the informal forms. Thank the people who serve you coffee, but do not force them into conversation. While you may be uncomfortable with the hierarchies, Latin Americans are uncomfortable violating them. It may be helpful to realise that status does not reflect on one's worth as a human being, but merely on one's role in a web of relationships. Be gracious to everyone but, to be accepted yourself, do not challenge these values.

Your position in the hierarchy does not by itself determine what you can accomplish. It is merely a signal about what you can offer in an interdependent relationship. As a foreigner you will have contacts and resources and knowledge that may be valuable. As you are building relationships, offer to share your bibliographic references, send an article or suggest an author whose interests complement your colleague's. Do not represent yourself as a superior scholar. This will irritate Latin American inferiority concerns and create resistance. The relationship you want to establish is reciprocity among peers.

Be careful not to *avança o sinal* or 'jump the gun' by making requests that are not in proportion to the strength of the relationship. Do not ask for logistic support, speaking opportunities, office space and data collection assistance unless they are offered. Even then, start small and accept offers of help incrementally and with displays of gratitude and reciprocity. Faculty and schools in Latin America operate with extremely limited resources. Offering to speak to classes or faculty may be seen as a burden in terms of logistics and hospitality rather than a benefit. Latin Americans may agree to help in order to be polite, but they may also resent being asked and may withdraw passively if they feel they are being exploited.

Developing reciprocal relationships with businesses is first based on the relationship between your mutual contact and a key person within the corporation. Second, it is based on affinity between you and your primary contact within the corporation. If you 'hit it off', you will find many doors opened to you for no practical reason whatsoever. People trust their instincts and will be helpful to those they genuinely like and respect. Additionally, in each contact with members of a corporation, you will be either building a base of trust or erecting barriers. It is important to be sincerely and consistently grateful, transparent and honest. Finally, businesses may be interested in some reciprocal benefits in exchange for their help. Some companies will appreciate being thanked in acknowledgements or having their name mentioned in the text of your work. Some may want a copy of your research findings, especially if they can see its practical applications for them. Some companies may actually expect a sort of free consulting benefit, and you should be careful not to mislead about what you can offer them. Be aware that some businesses may be generally wary and will not be willing to talk with you under any circumstances. This happens to the locals too.

Polychronic and Present Time

Time is not a simple concept in Latin America. The past, present and future all play a part (Kluckhohn and Strodtbeck 1961). Latin America is sometimes called the land of *manhna* (tomorrow) because the next day is for doing the things that were not accomplished today and because the hope is always for a better future. However, Latin Americans are not generally goal-oriented, focused on accomplishments to be realised at some later time. Some countries, such as Mexico, look respectfully to the past and proudly maintain traditions (Condon 1985). But this also has limited application. The situational focus on the present is really the strongest influence on the way Latin Americans perceive time. This region has a living memory of military coups, hyperinflation, democracies carved from dictatorships, and five Argentine presidents in two weeks. When change is the primary constant, we have chosen to focus on what is immediately relevant. The past and future are both beyond our control. The present is tangible and ours to do with as we can.

The other important time orientation in Latin America is the ability to do several things at once, a polychronic orientation (Hall 1959, 1983). It is not unusual to hold a meeting in your boss's office while he signs paperwork, takes phone calls, receives other visitors, and asks his secretary to book his next business trip. People arrive late to meetings not because they do not respect the other people who will attend but because they were showing respect to the people with them in the previous meeting. Time is measured by the task rather than by the clock.

As a researcher you should plan for extra time to accomplish things in Latin America. I generally estimate what it would take to accomplish a task in the USA and triple it to get a rough estimate of Latin American timetables. It is important not to judge this time difference as if it were the result of personal or cultural inadequacies. Infrastructure limitations alone can delay people with the best of intentions. Phone calls do not always go through, traffic backs up, pipes break, soccer games close businesses for the afternoon. Because Latin Americans do not internalise time pressure the way many northern Europeans and North Americans do, these frustrations are perceived differently. They are rolled into the process rather than being confronted as hurdles that must be overcome. Instead of exerting extreme efforts to meet a time limit that was, after all, arbitrary, deadlines are pushed back to accommodate crises.

A series of interviews that could be conducted in two days in the USA could take a full week in Latin America since both the logistics and conversations will tend to run longer. A good guideline is to schedule no more than one meeting in the morning and one in the afternoon. Take a book or some paperwork to occupy yourself in waiting room down times, but most of all settle in and follow the lead of your host. As people come in and out of the office, you will often be pleasantly surprised at the serendipitous encounters. Do not be offended by comings and goings and multiple phone calls. These are just the routine multi-tasking pace and not signals that you are unwelcome. However, you must also be careful not to stay after you have been signalled to leave. Checking a watch and apologising about not having more time are polite ways of signalling the end of a meeting.

Since Latin Americans can do many things at once, they often seem unfocused to people from monochronic cultures. Added to the natural tendency for multi-tasking is the economic necessity that forces many academics to hold two or three teaching and research positions, as well as at least one administrative or consulting job. One way to manage a schedule with a Latin American partner is to build lots of flexibility into the schedule and send frequent reminders. People who are oriented to the present will prioritise what is current. Agreements made in the past for commitments promised in the future are easier to put aside than reminders received today.

Passion versus Planning

'In Brazil it is better to be lucky than to work hard.' That's what my boss told me after my first public success in Brazil. I wanted to be recognised for my efforts. Brazilians kept praising me for being *pé quente* (hot foot – a soccer player who has success in a game). It is not that Latin Americans do not work hard; they do. And they reward and value effort. But, with so many things beyond one's control, it takes some luck to be successful. Imagine the beloved Brazilian racing car driver Ayrton Sena stuck in a São Paulo traffic jam when the river overflows. All of his driving skills in a Ferrari would not get him to the airport any faster than the driving student in a second-hand car. Skill matters, but fate is the ultimate locus of control.

In a competitive analysis of the Ayacucho region of Peru, various factors for success are listed including demand factors, government role, industry structure and strategy. Also listed is a factor labelled *azar* or bad luck. This factor includes things such as weather problems, natural disasters, insects, protectionism in export markets, and synthetic substitutes for natural raw materials (Indacochea 2001). While the same things affect businesses in other parts of the world, they would probably be called environmental factors, market forces and technological changes. In Peru, bad luck accounts for a wide range of issues.

Do not be surprised to find that your careful plans are not as carefully followed in Latin America, even by you. Flexibility is as valued as it is necessary. You will find broad objectives more productive than detailed operationalisations. Many things that one takes for granted in long-time industrialised countries (such as functioning phones and lifts) really are outside of your control among Latin American contradictions and extremes.

Creativity is also highly valued. It is more important than precision and rigour. In a critique of the published research on Latin American telenovelas, one author notes that the studies do not provide much justification for the research methods chosen and that the methods do not seem to be well suited for the research agendas proposed (McAnany and LaPastina 1994). Grand ideas are not always followed by actionable implementation. But for Latin Americans, this does not detract from the value of the idea. Creative perspectives, new visions and original ideas are valuable in themselves. Careful precision, protracted data collection and scientific replicability are met with respect but less enthusiasm.

These different priorities can lead to conflict among Latin American and foreign research partners. I heard both sides of a story from a failed research partnership. The North American had spent a sabbatical semester at the Latin American school. He was renowned in his field and widely published. Expectations were high on both sides for a partnership that would provide insights into Latin America and publications in international journals. The Latin Americans complain that the North American did not follow through on his obligations to publish what they produced. The North American complains that the data collected was not of a publishable standard. Passions were disappointed when plans were not carefully implemented. Neither side recognised what was actually motivating the other, and the common objectives were not met.

Conversation Patterns

Even for people who speak Spanish and Portuguese, Latin Americans can be difficult to understand because of their distinct non-verbal codes and speech patterns. Perhaps the most striking characteristic is the physical expressiveness. Latin Americans may wave their arms, raise their voices, stand up, and pound your shoulder as well as kiss you on both cheeks several times. These are like physical punctuation in a conversation: dashes, exclamation marks, ellipses and parentheses. In fact, some Latin Americans are convinced they feel more than people from some other countries because they express their feelings more than other people. The difference is between cultures which are Dionysian (exhibiting stoicism and control) and those which are Apollonian (emotionally expressive) (Albert 1996).

The order and content of speech is also characteristic of this region. It is considered rude and cold to 'get right to the point'. Discussion during meetings in Latin America is not primarily oriented towards an agenda but towards a relationship. Latin Americans generally start conversations with friendly banter, move on to some historical framing, touch on the meeting subject, back up to introduce a key figure, circle around to the subject again, thank you warmly for your participation, return to the subject briefly, make sure you are comfortable with the work progress so far, and close with an invitation for your family to visit at the beach house. If you are working from an agenda with three points, you may be surprised to find that you covered all three but simply did not approach them in the tidy order you had expected.

Ceremonial speech is important to show respect and establish the hierarchy. The circular agenda relates a broad range of perspectives to the main agenda item in a holistic fashion. Moving quickly through a variety of topics may be used as a 'light' way of giving negative views or even saying no without being confrontational. People must observe the context as much as the content in order to understand the message (Albert 1996; Hall 1981). Physical space and touching carry as much meaning as the words yes and no (Hall 1982).

Symbols and interpretations are vital for qualitative research. In the high-context speech of Latin America, researchers must hear the non-verbal messages. Many symbols can be explained, but many others must be experienced to be understood. The good news about culture as learned behaviour (Berry et al. 1992) is that it can be learned by foreign researchers as well as by natives. As the opening story demonstrates, partnerships between locals and foreigners can produce insights neither would have perceived alone.

Latin Americans are generally familiar with research techniques and do not mind participating in studies. The wide diffusion of television has created a familiarity with interviews such as those shown on news programmes and talk shows. Tape recorders and even cameras will produce only temporary self-consciousness. People do not have to be coaxed too much for self-disclosure. Expressiveness is already the norm. Once contacts have agreed to meet with researchers, establishing a rapport requires showing a personal interest in the subject and listening in a physically engaged manner. Remember that questions will not be answered directly to the point. The answer may involve a lot of background and associations that are not immediately clear to the interviewer. Questions may need to be asked several times in different ways before the intent of the subject becomes clear. Connections will often be assumed and follow-up questions are often necessary if the interviewer wants to be sure of his/her understanding.

CONCLUSION

This chapter has provided an introduction to the macro-level socio-political environment of Latin American business, from the extreme class differences to the infrastructure challenges. It has also explained some of the behaviours and social norms that are characteristic (though not universal) among Latin Americans such as hierarchies, relationships, particularism and passion. Together these should provide an initial understanding of Latin America for qualitative research design and analysis. Specific tips and recommendations should also provide a good start while the researcher develops enough personal experience to form his/her own set of adaptations.

Despite some of the unique challenges I face doing research in Latin America, living here also provides some significant benefits like a cheerful and energetic work environment, a field of almost limitless possibilities, and a certainty that my research and teaching make a practical difference in people's lives. More than anything else, the warmth and enthusiasm of the people is what makes Latin America such a dynamic and rich place for research. The rest of the world has much to learn from the people and practices here. By applying the material presented in this chapter, foreign researchers will have a good start towards appropriate, productive and pleasant work in Latin America.

ACKNOWLEDGEMENTS

The author wishes to thank the faculty, students and staff of Escola de Administração de Empresas de São Paulo da Fundação Getulio Vargas (FGV-EAESP) for their kindness, insights and friendship. Thanks also to the Latin American Studies programme of Cornell University and the US Department of Education for two Foreign Language and Area Studies Fellowships for Portuguese language studies.

REFERENCES

Albert, R.D. (1996), 'A framework and model for understanding Latin American and Latino/Hispanic cultural patterns', in D. Landis and R.S. Bhagat (eds), *Handbook of Intercultural Training*, Thousand Oaks, CA: Sage, pp. 327–48.

Berry, J.W., Y.-H. Poortinga, M.H. Segall and P.R. Dasen (1992), *Cross-Cultural Psychology: Research and Applications*, Cambridge: Cambridge University Press.

Burns, E.B. (1993), *A History of Brazil*, 3rd edn, New York: Columbia University Press.

Condon, J.C. (1985), *Good Neighbors: Communicating with the Mexicans*, Yarmouth, ME: Intercultural Press.

Craig, C.S. and S.P. Douglas (2000), *International Marketing Research*, Chichester: John Wiley & Sons.

Degler, C. (1971), *Neither Black nor White*, Madison, WI: University of Wisconsin Press.

Fleury, M.T.L. (2001), 'Diversidade cultural: gerenciando a pluralidade nas empresas', in T. Wood Jr. (ed.), *Gestão Empresarial: Oito Propostas para o*

Terceiro Milênio, São Paulo: Atlas, pp. 186–99.

Fleury, M.T.L., G.T. Shinyashiki and L.A. Stevanato (1997), 'Arqueologia teórica e dilemas metodológocos dos estudos sobre cultura organizational', in F.C.P. Motta and M.P. Caldas (eds), *Cultura Organizational e Cultura Brasileira*, São Paulo: Atlas, pp. 273–92.

Geertz, C. (1973), *The Interpretation of Cultures*, New York: Basic Books.

Gudykunst, W.B. and Y.Y. Kim (1997), *Communicating with Strangers: An Approach to Intercultural Communication*, Boston, MA: McGraw-Hill.

Hall, B.J. and M. Noguchi (1993), 'Intercultural conflict: a case study', *International Journal of Intercultural Relations*, **17**, 399–413.

Hall, E.T. (1959), *The Silent Language*, New York: Doubleday.

—— (1981), *Beyond Culture*, New York: Anchor Books.

—— (1982), *The Hidden Dimension*, New York: Anchor Books.

—— (1983), *The Dance of Life*, New York: Anchor Books/Doubleday.

Harrison, P.A. (1995), 'Behaving Brazilian', in G.H. Summ (ed.), *Brazilian Mosaic: Portraits of a Diverse People and Culture*, Wilmington, DE: Scholarly Resources Inc., pp. 177–81.

Heck, M. and R. Belluzzo (1998), *Cozinha dos Imigrantes: Memórias e Receitas*, São Paulo: DBA Artes Gráficas.

Hofstede, G. (1980), *Culture's Consequences: International Differences in Work-Related Values*, Beverly Hills, CA: Sage.

Indacochea, A. (2001), *Ayacucho Competitivo*, Lima: CARE Peru.

Kluckhohn, F. and F. Strodtbeck (1961), *Variations in Value Orientations*, Evanston, IL: Row, Peterson.

McAnany, E.G. and A.C. LaPastina (1994), 'Telenovela audiences: a review and methodological critique of Latin American research', *Communication Research*, **21** (6), 828–40.

Oliveira, J. (2001), *Brazil: A Guide for Businesspeople*, Yarmouth, ME: Intercultural Press.

Pizano, E.S. (2001), 'Gobernabilidad para la Globalización: el reto de América Latina in Globalización: Hacia una agenda para América Latina', paper presented at the Primer Encuentro de Ex Presidentes Latinoamericans, Cartagena, Columbia, September.

Prates, M.A.S. and B.T. Barros (1997), 'O Estilo Brasileiro de Administrar: Sumário de um modelo de ação cultural brasileiro com base na gestão empresarial', in F.C.P. Motta and M.P. Caldas (eds), *Cultura Organizational e Cultura Brasileira*, São Paulo: Atlas, pp. 55–69.

Rich, P.G. (2002), 'E-Commerce, Latin America and the WTO', in P.G. Rich (ed.), *Latin America: Its Future in the Global Economy*, Basingstoke: Palgrave, pp. 135–63.

Robles, F., F. Simon and J. Haar (2003), *Winning Strategies for the New Latin Markets*, Saddle River, NJ: Pearson Education.

Roett, R. (1995), 'The patrimonial state', in G.H. Summ (ed.), *Brazilian Mosaic: Portrait of a Diverse People and Culture*, Wilmington, DE: Scholarly Resources, pp. 181–4.

Strathern, M. (1995), 'The nice thing about culture is that everyone has it', in M. Strathern (ed.), *Shifting Contexts: Transformations in Anthropological Knowledge*, London: Routledge, pp. 153–76.

Tajfel, H. and J.C. Turner (1979), 'An integrative theory of intergroup conflict', in W.G. Austin and S. Worchel (eds), *The Social Psychology of Intergroup Relations*, Monterey, CA: Brooks/Cole, pp. 33–47.

Tharp, M.C. (2001), *Marketing and Consumer Identity in Multicultural America*, Thousand Oaks, CA: Sage.

Trompenaars, F. and C. Hampden-Turner (1997), *Riding the Waves of Culture: Understanding Cultural Diversity in Business*, London: Nicholas Brealey.

Wagley, C. (1995), 'A most personal people', in G.H. Summ (ed.), *Brazilian Mosaic: Portrait of a Diverse People and Culture*, Wilmington, DE: Scholarly Resources, pp. 148–53.

PART VI

From Analysis to Publication

Against Today's Fashion: Experiences from the 'Review Front'

Dirk Matten

It is perhaps a bit overstated to compare academia to the world of fashion. However, institutional scholars tell us that it is not reasoned thinking of rational actors in the first place which legitimises certain professional practices in an organisation. In the field of international business (IB) research it sometimes appears that 30 years of predominantly quantitative and contingency framework-oriented work have created a somewhat funny 'mimetic isomorphism' which regards this approach as the only legitimate take on research questions. This is certainly the experience of scholars working closer to the approach central to this volume.

Having said that, I of course concede that there is ample and rich opportunity to publish qualitative research in good journals. Many of the leading thinkers in the field – the list of contributors to this volume is certainly proof to that – see the richness and benefits of qualitative research as well as the limits of extant work in the field. But as with all shifts of paradigms, such a 'perestroika' takes a while to become common currency. An academic who wants to publish his/her qualitative research in reasonable journals therefore stands a fair chance of getting first-hand feedback from a multitude of reviewers who have dedicated most of their professional life to quantitative research and who are likely to regard any other take on IB research basically as some sort of heresy.

A first concern of mainstream reviewers would be that *qualitative approaches commonly draw on a broader array of social science theory* than quantitative work. While the latter mostly would prefer economic and – to a lesser degree – psychological theory, many qualitative scholars ground their theoretical framework in sociology, politics, philosophy, ecology, or even the arts, just to name a few. A typical reviewer then would, for instance, comment that 'the primary flaw of the study is that it doesn't build on, or accurately incorporate, management theories. It draws instead almost entirely on political science theories … rather than the terms that are more commonly used in the management literature'. Hence, such a deviation from the canonised collection of theories will be branded as 'quite dangerous'. One particular reviewer even argued that our theoretical approach in a particular paper could be equalled to basically defending communism (as a post-1968 German I took that as a compliment; Americans though will know that this is as bad a verdict as it gets)!

Another typical worry to encounter would be that normally *qualitative research is conceptualised somewhat differently to quantitative work*. There is a richer, verbal and sometimes more open definition of constructs as well as of links between constructs; model relationships are conceptualised by different ways of abstraction. 'Measuring' a phenomenon by numbers or, for instance, by narrative, of course results in completely different 'models' of reality. This will lead mainstream scholars to comment that 'the authors have interviewed members of these organisations without any theoretical model in mind' and that their study 'seems like a lot of mixed information rather than a clear theoretical analysis'. With such a rigorous (mostly economic) model in mind, no wonder that such a reviewer concludes that 'if this were a theoretical conceptualisation, rather than a mere polemic, then some hypotheses would be derivable'. Some reviewers are even so strongly tied to their typical methods of conceptualising a problem that they already see a deviation from established 'technologies' as a serious flaw: 'Figure 1, which the reader would expect to be a visual representation of a theory or a model is really *only a table*. Why is it labelled "Figure 1"? I can't imagine, unless the authors believe a figure is synonymous with a model' [emphasis added].

A very common anxiety of quantitative scholars in IB is fuelled by *different forms and modes of verification of qualitative research findings*. While not all would go to the extreme of judging that 'this manuscript is interesting and I would enjoy reading it in a popular press outlet' a typical comment with regard to qualitative research would be: 'Why not gather some quantitative data, especially when measures are available'. The obvious reason to do so for those reviewers lies in the fact that a particular paper is 'looking at a number of constructs for which measures exist' – and qualitative data obviously does not count as 'measuring' anything. This is particularly the case when research is based on a small number of case studies: as such research 'is not based on large data with statistical tests' the – allegedly unsatisfactory – work 'requires a clearly thought out research design and possibly either deeper or wider study to reach conclusions that would be acceptable'.

I should finish this brief foray with two comments. First, the editors invited this anecdote not as a lament over the unfair world of peer reviewed journals. After all, those quotes all relate to work which ultimately was published in fairly reasonable outlets, such as *Academy of Management Review, Journal of Management Studies, Human Relations* or *Journal of International*

Management. Second, my intention is not to make fun of esteemed colleagues from a different research tradition. Actually, we were quite thankful for many of these comments as those reviews actually helped my co-authors and me to improve our work. Some of them admittedly were triggered by a certain sloppiness in our way of writing, arguing and concluding. There is no point in being arrogant towards those 'number crunchers' while at the same time not living up to standards of solid qualitative research – which in fact are far higher with regard to verbal rigour, sharpness of argumentation and subtlety in qualifying statements.

23. Ensuring Validity in Qualitative International Business Research

Poul Houman Andersen and Maria Anne Skaates

INTRODUCTION

It is an obligation for all scientists to conduct rigorous studies, regardless of their research tradition. The process of validating studies based on qualitative research strategies is therefore a core issue for both the readers and producers of qualitative research. In international business (IB) research textbooks, validity is most often merely equated to measurement issues, if covered at all (see, for example, Craig and Douglas 2000; Kumar 2000). However, in essence, the validity issue concerns the intersubjective convincibility of a study: to what extent do scholars agree that a study and its results cover the phenomena they claim to cover (Easton 1998; Hammersley 1990)? On this more fundamental level, validity is related to the social research issues of ontology, that is, the nature of 'reality', such as the essence of the phenomenon under study, and epistemology, that is, assumptions about the grounds of knowledge, and how this knowledge can be grasped through methods of inquiry.

Qualitative researchers have been scolded for not taking the validity issue seriously (Miles and Huberman 1994). As will be shown, it is the exception rather than the rule that qualitative research contributions include a discussion of validity issues. This state of affairs fuels the default notion among reviewers and editors that qualitative research is suspect, lacking rigour and, in general, unscientific (Morse 1999). In addition, reviewers often lack sufficient heuristics for judging the quality of these studies (Cooper 2001). Moreover, qualitative research approaches sometimes implicitly carry with them an (at least partially) subjectivist stance towards ontology, due to, for example, the importance of getting an 'emic' or 'insider's' understanding of foreign business situations or cultures (see, for example, Beerman and Stengel 1996; Pike 1966; Usunier 2000) and of the enacted nature of human relations (see Easton 1992). The nature of knowledge within such subjectivist ontologies is different to that of objectivist-inspired ontologies. Rather than uncovering social regularities, research approaches based on subjectivist ontologies seek to provide the researcher with prerequisites for understanding processes of human sensemaking. They emphasise the theory(ies) being used by social actors (Morgan and Smircich 1980), and involvement in the studied field rather than observing it as an external actor (Morgan 1983). They tend to generate diagnosis/synthesis rather than explanation (Mittrof and Kilman 1982). As a result of these differences, quality claims raised by adherents of objectivist ontologies cannot be directly applied to research methodologies developed from a subjectivist or at least partially subjectivist stance. This, in turn, leads some qualitative researchers to discard the idea of quality control in social science altogether, since standard checks for validity and reliability are not pertinent to qualitative inquiry (see Agar 1986; Leininger 1994). Others have attempted to develop alternative or parallel concepts to the canons of validity and reliability, such as trustworthiness and authenticity (Lincoln and Guba 1985).

However, this rejection of basic objectivist assumptions should not lead us to assume that more subjectivist-oriented research need not deal with the issue of validity. On the contrary, in our view, which is consistent with the opinions of many users and producers of qualitative social and business administration research (see, for example, Eisenhardt 1989; Kvale 1989; Maxwell 1992; Miles and Huberman 1994; Silverman 1994; Yin 1994), one needs more than the researchers' claim of relevance when assessing the merits of a study's findings and conclusions. Moreover, when conducting research, qualitative, no less than quantitative, researchers need guidelines for ensuring rigour in their research process. Furthermore, we view the discussion of validity issue of qualitative studies as being especially important in IB research for two reasons: first, validity is especially difficult to achieve in qualitative international research, due to differences in researchers' and respondents' cultural assumptions (Adler 1983; Kvale 1994; Usunier 2000); and second, validity and other scientific argumentation principles are socially constructed and differ across cultural and institutional contexts (Clyne 1987; Sullivan and Weaver 2000). For instance, while researchers have continued to use the terminology of reliability and validity in qualitative inquiry in Britain and in the rest of Europe, those who do so in the United States are a minority voice (compare Morse et al. 2002). Therefore, qualitative research strategies that may be accepted models for producing valid science in, for example, a specific Scandinavian IB department may not be viewed as valid elsewhere.

The purpose of this chapter, then, is to provide an account of how the validity issue, as related to qualitative research strategies within the IB field, may be grasped from an at least partially subjectivist point of view. We shall therefore first assess the extent to which the validity issue has been treated in qualitative research contributions published in six leading English-language IB journals. Thereafter, we will discuss our findings and relate them to (1) various levels of the research process and (2) the existing literature on potential validity problems from a more subjectivist point of view (for example, Alasuutari 1995; Kirk and Miller 1986; Morgan and Smircich 1980). In subsequent sections, we shall present some strategies for ensuring validity during the research process, as well as illustrate various ways in which validity may be considered in IB articles, to allow for a greater extent of critical evaluation of validity claims. Finally, in the concluding section, we shall summarise our arguments and their implications for future qualitative IB research.

LITERATURE REVIEW

The aim of our literature review is to determine the extent to which the validity issue has been treated in qualitative research contributions published in leading outlets for IB research. We have chosen to restrict our focus to English-language publication outlets, despite the relevance and importance of IB insights from research published in other languages (see Holden 1998; Walters 2001).

Classification of Research Approaches

In daily parlance among business academics, the concepts of qualitative and quantitative research are often discussed as if these classifications were a matter of little dispute. However, there is no clear-cut definition of what comprises a research strategy and how it diverges from other approaches. For our present purpose, we have found it useful to group the contributions into three overarching categories, based on whether they present (1) a qualitative research approach, (2) a quantitative research approach, or whether they are (3) review-oriented, modelling or commentary papers.

By qualitative research we mean studies that seek to explore the nature of phenomena (as opposed to the quantification of given observations). Studies with a qualitative approach are usually based on open-ended interviews and the interpretation of other field data such as internal memos and archival texts, but may also convey quantitative data and (usually descriptive) statistics. By quantitative research, we mean studies that use mainly quantitative data, most usually to follow the validation strategy of proposition development and empirical testing. These studies aim at testing a theory-driven series of causal relationships, using formal propositions as a device for probing, and formal, statistical testing methods. Our third category – reviews, modelling and commentary – is concerned with theory development and general commentary. The encompassed contributions range from formal or normative model development based on reasoning (such as the present contribution) to essays from corporate elites establishing an overview of a current theoretical debate or situation. They may present empirical material as well (that is, both qualitative and quantitative data), but do so mainly for anecdotal or illustrative purposes.

The Data

In English-language IB research, article publication is the main mode of communicating research results. We have therefore chosen to examine qualitative research articles in the six English-language journals that were identified as leading IB journals in a recent study (DuBois and Reeb 2000): (1) *Journal of International Business Studies* (henceforth: *JIBS*); (2) *Management International Review* (*MIR*); (3) *Journal of World Business* (*JWB*), formerly *Columbia Journal of World Business* (*CJWB*);[1] (4) *International Marketing Review* (*IMR*); (5) *Journal of International Marketing* (*JIM*), which has been published since 1993; (6) *International Business Review* (*IBR*), which has been published since 1993, formerly known as *Scandinavian International Business Review*.

Our review covers journal articles appearing in these journals in the period from 1991 to 2001, or as long as the journal has existed within this time slot. We have left out contributions that did not lend themselves easily to our classification framework. These include personal memoirs of academic life, internal debates on a specific contribution, book reviews and interviews. Our first step involved surveying a total of 1783 journal articles in 297 issues of the journals.

Although all six surveyed journals focus on IB or international marketing and claim to be open to all relevant contributions regardless of methodologies applied, the three types of studies, that is, (1) qualitative, (2) quantitative, and (3) review-oriented, modelling or commentary contributions are not equally represented in the journals. Figure 23.1 provides an overview of the percentage of each study type found in the surveyed journals. Disregarding *CJWB*, the figure shows a consistent distribution in the sense that quantitative research strategies have a dominant position in English-language IB research. In contrast, qualitative research strategies are the road least followed. Taken together, approximately 10 per cent of all published IB research is of the qualitative variety. Approximately 50 per cent is based on quantitative inquiry, while the remaining 40 per cent of studies reviewed concern conceptual contributions dealing with model development and/or theoretical reviews. However, there are significant differences among the journals with respect to their propensity to publish qualitatively oriented research. At one extreme, only 3 per cent of the studies published in *JIBS* have been based on qualitative inquiry; at the other extreme, around 20 per cent of the studies in *JWB* have been based on a qualitative research approach.

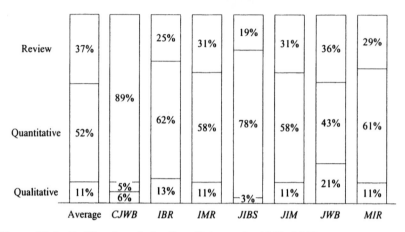

Figure 23.1   Publications in leading IB journals, 1991–2002

The second step of our analysis was to look at the 176 qualitative contributions alone, to determine (1) the number of instances in which validity was discussed, (2) the presence of an explicitly stated subjectivist or partially subjectivist ontology, and (3) the number of instances in which an 'emic' or 'insider's' perspective on the theme of the research (see, for example, Beerman and Stengel 1996; Pike 1966; Usunier 2000) was referred to. Our analytical data shows that only a minority, that is, around one-third of the reviewed qualitative contributions, discusses the validity issue at all. Moreover, there is no correspondence between those studies dealing with validity and a focus on cross-cultural issues. This is consistent with a prior review of qualitative research in IB (Yeung 1995). This relatively infrequent treatment of the subject of validity may be viewed as alarming, as any study involving cultural differences between the researcher and the culture in which the studied phenomena is embedded, must deal with the validity issue especially carefully, due to the potential for cross-cultural validity problems (for example, Adler 1983). In relation to the more specific issues (2 and 3, above) of subjectivist or partially subjectivist ontology and an 'emic' perspective, discussion of elements of either or both was only present in a small minority of the contributions, that is, around 3 per cent.

Thus we can conclude that it is the exception rather than the rule that qualitative research contributions include a discussion of validity issues. Moreover, while qualitative research approaches carry with them elements of a subjective stance to epistemology, this issue is not usually discussed in the presentation of the research. We share the view of, for example, Eisenhardt

(1989), Kvale (1989), Maxwell (1992), Miles and Huberman (1994), Silverman (1994) and Yin (1994), that one needs more than the researcher's claim of relevance when assessing the merits of a study's findings and conclusions. Obviously, we are very concerned about this very low level of discussion of validity-related issues in English-language IB articles based on qualitative research. In the following section, we shall therefore discuss the links in the components of the research process that need to be coherent and well considered, in order to ensure validity.

VALIDITY IN QUALITATIVE IB RESEARCH: DO WE SEE WHAT WE BELIEVE WE SEE?

As we initially stated in our introduction, the issue of validity can be posed in very general terms as: how well does the data set generated from this research approach reflect the phenomena it is intended to cover? However, more specific formulations of validity criteria vary somewhat according to the researchers' ontological and epistemological views. Yet there is a fixed relationship between ontology, epistemology and the other elements of the research process, as depicted in Figure 23.2. The figure shows that the choice of research strategy (that is, the specific methodological approach used in relation to the research questions, such as conducting a conceptual study and/or some type of qualitative or quantitative study to examine the research questions) is closely related to the researcher's general epistemological viewpoint (for example, preference for interpretivist or functionalist explanations),[2] which in turn is influenced by the researcher's general ontological beliefs (that is, about the mainly objective or mainly subjective nature of human reality). Most researchers[3] would adhere to Figure 23.2's hierarchy (see, for example, Schmidt 1994; Weick 1989).

Ontological and Epistemological Viewpoints and Research Strategy

In contrast, those researchers who adhere to the intermediate – that is, partially subjectivist, partially objectivist – ontological positions, such as the realists or the social constructivists, may make use of the classificatory framework of Figure 23.2 in their efforts to ensure validity.[4] In these intermediate positions, the concept of truth is more problematic and arbitrary than it is for pure objectivists. This is because rather than assuming an empirical world of universally causal mechanisms waiting to be uncovered, the social world, which may still contain some regularity, is subjected to an ongoing construction process conducted by reflexive actors, none of whom is able to completely objectively describe social reality.

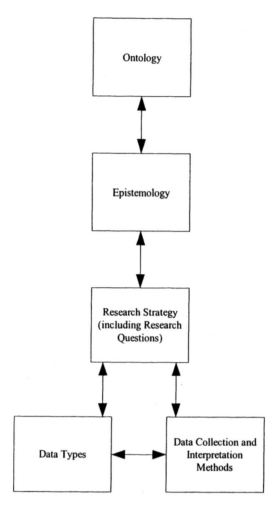

Figure 23.2   Ontology, epistemology and research process components

However, the adherents of the different intermediate ontological and epistemological positions often demonstrate varying preferences for research strategies that are often influenced by these positions. For example, many realists prefer to use research strategies that will result in generally applicable or middle-range functionalist explanations due to their quest to try to achieve as good an understanding of an agreed-upon reality as possible. In contrast, large numbers of social constructivists stick to strategies aimed at uncovering ongoing sensemaking and self- and other-construction processes in very specific contexts, due to their ontological and epistemological emphasis on enactment.

Research Strategy, Data Types, and Data Collection and Interpretation Methods

There are, of course, direct links between the types of data collected (for example, statements of respondents, surveys, statistics, written reports, and so on), the data collection process (for example, via interviews, observation, reading of reports and memos), the interpretation methods and the chosen research strategy in a specific research process. These connections are elucidated in a number of qualitative IB articles (for example, Festing 1997; Teigland et al. 2000; Tsang 2001).

In relation to these links, it is also important that the researcher recognise that most qualitative data can be interpreted in different ways, and that he or she makes carefully considered choices concerning the data collected and the way it is interpreted on the basis of this recognition. Alasuutari (1995) has identified three fundamentally different ways of interpretation: factist, narrative and rhetorical. From the factist perspective, the researcher aims at coming as close to an 'objective' reality as possible, for example, by critically examining the truthfulness of written information and/or the honesty of an interview respondent. In contrast, when interpreting from the narrative perspective, the truthfulness and honesty of statements and texts are not relevant; it is the argumentative structures and justifications of the written and/or oral statements and/or bodily action that are studied, often to create an overview of the patterns with which human beings present their statements and actions. Finally, in the rhetorical perspective, the interaction between the speakers, actors or the writers of texts and their audience becomes the object of interpretation. How are these communicators attempting to influence their audience, that is, how do they – perhaps implicitly – seek to speak to their audience's perceptions and preferences?

Sometimes, however, the above links and interpretation strategies do not add up well in cross-disciplinary and pre-paradigmatic areas of inquiry, such as IB, where researchers are often methodologically predisposed towards specific research strategies that may be less useful in certain contexts. For instance, as Parkhe (1997) points out, even though quantitative data sources are unlikely to be helpful in capturing and delineating the 'soft' core concepts of international joint venture research such as reciprocity or trust, researchers of international joint ventures are often biased towards quantitative multivariate data analysis. Such problems are perhaps also linked to the lack of discussion on validity in most qualitative IB articles. Easton (1998) stated that it is ultimately impossible to know what reality is. This is because both (1) all data types collected and (2) all measures of this data (see Figure 23.2) are in themselves mere indirect and interpretive constructs selected by researchers, which cannot be said to capture the essence of the phenomena being studied (Kant [1787] 1998). This is what makes the issue of validity a concern for the adherents of the intermediate ontological and epistemological positions. As Kirk and Miller (1986, p. 11) point out, 'The way we perceive and understand that world is largely up to us, but the world does not tolerate all understandings of it equally'. Therefore, readers of IB research need validity measures to evaluate and discern between different qualities of interpretive research results and to ensure that the reflections represented by the researcher also have merits in the social reality that the researcher intends to portray.

In relation to the construction and results of a specific research process (see Figure 23.2), validity problems may be the cause of three possible generic errors (Kirk and Miller 1986): type one error – believing a research result would be intersubjectively judged to be true when it would not be; type two error – rejecting a principle when it in fact would be intersubjectively assessed to be true; and type three error – fundamentally asking the wrong research question. Furthermore, as concerns data types, data collection and interpretation (see Figure 23.2) several additional types of errors are possible: choosing the wrong types of data or data collection methods or interpreting the data wrongly in its collection (Alasuutari 1995; Usunier 2000). In the following, we shall look more closely at each type of error. For the sake of argumentative coherence, we shall start with type three errors, as they are often related to discrepancies between the research strategy and the ontological and epistemological presumptions of the researcher. We shall then move to the errors concerning data types, data collection and interpretation, and end by discussing type one and two errors in research processes, because these types of errors are most closely related to mismatches between the research strategy, data types, data collection and interpretation.

Type Three Errors

In relation to the type three error of asking the wrong research question, research questions can be incorrectly formulated if there is a mismatch between the chosen research strategy and the ontological and epistemological presumptions of the researcher. As in Parkhe's (1997) example, the preference of researchers of international joint ventures for realist or pure objectivist ontologies often leads them to use less-than-ideal quantitative data sources. Consequently, they also tend to formulate less-than-ideal research questions when attempting to capture socially-constructed concepts such as reciprocity or trust.

Type three errors also often occur in IB if the researcher mistakenly assumes that the traits and categorisations of his/her culture are the same as those abroad. In international marketing research, this has been discussed as the problem of self-referent cultural influence when conducting research (Craig and Douglas 2000). This is because certain categorisations are culture specific in nature, and therefore either do not bear any merit or change meaning in other cultural settings (Usunier 2000). For instance, international marketing studies of 'teenage consumer habits worldwide' implicitly assume that 'teenagers' as a distinct social group is a universally applicable categorisation of humans. To speak of 'teenagers' in such a manner may be reasonable when conducting research in, for instance, the United States, but it is much less so in rural Vietnam.

Errors Concerning Data Types, Data Collection and Interpretation

As previously mentioned, many errors are the result of an improper match between data types and data collection and interpretation strategies. An example of this is found in Hellman's (1994, p. 204) explanation of the differences in the results about the internationalisation of Finnish banks and the results of two previous articles on this same topic (Sivonen 1983; Turkkila 1992):

> The difference in results may, at least party, be explained by the fact that in the previous studies, the banks themselves were allowed to state the motives for their internationalisation, and may for 'image' reasons have wanted to picture themselves as 'merely' serving their customers, not having intentions of expanding internationally or of taking part in international financial-market activities.

In the above example, Hellman (1994) suggests that in the previous studies by Sivonen (1983) and Turkkila (1992), the responses of Finnish bank officials were naively taken at face value for being 'facts', without consideration of the possible rhetorical reasoning behind the Finnish bank officials' answers.

A second problem in relation to data interpretation may be the researcher's non-native familiarity and mastery of the semantics and pragmatics of non-verbal and verbal communication strategies in the countries where the qualitative research is being undertaken. This may lead to the researcher misinterpreting, for example, some of the respondents' actions, gestures, humour, irony or indirect references to subjects considered taboo (Asante and Gudykunst 1989). For instance, a researcher from one nation who is interested in career processes in multinational corporations may see the removal of a middle-aged manager from a top position to a lower-ranking position within a company as a demotion, whereas in the national office being studied, that is, an office in another nation, this action may have been taken due to the request of the employee for more free time and may also be viewed as an acknowledgement of this person's efforts and a wish to retain him or her as a valuable staff member.

These problems of correctly interpreting communication may also be present when the researcher is conducting the research in another language than his or her native language and when he or she is using English as a lingua franca when interviewing non-native speakers of English. This is because even fairly proficient non-native speakers of foreign languages very often make some use of their native pragmatic cultural conventions when communicating in a foreign language (Asante and Gudykunst 1989). Thus, a Japanese communicating in nearly fluent Arabic may unconsciously intersperse at least a few elements of Japanese humour or politeness in his or her Arabic verbal communication; these elements may, in turn, well be misunderstood by the Saudi Arabian listener.

The expectations concerning the researcher's and the interviewee's roles in the research process may also vary across countries, and must be accounted for in the data collection and interpretation strategy. For example, Goodyear (1982) found that many respondents in developing countries considered market research interviewing to be a type of long-winded selling, which may have led to their giving less-than-honest responses, an issue that Usunier (2000, p. 228) may have also been confronted with, when he was met with the following question in Mauritania: 'What do you want us to tell the interviewee to answer?'. In connection with this issue, which is related to rhetorical elements, information about the sex, age, position, academic degrees, and ethnic or social background of the researcher may also affect the expectations of the foreign respondent in ways different from the case of a respondent in the interviewer's home country. For example, mention of an academic interviewer's full professor status carries very different assumptions and associations in Germany than is the case in the UK, given that German full professors usually also fulfil the same responsibilities as academic department heads in the UK university system.

Type One and Two Errors

From the above discussion, it should now be becoming clear to the reader that a majority of the aforementioned errors of type one (that is, believing a research result would be intersubjectively judged to be true when it would not be) and two (rejecting a principle when it in fact would be intersubjectively assessed to be true) are simply the result of mistakes in research strategy, that is, (1) choosing the wrong types of data or data collection methods, (2) interpreting the data wrongly in its collection, and/or (3) an improper match between data and interpretation choices. These problems, in turn, are sometimes a result of a lack of resources rather than deliberate negligence. For, in order to be carried out properly qualitative research strategies often call for substantial resources, which may not be available, which in turn often leads researchers to attempt interpretation of less well-developed sets of data.

A powerful example of error – specifically, type two error – occurs when researchers, eager in their quest to discover new unique features, fail to see similarities or may be lured by decoys imposed upon them by 'natives'. A case in point here is the famous incident concerning Margaret Mead, an American anthropologist who studied Samoan culture. Mead became renowned for her study of sexual behaviour among adolescents, showing that the Samoan community – unlike other societies such as the American society in the 1920s – did little to curb sexual activity among teenagers. However, as demonstrated by Freeman (1983), Mead's research was less than thorough and was essentially based on interviews with a few female Samoan companions, whom she questioned about sexual activities. Embarrassed by Mead's insistent probing about a forbidden topic, these women resorted to a customary Samoan practice of prankish hoaxing, and presumably had a great time fooling Mead into believing the opposite of the truth about their lives. With this somewhat extreme, admittedly non-IB example in mind, we shall present some strategies for ensuring validity during the IB research process, as well as illustrate various ways in which validity considerations may be written in IB articles, to allow for a greater extent of critical evaluation of validity claims.

STRATEGIES FOR ENSURING AND DEMONSTRATING VALIDITY

As argued here, the issue of validity as a measure of the rigour and quality of the research being presented is equally important for qualitative and quantitative IB research. Addressing validity issues is a way of ensuring rigour in research. Without rigour, research risks becoming fiction and thereby losing its value. However, as pointed out, the criteria for evaluating the validity of research efforts rely not on the methodologies themselves but rather on the underlying epistemological and ontological assumptions of the researcher, as well as the constraints of the qualitative methodology chosen. There is no single way of validating one's qualitative research findings, and consequently there exists more than one set of procedures to demonstrate validity when publishing qualitative research. However, below we present an overview of what we believe to be the key validity issues that must be addressed from a realist or interpretive perspective when conducting and presenting qualitative research in an IB setting.[5]

Existing contributions (Cooper 2001; Morse et al. 2002) would suggest that validity checks fundamentally must serve two purposes. The first purpose is to ensure validity during the research process and avoid problems emanating from self-deception of the researcher (Salner 1999). In relation to this purpose, Kvale (1989) regards the validation process more fundamentally as a process of sceptical questioning. According to him, the elements that must be questioned in connection with a scientific study include the subject matter investigated and the concept of true knowledge itself, according to the correspondence and coherence philosophical criteria of truth. This is in line with a key trend since the seminal work of the ontological realist Popper (1979): validation procedures associated with a broad range of epistemological and ontological positions have increasingly emphasised sceptical questioning and falsification, to the detriment in particular of 'pure objectivist' attempts at verification. The second purpose necessarily rests on the resolution of the first; it is to make it possible for readers and users (as well as journal editors and reviewers) to evaluate the rigour of the research results presented.

Process Validity Issues

As our literature review showed, issues of validity have been downplayed in most English-language qualitative IB research reporting. It has even been claimed that qualitative researchers do not need support from process validity criteria, as they can more easily assess whether they are capturing the phenomenon they are trying to measure when meeting the field (Cooper 2001). However, this is probably an overtly optimistic view of the mental abilities of a qualitative researcher. As pointed out by Salner (1999), qualitative researchers frequently stumble over problems such as psychological limits and a lack of strategies for handling anxiety, confusion, anger and so on during their research endeavours, and this pattern may be the rule rather than the exception. Qualitative researchers embarking on cross-cultural research in particular should constantly be engaged in critical self-questioning: to what extent are detected patterns a product of my expectations? Cooper (2001) points to problems such as the holistic fallacy (looking for congruence and emergent patterns when findings in reality are more heterogeneous and complex), the risk of interviewing and/or relying on elites only, and the problems of going native (not being able to detach from the views of informants). Thus, as concerns all levels of Figure 23.2 and the interactions between the levels, process validity can be described quite generally as 'to validate is to question' and 'to check' (Kvale 1989), that is, for intersubjective agreement about the correspondence of the researcher's data and data interpretation to the social world and for the level of coherence in logic and consistency of the researcher's theoretical arguments.

Clearly, procedures are needed for identifying and correcting errors before they are built into emerging models. Morse et al. (2002) suggest that, overall, these problems lie with the responsiveness of researchers, and the extent to which researchers remain open, use sensitivity, creativity and insight and are willing to relinquish ideas that are poorly supported. More precisely, qualitative researchers should look for methodological coherence concerning the congruence between the research strategy and the other components of research process (see Figure 23.2). Following Brinberg and McGrath (1985), research questions must match the data collection method, which again must match the data and interpretive procedures, as already suggested.

Although the aforementioned problem of type three errors (that is, asking the wrong research question) is equally present in both qualitative and quantitative research, qualitative researchers may engage in ongoing testing of reality, which may lead to modification or changes in research questions, to ensure the elimination of these type three errors. In contrast, researchers relying on quantitative methods, notably the testing of hypotheses, depend entirely on their ability to ensure a good fit between the research strategy and the underlying epistemology and ontology and to avoid culturally couched questions *ex ante* to their data collection activities. However, for researchers who use either or both types of methods, early entry into the field and interaction with researchers outside one's own cultural domain are highly recommended, in order to obtain a pre-understanding of emic perspectives within foreign research fields. Moreover, in order to pre-test and stimulate the search for research questions, which can stand the test of cultural bias, researchers using all methodologies need to take a flexible stance when initially formulating research questions. They must also try to initially tease out their (possibly taken-for-granted) culturally biased assumptions in the formulation of research questions.

After the research questions have either initially or finally been agreed upon, the issues of data types, data collection and interpretation become paramount. When qualitative researchers select data types (including the total amount of data), they should make sure that the area under study becomes saturated and that some replication occurs (Morse 1991). In some qualitative methodological procedures, such issues are incorporated (for example, grounded theory's use of extreme case sampling, see Strauss and Corbin 1990), whereas other methodological procedures do not state these issues explicitly. Moreover, concurrent data collection and theoretical analysis, where the researcher moves between data collection and more theory-related data analysis ('zipping', see Orton 1997, or 'abductive reasoning', see Dubois and Gadde 2002), may be an important means of ensuring process validity. In this instance, the researcher uses existing theory to identify puzzles and gaps in respondents' answers and return these questions in order to critically assess their obtained understanding of the observed phenomena.

Furthermore, if a clear pattern begins to emerge, the use of multiple sources of evidence – for example, via the various possible types of triangulation (Yin 1994) – that converge to support one explanation may be a suitable validation strategy and can entail one or more of the following (Jick

1979; Yin 1994):

1. the use of multiple data sources (data triangulation);
2. the use of multiple information collectors and/or evaluators, who must reach consensus about the truthfulness of the data (investigator triangulation; here, some experts, for example, Kvale (1994) also suggest that informants or the subjects of the research should be involved in this process, whereas others, for example, Sandelowski (1993), argue for the converse);
3. the use of multiple methods, that is, qualitative methods such as long interviews or participant observation, and/or quantitative methods, that is, analysis of economic, accounting or survey data (methodological triangulation).

Triangulation is also applicable when the research questions of the study call for analysis using the rhetorical perspective on data. Here, however, due to the rhetorical perspective's emphasis on the role of power in human discourse, it is important to include the involved informants and audience in the intersubjective process of validation (see Erlandson et al. 1993; Habermas 1981; Kvale 1994). In relation to narrative aspects of interpretation, triangulation is more controversial. However, here, following Alasuutari (1995), triangulation is understood a bit differently, as the use of multiple information collectors and/or evaluators, including the informants/subjects of the research, who must reach consensus about the written or oral statements studied. It may still be a useful strategy in achieving intersubjective agreement about the quality of the narrative treatment of data.

However, despite criticism of triangulation by the believers in strongly subjectivist ontologies, we maintain that triangulation can be viewed as relevant to them. In addition, the construction of explanations based on narrative and rhetorical interpretation of data also often includes some establishment of facts (see Alasuutari 1995). In these instances, the modified version of investigator triangulation for narrative interpretation can be supplemented by factist methods of triangulation (from, for example, Yin 1994).

Moreover, with specific regard to cross-cultural IB studies, investigator triangulation, that is, the use of both native and foreign investigators, may be an especially suitable validation strategy. This is particularly relevant in situations where the researcher is not fully familiar with the culture in which the research is taking place, regardless of whether the interpretation of data is to be mainly factist, rhetorical or interpretive. Clearly, this strategy is no quick fix for ensuring validity issues, as it also entails the pre-establishment of some intersubjective understanding among the investigators. Although this subject is (too) seldom dealt with, there are reports on some techniques for achieving this reported in the IB literature we have surveyed. For instance, O'Grady and Lane (1996) use inter-rater reliability measures, developing and comparing themes in a process of both reconciling discrepancies and achieving investigator triangulation. Others simply solve divergent issues by means of discussion (Bresman et al. 1999).

Finally, most qualitative researchers consciously work to develop specific communication styles for gaining access to respondents, by signalling and demonstrating trustworthiness, academic rigour, empathy, neutrality and so on. However, using a specific recipe for gaining access to and interviewing actors developed in one specific cultural context may be unsuccessful or lead to unintended and/or dysfunctional consequences for validity, if used in another cultural context. Thus we suggest that culture-specific communication strategies be developed to meet the role expectations and other pragmatic circumstances of each unique foreign research situation.

Outcome Validity Issues

As previously suggested, the discussion of outcome validity concerns how trustworthiness is communicated, both with regard to how findings are selected and interpreted (Sandelowski 1986) and how interpretations are presented (Miles and Huberman 1994). Guba and Lincoln (1981) and Lincoln and Guba (1985) have developed a set of criteria for ensuring the rigour of completed research, which have been seminal for the development of standards used to evaluate the quality of qualitative inquiry (compare Morse et al. 2002). The central problem of presenting qualitative findings is the lack of accessibility to the interpretation process itself. As pointed out by Miles (1979), qualitative data frequently consist of voluminous sets of material, which are practically inaccessible to outsiders. A number of guidelines and procedures can, however, be helpful to opening up this black box. The selection and interpretation of the findings may rely on:

1. Careful presentation of data collection details and procedures, as done by Levy (1995) in his study of international sourcing and supply chains, which also contained an imitable research site description. Two other examples of this are: (a) thoroughly explaining the multiple site interviews, as in the case of Michailova (2002), who interviewed more than 26 managers in two Russian companies with Western minority owners; and (b) explicitly describing the involvement of numerous researchers and the replication and verification processes, including extracts from case interpretations by participants (for example, García-Canal et al. 2002).

2. Explicit treatment of the contradictions between the study's results and any previous research results. An example of this is Hellman's (1994)

previously discussed explanation of the differences in the results about the internationalisation of Finnish banks and the results of two previous articles.

Various authors have also suggested other formal procedures for ensuring outcome validity. For instance, Wilson and Woodside (1999) recommend the use of external evaluators for reading through the material and checking findings in a so-called degrees-of-freedom analysis. Other methodologists (for example, Jorgensen 1989) purport that using a diary for tracking emergent themes and changes in theoretical focus during data collection may be helpful in both the authentication and the outcome presentation of the findings. Finally, Miles and Huberman (1994) suggest that the inclusion of artefacts and citations, descriptive statistics and graphical displays may help external evaluators assess the rigour of the analysis.

CONCLUSION

The purpose of this chapter has been to provide some advice to IB researchers embarking on qualitative procedures for empirical inquiry. First, as should be clear from our review of leading English-language IB journals, qualitative inquiry is still an underdeveloped area in IB, especially when contrasted to the frequency of quantitative contributions in leading IB journals. We believe, unfortunately, that the established norm of IB research rests primarily on a naive objectivist form of inquiry and that qualitative research may not be held in sufficiently high regard because it cannot adhere to the procedures of scientific validation inherent in this naive objectivism. Therefore, it is of utmost importance for IB researchers using a qualitative methodology to explicate their procedure and the background rationale for this procedure, to ensure validity both during the research process and in the presentation of results. We shall here briefly summarise our recommendations with respect to explicating procedures in order to improve outcome validity, along with references to some best practice examples from the literature:

1. explicate the rationale for using qualitative inquiry in your study (Parkhe 1997);
2. clarify data selection procedures (Brewer 2001; Brouthers and Bamossy 1997);
3. explain data handling procedures and how possible errors of the type one, two and three variety have been avoided during the data collection process (Hellman 1994; Tsang 1999);
4. clarify data analysis and interpretation procedures (Festing 1997; O'Grady and Lane 1996; Teigland, Fey and Birkinshaw 2000; Tsang

2001);
5. use your raw data as much as possible in supporting the claims made (Beechler and Yang 1994).

Furthermore, it is necessary that readers, reviewers and editors understand that even though validity in both interpretivist and realist approaches concerns ensuring rigour of the research carried out, validity procedures in qualitative inquiry cannot simply imitate quantitative realist or naively objectivist inquiry due to the presence of differing ontological and epistemological assumptions, as well as fundamentally different methodological pitfalls. In addition, procedures for ensuring scientific rigour do not only relate to the presentation of the results but are also fundamentally related to ensuring process validity. Qualitative IB researchers must also acknowledge the dangers of holistic fallacies and other evils of self-deception linked to qualitative enquiry in cultures alien to the researcher. However, we remain confident that even though challenges abound in rigorous qualitative enquiry into the IB area, the pursuit of rigour through validation is the most powerful way to enhance our understanding of the really tricky parts of exploring international business practices.

NOTES

1. In contrast to DuBois and Reeb (2000), we deemed it best to analyse *Columbia Journal of World Business* and *Journal of World Business* separately, because the journal title change in 1997 was also accompanied by substantial changes in journal content and editorial line.
2. The interpretive/subjective paradigm is concerned with understanding the nature of the social world at the level of subjective experience. It views the social world as an emergent and ongoing construction process and regards the social world as constructed by assumptions and intersubjectively shared meanings. In contrast, the functionalist/objective paradigm sees the social world as having an existence beyond individual cognition and as such suggests an epistemology allowing causal explanations of social events
3. With the exception of some postmodern and radical subjectivist researchers. However, these postmodernists and radical subjectivists will be eliminated from consideration in this chapter, as they do not believe in the relevance of the validity question. Moreover, researchers who adhere to pure objectivism, by, for example, believing that it is possible to observe the empirical world and its alleged social rules 'as they are', will also be excluded from our consideration, as these persons acknowledge neither any element of subjectivism in research nor the potential validity problems this subjectivism entails (Morgan and Smircich 1980).
4. Both social constructivists and realists embrace the idea that the social world has features which can take on an 'objective' existence (for instance, cultural institutions such as a language). However, their epistemologies regarding how this social reality can be grasped differ fundamentally.
5. The issues here primarily pertain to research strategies based on a partially subjectivist ontology, but may be adopted by researchers taking a realist ontology as well, due to this ontology's encompassing of an element of subjectivity. However, since the realist ontological perspective is also contingent on objectivism, realists may also want to subject

their research to validity checks relating to, for example, reliability and reversibility issues.

REFERENCES

Adler, N.J. (1983), 'A typology of management studies involving culture', *Journal of International Business Studies*, **14** (2), 29-47.

Agar, M. (1986), *Speaking of Ethnography*, Newbury Park, CA: Sage.

Alasuutari, P. (1995), *Researching Culture: Qualitative Method and Cultural Studies*, London and Thousand Oaks, CA: Sage.

Asante, M.K. and W.B. Gudykunst (eds) (1989), *Handbook of International and Intercultural Communication*, Newbury Park, CA: Sage.

Beechler, S. and J.Z. Yang (1994), 'The transfer of Japanese-style management to American subsidiaries: contingencies, constraints and competencies', *Journal of International Business Studies*, **25** (3), 467-91.

Beerman, L. and M. Stengel (1996), 'Werte im interkulturellen Vergleich', in N. Bergemann and A.L.J. Sourisseaux (eds), *Interkulturelles Management*, Heidelberg, Germany: Physica-Verlag, pp. 7-34.

Bresman, H., J. Birkinshaw and R. Nobel (1999), 'Knowledge transfer in international acquisitions', *Journal of International Business Studies*, **30** (3), 439-62.

Brewer, P. (2001), 'International market selection: developing a model from Australian case studies', *International Business Review*, **10** (2), 155-74.

Brinberg, D.L. and J. McGrath (1985), *Validity and the Research Process*, Beverly Hills, CA: Sage.

Brouthers, K. and G.J. Bamossy (1997), 'The role of key stakeholder in international joint venture negotiations: case studies from Eastern Europe', *Journal of International Business Studies*, **28** (2), 285-308.

Clyne, M. (1987), 'Discourse structures and discourse expectations: implications for Anglo-German academic communication in English', in L.E. Smith (ed.), *Discourse Across Cultures*, Hemel Hempstead: Prentice-Hall, pp. 73-83.

Cooper, C.D. (2001), 'Not just a numbers thing: tactics for improving reliability and validity in qualitative research', paper presented at the Academy of Management Research Methods Forum, available at http://www.aom.pace.edu/rmd/.

Craig, C.S. and S.P. Douglas (2000), *International Marketing Research*, 2nd edn, New York: John Wiley & Sons.

Dubois, A. and L.E. Gadde (2002), 'Systematic combining: an abductive approach to case research', *Journal of Business Research*, **55** (7), 553-60.

DuBois, F. and D. Reeb (2000), 'Ranking the international business journals', *Journal of International Business Studies*, **31** (4), 689-704.

Easton, G. (1992), 'Industrial networks: a review', in B. Axelsson and G. Easton (eds), *Industrial Networks: A new View on Reality*, London: Routledge, pp. 3-27.

——— (1998), 'Case research as a methodology for industrial networks: a realist apologia', in P. Naudé and P. Turnbull (eds), *Network Dynamics in International Marketing*, London: Pergamon, pp. 73-87.

Eisenhardt, K.M. (1989), 'Building theories from case study research', *Academy of Management Review*, **14** (4), 532-50.

Erlandson, D.A., E.L. Harris, B.L. Skipper and S.D. Allen (1993), *Doing Naturalist*

Inquiry: A Guide to Methods, Newbury Park, CA: Sage.

Festing, M. (1997), 'International human resource management strategies in multinational corporations: theoretical assumptions and empirical evidence from German firms', *Management International Review*, **37** (1), 43–63.

Freeman, D. (1983), *Margaret Mead and Samoa: The Making and Unmaking of an Anthropological Myth*, Cambridge, MA: Harvard University Press.

García-Canal, E., C.L. Duarte, J.R. Criado and A.V. Llaneza (2002), 'Accelerating international expansion through global alliances: a typology of cooperative strategies', *Journal of World Business*, **37** (2), 91–107.

Goodyear, M. (1982), 'Qualitative research in developing countries', *Journal of the Marketing Research Society*, **24** (2), 86–96.

Guba, E.G. and Y.S. Lincoln (1981), *Effective Evaluation: Improving the Usefulness of Evaluation Results Through Responsive and Naturalistic Approaches*, San Fransisco, CA: Jossey-Bass.

Habermas, J. (1981), *Theorie des kommunikativen Handelns*, Frankfurt am Main: Suhrkamp, translated into English by T. McCarthy as J. Habermas ([1981] 1997), *The Theory of Communicative Action*, Cambridge: Polity.

Hammersley, M. (1990), *Reading Ethnographic Research: A Critical Guide*, New York: Longman.

Hellman, P. (1994), 'The internationalization of Finnish financial service companies', *International Business Review*, **5** (2), 191–208.

Holden, N. (1998), 'Viewpoint: international marketing studies – time to break the English-language stranglehold?', *International Marketing Review*, **15** (2), 86–100.

Jick, T.D. (1979), 'Mixing qualitative and quantitative methods: triangulation in action', *Administrative Science Quarterly*, **24**, 602–11.

Jorgensen, D.L. (1989), *Participant Observation: A Methodology for Human Studies*, Newbury Park, CA: Sage.

Kant, I. ([1787] 1998), *Kritik der reinen Vernunft*, Hamburg: Felix Meiner Verlag, ed. J. Timmermann, translated into English by P. Guyer and A.W. Wood as I. Kant ([1782/1787] 1998), *Critique of Pure Reason*, Cambridge and New York: Cambridge University Press.

Kirk, J. and M.L. Miller (1986), *Reliability and Validity in Qualitative Research*, Newbury Park, CA: Sage.

Kumar, V. (2000), *International Marketing Research*, Upper Saddle River, NJ: Prentice-Hall.

Kvale, S. (ed.) (1989), *Issues of Validity in Qualitative Research*, Lund: Studentlitteratur.

―――― (1994), *InterViews. An Introduction to Qualitative Research Interviewing*, Thousand Oaks, CA: Sage.

Leininger, M. (1994), 'Evaluation criteria and critique of qualitative research methods', in J.M. Morse (ed.), *Critical Issues in Qualitative Research Methods*, Beverly Hills, CA: Sage, pp. 95–115.

Levy, D.L. (1995), 'International sourcing and supply chain stability', *Journal of International Business Studies*, **26** (2), 343–60.

Lincoln, Y.S. and E.G. Guba (1985), *Naturalistic Inquiry*, Beverly Hills, CA: Sage.

Maxwell, J. (1992), 'Understanding validity in qualitative research', *Harvard Educational Review*, **62** (3), 279–300.

Michailova, S. (2002), 'When common sense becomes uncommon: participation and empowerment in Russian companies with Western participation', *Journal of World Business*, **37** (3), 180–87.

Miles, D. (1979), 'Qualitative data research as an attractive nuisance: the problem of data analysis', *Administrative Science Quarterly*, **24**, 590–601.

Miles, M.B. and A.M. Huberman (1994), *Qualitative Data Analysis*, Newbury Park, CA: Sage.

Mittrof, I.I. and R. Kilman (1982), *Methodological Approaches to Social Science*, San Francisco, CA: Jossey-Bass.

Morgan, G. (1983), 'Research strategies: modes of engagement', in G. Morgan (ed.), *Beyond Method*, Newbury Park, CA: Sage, pp. 19–44.

Morgan, G. and L. Smircich (1980), 'The case for qualitative research', *Academy of Management Review*, **5** (4), 491–500.

Morse, J.M. (1991), 'Strategies for sampling', in J.M. Morse (ed.), *Qualitative Nursing Research: A Contemporary Dialogue*, 2nd edn, Newbury Park, CA: Sage, pp. 127–45.

—— (1999), 'Myth #93: reliability and validity are not relevant to qualitative inquiry', *Qualitative Health Research*, **19**, 717–18.

Morse, J.M., M. Barrett, M. Mayan, K. Olson and J. Spiers (2002), 'Verification strategies for establishing validity and reliability in qualitative research', *International Journal of Qualitative Methods*, **1** (2), 1–19.

O'Grady, S. and H.W. Lane (1996), 'The psychic distance paradox', *Journal of International Business Studies*, **27** (2), 309–34.

Orton, J.D. (1997), 'From inductive to iterative grounded theory: zipping the gap between process theory and process data', *Scandinavian Journal of Management*, **13** (4), 419–38.

Parkhe, A. (1997), '"Messy" research, methodological predispositions and theory development in international joint ventures', *Academy of Management Review*, **18** (2), 227–68.

Pike, K. (1966), *Language in Relation to a Unified Theory of the Structure of Human Behavior*, The Hague: Mouton.

Popper, K.R. (1979), *Objective Knowledge – An Evolutionary Approach*, Oxford: Clarendon.

Salner, M. (1999), 'Self-deception in qualitative research: validity issues', paper presented at the Association for Qualitative Research Conference, Melbourne, Australia, July.

Sandelowski, M. (1986), 'The problem of rigor in qualitative research', *Advances in Nursing Science*, **8** (3), 27–37.

—— (1993), 'Theory unmasked: the uses and guises of theory in qualitative research', *Research in Nursing and Health*, **16**, 213–18.

Schmidt, S.J. (ed.) (1994), *Der Diskurs des Radikalen Konstruktivismus*, Frankfurt am Main: Suhrkamp.

Silverman, D. (1994), *Interpreting Qualitative Data*, Los Angeles, CA: Sage.

Sivonen, S. (1983), *Suomalaisten palveluyritysten ulkomaiset toimintavaihtoehdot ja kansainvälistyminen*, Vientikoulutussäätiö, FIBO (Finnish International Business Operations) publications no. 14:24, Helsinki.

Strauss, A. and J. Corbin (1990), *Basics of Qualitative Research: Grounded Theory Procedures and Techniques*, Newbury Park, CA: Sage.

Sullivan, D.P. and G.R. Weaver (2000), 'Cultural cognition in international business research', *Management International Review*, **40** (3), 269–97.

Teigland, R., C.F. Fey and J. Birkinshaw (2000), 'Knowledge dissemination in global R&D operations: an empirical study of multinationals in the high technology electronics industry', *Management International Review*, **40** (1), 49–77.

Tsang, E.W.K. (1999), 'The knowledge transfer and learning aspects of international HRM: an empirical study of Singapore MNCs', *International Business Review*, **8** (5–6), 591–609.

———— (2001), 'Managerial learning in foreign-invested enterprises of China', *Management International Review*, **41** (1), 29–51.

Turkkila, A. (1992), 'Suomalaisten pankkien kansainvälistyminen', Bank of Finland Discussion Paper 19/92, Helsinki.

Usunier, J.-C. (2000), *Marketing Across Cultures*, 3rd edn, London: Pearson Education.

Walters, P.G.P. (2001), 'Research at the "margin": challenges for scholars working outside the "American–European" domain', *International Marketing Review*, **18** (5), 468–73.

Weick, K.E. (1989), 'Theory construction as disciplined imagination', *Academy of Management Review*, **14** (4), 516–31.

Wilson, E.J. and A.G. Woodside (1999), 'Degrees-of-freedom analysis of case data in business marketing research', *Industrial Marketing Management*, **28** (3), 215–30.

Yeung, H.W.-C. (1995), 'Qualitative personal interviews in international business research: some lessons from a study of Hong Kong transnational corporations', *International Business Review*, **4** (3), 313–39.

Yin, R.E. (1994), *Case Study Research: Designs and Methods*, 2nd edn, Thousand Oaks, CA: Sage.

24. Computer-assisted Qualitative Data Analysis: Application in an Export Study

Valerie J. Lindsay

INTRODUCTION

This chapter describes the use of computer-assisted qualitative data analysis software (CAQDAS) in the context of a qualitative study of export performance. The chapter focuses on the analysis of qualitative data, drawing particularly from principles described by Miles and Huberman (1994). This chapter describes the use of CAQDAS in an international business setting. It aims to provide a critical discussion on the practical application of CAQDAS, and illustrates how its use contributes to conceptual model building as an outcome of the qualitative analysis of research data.

Until recently, the focus of the literature on qualitative research has been on data collection methods, with relatively little attention being paid to qualitative data analysis or the interaction between different phases of qualitative research (Burgess 1995). With regard to data analysis, Eisenhardt (1989, p. 539) quotes Miles and Huberman (1984, p. 16): 'One cannot ordinarily follow how a researcher got from 3600 pages of field notes to the final conclusions, sprinkled with vivid quotes though they may be'. Because qualitative data cannot usually be easily quantified, it is not surprising that their analysis is accompanied by practical, technical and methodological problems (Fielding and Lee 1991). In response to these issues, and the need for better organisation of large data sets, awareness and use of CAQDAS have grown over recent years.

CAQDAS programs have been widely used in sociological and business research settings, but there remains considerable potential for their use in international business research. For example, researchers in the export field argue for more qualitatively-based methods (for example, Katsikeas 1994; Leonidou 1995b). These authors highlight the need for more adequate explanations of export performance and the role of its antecedents, through the application of qualitative research methods. Despite these views, there have been relatively few qualitative studies of export performance and, consequently, a limited contribution to theory building in this area.

The study described in this chapter utilised two CAQDAS computer software programs, NUD*IST4 (Non-Numerical Unstructured Data Indexing Searching and Theorizing), produced by QSR International, and Decision Explorer, produced by Banxia, to assist the data analysis process. QSR and Banxia have enabled data exchange via export functions, which facilitates mapping of NUD*IST coded data in Decision Explorer. The combined use of these programs enabled an approach to qualitative data analysis that provided a level of efficiency and rigour not normally associated with manual approaches.

The study is used in this chapter to illustrate the methodological issues associated with the application of CAQDAS. A qualitative, interview-based case study research design was used. Theory building was achieved by the use of a modified grounded theory approach (Glaser and Strauss 1967; Miles and Huberman 1994; Strauss and Corbin 1998). A conceptual model of export performance was developed, utilising multiple cases to provide robustness (Herriot and Firestone 1983) and internal validity (Eisenhardt 1989), as well as enabling replication logic, an important element in the development of theory (Yin 1994).

This chapter is structured as follows. The use of CAQDAS in qualitative research is discussed and an overview is then given of the two computer-assisted software programs used in the study, NUD*IST and Decision Explorer. Next, the application of the software tools to the export performance study is discussed. Results obtained from the analysis are briefly outlined, including the presentation of a conceptual model of export performance. Finally, conclusions and implications are discussed, noting practical advice on the use of NUD*IST and Decision Explorer in qualitative research.

CAQDAS – A MEANS OF STRENGTHENING QUALITATIVE METHODS?

Qualitative methods are generally well suited to studies looking at how change occurs over time or situations where it is important to understand meaning. Qualitative methods also support research that requires flexibility, fluidity and continual renegotiation (Easterby-Smith et al. 2002). Qualitative methods contribute to the development of new theories and enable the research process to be adjusted to new issues and ideas as they emerge.

CAQDAS supports the two ways of analysing qualitative data as identified by Easterby-Smith et al. (2002, p. 117): content analysis and grounded analysis. Content analysis 'goes by numbers', and grounded analysis 'goes by feel and intuition'. CAQDAS is well suited to the analysis of qualitative studies with large amounts of data and for longitudinal projects, both often associated with grounded analysis. The close affinity between many CAQDAS packages and a grounded theory approach has been noted (Lonkila 1995). CAQDAS can also assist in the 'scientific analysis' of qualitative data (White 2002), such as in content analysis, although different computer software programs (for example, Diction 5.0, C-I-SAID) are often used for these types of analyses. In addition, while statistical replication is not generally an objective of qualitative research, because of different contexts and approaches used in different studies, it can be part of an approach that includes both quantitative and qualitative research methods, and many types of CAQDAS support this (Bazeley 2002).

While the limitations or weaknesses associated with qualitative research methods have been extensively reported (for example, Miles and Huberman 1994), many can potentially be reduced by the use of CAQDAS. For example, the number of cases that can be studied is often limited by the constraints of manual approaches. By facilitating the organisation and analysis of large volumes of data, CAQDAS potentially overcomes this difficulty. Qualitative studies, particularly with large data sets, invariably take time, but CAQDAS can reduce the time taken, particularly in the data coding and analysis process (Seale 2000; Weitzman 2000).

CAQDAS can provide more rigour and traceability in the interpretation of transcripts and interview results (Seale 2000). CAQDAS software programs encourage similar and consistent processes of data handling among researchers, thus enhancing reliability. The processes and steps involved in data capture through questioning, application, reporting of interview results, and stages of analysis allow some measure of quality control through cross-checking and documentation. The data organising and managing capability of CAQDAS readily supports re-coding and reviewing of data to allow adjustments in data collection as the study progresses. This enables the researcher to gain insights through the interaction of the collection and analysis phases, thus meeting the demands of flexibility as well as consistency in research design.

Richards (1995) asserts that the use of CAQDAS changes the balance between data organisation and researcher's creativity, enabling the exploration of data to become less constrained because the data organisation is made easier. Application of CAQDAS also provides a measure of internal validity not easily achieved with manual methods. In particular, it allows for greater coherence and for systematic interrelationships between concepts to be drawn. CAQDAS provides versatility in the treatment of data, enabling them to be combined, viewed in new ways, and re-analysed as new perspectives emerge. Depending on the actual program, there may be an increase in sophistication and complexity of analysis through the use of automated Boolean and proximity searches on any code or combination of codes (Seale 2002), which enhances the analyst's ability to generate and test theory (in NUD*IST, this is enhanced through a process called 'system closure').

The concern that a computer-based process may detract from creative researcher input (Burgess 1995) is usually countered by the potential separation of data organisation and researcher creativity, increasing creative freedom overall. Richards (1995) points out that analysis is ultimately the responsibility of the researcher, and the software is primarily a tool for assisting the process. The balance of researcher responsibility and advantages of increased researcher control is illustrated in the following statement: 'Although software may invoke a new potential for an infinite array of connections between previously unconnected things, we maintain that it is the researcher who must still decide what is meaningful and how it is meaningful' (Bassett et al. 1995, p. 18).

Hesse-Biber (1995, p. 39) emphasises that it is important for the researcher to assess his/her own strengths and weaknesses, as well as the implications of using computer-assisted software to analyse quantitative data. She states that: 'It is clear that the interpretation of qualitative data is enriched by the use of computer software programs and that more dialogue is needed on other issues' to overcome common fears associated with this technology. More recent indications of researchers' experiences with CAQDAS suggest that these systems provide considerably more opportunity for interpreting and understanding qualitative data than is possible using a manual system (for example, Dolan and Ayland 2001; Lindsay 1999; Richards 1995). However, it is important for the researcher to not lose sight of the contextual nature of data coded with CAQDAS. This is the 'whole respondent' issue noted by Dolan and Ayland (2001). When data are disaggregated into potentially unrelated segments in the coding process, individual data segments become isolated from the overall context represented by the data from the complete transcript, or 'whole respondent'. Some CAQDAS programs (for example, NUD*IST version 4 and later releases of QSR NUD*IST, and ATLAS.ti) allow coded data to be viewed and analysed within a range of contextual settings presented in the 'whole respondent' document, as well as complete sets of documents. It is, however, incumbent on the researcher to ensure that analysis and interpretation of the data include consideration of the broader contexts in which the data sit.

This discussion has shown that while relatively new to the field of qualitative research, CAQDAS has both proponents and those who report shortcomings (for example, reviewed by Burgess 1995). It is generally accepted that the length of time involved in preparing the data and entering them into the system may be a disadvantage, although some newer versions of CAQDAS are less time-consuming in the data preparation stage. On the other hand, it is also generally accepted that CAQDAS lessens the otherwise labour-intensive aspects of coding and retrieval of data. While there is some divergence of views regarding the application of CAQDAS to theory building and hypothesis testing, there is more agreement on its effectiveness for data management and administration (for example, Kelle 1997).

My own field of study is export performance, to which I decided to apply CAQDAS. Current understandings of exporting, export performance and internationalisation have been significantly influenced by the research approaches taken (Leonidou 1995a). Reviews of the export literature highlight problems and inconsistencies in findings that result from differences and limitations of research approaches and methods of data analysis used (Katsikeas 1994). Export research is starting to move away from using the 'pure' quantitative method, which has been seen as 'bedevilling' the area (Kamath et al. 1987), towards the use of interviews and case studies, and other qualitative approaches, often in conjunction with quantitative techniques. Consequently, a number of researchers argue for more conceptual input into the design of export research and for more in-depth, focused research methods (for example, Cavusgil and Zou 1994; Matthyssens and Pauwels 1996). These approaches would enable a greater understanding of export performance and the ways in which the variables interact (Aaby and Slater 1989). Theory building through case study research and conceptual modelling can capture the complex relationships between export performance variables and provide some tentative explanation for the construct (for example, Andersen 1993; Katsikeas 1994). Those qualitative studies in exporting that are reported in the literature have tended to be exploratory in nature, largely because there is a limited qualitative research base from which to draw and develop more explanatory studies. The limited body of qualitative export research also means that there is a lack of guiding principles and materials, such as interview techniques, questionnaire designs, and general in-field 'familiarisation' with the subject (Miles and Huberman 1994). CAQDAS offers ways to strengthen the qualitative method, and help to address some of the limitations concerned with rigour and traceability of the researcher's interpretation of the data.

NUD*IST AND DECISION EXPLORER

Two main types of CAQDAS programs have been distinguished, those designed for descriptive–interpretive research and those that explicitly support theory building (Tesch 1991). The NUD*IST program is one of the earliest firmly supporting theory building, while also enabling descriptive–

interpretive approaches. A number of the other currently popular CAQDAS programs, such as ATLAS.ti and Ethnograph, have broadly similar characteristics, but vary in their complexity and sophistication.

Choice of which package to use depends on a number of factors. All programs facilitate the analysis of large data sets, but are generally chosen on the basis of their appropriateness to the task required, particularly on the methodological goals of the researcher and the nature and scope of the research (Flick 2002). While broadly similar, some contain more sophisticated analytical capability, while others enable the visual mapping of coded data. Some concentrate more on coding of very large data sets and others more on exploration and theory building. Specific characteristics are generally well described in the informational material provided with each package. In addition, comparative studies of different CAQDAS programs are worth consulting (for example, Barry 1998; Dolan and Ayland 2001; Lewis 1998).

The NUD*IST program was designed not only for the organisation of data, but also for exploring the relationship between data and ideas (Richards 1995). The early use of NUD*IST in live, longitudinal projects has been thoroughly documented by Richards (1995), and this program now has a long and successful history in a wide range of settings and situations requiring the analysis of qualitative data.

My own study, which was longitudinal over a period of six years, utilised QSR NUD*IST 4 (more recently known as QSR N4); this was the most recent version available at the commencement of the study. More recent versions are N6 and its sister program, NVivo. N4 incorporated major methodological advances from the earlier N3 version, and N6 has incorporated significant technological advances (Bazeley 2003, personal communication; QSR International 2003). Both NVivo and N6 support the following functions: coding, re-coding and editing of text; search and retrieval of data; automated data processing; data linking; memoing; and data displays (QSR International 2003); but they do this in different ways to suit different methodological approaches and research objectives.

N6 is particularly useful for research that requires primarily coding, searching, managing and tracking of documents. From its earlier versions of N4 and N5, N6 has incorporated new management tools for managing data, and new 'explorer' functions that fully integrate all document and node operations. It also includes automated formatting for selected text units, such as lines, sentences or paragraphs, which eases the document preparation process.

NVivo is one of a new generation of qualitative software tools, which includes other programs such as ATLAS.ti. NVivo is 'a fine detail analyzer, allowing fluid exploration and interpretation and integrating the processes of interpretation and questioning' (QSR International 2003). It is especially useful for exploration of ideas from the data, and theory building. Like ATLAS.ti, NVivo allows graphic modelling of data, and, like N6, NVivo supports export to Decision Explorer.

NUD*IST 4, which was used in this study, was designed to meet three key goals of qualitative research: managing documents, containing both textual and non-textual data; creating ideas and managing categories, minimising clerical routine and maximising flexibility; and asking questions and building and testing theories about data, by linking documents and ideas (QSR 1997). Many of the comparative studies and documentation about CAQDAS, some of which are discussed above, have utilised NUD*IST (until recently using versions QSR N3, N4 and N5), since it is one of the most widely used programs of this type.

Decision Explorer is a conceptual mapping tool that enables concepts (or variables) to be arranged spatially to show their linkages and interrelationships, and analytical procedures to be applied to assist in the interpretation of the conceptual maps. Among its various applications, Decision Explorer (and its earlier version, COPE) has been used to support research into strategic decision-making and in managerial cognitive mapping contexts (for example, Eden 1988; Jenkins and Johnson 1997). Decision Explorer structures linear sets of data into cognitive, or conceptual, maps that highlight the linkages and relationships between the variables, or concepts, concerned, and, thus, is a natural complement to NUD*IST. The interface between NUD*IST and Decision Explorer is managed by direct export/ import functions in both programs.

Decision Explorer provides 'an explicit picture of an issue which clearly shows the interrelatedness and interdependencies of different aspects of the issue, which can then be explored and debated' (Banxia 1997, p. 6). The conceptual maps provide construct validity and may be analysed to provide further insights into the data and areas for further investigation. Among the analytical techniques offered in Decision Explorer, and utilised in this study, are: explore, which assists the analysis of single concepts; centrality analysis, which provides some insight into the centrality of each concept in the map, or model; domain analysis, which examines the connectivity of concepts and identifies the 'busy' concepts in the map; heads and tails, which determines the single explanatory or consequential concepts; and set logic analysis, which assists the structuring of concepts into sets, whose differences and similarities can then be determined.

Use of this type of mapping process allows complex data to be organised into a coherent picture to improve understanding of the contextual situation. Through its association with NUD*IST, Decision Explorer maintains the richness of the data, also enabling the researcher to manage its complexity, rather than having to provide a summarised overview which, while helpful in providing context, limits the researcher's ability to examine the contributing elements (Banxia 1997), as would be the case with most manual methods of analysis. Model building from cognitive, or conceptual, maps supports a phenomenological approach to research: 'A map is not a reflection of some objective reality but rather a representation of an individual's perceptions of an issue' (Banxia 1997, p. 18). Model building in Decision Explorer is based on a body of cognitive psychology theory, known as 'personal construct theory' (Kelly 1955).

Since the researcher is the key agent in the mapping of concepts and the creation of links in Decision Explorer, the process is judgemental and interpretive. However, rigour is increased when there is transparent and accessible data coding supporting the mapping decisions, a clear benefit of the program's association with NUD*IST. Maps that involve many interlinked concepts may be quite overwhelming for the researcher; however, Decision Explorer allows the disaggregation of the maps to allow more 'manageable' viewing and analysis.

Use of Decision Explorer in the study enabled further development of the analyses undertaken in NUD*IST. Specifically, it provided an additional level of data organisation that supported the building of a conceptual model of export performance. Using Decision Explorer, the researcher was able to add a visually accessible interpretive and contextual dimension to the NUD*IST analysis, assisting the definition of multidimensional aspects of the export performance construct. The combined use of NUD*IST and Decision Explorer in this process appeared to provide a more rigorous and meaningful outcome than that possible from either software package alone. This type of data analysis and modelling provides an approach that is particularly appropriate for studying relational perspectives of exporting (for example, Styles and Ambler 1994), incorporating linkages, both internal and external to the firm, and enabling a more dynamic and process-oriented approach.

Notwithstanding the apparent benefits of this approach, there appears to be little, if any, research demonstrating the combined use of NUD*IST and Decision Explorer in the export field. This chapter describes in more detail the researcher's experience of using this dual approach in a qualitative study of export performance, highlighting the potential for wider application of CAQDAS in international business research, particularly in export research. The next section outlines the study and discusses the use of both NUD*IST and Decision Explorer in this context.

THE APPLICATION OF CAQDAS TO A STUDY OF EXPORT PERFORMANCE

The study aimed to determine the antecedents of export performance, and their interrelationships, and to develop a conceptual model that offers a tentative explanation for the export performance construct. The study was qualitative, and utilised CAQDAS (specifically NUD*IST and Decision Explorer) as qualitative data analysis tools. This section outlines the main components of the study, discusses the application of the CAQDAS, and illustrates how these assisted the researcher in the development of a conceptual model.

Research Design and Analytical Approaches

This study utilised a case study approach (for example, Eisenhardt 1989; Yin 1994), drawing on interviews as the primary data collection method, in a longitudinal study incorporating three time points over six years. The chapter draws on only the first part of this study, since this conceptual model-building component best illustrates the use of CAQDAS. Subsequent parts of the study aimed to test the model and analyse changes over time. Case studies look in depth at one, or a small number, of organisations generally over time in the form of longitudinal studies. Both quantitative and qualitative data may be involved, and Yin (1994) argues that the approach can allow for the application of rigorous comparisons (Easterby-Smith et al. 2002).

The study design was based on a modified grounded theory approach. Locke (1997) notes that methods associated with grounded theory have evolved and developed since their original presentation, with somewhat divergent views having emerged between the original proponents of grounded theory, Glaser and Strauss (1967). Glaser's view is that researchers 'should start with no pre-suppositions, and should allow ideas to "emerge" from the data'. Strauss, by contrast, recommends 'familiarizing oneself with prior research and using structured, and somewhat mechanistic, processes to make sense of the data' (Easterby-Smith et al. 2002, pp. 46–7). Miles and Huberman (1994) tend to follow a Straussian view, suggesting some prior conceptualisation of issues, rather than a pure grounded theory approach that builds theory from a base of zero conceptualisation. Prior conceptualisation about export performance was attained in this study from a detailed literature review and a brief prior familiarisation study of a small sample of exporters, which led to the formulation of research questions. Overall, this study tended more towards a Straussian approach, although this still means that theoretical concepts were shaped primarily from the data, rather than starting from a logically deduced theoretical framework.

The research sample

The unit of the research was the firm, with each case representing a single firm. Purposive sampling was applied to a population of exporters to select 16 companies with the following characteristics. They were manufacturing companies, small to medium sized, located in various parts of New Zealand, and currently exporting. They were also recent export award winners, an indication of export success used by others (for example, Styles and Ambler 1994).

Data collection and analysis

Data were collected from managers of the export companies using an interview technique. A semi-structured interview questionnaire was developed, having been informed by an earlier detailed literature review and a brief familiarisation process (Miles and Huberman 1994) with a small number of exporting firms. The focus of the questionnaire was on determining the antecedents of export performance, but the interview process was open-ended to allow exploration of additional aspects of exporting as they arose in the interviews, in a process of cooperative inquiry (Reason 1988).

In all cases, in-depth interviews were conducted with the managing director and/or general manager and/or export manager of the firms, with interviews lasting from 2–4 hours. Interviews were documented by the researcher in shorthand note form, and a number were also tape-recorded. Several companies, however, did not agree to tape-recording of interviews, and so only the shorthand notes were used for the analysis, in order to avoid bias. The researcher also generated notes immediately after each interview, capturing impressions and contextual information relevant to the interview.

After the interview notes were transcribed by the researcher the data were formatted and entered into NUD*IST for analysis. From this point, the process broadly followed the seven-step process for grounded theory approaches to qualitative data analysis described by Easterby-Smith et al. (2002). This is a significant development of the four-stage approach to grounded theory originally laid out in Glaser and Strauss (1967), and follows the approaches later reported by Strauss (1987) and Strauss and Corbin 1990, 1998). The seven-step process is described below with the key part highlighted in italics. The first three steps involved a process of *familiarisation* with the data (and additional notes made by researcher after each interview), *reflection* and then preliminary *conceptualisation* of the data (Easterby-Smith et al. 2002), all informing the coding stage of the analysis.

Coding (Step 4) was then conducted on the data on the basis of each sentence; in other words, data were reviewed sentence by sentence, within a wider section of the interview transcript data, which reflected the topic relating to the sentences being coded. The inclusion of such 'sections' in NUD*IST allowed coded single sentences to be reviewed within their immediate context. The data were coded in this way into hierarchical trees of nodes and sub-nodes in NUD*IST in a process that was largely inductive, but incorporated some prior perceptions of codes from the earlier preconceptualisation stage. Accordingly, the naming of nodes was mostly determined by the researcher, rather than from the exact language of the interview subjects (that is, '*in vivo* coding'), which tended to be quite varied. Using researcher-named nodes also facilitated easier comparisons with terminology used in the literature (Easterby-Smith et al. 2002). For example, 'strategy formulation', a key code and theme in the conceptual model, captured discussions in the case materials about how strategy was developed within each particular case setting. However, the concept was reflected in the cases in a variety of ways, and there was no common terminology among the interviewee managers. The term was chosen by the researcher because it reflected the meaning of the discussions, and allowed easy comparison with terminology in the literature.

Coding is central to grounded theory analysis, and this is where the strength of CAQDAS becomes most evident. As this coding phase of the analysis progressed, the researcher also engaged in *recoding* (Step 5), renaming and *linking* (Step 6) of the codes and data, leading to the emergence of patterns and themes associated with the data. The coding thus moved from general or open coding, where broad themes were identified, to axial coding, which provided more focus, for example, in the development of sub-themes, and finally to selective coding. This provided highly focused coding around the emerging theme, for example, in the further refinement of sub-themes, or the linking between specific codes sharing detailed aspects of the theme concerned. These results were subject to *re-evaluation* (Step 7), by reference back to the original data and consideration of advice from experts in the field of export research. In the context of the study, the resulting nodes represented variables relating to the export performance of the firms concerned. Many of these were identified directly by managers of the companies, and others through inference and interpretation of the data by the researcher.

Lincoln and Guba (1985) suggest that coding and recoding reach completion when 'the analysis itself appears to have run its course – when all of the incidents can be readily classified, categories "saturated", and sufficient numbers of "regularities" emerge' (Miles and Huberman 1994, p. 62). In this study, the completion of coding and recoding for single cases tended to coincide with the point at which further iterations involving review of the full transcript provided no additional codes, or sub-codes, and no further meaningful rearrangement, or renaming of existing codes to assist the interpretation of the data. However, new insights were frequently provided by the coding of subsequent cases. For example, a subsequent case might throw up a new code, which then provided an opportunity for re-examination of earlier cases. The coding process did not, therefore, reach its full conclusion until all cases had been coded.

Data displays   Both within- and cross-case analysis was conducted, enabling both variable- and case-oriented approaches to the data analysis (Miles and Huberman 1994). According to Miles and Huberman, the use of data displays is an essential part of the qualitative data analysis process, particularly in assisting with the interpretation of interview data and codes. They suggest various types of matrix formats displaying data and the results of data analysis in ways that allow the complexity of a mass of qualitative data, in a wide range of circumstances, to be captured. Miles and Huberman (1994, p. 91) describe data displays as 'visual formats that present information systematically, so that the user can draw valid conclusions and take needed action'.

Data display types used for interpreting and presenting within- and cross-case analyses in the study were: checklist matrices, for initial comparisons between the data and findings from the literature; content-analytic matrices for examination and verification of the data and its organisation into patterns and themes; and conceptual (cognitive) causal maps (created in Decision Explorer), for providing preliminary explanation of the data.

Checklist matrices draw from the initial broad themes identified in the coding process, and allow a high-level comparison with similar broad themes in the literature. In this study, the checklist matrix provided the initial comparison between key factors emerging from the data and those represented by existing studies. Early similarities and differences between broad findings from the study and the literature were therefore noted.

Content-analytic matrices provide a finer level of data interpretation, displaying the data as they are organised from multiple cases into patterns and themes that form the basis for subsequent mapping. This provides an indication of the core data underlying the interpretive analysis. Particularly important in this type of matrix is the display of data from the original transcripts, which illustrate the pattern or theme being noted. The matrix offers information on the cross-case analyses, indicating the number of cases containing data that support a particular pattern or theme, which provides inferences as to its potential importance (Miles and Huberman 1994) in the conceptual model. The content-analytic matrices developed in this study in some cases included substructured variables. Substruction is a way of locating underlying dimensions of variables in a systematic way (Miles and Huberman 1994). In the study's cases, some variables (codes) had more than one dimension (for example, Table 24.1 shows 'exchange rates' and 'interest rates' as posing a 'problem' or 'no problem' in the cases concerned). The content-analytic matrices developed in the study supported a more detailed written commentary on the single- and cross-case coded results and their analyses. An example of part of the content-analytic matrix for the factor, external environment is shown in Table 24.1; the notes to the matrix explain the meanings and interrelationships between the columns in the table.

Mapping   While maps are also important means of displaying data, they can also provide an interpretive and analytic platform of their own. Mapping of the data follows from the earlier described data displays, representing a relational, and potentially explanatory, interpretation of the data and their relationships. The detailed written commentary is also important in supporting the relational representations in the map. Maps can be subject to a range of analyses, depending on the mapping process or tool used – some of these are described below.

An example of the conceptual maps developed in this study is illustrated in Figure 24.1, below. Nodes were imported directly from NUD*IST into Decision Explorer, using the specific export function in NUD*IST. In Decision Explorer the nodes are referred to as 'concepts'. Existing links between nodes and sub-nodes were carried over from the NUD*IST analysis, while other inter-node and inter-sub-node links were constructed manually by the researcher, based on an in-depth understanding of the data and its organisation in NUD*IST. Decision Explorer was used by the researcher to organise and link all three levels of coding from NUD*IST, reflecting the patterns and themes identified earlier. Rearrangement of the resulting concepts and their link was part of the reflective process of the researcher as the map and its contextual elements developed.

This facilitated the creation of a conceptual model of the relationships between variables and the processes involved in export performance, through an approach driven by the researcher, but utilising data coded and analysed in NUD*IST. Mapped concepts were relabelled as factors (high-level components, largely reflecting the first-level coding in NUD*IST), variables (mid-level components, largely reflecting the second-level coding in NUD*IST) and indicators (lowest-level components, largely reflecting the third-level coding in NUD*IST), consistent with the terms used in other export performance models (for example, Aaby and Slater 1989).

Table 24.1   *External environment: domestic market environment sub-factor:*
illustrative example from content-analytic matrix (cross-case) [a]

First-level factor [b]	Variable [c]	Examples of data from cases [case reference] [d]
Political/ Economic Environment – General 16 (100%)		Not been affected by anything associated with NZ economics or politics. Because small, they are insulated. [B #69-70]
		Inflation major worry. Industry cost structures include government taxes, especially resource rentals and fuel tax, which is 100% and a major cost. [L #38, 42]
Exchange Rates 15 (94%)	Problem 13 (81%)	Exchange rates a major roadblock. Exchange rates change too quickly, especially the end of the 1970s and the early 1980s. [A #70-71]
		Exchange rates are the biggest worry – they caused a lot of grief last year and they would have folded without the domestic business. Exchange rate changes upset the asset ratios. [F #81-82]
		They deal in the export market currencies, or USD; this is by far the biggest negative influence. Prices can be flexible, but not too much (to overcome exchange rates). Customers are not interested in NZ's exchange rate problems. [G #77, 80-81]
	No Problem 4 (25%)	Exchange rates not a problem. Price varies with each exchange rate and customers are OK about this. Usually quote on the present exchange rate. [N #116-118]
		They can live with the exchange rate. Major exporting countries have strong currencies. The main problem is fluctuations in exchange rates. [B #98-100]
Interest Rates 13 (81%)	Problem 9 (56%)	They do a lot of R&D, but the risk and high interest rates make it difficult. [M #70]
		These are a major expense. [O #34]
		They are undercapitalised and rely on borrowed capital, therefore interest rates are a problem. [A #105]
		Interest rates are a major factor in investment decisions. [P #143]
	No Problem 4 (25%)	They can use the export markets for loans, which gives them a choice as to where they borrow from. Export markets are not concerned with NZ's problems and with its internal economy. Interest rates are not as important as exchange rates. [D #100-102]

Notes:

a.   The table is an illustration of a detailed narrative that discussed each of the variables, their dichotomies, contexts, and interrelationships. Since the chapter is concerned mainly with the application of CAQDAS, rather than the detailed results of the export study, this narrative is not presented here

b.   This column notes the variables identified in the NUD*IST analysis, associated with the theme, or first-level factor, Political/Economic Environment – General. The number of cases providing information about the particular variable is presented, along with the percentage of total cases that this number represents, providing an indication of the extent to which this variable featured among the cases.

c.   This column separates the total number and percentage of cases providing information about the variable, as either a 'problem' or 'no problem', that is, reflects substructured coding.

d. This column provides examples from the interview data associated with the case studies. NUD*IST references to the case studies and the location of the illustration in the coded data are provided in square brackets, enabling access to the wider context of the data, and the coding framework.

The links determined by the researcher also showed the explanations for, and consequences of, each variable (concept) associated with the higher-level factors, or lower-level indicators. These reflected the key decision points and factors involved in the organisational decision-making process at various stages of the export performance pathway. The mapping of the variables, with explanations, consequences and key decision-making points, highlighted the process-oriented and dynamic nature of the export performance construct. In particular, it enabled the underlying elements of strategy and the strategy process to be identified as core strands through the export performance process. In other words, the mapping enabled the representation of a core strategy process identified through the coding of data in NUD*IST, and conceptualised in the mapping with Decision Explorer, reflecting the move from individual nodes to a theme of interconnected factors, variables and indicators. Preconceptualisation from the research literature and an initial small familiarisation study also supported the interpretation and representation of the nodes and patterns around a strategy process theme, which was reinforced as the analysis progressed.

As with the coding, the mapping process was iterative, with frequent reference back to the data coded in NUD*IST, and cross-checking of researcher assumptions about these data. Reference to the detailed written commentary from the original interview data was particularly important for providing insights to the mapping process, and verification of relational representation. The earlier checklist and content-analytic matrices also provided ways of checking elements of the resulting model against those in the extant literature, and the researcher's assumptions being used in the conceptualisation of the map. Where indicated from these processes, adjustment of the concept linkages was made, and the process was continued until the map appeared to represent a robust interpretation of the data and patterns that had emerged in the NUD*IST analysis around a core theme.

At this point, the map was considered to be a preliminary conceptual model of export performance.[1] Although the model arose from the judgemental analysis and interpretation of the data by the researcher, the process provides transparency and traceability that enables others to understand the basis for the model and its components. In other words, the processes supporting the model provide a logical trail of explanation (Yin 1994) back to the original data.

The Conceptual Model

The conceptual map ('master map') produced in Decision Explorer showed all 82 concepts (nodes from NUD*IST) and each of the three coding levels (that is, factors, variables and indicators). For ease of visual display and interpretation of separate components of the map, the master map was disaggregated into two other maps. Figure 24.1 depicts the simplest form of the conceptual model, showing the total number (12) of factors, that is, the highest-level concepts.

The second-level map illustrated variables associated with the key factors in the model, while the master map (neither shown) includes the third-level indicators, in the context of all the variables and factors, and is relatively complex. The model's complexity highlights the need for researchers to consider the antecedents of export performance as interrelated, rather than unconnected, entities. It also demonstrates the importance of process – in this case, strategy process – as a core integrating strand. The visual and analytical complexity of the model may be one reason why there have been relatively few attempts to investigate relationships between variables in export performance models, particularly where researchers have had to rely on manual approaches to qualitative data analysis.

In order to determine key influences and tentative paths of cause and effect, the model was subjected to a number of the analytical techniques available in Decision Explorer, as outlined earlier in this chapter. Centrality analysis identifies the models' most central concepts, based on the relative numbers of inward and outward links to each concept, at various levels of connectivity of the links. This analysis was applied to the entire model containing 82 concepts, and confirmed the central importance of all the first-level factors, except for Firm Strategy, in the conceptual model (Figure 24.1). Export Strategy Implementation was determined as the most important factor. Although Firm Strategy was not one of the most important central concepts in the model, an analysis of connectivity, domain analysis, identified Firm Strategy as a key component of the model. This analysis considers the overall connectivity of the concepts, and highlights that Firm Strategy plays a key high-level integrating role in the model, rather than a high-level representation of many deeper concepts. These key factors were confirmed in subsequent phases of the study, which tested the model over two further time points.

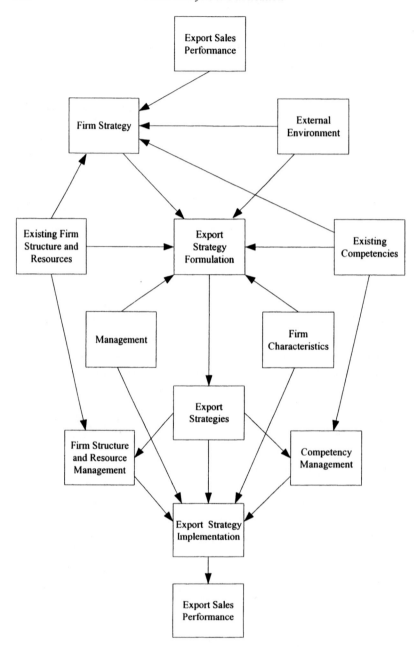

Figure 24.1   Conceptual model of export sales performance (first-level factors)

CONCLUSIONS AND IMPLICATIONS

This chapter has focused on the contribution of CAQDAS to the analysis of qualitative data. Description of the techniques applied to the analysis of qualitative data generally receives less attention in the literature than the collection of qualitative data (Miles and Huberman 1994). The chapter has considered the application of CAQDAS in an international business setting, namely in a study of export performance. In particular, the complementary use of two CAQDAS programs, NUD*IST and the decision-mapping software, Decision Explorer, has been described. Working with interview data from a number of case studies, these programs provided the researcher with tools able to assist theory building through the development of a conceptual model of export performance.

The combined use of NUD*IST and Decision Explorer contributed significantly to the qualitative data analysis process in the study. Miles and Huberman (1994) note the issue of subjectivity and reliance on an individual's interpretation of data for meaning. However, through examination and review of data coding and the analytical steps undertaken by the researcher in NUD*IST, a logical chain of evidence (Yin 1994) is made explicit. This allows for validation and/or reinterpretation of the data by another researcher to test and challenge the conclusions drawn, as part of a more rigorous triangulation procedure. As part of this, for example, the researcher may develop further analyses, add more data as desired, or investigate evolving research interests, or new lines of inquiry. The use of Decision Explorer enabled an in-depth analysis of the data and a visual representation of the complexity of relationships involved, the latter greatly assisting the understanding of the export performance construct. Application of these software programs, therefore, enhanced the research process and provided a level of rigour and validity not usually possible with manual methods.

There is an increasing recognition of the need for qualitative methods to be applied in many areas of international business research, particularly those that require an in-depth understanding of interacting influences and dynamic processes. For example, research in international alliances and joint ventures, social networks, internationalisation processes, services internationalisation, multinational corporation–subsidiary relationships, and many others could draw more on qualitative methods to enhance understanding in these areas. In this study of one branch of international business, export performance, the application of NUD*IST and Decision Explorer assisted the researcher in conducting an in-depth, qualitative approach that is widely called for by other researchers in this field. The results of the study contribute to a theory of export performance, through the development of a conceptual model with strategy process as its core. The use of CAQDAS in the study strengthened the qualitative approach used, providing rigour, transparency, and traceability from the conceptual model back to the original data. The key practical contribution of the CAQDAS programs used lay in their contribution to coding and organisation of the large amounts of data involved in the study.

ACKNOWLEDGEMENT

The author is grateful for the helpful comments from Pat Bazeley.

NOTE

1. Technically, the export performance measure was export sales performance, since this was operationalised using sales-related measures (export sales, export sales growth, export intensity and export intensity trend), dictated primarily by the data available from the study firms.

REFERENCES

Aaby, N.E. and S.E. Slater (1989), 'Managerial influences on export performance: a review of the empirical literature 1978–88', *International Marketing Review*, **6** (4), 53–68.

Andersen, O. (1993), 'On the internationalization process of firms: a critical analysis', *Journal of International Business Studies*, **24** (2), 209–31.

Banxia Software (1997), *Decision Explorer Manual*, Glasgow: Banxia Software Ltd.

Barry, C.A. (1998), 'Choosing qualitative data analysis software: Atlas/ti and Nudist compared', *Sociological Research Online*, **3** (3), http://www.socresonline.org.uk/socresonline/3/3/4.html.

Bassett, R., S. Cox and U. Rauch (1995), 'The emperor's new clothes: is there more to NUD*IST than meets the eye?', *Society/Société*, **19** (2), 18–23.

Bazeley, P. (2002), 'The evolution of a project involving an integrated analysis of structured qualitative and quantitative data: from N3 to NVivo', *International Journal of Social Research Methodology*, **5** (3), 229–43.

Burgess, R.G. (ed.) (1995), *Studies in Qualitative Methodology: Computing and Qualitative Research*, London: JAI Press.

Cavusgil, S.T. and S. Zou (1994), 'Marketing strategy–performance relationship: an investigation of the empirical link in export market ventures', *Journal of Marketing*, **58** (January), 1–21.

Dolan, A. and C. Ayland (2001), 'Analysis on trial', *International Journal of Market Research*, **43** (4), 377–89.

Easterby-Smith, M., R. Thorpe and A. Lowe (2002), *Management Research: An Introduction*, 2nd edn, London: Sage.

Eden, C. (1988), 'Cognitive mapping', *European Journal of Operational Research*, **36**, 1–13.

Eisenhardt, K.M. (1989), 'Building theories for case study research', *Academy of Management Review*, **14** (4), 523–50.

Fielding N.G. and R.M. Lee (eds) (1991), *Using Computers in Qualitative Research*, London: Sage.

Flick, U. (2002), *An Introduction to Qualitative Research*, 2nd edn, London: Sage.

Glaser, B.G. and A.L. Strauss (1967), *The Discovery of Grounded Theory: Strategies of Qualitative Research*, London: Weidenfeld & Nicolson.

Herriot, R.E. and W.A. Firestone (1983), 'Multisite qualitative policy research: optimizing description and generalizability', *Educational Researcher*, **12** (2), 14–19.

Hesse-Biber, S. (1995), 'Unleashing Frankenstein's monster? The use of computers in qualitative research', in R.G Burgess (ed.), *Studies in Qualitative Methodology: Computing and Qualitative Research*, **5**, 25–42.

Jenkins, M. and G. Johnson (1997), 'Linking managerial cognition and organisational performance: a preliminary investigation using causal maps', *British Journal of Management*, **8**, special issue, S77–S90.

Kamath, S., P.J. Rosson, D. Patton and M. Brooks (1987), 'Research on success in exporting: past, present and future', in P.J. Rosson and S.D. Reid (eds), *Managing Export Entry and Expansion: Concepts and Theory*, New York: Praeger, pp. 398–421.

Katsikeas, C.S. (1994), 'Perceived export problems and export involvement: the case of Greek exporting manufacturers', *Journal of Global Marketing*, **7** (4), 29–57.

Kelle, U. (1997), 'Theory building in qualitative research and computer programs for the management of textual data', *Sociological Research Online*, **2** (2), http://www.socresonline.org.uk/socresonline/2/2/1.html.

Kelly, G.A. (1955), *The Psychology of Personal Constructs*, New York: Norton.

Leonidou, L.C. (1995a), 'Export stimulation research: review, evaluation and integration, *International Business Review*, **4** (2), 133–56.

────── (1995b), 'Empirical research on export barriers: review, assessment and synthesis', *Journal of International Marketing*, **3** (1), 29–43.

Lewis, R.B. (1998), 'Atlas/ti and NUD*IST: a comparative review of two leading qualitative data analysis packages', *Cultural Anthropology Methods*, **10** (3), 41–7.

Lincoln, Y.S. and G. Guba (1985), *Naturalistic Inquiry*, London: Sage.

Lindsay, V.J. (1999), 'Measuring export performance: challenges and implications for policy-makers', *Proceeding of the Australia–New Zealand International Business Academy*, Sydney, October.

Locke, K. (1997), 'Rewriting the discovery of grounded theory after 25 years?', *Journal of Management Inquiry*, **5**, 239–45.

Lonkila, M. (1995), 'Grounded theory as an emerging paradigm for computer-assisted qualitative data analysis', in U. Kelle (ed.), *Computer-Aided Qualitative Data Analysis: Theory, Methods and Practice*, London: Sage, pp. 41–51.

Matthyssens, P. and P. Pauwels (1996), 'Assessing export performance measurement', *Advances in International Marketing*, **8**, 85–114.

Miles, M.B. and A.M. Huberman (1984), *Qualitative Data Analysis: A Sourcebook of New Methods*, Thousand Oaks, CA: Sage.

────── (1994), *Qualitative Data Analysis: An Expanded Sourcebook*, Thousand Oaks, CA: Sage.

Qualitative Solutions and Research (QSR) (February 1997), *NUD*IST 4 Manual*,

Latrobe, Melbourne: Qualitative Solutions and Research Pty Ltd.

QSR International (2003), 'NVivo or N6? Comparison tables', available from www.qsr-software.com.au/products/productoverview.

Reason, P. (1988), *Human Inquiry in Action*, London: Sage.

Richards, L. (1995), 'Transition work! Reflections on a three-year NUD*IST project', in R.G. Burgess (ed.), *Studies in Qualitative Methodology: Computing and Qualitative Research*, London: JAI Press, pp. 105–40.

Seale, C. (2000), 'Using computers to analyse qualitative data', in D. Silverman (ed.), *Doing Qualitative Research: A Practical Handbook*, London: Sage, pp. 154–74.

———— (2002) 'Computer-assisted analysis of qualitative interview data', in J.F. Gubrium and J.A. Holstein (eds), *Handbook of Interview Research: Context and Method*, Thousand Oaks, CA: Sage, pp. 651–70.

Strauss, A.L. (1987), *Qualitative Analysis for Social Scientists*, Cambridge: Cambridge University Press.

Strauss, A.L. and J. Corbin (1990), *Basics of Qualitative Research: Grounded Theory Procedures and Techniques*, Thousand Oaks, CA: Sage.

———— (1998), *Basics of Qualitative Research: Techniques and Procedures for Developing Grounded Theory*, 2nd edn, Thousand Oaks, CA: Sage.

Styles, C. and T. Ambler (1994), 'Successful export practice: the UK experience', *International Marketing Review*, **11** (6), 23–47.

Tesch, R. (ed.) (1991), 'Computers and qualitative data II', *Qualitative Sociology*, **14** (3 & 4), special issues, Parts 1 & 2.

Weitzman, E.A. (2000), 'Software and qualitative research', in N. Denzin and Y.S. Lincoln (eds), *Handbook of Qualitative Research*, 2nd edn, Thousand Oaks, CA: Sage, pp. 803–20.

White, H. (2002), 'Combining quantitative and qualitative approaches in poverty analysis', *World Development*, **30** (3), 511–22.

Yin, R.K. (1994), *Case Study Research: Design and Methods*, Thousand Oaks, CA: Sage.

25. Writing About Methods in Qualitative Research: Towards a More Transparent Approach

Tatiana Zalan and Geoffrey Lewis

INTRODUCTION

Much qualitative research has been criticised for its lack of objectivity, replicability, validity and generalisability, and has been relegated to the role of the 'poor cousin' of quantitative research. Unfortunately, this criticism is often well founded. According to Huberman and Miles (1994), one of the main weaknesses of qualitative research has been the inability or reluctance of researchers to give a detailed and transparent account of the research procedures and methods they employed. Researchers using qualitative methods often restrict their 'methods' sections to statements such as 'The study employed the constant comparative method', with no further explanation. Inevitably, such research practices raise questions about the credibility and plausibility of findings.

One of the views about writing a methods section holds that it is the easiest part of a research report to write, if the study has been well planned (van Wagenen 1991). International business (IB) researchers who have had previous exposure to qualitative research would challenge this view: in fact, their experiences might prove exactly the opposite. Part of the problem is that, unlike with quantitative research, there are no strict guidelines on how to structure the methods section in such a way so as to convince the user of the study that the research *is*, after all, a scientific endeavour. The problem is exacerbated by the fact that there are few detailed guidelines regarding what a 'good' methods section in a study using qualitative methods should look like, as noted by Huberman and Miles (1994). Many of the existing guidelines for a doctoral dissertation (for example, Perry 1994) seem to be written by researchers who are more familiar with quantitative methods and who tend to be less sensitive to the specific challenges faced by researchers using qualitative methods. In our experience, some of these guidelines are not only unhelpful, but very often misleading.

The purpose of this chapter is to present a suggested structure of the methods section in a study using qualitative methods by outlining a standard set of expectations of what should be included in such a section. The discussion builds on the recommendations and experiences of other researchers (for example, Berg 1979; Miles and Huberman 1994; Pauwels 2000) as well as our own experiences and judgement (Lewis 1988; Zalan 2003). Although the chapter focuses on the methods section of a doctoral thesis or a dissertation, it can also be used as a guideline by researchers working on more or less extensive projects.

This chapter distinguishes between *methodology* as a subfield of epistemology, or 'the science of finding out' (Babbie 1992, p. 18), and *research methods* as systematic, focused and orderly collection and analysis of data (Ghauri et al. 1995, p. 83) to solve the research problem and develop or test theory. Because 'methodology' refers to the general study of methods and involves discussions about which methods are appropriate, the correct heading for this section in a research project should probably be 'method(s)' or 'research design', rather than 'methodology', as is often the case, unless methodological considerations are explicitly addressed. The distinction between 'methods' and 'methodology' is more commonly made in Europe than in the USA (Berg 1979). This distinction, however, is frequently difficult to make and is often a matter of convention.

Writing up a methods chapter in a dissertation or a book using qualitative methods is, as mentioned earlier, a challenge. Writing on how to write a methods chapter is no less challenging. Qualitative methods, by their very diverse and fluid nature, defy codification (Tesch 1990), and the research process using these methods is equally difficult to capture. The writing process for this chapter involved comparisons with quantitative methods, from which qualitative research can borrow to its advantage, and, inevitably, discussion of specific issues in qualitative research. It should be noted, however, that borrowing from quantitative research should proceed with caution, and it is erroneous to assume that what applies to quantitative research would necessarily apply to qualitative research. We have also frequently drawn from, and referred to, what we believe is quality organisational, strategic management and IB research to illustrate major points. We suggest that an IB researcher concerned with presenting a transparent account of methods can benefit from detailed descriptions in Bartlett and Ghoshal (1989), Berg (1979), Haspeslagh and Jemison (1992), Lewis (1988), Pauwels (2000) and Sharpe (1998). The discussion in the chapter follows the structure of a sample methods chapter presented in the appendix.

A brief mention of writing style in the methods chapter is warranted here.

While quantitative researchers tend to use the passive voice (for example, 'the data were collected'), the personal pronoun 'I' or 'the researcher(s)' appear to be more appropriate for studies using qualitative methods. However, as the use of active or passive voice is also a matter of academic conventions, the researcher may need to justify the use of the personal pronoun.

PART 1: JUSTIFICATION OF THE METHODOLOGY

Why Should Qualitative Researchers Justify their Methodology?

The need for a section which outlines the ontological, espistemological and methodological tenets of the research project goes well beyond impressing the examiner and fellow researchers with the usage of complex terms: it justifies the choice of methodology and research methods that underpin subsequent analysis and interpretation of the data in Part 2. Not only should the research problem, research design, methods of observation, measurement and types of analysis fit together (Kerlinger 1973), they should also be congruent with the ontological and epistemological position of the researcher. As stated by Guba and Lincoln (1994), questions of method are secondary to questions of the paradigm which guides the researcher, not only in choice of method, but also in terms of their ontological and epistemological foundations. Different researchers may have diverse views of what is real, what can be known, and how facts can be faithfully rendered (Miles and Huberman 1994). For example, the epistemological frame of reference may have implications for the choice of either the etic (outsider's) or the emic (insider's) approach to conducting international management research (see Roffey 1998).

The prevailing methodological approach for the social sciences – and particularly for management research – is based on the positivistic, hypothetico-deductive model of reasoning, as management research has been trying to establish legitimacy within the broader scientific community. Researchers in the social sciences looked to the physical sciences in order to deal with theory-building and theory-testing issues, because this 'scientific method' had been proven to work exceptionally well for centuries, providing a foundation on which much of Western culture's intellectual tradition is built (Kuhn 1962).[1] It is understandable that management research has tried to emulate the physical sciences, and it is not necessarily a bad approach. However, just as physical sciences take the philosophical underpinning of the scientific method for granted, so do social science researchers using quantitative methods: in most such studies, the ontological (objectivism), epistemological (positivism) and methodological (quantitative statistical methods) underpinnings are implicitly assumed. As a result, very few 'methods' chapters in doctoral theses or other academic work deal with anything other than methods. Quantitative researchers thus seem to conveniently avoid the issue of methodological justification, even though they often go to extreme lengths to justify their methods (for example, sampling and data collection instruments), as if they were doing 'real science'.[2] Too often, using a quantitative *method* in social sciences seems to provide the justification for using a quantitative *methodology*.

In qualitative research, this cannot, and should not, be the case. Qualitative researchers have to justify what they are doing because they need to explain why they have not used quantitative methods. Dealing with methodological issues also provides the researcher some reassurance that the investment he or she is making in qualitative research is worthwhile, while at the same time being able to satisfy examiners, reviewers and other researchers. As qualitative researchers are more driven by the nature of the problem than the method (that is, 'will this approach allow me to understand the phenomenon?'), they tend to be interested in ontological and epistemological issues. For this reason, consistent with the recommendations by Miles and Huberman (1994), it makes sense to state ontological assumptions expressly, and the theories of knowledge and method that inform the researcher.

Ontology and Epistemology

The fundamental ontological question facing management researchers is whether reality is of an objective nature and external to the individual (that is, is independent of the mind) or the product of individual cognition and mind (Babbie 1992). Most management researchers, regardless of their paradigmatic preferences, will have little to contribute to this philosophical debate,[3] yet some prefer to make their ontological and epistemological stance clear. For example, Miles and Huberman (1994, p. 4) subscribe to 'transcendental realism' – that is, they believe that social phenomena exist not only in the mind, but also in the objective world and that there are some repeatable regularities and sequences that link these phenomena. This stance allowed them not only to produce high-quality research in the area of education, but also set a standard in rigorous analytical procedures for the social sciences in general.

Epistemology – that is, the philosophical theory of knowledge – is concerned with such central issues as explanation, causality, generalisation and external validity. Although the boundaries between the epistemological paradigms are becoming increasingly blurred – particularly in IB research which is multi-paradigmatic by nature (Toyne and Nigh 1998) – positivist and interpretivist paradigms remain competing claims regarding what constitutes warrantable knowledge (Henwood and Pidgeon 1999). Even within the interpretivist paradigm, there may be several answers to what can be known (see, for example, Guba and Lincoln 1994). Researchers coming from the positivist perspective (who are likely to be the external reviewers of a thesis) may not be familiar with these distinctions, so it makes sense for the researcher to discuss them at some length. Useful points of departure on the issues of explanation and causality are Kaplan's (1964) book *The Conduct of Inquiry* and Huberman and Miles (1994), while a careful treatment of the issues of generalisability and validity in qualitative research is provided by Guba and Lincoln (1989), Miles and Huberman (1994), Tsoukas (1989) and Yin (1984).

Methodology

Methodology is perhaps the most important section in Part 1. The purpose of this section in a study is twofold: to demonstrate the grasp of the theory of method and to lay out general methodological considerations consistent with the research problems, ontological and epistemological positions and underlying theories. The knowledge of methodology will then be applied by the researcher in Part 2 (Research Design). Researchers should take care not to describe the body of knowledge about the theory of method *per se*, but to provide justification of why a particular methodology is preferred over a wide array of other available alternatives. It appears that at least three aspects need to be addressed in this section: (1) research methods in previous studies and their limitations; (2) justification of the methodology used by focusing on its advantages over other methodologies; and (3) a brief description of the methodology.

In all probability, researchers committing themselves to qualitative studies are doing this at least in part because of an appreciation of the limitations of quantitative methodology with regard to the phenomenon they are concerned with studying, so they will have little difficulty in addressing these limitations. The field of management theory, as noted by Mintzberg (1979, p. 583), has paid dearly for its obsession with rigour in the choice of methodology, leading to statistically significant but largely useless results. In the area of international diversification and performance, for example, the more studies are done, the more confusing the results become, which is why qualitative methods may shed more light on this 'overworked' area (Zalan 2003). A similar observation is made by Parkhe (1993) in relation to research on international joint ventures, which has generated a significant number of individually useful quantitative studies, yet has not produced a coherent body of work with an underlying theoretical structure.[4] However, researchers should take care to provide a balanced view of the state of knowledge in the area, bearing in mind that in many cases statistical methods would be the most appropriate approach.

The choice of methodology is determined not only by ontological and epistemological stance of the researcher, but also by (1) the objective of the study; (2) the nature of the research problem; and (3) the theoretical frameworks that inform the study. These should be the *primary* concerns and will often shape the ontological and epistemological stance adopted by the researcher. The researcher thus needs to discuss how the chosen methodology is driven by each of these considerations. If the objective of the study is, for example, to build a new theory, then qualitative methods, such as case study research, would be an appropriate option. Qualitative methods are particularly well suited to finding causal relationships, looking directly and longitudinally at processes, states and events, and showing how these led to specific outcomes (Huberman and Miles 1994). IB researchers can also present a convincing argument that qualitative methods are most effective in those areas of IB research which require a longitudinal perspective, such as the internationalisation process of the firm or studies of organisational change in multinational corporations. Qualitative methods may offer a unique advantage when the IB researcher is trying to observe, describe and explain dynamic processes, such as international negotiations or decision-making by top management teams, which are best captured in close proximity to the phenomenon. In general, whenever a holistic, dynamic and contextual explanation of the phenomenon is required, qualitative methods would be the most appropriate methodological choice (see Pettigrew 1990, 1992).

Finally, the chosen methodology should be consistent with underlying theoretical frameworks: even though some researchers may engage in highly inductive research from an atheoretical position (for example, Brown and Eisenhardt 1997), it is difficult to conceive that any study can be completely theory-free from the beginning. To illustrate the point, while the theory of the transnational has been built inductively (Bartlett and Ghoshal 1989), it has eminent theoretical antecedents – the integration/responsiveness framework (Prahalad and Doz 1987) and the strategy-structure literature. It is, therefore, critical for the researcher to explicate why a particular methodology is more appropriate for the study of the phenomenon, given its theoretical underpinnings and the limitations of the previous methodologies. In addition, as suggested by Perry (1994), researchers need to show familiarity with controversies with regard to a particular methodology.

The examiners or reviewers, in all probability, will have a broad understanding of the methodological approach chosen by the researcher. Grounded theory or case study research, for example, are fairly common approaches in organisational and IB research which require little explanation, unless the researcher introduces a major modification. Even so, to paraphrase Perry (1994), the researcher needs to show familiarity with the method. Moreover, it is not uncommon for qualitative researchers to use more 'exotic' methods, a new method or multiple methods, dictated by their concern for the phenomenon they are investigating. In such cases, a more detailed explanation will probably be required – to some extent the researcher's contribution may be methodological as well as substantive. For example, the ethnographic approach, which has long traditions in management research generally, has not been used extensively in IB and will thus require some elaboration in this section of the methods chapter. In fact, it is highly likely that an IB researcher will make a methodological contribution, because the field of IB is characterised by methodological complexity (Adler 1983) and on many occasions the researcher will be stepping into unknown territory.

In conclusion, a word of caution is warranted. Despite the obvious need to address the issues of ontology, epistemology and methodology in Part 1, researchers should be careful not to turn their discussion into a philosophical treatise in an attempt to present their work as a worthy scientific endeavour. If they do, they will probably have the effect of boring and exasperating the reviewer, rather than anything else. After all, the purpose of this section is to justify and explain the methodology and method, and it should be limited to that.

PART 2: RESEARCH DESIGN

Unit and Levels of Analysis and Sampling Decisions

Reviewers and fellow researchers coming from the positivist perspective often feel uneasy about the fact that qualitative researchers are operating with small samples, sometimes with a sample of one. In the experience of one of the authors, on a number of occasions she was advised to increase the number of firms in her study, as if it would improve the validity or generalisability of her findings. One of the ways of dealing with these perceptions is to remind the readers that some of the best studies in management and IB which have had lasting and profound impact were done on very small samples. The path-breaking study on the internationalisation process of the firm by Johanson and Wiedersheim-Paul (1975), developed from the small sample of four Swedish firms, is a good case in point. In writing up their work, researchers should never be 'apologetic' for a sample of one, as it is far better to have an in-depth understanding of one case, rather than a superficial understanding of 100 cases (Mintzberg 1979). However, given the widespread scepticism that prevails toward small-sample studies, researchers need to carefully justify the sample size and explain the effect of adding one or more cases to the sample on the quality of the conclusions.

Similar to quantitative researchers, qualitative researchers need to describe, define and justify the units and levels of analysis, the settings and characteristics of the sample. The issues of units and levels of analysis and sampling procedures are well developed, so researchers should have few problems dealing with them (refer, for example, to Yin 1984). These issues are of critical importance to qualitative studies, because the choice of a case may well influence the results of the study, given that it is chosen for theoretical, not statistical, reasons. The purpose is to satisfy the reviewer and make it possible for other researchers to use the results of the study as a basis for comparison, thus ensuring comparability and transferability of the results to other similar settings (Goetz and LeCompte 1984). The issue of settings is particularly relevant to IB research, where settings differ dramatically, shaped by a host of contextual factors. We thus support both Hofstede's (1980) and Boyacigiller and Adler's (1991) recommendation that researchers should explain the geographical, national and cultural characteristics of their sample so that the reviewers, readers and researchers themselves could recognise potential limitations – otherwise IB scholars might inappropriately promulgate universal applicability of their findings.

Data Collection

In this section, the researcher needs to describe the sources of data used (together with their advantages and disadvantages); data collection procedures (for example, how interviewees were identified and approached); issues in the researcher–research participants' relationships and how these issues were resolved; research protocols (if appropriate); specific procedures employed to ensure the quality of the data, and data limitations.

Most qualitative researchers should have few problems with describing the sources of data or data collection methods and protocols: comprehensive guidelines are given in almost any book on qualitative research methods. However, one problem in IB research is that such guidelines might be useful in Western, or even Anglo-American, settings, but may not be appropriate or feasible in other parts of the world (Michailova, Chapter 18 this volume). Therefore, if the researcher has modified such general guidelines to suit the particular context in which the study was conducted, these modifications should be discussed and explained. Books on qualitative research methods typically do not cover these issues, so the researcher may be entering into unchartered territory. A further IB-specific issue in data collection is dealing with the language barrier, and researchers should be prepared to explain if, and how, they handled this issue through the use of interpreters or of English as a 'lingua franca', and the resulting translation and equivalence problems (for more details, see Marschan-Piekkari and Reis, Chapter 11 this volume).

While quantitative research is concerned with issues such as response rates, in qualitative research a major challenge is dealing with the nature and quality of the data and acknowledging their limitations. These issues should receive special consideration in this section, because they have direct impact on the soundness of findings and credibility of the research process. Despite the heroic data collection efforts that qualitative researchers often make to assemble the necessary data set, the quality of the data may not be as high as desired. This is because the data collection approach in qualitative research frequently tends to be opportunistic: it is impossible to interview managers who refuse to be interviewed, while getting access to organisations and their documentation may be difficult because of confidentiality reasons. Interviewing managerial elites also presents formidable challenges (see Welch et al. 2002). Further, IB researchers may be faced with constraints imposed by physical distance, as it can often be too expensive to travel to meet all relevant informants.

Finally, even if researchers do get access to organisations, some issues may be of a highly political or emotionally charged nature. For example, Pauwels (2000) reports reluctance of managers to comment on certain aspects of international market withdrawal, because withdrawal may be interpreted as a failure of international strategy. On the other hand, in the experience of Berg (1979), informants can be very open with the researcher about 'secret' documents and even personal matters, which may suggest that they are pursuing hidden agendas, going well beyond provision of data. Lewis (1988) shows that these issues can be overcome by investing enough time in building relationships and demonstrating trustworthiness, which in the case of IB research may also mean encountering and overcoming cross-cultural differences. The danger is that the researcher may 'go native' and no longer be a relatively objective collector of data.[5] In such cases, data contamination may become a real problem. Therefore, the researcher should explicate how problems of getting access to data were overcome and how data quality was assured. Ways to deal with these data limitations are triangulation by data sources, data collection methods and investigators, as well as effectively managing the researcher–research participant relationship (see Lewis 1988; Neuman 2000).

Data Management, Displays and Use of Computers

One of the major challenges of qualitative research that all researchers confront is dealing with complexity – otherwise, as cogently noted by Pettigrew (1990, p. 281), 'death by data asphyxiation' would be inevitable. The literature on qualitative methods suggests several alternatives for dealing with this problem at both strategic and operational levels (see Miles and Huberman 1994; Pettigrew 1990; Strauss 1987).

Because reviewers and examiners are well aware of the problem, they are curious to find out how a researcher, from masses of interview and other field data, arrived at half a dozen major concepts or patterns. For example, during the course of his strategy process research, Lewis (1988) collected some half a million words of notes that were eventually distilled into a one-page schematic representation of the process of strategic change. To satisfy this natural concern of readers, qualitative researchers need to explicate what specific and systematic procedures they used to reduce the data as well as how the data were stored and managed for easy retrieval. A diagram reflecting the data reduction and analysis procedure may prove useful in this regard (see Figure 25.1).

This section should also contain a description of the way the data were presented through data displays, with some justification of why certain types of displays (for example, field notes) were preferred over the others (for example, matrices and networks). These displays should support the main conclusions of the study. Although the traditional way of presenting data has been the narrative text (Huberman and Miles 1994; Miles and Huberman 1984), it may have the effect of 'bludgeoning' the reader into submission because it can be dispersed, sequential, poorly ordered, monotonous and overloading.

As computer software for qualitative data analysis (QDA) is becoming increasingly popular in management research (see Lindsay, Chapter 24 this volume), it is advisable to explain why the researcher used – or did not use – a specific software package. Contemporary statistical research is unimaginable without computer software usage, and the expectation is that qualitative researchers should go this way, despite the limitations of computers for data analysis and particularly interpretation. Researchers who are *not* using QDA software in their study should justify why they have made this choice – reasons may vary from heterogeneity of data, inability of computers to deal with specific types of analysis (for example, semiotic and discourse analyses) or simply the cost–benefit considerations in the case of a small volume of data. In the earlier days of computer software for QDA, researchers were advised to elaborate on the programs they were using. With the increasing familiarity of the scientific community with QDA, this description is probably redundant in contemporary qualitative studies. However, given the proliferation of software packages, researchers should explain *why* they chose a particular package over another.

Analysis and Interpretation

Because the constant iteration between data collection and analysis is a key feature of much of qualitative research, it is difficult and even misleading to separate a discussion on data collection from that on analysis (Welch 2001). However, for reasons of methodological clarity and, more pragmatically, for the reviewer, it may be necessary for the researcher to describe the two processes separately.

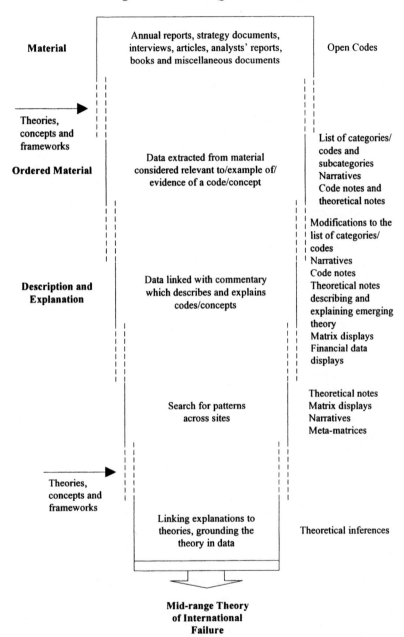

Source: This figure draws on Zalan's (2003) study. Adapted from Lewis (1988, p. 232).

Figure 25.1 Funnel of data collection, management and analysis

Specific analytical techniques for qualitative analysis are reasonably well formulated (see Miles and Huberman 1994; Pettigrew 1990; Strauss and Corbin 1990; Yin 1989). What is often missing from these descriptions, however, is the cognitive process by which the researcher arrived at certain interpretations or conclusions about the data. The entire process school in IB strategy – exemplified by Doz and Prahalad's (1984) research into patterns of strategic control in multinational firms – has been criticised precisely because it is difficult to establish a link between empirical work and conceptual development (Melin 1992). Qualitative research is intellectual craftsmanship (Tesch 1990) and utilises a different logical system for establishing cause–effect relationships from quantitative research. Quantitative research is primarily concerned with verification or falsification of a priori theory. By contrast, in qualitative research the process of *discovery* is the more important element of theory development (Henwood and Pidgeon 1999).[6]

Discovery is, undoubtedly, the most exciting part of qualitative research for the researcher, the reviewer and fellow academics – without discovery, there is no scientific advance. The process of inductive discovery falls short of detective work (Mintzberg 1979) and is blended with intuition (Berg 1979), which is a legitimate element of discovery in any science. This is the point that Kuhn (1962) makes about physical science research – a lot depends on intuition. It is, therefore, unfortunate that researchers are often unwilling to communicate this process to the readers, and these practices may well undermine the credibility of their findings. By contrast, quantitative researchers tend to be far better at systematically explaining how their constructs and instruments were developed, defined, improved and tested. Surely, verbalising the creative process is a daunting task and an art in itself, but given that the qualitative researcher is an instrument in the process, it is critically important to show how the 'instrument' functions.

Because of the differences in the logical systems of induction and deduction, qualitative researchers are urged to reveal the actual course of decision-making, breakthroughs and dead-ends in conceptualisation and the development of their thinking and interpretation (Silverman 2000). For example, in the methods section of their research on managing acquisitions, Haspeslagh and Jemison (1992) describe not only how they analysed the data, but also how their thinking about constructs evolved over time.

It may also be useful to discuss how the analysis of a 'negative case' or new data helped the researcher to modify the emerging construct or model. Exploring evidence which does not fit the model serves as a device for challenging initial assumptions and categories (Henwood and Pidgeon 1999). This will also convince the examiner or reviewer that the researcher was honest about altering the model faced with conflicting evidence, rather than fudging the data to fit the model.

IB researchers are also likely to face challenges of developing analytical categories and interpretations across cultures not common to within-culture studies. For example, much of the meaning of messages in high-context cultures comes from the paralanguage, facial expressions, setting and timing, rather than from the spoken word (Boyacigiller and Adler 1991). Paralanguage, in itself, can be interpreted differently by the researcher and research participants socialised in different cultures. The meaning of concepts, such as 'power' or 'organisational commitment' vary significantly across cultures, while certain concepts, such as 'achievement', have no direct equivalent in some languages (Wright 1996). All these issues have important implications for qualitative data analysis and interpretation, and hence on the soundness of the conclusions, which IB researchers should be prepared to communicate to the reader.

Analysis and interpretation can also be extended to the decisions researchers make about presenting and writing up their data. Some qualitative researchers follow the quantitative and realist traditions of presenting a theoretical framework and research questions followed by the corresponding findings. Other researchers may take a more reflexive stance to theory development, constructing their text around their own voyage of discovery, sensemaking and interpretation (Denzin 1994).

Ethical Issues

Ethical considerations are a critical issue in any qualitative research. The collection of much good qualitative data relies on building trust between the researcher and the researched or using the credibility of colleagues in gaining access to organisations. If any of these are abused, the opportunities for future researchers will be spoiled. The ethics of qualitative research give rise to a number of tensions, such as the need for the researcher to build close relationships with the researched versus the imperative to remain a relatively neutral observer. The researcher's willingness to report the data as he or she sees them may often conflict with the interpretation of the same data by the participants in the study. Issues of anonymity, confidentiality, openness of the participants, as well as providing feedback to the organisations and getting clearance from the informants also need to be addressed in this section (see, for example, Babbie 1992 and Emory and Cooper 1991, who discuss general ethical considerations).

In the international context, ethical considerations become even more important, not in the least because the IB researcher is likely to deal with two or more sets of values (Punnett and Shenkar 1996).[7] Even the straightforward matter of signing an informed consent form by research participants – a typical requirement in such research cultures as North America and Australia – may be undesirable, impolite or impossible in certain locations (Punnett and Shenkar 1996). Given that there are no clear guidelines to follow in dealing with many of these situations, researchers will often need to use their own judgement (Wright 1994). These issues need to be specifically addressed by the researcher in this section of the methods chapter, thus adding to the credibility of the research process.

PART 3: ASSESSMENT OF THE STUDY

Validation of the Study

How sound are the findings of the study? This question is likely to worry the researcher and the reviewer alike, and even sometimes the subjects of the study. Validation of the study is one of the most critical – yet frequently missing – parts of a research project which uses qualitative methods. This is despite the fact that validity, and particularly *external validity*, or transferability (Lincoln and Guba 1985), has been acknowledged as a major challenge in qualitative research and indeed its major limitation. Validation, however, is a somewhat broader concept than validity and may include such issues as objectivity, freedom from bias, replicability and internal reliability. Attempting to avoid careful treatment of this subject in a thesis is simply to avoid confronting a pertinent methodological issue and thus cast serious doubts in the reviewer's mind about the plausibility of the study's findings.

Although this section appears at the end of the methods chapter, validation is not a separate – and certainly not the last – stage of the study. As observed by Pauwels (2000, p. 142), 'validation is a dynamic effort which is performed through the entire research process'. Because standards for the quality of conclusions tend to differ among methodologists, in part reflecting their divergent epistemological positions, the researcher needs to select the criteria that are most appropriate for the methodology he or she is using. A set of guidelines to validate a study using qualitative methods proposed by Guba and Lincoln (1989) and criteria for grounded methodology suggested by Strauss and Corbin (1990) could be a useful starting point for qualitative researchers. Depending on the epistemological position of the researcher, sometimes even criteria for quantitative research would be appropriate (see Kidder 1981; Miles and Huberman 1994): for example, the external validity criterion is not incompatible with the scientific realism epistemology (Tsoukas 1989). Researchers are thus strongly advised to explicitly address the criteria for validation – not just by stating what the issues were, but how each of them was specifically dealt with in the study (see also Andersen and Skaates, Chapter 23 this volume).

Limitations of the Study

There is little doubt that quantitative research is more amenable to validation than qualitative research. Despite qualitative researchers' increasing concern with rigour and validity, qualitative research is so detailed and time-consuming that it is unlikely that other researchers would be willing to replicate it. In writing up their work, qualitative researchers should come to terms with the inherent limitations of the methods they use and always put conditional statements around their findings. The more carefully the limitations are acknowledged, the more sound and valid their findings will be. Some of these potential limitations – such as an opportunistic approach to data collection; lack of negotiation of 'joint reality' among the researcher and the participants in the study; and relationships of power with corporate elites – have been discussed earlier in the chapter. Other common limitations, such as researcher bias, transferability to other contexts and the exploratory nature of the study, will be briefly addressed below.

Every organisational researcher subscribing to a particular ontological and epistemological paradigm indicates a predisposition towards that view of the world and is, therefore, subject to researcher bias, even though quantitative researchers have been conditioned to believe that their research is somehow bias-free. Qualitative IB researchers, and particularly those who pursue direct, prolonged and reflexive engagement with informants, are encouraged to disclose how their education, disciplinary focus, theoretical frameworks, nationality, and personal interests and beliefs might have influenced the results of the study. For example, in cross-cultural research it is almost certain that researchers will interpret their findings through the lens of their own cultural values. Rather than disguise their biases, IB researchers can wisely use them to produce higher-quality research outcomes.

The IB researcher should take special care in explicating the extent of transferability of research findings to other language and cultural settings. In IB research, it is not uncommon that the researcher and/or the informants are not operating in their native language, or even lack cultural sensitivity. When informants are not comfortable with using a foreign language, they tend to either restrict themselves to short answers, depriving the researcher of valuable information, or withdraw from the research to avoid embarrassment, introducing another source of error in the data (Wright 1996). Language barriers may not only impact on data analysis and interpretation, but also put certain constraints on the sampling frame and procedures: for example, the choice of English as an interview language in a South-East Asian country is likely to restrict the sampling frame to the more educated stratum of the society. Greater transparency about the boundaries of the research findings, cultural biases and other limitations of the research design will serve the dual purpose of preventing IB researchers from laying unrealistic claims to the universality of their findings while simultaneously assuring the readers of the usefulness of these findings in comparable settings.

We believe that the exploratory nature of a qualitative study cannot be, strictly speaking, a limitation. As emphasised throughout this chapter, idiographic inquiry is driven by the phenomenon and if the phenomenon is poorly understood, then the exploratory research design would be the only logical choice. Nevertheless, there has been a tendency within the positivist paradigm to confine idiographic research to the initial stages of scientific inquiry (for example, Babbie 1992), stemming from a lack of familiarity with the ontological, epistemological and methodological principles of qualitative methods. For this reason, exploratory qualitative research may be viewed by reviewers and examiners as purely descriptive and thus somewhat inferior to explanatory research, even though both description and explanation are legitimate contributors to theorising in organisational science (see Whetten 1989). It is worth noting that exploratory qualitative research can in fact extend the possibilities of theorising beyond grand or mid-range theories to include metaphors, typologies and concepts used by the researcher to characterise a poorly understood phenomenon (see Llewellyn 2003, on levels of theorising in qualitative research).

CONCLUSION

A quote from Berg (1979, p. 165) seems an appropriate way to conclude the discussion on how to write a methods chapter in a doctoral dissertation or other study using qualitative methods. In his words,

> The task of the researcher is not ... to show whether his findings, models or hypotheses are right or wrong, but to convince the reader that they are reasonable conclusions, drawn from material, which has been processed by methods which can be explicitly described.

This quote underscores the importance of greater transparency in writing about methods by qualitative researchers, which in turn will lead to greater credibility and, hopefully, a wider acceptance of their work.

In the past, qualitative research tended to suffer from the fact that analytical techniques were not well developed and, consequently, not adequately disclosed by researchers. Now, through joint efforts of many distinguished management scholars and methodologists, the problem of developing appropriate qualitative data analysis techniques is being addressed. There is also a growing recognition that many of the most pressing problems in IB and management research can be more effectively addressed using qualitative methods. This trend is matched by a growing frustration with the overuse of quantitative methods leading to studies reporting results with marginal levels of statistical significance and often zero levels of practical importance. We thus urge IB researchers to be more transparent about their methods, as this will not only increase the legitimacy of qualitative research within the scientific community, but also allow fellow researchers to build on their experience.

NOTES

1. Interestingly, 'real' scientists, that is, those who devote their lives to research in the physical and life sciences, do not seem to suffer the same preoccupation with methodology as social science researchers. Kuhn's work dispels the myths of how physical science researchers work. For physical and life science researchers, the philosophical underpinnings of the way they go about their work can largely be taken for granted. Research *methods* must be carefully thought through and repeated in a way that enables others to replicate their work, but they do not have to justify their *methodology*.
2. We believe that researchers using quantitative methods should also justify the choice of their methodology based on the ontological and epistemological assumptions they are making. While quantitative methods are appropriate in many cases, there is ample evidence to suggest that they have been used incorrectly and uncritically: see, for example, the discussion by Rouse and Daellenbach (1999) on the inappropriateness of quantitative methods to study competitive advantage using the resource-based view of the firm.
3. Philosophers, for whom the issue of reality is central to their inquiry, have been debating what is 'real' for thousands of years, without yet coming to a satisfactory conclusion (see Babbie 1992, pp. 54–5, on the issue of reality and objectivity in social sciences).
4. Contrary to the popular view that qualitative methods are most appropriate when there is little prior research on the topic, Eisenhardt (1989) suggests that qualitative methods may also work well when the research topic is well studied, but a fresh perspective is needed.
5. Even though some researchers using qualitative methods may argue that 'objectivity' should not be a criterion in qualitative research, we would contend that 'objectivity' should be a standard in any science, including management and IB. We acknowledge, however, that in qualitative research it is a particularly difficult standard to achieve.
6. It is assumed that theory (whether grand or mid-range) is a primary concern of both qualitative and quantitative research. However, the outcomes of qualitative research may include concepts, conceptual frameworks and propositions (Eisenhardt 1989).
7. Punnett and Shenkar (1996) provide a useful account of what ethical issues a cross-cultural researcher might face and suggest how to deal with them.

REFERENCES

Adler, N.J. (1983), 'Cross-cultural management research: the ostrich and the trend', *Academy of Management Journal*, **8** (2), 226–32.
Babbie, E. (1992), *The Practice of Social Research*, Belmont, CA: Wadsworth.
Bartlett, C. and S. Ghoshal (1989), *Managing Across Borders: The Transnational Solution*, Boston, MA: Harvard Business School Press.
Berg, P.-O. (1979), *Emotional Structures in Organisations: A Study of a Process of Change in a Swedish Company*, Lund: Studentlitteratur.
Boyacigiller, N.A. and N.J. Adler (1991), 'The parochial dinosaur: organisational

science in a global context', *Academy of Management Journal*, **16** (2), 262–90.

Brown, S.L. and K.M. Eisenhardt (1997), 'The art of continuous change: linking complexity theory and time-paced evolution in relentlessly shifting organizations', *Administrative Science Quarterly*, **42** (1), 1–35.

Denzin, N.K. (1994), 'The art and politics of interpretation', in N.K. Denzin and Y.S. Lincoln (eds), *Handbook of Qualitative Research*, Thousand Oaks, CA: Sage, pp. 500–515.

Doz, Y. and C.K. Prahalad (1984), 'Patterns of strategic control within multinational corporations', *Journal of International Business Studies*, **15** (Fall), 55–72.

Eisenhardt, K.M. (1989), 'Building theories from case study research', *Academy of Management Review*, **14** (4), 532–50.

Emory, C.W. and D.R. Cooper (1991), *Business Research Methods*, 4th edn, Boston, MA: Richard D. Irwin.

Ghauri, P., K. Grønhaug and I. Kristianslund (1995), *Research Methods in Business Studies: A Practical Guide*, Hemel Hempstead: Prentice-Hall.

Goetz, J.P. and M.D. LeCompte (1984), *Ethnography and Qualitative Design in Educational Research*, Orlando, FL: Academic Press.

Guba, E.G. and Y.S. Lincoln (1989), *Fourth Generation Evaluation*, Newbury Park, CA: Sage.

—— (1994), 'Competing paradigms in qualitative research', in N.K. Denzin and Y.S. Lincoln (eds), *Handbook of Qualitative Research*, Thousand Oaks, CA: Sage, pp. 105–17.

Haspeslagh, P.C. and D.B. Jemison (1992), *Managing Acquisitions: Creating Value Through Corporate Renewal*, New York: Free Press.

Henwood, K.L. and N.F. Pidgeon (1999), 'Qualitative research and psychology', in M. Hammersley (ed.), *Social Research: Philosophy, Politics and Practice*, London: Sage, pp. 111–35.

Hofstede, G. (1980), *Culture's Consequences: International Differences in Work-Related Values*, Beverly Hills, CA: Sage.

Huberman, A.M. and M.B. Miles (1994), 'Data management and analysis methods', in N.K. Denzin and Y.S. Lincoln (eds), *Handbook of Qualitative Research*, Thousand Oaks, CA: Sage, pp. 428–44.

Johanson, J. and F. Wiedersheim-Paul (1975), 'The internationalisation of the firm: four Swedish case studies', *Journal of Management Studies*, **12** (3), 305–22.

Kaplan, A. (1964), *The Conduct of Inquiry*, San Francisco, CA: Chandler.

Kerlinger, F.N. (1973), *Foundations of Behavioural Research*, 2nd edn, New York: Holt, Rinehart & Winston.

Kidder, L.H. (1981), 'Qualitative research and quasi-experimental frameworks', in M.B. Brewer and B.E. Collins (eds), *Scientific Inquiry and the Social Sciences*, San Francisco, CA: Jossey-Bass, pp. 226–56.

Kuhn, T.S. (1962), *The Structure of Scientific Revolution*, Chicago, IL: University of Chicago Press.

Lewis, G.P. (1988), *Corporate Strategy in Action: The Strategy Process in British Road Services*, London: Routledge.

Lincoln, Y.S. and E.G. Guba (1985), *Naturalistic Inquiry*, Newbury Park, CA: Sage.

Llewellyn, S. (2003), 'What counts as "theory" in qualitative management and accounting research: introducing five levels of theorising', *Accounting, Auditing and Accountability Journal*, **16** (4), 662-88.

Melin, L. (1992), 'Internationalisation as a strategy process', *Strategic Management*

Journal, **13**, 99–118.

Miles, M.B. and A.M. Huberman (1984), *Qualitative Data Analysis: A Sourcebook of New Methods*, Newbury Park, CA: Sage.

——— (1994), *Qualitative Data Analysis: A Sourcebook of New Methods*, Newbury Park, CA: Sage.

Mintzberg, H. (1979), 'An emerging strategy of "direct" research', *Administrative Science Quarterly*, **24** (4), 582–9.

Neuman, W.L. (2000), *Social Research Methods: Qualitative and Quantitative Approaches*, Boston, MA: Allyn & Bacon.

Parkhe, A. (1993), '"Messy" research, methodological predispositions, and theory', *Academy of Management Review*, **18** (2), 227–68.

Pauwels, P. (2000), 'International market withdrawal: a strategy process study', PhD thesis, Diepenbeek: Limburgs Universitair Centrum.

Perry, C. (1994), 'A structured approach to presenting a PhD thesis: notes for candidates and their supervisors', paper presented at the ANZ Doctoral Consortium, University of Sydney, February.

Pettigrew, A.M. (1990), 'Longitudinal field research on change: theory and practice', *Organization Science*, **1** (3), 267–92.

——— (1992), 'The character and significance of strategy process research', *Strategic Management Journal*, **13**, 5–16.

Prahalad, C.K. and Y.L. Doz (1987), *The Multinational Mission: Balancing Local Demands and Global Vision*, New York: Free Press.

Punnett, B.J. and O. Shenkar (1996), 'Ethics in international management research', in B.J. Punnett and O. Shenkar (eds), *Handbook for International Management Research*, Cambridge, MA: Blackwell Business, pp. 145–54.

Roffey, B.H. (1998), 'Women and business leadership in the Philippines: a study of Filipino managers and entrepreneurs', PhD thesis, Adelaide: School of Commerce, Flinders University of South Australia.

Rouse, M.J. and U.S. Daellenbach (1999), 'Rethinking research methods for the resource-based perspective: isolating sources of sustainable competitive advantage', *Strategic Management Journal*, **20**, 486–94.

Sharpe, D.R. (1998), 'Shop floor practices under changing forms of managerial control: a comparative ethnographic study', PhD thesis, Manchester: Manchester University.

Silverman, D. (2000), *Doing Qualitative Research: A Practical Handbook*, London: Sage.

Strauss, A. (1987), *Qualitative Analysis for Social Scientists*, Cambridge, New York: Cambridge University Press.

Strauss, A. and J. Corbin (1990), *Basics of Qualitative Research: Grounded Theory Procedures and Techniques*, Newbury Park, CA: Sage.

Tesch, R. (1990), *Qualitative Research: Analysis Types and Software Tools*, New York: Falmer Press.

Toyne, B. and D. Nigh (1998), 'A more expansive view of international business', *Journal of International Business Studies*, **29** (4), 863–76.

Tsoukas, H. (1989), 'The validity of idiographic research explanations', *Academy of Management Review*, **14** (4), 551–61.

van Wagenen, R.K. (1991), *Writing a Thesis: Substance and Style*, Englewood Cliffs, NJ: Prentice-Hall.

Welch, C. (2001), 'Firm-government relations in international business networks: a longitudinal case study', PhD thesis, Sydney: University of Western Sydney.

Welch, C., R. Marschan-Piekkari, H. Penttinen and M. Tahvanainen (2002), 'Corporate elites as informants in qualitative international business research', *International Business Review*, **11** (5), 611–28.

Whetten, D.A. (1989), 'What constitutes a theoretical contribution?', *Academy of Management Review*, **14** (4), 490–95.

Wright, L.L. (1994), 'Indonesia: myth and reality in the land of the shadow puppet', *International Studies of Management and Organization*, **24** (1–2) Spring/Summer, 35–60.

——— (1996), 'Qualitative international management research', in B.J. Punnett and O. Shenkar (eds), *Handbook for International Management Research*, Cambridge, MA: Blackwell Business, pp. 63–81.

Yin, R.K. (1984), *Case Study Research*, Beverly Hills, CA: Sage.

——— (1989), *Case Study Research: Design and Methods. Revised Edition*, Newbury Park, CA: Sage.

Zalan, T. (2003), 'Internationalisation of Australian firms: toward a theory of international failure', PhD thesis, Adelaide: School of Commerce, Flinders University of South Australia.

APPENDIX: STRUCTURE OF A SAMPLE METHODS CHAPTER

Part 1: Justification of Methodology

Ontology and Epistemology Justification of the choice of ontology and epistemology

Methodology Research methods in previous studies and their limitations
Justification of the methodology (advantages and disadvantages)
Description of the methodology

Part 2: Research Design

Unit and Level of Analysis, and Sampling Decisions Description, definition and justification of the unit and level of analysis
Sampling procedures
Settings and characteristics of the sample

Data Collection Sources of data (including their advantages and limitations)
Data collection procedures (e.g. how interviewees were identified and approached)
Researcher–research participants interaction
Research protocols
Quality and reliability of data
Data limitations

Data Management, Displays and Use of Computers Data reduction and complexity management procedures
Database size, storage and retrieval of data
Data displays
Computer software used (if any)

Analysis and Interpretation Analytic procedures
Interpretation of data
Stages in conceptual development
Negative case analysis
Culture-specific issues in analysis and interpretation (e.g. conceptual equivalence)

Ethical Issues   Building trust between the researcher and the researched
Confidentiality, anonymity, openness of informants
Providing feedback to/getting clearance from informants
Culture-specific ethical issues (e.g. a higher degree of anonymity required in some cultures)

Part 3:   Assessment of the Study

Validation of the Study   Validating the study using criteria developed for qualitative and quantitative research

Limitations of the Study Issues related to the nature of the study (exploratory vs explanatory), data collection procedures, researcher bias, boundaries of the study, transferability to other contexts, settings and timeframes, relationships of power between the researcher and the researched, language and cultural barriers

26. 'Writing It Up': The Challenges of Representation in Qualitative Research

Sara L. McGaughey

INTRODUCTION

The ability to capture context – the set of circumstances surrounding an event or situation that help in its interpretation – is considered a particular strength of qualitative research and writing. This strength arises by virtue of the central role that narrative plays in the various phases of qualitative research. Narratives construe reality not as snapshots in time within which reified causes affect one another, but as stories, cascades of related events (Abbot 1994). Narratives thus embody an assumption of path dependence, and interconnected levels of context – both temporal and spatial – are given primacy. Quantitative studies do not, of course, ignore context completely, but it is often pared down and simplified in the search for universal truths. Indeed, the notion of context is always relevant when different sets of data or examples are being compared, and one is interested in identifying and explaining similarities and differences (Hodder 1994). Without context, there is no meaning (Bateson 1978).

Discussions of methods used in international business (IB) articles published in our leading journals tend to focus on research design, data collection and analysis. The implicit assumption is that by taking account of context in these stages of the research process, a deeper understanding of complex, poorly understood phenomena can be gained. Yet our choice of research *representations* – the portrayals of our approach to inquiry and related findings that we construct and present to others through various media – also play a critical role in conveying context and meaning. While organisational research over the last decade has been characterised by increased attention to representation, including concerns for authorship and authority (that is, whose truth?) and for rhetorical style in conveying meanings (Jeffcut 1994), these concerns have received little explicit attention in the field of IB.

The focus of this chapter is, therefore, the challenge of how we represent our research when we write for various audiences – including reviewers, other scholars, practitioners, and those actively participating in our studies as, for example, interviewees. I begin with a short overview of several traditions that shaped my own approach to the representation of knowledge and experience in a recently completed longitudinal study of the internationalisation of knowledge-intensive, small and medium-sized enterprises (SMEs) (McGaughey 2003). Representational strategies used in 'writing up' the study included autobiographical narratives, a cartoon, dramas, a confessional tale from the field, a visual process map, newspaper headlines, reproduction of archival extracts (for example, from diaries, telexes and advertisements from two decades ago), and verbatim quotes, among others. I offer two examples of the representational strategies used. The first representation relates to 'findings', and the second to the research process itself. For each example, I discuss the purpose of the representation and the methods of construction used. I conclude with a short discussion of ethical considerations in crafting and re-crafting such representations, and some general observations based on my own trial-and-error learning.

I view understandings of research practice as 'embedded knowledge'. My early understandings of off-the-shelf prescriptions for research methods and their philosophical underpinnings have been modified, refined, and converted into highly personal forms of knowledge through practice and experience. What I offer below, then, is not a recipe that should be followed in the pursuit to capture context and meaning, but an invitation to open up the conversation about representations of *what* we find (or create) through our research, as well as representations of *how* we conduct our research.

INFLUENCES IN 'WRITING' QUALITATIVE RESEARCH

The field of IB has been challenged by calls for new approaches to inquiry throughout the 1990s, and these continue unabated. Dissatisfaction with the dominant objectivist epistemologies, positivist theoretical perspectives, and static, cross-sectional research designs that ignore unfolding processes and richly textured contexts is evident across a number of fields in IB (for example, Buckley and Chapman 1997; Redding 1997). The ensuing debates are not simply at the level of method, at which the qualitative/quantitative distinction resides. Rather, they delve into the very foundations of research by asking questions about the nature of truth, knowledge and reality. While quantitative research is typically associated with an objectivist epistemology and positivist theoretical perspective, much 'qualitative' research is similarly endowed. The early realist tales in ethnography are one example (see Van Maanen 1988). What is at issue, then, is the philosophical foundations of the research.

My own approach to portraying to others findings derived from my research and the research process itself has been increasingly influenced by an epistemology of social constructionism, an interpretive theoretical perspective, and ethnography as methodology. Social constructionism is the view that all knowledge – and hence all meaningful reality – is contingent upon human practices. Knowledge is constructed through interaction between human beings and their world, being developed and transmitted within a social context (Crotty 1998). Knowledge thus has a communal basis. The objectivist epistemology that seems to permeate much IB research holds an assumption that truth or reality can be carried by language, and that 'scientific' languages are closer to the truth than others. Passive voice, dispassionate and objective rhetoric – what Van Maanen (1995, p. 9) has called 'the style of non-style' – characterises scientific writing through which knowledge is constituted as a problem- (hypothesis-) centred, linear and straightforward (Paget 1995; Richardson 1995). Social constructionism, however, affords no such privilege between the 'world' and the 'word' (Czarniawska 1997; Gergen 1999). Language, and indeed all forms of representation, gains meaning from how it is used in relationships. Different communities of people may embrace distinct systems of meanings, and description and narration cannot be considered as straightforwardly representational of reality. As Richardson (1993, pp. 704–5) notes, 'everybody's writing is suspect'. Concern with the blinding potential of the taken-for-granted leads constructionists to the celebration of reflexivity: a willingness to place one's premises into question, including one's assumptions about representations.

Interpretivist theoretical perspectives are those that are primarily concerned with rendering accounts of human meaning systems (Gergen 1985), with a focus on processes by which meanings are created, negotiated, sustained and modified within the context of human interaction. Within this broad approach, narrative, sensemaking and dramaturgical schools of thought – that reflect the social constructionist understandings of knowing and knowledge and, in turn, inform the chosen methodology – have been influential in crafting representations of findings and methods.[1] Narrative, or story-telling, is a ubiquitous form of 'meaning making' in organisational life (Bruner 1986, 1996; Czarniawska 1997; Polkinghorne 1988, p. 36). A narrative is a meaning structure that organises human events, actions and artefacts isolated from the stream of experience into a whole, with significance attributed to events and actions according to their effect on the whole. Emplotment, a term referring to the act of configuring order in a story, is the most fundamental element of narrative construction. The act of emplotment 'extracts a configuration from a succession' and mediates between the two poles of event and story (Ricoeur 1984, p. 66). As explained by Ricoeur (1984, p. x), the plot 'grasps together and integrates into one whole and complete story multiple and scattered events'. Narratives are fundamental to sensemaking activities (Weick 1995).

Sensemaking perspectives present the reality of everyday life as an ongoing accomplishment, which takes particular shape and form as individuals attempt to create order and make sense of the situations in which they find themselves (Morgan et al. 1983). Sensemaking perspectives of organisational life are premised on the equivocality of meanings to be extracted from elapsed experience (Weick 1995). The recounting of past experience to oneself or another is not simply the telling of a story, but part of a *continual* effort to organise the experience in meaningful terms. Constructing a story involves a degree of narrative smoothing: the process of creating clean, unconditional plots with no ambiguity of meaning. From a dramaturgical perspective, the question of how a story unfolds can be construed as how one episode of interaction, or event, conditions another. Concerned with social acts and emergent meaning, the dramaturgical perspective posits that the meaning of people's doings is to be found in the manner in which they express themselves through symbolic communication in interaction with similarly expressive others (Brissett and Edgley 1990; Wexler 1983). Meaning is *established* through interaction, not simply reflected in it. The aim of ethnographic description is to capture this meaning and 'present phenomena in new and revealing ways' (Hammersley 1992, p. 13).

Three elements central to interpretive ethnographic description were particularly important in the representations of SME internationalisation: thick description, holism and polyphony. Gilbert Ryle (1968) coined the term 'thick description' for description that captures the meaning or intent of an action, with Geertz (1973) adopting and popularising it for ethnographic endeavours. Thick description is not just rich description, and certainly not endless description (Wolcott 1999). Rather, it is description that reflects socially established codes or structures of meaning. With reference to discourse, it is not the saying, but the *said* of speaking. It is through thick descriptions that the constructs of social scientists (for example, legitimacy, charisma, trust) can be thought about concretely, and applied imaginatively (Geertz 1973).

A holistic approach is one that emphasises the wholeness of phenomena by integration of its parts. Wolcott (1999) argues that the 'completeness' that ethnographic holism points to is really a call for making connections between things and for attention to the wider context in which they are situated, rather than the fragmentation arising from the classification of everyday life into the universal categories of functionalist ethnographies. Connections are also the strong suit of narrative, with its emphasis on spatial and temporal contexts and emplotment. This wider context to which holism points may include multiple perspectives and polyphonic representations. Polyphony (or multivocality) is a method of representation that attempts to allow people to speak for themselves, and thus concerns the relationship between author(ity) and text. The quality of polyphony is achieved by the academic-author sharing the role of authorship with research participants, typically employing extensive verbatim quoting (Martin 1995) without abandoning the authorial and interpretive role (Bate 1997). The use of polyphony is particularly appropriate in settings where there exist a rich diversity of perspectives, understandings or interpretations.

In summary, constructionism brings recognition of the constructed and communal nature of knowledge. Associated with this is a posture of reflexivity and willingness to question and perhaps challenge existing, more orthodox conventions for representation.[2] Interpretive narrative, sensemaking and dramaturgical perspectives are concerned with ways in which meaning is constructed, and embody assumptions that inform how this meaning is displayed through ethnographic descriptions infused with thick description, holism and, at times, polyphonic representations.

CRAFTING AND CRITIQUING REPRESENTATIONS

The choice of representation used is dependent upon the nature of the research phenomenon, the goals of the researcher, the wishes of those participating in the research, and the intended audience. For example, in the study of SME internationalisation (McGaughey 2003) a central place was afforded to the autobiographical stories of key individuals and their organisational activities. In these, the narrator is the primary character in the story, and the narrator considers the story recounted to be, for the most part, 'true'. In addition to introducing important events or activities, the telling of the story allows individuals to express their own uniqueness (Anderson and Jack 1991), and reveals personal values and traits that 'set the stage' for further interactions between the reader and this 'character'.

Autobiographical narratives speak of a time past, and were not intended to convey to the reader the immediacy of the events being recounted. More experimental forms of representation, including a cartoon, dramas, transcripts from diaries and dramaturgical tales from the field were used to draw the reader into the world of the 'other'. Writing monologues or dialogues that sound authentic is not an easy undertaking (Ely et al. 1997). While the autobiographical narratives used solely the words and sentences of the narrator, this was not always possible or desirable in other forms of representation. I thus perused books on creative writing of fiction, non-fiction and script writing (for example, Gutkind 1997; Wood 1995) to identify and develop appropriate techniques. Each experimental representation was crafted around the seven questions listed below, the first five of which were drawn from Yordon's (1997) prescriptions regarding experimental theatre: (1) What is the representation about? (2) Why is it presented? (3) Who is speaking and/or addressed? (4) Where and when does it take place? (5) How is the representation constructed? (6) What are the data sources and who is the 'author'? (7) What ethical considerations might arise in the construction of this representation, and how can they be addressed to minimise potential harm to others?

In addition to the ethical considerations discussed later, two broad criteria guided the construction and my own evaluation of the representations: verisimilitude and interpretive richness. An account's *verisimilitude* (or *vraisemblance*) refers to its appearance of reality, and reflects its ability to draw the reader so closely into the world captured in the account that it can be 'palpably felt' (Adler and Adler 1994, p. 381). An account that is accorded such a high level of authenticity by the reader tends to have a high degree of internal coherence and plausibility. Coherence is a criterion found in its own right across disciplines for explanatory narratives. Atkinson (1978, p. 131), with reference to the discipline of history, describes this coherence as 'comprehensiveness with unity, nothing relevant omitted, everything irrelevant excluded', although he does not claim 'to be able to fully articulate this conception'. What is at issue is the way in which the whole research endeavour 'hangs together'. Agar and Hobbs (1982), with reference to ethnographic interviews, explicate three forms of coherence that can be adapted to written accounts: global coherence (that is, the extent to which elements of a narrative contribute to the overall goal of the narrator); local coherence (that is, the structure of the text, effected through drawing relationships between text segments and employing devices such as chronology, juxtaposition, explanation and elaboration), and thematic coherence (that is, the existence of chunks of text or themes that repeatedly figure as important. Coherence is not, however, unproblematic as a criterion for the appraisal of scholarly texts. In the writing of any narrative, there is a powerful temptation – and often a seeming imperative – to simplify and make explicable the connectedness of events for the reader. A challenge in writing is thus to maintain and convey a sense of the unexpected, of the unpredictability of human life, of the tentativeness and ambiguity of meaning – and to thus balance the smoothing contained in the plot that leads to coherence with what might be obscured in the smoothing (Clandinin and Connelly 2000).

The coherence of a narrative account adds to its plausibility, or the extent to which the reader is able to believe that it conforms to a socially constructed meaningful reality and not its own laws (Atkinson 1990). This naturally draws, in part, on the prior knowledge or experiences of the reader. A requirement for plausibility in research has been criticised as condemning us to reproduce existing models of the world (Silverman 1993, p. 155). Where interpretations do not conform to common beliefs or understandings of a phenomenon, plausibility may still be achieved through attention to holism and thick description. In many cases, albeit perhaps not all, the surprising may still be plausible when sufficient context is provided. Explicitly describing the nature of empirical material acquired and how interpretations are made (that is, trustworthiness), along with a posture of reflexivity, may also enhance the plausibility of the study in the eyes of many readers (Lather 1986; Riessman 1993).

Verisimilitude speaks to how lifelike an account is taken to be, with coherence and plausibility essential features of this. What, however, makes an account *worth* telling and, perhaps more importantly, worth reading? A worthwhile account is often thought to be one that offers something remarkable (Robinson 1981). A story that is remarkable deviates from shared norms of experience and challenges one's model of reality, thereby attracting attention. What is seen to be remarkable is, however, determined by the people in a community and their shared system of meaning, and may change over time (Gergen 1999). Thus, remarkableness with reference to a spatio-temporally situated audience may be a desirable criterion to the extent that we are interested in the current worth of what we write or read, but is not *essential* to the longer-term worth of the narrative. Guiding my construction of representations is another criterion that I see as subsuming remarkableness: interpretive richness. Research rich in points usually avoids definite statements about 'how things are' and emphasises the importance of looking at things in a particular way. It thus offers new insights, often through the problematisation of established ways of thinking (Alvesson and Skölberg 2000). A representation rich in points opens itself to reinterpretation, rather than closing off avenues of inquiry. This, of course, echoes the social constructionist call for generative discourses and theories.

REPRESENTATIONS OF CONTEXT

Below I offer two examples of what might be considered less-than-conventional representations in IB research: a drama and a tale from the field. Each example was originally embedded within a broader narrative of a focal firm's growth and internationalisation (McGaughey 2003). Because the representational examples are presented out of context – that is, extracted from the broader narrative in which they were embedded – I have altered the names of the companies and individuals.

The focal organisation was a privately owned cluster of companies (referred to hereafter as the Group) based in the southern-most state of Australia – Tasmania. In 1996 it was in the business of lightning, transient and surge protection, and in high-performance power-conditioning technologies. The Group had its origins in a venture started in 1975. By 1996 it employed approximately 125 people throughout Australia, with strong financial performance over the preceding four years. The technologies embodied in the products manufactured and exported by the Group were supported by a number of patents worldwide, and throughout the 1990s it had been recipient of a number of research and development (R&D) awards. In 1996 it won the Australian Export Award, and was exporting to over 29 countries. The Group was, in the words of the Tasmanian Premier quoted in the State's main newspaper, an 'inspirational Tasmanian success story' *(The Mercury* 1996, p. 79).

Emotion and Polyphony Through Drama

Despite its success, the history of the Group was filled with moments of turmoil and crises where the survival of the Group – or of some of its core activities – was threatened. In crises, ambiguity of cause, effect, and means of resolution lead to disillusionment and a shattering of commonly held beliefs, values and basic assumptions. Crises may be experienced by those involved as personally and socially threatening (Pearson and Clair 1998). Even though emotion is an intrinsic part of organisational life – and comes to the fore in moments of crisis – it is typically suppressed in social science texts (Paget 1995). Written or staged dramas that are intended to be evocative may more readily capture experiences and events that are multisided, unruly and ambiguous in meaning (Denzin 1996) than conventional formats of reporting. I use dramatic forms of writing to convey a sense of event, recover emotionally laden experiences, and give voice to diverse perspectives.

One of the dramas used in the study of SME internationalisation was set in June 1986, approximately a decade after the founding of the firm. By 1986, Group employees numbered 28. Four years prior, in 1982, the export activities had received strong endorsement when the company was honoured with its first Australian Export Award. Significant investments across the organisation were to underpin future growth, and exciting new directions in lightning research were being pursued. Overall, the future appeared bright for the Tasmanian entrepreneurs. The events of May and June 1986, however, were to cast a shadow over the entrepreneurs' activities.

On 28 May 1986, the Independent Member for Franklin in the Tasmanian Senate wrote to the Minister for Health in the State Government expressing concerns about the export from Tasmania of lightning arrestors containing

Americium by a firm in the Group, the return of damaged lightning rods to Tasmania in civil aircraft, and inadequate storage facilities for such radioactive material. Received by the Minister on 30 May, the letter somehow found its way into the hands of the press, with the story making headlines in a flurry of Tasmanian newspapers only four days later, on 3 June. In response, the CEO of the Group issued a press release. That same afternoon, the issue was raised in Federal Parliament, and on 4 June the firm was named in parliament as the company involved. It was not long before the national media picked up the story, including segments on radio stations and national television. A decade later, the CEO of the Group remembered the period as 'a horrible year' with 'the first lining up of some of the bigger forces in business' leading to 'a very big mortal wounding on the psychology of the infant company'.

I used a drama to introduce these events and, more specifically, provide background information, display the diverse perspectives and equivocality of meaning, evoke the strength of stakeholder emotions that came to the fore during this period, and reflect the sense of being under siege felt by executives of the focal firm. In reflecting diverse perspectives, the drama portrays contrasting legitimacy assessments of the firm's actions in exporting radioactive lightning rods. The setting for the drama is a TV studio. The guests are the Independent Member for Franklin of the Tasmanian Senate, an academic from the university in Tasmania, and the CEO of the firm in question. The date is 4 June 1986, little more than one month after the Chernobyl disaster. The drama opens as follows:

Reporter: First tonight the horrifying news that hazardous radioactive material has been shipped to Hobart and kept in storage in the heart of the city with no adequate precautions. What's all the fuss about? Well, it's over something called Americium. To discuss the issues, I'm joined now by Dr Gerry Waters, recently elected to the Tasmanian House of Assembly as a Green Independent Member for Franklin. Also with me is Dr John Turner, a lecturer in Physics at the University of Tasmania, and Dr Stephen Jones from [the Group] – the firm at the centre of this controversy. Gentlemen, thank you for joining us ... Dr Turner, if I can start with you. What is this 'Americium'?

Academic: It's a trans-uranic compound, which comes out of nuclear power stations. It's part of the waste from nuclear power stations. It's very similar in radioactive hazard to plutonium. It's one of the most dangerous radio chemicals known to man and micrograms – the tiniest microscopic particles of dust – could cause cancers.

Reporter: So it's waste from nuclear power stations. It's used in lightning conductors. Is it used in anything else?

In the first few paragraphs of the drama the characters are introduced, and basic information about the event is given. Fear is introduced from the outset of the drama by both the reporter ('first tonight the horrifying news') and the academic ('the tiniest microscopic particles of dust ... could cause cancers'). As the drama progresses, diverse perspectives are aired and countered by the participants, with the statements made by the guests – the politician, academic and the CEO – becoming more and more emotionally charged. The following statements, drawn from the closing stages of the drama, are illustrative of the diverse judgements made regarding the legitimacy of the firm's actions and strength of emotions. Embedded in the statements of the CEO is an array of legitimacy management behaviours (for example, justifications (Scott and Lyman [1968] 1990), factual distortion (Allen and Caillout 1994)) as he strives to establish the meaning of the event and actions.

> *Politician:* I've drawn it to [the Minister for Health's] attention. If the seal on any of these radioactive sources is broken, then they are potentially deadly to anyone exposed to them. Not surprisingly, the manufacture of such arrestors is banned in Switzerland, and their use within Australia, including Tasmania, is also banned. Yet they are being produced in Tasmania and exported to South East Asia, contrary to the recommendation of the Tasmanian Radiation Advisory Council in 1982 that exports should cease. If they are too dangerous to be used here in Australia, why are they safe enough to export to South East Asia? This attitude seems to me to be comparable to the dumping of dangerous pesticides banned in more enlightened Western countries on the unsuspecting third world.
>
> *CEO:* Hang on a minute. Most Asian countries have different perceptions of the relative risks of lightning and radiation. Most areas in Asia have intense lightning storms through the year and lightning induced death and damage is much higher than in Australia. It's not surprising that the governments of Asian countries assess the risks of lightning to be greater than the risks of radiation. I want to stress that [we have] not breached any regulations or statutory procedures. Even the Tasmanian Department of Health have declared that we have not broken any law.
>
> *Politician:* [... Further statements by the politician are omitted ...]
>
> *Reporter:* Dr Turner, one last comment?
>
> *Academic:* I'm very concerned that this has been allowed to go on for so long. I think they should have been banned years ago. I'm very concerned about the morality of exporting these things to South East Asia. I mean, they are in gold foil with no labels on them. People might souvenir them and even before the seals are broken they are dangerous. If you carry them around in your pocket for very long, you'd be seriously irradiated. Ethically it's incredible that we're not allowed to use them here yet we can send them off to South East Asia. I think we're getting our own back, frankly. Somebody perhaps over there is sending us a message.
>
> *Reporter:* Gentlemen, we'll have to leave it there. Gerry Waters, John Turner, Stephen Jones – thank you for joining us.

A radio transcript of an interview involving the politician and the academic, but not the CEO, provided the initial structure for the drama, and was embellished considerably. Discrete utterances woven into the drama ranged from a short turn of phrase to a lengthy paragraph embodying several ideas. Using the natural language and configuration of ideas used by the participants as much as possible enhanced the verisimilitude of the drama. The final drama is a collage of verbatim statements drawn from a variety of primary sources, including: transcripts of television and radio interviews; personal and official correspondence to, for example, the editor of the local newspaper, politicians, and each other; and press releases. Through these verbatim extracts, the role of authorship was in part shared with the characters in the drama. Importantly, the statements in the drama made directly by these three characters are drawn only from primary sources, and not from second-hand reports that quoted or paraphrased their actual words, with the exception of several bridging phrases attributed to the CEO (for example, 'Hang on a minute') to maintain local coherence in the drama as the views of the CEO were juxtaposed against those of the politician and academic. The CEO's script was a synthesis of statements made at the time by the CEO and the Group's Chairman. Where a concern took on particular prominence, repetition was used across characters, thereby enhancing thematic coherence. For example, the risk of cancer was a prominent concern, and the word 'cancer' is thus mentioned three times in the drama. This repetition across speakers implies a process of constructing – or at the very least re-presenting – a shared understanding between the politician and the academic. The drama also developed the themes of legitimation and organisational crises that had been introduced earlier in the narrative of internationalisation – including an earlier discussion of the initial decision to export radioactive lightning rods – thereby contributing to the global coherence of the overall narrative.

The reporter's script was constructed using different guidelines from those used for other characters. It comprises statements reported in a variety of media and by different authors (for example, newspaper reporters, government scientists), along with a number of statements designed to give the reader the necessary context, or to achieve local coherence between segments of the drama. Through the reporter it was possible to provide readers with the wider historical context, and to present concerns or statements reported 'second-hand' in the mass media. These statements were important to understanding the context and experience of the focal firm: news media are relatively entrenched, pervasive and influential elements of the broader environment (Weaver et al. 1999), and thus influenced public perception of the events and the legitimacy of the firm's actions. When first presented, references to the original and secondary sources of the statements were given in the drama to enhance its plausibility and trustworthiness in the eyes of the reader.

Apart from what was actually said, the construction of this drama also involved deliberate choices about the prominence of each voice. 'Prominence' is used here to refer to a character's position in the sequence of voices heard and the amount of 'air time' (measured here in terms of number of words uttered) it received. The entire drama was more than 1300 words in length. Forty-eight per cent of the words uttered were those of either the politician or the academic, both of whom were in opposition to the CEO. Utterances of the CEO account for only 18 per cent of all words, and he was not invited to speak until half way through the drama. Over 60 per cent of the utterances made by the reporter recounted criticisms made by the politician or fears in the broader community, and thus add to the voices of the politician and academic. This imbalance in the prominence of each voice was intended to evoke the feelings expressed by the Group's executives in correspondence at the time (that is, mid-1986), and in interviews a decade later. These included chagrin at the manner in which the politician had been able to 'obtain headlines in the media' without the company being notified or even contacted to 'check the facts', and a belief that the company had been subjected to 'exaggeration and emotional publicity' and 'unfairly singled out for attention', without being afforded the opportunity to adequately present their position. The *form* of the drama is thus intended to convey more than what is actually stated.

Method: A Tale from the Field

The use of more evocative and polyphonic representations need not be limited to research findings, but can also be useful in conveying aspects of the research process itself. A peculiarity of much IB research – and, indeed, much research in the social sciences in general – is a failure to acknowledge deviations, emotions, personal preferences, or any element of the research process that may make the researcher vulnerable to criticism or ridicule from the dominant community of scholars. In research underpinned by an objectivist epistemology and positivist theoretical perspective, research conclusions are treated as independent of those who are conducting the research and of the audience to whom the results are presented. In the interests of surviving the examination or journal review process, younger scholars are often advised to follow an approved 'methodological algorithm' (Polkinghorne 1997, p. 4), even to the extent of perpetuating a perception in the final research report or article that what was done was precisely what was planned (for example, Perry 1998). It is not my intention here to dissuade readers from following such advice, but to observe that this conventional format of reporting research methods is not designed to communicate a knowledge claim so much as to communicate its validity (Polkinghorne 1997). 'Hygenic research' in which problems do not arise and emotions are not involved is typically research as it is reported, rather than research as it is experienced (Paget 1995; Stanley and Wise 1983, p. 153). A danger of such an approach is that it masks the temporal character of the research endeavour (Lincoln 1997) and perpetuates a myth that 'good' research is never messy, should never openly challenge established views, and is value-free and emotionless. Bochner's (2000, p. 267) observations concerning ethnographers more generally are, I suspect, also relevant to scholars of IB:

> In our hearts, if not our minds, we know that the phenomena we study are messy, complicated, uncertain, and soft. Somewhere along the line we became convinced that these qualities were signs of inferiority, which we should not expose ... Traditionally we have worried much more about how we are judged as 'scientists' by other scientists than about whether our work is useful, insightful or meaningful – and to whom.

Polkinghorne (1997, p. 9) has, 'in the spirit of experimentation', suggested the use of a narrative research report to capture the temporal context of the research process. The narrative configures into a story of diverse events, actions, deliberations and choices that emerged as the research evolved. It takes into account the planned as well as the unplanned, and thus recognises the role of improvisations in the research process as the researcher strives to fulfil certain goals. In such reports, the researcher uses the voice of the story-teller, telling his/her own tale in the first person, rather than using the impersonal, passive voice. As with any story, not all events, actions, deliberations or choices will be included in the final story, but are selected according to their contribution to the progression of the plot – or, in the case of a research report, their contribution to the research findings. I adopted Polkinghorne's (1997) advice concerning the reporting of the research process in my study of SME internationalisation. Embedded within my narrative of the research process was a drama that could be likened to a confessional tale from the field (Van Maanen 1988). The tale was used to open a discussion of my approach to inquiry, and portions of it are reproduced below (McGaughey 2003, pp. 27–9):

> I took my seat opposite the CEO ... and once again admired the tranquil, almost opulent, vista of the Derwent River through his expansive window ... It was ten months since I had become involved with the company, and exciting times were afoot ... Discussions with Steve had always been interesting, even if they invariably left me feeling like a slow-witted sloth. But on this occasion, he seemed somewhat hesitant to begin. 'Sara, before we start, I wanted to ask you about your research ...'
>
> I was struck with horror. *Oh no*, I thought, *he's going to ask me what I've decided to focus on for my dissertation, and I'm still so unsure ... I knew this was going to happen sometime. I'm going to have to confess that I can't get a grip on things ... Where to start? So many choices. So much damn uncertainty – I hate uncertainty. This 'international standards' stuff keeps rearing its head, but gosh it's techy ... Ironic I chose a high-tech firm to study! Bloody hell – I should have*

nailed my core themes in the first month or two. Three at the most. He'll think I'm incompetent. Hmpf. He's probably right. 'Ah-ha?' I asked with an inquiring smile.

'Well, you've been doing a fair few interviews, talking to a lot of people – and I'm happy with that. There's no problem there. But how do you know that what someone says to you is true? How do you know that what you'll write in your thesis is accurate?'

Ahh. Is that all? 'Well … it's not really a case of just reporting what someone says. I mean, I go to some length to get a variety of views or perspectives on [the Group's] internationalisation, and try to weigh them up, so to speak, to work out what really happened. Then there's all that archival information that I'm using in my analysis to get a more accurate picture of how the firm has evolved.' *Does that answer your question?*

'Yes, but there's a lot of self-interest running at the moment, Sara … We're all pretty tense at the moment, and some people are expressing views they wouldn't normally – views that could damage [the Group] at this point in time. From my perspective, I need to know that you're getting the real picture, what's really going on, and not just one person's view.'

Stephen's concerns seemed quite reasonable to me, and I tried to reassure him. 'Hmmm … I can see your difficulty, Steve, but there are methods and criteria by which qualitative research is judged that help in overcoming such problems. For example … throughout the research process, we try to maximise what's called the validity and reliability of findings, minimising bias, trying to remain objective, documenting …' *This isn't what he wants to hear. I'm missing something. What have I missed?*

'As far as I can see, Sara, the easiest way to avoid these problems of inaccuracy is for me to listen to the taped interviews.'

What?! Like hell!! I was shocked. *OK, sometimes people 'download' on my tapes, but you've never questioned the privacy of my interviews before. Never. This doesn't make sense. There have always been divisions, tensions: marketing–production; old building–new building; personalities in friction. That's not new. So, where's this all coming from?* I collected my thoughts …

Following this climax, the tale continues for several more paragraphs before a resolution to the crisis is reached. In contrast to the drama presented earlier concerning the return of radioactive lightning rods exported from Australia, the above tale from the field was reconstructed from field notes some time after the event. There was no verbatim record of the interaction with Stephen. I thus found it far more difficult to capture a sense of natural speech and dramatic tension present. Speech is encased in quotation marks, and my stream-of-consciousness or real-time thoughts appear in italics (for example, *He'll think I'm incompetent. Hmpf. He's probably right.*). Otherwise, I use the voice of the story-teller reflecting on events (for example, Stephen's concerns seemed quite reasonable to me). Although the narrative has two main characters, it is a highly personal tale in which authorship was not shared with the CEO, although he read the final version.

The above drama is intended to convey a number of aspects about the research process including: some of the challenges of maintaining access; the uncertainty, confusion, and even anxiety I faced in the field; my self-directed annoyance at being unable to 'perform'; and my personal bias against pursuing the persistently important issues surrounding technology standards. It is also deliberately open to further interpretations. The primary reason, however, why I chose to position this tale up front as the introduction to a discussion disclosing the beliefs and assumptions that informed my research, rather than tucked away as an embarrassing episode or even left out entirely, was to demonstrate my own implicit, unquestioned theoretical perspectives and epistemic beliefs.

Accuracy. Validity. Reliability. Objectivity. This is the language I used in trying to describe to the CEO the criteria by which my research would be judged in my attempt to reassure him that I would endeavour to report what had 'really happened'. It was a language shared with the CEO, a previous Rhodes scholar with a PhD in engineering. It is a language informed by a thoroughly objectivist epistemology; the language and associated philosophy with which I was familiar (see, for example, McGaughey et al. 1997). In the course of this study, my implicit beliefs were challenged in a way previous research had not done, with significant implications for the conduct of the inquiry and the nature of possible contributions. In the narrative of research method, this tale from the field served as a temporal anchor for the reader, identifying how the research was initially conceptualised and conducted. The subsequent research narrative described how my approach to inquiry then evolved. The tale also afforded me the opportunity to laugh at myself, to share my folly and amusement with others, and to be a basis for reflection.

ETHICS OF REPRESENTING 'THE OTHER'

The conduct of fieldwork, and the subsequent representations, are filled with moral decisions. Scholars of IB are not the only audience of our research representations. Apart from possible interest from practitioners, policy makers, students and other scholars, those who have participated in the study may also take a keen interest in what is written – either now or in the future. The representations we make of others may not only have commercial implications, but can also affect the sense of self that is held by those portrayed. It is at times an inadequate defence for scholars to claim that participants in the study will never read the work, and thus will not be harmed. Participants themselves may also believe this. Once an idea or representation is in print, however, it has an enduring quality. It can be revisited. It can be discovered for the first time years hence. It can be readily passed to others in the organisation, broader networks, and around the globe. When in print – particularly where direct quotes and identifying information is used – deniability becomes more difficult for participants. Disguising individuals and firms is often proposed as a means by which these ethical dilemmas can be largely overcome. Depending on the nature of the study, however, substantive anonymity may only be possible if the study is stripped of virtually all context. In doing so, we risk that the study will become meaningless. Achieving balance between the pursuit of meaningful scholarship and respecting the needs of 'the other' can be challenging.

In the study of SME internationalisation, a number of factors impeded any substantive anonymity, including an emphasis on the Group's patented technology, the nature of the industry, and the position of the Group within it. I thus sought the informed consent of participants in the study concerning representations of the research outcomes. Informed consent refers to the voluntary agreement of an individual or group, based on sufficient knowledge and understanding of all relevant information, to participate in the research. Although I had secured consent at the commencement of the research, the study had evolved sufficiently that I felt it unlikely that participants had anticipated how I might report my findings. After all, I had not! What impact would what I had written have on the companies and individuals portrayed? Had I betrayed their trust?

I began the process by seeking informed consent for a cartoon I had crafted to depict the initial outward internationalisation of the Group. The story depicted in the cartoon drew on an account of events first given to me by 'Dennis'. This account was also told by others in the organisation, and supported by substantial amounts of archival data. In crafting the cartoon, I intended to share authorship with the main character in the story. Indeed, I believed I was honouring Dennis's account, and capturing the essence of his recollections of the early years.

The cartoon and a short explanation were faxed to Dennis, and I awaited his reply. It was not favourable. Libel and lawyers were mentioned. I was devastated. I was certain that nothing I had portrayed was libellous, but was disturbed that I could have so insulted a participant in the study and misjudged his likely reaction. I consulted the chairman of the company, who initially proposed changes to the cartoon that impinged on elements that were central to the interpretations of the events. I thus provided the chairman with the full context of the cartoon, including its purpose in the overall narrative of internationalisation and a description of the discussion that followed the cartoon. With the context and meaning of the cartoon now apparent, the chairman accepted its form and content with only a minor alteration that was peripheral to the meaning I sought to convey. I soon came to realise that my mistake with Dennis had less to do with what I had crafted than with how I had sought informed consent: I did not send the cartoon *in context*. The full context had been withheld only because I did not think Dennis would be interested in my academic prose, and feared irritating or boring a busy, senior executive with my interpretations of events. It is ironic that I made these assumptions given the emphasis that qualitative researchers place on context when seeking to convey meaning. In the final reviewing of the cartoon – presented in context – informed consent was granted by Dennis, and an invitation to visit his new start-up extended.

The point is that we cannot always anticipate how our work may be used or how others may react to it. In subsequent rounds of seeking of informed consent for representations, I provided respondents not only with the directly relevant section of the overall narrative but also, where possible, with the surrounding context. Embedded in the prose were references to sources of my information to give my interpretations added authority. I extended this process to include individuals who were not, strictly speaking, participants, but who were named in the study by virtue of prior or current associations with the Group. In the newsroom drama above, for example, the politician and academic were not initially interviewed. Each was thus provided with the full drama, an additional 15 pages of associated text, and a description of how the research might be used in the future. As contentious as the drama is, in the ensuing discussions the academic asked only that I mention in a footnote that an interview with all three characters in one room had not taken place. The politician only noted that 'senator' should be replaced by the abbreviation 'MP' in one place of the associated text. Otherwise, informed consent was granted.

Qualitative researchers must, of course, be wary of having their studies held 'hostage' to the whims of participants or even non-participants. Only one non-participant of those contacted threatened me in writing with an injunction and defamation proceedings if I made *any* mention of certain events that occurred more than a decade ago. It was, apparently, not negotiable. The incident was pivotal to my study. I thus addressed this threat by limiting reference to this individual to only those elements essential to my study, and reporting only public domain information. I also suppressed his name and current activities as these were unimportant to my study. Perhaps even more difficult to manage are instances where respondents who have been supportive of the research process – through, for example, access or funding – wish to impress their version of events. The process of informed consent of representations can generate a wealth of potentially valuable new data, but carries with it a host of issues about how this new data should be treated.

The management of the informed consent process involves not only negotiations with those 'in the field', but also other scholars. In my experience in Australia, not all academics administering advice (at the departmental level) on the ethical conduct of research are able to conceive the particular challenges surrounding how richly contextualised qualitative research is written up. Added to this, the codes governing the conduct of ethical research in the social sciences in Australia have historically been based on those derived from the medical sciences or survey-based research, and are not always easy to translate across to qualitative studies. Even where tendencies in particular countries are less litigious, or where the laws of defamation and free speech better protect scholarly research, the ethical concern for how others are represented is *not* diminished. Interestingly, even senior scholars generally supportive of my approach to representations sought to impose rules of silence and taboo when I chose to *in writing* make mention of the threat of legal proceedings I had received from one non-participant. These issues clearly need to be discussed, rather than swept under the carpet. They also need to be kept in perspective. Despite my cautionary comments, the process of seeking informed consent for representations revealed that most participants actually *wanted* to have the story told with them *named* in it, even when opposing views were also expressed.

CONCLUDING REMARKS

The central concern of this chapter has been the means by which we represent both research findings and the research process. These representations are influenced not only by the role context plays in establishing meaning – a role that is particularly prominent in much qualitative research – but also the philosophical basis of one's approach to inquiry. These beliefs may, at times, be only implicitly held and unquestioned as we adhere to 'taken for granted' conventions. A constructionist epistemology, however, invites continuing reflection about our research representations. Yet constructionism does not choose a victor between competing approaches: all conventions are constructions. Because knowledge systems are dependent upon shared intelligibility, research activity will continue to be governed by normative rules (Gergen 1985). The process of hiring, tenure and promotion that exists in many business schools – with publication in discipline-based journals and statistical analyses being prized – reinforces the status quo, positivist methodologies (Paquet 1998; Rumelt et al. 1991) and, as a consequence, 'scientific' representations of findings and process. Even the structure of this chapter, written for a particular audience, purposely follows some well-established conventions. This chapter should not, then, be seen as a call for radical experimentation at one's own peril. Rather, it is an appeal for all of us to engage in considered deliberation about how we choose to represent our research findings and practices, and to what ends. The norms governing representations in IB scholarship will, inevitably, be shaped by the choices we make.

ACKNOWLEDGEMENTS

I am grateful to Catherine Welch and Rebecca Marschan-Piekkari for helpful comments on an earlier draft of this chapter.

NOTES

1. Not all approaches to narrative understanding are underpinned by an interpretive theoretical perspective.
2. The notion of orthodoxy is, of course, a relative one. My own representations are limited to pen and paper, and have not yet extended to the live performance of poems, scripts, narratives or dramas. For a brief overview of performance texts, see Denzin (1996).

REFERENCES

Abbot, A. (1994), 'History and sociology: the lost synthesis', in E.H. Monkkonen (ed.), *The Uses of History Across the Social Sciences*, Durham, NC and London: Duke University Press, pp. 77–112.

Adler, P.A. and P. Adler (1994), 'Observational techniques', in N.K. Denzin and Y.S. Lincoln (eds), *Handbook of Qualitative Research*, Thousand Oaks, CA: Sage, pp. 377–92.

Agar, M. and J.R. Hobbs (1982), 'Interpreting discourse: coherence and the analysis of ethnographic interviews', *Discourse Processes*, **5**, 1–32.

Allen, M.W. and R.H. Caillout (1994), 'Legitimacy endeavours: impression management strategies used by an organisation in crisis', *Communication Monographs*, **61** (March), 44–62.

Alvesson, M. and K. Skölberg (2000), *Reflexive Methodology: New Vistas for Qualitative Research*, Thousand Oaks, CA: Sage.

Anderson, K. and D.C. Jack (1991), 'Learning to listen: interview techniques and analysis', in S. Gluck Berger and D. Patai (eds), *Women's Words: The Feminist Practice of Oral History*, New York: Routledge, pp. 11–26.

Atkinson, P. (1990), *The Ethnographic Imagination: Textual Constructions of Reality*, London and New York: Routledge.

Atkinson, R.F. (1978), *Knowledge and Explanation in History: An Introduction to the Philosophy of History*, London: Macmillan.

Bate, S.P. (1997), 'Whatever happened to organizational anthropology? A review of the field of organizational ethnography and anthropological studies', *Human Relations*, **50** (9), 1147–75.

Bateson, G. (1978), 'The pattern which connects', *Coevolution Quarterly*, **18** (Summer), 5–15.

Bochner, A.P. (2000), 'Criteria against ourselves', *Qualitative Inquiry*, **6** (2), 266–72.

Brissett, D. and C. Edgley (1990), 'The dramaturgical perspective', in D. Brissett and C. Edgley (eds), *Life as Theatre*, 2nd edn, New York: Addine de Gruyter, pp. 1–46.

Bruner, J. (1986), *Actual Minds, Possible Worlds*, Cambridge, MA: Harvard University Press.

―――― (1996), *The Culture of Education*, Cambridge, MA: Harvard University Press.

Buckley, P.J. and M. Chapman (1997), 'The perception and measurement of transaction costs', *Cambridge Journal of Economics*, **21**, 127–45.

Clandinin, D.J. and F.M. Connelly (2000), *Narrative Enquiry: Experience and Story in Qualitative Research*, San Francisco, CA: Jossey-Bass.

Crotty, M. (1998), *The Foundations of Social Research: Meaning and Perspective in the Research Process*, St Leonards, Australia: Allen & Unwin.

Czarniawska, B. (1997), *Narrating the Organization: Dramas of Institutional Identity*, Chicago and London: University of Chicago Press.

Denzin, N.K. (1996), *Interpretive Ethnography: Ethnographic Practices for the 21st Century*, Thousand Oaks, CA: Sage.

Ely, M., R. Vinz, M. Downing and M. Anzul (1997), *On Writing Qualitative Research: Living by Words*, London: Routledge Flamer.

Geertz, C. (1973), *The Interpretation of Cultures*, New York: Basic Books.

Gergen, K.J. (1985), 'The social constructionist movement in modern psychology', *American Psychologist*, **40** (3), 266–75.

―――― (1999), *An Invitation to Social Construction*, London: Sage.

Gutkind, L. (1997), *The Art of Creative Non-Fiction*, New York: John Wiley & Sons.

Hammersley, M. (1992), *What's Wrong with Ethnography? Methodological Explorations*, London: Routledge.

Hodder, I. (1994), 'The interpretation of documents and material culture', in N.K. Denzin and Y.S. Lincoln (eds), *Handbook of Qualitative Research*, Thousand Oaks, CA: Sage, pp. 393–402.

Jeffcut, P. (1994), 'The interpretation of organisation: a contemporary analysis and critique', *Journal of Management Studies*, **31** (2), 225–50.

Lather, P. (1986), 'Issues of validity in openly ideological research', *Interchange*, **17** (4), 63–84.

Lincoln, Y.S. (1997), 'Self, subject, audience, text', in W.G. Tierney and Y.S. Lincoln (eds), *Representation and the Text: Reframing the Narrative Voice*, Albany, NY: State University of New York Press, pp. 37–55.

Martin, J. (1995), 'The style and structure of cultures in organizations: three perspectives', *Organization Science*, **6**, 230–32.

McGaughey, S.L. (2003), 'New descriptions and understandings of internationalisation: a tale of knowledge-intensive SMEs', PhD thesis, University of Queensland, Brisbane.

McGaughey, S.L., R.D. Iverson and H. DeCieri (1997), 'A multi-method analysis of work-related preferences in three nations: implications for inter- and intra-national human resource management', *International Journal of Human Resource Management*, **8** (1), 1–17.

Mercury, The (1996), 'Firm's expertise sparks worldwide interest', 16 February, p. 79.

Morgan, G., P.J. Frost and L.R. Pondy (1983), 'Implications for management theory', in L.R. Pondy, P.J. Frost, G. Morgan and T.C. Dandridge (eds), *Organizational Symbolism*, Greenwich, CT: JAI Press, pp. 3–35.

Paget, M.A. (1995), 'Narrative and sociology', in J. Van Maanen (ed.), *Representation in Ethnography*, Thousand Oaks, CA: Sage, pp. 222–44.

Paquet, G. (1998), 'Evolutionary cognitive economics', *Information Economics and Policy*, **10** (3), 343–57.

Pearson, C.M. and J.A. Clair (1998), 'Reframing crisis management', *Academy of Management Review*, **23** (1), 59–76.

Perry, C. (1998), 'A structured approach for presenting theses: notes for students and their supervisors', www.scu.edu.au/schools/gcm/ar/art/cperry.html, 28 May.

Polkinghorne, D.E. (1997), 'Reporting qualitative research as practice', in W.G. Tierney and Y.S. Lincoln (eds), *Representation and the Text: Reframing the Narrative Voice*, Albany, NY: State University of New York Press, pp. 3–21.

―――― (1988), *Narrative Knowing and the Human Sciences*, Albany, NY: State University of New York Press.

Redding, S.G. (1997), 'The comparative management theory zoo: getting the elephants and ostriches and even dinosaurs from the jungle into the iron cages', in B. Toyne and D. Nigh (eds), *International Business. An Emerging Vision*, Columbia, SC: University of South Carolina Press, pp. 416–39.

Richardson, L. (1993), 'Poetics, dramatics, and transgressive validity: the case of the skipped line', *Sociological Quarterly*, **34** (3), 695–710.

―――― (1995), 'Narrative and sociology', in J. Van Maanen (ed.), *Representation in Ethnography*, Thousand Oaks, CA: Sage, pp. 198–221.

Ricoeur, P. (1984), *Time and Narrative*, Chicago, IL and London: University of Chicago Press.

Riessman, C.K. (1993), *Narrative Analysis*, Thousand Oaks, CA: Sage.

Robinson, J.A. (1981), 'Personal narratives reconsidered', *Journal of American Folklore*, **94**, 58–85.

Rumelt, R.P., D. Schendel and D.J. Teece (1991), 'Strategic management and economics', *Strategic Management Journal*, **12** (special issue, Winter), 5–29.

Ryle, G. (1968), 'The thinking of thoughts: what is "*le Penseur*" doing?', *University Lectures*, (no. 18), Canada: University of Saskatchewan.

Scott, M.B. and S. Lyman ([1968] 1990), 'Accounts', in D. Brisset and C. Edgley (eds), *Life as Theatre*, 2nd edn, New York: Addine de Gruyter, pp. 219–42.

Silverman, D. (1993), *Interpreting Qualitative Data: Methods for Analyzing Talk, Text and Interaction*, Thousand Oaks, CA: Sage.

Stanley, L. and S. Wise (1983), *Breaking Out: Feminist Consciousness and Feminist Research*, London: Routledge & Kegan Paul.

Van Maanen, J. (1988), *Tales of the Field. On Writing Ethnography*, Chicago, IL and London: University of Chicago Press.

―――― (1995), 'An end to innocence: the ethnography of ethnography', in J. Van Maanen (ed.), *Representation in Ethnography*, Thousand Oaks, CA: Sage, pp. 1–35.

Weaver, G.R., T.L. Klebe and P.L. Cochran (1999), 'Integrated and decoupled corporate social performance: management commitments, external pressures, and corporate ethics practices', *Academy of Management Journal*, **42** (5), 539–52.

Weick, K.E. (1995), *Sensemaking in Organizations*, Thousand Oaks, CA: Sage.

Wexler, M.N. (1983), 'Pragmatism, interactionism and dramatism: interpreting the symbol in organisations', in L.R. Pondy, P.J. Frost, G. Morgan and T.C. Dandridge (eds), *Organizational Symbolism*, Greenwich, CT: JAI Press, pp. 237–53.

Wolcott, H.F. (1999), *Ethnography: A Way of Seeing*, Walnut Creek, CA: AltaMira Press.

Wood, M. (1995), *Description: Elements of Fiction Writing*, Cincinnati, OH: Writer's

Digest Books.

Yordon, J.E. (1997), *Experimental Theatre: Creating and Staging Texts*, Prospect Heights, IL: Waveland Press.

27. Getting Published: The Last Great Hurdle?

Denice E. Welch and Lawrence S. Welch

INTRODUCTION

The care and thoroughness, the uniqueness, innovativeness and even brilliance of research will mean little if it is never published. One of the primary aims of research is to contribute to the development of knowledge in one's field and for this to happen, others need to be informed. Moreover, for those in the academic profession, research output is part of the job description, and promotion and/or tenure of appointment depends on a demonstrable track record of research publications. While there are many ways of broadcasting one's research – conferences, staff seminars and the like – the journal article remains the major means of scientific communication and is therefore the main focus of this chapter. Books and book chapters are other important avenues and some of the comments about publications in journals apply equally to the process pertaining to books, given that often there is a similar review exercise involved.

Getting published is becoming harder. With the increasing numbers of academics entering the field of international business (IB), getting one's work published in reputable journals has become a highly competitive process placing additional stress on all involved in the process. It is not just the sheer number of manuscripts being submitted to IB and related journals. As we discuss later, there is pressure on researchers attempting to gain acceptance in journals to conform to what is perceived to be the most appropriate format, in terms of research methodology, article structure and writing style. This peer pressure is even more of an issue for those taking an idiographic approach, given the prejudice against qualitative methods often encountered in the journal review process.

The review process is subjective and, as a result, often flawed, despite the good intentions of journal editors, editorial board members and the array of conscientious reviewers involved. This is perhaps illustrated by Gans and Shepherd (1994, p. 166), who surveyed 140 leading economists to gauge their publication experience. Based on a 60 per cent response rate, they concluded:

'our survey demonstrates that many papers that have become classics were rejected initially by at least one journal – and often by more than one'. They note that some prominent economists have focused on books as outlets rather than enduring the tortuous journal publication route.

As an indication of the difficulties of getting published, in an earlier study, Peters and Ceci (1982) sent out disguised but already published articles and found that reviewers recommended rejection of these articles (cited in Beyer et al. 1995). The blind review is an attempt to mitigate bias by not revealing the author's name (or names) so that reviewers are not influenced by factors such as standing in the field, or lack thereof. However, there are other elements to bias. As Patton (1990, p. 38) reminds us: 'Routine ways of thinking and paradigmatic blinders constrain flexibility and creativity by locking researchers into unconscious patterns of perception and behavior that disguise the biased, predetermined nature of their methods "decisions"'. Schooled in a particular methods tradition, many reviewers seem unable to appreciate an alternative approach and will recommend non-publication of a manuscript that does not conform to their perception of what constitutes proper research. Prejudice is not only a major barrier to the advancement of scientific knowledge, but using the review process in such a manner is a form of hegemony – though those engaging in such practice would not necessarily regard their behaviour in that light. Rather, they would see it as a legitimate means of preserving scientific standards. However, as Cummings and Frost (1995, p. 7) point out: 'most journals reward caution and punish risk taking, making it likely that editorial decisions are conservative. As a result, journals yield products that are standardized and predictable'.

This chapter, then, deals with what is perhaps the most difficult stage in the research process – that of getting research results published in reputable international periodicals and books. Some knowledge of the dynamics of the review process may assist in handling what can be a frustrating exercise. The following sections discuss the roles of journal editors and reviewers and key aspects of the blind peer review process. In so doing, we use examples not only from our own experiences, but that of colleagues who have kindly forwarded us correspondence pertaining to their encounters with editors and reviewers. Further, we draw on the results of a simple content analysis of three major IB journals to illustrate disparity between espoused editorial policy and actual publication practice, and discuss the impact this may have on idiographic researchers' ability to achieve article publication in leading journals in their field. We then suggest some approaches and strategies to handle the publication process.

THE PATH TO PUBLICATION

The starting point to journal publication is, of course, submission of a manuscript to the editor of the target journal. Editorial judgement of the article's potential suitability is then exercised: by the editor alone, or in consultation with members of the editorial board and assistant editors. If the manuscript passes this initial hurdle, it becomes part of the review process. The path to publication sometimes may be smooth, where the manuscript is accepted with little or no modification. But for most, getting even the most carefully crafted article through the review process can be difficult. It is not uncommon for an article to undergo at least two revisions before it is accepted for publication. Revising an article on the basis of reviewers' comments does not necessarily guarantee publication.

Why is the process becoming so difficult? In order to shed light on the process, we shall begin with the negative: why a manuscript is rejected.

Journal Ranking and the Rejection Rate

The burgeoning community of global scholars is generating copious articles, with numerous hopeful authors targeting publication in highly ranked journals. The volume of submissions generates a competitive environment that of itself necessarily results in a high rejection rate, as there are more articles than journal outlets. The level of competition is linked to the standing or ranking given to the various journals. It is considered highly desirable to have one's work published in a prestigious international journal and determining journal rankings becomes an important part of the publication 'game' (see DuBois and Reeb 2000 as an example of articles relating to journal ranking).

The rejection rate of submitted articles is often used as a criterion for ranking journals – that is, the higher the rejection rate, the better the journal. Given this link, it is not surprising to find a vested interest by parties to the review process to ensure a high rejection rate. Editors presiding over 'quality' journals will be more than keen to protect their journals' standings, and overtly encourage a high rejection rate in the instructions given to journal reviewers. Likewise, editors of new journals eager to establish a claim to 'quality' can similarly instruct reviewers to be mindful of the need to maintain quality through the rejection rate. Some journals include rejection rates in the information presented on their Web pages.

Further, the highly competitive publication environment is compounded by an increasing trend for publicly-funded universities in many countries is to have research funding linked to output indices, such as the number of articles published in international journals. Such an environment naturally encourages a greater volume of submissions to journals, fuelled by the additional link between career advancement and the number of journal publications (the 'publish or perish' mantra). There may be also an element of self-comparison involved. An author who has been subjected to the drawn-out, even tortuous, review process that tends to be associated with publication in a high-ranking journal may become a zealous reviewer only too happy to act in the role of preserver of the journal's standing.

The Role of the Editor

Editors are pivotal actors in the publication process. They decide on a manuscript's suitability for the journal. They shape the list of reviewers and make the final decision regarding publication. From our experience, editors can be separated into two groups: those that are hands-on and those who are non-interventionist. The hands-on editor tends to play an active role throughout the review process. They will step in and provide guidance for those confronting conflicting reviewers' comments. Such editors can direct authors to the weighting that should be placed on certain reviewers' comments, and may even override a reviewer's opinion if it is deemed inappropriate or even unhelpful. In other words, they exercise editorial judgement. 'Non-interventionists' on the other hand are more passive, even when it is obvious that reviewers' comments are conflicting or inappropriate. The consensus of the reviewers prevails. One can often be left with the impression that the editor's attitude is: 'my reviewers right or wrong'.

One would expect editors to adhere to the stated editorial policy of their own journal, but this is not always the case. Take one of the leading journals, the *Journal of International Business Studies*. Its stated editorial policy reads: 'As a methodologically pluralistic journal, *JIBS* welcomes conceptual and theory-development papers, empirical hypothesis-testing papers, mathematical modelling papers, case studies and review articles'. However, a review of the journal's published articles over a decade (see Table 27.1 below) found a definite bias against qualitative-based articles. In one case, an article submitted to *JIBS* was rejected primarily on the basis of its lack of positivistic methodology. The author appealed to the editor, drawing his attention to the anti-qualitative comments made by the reviewers. The editor's response was to reiterate that *JIBS* accepted manuscripts using qualitative methodologies and did not 'wish to give you or anyone else the impression that it does not'. He added: 'It does appear as if some of the statements made regarding your paper were unduly harsh. Therefore I will take into consideration your suggestions and try to be as careful as possible to ensure fairness to all methodologies, and a proper mix of reviewers to fairly match the paper'. There was no mention of reviewers acting against editorial policy nor a suggestion that the paper could be sent to more appropriate reviewers. The article was published later in the more pluralistic *Journal of Management*

Studies.

A recent trend at some journals is for editors to ask authors to suggest the names of potential reviewers. While this might be seen as a counter to the above problem, it remains the prerogative of the editor to select reviewers. Editors also are responsible for designing the form sent to reviewers as a guide to assessing the suitability of the manuscript. It is instructive to see how many of these forms reflect a positivistic, hypothesis-testing bias.

Reviewers: Friends or Foes?

The blind, peer review process relies on editors being able to draw upon a body of suitable reviewers. One would assume that as international business blossoms as a field of scientific inquiry the pool of potential qualified reviewers would have increased. While this is perhaps true in terms of availability, locating suitable reviewers is another issue. By its nature, IB is a broad discipline, with researchers from many different backgrounds – economics, marketing, finance, psychology, organisational behaviour and so on – with different perspectives on the research process. In the extreme case, an economist might be called upon to review an article submitted by an anthropologist. While most editors endeavour to avoid this, examples abound of mismatches and their consequences in terms of publication. Apart from academic discipline, reviewers differ in their view of, and approach to, research and this frame of reference constrains how they react to various manuscripts. Few reviewers are competent to judge all types of data analysis techniques. Reviewers will also have differing views on the role of the reviewer. For example, they may regard their role as a coach providing constructive comments, or as a critic whose role is to point to the deficiencies and weaknesses of a manuscript, or both (Beyer et al. 1995).

Increasingly, for academics, review work is an addition to an already heavy workload. Also, the same individual may be asked to comment on a number of articles at the same time. Consequently, review work may be accorded a lower priority, manuscripts not given as careful a scrutiny as reviewers may like given time constraints, or the return of the reviewed manuscript is delayed. Reviewers may simply return the manuscript, declining to act as a reviewer, which forces the editor to find a substitute, adding to the length of time involved in the process, as well as increasing the risk of non-suitability, depending on the size and composition of the pool of potential reviewers that the editor may call upon. Who reviews what manuscript can become a game of chance.

Research that not only takes a different methodological approach but also crosses disciplinary boundaries faces additional difficulties. This is particularly so for research that concerns a specialised topic or functional area that draws on a spread of disciplines and a wide body of supporting literature.

It is difficult for editors to find reviewers who are competent in a wide range of disciplines within international business, and therefore equipped and confident to review such papers. Authors of such papers often end up with divergent reviews and are faced with a major challenge to revise in a way that enables successful reconciliation of disparate, and sometimes conflicting, comments and expectations. This is despite the call that is made frequently for more papers to reflect the multi-disciplinary character of IB issues.

A final comment on the review process is that of the difficulties of writers from non-English-speaking countries. English has become the language of IB journals. Academics from a non-English-speaking background are often in the somewhat invidious position of encountering English-as-a-mother tongue reviewers who have little understanding of what is involved in writing in a second language. Some reviewers can be highly intolerant of what they perceive as sloppy English, and reject an article on the grounds of it being 'poorly written' (Beyer et al. 1995). It pays to have a manuscript checked by a competent English speaker before submission to avoid this fate.

Stated versus Actual Editorial Policy

For idiographic researchers, reviewer bias is of particular concern despite protestations or claims from editors that they seek contributions from the full range of research methods. To support this contention, we conducted a simple content analysis of three of the major IB-dedicated journals. We chose first the *Journal of International Business Studies* (*JIBS*). *JIBS* is considered a high-ranked journal in the field, its influence in part due to its role as the organ of the Academy of International Business and journal subscription is a membership side-benefit. The *Management International Review* (*MIR*) journal was an obvious choice given its status as the oldest IB journal (in its 42nd year). It is a European-based journal. The third journal – *International Business Review* (*IBR*) – is a comparatively new journal, founded in 1992 as the *Scandinavian Journal of International Business*, but underwent a name change the following year. Also based in Europe, *IBR* recently became the organ of the European International Business Academy, reflecting its growing influence and standing in the field. All three journals share a common stated editorial policy of accepting an eclectic range of articles from the various streams of IB research.

We took a ten-year timeframe (eight years for *IBR*) – the last decade of the last century – to see if these journals adhered to their editorial policy, and whether there was some truth to a growing perception of IB researchers of a strong bias towards quantitative, hypothesis-testing articles. Articles submitted for normal consideration only were included as our purpose was to try and identify possible reviewer bias. Special issues and symposia, invited papers, research comments and rejoinder papers were omitted. We divided articles into three categories: empirical-based quantitative – those using survey or interview data analysed using statistical packages; empirical-based qualitative – theory-building and theory-testing approaches based on qualitative data; and conceptual articles – including literature reviews, conceptual frameworks, mapping and economic/financial modelling. The results are presented in Tables 27.1, 27.2 and 27.3. When considering the tables, one should bear in mind that we have no data regarding the rejection rates of articles of each persuasion – we can only present the outcomes of the review processes of the three selected journals.

Turning firstly to *JIBS*, the editorship changed twice during the ten-year period, indicated in Table 27.1 by the # symbol. However, this does not appear to have affected the seemingly consistent heavy bias towards quantitative articles (83.2 per cent) at the expense of conceptual (13.8 per cent) and qualitative papers (3 per cent). Of the eight qualitative papers identified over the ten-year period, only two articles could be described as purely qualitative, using idiographic techniques for data collection and analysis. The remainder, though based on qualitative data, used quantitative analysis techniques – for example, data quantified for hypothesis testing and, in one instance, a combination of cases with a simulation model.

Table 27.1   Analysis of articles published in JIBS, *1990–1999*

Year	Quantitative	Qualitative	Conceptual	Total
1990	27	1	1	29
1991	24	0	5	29
1992	23	1	6	30
1993 #	23	1	4	28
1994	15	1	4	20
1995	25	1	4	30
1996	22	1	4	27
1997	28	1	1	30
1998 #	17	0	3	20
1999	19	1	5	25
Total	223	8	37	268
	(83.2%)	(3%)	(13.8%)	

Table 27.2 shows a similar bias towards quantitative articles (75.6 per cent of the total) in *MIR* over the 1990s, although somewhat less pronounced than for *JIBS*. Likewise, very few qualitative-based articles were published (5 per cent). The main difference between *MIR* and *JIBS* is in the greater inclusion of conceptual articles (19.4 per cent compared with 13.8 per cent). The qualitative articles were single and multiple case studies using qualitative data

analysis. The *MIR* editorship remained unchanged during the decade.

Table 27.2   Analysis of articles published in MIR, *1990–1999*

Year	Quantitative	Qualitative	Conceptual	Total
1990	18	0	5	23
1991	14	0	5	19
1992	18	0	3	21
1993	13	1	4	18
1994	11	1	2	14
1995	13	2	2	17
1996	14	2	1	17
1997	11	1	5	17
1998	14	1	3	18
1999	10	1	5	16
Total	136	9	35	180
	(75.6%)	(5%)	(19.4%)	

There is a somewhat more balanced distribution in *IBR* compared to the other two journals. However, as Table 27.3 shows, as the journal grew in size, with the number of issues per year increasing from three to six, as well as growing in standing within the academic community, there has been a drift towards quantitative papers (37.5 per cent in the first year, compared to 68.1 per cent in 1999). Overall, quantitative papers represented 65.1 per cent of the total number of papers published, compared to 9.6 per cent qualitative, and 25.3 per cent conceptual. The year 1998 is somewhat of an aberration in that all articles were of a quantitative nature. The qualitative papers were predominantly case studies (single and multiple). One used the critical incident technique for data collection. Another study quantified the qualitative data for statistical testing. The founding editor remained at the helm throughout the eight years investigated.

So, what can we deduce from the three tables? The figures suggest that the two European-based journals appear to be more sympathetic towards qualitative and conceptual papers, but the preponderance of positivist, quantitative methods articles is noticeable across the three journals. Of course, the bias may just reflect the number of quantitative articles submitted for review, compared with those following a qualitative approach, which, in turn, may reflect the general research environment. Young scholars are being advised against taking a qualitative methods approach, or at least to use a combination of qualitative and quantitative methods, if they want their work published in leading, prestigious international journals. Another explanation may be that researchers trained in a positivistic scholastic atmosphere are dominant in international business and therefore more articles taking a positivist approach are accepted relative to those taking an idiographic approach. Reviewers' perceptions about journal policy, based on practice rather than stated editorial policy, reinforce the bias leading to an entrenched view.

Table 27.3   Analysis of articles published in IBR, *1992–1999*

Year	Quantitative	Qualitative	Conceptual	Total
1992	6	2	8	16
1993	5	2	6	13
1994	11	1	6	18
1995	10	1	9	20
1996	19	3	5	27
1997	23	3	5	27
1998	19	0	0	19
1999	15	4	3	22
Total	108	16	42	166
	(65.1%)	(9.6%)	(25.3%)	

The reviewer's frame of reference is a major issue. Even where the journal is sympathetic to qualitative methodology, there is often confusion in the minds of reviewers about what constitutes good qualitative research. For example, grounded exploratory research may produce unanticipated but important findings. This is the world of exploratory research. Yet, some reviewers regard this as sloppy research because the findings are not derived from clear, a priori research questions. The trained qualitative researcher can see that this is an illogical position to take, as one cannot – indeed, should not – frame questions that seek to anticipate the unanticipated. However, a reviewer trained in the hypo-deductive, positivistic school may find it difficult to conceive of research findings that are not systematically linked to propositions or hypotheses. Unfortunately, we have encountered cases where researchers with little or no experience of qualitative methods have been approached to act as a reviewer of qualitative papers and, instead of declining, appear to relish the opportunity to reject the paper on the grounds of its methodological approach. Of course, this methods bias is not declared but often can be identified in the way the reasons for the rejection of the article are couched. A colleague forwarded the following comment to us as an example. The paper dealt with the conduct and results of an exploratory case study. The reviewer concludes with: 'My recommendation to the author would be to start by constructing a typology ... then by using existing theory hypothesising on most likely explanations and present empirical results'.

Another example comes from the review of an article submitted to *JIBS*. One reviewer commented:

> The case study part [of the paper] could go to *Human Resource Management* for review since they are comfortable with case studies [by implication, *JIBS* is not]. If the conceptual framework part of the study is to be published as a separate piece, it needs more reworking before submitting it to a journal like the *Academy of Management Review*. You need to state specific propositions ... The best article, of course, would be to present and test fully the model with a large enough sample of firms that vary on both your independent and dependent measures. That kind of article could be submitted to *JIBS*.

No action was taken by the editor in the light of the clearly espoused methods bias. The paper later appeared in the *Journal of Management Studies*.

The bias against non-quantitative articles is often extended to conceptual work, as the following instances highlight:

> This paper deals with a good topic, but is too descriptive and conceptual. The author should include some data and analysis before it can be considered for publication in an academic journal. (*JIBS* reviewer. This paper was published by *MIR*)

> As *JIBS* does not publish conceptual pieces, I suggest you follow the *Academy of Management Review* guidelines and include propositions. (instruction given by a *JIBS* special issue editor)

Such ingrained attitudes add to the difficulty of getting theory-building articles through the review process. Indeed, Sutton (1997) has suggested that there may be circumstances where the best approach is not to mention the fact that some form of qualitative research has formed the basis for the development of concepts/ideas. This may seem to be highly instrumental, even cynical, but in the light of the rate of publication of qualitative versus conceptual articles in IB journals (see Tables 27.1–3), it may be an expedient path to publication.

It is little wonder that many identify with the following comment by Henry Mintzberg (McCarthy 2000, p. 32): 'God invented Americans to test theories but she never realized that there would be so many Americans and so few theories worth testing'.

The presentation of the paper itself is another barrier. Those trained in the positivist approach relate to a standard format. Research papers are set out in distinct sections: introduction, theoretical context, methodology, findings, discussion, conclusion and, more recently, managerial implications. Some qualitative papers fit into such a structure, but many do not. A busy reviewer can easily flip through the manuscript, notice that the expected signposts are missing and reject it on the grounds of being unscientific, even sloppy, research.

OVERCOMING THE BARRIERS

Despite the uneven playing field that qualitative researchers appear to face, publication in reputable quality journals, and other outlets, is possible. In this section, we outline a range of considerations in developing a strategy for trying to overcome the obstacles to publication of qualitative research in international business. The strategy adopted will be a by-product of factors such as those depicted in Figure 27.1. Clearly, these are not mutually exclusive, as the following discussion reveals.

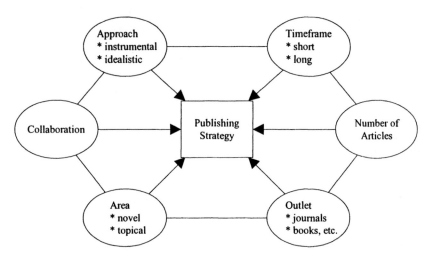

Figure 27.1 Factors involved in developing a publishing strategy

In seeking publication of a manuscript, there is a natural tendency to focus on preserving the integrity of the research and its findings in a non-compromising manner – what might be called an *idealistic approach*. However, such an approach may court rejection, especially in higher-ranked journals, given that the demands of the review process typically require a number of compromises, in part due to the bias against qualitative research, as identified in Tables 27.1–3. Thus, an author taking a non-compromising approach may find it necessary to seek a more sympathetic outlet, even if this may be seen as a lesser-ranked journal, or one that is not considered mainstream international business. It also requires a preparedness to withdraw the manuscript, and submit it to another journal, until it eventually finds a home. An idealistic approach usually means that the author has to be persistent and prepared to accept a longer timeframe.

An *instrumental* approach, as the term implies, means a willingness to conform to what is seen to be required in order to get published, bearing in mind the limitations of presenting an article based on qualitative research. Instrumentalism means studying the target journal to determine the preferred type of article in terms of style and methodological techniques. For example, a conceptual, theory-building piece aimed at the *Academy of Management Review* would need to recognise a preference for carefully crafted propositions as the accepted way of building an article. By conforming to expectations about what qualifies as an appropriate format for a potential contribution, the chances are increased of the editor (or the staff involved) accepting a manuscript for review, as well as avoiding a reflexive, negative response from the reviewers. Noting the composition of the editorial board from whose membership likely reviewers may be drawn, as well as those authors whose work has been published in the journal and are likely to be potential reviewers, assists in determining appropriate presentation and content. Authors taking the instrumental approach will consider the relevant published work of the editor and board members, and ensure that where possible potential reviewers' work is acknowledged in the manuscript, recognising that reviewers tend to look for whether and how their own work is cited, if such work is relevant. In one case, the editor of *JIBS*, in his initial letter advising that the manuscript had been sent to reviewers, indicated that the authors should consult one of his articles that he considered relevant to the topic of the manuscript.

Idealism and instrumentalism can be seen as extreme positions on a continuum. In reality, the majority of qualitative researchers tend to adopt a mixture: seeking to retain as much of the core of their ideas while leavening their approach with a measure of instrumentalism. Of course, the degree to which authors conform and compromise is related to decisions around other factors, as shown in Figure 27.1.

One of these factors is *collaboration*: linking up with another author/s, preferably with some standing in the field through publications and editorial board memberships. Collaboration can be an important way of enhancing the chances of publication from a number of perspectives. Tapping into others' experience, through writing with prominent or better-known colleagues in the field, may involve trading one's own research for another's publication experience and contacts to enhance the chances of publication. Collaboration can be a way of spreading the workload to handle time constraints, and getting into new areas (for example, post-doctorate work). Joining an existing project team can be an effective way of shortening the *timeframe* involved in generating publications, compared with commencing a new line of research from scratch. Of course, one needs to weigh up the costs as well as the benefits of taking a collaborative strategy. For example, single-authored articles have the advantage of carrying weight for academic promotion and tenure decisions, while collaborative work is valued for its evidence of team work in a research context. As well, collaboration can prolong the time taken to initiate and carry out the project because of the additional time taken in consulting and agreeing on approaches, analysis and write up – a process which can be accentuated in the case of an international team.

A related aspect in determining publication strategy is the *number of articles* that an author seeks to submit to the review process (see Figure 27.1). As noted earlier, to seek to publish in a highly ranked journal may be a lengthy process, with a high probability of this ending in a negative outcome anyway. A manuscript may survive up to two rounds of the revision process and still be rejected. Even if acceptance is a final outcome, the process may take three years or more. In situations where a manuscript has been rejected by more than one major journal before its final acceptance, the time involved may be very lengthy. Gans and Shepherd (1994, p.170) relate the experience of Paul Krugman, a prominent economist, who experienced considerable delay in having one of his important articles accepted as a result of rejection from at least two major economic journals. Because of the delay in publication, when the article finally appeared Krugman's concept had been picked up by others in the field. At least 100 published and unpublished pieces based on these ideas appeared well before his original piece was finally printed by the journal. This forced him to add a postscript to the original manuscript referring to this subsequent literature. An additional concern with publication delays may be the ageing of the data. Unlike wine, old data are not appreciated always by reviewers, and may provoke comments such as: 'this study needs to be updated'.

Given the difficulties associated with publication in highly ranked journals, therefore, a more appropriate approach may be to seek to generate a series of articles. For instance, one can aim a piece at a highly ranked journal while others are written for journals where there is a higher chance of publication and in a shorter space of time. Qualitative researchers often have access to a very large data bank which may enable them to take their analysis and theory development in more than one direction depending on the nature of the themes that emerge from the data iteration process. A stream of publications does not mean recycling the same article, but picking up different ideas, issues and perspectives and recognising that not everything can be adequately treated in one article. Some of the work of Bartlett and Ghoshal in international management could be regarded as a series of work dealing with key ideas arising from their case studies of a number of large multinationals (see, for example, Bartlett and Ghoshal 1987a, 1987b, 1988, 1990, 1995; Ghoshal and Bartlett 1990, 1995). This approach is assisted through targeting journals in different disciplines, as well as utilising practitioner-oriented journals. In some cases, there may be scope for considering the research findings from a government policy perspective rather than a managerial focus. However, the experience of Krugman and others demonstrates that no matter how carefully crafted a manuscript is, and appropriately positioned it is in terms of a targeted journal, the chances of rejection are still considerable, bearing in mind the earlier discussion on journal rejection rates. Having a series of articles under review in various journals is an important counter.

As already noted, the *choice of journal* is an important step on the path to publication. In fact, many would argue that it should be the starting point to the whole process. Many IB articles are not published in journals dedicated to the area, but in broader journals such as *Academy of Management Journal/Review/Executive*, *Journal of Management Studies*, *Journal of Business Research*, *Journal of General Management*, *Journal of Marketing* and the like. With the plethora of journals on offer, selecting a suitable journal may be difficult. An article on a specific aspect of international business may not be appreciated in a broad-based journal such as *JIBS*. Rather, one could target a specialist journal, that may not have the same status as *JIBS*, nor even have the word 'international' in its title. For example, an article dealing with the role of information in export behaviour might receive a more sympathetic treatment in the *International Journal of Information Management* or *Prometheus* (which focuses on information issues) rather than the more marketing-oriented *Journal of International Marketing*.

Apart from taking a wider approach to journal selection, special issues of journals may represent an appropriate avenue. Special issues typically accept a broader range of articles; for example, there is an interest in survey and theory development pieces which expose development in a particular area. Special issue topics in international business are chosen often as a response to emerging research areas and issues, such as e-business and the impact of the Internet, or to growing interest in certain countries or regions. Special issues may develop as a result of conferences. It is not uncommon for session chairs to suggest to editors the possibility of a special issue devoted to the topic of a particular conference session. If there are no relevant special issue topics available at a given point in time, it is possible to suggest to journal editors a topic that would encompass one's research, and perhaps offer to act as special issue editor.

Journal editors attending conferences may respond to emerging themes or research areas and approach authors – either for special issue editorship, or invite submission to their journal for a special issue or as a 'normal' paper. Some editors are active in soliciting paper submissions in areas that they regard as important topics but have not been included in their journals. Conference presentations therefore may be important as an avenue to publication.

As a general comment, papers that cover old ground in any field tend to have more difficulty in being accepted as journal articles than those that address new *areas* and are seen to advance knowledge. Articles dealing with *novel ideas* or new ways of examining issues and those that are topical often are more readily accepted. For example, journals were keen to publish some of the early work on companies' experiences in China, and articles dealing with the impact of the Internet in international business. Journals often include in pro forma review sheets a criterion related to a manuscript's contribution to knowledge advancement. Of course, a new topic or idea may take the journal's reviewers out of their comfort zone. Much depends on the preparedness of journal editors to support novel approaches and topic areas.

While we have been focusing on journal publication, *books* still represent an important outlet for research and sometimes a faster path to publication. As with special issues of journals, books can comprise a selection of papers that have been presented at conferences dealing with a special theme or area. Opportunities to publish chapters in books may arise from open invitation or from personal approaches through one's scholarly network. The review process for chapters published in books can be highly varied, though in general it tends to be less demanding than in most journals and more closely directed by the editor. Edited books sometimes are a collection of previously published work, including articles published in lower-ranked journals, on the grounds of their influence in, or relevance to, the field in question. Such compilations may be used in classroom teaching, doctoral programmes and the like, and can be an important vehicle for an author's ideas to be advanced, bringing authors' work to the attention of a broader audience of potential and current researchers.

Given the vagaries of the journal publication route, and the perceived limitations of book chapters, complete books – sole or joint authored – represent an outlet favoured by some researchers as a way of ensuring that the integrity of the research is maintained, and in a more substantial form. The problem with this strategy is that completing a book requires considerable time, particularly if sole authored – time that could have been spent on writing and revising a number of journal articles – and without prior agreement from the publisher, the book could still be rejected. Gans and Shepherd (1994, p. 174) quote the experience of Oliver Williamson whose book, *Markets and Hierarchies: Analysis and Antitrust Implications*, was initially rejected by one publisher. The referees used by this publisher 'did not see much merit in the exercise'. The book was eventually published by the Free Press. Publishing houses have to be convinced of a suitable volume of sales before proceeding and will forward a book proposal to various reviewers in the field.

A form of publication that should be considered carefully is that of *working papers.* Given that they carry limited weight in terms of academic standing, and for promotion purposes, few academics would see them as an end to the process. Their impact partly depends on the extent of circulation of the working paper series and the regard for the institution involved. Some researchers use working papers as a way of ensuring early release of their work, or of seeking a reaction by others in the field, with the ultimate aim of publication in a reputable journal. A concern mentioned by many academics, particularly with the rise in Internet use as a means of making working papers accessible, is that ideas revealed in a working paper can be picked up by others and rapidly incorporated in articles submitted to journals, pre-empting the original author who has only the working paper as evidence of priority.

Handling the Review Process

As already noted, an author can accept the editor's rejection of a manuscript and submit the article to another journal as quickly as possible, thereby seeking to minimise the delay in getting the article finally published. However, it is possible to appeal against the decision. Editors have been known to respond positively to well-argued feedback about the review process, although anecdotal evidence suggests that mostly they do not, particularly the non-interventionist editor we discussed earlier. Again, the decision about whether to appeal or not may be influenced by the time factor, and the strength of one's case. Engaging in a dialogue with an editor, with no certainty of influencing the outcome, will add to publication delay. If arguments are convincing, the editor may elect to send the manuscript out for another review round with new reviewers. In the extreme case, the editor may override the reviewers' recommendation for rejection and accept the manuscript as it stands. Some colleagues have been known to ring the editor personally and 'discuss the matter'. This last approach may work for those with an established reputation in the field and are known to the editor, but may backfire. However, it is important that reviewers' comments are not accepted uncritically when the basis for rejection is mainly due to the use of a qualitative research methodology. Editorial attention needs to be drawn to any bias encountered during the review process.

In cases where the manuscript is considered to require revision before a final decision is made, the handling of reviewers' comments and suggestions can be pivotal. Reviewers unfamiliar with qualitative research methods may suggest the author make changes that follow a more positivistic path. For example, a reviewer may suggest that the author should develop hypotheses and test them. This suggestion is effectively a rejection and should be treated as such, in the manner noted above. Other comments often encountered are: requests for propositions, queries about generalisability (particularly where a single case study is concerned), and questions about qualitative techniques such as data iteration, data triangulation and data reliability.

The methodology section of an article is of key importance, and frequently it is the area where reviewer questions arise. As far as possible, these should be anticipated and addressed in the initial version of the article submitted for review. While qualitative research lacks the parsimony and shorthand of the quantitative, that does not mean one cannot present a succinct yet comprehensive account of how the research was undertaken, the protocols followed, and how the data were analysed – in effect, to demonstrate the full rigour of good qualitative research. Nevertheless, reviewers may demand further justification of aspects of the methodology, so authors should be prepared to extend the methodology section. The use of software packages (for example, NUD*IST and ATLAS.ti) in some cases will enhance the credibility of the research in the eyes of reviewers, but these packages can pose problems for others who are not familiar with their role in qualitative research.

Clearly, the way qualitative data is presented is important. The use of quotations may cause some concern, particularly where a seemingly large number are included in the text. It is not uncommon for reviewers to express concern about becoming lost in a forest of quotations from interviews and request that the use of interview data be reduced. When interviews form the bulk of the research, it can be difficult to present empirical data in a way that allows the reader to judge the findings, but the impact can be lost if verbatim quotations are not carefully pruned and organised. The reader needs to get a feel for the whole picture, as well as the weight of the evidence. Ways of assisting this include tables, figures, sketches and flow charts that can be useful in summarising, illustrating and clarifying the data. Nevertheless, interview data are critical and revising to meet reviewers' concerns should not be taken to the point where changes will affect the integrity of the evidence the interview data represents.

Generation of testable propositions is emerging as almost a reflex demand by reviewers considering qualitative work of a conceptual or theory development nature. In a broader sense, the demand for propositions appears to be a manifestation of a prescriptive format for developing ideas and concepts that arise through qualitative research methods. Authors who have used a different form of presenting research outcomes may be faced with the question of why they have not generated testable propositions. In such cases, authors face the difficult task of convincing editors and reviewers as to why testable propositions are inappropriate. Not surprisingly, many take the path of least resistance and concoct a set of propositions as a way of overcoming this barrier to publication.

CONCLUSION

'I would estimate that 60 per cent of my papers sent to refereed journals have been rejected on the first try ... I still open return letters from journals with fear and trembling, and more often than not receive bad news' (Gans and Shepherd 1994, pp. 169 and 178). These comments by Paul Krugman, a well-known and highly successful international economist, are a stark reminder of how tough the publication game can be.

Our analysis has suggested that using qualitative research methodology tends to increase the difficulties of getting published, particularly in highly-ranked journals such as *JIBS*. Combined with the length of time involved in the review process, it may be necessary for authors to be prepared to submit articles to a range of journals. Some may pass muster in a short period of time, others may turn into 'problem' papers in terms of getting through review rounds. Regardless, one requires patience, persistence, and some luck. Gans and Shepherd (1994, p. 177), reviewing the publication experience of prominent economists, conclude that: 'A rejection usually does not kill a paper; among our examples, a rejected paper usually finds life at another journal, even if the paper is unorthodox'. The message from all involved in the publication game would concur that persistence and patience ultimately bear fruit, even though the end result might not be the preferred journal or that, because of the time taken in finding a home, the impact of one's work has been somewhat diminished. For this reason, having a number of articles in the review pipeline ensures that one is not so dependent on a given problem paper.

Being prepared to withdraw a paper from a journal review is still important, especially in cases where it is clear that the article will be rejected unless the author is prepared to undertake major changes that require considerable time, without the certainty of the final product being acceptable to the reviewers. In addition, the required changes may interfere with the integrity of the research.

A final rallying call is for qualitative researchers to remain persistent: to continue submitting their research to all relevant journals, especially those that evince a bias against qualitative research methods; and to engage in dialogue with journal editors, pointing out instances of bias and cases where reviewers have breached editorial guidelines in their assessment of manuscripts using qualitative research. These actions are important to ensure that editors support the diversity of IB research approaches. Otherwise, we shall reach the point where qualitative IB research is never published in major journals, thus completing a self-reinforcing cycle. The further danger is that with major outlets virtually closed, why do qualitative research? Furthering the development of IB theory, ideas and knowledge depends in part on the contribution of qualitative research – by itself as well as in conjunction with quantitative methods. The field of international business will be poorer without researchers prepared to conduct qualitative research.

REFERENCES

Bartlett, C.A. and S. Ghoshal (1987a), 'Managing across borders: new strategic requirements', *Sloan Management Review*, **28** (4), 7–17.

—— (1987b), 'Managing across borders: new organizational responses', *Sloan Management Review*, **29** (1), 43–52.

—— (1988), 'Organizing for worldwide effectiveness: the transnational solution', *California Management Review*, **31** (1), 54–74.

—— (1990), 'Matrix management: not a structure, a frame of mind', *Harvard Business Review*, **68** (4), 138–45.

—— (1995), 'Rebuilding behavioural context: turn process reengineering into people rejuvenation', *Sloan Management Review*, **37** (1), 11–23.

Beyer, J.M., R.G. Chanove and W.B. Fox (1995), 'The review process and the fates of manuscripts submitted to *AMJ*', *Academy of Management Journal*, **38** (5), 1219–60.

Cummings, L.L. and P.J. Frost (1995), 'Conceptual perspectives: introduction', in L.L. Cummings and P.J. Frost (eds), *Publishing in the Organizational Sciences*, 2nd edn, Thousand Oaks, CA: Sage, pp. 3–12.

DuBois, F.L. and D.M. Reeb (2000), 'Ranking the international business journals', *Journal of International Business Studies*, **31** (4), 689–704.

Gans, J.S. and G.B. Shepherd (1994), 'How are the mighty fallen: rejected articles by leading economists', *Journal of Economic Perspectives*, **8** (1), 165–79.

Ghoshal, S. and C.A. Bartlett (1990), 'The multinational corporation as an interorganizational network', *Academy of Management Review*, **15** (4), 603–25.

—— (1995), 'Changing the role of top management: beyond structure to processes', *Harvard Business Review*, **72** (1), 86–96.

McCarthy D.J. (2000), 'View from the top: Henry Mintzberg on strategy and management', *Academy of Management Executive*, **14** (3), 31–42.

Patton, M.Q. (1990), *Qualitative Evaluation and Research Methods*, 2nd edn, Beverly Hills, CA: Sage.

Sutton, R.I. (1997), 'The virtues of closet qualitative research', *Organization Science*, **8** (1), 97–106.

28. Publishing Qualitative Research in International Business

Julian Birkinshaw

INTRODUCTION

This book has provided many useful perspectives on qualitative research methods in different aspects of international business, and in different parts of the world. In this final chapter, I want to take a rather different approach. My purpose is to provide some insights into how one publishes qualitative research in the field of international business. And my approach to doing this is to offer some very personal reflections on what I have done well, and not so well, over the last eight years or so.

Because this is a rather introspective piece, it is important to surface my biases at the outset. First, I believe strongly in the value of qualitative methods as a means of advancing knowledge. My first degree, many years ago, was in geology, and an eminent professor in the field was famous for saying that 'the best geologist is the one who has seen the most rocks'. The same can be said for the field of business studies: the best business scholar is the person who has talked to the most managers (and perhaps other employees as well) or seen the most companies. It is only by spending time 'in the field', I believe, that we as business academics can get the depth of understanding of subject matter that we need to advance knowledge. My training at the Richard Ivey School helped to reinforce this belief, but it was there all along.

Second, I do not believe the academic journals will ever fully embrace qualitative research methods. Of course, all the major journals publish *some* qualitative studies, and they all cry out for more. But the reality is that analysing and writing up qualitative studies is simply harder than working through quantitative material. And most of us are not well enough trained in the techniques to be able to reach the standards the journals demand.

Third, my approach to research design is emergent. That is, I tend to focus first on the phenomenon I am interested in, I undertake a series of interviews to make sense of it, and only then do I start thinking about the best way of designing a research study. I am not recommending this approach, but it has worked well for me. And more to the point, it has resulted in a number of fairly interesting hybrid designs that combine to varying degrees the best of qualitative and quantitative methodologies.

Taken together, these biases suggest a simple theme to this chapter. Publishing qualitative research is difficult, but it is worth the struggle. My experiences, both positive and negative, can hopefully provide you with some ideas that will help you in your quest to get your qualitative research into the major journals.

The main body of this chapter focuses on five different research designs that can be used to present qualitative research (often with complementary quantitative data) in a journal-friendly way. For each one, I provide a detailed example from my own research, with some of the reviewers' comments and my responses to those comments. Then in the latter part of the chapter I examine some of the broader themes around publishing qualitative research.

APPROACHES TO PUBLISHING QUALITATIVE RESEARCH

There are a variety of ways of analysing and writing up qualitative research. One approach which will not be considered further here is ethnography, in which the researcher describes his/her findings through thick description, quotations and references to his/her own field notes. This approach is seldom used in international business (though there is no reason why it should not be), and moreover it is an approach I have never used myself. For examples of how it is done, and some guides to the methodology see Barley (1990, 1996), Barley and Kunda (1992), Van Maanen (2000) and Sharpe (Chapter 15 this volume).

All other approaches to analysing and writing up qualitative research tend to take a rather positivist perspective. That is, they attempt to impose some sort of order on the data so that it can be evaluated using the standard criteria of reliability and validity. This can be done entirely in a qualitative way (for example, through creating lengthy tables of text to allow cases to be compared with one another) or it can involve some level of quantification (for example, text analysis techniques or complementary numerical data).

My own approach has always fallen somewhere within this spectrum, and most usually with a deliberate strategy of collecting both qualitative and quantitative data and writing up the study using both. This approach has been driven by my own personal belief that we need both case studies and large-sample data to fully inform our understanding of a phenomenon. But it has also been driven by a pragmatic recognition that pure qualitative research is very hard to publish in the top journals. As a result, I have ended up adopting a number of different designs, all of which have sought to get around, in various ways, the traditional weaknesses of qualitative case-based research (that is, hard to replicate, hard to generalise). Reviewing my work over the last eight years or so, I can identify five different designs.

Design 1. Pure Qualitative Case Studies

I learned fairly quickly that pure case study research is very hard to publish. While I tried several times to get such studies published, only one ended up in a peer-reviewed journal, *International Business Review* (Birkinshaw and Ridderstråle 1999). I shall make a few comments about my experiences shortly, but before doing so it is worth noting that this methodology has produced some of the most influential studies in the field of business studies. Many of these are written up in books (for example, Bartlett and Ghoshal 1989; Prahalad and Doz 1987) but there are also plenty of examples of case study research in the major journals. Examples include Burgelman (1983, 1991, 1996), Galunic and Eisenhardt (1996), Ghoshal and Bartlett (1994) and Malnight (1994, 1996). These studies conform to one of two models. The first is the one-company case study, as popularised by Yin (1984), in which the single company is described in great detail to work through a new theory or framework (though Yin also discussed multiple case studies as well). It typically ends up with a set of research propositions that in theory at least should be tested on a large-sample data set (for example, Burgelman 1991; Malnight 1996). The second model is the comparative analysis of 4-6 companies, which has been perfected by Kathy Eisenhardt and her co-authors (for example, Brown and Eisenhardt 1997; Eisenhardt and Tabrizi 1995; Eisenhardt and Zbaracki 1992; Galunic and Eisenhardt 1996). This approach uses the case studies to draw out interesting new insights, which are then presented in comparative form, essentially as a series of large tables with the core categories along the top and the 4–6 cases down the side.

My own experience of pure qualitative case studies is relatively modest. My first three forays, all using the comparative case approach, were all rejected from their target journals. One eventually died, one eventually got published (Birkinshaw and Ridderstråle 1999), and the third was repackaged with some additional quantitative data and then published (Birkinshaw 2000). What I learned from these experiences was perhaps surprising. The overall attitude among reviewers towards qualitative research was overwhelmingly positive. For example, one reviewer began in the following way, before recommending rejection:

> You are to be congratulated on the depth of your case based research and your attempt to write this up for a journal such as *SMJ* [*Strategic Management Journal*]. Papers on such research should be encouraged. In addition you are correct in pursuing a case based methodology for this sort of research.

But while they praised the approach in principle, they were very hard to please in practice. Typical comments requested 'much more detailed case analyses' or observed in cases where I had provided a lot of detail that 'the argument on these pages is hard to follow'. To some degree these comments were a function of my own experience and capabilities as a researcher, but looking back on it, I think the underlying point is simply that *writing up qualitative research is harder than writing up quantitative research*. The reviewer does not reject the qualitative study; he/she just imposes strict standards that most researchers are not well equipped to meet. It is far easier, by comparison, to write up a quantitative study because there are well-understood techniques and norms around how it is done. And by the same token, often the criteria for assessing qualitative research are not well understood among reviewers.

My early experiences with this approach led me to seek out alternative methods, all of which ended up as a combination of qualitative and quantitative methods. These are described in the paragraphs that follow.

Design 2. Case Study Analysis with 20–30 Observations

This approach is still qualitative, in that each observation is a 'story' about a company, or about a subsidiary or a project within a company. However, there are enough of them that one can begin to infer some generalisable patterns. It is, in effect, an extension of Eisenhardt's 4–6 company design. With a sample of only 20–30 it is difficult to do worthwhile statistical analysis, but depending on the phenomena being researched it can yield some very interesting findings.

Take my *Journal of International Business Studies* paper looking at the evolution of world product mandates (Birkinshaw 1996). This paper was built on my doctoral research, and in particular on the 34 cases of 'world mandates' granted to the six subsidiary companies I studied. It proposed a simple life cycle model whereby the mandate was gained, developed, and then (sometimes) lost. Using my case material I identified 31 incidences of mandate gain, 24 incidences of mandate enhancement and seven incidences of mandate loss, and for each one I identified the conditions under which the life cycle event occurred. This allowed me to construct three giant tables of data, with the cases down one side and the categories along the top. This approach essentially allowed me to present the entire body of data to the reader, so that he/she could evaluate it for him/herself.

To my pleasant surprise, the reviewers bought this approach immediately. Of the four reviewers, one said publish as is, one said it should be a research note, and the other two were positively inclined but with detailed concerns, all of which were easily sorted out. Indeed, one even went out of his/her way to praise the methodology, 'Overall I like the paper very much. It is a good example of how careful case research can build useful knowledge on interesting phenomena. However, there are a number of specific points ... '

My sense is that this is a very effective research design *if* the phenomenon under investigation is relatively novel. While world product mandates had been studied many times, no-one had previously modelled them in terms of a life cycle. Hence, this was an effective way of establishing the validity of such a model. The design also has the important benefit over classic case research that it is relatively easy to write up. The tables of data provide the structure, and it is also possible to do basic numerical analysis, as the example in Table 28.1 illustrates.

Table 28.1   Characteristics of mandate developments, 25 cases

Characteristic	Categories	Number of Cases
Prime mover	Subsidiary	12
	Subsidiary and parent company together	11
	Parent company	2
Source of charter	*de novo*, i.e., not previously in existence	15
	From a parent company entity or sister subsidiary	10
	From an independent entity, e.g., an acquired firm	–
Strategic motivations	Market seeking (i.e., where the subsidiary offers a leading-edge customer base); includes global customers	10
	Resource seeking (i.e., where subsidiary offers the most attractive location for a business activity)	7
	Efficiency seeking (i.e., associated with the rationalisation of existing corporate assets)	8
	Strategic asset seeking (e.g., acquisitions)	–
Geographical scope	North America only	4
	North America with nominal exports beyond	3
	Global	18
Functional scope	Full business accountability	4
	Full business accountability excluding sales	8
	Product management (and other support) only	2
	Manufacturing (and associated engineering) only	7
	Manufacturing and development only	4

Source: Birkinshaw (1996).

Design 3. Case Study Analysis with 20–30 Observations plus Follow-up Questionnaire

This is similar to design 2 above, but with a follow-up questionnaire sent out to the respondents from the 20–30 companies/units/projects. The purpose of the follow-up questionnaire is essentially to validate and expand on the case study findings. Particularly in cases where the study has evolved over the period of data collection, you often find that there are questions you wish you had asked the first set of respondents. So rather than re-do the interviews, my approach is typically to put together a brief questionnaire and send it out to the key individuals. And because these people already know me, I typically get a 90 per cent or more response rate.

My doctoral thesis research, reported in the *Strategic Management Journal* (Birkinshaw 1997), is a good example of this design. The analysis focused on 39 strategic initiatives by subsidiary managers. I had detailed qualitative information about each case from 100 respondents, but I also had quantitative responses to about 40 questions.

In writing up this study, I opted for a deductive framing, whereby I first developed a set of hypotheses around the types of subsidiary initiatives and their distinctive characteristics, and then I used both qualitative and quantitative data to support those hypotheses. But the reviewers were not entirely convinced by this approach. They did not like the hypotheses at all, so I ended up reverting to more open-ended research questions. And they were suspicious of my mixed methods. Here are a couple of the key comments:

> I would recommend that you drop the propositions and the 'quantitative' analysis and focus your efforts on developing a typology of MNC [multinational corporation] initiatives based on the various dimensions you have identified through the literature review together with your field observations.

> I appreciate your efforts to use multiple data sources and triangulation, but I am concerned about [one] key issue. You seem to believe that since you use Likert scales and used complementary qualitative data that you do not need to develop multi-items scales. This is not so. Either the questionnaire is valid on its own as an instrument or it adds nothing of great value. If you simply wanted to attach numbers to your qualitative data collection then you can do that by coding the transcripts. However, valid measurements are based on more than adding a numerical scale. Issues of construct validity and reliability must be addressed.

These were fair comments. My decision to provide qualitative *and* quantitative evidence was based in part on a concern that each was somewhat weak, so they supported each other. But the reviewers saw through this ploy in an instant, and suggested that I drop the quantitative material (which could be challenged very easily because I had neglected to build multi-item scales for some constructs). However, I decided to persist with both sets of evidence and managed to convince the reviewers that both sets of data should be retained. The argument I used was essentially one of triangulation in that, by providing both quantitative and qualitative data, I was providing a more rigorous treatment than would have been possible with either one set of data or the other.

I took a couple of points of learning away from this. First, complementary qualitative and quantitative measures can be informative, and can be extremely useful for addressing certain sorts of research questions. Second, you must still take care with each part of the design. I got away with rather marginal quantitative data in the paper described above, but many reviewers would not have been so accommodating.

Design 4. Case Study Analysis plus Follow-up Large-sample Study

This is a classic research design, with an exploratory phase based on qualitative interviews and then a second phase in which the propositions from the first phase are formally tested in a large-sample setting. The exploratory phase is often treated simply as a means of understanding the phenomenon under investigation, with the second phase providing the actual data for the research paper. My preference is to see them as equally important elements in a study, and to do the qualitative phase carefully enough that it can be written up alongside the quantitative study in a single paper. This may seem like a rather inefficient way of using lots of data, but depending on the specific focus of the paper it can work well.

Consider my co-authored paper on knowledge transfer in acquisitions which appeared in the *Journal of International Business Studies* (*JIBS*) (Bresman et al. 1999). This paper used detailed longitudinal case study evidence on three acquisitions as well as questionnaire data on a further 50 acquisitions. Here again, if I am to be honest, the mixed-method strategy was partly to alleviate a concern that neither body of data on its own was sufficiently strong to warrant publication. The cases were certainly interesting, but I was not confident that they would be well received on their own. The questionnaire data were okay, but the sample size was small and there was a common method bias problem in that all the data had been collected from the same source (the head of the R&D unit). The reactions of the reviewers to this design were mixed. Here are the relevant comments:

Frankly I feel the empirical results of this study were a little underwhelming.

To add longitudinal case study information to statistical analysis is a good research strategy. However, in this study we don't get very much of the insight, texture, richness or dynamics that such a technique is capable of providing. This part of the manuscript doesn't add so much.

This paper takes up an important question in a field of inquiry that needs strong new contributions. The quantitative methods are fine. The study does make a contribution. The question is whether the contribution is substantial enough to warrant publication in *JIBS*.

There were, in other words, concerns about the quantitative results (comment 1), the qualitative results (comment 2) and the overall contribution (comment 3), but I think the strategy of combining two different bodies of data actually worked because I was ultimately able to persuade the reviewers to buy in (after two rounds of revisions).

I have used this strategy on a number of other occasions. In one case I started with a purely qualitative analysis, rewrote it with some quantitative back-up material, and then rewrote it again as a combined qualitative–quantitative paper. It was eventually published in *Entrepreneurship Theory and Practice*, with the international angle downplayed almost entirely (Birkinshaw 2000). In a more recent case, which is still under review, I focused mostly on the quantitative material, and then used the case study data to help interpret the results and play out some of the more interesting findings. One reviewer commented as follows:

> I don't think that your 'qualitative insights' helped much. Why would the results of the interviews differ from the survey results anyway? And some of the comments seem more like uninformed theorizing. I suggest you should consider shortening this section considerably – basically to report that the interviews replicated the survey results (for what this is worth).

Needless to say, I left the qualitative insights in. I wrote a polite reply explaining that I felt there were insights to be gained through talking to managers that cannot be gained through a questionnaire. And I made some small amendments to the paper to ensure that my 'uninformed theorizing' did not drown out the findings from the large-sample analysis. But this reviewer's comment is important because it highlights the usually unstated bias of many of our academic colleagues against qualitative research. Anyone reading this book believes in qualitative research almost as a matter of definition. But we still need to convince others that it is worthwhile.

Incidentally, I have never used this design the other way round, that is, with a questionnaire first and then case studies to follow. The reason for this is simply that designing a good questionnaire (and gaining a good response rate) is extremely difficult, and only possible – in my experience – when the questionnaire reflects a detailed understanding of the issues and perspectives of the respondent. So I always conduct a round of case study interviews before attempting to design a questionnaire, and I think this has served me well.

Design 5. Case Study Analysis plus Survey Work within the Cases

This design focuses on a relatively small number of case studies, but it uses some forms of quantitative analysis (typically from questionnaires) *within* the cases to make specific points. The best example from my own work is a study of post-acquisition integration in three Swedish multinationals (Birkinshaw et al. 2000) that was published in the *Journal of Management Studies* after being rejected by *Strategic Management Journal*.

Unlike some of the earlier studies mentioned, I was enormously proud of the data collection work here. We had done extensive interviews in both acquirer and acquired units in three different companies, at two points in time (1992 and 1996). We collected extensive archival material on the three acquisitions. And we did a questionnaire of managers in both acquirer and acquired units, again at two points in time to see how attitudes towards the acquisitions had evolved. We wrote the study up in a deductive style, building up a framework and three research questions, and then interweaving qualitative and quantitative data to answer those questions.

How was the paper received? *Strategic Management Journal* came back negative. There were some compliments from the reviewers, such as 'the authors are to be commended for their patience and diligence in the research process'. But we also got many of the typical concerns: 'The manuscript as it now stands needs much work before it could be considered for publication' and 'the common themes among the three case studies do not seem to offer particularly unique or new insights'.

After a few minor changes we sent it to the *Journal of Management Studies*, and we received very positive reviews. Indeed, one of the comments on this paper stands out as the all-time most positive thing I have ever heard a reviewer say:

> This paper is a very worthwhile piece of research. Its main strengths are the quality and extent of the data gathering, the grounding in the existing literature, the soundness of the main research approach, the face validity of the extensive descriptive data, and the modesty in inferences and generalisability. It is a pleasure to see high quality access, a longitudinal approach, the competent use of both standard scales and qualitative data, very good comparability across cases, and a t-shaped design that combines breadth with depth. I would encourage the authors to also contemplate additional efforts such as a paper directed at *AMJ* [*Academy of Management Journal*] or *SMJ*.

A couple of points are worth underlining here. First, publishing is a stochastic process. Most journals only use two reviewers, and it is often the luck of the draw whether they end up being positively or negatively disposed. And this is particularly so with qualitative research where the epistemological biases of the reviewer weigh heavily in the overall decision. The second point here is that our multi-method approach was ultimately a success. It brings us full circle to the point I started with, namely that writing up qualitative research is difficult, so any efforts you make to bolster the text with quantitative elements are likely to be well rewarded. For other examples of this approach, see Adler et al. (1999), Dougherty (1992) and Dyer (1996).

To sum up, these five designs are all approaches I have used, and all have met with some degree of success. But I do not think this is an exhaustive list. Leonard-Barton (1990) for example, describes a design in which she pursued one case study in real-time and then a series of others in less detail and on a retrospective basis. And other combinations are no doubt possible as well.

OTHER METHODS AND USES OF QUALITATIVE RESEARCH

So far I have emphasised the designs you can use to write up qualitative or mixed-method research. But qualitative research can also be used in other ways:

- As an input into a large sample quantitative study (see design 3 above). Here the qualitative research is never actually written up, but it informs the development of the questionnaire, and the interpretation of the results.
- As an input into a theoretical paper. Often the insights gained from a qualitative study are easier to write up in the abstract than as case studies. In such a situation, the output from a qualitative research project may be a theoretical paper for the *Academy of Management Review* or similar. This is what Sutton (1997) calls 'closet qualitative research'.
- As the data for a practitioner-oriented paper. Writing for the *Harvard Business Review* and similar journals requires detailed case study examples, and it is far less bothered about issues of methodology and rigour. Most qualitative research therefore lends itself very nicely to being written up for such journals.

These are all fairly obvious points, but I think it is important not to underplay them. Most business schools are looking for a broad set of skills in their faculty. They demand high-quality academic publications, but they are also looking to influence the wider business community, and they require effective classroom teaching. I do not believe it is possible to deliver on all of these different demands if you spend your working life interacting with an SPSS dataset. The real insights come from the field – through interviews with people at all levels of an organisation. And the real payoff comes when these field-based interviews become the basis for your research, teaching, writing *and* consulting.

SOME BROADER THEMES

In the final part of this chapter I would like to discuss a number of broader issues around publishing qualitative research, and then finish up with some specific tips that you may find useful.

The first is the overall status of *international* business research within the field of business studies. There is a clear sense of concern among those of us who believe in international business research that it is still seen as something of a specialty field by 'mainstream' strategy and organisational behaviour researchers. Our research tends to be cross-disciplinary in nature, so it does not slot neatly into the traditional departments of a business school. It tends to rely on theories that we have imported from economics, sociology and other disciplines. And it often requires non-traditional research designs to address the complex, multi-faceted phenomena we study. All of this creates additional challenges to those doing qualitative research. It is difficult to publish qualitative research in top journals; and it is difficult to publish international business research in top journals. So publishing qualitative international business research is doubly difficult. And to make matters worse, the specialty nature of the field of international business means that our journals do not have the same status as their counterparts in the mainstream fields. In my own school (London Business School), the *Journal of International Business Studies* does not rank as an 'A' journal, which means we are essentially being discouraged from publishing in it.

How can the field of international business increase its status with the mainstream disciplines? There are no simple answers of course, but a large part is around the quality of the research we do. To be frank, some of the research that gets published in the specialty international business journals (including my own work) is not of the highest standard in terms of theory and methodology. There is plenty of scope to increase our rigour and our attention to detail, and in so doing to generate greater acceptance of our work from other disciplines. Hopefully this chapter has provided some insights into how this can be done for qualitative methodologies.

Let me also address the issue of which journals to publish qualitative research in. These comments apply only to what we might call 'macro' international business – issues of strategy, organisation, market entry, internal organisational relationships and so forth. Unfortunately I have no experience of publishing individual level or 'micro' international business research (for example, cross-cultural leadership styles), so I cannot comment on the appropriate journals for such work.

I have had most of my success with the *Strategic Management Journal* and the *Journal of International Business Studies*. To generalise enormously, these two journals seem to find a way of trusting in an interesting or novel piece of research, and making some concessions to the methodology if the issue warrants it. Some of the other top journals, including the *Administrative Science Quarterly* and the *Academy of Management Journal*, are much less forgiving. For both these two, the data and methods have to be of the highest quality for a paper to be seriously considered. They are certainly open to publishing qualitative research, but they have a very clear, almost formulaic, sense of how it should be done. *Organization Science*, by contrast, has a much more open-minded approach to what constitutes good qualitative research, and I have seen many different types of studies published there. Of the specialist international business journals, all have some openness to qualitative research but none exactly seeks it out either. I have experience with the *International Business Review*, the *Management International Review* and *Thunderbird International Business Review*. I have never tried publishing in the *Journal of International Management*, but I sense that it has a similar approach to the others. There are also a number of other mainstream journals that are interested in qualitative international business research, including the *Journal of Management Studies*, *Organization Studies* and the *Journal of Management*.

In terms of the different attitudes on either side of the Atlantic, the rule of thumb here is that the European journals are more accommodating of qualitative methodologies, while the American journals are more comfortable with the classic quantitative hypothesis testing model. But this distinction may be blurring, with some American journals like *Organization Science* becoming more pluralist in its approach to methodology, and some of the European journals adopting American standards.

SUMMARY

This chapter has covered a number of issues concerned with publishing qualitative research. It is by no means exhaustive, and it is highly idiosyncratic in that it draws on my own personal experiences – and my clear biases – as a researcher in the field of international business. But hopefully I have provided some useful insights into the art of publishing qualitative research, and helped some of you to avoid making easily avoidable mistakes. Let me end with a few specific tips as you contemplate working on or writing up your own qualitative research.

Invest in design early on. Most of the 'fatal flaws' in articles submitted for publication could have been resolved with a little more care at the research design phase. This includes such things as defining your sample more carefully, collecting data from the right people (for example, making sure that you speak to both subsidiary and head office managers), and using existing measures for questionnaire items. It goes against my nature to do this, but there are many times I wished I had taken a bit more care in these early stages. However, I also believe it is important to be flexible in one's research approach, and to be prepared to 'repackage' an article as appropriate, perhaps even by getting hold of new empirical material.

Focus on the phenomenon not the theory. I do not think everyone will agree with this, but it is my strong belief that good research starts with a real-life managerial problem or phenomenon. And this approach really lends itself to qualitative research because if there is a new phenomenon or problem to be investigated, the obvious starting point is to talk to the managers or other individuals who are grappling with it.

Look for new levels of analysis. One of the key advantages of qualitative research is that it can be done at multiple levels of analysis. In my doctoral research I began by studying subsidiary-level issues, but as I got deeper into it I realised from my interviews that the 'world mandate' and the 'initiative' were both interesting and valid units of analysis in their own right. I could not easily have done this had I taken a questionnaire or archival approach to my study, because it was only through the interviews that these new possibilities emerged.

Measure what you can. While qualitative data provide the important research insights, it is often hard to convey those insights to others. So as you proceed with your research, it is useful to quantify anything that lends itself to such an approach. For example, in one study changes in organisation culture were important to my understanding of the acquisition process, so I conducted a culture survey in the acquired and acquiring companies. You never know for sure how these data will be used, but it is much harder to go back and collect them afterwards.

Persevere with reviewers. While qualitative methods come under careful scrutiny, it is very unusual for a reviewer to challenge a paper purely on the grounds that it uses the wrong methodology. Indeed, a good journal editor will always select reviewers who have at least some interest or experience with qualitative methods. So when you receive the inevitable questions about your use of a qualitative or hybrid methodology, it is often worth standing your ground, and explaining more carefully why it was the right methodology. I typically make the rather hackneyed argument that I am researching relatively new or poorly understood phenomena, so it is valuable to utilise all the different potential sources of data in order to make sense of them. Ultimately, if the reviewers' major concerns in other areas have been satisfied, they will typically accept the authors' prerogative and *not* demand that the qualitative material be removed.

Take a portfolio approach to publishing. This is a fairly generic comment, but for those with an interest in qualitative research it is particularly relevant. What I mean by this is two things. First, there is always a stochastic element to the review process, so rejection from one journal does not mean your paper is no good. Send it out again, and you may be surprised how different a response you receive. Taking your portfolio as a whole, sometimes you will get lucky with your reviewers, and sometimes you will not. The second point about the portfolio perspective is that qualitative research can be taken in a number of different directions. It can be written up for a major journal, but it can also be written up for a managerial audience or a public policy audience, and it may spawn an academic book or a text. My aim nowadays is always to write up my research for as many audiences as possible.

There is much more to say on this subject, but I shall finish here. This chapter has taken a fairly informal look at issues of publishing in quality journals. It has described, in a sense, my own voyage of discovery in terms of the techniques one uses to undertake and write up qualitative research. It has shown the benefits of taking a flexible, open-minded approach to research design, and the value of experimenting with different presentation formats. Hopefully you can pick up on some of these ideas and apply them to your own qualitative research.

REFERENCES

Adler, P., B. Goldoftas and D. Levine (1999), 'Flexibility versus efficiency? A case study of model changeovers in the Toyota production system', *Organization Science*, **10** (1), 43–68.

Barley, S.R. (1990), 'Images of imaging: notes on doing longitudinal field work', *Organization Science*, **1** (3), special issue, 220–47.

——— (1996), 'Technicians in the workplace: ethnographic evidence for bringing work into organizational studies', *Administrative Science Quarterly*, **41** (3), 404–41.

Barley, S.R. and G. Kunda (1992), 'Design and devotion: surges of rational and normative ideologies of control in managerial discourse', *Administrative Science Quarterly*, **37** (3), 363–99.

Bartlett, C.A. and S. Ghoshal (1989), *Managing across Borders: The Transnational Solution*, Boston, MA: Harvard Business School Press.

Birkinshaw, J.M. (1996), 'How subsidiary mandates are gained and lost', *Journal of International Business Studies*, **27** (3), 467–96.

——— (1997), 'Entrepreneurship in multinational corporations: the characteristics of subsidiary initiatives', *Strategic Management Journal*, **18** (2), 207–30.

——— (2000), 'The determinants and consequences of subsidiary initiative in multinational corporations', *Entrepreneurship Theory and Practise*, **24** (1), special issue, 9–35.

Birkinshaw J.M., H. Bresman and L. Håkanson (2000), 'Managing the post-acquisition integration process: how the human integration and task integration processes interact to foster value creation', *Journal of Management Studies*, **37** (3), 395–426.

Birkinshaw, J.M. and J. Ridderstråle (1999), 'Fighting the corporate immune system: a process study of peripheral initiatives in large, complex organizations', *International Business Review*, **8,** 149–80.

Bresman, H., J.M. Birkinshaw and R. Nobel (1999), 'Knowledge transfer in acquisitions', *Journal of International Business Studies*, **30** (4), 439–62.

Brown, S.L. and K.M. Eisenhardt (1997), 'The art of continuous change: linking complexity theory and time-paced evolution in relentlessly shifting organizations', *Administrative Science Quarterly*, **42** (1), 1–34.

Burgelman, R.A. (1983), 'A process model of internal corporate venturing in the diversified major firm', *Administrative Science Quarterly*, **28,** 223–44.

——— (1991), 'Intraorganizational ecology of strategy making and organizational adaptation: theory and field research', *Organization Science*, **2,** 239–62.

——— (1996), 'A process model of strategic business exit: implications for an evolutionary perspective on strategy', *Strategic Management Journal*, **17,** 193–214.

Dougherty, D. (1992), 'Interpretive barriers to successful product innovation in large firms', *Organization Science*, **3** (2), 179–202.

Dyer, J.H. (1996), 'Specialized supplier networks as a source of competitive advantage: evidence from the auto industry', *Strategic Management Journal*, **17** (4), 271–91.

Eisenhardt, K.M. (1989), 'Building theories from case study research', *Academy of Management Review*, **14** (4), 532–50.

Eisenhardt, K.M. and B.N. Tabrizi (1995), 'Accelerating adaptive processes: product innovation in the global computer industry', *Administrative Science Quarterly*, **40** (1), 84–110.

Eisenhardt, K.M. and M.J. Zbaracki (1992), 'Strategic decision making', *Strategic Management Journal*, **13,** special issue, 17–37.

Galunic, D.C. and K.M. Eisenhardt (1996), 'The evolution of intracorporate domains: divisional charter losses in high-technology, multidivisional corporations', *Organization Science*, **7** (3), 255–82.

Ghoshal, S. and C.A. Bartlett (1994), 'Linking organisational context and managerial action: the dimensions of quality of management, *Strategic Management Journal*, **15,** 91–112.

Leonard-Barton, D. (1990), 'A dual methodology for case studies: synergistic use of a longitudinal single site with replicated multiple sites', *Organization Science*, **1** (3), special issue, 248–66.

Malnight, T. (1994), 'Globalization of an ethnocentric firm: an evolutionary perspective, *Strategic Management Journal*, **16,** 119–41.

——— (1996), 'The transition from decentralized to network-based MNC structures: an evolutionary perspective, *Journal of International Business Studies*, **27** (1), 43–66.

Prahalad, C.K. and Y.L. Doz (1987), *The Multinational Mission*, New York: Free Press.

Sutton, R.I. (1997), 'The virtues of closet qualitative research', *Organization Science*, **8** (1), 97–106.

Van Maanen, J. (2000), *Qualitative Studies of Organisations*, Thousand Oaks, CA: Sage.

Yin, R.K. (1984), *Case Study Research*, Beverly Hills, CA: Sage.

Case Studies in Construction:[1]
Recollections of an Accidental Researcher

Stewart R. Clegg

Many researchers, I suspect, find their path into the research field prefigured by small acts of randomness. In my case, it was getting married. Of course, almost all marriages are random – there are an infinite number of people whom one might choose to marry but, once that randomness is settled, however provisionally, some patterning begins as we socially construct the nature of the new relationships that we enter into. In my case, I gained a father-in-law who was a police sergeant in Huddersfield, a small town in the North of England. I married between graduating as an undergraduate and starting as a PhD student, in a window of opportunity for earning some money with which to establish a new life together with my wife. I needed a job but did not know where to look: fortunately my prospective father-in-law did. He had been liaising with a construction site in the city, which necessitated some disruption to travel flows, and, at his suggestion, I went to ask them if they had any labouring jobs available.

The next day I started work as a labourer on the site, where I spent the next three months. It was hard work but I enjoyed the atmosphere, the camaraderie and the money.

About 18 months later I was in a desperate situation: my PhD supervisor was insisting that I get stuck in to some fieldwork. All my attempts at access in the industry I had chosen had failed, for one reason or another. In desperation my supervisor asked me, 'Isn't there any industry that you know anything about or have contacts in?'. 'Construction', I replied.

Three months later I found myself at the start of a lengthy period of fieldwork tape-recording and noting meetings, interactions and scenes from everyday life on a construction site. Randomness had me doing a social constructivist study of construction (Clegg 1975).

For many years after that I studiously avoided fieldwork – there was always another theory paper or book to write and in many ways it was so much easier to dwell in the relatively more settled inter-textual spaces of the bibliography than the contextual spaces of the construction site.

Twenty-five years passed quickly, most of them in Australia (another story of randomness), where one day, after presenting a paper on 'intelligent organisations' to new colleagues at the university I had just joined, one of them said 'would I like to meet a friend [of his] who would be very interested in the issues that I had addressed?'. 'Of course', I said.

Thus began a friendship that proved enormously influential. Kevin Foley, the person in question, was a leading light in the Australian 'quality movement'. Quality management had had an enormous impact in Australia since the 1980s as a result of both Kevin's zeal in leadership and government sponsorship of the process. I was interested in what happens when organisations collaborate and so, it seems, were Kevin and some of his fellow members of QAS (Quality Assurance Services). Between us we talked the notion of 'collaborative quality' into existence – how do organisations that collaborate to provide an outcome do so? We applied for a joint industry/university research award and were fortunate enough to receive the funding requested.

One of the two industries that we selected for analysis was the construction industry. As a project managed industry it was an ideal choice and I knew a little about it from my earlier doctoral work.

We planned to spend some time doing qualitative research in the field and some time doing a subsequent survey. We spoke to a number of construction firms about the possibilities of access and at one of them we heard about a new alliance that had been put together between Sydney Water and three construction companies, to build a major piece of Sydney Olympics infrastructure – a stormwater and sewerage retention tunnel designed to stop overflow of raw sewage and street-litter into the harbour and ruining the televisual charm of Olympic events on Sydney Harbour through the sight of unsightly shit-brown tinged water.

What followed was nearly 18 months experience back in fieldwork, this time with a very able research assistant, Tyrone Pitsis, in the milieu of construction, once again looked at from a constructivist point of view. So the random cycle returns: as a result of this earlier research we have been approached by Sydney Water and their alliance partner, Transfield, to do further research on a new alliance venture, on the basis of our earlier work (Clegg et al. 2002, forthcoming; Pitsis et al. 2001).

Marrying a wife and gaining a father-in-law who was a police sergeant led to quite accidental outcomes and surprising decisions: in my case, a career-long interest in how constructors construct construction.

I suspect many research careers are equally as accidental.

NOTE

1. I like puns – and the title should be read as an evident pun. Case studies are always constructed and a number of the more significant ones that I have conducted have been on the construction industry: hence the pun.

REFERENCES

Clegg, S. (1975), *Power, Rule and Domination: A Critical and Empirical Understanding of Power in Sociological Theory and Organizational Life*, London and Boston: Routledge and Paul Kegan.

Clegg, S., T. Pitsis, T. Rura-Polley and M. Marosszeky (2002), 'Governmentality matters: designing an alliance culture of inter-organisational collaboration for managing projects', *Organization Studies*, **23** (3), 317–37.

Clegg, S., T. Pitsis, T. Rura-Polley and M. Marosszeky (forthcoming), 'Constructing the Olympic dream: managing innovation through the future perfect', *Organization Science*.

Pitsis, T., S. Clegg, T. Rura-Polley and M. Marosszeky (2001) 'The odyssey of project management: from quality culture to quality cult', *Quality Australia: The Business Improvement Journal*, **16** (1), 22–4.

Index

abductive reasoning 477
abstracting
  labels 59
  phenomena 72
academic
  competitive environment 7, 191,
    553–4
  culture 269–70
  journals 259, 276
  payment for research 385–6
  reviewers 555
  rigour 276, 277
  status 389–90
academic research, nature and value
  385–6
academic versus business world
  269–70
accents 219, 230, 233
access to organisations
  communication styles in 479
  determinants of 113
  India 423–4, 435
  Japanese multinationals 314–15
  language in 232
  multinationals 251–4
  negotiating 368–70
  organisations 267–8, 291–4
  personal contact 34, 448–9
  problems of 300–302
  Vietnam 385, 389–91
acculturation 435
accuracy of information 391–3
acontextual questions 409, 417
across-case analysis 130, 135–6, 140
across-method triangulation 165
Africa
  history 145
  relations with Latin America 446
  traditions 86–7
  Western representations of 58

see also Nigeria; Senegal; Sudan;
    Zimbabwe
age issues 219, 292–3, 374–5
alternative research paradigms, lack of
  14–15
ambiguities 199–200
analysis of data see data analysis
analytical
  approaches to research design 494
  generalisation 130–31, 138–40
anonymity 195, 201, 259–60, 274, 300,
  544
anthropological methodology 58
Antoniou, Christos 292, 293, 295–6
appropriation strategies 59–60
Ardener, Edwin 299
articles
  brevity of 259
  flaws in 581–2
  methodology sections of 567
  review of 6–7, 25–6, 40
Asia
  foreign language usage 234
  HRM research in 34
  links with Latin America 446
  multinational companies research
    232–3, 254
  relationship building 394–5
  see also China; Hong Kong; India;
    Indonesia; Japan; Singapore;
    South Korea; Sri Lanka; Taiwan;
    Thailand
Association of Social Anthropologists
  299
'assortments' of information 208–9
Aston Studies 71
ATLAS.ti 489, 491, 492, 567
attitude research 407–8
atypical cases in theoretical sampling
  129

Index